Countries Austria
Belgium and Luxembourg
Channel Islands
Corsica
Crete
Cyprus
Egypt
England
France
Germany
Greece
Holland
Hungary
Ireland
Northern Italy
Southern Italy
Malta and Gozo
Morocco
Portugal
Scotland
Sicily
Spain
Switzerland
Turkey: Bursa to Antakya
Wales
Yugoslavia

Cities Boston and Cambridge
Florence
Istanbul
Jerusalem
London
Moscow and Leningrad
New York
Oxford and Cambridge
Paris and Versailles
Rome and Environs
Venice

Themes Churches and Chapels of Northern England
Churches and Chapels of Southern England
Literary Britain and Ireland
Museums and Galleries of London
Victorian Architecture in Britain

The palm house, one of several display houses in the Birmingham Botanic Gardens

BLUE GUIDE

GARDENS
OF
ENGLAND

Frances Gapper, Patience Gapper
and Sally Drury

Atlas and garden plans by John Flower

A & C Black
London

WW Norton
New York

First edition 1991

Published by A & C Black (Publishers) Limited
35 Bedford Row, London WC1R 4JH

© A & C Black (Publishers) Limited 1991

Apart from any fair dealing for the purpose of research or private study, or criticism or review, as permitted under the Copyright, Designs and Patents Act, 1988, this publication may be reproduced, stored or transmitted, in any forms or by any means, only with the prior permission in writing of the publishers, or in the case of reprographic reproduction in accordance with the terms of licences issued by the Copyright Licensing Agency. Inquiries concerning reproduction outside those terms should be sent to the publishers at the abovementioned address.

A CIP catalogue record of this book
is available from the British Library.

ISBN   0–7136–3389–1

Published in the United States of America by
WW Norton and Company, Inc.
500 Fifth Avenue, New York, NY 10110

Published simultaneously in Canada by
Penguin Books Canada Limited
2801 John Street, Markham, Ontario, LR3 1B4

ISBN   0–393–30777–8   USA

Born in Stockport, **Frances Gapper** now lives in London. She has worked as a horticultural journalist on the magazines *Horticulture Week* and *Gardening Now* and the partwork *Successful Gardening*. She also writes fiction.

Patience Gapper was born in Devon and comes from a family of keen gardeners and intermittent writers. She is a member of the RHS, the NCCPG and a Friend of Kew Gardens and counts the exploration of gardens as one of life's major pleasures. At present she works for an Outer London borough, producing information for the public about social services.

Sally Drury graduated in Horticulture in 1982 from Reading University. She was Technical Editor on the *Gardeners' Chronicle* and *Horticultral Trades Journal* before becoming a freelance horticultural writer in 1988.

Printed and bound in Great Britain by
William Clowes Limited, Beccles and London

PREFACE

Writing a gardens guide is an exciting and rewarding occupation, but one with natural hazards. Since gardens are always changing, the notable feature or plant described on one visit may well be gone by the next. Recent extraordinary weather conditions have magnified this state of impermanence, with ancient trees uprooted and flung about like matchsticks and whole pleasure gardens and avenues wrecked overnight. We began researching this guide in spring 1987 in Sussex and Kent; in the October of that year came the great gale, which changed the face of many gardens in southern England. The countrywide storms of January and February 1990 caused wider havoc.

We would like to put on record our thanks to those generous gardeners and garden owners who took time to accompany us on our initial visits and painstakingly updated our notes—even pausing in the massive task of clearing and restoration to discuss their future plans.

Gardens rooted deep in history have many hidden resources and can produce surprises. In the drought of summer 1989, dry patches appearing at regular intervals on a lawn led to the discovery of a Lutyens pergola at Knebworth in Hertfordshire, and recent excavations at Castle Bromwich near Birmingham have uncovered the remains of at least four separate garden designs dating back to the sixteenth century, as well as a large medieval cesspit. Many other gardens have been faithfully recorded and maintained through centuries and can be experienced as living pieces of history. Almost 1100 parks and gardens in England are classified as historically interesting and can be found in the *Register of Parks and Gardens of Special Interest in England* produced by English Heritage.

The best gardens remain true to the spirit of their original creators while continuing to develop, maintaining a fruitful and energetic relationship between past and present. Gardens planted in this century, though drawing to some extent on the past, present a contemporary vision. We have tried to honour both the influential achievements of the great landscapers of past centuries—Lancelot Brown, William Kent, Humphry Repton—and the unique insights of gardeners such as Gertrude Jekyll and Vita Sackville-West. We have also explored the work of notable present-day gardeners and garden writers including Graham Stuart Thomas, Beth Chatto, Penelope Hobhouse, Christopher Lloyd and Rosemary Verey. We have attempted to reflect the huge diversity of English gardens: herb gardens, botanic gardens, cottage gardens, water and woodland gardens, gardens in Japanese, Dutch or Indian style, formal, architectural, romantic, picturesque and classical gardens, landscaped parks—and those eluding any classification.

Because we chose to focus mainly on gardens open frequently and regularly to the public during the season, many unique and beautiful gardens have had, with regret, to be excluded from this book. To keep it pocket-sized, others that open regularly had to be described more briefly—see the section at the back of the book. Choices have been hard to make. The enthusiastic garden visitor should refer to *The National Trust Handbook* and to *Gardens of England and Wales*, a listing of over 2500 private gardens opened occasionally through the National Gardens Scheme Charitable Trust. The selections of gardener writers are another valuable source of information. We hope that readers of this guide will be encourage to make their own discoveries in gardens that we had to pass by, or which are now being designed and planted for the future.

Grateful thanks to Gemma Davies, our Blue Guide Editor, for her patience, tact and helpful advice; and to Ronald Joyce, her assistant.

Frances Gapper, Patience Gapper and Sally Drury

For permission to reproduce the photograph on p 275 the publishers would like to thank Roddy Llewellyn, author of *Water Gardens: a connoisseur's choice*, the photographer Bob Challinor and Ward Lock (a division of Cassell plc).

The photograph of Overbecks Garden, Devon, is by Tony Murdoch, and that of Painshill Park, Surrey, by Jack Chinn.

A Note on Blue Guides

The Blue Guide series began in 1918 when Muirhead Guide-Books Limited published 'Blue Guide London and its Environs'. Finlay and James Muirhead already had extensive experience of guide-book publishing: before the First World War they had been the editors of the English editions of the Germany Baedekers, and by 1915 they had acquired the copyright of most of the famous 'Red' Handbooks from John Murray.

An agreement made with the French publishing house Hachette et Cie in 1917 led to the translation of Muirhead's London Guide, which became the first 'Guide Bleu'—Hachette had previously published the blue-covered 'Guides Joannes'. Subsequently, Hachette's 'Guide Bleu Paris et ses Environs' was adapted and and published in London by Muirhead. The collaboration between the two publishing houses continued until 1933.

In 1933 Ernest Benn Limited took over the Blue Guides, appointing Russell Muirhead, Finlay Muirhead's son, editor in 1934. The Muirhead's connection with the Blue Guides ended in 1963 when Stuart Rossiter, who had been working on the Guides since 1954, became house editor, revising and compiling several of the books himself.

The Blue Guides are now published by A & C Black, who acquired Ernest Benn in 1984, so continuing the tradition of guidebook publishing which began in 1826 with 'Black's Economical Tourist of Scotland'. The Blue Guide series continues to grow: there are now more than 40 titles in print with revised editions appearing regularly and many new Blue Guides in preparation.

'Blue Guides' is a registered trademark.

CONTENTS

SHORTER DESCRIPTIONS

Maps and Plans

Key to symbols

P	Car Park	R	Refreshments
CP	Coach Park	S	Shop
E	Entrance	☎	Telephone
▨	Glasshouses	T	Toilets
✳	Picnic areas	⌁	Viewpoint
♠	Plant Sales	V	Visitor Centre

A HISTORY OF ENGLISH GARDENS

Changing fashions and tastes in gardening reveal the deeper undercurrents of a nation's development: reflecting, besides the state of its economy, its preoccupations and priorities; its relation to the natural world—and what is conceived as 'natural'; its sense of beauty; even its spiritual values. Hence the interest of comparing the garden art and gardening history of different nations, which is not our purpose here—for an introduction, the reader is referred to Christopher Thacker's 'The History of Gardens' (Croom Helm, 1985). But the study of English gardens inevitably extends outwards, acknowledging the considerable influence of other European gardens—French, Italian, Spanish, Dutch, German—besides those of Japan and China.

Gardening flourishes in peaceful, settled periods, when people have leisure, opportunity to experiment and (often but not necessarily) money to spend and gardeners to employ; as witness the number of great gardens almost destroyed by neglect in the 1939–45 war, and retrieved from the wild only through years of hard work. English gardening art reached a high point of development in the eighteenth century, that most civilised of periods, when gardening—or the creation of a beautiful landscape infused with ideas, specific values, poetic and classical references—became *the* occupation of the aristocracy, and for many noblemen a life's work, an obsession. The inspired and magnificent garden landscapes of this period crowned the achievements and developments of many centuries.

Roman gardens. Invading Britain in the first century AD, the Romans brought many new plants—vegetables such as cabbages, cucumbers and radishes; trees and shrubs including sweet chestnuts, limes and mulberries; also the vine grape and garlic.

The Romans created symmetrical pleasure gardens around their British villas, with rectangular beds and lawns and straight walks and alleys; modest versions of the huge and splendid gardens created around villas in Italy at this period.

Early gardens in castles and monasteries. The Roman withdrawal in the early part of the fifth century was followed by the Dark Ages, when the wars and feuds of the Anglo-Saxons, Picts, Scots and others would have tended to curtail any attempts at gardening. However, small gardens within the inner walls of fortified castles were planted with herbs to season meat and fish; and some vegetables and fruit may have been grown, to supplement an otherwise monotonous diet.

The monasteries provided another peaceful refuge, where herb gardens flourished alongside orchards and vegetable grounds, providing vital food resources. Herbs were also important for medicinal purposes.

Monastic gardens kept plants in cultivation that might otherwise have been lost. Plants were grown primarily for their usefulness. Lilies, roses and irises were valued as herbs; but these and other flowers would also have been used to decorate the altar and to make chaplets and garlands for the clergy to wear on festival days.

Monastic gardens continued through medieval times, their design remaining simple and utilitarian.

Medieval gardens. The first medieval pleasure gardens developed behind castle walls, and would have offered a pleasant antidote to the stench and overcrowding of the baronial hall; in times of peace, orchards were planted beyond the walls, and small plots of land hedged or fenced about to make gardens.

These medieval secular gardens were square or rectangular, following the shape of the cloister, and providing a similar atmosphere of seclusion. The garden would often be divided into smaller square or geometric shapes, with cross paths. Trees were clipped to form roofs and divisions. There would perhaps be trellis work, arbours and pergolas. Early medieval gardens had 'flowery medes' or grassy lawns, and raised beds of scented plants. Arbours were popular, overhung with vines or roses. Turf seats, or raised banks, provided resting points, and these were often planted with flowers.

Mounts, or small hills, either round or square, became common in the later Middle Ages. These were designed to give a better view of the garden itself, not the surrounding countryside. The medieval garden was primarily a refuge from the world's ills, the 'paradyse erthly' of much medieval poetry.

Tudor and Elizabethan gardens. The Tudors brought times of peace, stretching from the late fifteenth through the sixteenth century; and increased wealth among the nobility, resulting from the Dissolution of the Monasteries. Large and splendid houses were built, often from the stones of ruined religious buildings, and extensive pleasure gardens gave evidence of the wealth and power of their owners. They also bore witness to the adventurous, extravagant spirit of the Italian Renaissance.

Many of the great Tudor and Elizabethan houses were built around a central courtyard, laid out and planted in formal style, with elaborate raised beds. These beds evolved into knot gardens of complex design—low evergreen bushes forming the intricate patterning and the gaps between filled with bright flowers or herbs, occasionally with coloured sand or brick dust, and usually edged with scented herbs, such as lavender or rosemary. Designed to be viewed from above, they were typically laid out below the house windows.

Modern knot gardens—such as the splendid one at Hampton Court Palace in Greater London—are seldom exact recreations; but one fine 'in period' example, using plants known to have been grown in the sixteenth and seventeenth centuries, can be seen at Cranborne Manor in Dorset, another at Little Moreton Hall in Cheshire; and there is a large sunken knot garden at Hatfield House in Hertfordshire.   Mounts remained in fashion and these, too, grew increasingly elaborate—Sir Francis Bacon, in his essay 'Of Gardens', published in 1625, recommends the 'cockleshell' turnings of the mount at Wressel Castle, which made it a puzzle to climb; however, Bacon disapproved of knots and elaborate topiary. Mounts would often be crowned with a gazebo or banqueting room. Mazes also became popular, the patterns laid out in turf or low shrubs and herbs (hedge mazes did not appear until the seventeenth century). Bowling greens were included in many gardens of great houses.

These were also, however, 'working gardens', with orchards and stew ponds, dovecots and beehives, supplying the needs of the table. Fruit was grown in variety, including apricots and peaches, mulberries and medlars.

Many new plants and trees were introduced to Britain and Europe from the East and the Americas in the sixteenth and seventeenth centuries: in the late sixteenth century, besides potatoes, tomatoes and tobacco, we gained hyacinths, tulips, the oriental plane (*Platanus orientalis*), yuccas, sunflowers and nasturtiums.

The seventeenth century. French formal gardens had a considerable influence on British gardening conceptions, mingling with the Italian Renaissance tradition and joined by the Dutch style. The kitchen garden became a separate entity, often situated at some distance from the house, and freeing the rest of the garden for display, pleasure and surprise.

The Elizabethan knot evolved into the parterre, a distinctive French feature, much larger than the knot, laid out as part of a total design with the house and distinguished by its orderly elegance and balance of graceful patterns. The huge weaves and scrolls of the parterre were planted in box and the spaces filled with coloured stones, brick dust, sand or coal. Complex broderies of box were laid out at Hampton Court in the reign of William of Orange; but removed in the early eighteenth century, on the order of Queen Anne, who could not abide the smell.

Statues, avenues, canals and elaborate waterworks were all popular, showing the Italian influence, but formal gardening received fresh impetus with the Restoration of Charles II in 1660 and the return of exiled Royalists from France. Versailles, laid out by Le Nôtre for Louis XIV from the early 1660s onwards, made an indelible impression on the European gardening imagination: magnificent, ostentatious, huge, with its straight avenues leading off into the endless distance. Although the English could not hope to imitate the god-like scale of Versailles, Le Nôtre's influence was soon to be seen in long avenues, *allées* cutting through woodland, alignment of the garden's central axis with that of the house, canals, statues and fountains. On a more domestic scale, the formal Dutch garden style came into vogue in the reign of William and Mary.

The seventeenth century formal garden would often include a Wilderness, crossed by straight paths, planted with flowering trees and shrubs and only 'wild' in contrast with the rest of the garden; one example can be seen at Ham House in Surrey.

Topiary work flourished in this century; one fine surviving example is Levens Hall in Cumbria, where box-edged parterres frame massive and extraordinary topiary shapes. The gardens were laid out in 1692 by M. Beaumont, a pupil of Le Nôtre. Orangeries, built to overwinter citrus and evergreen trees and tender exotics, became increasingly sophisticated in construction. By the end of the century, most had large windows on the south-facing side, but glass roofs took much longer to catch on; the first British glass-roofed orangery was built in 1696.

Most famous among seventeenth century plant hunters were the

Tradescants, John the Elder and John the Younger, who introduced a great number of important plants to England—orange trees, cypresses, figs, broom, the tulip tree, swamp cypress and Virginia creeper, among many others. The influx of new plants from abroad prompted the setting up of a number of nurseries. One of the most important was that of London and Wise, who were both nurserymen and garden designers (they laid out the gardens at Melbourne Hall in Derbyshire).

Oxford University Botanic Gardens were founded in 1621 as physic gardens; followed half a century later by the Chelsea Physic Garden.

The eighteenth century. Around 1710 began a reaction against the seventeenth century formal garden which was to have far-reaching effects, for this was the century in which man discovered Nature. Poets and writers such as Shaftesbury, Addison and Pope were the first to attack the previous century's achievements, and to uphold the 'natural' over the formal, although ideas as to what was 'natural' changed as the century progressed. The garden thus held an important place in culture and thought. This was a great age for gardening—and an age of great gardeners, both professional and amateur.

Pope, in his 'Epistle to Lord Burlington', exhorts the garden planner never to forget Nature, to consult 'the Genius of the Place', eschewing pompous artificiality and unnatural attempts at symmetry. Richard Boyle, the 3rd Earl of Burlington, was a great patron of the arts and a friend of artists and writers. His first layout (1718–1735) for his gardens at Chiswick was of the kind popular since the Restoration—formal, grand and geometrical, including a huge *patte d'oie* or goosefoot of avenues. William Kent (1685–1748), a leading exponent of the 'natural style', was given a free hand at Chiswick and made many changes, introducing kinks and bends into the artificial river, creating a wilderness with winding sinuous paths and placing small temples, grottoes and statues at strategic points.

Kent was trained as a painter, and had studied in Italy, only later becoming an architect and garden designer. He was greatly influenced by the works of the seventeenth century Italian painters Claude Lorrain and Gaspard Poussin, depicting Arcadian scenes in the Italian countryside—particularly the steep hilly terrain around Rome. Taking these as the basis for an idealised conception of Nature, he introduced reminders of an idyllic, Elysian past, an era of classical antiquity, into his landscapes: classical buildings, ruins and other romantic or symbolic features. Rousham Park in Oxfordshire is one of the best remaining examples of Kent's work, and shows how carefully, with great artistic effect, such features were 'placed', designed to be revealed in sequence and to evoke particular emotions.

West Wycombe Park, Sir Francis Dashwood's inspired creation in Buckinghamshire, is another fine example of the early landscape movement; semi-formal rather than informal, filled with classical buildings and references. Vistas unfold as you progress round the garden, with buildings and temples acting as focal points. Henry Hoare's Stourhead in Wiltshire—in time of conception, between

Kent and Brown—also shows Kent's influence in the use of buildings and classical references.

The 'total landscape garden' developed in the second half of the eighteenth century and was almost entirely the work of Lancelot 'Capability' Brown. Nicknamed for his ability to appreciate the capabilities, or natural potential, of a landscape, Brown followed a far purer, simpler and more open conception of Nature than Kent's. His landscapes are characterised by wide stretches of grass leading right up to the house, the complete absence of formal gardens and a seeming lack of boundaries. Huge lakes are shaped to give the impression of winding rivers, and belts of woodland or isolated groups of trees are used to ornament hillsides and direct the eye towards distant prospects.

These open sweeps of landscape were made possible by the ha-ha, a boundary ditch which kept animals from straying past a certain point, but which was invisible from any distance, giving the illusion of an unbroken line between garden and countryside. Probably introduced by Charles Bridgeman (died 1738), ha-has can still be seen in a number of gardens, including Rousham, West Wycombe, Bowood and Blenheim.

Ideas of the sublime and the picturesque in the late eighteenth century brought a reaction against smooth lawns and serpentine lakes, in favour of the savage, the rude and the untamed. The wild and gloomy Italian landscapes of a third seventeenth century painter, Salvator Rosa, were now preferred to the peaceful 'Golden Age' paintings of Claude and Poussin. The 'natural' was equated with the primitive. Grottoes and hermitages, Gothic buildings, ruins and arches—even 'Swiss cottages'—were the order of the day.

Around the turn of the century, English gardening lost something of its buoyancy and extravagance of spirit; the excesses of the picturesque style fell from favour, and certain formal, 'unnatural' elements crept back into the garden, on a small scale. Humphry Repton (1752–1818) was responsible for reintroducing beds of flowers near the house, fountains and balustrades.

The nineteenth century. The landscape garden remained without any strong successor for the first few decades of the nineteenth century. Various styles were tried out here and there, such as the Indian style at Sezincote in Gloucestershire. The Chinese style was most successful, as exemplified by the fine pagoda at Alton Towers in Staffordshire, designed by Robert Abrahams, and the 'China' area at Biddulph Grange in the same county. Alton Towers, with its mixture of many styles—its Swiss cottage, Italian garden and Dutch garden, Roman bath and colonnade—may seem eccentric today, but reflects very well what Christopher Thacker has named the 'eclectic impulse' of the early nineteenth century.

New plant species had been flooding into the country throughout the eighteenth century, and thousands more arrived during the nineteenth century. The ending of the Napoleonic wars in 1815 brought far greater freedom of travel than had been possible for the previous 20 years. The Horticultural Society (later the Royal Horticultural Society), founded in 1804, financed a number of expeditions. Intrepid Victorian plant hunters found their task of transferring seedlings and young plants across the seas greatly facilitated by the invention of the Wardian case.

New, exotic and tender plants appeared, not only in botanic gardens such as Kew, but in private collections and gardens across the land. Elaborate glasshouses of ingenious design appeared in gardens and estates, culminating in the building of the Crystal Palace by Sir Joseph Paxton (1801–65).

Gardening periodicals and manuals proliferated in the first half of the nineteenth century, with the rise of the middle classes. The cylinder or reel lawnmower, invented in 1830 by Edwin Budding, soon replaced the scythe and the sheep, making a smooth lawn easy to achieve.

The Victorians eventually settled for preference on the neo-Italianate style, for the gardens of great houses and middle class villas. This style was distinguished by its rigidity and formality, and featured long gravel walks, closely mown lawns, clipped hedges, fountains and statues and decorated terraces with balustrades. Both Sir Charles Barry (1795–1860) and W.A. Nesfield (1793–1864) favoured gaudy parterres laid out on Italianate terraces. This accorded with the Victorian taste for labour intensive massed bedding in riotous bright colours.

A move towards greater informality taking place in the last quarter of the century, accompanied by a new appreciation of the individual plant and its qualities, the herbaceous border came into prominence. Gertrude Jekyll (1843–1932), approaching border planting with the eye of an artist, popularised the planting of informal drifts of colour, the gradation of warm and cold colours, and one-colour borders. William Robinson (1838–1935) advocated the planting of 'natural' and wild gardens, alpine and rock gardens and led the reaction against bedding-out plants, which he abhorred. Robinson and Jekyll turned away from grand movements and styles, looking for inspiration to the English country or cottage garden, as it had existed for many centuries, without interruption or change, in peaceful obscurity.

The twentieth century. Gertrude Jekyll's 'presence looms over twentieth century gardening' (Jane Brown, The English Garden in our Time) and her influence is still felt. Lawrence Johnston's Hidcote also made an important impact on garden-making style in the early part of this century, combining and juxtaposing formal features and skilfully arranged vistas with informal and cottage garden planting. Hidcote was a direct predecessor of Sissinghurst, a garden of 'compartments' laid out and planted in the 1930s by Vita Sackville-West and Harold Nicolson. Percy Cane was another influential garden designer, who also linked formal and natural styles within a strong overall structure: his work can be seen at Dartington Hall.

The two wars brought drastic changes. Labour shortages following the 1914–18 war made it impossible to maintain the labour-intensive gardening schemes beloved by the Victorians; and the bombings of the 1939–45 war necessitated much landscaping and replanting of public spaces. Landscape architects such as Sylvia Crowe and Geoffrey Jellicoe contributed to this work. Examples of

Geoffrey Jellicoe's work can also be seen at Mottisfont Abbey, Wisley and Pusey.

Proving too costly to maintain, many large estates passed from private ownership into the hands of local authorities—such as Newstead Abbey, once the home of Lord Byron and now owned by Nottingham City Council. A number of fine gardens are now owned and administered by local authorities, and they vary a great deal in style and planting—from Highdown, the Sussex chalk pit garden (Worthing Borough Council) to the spacious gardens of Temple Newsam (Leeds City Council).

The National Trust, founded in 1895, now owns and opens to the public more than 130 gardens; its Gardens Committee was formed in 1948, and Hidcote was taken over by the Trust in that year. The Gardens Scheme, established in 1927, opened 600 private gardens to the public on an occasional basis; now called the National Gardens Scheme Charitable Trust, it opens more than 2500 private gardens each year (listed in its invaluable Yellow Book).

Horticulture became a booming industry in the 1950s and 1960s, and garden centres achieved immediate popularity. Gardening programmes on television and radio and gardening magazines and journals continue to fuel amateur enthusiasm. The first Chelsea Flower Show was held in 1913, and this show is still a popular mecca for gardeners.

Much important hybridisation and breeding work has been done this century, resulting in new, stronger and disease resistant varieties of plants. Hybrid tea and floribunda roses were first bred at the turn of the century, to give a longer flowering period, and soon took pride of place in British gardens. Now, however, old-fashioned shrub roses are being reintroduced, as well as new English roses, hybrids of modern varieties and shrub roses.

Wild flowers, no longer despised as weeds, are encouraged to flourish in many gardens, and nature conservation has become a priority. The National Council for the Conservation of Plants and Gardens in Britain (NCCPG) has established reference collections in gardens throughout Britain, with the aim of safeguarding endangered varieties.

Reference Books

Encyclopaedia of Garden Plants and Flowers, Reader's Digest 1975, 3rd ed. 1978

Hillier Manual of Trees and Shrubs, David and Charles

The Oxford Companion to Gardens, by Geoffrey and Susan Jellicoe, Patrick Goode and Michael Lancaster, Oxford University Press, 1986

The Royal Horticultural Society Gardeners' Encyclopaedia of Plants and Flowers, Brickell C. (Editor-in-Chief), Dorling Kindersley, 1989

Coombes, A.J., *The Collingridge Dictionary of Plant Names*, Collingridge Books, 1985

Hobhouse, P., *The National Trust; a Book of Gardening*, Pavilion/Michael Joseph, 1986

Keble Martin, W., *The Concise British Flora in Colour*, George Rainbird, 1965

Thomas, G.S., *Gardens of the National Trust*, The National Trust, Weidenfeld & Nicholson, 1979

Wright, M., *The Complete Handbook of Garden Plants*, Michael Joseph, 1989

Further Reading

Adams, W.H., *The French Garden 1500–1800*, Scolar Press, 1982

Brookes, J., *The Small Garden*, Tiger Books International PLC, 1989

Brown, J., *Gardens of a Golden Afternoon—Story of a Partnership:Edwin Lutyens and Gertrude Jekyll*, Penguin, 1985

Brown, J., *The English Garden in Our Time*, The Antique Collectors' Club, 1986

Chadwick, G.F., *The Works of Sir Joseph Paxton*, Architectural Press, 1961 (out of print)

Chatto, B., *The Dry Garden* J.M. Dent & Sons Ltd, 1981

Chatto, B., *The Damp Garden*, J.M. Dent & Sons Ltd, 1986

Clifford, D., *History of Garden Design*, Faber, 1962 (out of print)

Coffin, D.R., *The Italian Garden*, Dumbarton Oaks, USA 1972

Fish, Margery, *An All the Year Garden*, Collingridge, London, 1964 (out of print)

Hadfield, M., *A History of British Gardening*, John Murray

Harvey, J., *Medieval Gardens*, Batsford, 1990

Hobhouse, P., *Colour in Your Garden*, Collins, London, 1988; Little Brown Boston, 1985

Hobhouse, P., *Garden Style*, Windward/Frances Lincoln, 1988

Hunt, J.D. and Willis, P. ed., *The Genius of the Place: English Landscape Gardens 1620–1820*, Elek, 1975

Jekyll, G., *Colour Schemes for the Flower Garden*, Antique Collectors' Club, 1990 (reprint of 1912 original)

Jekyll, G. and Sir L. Weaver, *Gardens for Small Country Houses*, Antique Collectors' Club, 1985

Jones, B., *Follies and Grottoes*, Constable & Co Ltd, 1989

Lloyd, C., *The Well-Chosen Garden*, Elmtree Books/Hamish Hamilton, 1984, Mermaid Books, 1985

Lloyd, C. *The Well-Tempered Garden*, Penguin Books, 1987

Massingham, B., *Gertrude Jekyll*, Shire Publications, 1975

Repton, H., *Observations on the Theory and Practice of Landscape Gardening*, 1803. Reissued by Phaidon, 1981

Robinson, W., *The English Flower Garden*, John Murray 16th ed. 1986 (out of print)

Rushford, K., *The Hillier Book of Garden Planning and Planting*, David and Charles, 1988

Stroud, D., *Capability Brown*, Faber, 1984

Thacker, C., *The History of Gardens*, Croom Helm, 1985

Lees-Milne, A. and Verey, R., The Englishman's Garden, Viking Penguin, 1987
Lees-Milne, A. and Verey, R., The New Englishwoman's Garden, pub Chatto & Windus, 1987
Verey, R., *Classic Garden Design*, John Murray, 1989
Verey, R., *The Garden in Winter*, Frances Lincoln, 1988
Verey, R., *The Scented Garden*, Mermaid/Michael Joseph, 1982.

Glossary of Terms

ALLÉE, a walk usually cut through woodland or enclosed by dense plantings of trees and shrubs

ALPINE, by botanical definition, a plant found in pastures between the tree line and snow line of mountainous districts. Often generally applied to plants suitable for growing in rock gardens

ANNUAL, a plant that germinates from seed, grows, flowers, sets seed and dies within a year or less

ARBORETUM, a collection of trees including exotic, unusual or scientifically interesting specimens

BALUSTRADE, a long row of posts or pillars, usually stone, surrounded by a rail. Generally decorative to terraces

BEE-BOLES, niches or alcoves set into walls, to house small straw beehives. Date from Tudor times

BIENNIAL, a plant that completes its life-cycle over two years. In the first year it produces leafy growth, in the second it flowers and then dies

BRACT, a modified leaf at the base of the flower stalk or flower cluster. In some plants it appears to form part of the flower itself

CLOCHE, a cover used to protect young plants, or in propagation. Early cloches were bell-shaped

CORDON, generally applied to fruit trees that are trained by removing all the lateral branches to leave a single main stem growing upright, horizontally or more often at an oblique angle

CULTIVAR, correctly, cultivated variety. A horticulturally selected plant

ERICACEOUS, any plant in the family Ericaceae, including heathers and rhododendrons

ESPALIER, generally applied to fruit trees. A method of training trees on spurs by selecting lateral branches to grow horizontally in opposite pairs on each side of the main stem

FASTIGIATE, describes trees and shrubs with branches erect and close together rather than spreading

FORCING, the practice of hurrying plants into flower or to produce fruit early by means of artificial conditions

GAZEBO, a building, pavilion or similar structure, often two storeys high. Used as a focal point in a garden or as a shelter from which to view the garden.

GLAUCOUS, dull greyish-green or blue, referring to leaves or stems; covered with a powdery bloom

GRAFTING, the practice of binding parts of two different plants together. Sucessful grafts unite and become a single plant

GROTTO, a cave-like structure, often decorated with shells or fossils. A popular feature in 18C landscape gardens, often intended to induce feelings of poetic melancholy in the visitor

HA-HA, a sunken wall and ditch, forming an invisible barrier between parkland and garden, to keep animals out

HERBACEOUS, a plant that does not form a persistent woody stem (as shrubs do). A term usually applied to perennials

HYBRID, a plant resulting from a cross between two different species

ICE HOUSE, a man-made underground cavern used for the storage of ice. Dates from late 17C. Usually sited some distance from the house and often close to a lake from which the ice was taken. Generally mounded over with earth

KNOT, intricate pattern formed by the planting and clipping of low shrubs. Popular in the 15C and 16C

LOGGIA, a gallery, arcade or shelter, open on one or both sides. Originally designed as a shady walk or viewing point

MOUNT, an artificial mound or bank of earth, used as a vantage point from which to view the garden, or see over defensive walls into the surrounding countryside. A feature of many medieval and Tudor gardens

MULCH, generally a bulky organic material, such as bark chippings or peat, spread on the soil surface to aid water retention and to stop weeds growing

OBELISK, a tall, thin, tapering structure or monument. Popular as focal points in 18C landscape gardens

ORANGERY, elaborate forerunner to the greenhouse. Primarily used to overwinter oranges and exotic plants

PAGODA, a Chinese building, usually tall and slender, surmounted by a peaked roof and often with more roofs at each storey. Popular as ornaments in gardens of the late 18C and 19C

PANICLE, branched cluster of individually stalked flowers

PARTERRE, French word meaning 'on the ground'. Generally a level space divided to form a symmetrical pattern of matching flower beds or scroll work, depicted in small evergreen shrubs such as box. May be elaborate or simple. Intended to be viewed from above. Developed in France in late 16C and early 17C

PERENNIAL, a plant that lives for more than two years, dying down in autumn and reappearing the following spring

PERGOLA, a walk covered by pillars and cross members, which support plants

PINETUM, a collection of coniferous trees, including exotic, unusual or scientifically interesting specimens

PLEACHING, the practice of forming a dense hedge by interweaving the branches of well-spaced trees but leaving the trunks prominent. Generally applied to limes and hornbeams

PLUNGE, the practice of sinking pots or other plant-holding containers up to the rim in soil, so as to hide the pots from view and protect the plants from fluctuating temperatures, or from drying out. The sites are called plunge beds

PROCUMBENT/PROSTRATE, plants with a spreading habit, growing horizontally close to or on the ground

RACEME, an unbranched, elongated flower head, comprising short-stalked flowers, spirally arranged

SPECIES, a group of plants bearing the same unique characteristics, breeding true from seed

STEW PONDS, ponds stocked with fish for the table. A feature of medieval gardens, especially monastic

TEMPLE, garden architecture, ornamental or functional, designed along classical lines. Popular in 18C landscape gardens

TOPIARY, the art and practice of clipping trees and shrubs into ornamental shapes. Best performed in box or yew. Developed in Roman times, revived in the Middle Ages and popular in 17C and 19C

TUFA, a porous type of stone, which can retain water and support plant growth

VISTA, a view framed by trees and shrubs

WILDERNESS, in the 17C, a dense planting of trees and shrubs, crossed through by a network of intersecting paths. Now, any part of a garden that is uncultivated and left to nature

AVON

University of Bristol Botanic Garden

ADDRESS AND TELEPHONE: Bracken Hill, North Road, Leigh Woods, Bristol BS8 3PF. Tel. Bristol (0272) 733682

OWNERS: The University of Bristol

DIRECTIONS: first right after crossing Clifton Suspension Bridge from Bristol. Proceed 500 yds, garden on left. Public Transport: BR to Bristol Temple Meads, then take Cityline bus 8 or 9 (circular route leaving every 10 minutes) either to Clifton (alight Christchurch), walk over Suspension Bridge, small toll, to North Road or to bottom of Park Street (alight College Green) cross to bus stop opposite outside the Cathedral and take the Badger Line 358, leaving every 20 minutes, to Ashton Park Lodge at the top of Rownham Hill and walk from there to North Road.

OPENING TIMES: 9–5 daily except during Christmas week, Easter week or on BH. Access on Sat and Sun restricted to Friends of the garden and affiliated groups, or to parties by special arrangement with the curator.

ADMISSION: free. Coach parties by arrangement with the curator

CAR PARKING: in North Road or adjacent roads

TOILETS: yes

REFRESHMENTS: teas supplied for parties by arrangement

SHOP: no

DOGS: no

WHEELCHAIR ACCESS: yes, to most of the garden. Toilets for the disabled: yes

PEAK MONTHS: May to September

NOTABLE FEATURES: glasshouses with fine collections of tender plants, mature formal and landscaped garden, ponds, rock garden, nursery area, plant collections, including range of plants from south-western region under threat of extinction

The University of Bristol Botanic Garden was established at Bracken Hill in 1959, two previous gardens (the first begun in 1882 by Adolph Leipner, the University's first professor of botany, and the second developed in 1938 as a field garden) having been sacrificed for the development of university buildings.

The original layout and some mature trees in the 5-acre garden at Bracken Hill (a sizeable house built for a Mr Melville Wills in 1886) have been largely retained, but since 1970 very extensive development has been carried out, all the wooden-framed plant houses being replaced with low-maintenance aluminium structures. Areas of the garden have been modified to provide ecological and conservation displays, with the aim of presenting the widest possible range of plants for educational and research purposes.

In spite of its pleasant surroundings in a spacious, wooded Victorian suburb, the climate and soil of the garden are not ideal; the soil is a silty clay of pH 7.8 (which necessitates a specially prepared bed of more acid soil for the garden's small collection of ericaceous plants) while the climate tends to cold wet winters and dry summers. Moreover, the location of the garden on high ground above the gorge of the River Avon means that it is exposed to high winds. Nevertheless, the garden flourishes under the care of the curator and his 2 full-time staff, helped by 2 horticultural students and some devoted volunteers.

Additions are constantly made to the garden's 4000 species and the planting is pushed to its limits, with many tender specimens growing out of doors in summer and taken inside in winter. The garden also maintains an extensive seed store, sending out and receiving seeds from 200 botanic gardens throughout the world. An advice and teachin centre within the grounds provides a range of courses in horticulture, botany and conservation.

Because its purpose is to engage the mind as well as to please the eye, the garden is always interesting, as there will always be some species of plants flourishing even in the extremes of weather. When we visited, late in an exceptionally hot dry summer, the Australasian yuccas, cordylines and phormiums in the monocotyledon beds were, not surprisingly, doing well, as were the windmill palms (*Trachycarpus fortunei*) near the entrance. Some of the rare English wetland plants in the pond areas nearby were not at their best but we could still see some interesting native specimens, such as the greater fen sedge, marsh pea and milk parsley as well as the more exotic *Gunnera manicata* from South America.

The recommended route leads on from this damp garden through stone arches, under the shade of a copper beech and a Chinese poplar (*P. lasiocarpa*) which has heart-shaped, red-veined leaves. You emerge on to a wide lawn sloping down from the north face of the house, which contains beds and borders and a deep pool flanked by a high peat mound. This provides a home to acid lovers, notably the Chilean flame tree (*Embothrium coccineum*).

In the bed along the wall at the foot of the lawn is a selection of plants which spread before setting leaves; among them, the musk thistle (*Carduus nutans*) with spiky leaves and *Morina betanicoides*, a member of the scabious family, with pale pink hanging tubular flowers, spiny bracts and leaves.

This area also features a bed of bamboos (arundinaria species) and grasses (carex and festuca spp.). Walking past these beds you come to one of the original features—a large Victorian rock garden, rather overshadowed by a Californian redwood, a Deodar cedar and a cedar of Lebanon.

The main lawn above the house, to the south, is laid out with attractive specimen trees: among others, a tulip tree (*Liriodendron tulipifera*), a blue cedar (*C. Atlantica glauca*) a silver wattle (*Acacia dealbata*), a paperbark maple (*Acer griseum*) and a loquat or Japanese medlar (*Eriobotrya japonica*). Here too are specialist rock beds containing plants and shrubs from New Zealand, South Africa and Mexico and Australia. In one Australian bed is a blue foliaged *Eucalyptus perrinniana*, a callistemon (bottle brush bush) and a spider flower (*Grevillea sulphurea*) with needle-like leaves and canary yellow flowers. Other beds contain rare and endangered species from the locality, including the Bristol onion (*Allium sphaerocephalon*).

In this area there are also collections of plants from other parts of the British Isles, including Cornwall and Wales, and further on specialist beds including a large border of hebes. Nearby, on the lawn, is a mulberry (*Morus nigra*) and a golden rain tree (*Koelreuteria paniculata*).

The garden's emphasis on local plants continues in the formal garden, a peaceful area with a rectangular lily pond. Near the semicircular Hiat Cowles Baker memorial (moved from the original Field Garden) are more scarce species from the south-west counties. There are also raised beds of shrub roses and herbaceous plants, and Australian acacias against the wall.

Beyond the formal garden a long herbaceous border runs the length of a series of glasshouses. Many seeds used for propagation and exchange are grown in this border, which forms a link between the garden areas surrounding the house and the more obviously educational and nursery features. Branching left, you can see new plantings of native trees and shrubs including the local Bristol whitebeam. Near here is a nursery for young trees, including more exotic species, such as a young *Sequoiadendron giganteum* and a sweet gum (*Liquidambar styraciflua*). The beds along the wall provide a well-labelled display of poisonous native plants including the curious thornapple (*Datura stramonium*) with its hard, green, prickly seed head. This collection merges, perhaps somewhat riskily, into a herb bed. These borders are laid out for interest and instruction, rather than combinations of form and colour.

After passing a triangular bed of young conifers, which have to be replaced frequently when they grow too large, you enter the kitchen garden area where there are beds for seed production and displays of annuals, perennials and wild flowers. A sizeable fruit cage is arranged to demonstrate different pruning methods used on fruit trees, fruit bushes and vines. Nearby are terraces with narrow pools and ditches where you can find a variety of aquatics and near these, in appropriately dry sections, an unusual display of sand dune plants as well as alpines and a large collection of houseleeks (sempervivums). Along the south-facing wall at the bottom of the kitchen garden is an interesting range of shrubs and flowering plants from warm climates, many of which have to be brought indoors in the winter.

The glasshouses have been put last on the itinerary and they make a spectacular finale to the tour. The first (lean-to) house is filled to its limits with plants which enjoy tropical heat: colourful bromeliads and orchids, bougainvillea (a deep purple was in bloom on our visit) and papyrus. There are examples of many foliage plants now commonly used as house plants (coleus and impatiens) and under the stagings, shade-loving plants suitable for the home. Creepers and hanging baskets flourish overhead, and ferns and mosses underfoot, in the waterbeds below the gratings.

The range and variety of cacti and succulents in the central glasshouse bears comparison with those in many larger gardens. Insectivorous plants, grown in sphagnum moss, shaded in summer and fed only with rain water are another specialist group in this house, which caters for plants that can stand low winter temperatures. There are stinging plants (well labelled) and plants that move in response to touch.

The top house, largely used for propagation, displays unusual types of houseplant. The fern house, on the other side of the path, offers many graceful and distinctive varieties from the wood fern (dryopteris), spleenwort (asplenium) and maidenhair (adiantum) species to the curious one-leaved South African streptocarpus.

On your way back to the entrance gate, you can see one of the garden's specialist interests: a collection of cistus planted on rocky banks.

The botanic garden provides a thriving resource centre for the university, the town and the surrounding areas, and is also a pleasant and stimulating place for anyone to visit.

Enquiries concerning becoming a Friend of the Garden can be made by post direct to the curator, or on visiting the garden, by approaching any of the garden staff.

The Manor House

ADDRESS AND TELEPHONE: Walton in Gordano, Clevedon, Avon BS21 7AN. Tel. Clevedon (0272) 872067

OWNERS: Mr and Mrs Simon Wills

DIRECTIONS: entrance by first house on N side of B3124 from Clevedon. Public Transport: Clevedon to Portishead buses stop in the village

OPENING TIMES: mid April to mid September, Wed and Thurs 10–4, Sun and Mon, May and August BH weekends 2–6. Open by appointment all year. House not open

ADMISSION: £1, accompanied children under 14 free. Coach parties by prior arrangement

CAR PARKING: yes

TOILETS: yes

REFRESHMENTS: no

SHOP: no, but plants for sale

DOGS: no

WHEELCHAIR ACCESS: yes to most of garden. Toilets for the disabled: no

PEAK MONTHS: May to June

NOTABLE FEATURES: plantsperson's garden with many unusual trees and plants; formal paved pool garden, lawns with specimen shrubs and trees, white garden, silver garden, background of established conifers and broadleaved trees

This garden is an outstanding example of the high standard of planting to be found in many of the 2000 gardens open under the National Gardens Scheme. Rare specimens are planted here, many of them grown from seeds collected by the owners on their travels to Nepal, South America, North America, Greece and Turkey. The garden also has a very beautiful setting—a peaceful valley not far from Bristol.

The Manor House was built c 1700. In the 1770s it was owned

by Sir John Durbin, the Lord Mayor of Bristol, and later passed to the Miles family, who were Bristol bankers. The pillared porch was built by the present owners, Mr and Mrs Wills, who came to live here in 1976. With its grey stone façade and elegant windows (the south windows date from the 18C) it provides an unobtrusive but distinctive background for the front gardens.

The visitor enters through an avenue of cypress oaks (*Quercus robur* 'Fastigiata'). A tulip tree (*Liriodendron tulipifera*) stands on the lawn to the left and a 103ft London plane (*Platanus* x *acerifolia*) to the right. On the lawn near the house an outstanding specimen of *Cornus controversa* 'Variegata' creates a sculptural effect with its layers of dappled foliage.

To the right of the porch lies a gravelled bed of silver shrubs and plants: a tall globe artichoke, a giant thistle, rosemary, lavender and mounds of the blue grass *Heliciorichon sempervirens*. There are also many different forms of *Iris unguicularis*, the Algerian iris. An unusual specimen here is the bead tree (*Melia azederach*), which has lilac flowers and yellow, egg-shaped (poisonous) fruits. Also growing against the wall we saw the yellow flowers of *Fremontodendron californicum* 'California Glory' and a ceanothus backed by *Vitis vinifera* 'Purpurea', the decorative purple and silver vine.

In the White Border the other side of the porch we noticed a snowbell tree (*Styrax wilsonii*) grown from seed, an American tree anemone (*Carpenteria californica*) and on the house wall above the bright orange tubular flowers of the Chilean glory flower (*Eccremocarpus scaber*). There is an unusual gold variety of *Iris pallida*, the variegated iris, and a most attractive campanula, *C. alliariifolia* 'Ivory Bells'. Later in the summer the white bells of *Galtonia candicans* replace the earlier flowers. The evergreen clematis *C. armandii* displays its pink and white apple-blossom flowers against the wall in early summer, with the green, pink and white leaves of *Actinidia kolomikta*, succeeded by the bright trumpet flowers of the trumpet creeper (*Campsis radicans*).

Also to the front of the house are an orchard and a spring garden, where you can see hellebores, trilliums, primulas and the hooded spathes of arisarums. Arisarum flowers are insignificant, but the berries are usually bright orange or red. These slightly menacing but fascinating plants are a speciality which Mr and Mrs Wills grow in rich soil in a cold frame for transplanting to the garden.

The main, North Garden lies on a slope to the side of the house, sheltered by a substantial belt of trees, both broad-leaved and coniferous. These are not just background; shrubs have been added to give brilliant foliage effects. In one grouping, gold conifers are set against blue spruce and a purple-leaved filbert (*Corylus maxima* 'Purpurea'), with bamboos and a pink-flowering deutzia. Further down the slope the bright lime-green leaves of *Robinia pseudoacacia* 'Frisia' contrast with a purple smoke tree (*Cotinus coggygria*) and a silver and green euonymus. A white single climbing rose has grown up into a blue *Chamaecyparis lawsoniana*, above a variegated, pink-flowering weigela. A blue-grey *Eucalyptus gunnei* nearby contrasts with a golden Irish yew.

Within this protective barrier lie the French lawns: wide expanses of grass containing island beds of shrubs and plants and individual specimen trees. The grass is cut to two mowing heights, so that clipped paths lead between the 'wilder' areas. On the north lawn we saw a dawn redwood (*Metasequoia glyptostroboides*), three silver-leaved buffalo berries (*Shepherdia argentea*), a crab apple with bright and tasty fruits (malus 'John Downie'), the Chinese paper birch (*Betula albo-sinensis*) and a sweet gum (*Liquidambar styraciflua*), which produces orange, crimson and purple leaves in autumn. There are birches and willows, a tooth-leaved zelkova, an unusual horse chestnut (*Aesculus discolor*), several different cercis species, Judas trees and many more.

The south lawn shows the same profusion of planting, including a silver leaved pear of erect habit (*Pyrus elaeagrifolia*), with the vivid pink-barred clematis 'Capitaine Thuilleaux' growing through it, and a graceful Himalayan cedar (*Cedrus deodara*). In this area we noticed two red Dawyck beeches and nearby a true blue iris (*I.songarica*), purple violas and the gold hosta 'Sunpower'. Also here are the pale green starry bracts of *Cornus kousa* and two *Parrotia persica*—graceful spreading members of the witch-hazel family which colour brilliantly in autumn. Everyone will make their own voyage of discovery in these lawns, finding the unexpected specimen, the unanticipated combination of familiar and unfamiliar plants. Helpfully, most of the trees and shrubs are labelled.

In a sheltered spot beneath the east bank is the Old Rockery, planted in brilliant colours: mauve Jerusalem sage (*Phlomis purpurea*) teamed with a purple rock rose (*Cistus albidus*) and a flame red helianthemum. Nearby we saw pale lilac parahebe 'Lyallii'.

At the foot of the two lawns, separated from them by a grass path and a drystone wall planted with alpines, lies the Pool Garden, surrounded by yew hedges. This is the only formal area and is dominated by an 85ft monkey puzzle tree (*Araucaria araucana*), with a straight knotted trunk and an umbrella head of dark foliage. The centrepieces are rectangular lily ponds with red, pink and white water lilies. They are flanked by gravel beds, rectangles of grass and four standard wisteria. Sun-loving plants grow through the gravel, with the emphasis on pinks, blues and whites. There is much silver foliage and many varieties of sweet smelling dianthus: red, pink, white, pink splashed with red and pink striped with cherry. The seat at the eastern end gives a full view down the length of this orderly and pleasant garden.

Behind the Pool Garden lies the North Wall Border, which has a small carob (*Ceratonia siliqua*) and a loquat (*Eriobotrya japonica*), both grown from seeds collected in Crete by Mr and Mrs Wills. Nearer the house there is a further lawn with a mixed bed planted for autumn colour: *Sorbus hupehensis* with pink and white fruits and orange and red leaves and *Hoheria sextylosa*, a glossy evergreen, both show up well against the blue-green of a *eucalyptus*. There are bunker beds, fruit beds and a red bed, and against the house a pergola with wisteria and a dark-foliaged jasmine growing over it. *Actinidia chinensis*, the Chinese gooseberry, grows on the house wall nearby.

It is only possible in a brief account to give an indication of the rewards to be found when visiting this garden. Mr and Mrs Wills are constantly making additions and alterations, so there will always be more to see.

BEDFORDSHIRE

Luton Hoo

ADDRESS AND TELEPHONE: Luton Hoo, Luton, Bedfordshire. Tel: Luton (0582) 22955

OWNERS: The Wernher Family

DIRECTIONS: 2 miles SE of Luton (30 miles from London) off A6129. Public Transport: Luton BR, 2 miles

OPENING TIMES: 26 March to 13 October, Tues to Sun. Closed Mon, except BH when opens 10.30. Gardens 12–6, house 1.30–5.45

ADMISSION: house and garden £3.70, OAPs £3.20, children £1.50; garden only £1.60, OAPs £1.35, children 50p. Reduced rates for pre-booked parties

CAR PARKING: yes

TOILETS: yes

REFRESHMENTS: restaurant

SHOP: yes

DOGS: no, except guide dogs

WHEELCHAIR ACCESS: limited because of steps. Toilets for the disabled: yes

PEAK SEASON: June and July for terraced gardens. Rock garden no special peak

NOTABLE FEATURES: parkland by Lancelot Brown with lake, lawns and trees; terraced gardens with herbaceous and rose garden; rock garden; fine trees

Luton Hoo is well known as the home of the Wernher Collection, which was begun late last century by Sir Julius Wernher and now includes masterpieces by Rembrandt, Titian and others; magnificent tapestries and furniture, medieval ivories and 16C jewels, bronzes, majolicas and English porcelain. It also houses a unique collection of jewelled objects by Carl Fabergé—the only collection of Fabergé's work on public view in Great Britain—brought to Luton Hoo by the late Zia Wernher, daughter of the Grand Duke Michaël Mikhailovitch and Countess de Torby.

The 3rd Earl of Bute, on returning to Luton Hoo in the 1760s, commissioned the architect Robert Adam to build the house. Remodelled again c 1827 by Smirke, largely rebuilt after a fire in 1843 and altered again in 1903 by Mewes and Davis, it remains a very impressive mansion.

The 1500-acre parkland was landscaped as a setting for the 3rd Earl's new mansion between 1764 and 1770 by Lancelot 'Capability' Brown and is a good example of his work. By damming the River Lea, Brown created a long serpentine lake to the east. He also planted clumps or 'rounds' of oak, ash and beech trees on the lawns sweeping down to the lake and merged the park into the surrounding countryside with more tree planting. Further tree planting, especially of cedars, was carried out in the 18C.

Two large formal terraces were laid out to the south of the house early this century, to designs by the architect Romaine-Walker. Both feature a clever combination of stonework, balustrading and ornaments, with intriguing planting designs.

The upper terrace comprises two rectangular lawns, each with a stone vase of colourful bedding and framed by gravel paths. Surrounding the whole are deep, lush herbaceous borders brimming with phlox, sedums, peonies, dahlias and other flowers of mostly soft colours, but with occasionally dark shades—port-wine-coloured penstemons for instance. Nicotiana, petunias and other annuals fill in any spaces to give an attractive summer display beneath the enclosing low walls. Light coloured stone vases along the top of the walls are set off by dark yew hedges behind.

Access to the lower terrace is gained by a broad, central, flight of steps, concave for the first part of the descent, convex for the second and interrupted half-way down by a circular landing with sundial. This brings you into one of the most beautifully designed rose gardens in England. Large geometric-shaped beds of soft pink, peach and lemon- coloured hybrid tea roses are surrounded by low box hedging, parterre-style. Box topiary and standard roses lend height to each bed and the design centres on an ornate fountain and round pool with water lilies.

Domed gazebos in the two far corners of the rose gardens overlook the parkland. Nearby, gate piers perfectly frame a cedar tree, which has unfortunately lost its main branch.

A feature frequently overlooked at Luton Hoo is the rock garden which lies hidden in trees and tall shrubs in the park. This garden was designed in the 1920s for Sir Julius Wernher as a surprise for his wife, and is reached by a path which meanders across the lawns from the terraced gardens.

Made in a dell, it features artificial cliffs and caverns with pools, streams and an arched stone bridge. There are dwarf conifers and brightly coloured acers, saxifrages, rock roses (helianthemums), small rhododendrons and so on. Hostas, primulas and other marginal and aquatic plants grow by the water. The garden includes a cool cave with boulder-like seats.

The Swiss Garden

ADDRESS AND TELEPHONE: The Swiss Garden, Old Warden, Biggleswade, Bedfordshire. Tel. Bedford (0234) 228330

OWNERS: leased to Bedfordshire County Council

DIRECTIONS: 2½ miles W of Biggleswade. On the Biggleswade to Old Warden Road

OPENING TIMES: April to October, Wed to Sun and BH Mon 1.30–6; last admission 5.15

ADMISSION: £1, OAPs and children 50p. Special rates available for parties on application

CAR PARKING: yes

TOILETS: yes

REFRESHMENTS: at adjoining Shuttleworth Aeroplane Collection and nearby Old Warden Village

SHOP: kiosk for guidebooks

DOGS: only in woodland walk

WHEELCHAIR ACCESS: yes. Toilets for the disabled: yes

PEAK SEASON: no special peak

NOTABLE FEATURES: thatched cottage, miniature chapel, grotto in informal setting; ornamental ponds and bridges; variety of trees and shrubs

The Swiss Garden was developed by the Ongley family, the 19C owners of Old Warden Park, and survives as an example of an early 19C garden showing strong influences of the Picturesque and Romantic.

The design and layout of this 8-acre garden reflect the fantasies and moods of the time, with shrubberies, groves and ponds used to separate or highlight numerous architectural features—chapel, well, grotto, summerhouse and so forth—and meandering paths connecting a series of intimate vistas. The Swiss Cottage itself stands on a knoll, near the centre of the garden.

Local tradition has it that the Swiss Cottage and Garden were built for a Swiss mistress of one of the Lords Ongley, but more probably the cottage and garden were created during the wave of enthusiasm for things Swiss that swept through England in the 1820s.

The 3rd Lord Ongley (1803–77) was mainly responsible for the early development of the garden. In 1872, he sold Old Warden Park to Joseph Shuttleworth, following which the Swiss garden was 'Victorianised' with bright flower beds near to the cottage, some remodelling of structures and further planting of specimen trees. Luckily neither the romantic layout or mood of the earlier garden were lost, but the 1939–45 war and the post-war period of economic hardship both left their mark.

Shortly after the war, the Shuttleworth Trust was established to manage the Old Warden estate and the famous Shuttleworth collection of historic aeroplanes on land adjoining the garden. But the garden itself, and particularly the structures, inevitably suffered from many years of minimal maintenance.

Little or nothing was done until 1976, when the garden was leased to the Leisure Committee of Bedfordshire County Council, which then assumed responsibility for its upkeep, restoration and management. While some of the smaller elements, such as bridges, still need attention, most of the major features have been restored and the garden is now open to the public.

The approach to the Swiss Garden is by a footpath, about 200 yds long, which runs through woodland before arriving at the garden entrance.

On a small grassy mound to the left of the entrance is one of the garden's most striking curiosities—a thatched kiosk, glazed in vivid colours—while on the opposite bank of the pond is the inevitable Victorian dog's cemetery, beneath a canopy of oak trees.

The route continues towards the three ornamental ponds. The upper pond drains into the middle, and the middle into the lower.

Little islands of hypericum and bergenias help to maintain the small scale and intimacy of this part of the garden. There are several humpbacked bridges, notably one between the upper and middle ponds, which is flanked by a pair of splendid Lawson cypresses (*Chamaecyparis lawsoniana* 'Erecta'). Elsewhere on the pond banks you can see a willow-leaved pear (*Pyrus salicifolia* 'Pendulaq) and a 70ft Swiss or Arolla pine (*Pinus cembra*).

From the ponds the East Walk follows the line of the garden boundary, skirting around the open expanse of the east lawn. Here you can see a huge English oak (*Quercus robur*); also a locust tree (*Robinia pseudoacacia*) and *Acer japonicum* 'Vitifolium'. On the opposite side of the path is the rock garden, planted with saxifrages, sedums and lilies.

The East Walk turns right into the South Walk, which features a huge cast iron urn dating from the last century, and continues past a splendid Wellingtonia (*Sequoiadendr giganteum*) to the Swiss Cottage itself.

The cottage is thought to date from the 1820s, although modifications have been made over the decades. The path leads directly onto the verandah, from which the main room can be viewed. The lower floor is reached by a sloping path to the rear of the cottage. Meals were probably prepared here by servants—as witness the bell pull.

The next garden feature is the tree shelter—a round seat and thatched canopy—constructed around the trunk of a huge oak tree. As well as the trees and shrubs already mentioned, you may also observe a fine specimen of the eastern hemlock (*Tsuga canadensis*) near to the terrace; elsewhere in the garden are incense cedars (*Calocedrus decurrens*) and deodar cedars (*Cedrus deodara*).

The well grove lies just a few steps past the wrought iron garden screen, marking the garden boundary, and from here you get an intriguing and 'prepared' view of the Swiss Cottage, on first appearance a single storey chalet. The well from which this glade takes its name is capped by a large Venetian-type Istriam marble well head, thought to be of early 19C origin.

Having walked through a shady yew tunnel, you arrive at a small chapel-like structure, in a dark setting of high embankments and heavy planting. Dating from the early 19C, this building is really a garden house, but its stained glass window and arched doorway give a somewhat ecclesiastical impression, which combines well with the melancholy atmosphere.

Continuing beyond the garden house or chapel, you follow a path that appears to end at a late Victorian wooden summerhouse. In fact it turns at right angles and leads onto an elevated walk or terrace, via cobbled steps. The terrace provides a further opportunity to view the Swiss Cottage, this time across domes of colourful pieris on the Cottage Lawn and with a fine backcloth of cedars and a Chilean pine or monkey puzzle (*Araucaria araucana*).

Next come the grotto and fernery, which are integrated in a large cruciform structure. Before 1977 this site was overgrown with self-set trees, which overhung and threatened the building, but these have been cleared and the exterior restored. A mysterious cave-like effect inside is created by the use of tufa stone, while the centrepiece or cross structure is a light glass and ironwork conservatory-style fernery. Do not be confused by the date of 1876 carved above the entrance doors—the grotto and fernery actually date from the early 1930s.

Emerging again into the daylight from the southern end of the grotto, you see the Swiss Cottage again, at the centre of the garden.

By turning left and following the path past the ponds, or right and past the cottage you will arrive back at the entrance kiosk.

Wrest Park

ADDRESS AND TELEPHONE: Wrest Park, Silsoe, Bedfordshire. Tel. (0525) 60718

OWNERS: English Heritage

DIRECTIONS: mid-way between Luton and Bedford (A6). Entrance via Silsoe village. Public Transport: Luton BR 9 miles. Buses from Luton, Bedford, Kettering to Silsoe. Sun and BH 'Leisure Link' direct to the door. Tel. (0234) 228336

OPENING TIMES: April to end September, Sat, Sun and all BHs 10–6. The Library, Entrance Hall and other state rooms are also open

ADMISSION: £1.35, OAPs and students 95p, children 60p. English Heritage members free. Coach parties welcome. Reductions for parties of 11 or more

CAR PARKING: yes

TOILETS: yes

REFRESHMENTS: yes

SHOP: yes

DOGS: on leads

WHEELCHAIR ACCESS: yes to gardens; steps to house. Toilets for the disabled: no

PEAK SEASON: no special peak

NOTABLE FEATURES: early 18C French style formal garden on grand scale; parterres; river by Brown; fine trees; herbaceous borders

Wrest Park is one of the few gardens in Britain to display 18C French formality on a grand scale—a style well suited to the flat landscape of this part of Bedfordshire. It was begun in 1706 by the 12th Earl of Kent (later created 1st Duke of Kent), its centrepiece being a formal canal known as the Long Water, framed either side by lawns and formal woodland. Through this woodland the Duke made a complex pattern of rides or *allées* focusing on urns, statuary or summerhouses at the various intersections. Thomas Archer designed the magnificent domed pavilion, which terminates the vista at the end of the canal, in 1710.

The house·for which this grand scheme was made no longer stands. By the 1830s it was falling into decay; its owner, Philip Yorke, 2nd Earl de Grey, had it demolished and a French Renaissance style 'château', designed by Clephane, was built some distance further back. New gardens were then created, to link this grand mansion with its old setting.

From the terraces, you get a fine view over the magnificent parterres. Scrolls of gravel and turf are highlighted with intricately patterned box-edged beds. Four large statues depicting mythological subjects add to the formal effect.

The broad central walk, flanked by more Portuguese laurels and statuary brought from the Great Exhibition of 1861, stretches across immaculate formal lawns to an ornate marble fountain, and beyond this to the Long Water. Woodland narrows the view and Archer's beautiful pavilion stands at the end of the vista.

The park covers some 90 acres in total. It is well worth walking down the long central vista to Archer's pavilion, which is considered one of the best examples of garden architecture in Britain. This temple-like structure is open to the public. The large middle room is painted with architectural features and figures in niches in *trompe d'oeil.*

Various features of architectural interest can be seen in the mature mixed woodland either side of the Long Water, including two large summerhouses known as the Half Houses and a variety of statues and monuments. Many of the rides are now in process of being freed from their overgrowth, to reveal the original sequence of vistas.

More architectural features can be seen in the gardens: about half-way down the western side stands an 18C Bowling Green House in Palladian style and decorated inside with superb plaster work. A little nearer the mansion, on a grass terrace, is the orangery, completed in 1836 and designed by the 2nd Earl de Grey.

Further west from the orangery is the Bath House, comprising two rustic circular buildings of rough hewn stone, one of deliberately 'ruined' appearance. Dating from about the mid 18C, the Bath House was possibly used for plunge bathing and has an intriguing patterned floor inlaid with bones. Outside, amid a dense growth of reeds and marginal plants, a cascade marks the start of Capability Brown's river.

Brown was commissioned to alter the garden between 1758 and 1760. Uncharacteristically, he left the formal gardens virtually untouched, and concentrated on making a serpentine river. This artificial water course almost encompasses the gardens, separating them from the parkland beyond and contributing an aspect of the 18C English landscape gardening style while maintaining the earlier French-style formality.

Brown also made a bridge across the river, but this was replaced in the late 19C. The nearby Chinese pavilion has been completely rebuilt within the last few years.

Visitors unable to explore the garden to its fullest extent will find other attractions closer to the house. The conservatory contains a selection of mainly flowering plants, and the adjacent Italian garden has been fully restored. The walled garden, built by the Earl de Grey, is not open to the public, but the fine wisteria, reputed to be one of the oldest in the country, spanning some 100ft, may be seen. Below the outer walls is a deep border of shrubs and herbaceous plants with climbing plants on the wall, including the

Judas trees (*Cercis siliquastrum*) which in May are smothered with rosy-lilac-coloured flowers.

In 1947 Wrest Park House and Gardens were purchased by the Ministry of Public Buildings and Works and leased to the ARFC Institute of Engineering Research. The gardens are cared for by English Heritage and the Research Institute. An ongoing programme of restoration is being undertaken by these two organisations and Land Use Consultants to ensure that Wrest Park will retain its important place in the history of British garden design.

BERKSHIRE

Savill Gardens

ADDRESS AND TELEPHONE: Crown Estate Commissioners, The Great Park, Windsor, Berkshire. Tel. Windsor (0753) 860222

OWNERS: Crown Estate Commissioners

DIRECTIONS: 4 miles S of Windsor, off A30 via Wick Road and Wick Lane in Englefield Green. Public transport: Egham station (Southern Region) 3 miles

OPENING TIMES: all year, except 25–26 December, daily 10–6 or sunset if earlier. House not open

ADMISSION: £2.20, accompanied children under 16 free. Reductions for pre-booked parties

CAR PARKING: yes; free if visiting gardens. Coaches by arrangement

TOILETS: yes

REFRESHMENTS: café

SHOP: yes

DOGS: no

WHEELCHAIR ACCESS: yes but difficult in parts. Toilets for the disabled: yes

PEAK MONTHS: peaks throughout the year but especially spectacular in spring

NOTABLE FEATURES: woodland garden with spring shrubs; herbaceous borders; rose garden; dry garden and peat garden; temperate house; water and stream garden; alpine meadow; autumn colour

The Savill Gardens lie just within the county boundary of Surrey in Windsor Great Park—35 acres of woodland planted with rhododendrons, shrubs and flowers. The park itself covers some 4500 acres and it is difficult to believe that its great plantings of forest trees have existed for only a couple of centuries. Before the 18C this area was a swampy wilderness; William, Duke of Cumberland, turned it into parkland, draining the swamp for landscaping and planting and in the process creating ponds and lakes, including the magnificent Virginia Water. During this period, many of the great forest trees were planted—beeches, oaks, and sweet chestnuts.

Eric Savill arrived in 1932 as deputy surveyor. A great horticulturist and landscaper, he created glades and vistas throughout the woodland and planted meadows of flowers. He also widened the stream and made the Upper and Lower Ponds. As a tribute to his work, King George VI declared, in 1951, that the gardens should be named after him.

The willow garden was one of the first areas that Savill tackled. Situated in the far north-west corner of the garden, it can be reached by following the richly planted stream uphill from the Upper Pond through the woodland beds—containing groups of azaleas and Japanese maples. The willow garden, beside the stream, is dominated by a large weeping willow, planted by Savill in 1932. Hundreds of drumstick primulas (*Primula denticulata*) flower to spectacular effect in spring. In March and April the skunk cabbages or bog arums are a striking sight with their golden (*Lysichiton americana*) and white (*L. camtschatcensis*) spathes.

Windsor Great Park has the National Collection of magnolias—as well as those of holly, dwarf conifers, rhododendron species, pieris, mahonia and hardy ferns. Here in the willow garden you can see *Magnolia cylindrica* (very rare), M. *campbellii mollicomata* and M. *liliiflora* 'Nigra'. In May, the latter bears flowers of deep purple outside, creamy-white and stained purple inside. The shrubs include several corylopsis and large mahonias. The callicarpas and acers are beautiful in autumn, with their colourful fruits and foliage.

Among the rhododendrons in the willow garden are attractive specimens like 'Blue Tit' and 'Elizabeth', but for a really spectacular and scented display, you should visit the temperate house between March and May. Here tender rhododendrons and various forms of *Camellia reticulata* can be seen, and the Tasmanian tree fern (*Dicksonia antarctica*). Tender ferns used as ground cover set off the rich colours.

West of the temperate house are herbaceous borders and rose gardens, planted on a site once used as a tree nursery. A long, broad, grassy walk runs between two wide herbaceous borders, planted for maximum effect of colour from July through to October. Herbaceous plants are staked unobtrusively with peasticks, and framed by foliage plants and ornamental grasses. In the middle of the broad walk is a willow-leaved podocarp (*Podocarpus chilinus*)—now an important focal point although it came from a box of unwanted seedlings left in a corner of the tree nursery.

The dry garden to the south of the herbaceous borders was begun in 1978, replacing an area of shrub roses. Tonnes of sandy gravel were dug into the previously moist soil, to accommodate a range of shrubs, herbaceous plants and bulbs from hotter, drier climates. To the west of the dry garden is a border containing a collection of day lilies (*hemerocallis sp*), and further on is an area of mixed roses, colourful in summer. A border of agapanthus 'Headbourne Hybrids' flowers blue and white in August and September.

On the other side of the broad walk an area of lawn is devoted to the display of modern hybrid tea roses in formal beds. These include the pretty coral pink fragrant 'Blessings', the beautiful golden yellow 'Freedom', and the coppery salmon pink 'Silver Jubilee'. A yew hedge and flowering shrubs forms a backcloth along one boundary and roses are trained along ropes and between pillars on the southern edge.

The northernmost boundary of Savill's garden is marked by a high brick wall richly draped with clematis, roses and many other climbing plants: purples, pinks, yellows and white. At the foot of the wall, raised beds provide suitable conditions for an extensive and well-labelled collection of alpines and other small plants. These are worth a look at any time of year.

This formal part of the garden, with its herbaceous borders, roses and raised beds, merges into the woodland beyond beds of floribunda roses on the western edge.

Grassy paths then tempt you off into the trees to enjoy the much more informal and natural plantings of rhododendrons, camellias and hydrangeas.

In the woodland garden, care has been taken to maintain the three-storey system of plantings. The magnificent tall trees which form the top storey have been thinned to provide perfect shade conditions for the plants below. The middle layer is formed by dramatic arrangements of the finest flowering and foliage shrubs, including rhododendrons, azaleas, camellias, magnolias and Japanese maples. The lowest storey consists of ground cover plants such as hostas, ferns and pulmonarias, and sub-shrubs like small evergreen azaleas, hydrangeas and gaulterias. Daffodils bloom here in spring.

Although the acid woodland soil is ideal for growing rhododendrons, the low annual rainfall of 22in. means they need a lot of watering. The true diversity of the genus can really be appreciated here, some with tiny, others with long paddle-shaped leaves; some forming small hummocks and others growing as trees 30–40ft tall.

The woodland garden also includes winter trees and shrubs such as *Hamamelis mollis* 'Pallida' with its large sulphur yellow flowers densely crowding the naked stems. In early spring the woods are set alight by scarlet pieris. In summer it is the turn of the hydrangeas and eucryphias and in autumn there are Japanese maples, liquidambars, linderas and other colourful trees and shrubs.

The alpine meadow is in full flower in March, with the nodding yellow heads of the Lent lilies (*Narcissus pseudonarcissus*), the cyclamen flowered *Narcissus cyclamineus* and lemon-yellow *Narcissus bulbocodium citrinus*.

Other striking areas are the peat garden (best in spring) an area of moisture-loving plants near to the lower pond, and the Jubilee garden, which you can reach by crossing the Jubilee bridge over the lower pond. Planted to commemorate the Silver Jubilee of Queen Elizabeth II, this garden features plants good for autumn foliage and berries.

The Savill Gardens demonstrate very high standards of horticultural practice and garden design. Considerable efforts are made to keep the garden well stocked, and planted. Although many trees and shrubs were lost in the storm of October 1987, the damage was quickly dealt with, and areas such the Friends Grove of silver lime trees (*Tilia tomentosa*) have been extensively redeveloped.

Swallowfield Park

ADDRESS AND TELEPHONE: Swallowfield Park, Reading, Berkshire RG7 1TG. Tel. (0734) 883815

OWNERS: Country Houses Association Ltd

DIRECTIONS: in village of Swallowfield, 6 miles SE of Reading. Public transport: Reading BR 6 miles. Buses from Reading

OPENING TIMES: May to September, Wed and Thurs 2–5. House also open

ADMISSION: £1.50, children 50p. Coach parties by prior arrangement

CAR PARKING: yes

TOILETS: yes

REFRESHMENTS: no

SHOP: no (guidebooks available)

DOGS: no

WHEELCHAIR ACCESS: yes. Toilets for the disabled: no

PEAK SEASON: no special peak

NOTABLE FEATURES: walled garden with wild garden and ornamental garden; 25-acre grounds with various mature trees

Swallowfield has a long history; it was mentioned as Soanesfelt or Swalfelle in the Domesday survey. The fine country house dates from 1678, although it has since been considerably altered, and is now converted into apartments.

John Evelyn visited Lord and Lady Clarendon at Swallowfield in 1685. He wrote:

> ...the gardens and walks are as elegant as 'tis possible to make by art and industrie and no meane expense, my Lady being extraordinarily skill'd in the flowering part, and my Lord in diligence of planting so that I have hardly seen a seate which shows more tokens of it than what is to be found here, not only in the delicious and rarest fruite of the garden, but in those innumerable timber in the ground about the seate, to the greatest ornament and benefit of the place.

There is one orchard of 1000 golden and other cider pippins; walks and groves of elms, limes, oaks and other trees. The garden is so beset with all manor of sweete shrubbs that it perfumes the aire. The distribution of the walk and parterres is excellent; the nurseries, kitchen garden, full of the most desirable plants; two very noble orangeries, well furnished.... There is also a certaine sweete willow and other exotics, also a very fine bowling greene, meadow, pasture and wood; in a word, all that can render a country seate delightful.

Today there are neither parterres nor orangeries. Swallowfield's chief feature is its walled garden west of the house. This was partially restored in June 1989 as part of the BBC 'Challenge Anneka' programme.

When the BBC team arrived, large parts of the wall, dating from 1722, needed rebuilding, and some sections had crumbled away.

The wild garden was a wilderness and the ornamental garden an overgrown jungle of grasses and brambles.

The BBC called in the television and radio garden expert, Alan Titchmarsh, garden designer David Stevens, a team of volunteer students from the Capel Manor Centre of Horticultural Education and trainee builders from the Reading College of Technology.

Damaged sections of the surrounding wall were rebuilt, brambles and weeds cleared, turf laid and the dilapidated pergola repaired. Hilliers' Nursery at Winchester supplied 30 bush apples, 25 flowering cherries, 30 laburnums, 20 wisteries, 50 mixed shrubs, 25 climbing roses, 175 rose bushes, 4 standard roses, 150 herbaceous plants, 200 santolinas and lavenders and 300 ground cover plants.

The walled garden is approached by a broad gravel walk flanked by old Irish yews clipped as cylinders and leading to the Italian Gate. This imposing and highly ornate archway is believed to have been brought from Italy by the 2nd Baronet, Sir Henry Russell, in the early 19C.

The wild garden, directly inside the gate, is filled with fruiting and decorative trees, including many apples and oaks, underplanted with a dense mixture of mahonias, berberis, shrub roses, hypericums and other flowering shrubs. Primroses, daffodils and bluebells appear in spring through a carpet of ground ivy and dog mercury. A central path leads straight through the wild garden, other paths meandering off to either side.

The walled garden is divided into two by a row of yew trees which forms a loose boundary between the wild garden and the ornamental garden created by the 'Challenge Anneka' team, which now features a hexagonal shaped conservatory surrounded by lawns and colourful beds of shrubs, roses and herbaceous plants.

Behind the conservatory is the newly restored pergola, now supporting a mixture of laburnums and wisterias interplanted with climbing roses for colour. Among the roses is 'Swan Lake', perhaps the best of all white climbers, with blooms that are unlikely to spoil in wet weather. The rose pink flowering 'Aloha' is also here, along with the orange-scarlet 'Danse du Feu' and the fragrant primrose yellow blooming 'Mermaid'. At the end is a statue of a boy holding a bird's nest.

Much of the remainder of this garden is laid out as orchard. Some old fruit trees have been saved, with 'Blenheim Orange' and 'Cox's Orange Pippin' added for variety, and a plentiful sprinkling of wild flowers beneath.

As late as 1917, Swallowfield had a staff of 16 gardeners and the park was famous for its exhibits of fruit at London shows. The grounds were well kept, with tended flower beds and greenhouses; even the driveway was swept twice weekly. Now there are just two handymen, who have duties other than gardening. Maintenance work has to be kept to a minimum, so lawn areas planted with clumps of rhododendrons and shrubberies take preference over flower beds and borders.

The south front overlooks broad sweeps of lawn with fine mature cedars of Lebanon (*Cedrus libani*). Northwards, behind the house, is a croquet lawn, and to one side of this is an Indian bean tree (*Catalpa bignonioides*) which, having fallen over, has re-rooted itself in several places. Other trees can be seen along the gravel walks leading northwards to the lake. These include fine specimens of holm oak (*Quercus ilex*) and lucombe oak (*Quercus* x *hispanica* 'Lucombeana'), weeping ash (*Fraxinus excelsior* 'Pendula'), walnut (*Juglans regia*), false acacia (*Robinia pseudoacacia*) and several beeches and magnolias. More recent planting includes a sweet gum (*Liquidambar styraciflua*) and a Persian ironwood (*Parrotia persica*), which are renowned for their autumn colours.

Among the conifers are Austrian pines (*Pinus nigra*), Douglas fir (*Pseudotsuga menziesii*), Lawson cypress (*Chamaecyparis lawsoniana*), Nootka cypress (*Chamaecyparis nootkatensis*), and swamp cypress (*Taxodium distichum*). There are also fine Atlas cedars (*Cedrus altantica glauca*) and around the lake itself are limes, poplars and laburnums. For the adventurous visitor there is a woodland walk to the River Loddon.

Since 1965 Swallowfield Park has been owned by the Mutual Households Association, now known as the Country Houses Association. This independent charity is concerned with the restoration and preservation of historic houses.

Valley Gardens

ADDRESS AND TELEPHONE: Crown Estate Commissioners, The Great Park, Windsor, Berkshire. Tel. Windsor (0753) 860222

OWNERS: Crown Estate Commissioners

DIRECTIONS: 4 miles S of Windsor. Entrance in Wick Road off the A30 near Egham

OPENING TIMES: all year round, daily, dawn to dusk. House not open

ADMISSION: no charge for pedestrians (garden is about a mile walk from Wick Road entrance).

CAR PARKING: yes, £2. Coaches by prior arrangement

TOILETS: yes

REFRESHMENTS: no, but available at nearby Savill Garden

SHOP: no, but at nearby Savill Garden

DOGS: yes

WHEELCHAIR ACCESS: difficult because of lawns, dirt paths and steep slopes. Toilets for the disabled: yes

PEAK MONTHS: peaks throughout the year but especially spectacular in spring (rhododendrons and azaleas) and for autumn colour

NOTABLE FEATURES: displays of rhododendrons and azaleas; National Collection of hollies, dwarf conifers and magnolias; National Collection of rhododendron species; woodland garden; heather garden; spring shrubs and plants; autumn colours

The Valley Gardens of Windsor Great Park were developed from 1947 onwards by Eric Savill (who also created the Savill Garden, half a mile away). Gently sloping and undulating, they lie on the northern side of Virginia Water Lake. During the 1939–45 war the lake was drained, to prevent it being used by bombers as a landmark. At that time the northern banks were a dense impenetrable jungle of *Rhododendron ponticum* and seedlings of birch and sycamore below a canopy of tall trees—oaks, chestnuts and pines—many planted by the Duke of Cumberland in the 18C. Helped by other leading gardeners, Savill cleared the land and established an informal woodland garden.

A canopy of mature trees now shelters a wide range of woodland shrubs and plants, selected to provide colour and interest all the year round. Spring and autumn are the peak seasons but summer is brightened by masses of hydrangeas, and witch-hazels (hamamelis) bloom delicate and fragrant in winter, along with winter-flowerlng viburnums and mahonias. Windsor Great Park also houses the National Collections of magnolias, rhododendron species, dwarf conifers and hollies.

The Valley Gardens are divided into three main areas, connected by rides and walks. Besides the main Valley Garden, there is a heather garden (created in a former gravel pit in 1954), and a third area containing the rhododendron species collection.

Rhododendrons, both species and hybrids, dominate the gardens. Spectacular displays begin in January, peak in May and June and linger into July and August. Windsor-raised hybrids can be seen in one part of the valley while another area is devoted to older hybrids. All the *Rhododendron* x *loderi* hybrids have been grouped together, as have June-July flowering hybrids. There is an important conservation aspect to the planting since many of these rhododendron species and hybrids are in danger of disappearing.

Thousands of evergreen azaleas have been planted in a natural amphitheatre known as the Punch Bowl over looking Virginia Water Lake and many more, including the taller deciduous types, can be found in the azalea valley. The Knaphill and Exbury varieties grow here as well as the Ghent hybrids from Belgium. Between March and May, camellias blossom in white, pink and scarlet; some are low and compact bushes, others grow as tall as 18ft.

Magnolias are planted throughout the gardens, sometimes singly and sometimes in groups. *Magnolia stellata* and *M. salicifolia* are among the first to flower, in March, followed by *M. campbellii* and *M.* x *soulangeana*. *M. sieboldii* produces its fragrant white flowers from May to August, accompanied in June by *M. sinensis*, with red-stamened white flowers, smelling of lemon. In April the striking affect is added to by flowering cherries such as *Prunus avium* 'Plena' and *P. sargentii*. On the north-western edge of the gardens are several acres of hydrangeas—a dramatic sight in July and August.

Japanese maples (*Acer japonicum* and *A. palmatum*) are scattered throughout the garden and sweet chestnuts, cherries and liquidambars contribute further glorious autumn colour, as do bright-berried cotoneasters and rowans. To the west of the azalea garden is the National Collection of hollies, which includes many hardy species and different forms of *Ilex aquifolium* and several new American-raised hybrids. Just beyond this, you can find the National Collection of rhododendron species—first established between 1900 and 1950 by John Barr Stevenson at Tower Court, Ascot, and acquired on Stevenson's death in 1951 by the Crown

Estate Commissioners. All the species have been indexed—very important for conservation purposes.

From the rhododendron collection it is a short walk via the pinetum to the heather garden. This was the site of a gravel pit until the 1914–18 war, after which it was slowly colonised. Informal plantings of heathers and heaths were made in 1954 with conifers. Between January and April you can see rose-red *Erica carnea, E. mediterranea* and several hybrids in flower. The second peak comes from June to October with varieties of *Calluna vulgaris*, the Cornish heath *E. vagans* and rose-purple Connemara heath (*Daboecia cantabrica*). More conifers, this time dwarf and slower growing types, can be found in a collection to the north-east.

BUCKINGHAMSHIRE

Ascott

ADDRESS AND TELEPHONE: Wing, near Leighton Buzzard, Buckinghamshire LU7 OPS. Tel. Aylesbury (0296) 688242

OWNERS: The National Trust

DIRECTIONS: ½ mile E of Wing, 2 miles SW of Leighton Buzzard, on S side of A418. Public transport: bus from Aylesbury, Leighton Buzzard (passing close Aylesbury BR and Leighton Buzzard), alight house on some services, or Wing Village Hall, ½ mile. Leighton Buzzard station, 2 miles

OPENING TIMES: house and gardens, mid April to mid May and September, Tues to Sun 2–6 and 2 BH Mons; also gardens only mid May to late August, every Wed and last Sun in each month and August BH Mon 2–6. Last admission 5.30. Closed Tues after BH Mon. Other open days vary; ring for exact details

ADMISSION: gardens only £2.20, children £1; house and gardens £3.80, children £2. Coach parties must book in advance (no reductions)

CAR PARKING: yes, 220 yds

TOILETS: yes

REFRESHMENTS: no

SHOP: no

DOGS: in car park only

WHEELCHAIR ACCESS: limited. Toilets for the disabled: no

Although not one of the National Trust's most famous gardens, Ascott is certainly one of the most striking. Notable for its many lovely mature trees and shrubs and its wide lawned terraces, it is also beautiful in spring, alight with daffodils and many other naturalised bulbs—crocuses, anemones, tulips, fritillaries and scillas.

Both gardens and house date mainly from the late 19C, although parts of the house survive from 1606. Leopold de Rothschild laid out the gardens, advised by the horticulturist Sir Harry Veitch of

Chelsea; and Mr and Mrs Anthony de Rothschild donated Ascott to the National Trust in 1950.

Two anguished-looking dog statues guard the entrance drive, which curves through trees towards the stableyard and house. Eight umbrella-shaped Portuguese laurels form a sedate avenue directly in front of the house: fuchsias, rugosa roses and cotoneaster grow near the door.

If you plan to visit the enormous fish pond, be warned: this part of the garden is isolated from the rest by a curious trick of design and you will have to retrace your steps back to the house. However, the grassy walk is pleasant, bordered by yew hedges and a steep sloping bank, with pines and other conifers above. The shrubs include potentillas, cotinus (smoke bush) and pinky-red *Berberis thunbergii*.

The pond itself is well stocked with fish, including valuable Koi carp, crammed with waterlilies (these were being cleared at the time we visited) and bordered by moisture-loving plants, such as astilbes, primulas and hostas. Willows overhang the water, backed by copper beeches and making a fine foliage contrast with tall bushes of golden privet.

Walking round the east side of the house, through new plantings of shrubs, you come to a series of grassy terraces, planted with superb specimen trees, including a weeping beech, copper beeches and a blue cedar (*Cedrus atlantica glauca*). A golden cedar (*C. atlantica* 'Aurea'), unusually well grown and spectacular, stands further down the slopes, shimmering gold and green. Beyond this, to the east, is a remarkable topiary sundial, featuring the quotation—'Light and shade by turn but love always'. The views to the south are superb, over fields and countryside.

Formal and informal areas are effortlessly combined at Ascott, with the help of well-placed hedges and topiary. A hedge of gold variegated holly runs along the lower terrace, with golden yew cones at each end: from here you can look down onto the Madeira Walk, with its straight flower borders and summerhouse. The wall directly below is well dressed with tender shrubs and climbers such as roses and honeysuckle.

The border flowers are mainly delicate shades of purple, pink and blue. In late summer, we saw elegant purple statice (sea lavender) and delicate rosy-purple thalictrum (dwarf meadow rue), *Romneya coulteri*, the California tree poppy, with brilliant white flowers and a central boss of golden stamens and agapanthus, the African blue lily. Sedum 'Autumn Joy' was just flushing pink, near to *Campanula lactiflora*, the milky bellflower, and *Abutilon vitifolium*, a vigorous climber with saucer-shaped flowers and felted leaves. The roses include creamy-pink 'Gruss an Aachen', with double flowers fading to creamy-white, and *Rosa violette*, a rambler with tiny purplish-mauve flowers.

Steps lead down to the small pool and a magnificent fountain by Waldo Storey. The steps are accompanied by low box hedging, punctuated with golden domes of yew and underplanted with artemisia. Golden yew hedges surround the circular fountain area: the beds beneath were planted with cosmos, delicate and colourful.

The fountain itself is extraordinary, in true Waldo Storey style (more examples of his work can be seen at nearby Cliveden). Two enormous sea horses, spouting water from their mouths, drag a huge shell containing a vigorous Venus attended by winged cherubs. In the Dutch garden, to the west, you'll find another very interesting though less extravagant bronze fountain: a three-tiered affair surmounted by a cupid, decorated with lion heads and dolphins and set in a scalloped pool.

The Dutch garden is situated at a considerable distance from the house. Walking westwards across the lawned terraces from Madeira Walk, past blue cedars tastefully interspersed with topiary pieces, we came across a very lovely small specimen of *Betula albo-sinensis septentrionalis*, a Chinese tree with very attractive bark and silky leaves. This whole area was planted with young specimens, including cedars, weeping and copper beeches, clipped golden yew and variegated holly.

The Dutch garden itself is distinguished by geometric beds of bright flowers, renewed twice a year, and straight gravel paths. The fountain stands in a big sunken circle at the north end, the surrounding banks crowned with cedars and red acers. The rockery bank, of tufa and Cheddar limestone, was completed in 1896. Tufa (a porous rock formed around mineral springs) was also used to create the small grotto above the Dutch garden to the north.

Leaving this formal area, you will find yourself on the very southernmost slopes of the garden. Two swamp cypresses (*Taxodium distichum*) mark the site of a vanished pond—these grow quite well in wet soils and large specimens sometimes produce knee-like growths from the roots. Young cedars stand nearby—cedars of Lebanon (*C. libani*), blue cedars (*C. atlantica glauca*) and the golden-yellow *C. atlantica* 'Aurea'. Further on is a golden Indian bean tree, *Catalpa bignonioides* 'Aurea', with soft yellow, velvety leaves, three weeping cedars (*C. atlantica* 'Pendula') and many other specimens. Fortunately, Ascott was little affected by the hurricane of October 1987, but considerable damage occurred in the January 1990 storms when several trees were lost or damaged. However, many specimen trees survived undamaged and these lovely trees have many years of life ahead.

Cliveden Gardens

ADDRESS AND TELEPHONE: Taplow, Maidenhead, Berkshire, SL6 OJB. Tel. Burnham (0628) 605069

OWNERS: The National Trust

DIRECTIONS: leave M4 at Junction 7 or M40 at Junction 4. Entrance by main gates opposite Feathers Inn (B476). Public transport: Taplow station, not Sun, 2½ miles; Burnham 3 miles. Bus: Bee Line 68 Slough to Maidenhead (passes close BR Taplow and Slough)

OPENING TIMES: grounds March to end October, daily 11–6; November and December, daily 11–4

ADMISSION: grounds £2.80, house £1 extra. Party rates on application to the Administrator. Parties must book

CAR PARKING: yes, 400 yds from the house

TOILETS: yes

REFRESHMENTS: café

SHOP: yes

DOGS: not in gardens

WHEELCHAIR ACCESS: partial; maps with suggested routes available. Toilets for the disabled: yes

PEAK MONTHS: none

NOTABLE FEATURES: fine views of Thames

The grand and magnificent garden landscape of Cliveden, on the Buckinghamshire/Berkshire border, has been impressing visitors for over 400 years, though it reached its peak of fame in Victorian times. Queen Victoria herself made frequent visits, as did the statesman George Canning. Perched on a well wooded cliff high above the Thames, Cliveden commands breathtaking views from the south front: and there are many fine features.

Cliveden was originally built for George Villiers, 2nd Duke of Buckingham, in about 1666. After his death, it was bought by George Hamilton, the Earl of Orkney, one of Marlborough's generals. Frederick, Prince of Wales, rented it from 1739 to 1751. The original 17C house was unfortunately destroyed by fire in 1795, and its replacement suffered the same fate in 1849; the present house was built around 1850 by Sir Charles Barry. In the late 19C, Cliveden was bought by William Waldorf, who later became the 1st Lord Astor, and it is still associated in many people's minds with the Astor family. Though given to the National Trust in 1942, it remained their home until 1966. The house is now run as a hotel.

One unforgettable feature is the huge parterre on the lawn to the south (best viewed from the 17C terrace above). In Victorian times, the beds were filled with many thousands of spring and summer bedding plants, accompanied by gladioli, hollyhocks and foxgloves and permanent plantings of azaleas and rhododendrons. According to *The Gardener's Chronicle*, the beds were designed by Mr J. Fleming, the head gardener of that period, and this seems most likely, though other sources favour Barry.

Whatever the case, the parterre was poorly maintained during the early 20C and had declined considerably by the time the National Trust took over. Today it is a picture of health and elegance, with its boldly designed wedge-shaped beds, edged with box, set around with sentinel clipped yews and filled with silver-grey, shrubs (santolina and senecio). A cast of Giovanni da Bologna's Pluto and Proserpine, acquired by Lord Astor from the Borghese collection, has been removed for restoration.

The terrace itself is obviously a solid architectural achievement, having survived two great houses and for 400 years. It includes 18 blank arches, echoed by the arched windows of the house above, and a magnificent central double staircase, flanked on either side by two equally impressive specimens of *Magnolia grandiflora*, underplanted with mahonia. Also along the walls grow *Celastrus orbiculatus, Actinidia chinensis* and *Rosa banksiae lutea*, double white and yellow.

A second balustrade runs below, built in quite a different style, graceful and decorative, incorporating stone seats and fountain basins. This is another of W.W. Astor's Borghese acquisitions: the Italian government tried unsuccessfully to prevent its purchase.

William Waldorf Astor's habit of collecting and importing foreign antiquities may be open to ethical debate, but he was certainly a great patron of the arts. He commissioned Thomas Waldo Story, an American sculptor living in Rome, to make the great Fountain of Love, which stands at the top of the main drive, near the car park. Three female figures, attended by winged cherubs, surround a giant shell, drinking and revelling in the elixir of love.

From the promonotory you can look right down over the river, hundreds of yards below. The Lombardy poplars on the far bank were planted by the 2nd Lord Astor, a great lover of trees. If you feel in need of exercise, a yew walk leads from the house down to the river, bordered on the right-hand side by a sheer drop—watch your step on a wet day! The riverside walk is shaded by mature trees, such as *Taxodium distichum* and tulip trees: poplars, oaks, beeches and various conifers make up the woodland. One tree of particular historic interest is Canning's Oak (just off one of the higher paths): apparently George Canning spent many pleasant hours seated under its branches, gazing down on the Thames.

A number of small (or relatively small) gardens have been established at Cliveden, providing welcome focal points within the larger landscape. The sunken memorial garden lies west of the house, close to one of the main woodland paths, but very well concealed. Cut into the hillside by the 1st Viscount Astor, it was originally planned as an Italian garden—some statues and a balustrade remain. It became a cemetery during the 1914–18 war, when Cliveden house was used as a gymnasium for Canadian soldiers. Memorial tablets are set into the turf. The walls are lined with porous tufa rock. Yew, laurel and ivy create an appropriately sombre atmosphere, lightened by variegated holly and an autumn blaze of Virginia creeper.

Lord Astor's love of the Italian Renaissance and Seicento garden-ing came to better fruition in the long garden (to the far north, just inside the boundary wall). Here are long undulating beds of euony-mus, edged with box, and some fine topiary pieces, along with lively 18C Commedia dell'Arte and Venetian statues. The shrub bed along the south-facing wall contains some unusual varieties of bay, and many lovely scented specimens, such as red-flowered *Calycanthus occidentalis* and *Carpenteria californica* with dark glossy leaves and white anemone-like flowers.

The rose garden lies just north of the house and west of the main drive, surrounded by a circle of yews, some dating back to the 18C. Both old and new roses grow here, in curving irregular flowing beds designed by Sir Geoffrey Jellicoe. The pretty painted wooden arches are covered with climbing roses, clematis and honeysuckle. This garden took much time and trouble to establish, especially as the thin gravel soil had to be replaced with loam: the story is told in Penelope Hobhouse's *A Book of Gardening* (The National Trust).

The water garden is particularly charming; you'll find it beyond the car park, to the east. This garden also was created and developed by the Astors. It features a very pretty pagoda, used in the Paris Exhibition of 1867, and flat stepping stones over the water, besides all kinds of water-loving plants and graceful flowering trees such as Japanese cherries and magnolias. In spring, the grass is flooded with bulbs—white daffodils, colchicums, bluebells and primroses.

If you feel in need of refreshment, head for the conservatory, east of the house, which has been converted into a large tea room. Outside stand eight decorative earthenware pots, planted with geraniums and helichrysum, and directly opposite a long shrubbery backed by trees.

Just south of here is the sword terrace, commemorating a famous duel between the 2nd Duke of Buckingham and the Earl of Shrewsbury, for possession of the latter's wife. Bedding plants were formerly used to create the sword design, but this proved too labour-intensive: the swords will henceforth be laid out in knapped flint.

The main approach to the house is imposing, though not so attractive as the south side. The lime avenue has obviously seen better days: it was first planted in the early 18C. As you approach the forecourt, note the elaborate clock tower, built by Clutton in 1861 for the Duchess of Sutherland; he also made the dovecot across the court.

The long flower borders were designed by Graham Stuart Thomas in the style of Gertrude Jekyll, with warm shades of red and yellow predominating to the east and cool shades of blue, mauve and white to the west. Eight sarcophagi span the width of the lawn, dating from the 2nd and 3C AD, and appearing to good effect against the great yew hedges behind.

West Wycombe Park

ADDRESS AND TELEPHONE: West Wycombe, Buckinghamshire, HP14 3AJ. Tel. High Wycombe (0494) 524411

OWNERS: The National Trust

DIRECTIONS: at W end of West Wycombe, S of the Oxford road (A40). Public transport: bus from surrounding areas (passing close High Wycombe BR). High Wycombe BR 2½ miles

OPENING TIMES: house and grounds, June, July and August, Sun to Thurs 2–6. Last admission 5.15. Grounds only, April and May, Sun and Wed 2–6; and Easter, May and Spring BH Sun and Mon 2–6

ADMISSION: house and grounds £3.80; grounds only £2.20. NT members free. Parties by prior arrangement. No reductions

CAR PARKING: yes, 250 yds

TOILETS: yes

REFRESHMENTS: no

SHOP: no

DOGS: no

WHEELCHAIR ACCESS: grounds only

NOTABLE FEATURES: 18C park and lake

Praised by one of our most eminent garden historians, Dr Christopher Thacker, for its 'original and daring thought', West Wycombe Park is an 18C landscape set about with classical buildings and references, but also conveying a spirit of lightheartedness and gaiety. A fine example of the style of the early landscape movement, it also reflects the complex character of its creator, the 2nd Sir Francis Dashwood.

In his wild and debauched youth, Sir Francis Dashwood was a member of the Prince of Wales' circle and a founder of the Hell Fire Club, also known as the 'Monks of Medmenham' and the 'Society of St Francis of Wycombe'. These young gentlemen held their meetings at Medmenham Abbey on the Thames and also used the labyrinth of chalk caves, excavated under West Wycombe Hill. Sir Francis made the Grand Tour and visited Italy four times. He co-founded the Dilettanti Society, of which Walpole wrote in 1743, in a letter to Horace Mann, '... the nominal qualification is having been in Italy, and the real one, having been drunk, the two chiefs are Lord Middlesex and Sir Francis Dashwood, who were seldom sober the whole time they were in Italy.'

However, Sir Francis was also capable of serious interests and endeavours. He was a Fellow of the Royal Society and the Society of Antiquaries, and was given an honorary Doctorate of Law at Oxford. He was Chancellor of the Exchequer in 1762 and in 1773, with Benjamin Franklin, produced a revised 'Book of Common Prayer' for the Church of England. He succeeded to the barony of le Despencer and became Lord le Despencer.

The park lies in a valley of the Chilterns, enclosed by rising slopes to the north and south. It incorporates the Dashwood mansion, which was rebuilt in a variety of classical styles in the mid 18C, and is set on high ground to the south. On its north side, the park is overlooked by West Wycombe Hill, on which stand the parish church of St Lawrence, crowned with a golden ball, and the hexagonal Dashwood mausoleum. West Wycombe village also lies to the north, out of sight.

A central feature of the park is its great lake, formed by damming a stream. This is reached from the entrance by following the Broad Walk. On either side of the Broad Walk are serpentine streams, with delightful flint bridges, and winding paths which lead through the woods. Vistas unfold as you progress, with classical buildings and temples acting as focal points.

As the National Trust guidebook points out, the semi-formal style of this landscape is 'far nearer Pope's ideal than Capability Brown's'. However, Sir Francis employed a pupil of Brown's, Thomas Cook, to work on the landscape between 1770 and le Despencer's death in 1782. Humphry Repton also visited the park three times in the late 18C, and advised Sir John Dashwood-King, Lord le Despencer's successor, to demolish some superfluous buildings and thin the trees.

The Music Temple stands on a lush wooded island on the lake, the central island of three. Designed by Nicholas Revett, who worked at West Wycombe from 1770 until 1781, it has a splendid Doric colonnade, and provides the main focal point in the landscape as seen from the house. Crossing one of the little flint bridges over the serpentine streams, you can walk along the south side of the lake, to the cascade. The land slopes steeply upwards from here to West Wycombe house and its lawns. Boat-house island, graced by willows, can be reached via another twin-arched bridge. The two fibreglass nymphs, on piers either side of the cascade, are replacements for the original lead statues. Thomas Cook probably modified and simplified the design of the cascade, which was far more ornate in the mid 18C. There are open views to the east, across fields.

North of the lake are Daphne's Temple and Kitty's Lodge, both probably designed by John Donowell (who remodelled much of the house for Sir Francis, but was dismissed by him in 1764). These stand either side of what was once the main entrance to the park—the main drive led southwards, up the southern slope to the Temple of the Winds, and then west, following the line of the ha-ha wall, to the house. In about 1770, Sir Francis repositioned the entry and drive. To the north-west is the Temple of Venus, a modern replacement for the original 18C temple (also probably built by Donowell).

The Temple of the Winds is based on the Tower of the Winds in Athens, and was one of the earliest English attempts at replicating an antique building. It is a strangely ugly construction, with its vast doorway (this was moved from the south front of the house and predates the rest of the temple by 50 years); but the views are pleasant, over cornfields. The ha-ha hall leads westwards to the Round Temple and the Temple of Apollo, close by the house. The latter, a massive arch of stone and flintwork, bears the motto of the Hell Fire Club.

The south front of the house is especially impressive, with its double colonnade of Tuscan and Corinthian pillars—these are made of plastered wood, not stone. The east portico is flanked by a lead lion and lioness and commands a good view down to the lake.

The present Sir Francis Dashwood lives in the house and has overseen its restoration. The house and grounds were given to the National Trust in 1943, but Sir Francis owns and runs the 4000-acre estate.

CAMBRIDGESHIRE

Anglesey Abbey

ADDRESS AND TELEPHONE: Anglesey Abbey, Lode, Cambridge, CB5 9EJ. Tel. Cambridge (0223) 811200

OWNERS: The National Trust

DIRECTIONS: in village of Lode on B1102 6 miles NE of Cambridge. Public transport: Cambridge BR 6 miles. Buses from Cambridge and Newmarket

OPENING TIMES: 30 March to 14 July, Wed to Sun and BH Mon 11–5; 15 July to 10 September, daily 11–5.30; 11 September to 13 October, Wed to Sun 11–5. House also open

ADMISSION: house and garden £4.50; garden only £2.

CAR PARKING: yes

TOILETS: yes

REFRESHMENTS: yes

SHOP: yes

DOGS: no

WHEELCHAIR ACCESS: yes, although house difficult. Toilets for the disabled: yes

PEAK SEASONS: no peak season

NOTABLE FEATURES: outstanding 100-acre 20C garden; majestic avenues; herbaceous, dahlia and hyacinth gardens; unrivalled collection of garden statuary and ornaments

Strolling around the gardens at Anglesey Abbey, you could easily make the mistake of thinking that you had stepped back into the 17C or 18C, so strong is the historical atmosphere and so grand the scale and manner of design. However, these impressive gardens are entirely a 20C creation.

An Augustinian priory was founded here in the 12C, and lasted for 460 years until the Dissolution of the Monasteries in the 1530s, when it was rebuilt as a Tudor house. The property then passed through the hands of a succession of families until it was purchased in a partly ruined state in 1926 by Huttleston Broughton, later Lord Fairhaven, the son of an industrialist.

During the next 40 years, Lord Fairhaven restored and extended the house and set about landscaping the flat, monotonous, wind-swept fenland countryside to accommodate his vast collection of art treasures. He laid out walks and avenues of trees in the manner of the 17C—a period he admired—and linked them by winding paths through belts of trees. Closer to the house he made smaller, more intimate gardens enclosed by hedges.

Fine statuary and garden ornaments of marble, stone, lead, bronze and copper were set at intervals throughout the grounds, providing interest in the otherwise undramatic and level terrain. This collection of historic statuary is one of the finest in the country.

One of the first parts of the garden to feature garden sculpture is the Emperor's Walk, so named because of the 12 busts of Caesars ornamenting its western side. About a quarter of a mile in length, this wide grassy walk was first planted with Norway spruce in 1955, but these were destroyed by gales in 1979 and the walk has since been replanted. The young trees have yet to achieve the effect desired by Lord Fairhaven but they make a good background to the statues.

On the opposite side of the walk are four enormous urns, two of bronze and two of copper, dating from about 1700 and in a bay set centrally along this side are two lead figures, representing Painting and Sculpture and two Roman women. All these were brought from the Temple of Victory at Stowe. Facing them is an unusual open temple with a Chinese-style canopy set on classical pillars. It encloses a large Roman urn made of Egyptian porphyry.

A short walk westwards brings you to the arboretum, at the

southern end of the lime avenue. The avenue of red twigged limes (*Tilia platyphyllos* 'Rubra') was planted in 1937, to commemorate the coronation of King George VI, and the arboretum was later established within the avenue to increase horticultural interest and to soften the straight lines of the original design. Among the trees here are a huge specimen of Hungarian oak (*Quercus frainetto*), a scarlet oak (*Quercus coccinea*), a large Japanese pagoda tree (*Sophora japonica*), Oliver's lime (*Tilia oliveri*) and a beautiful specimen of *Acer saccharinum laciniatum*, a graceful tree with finely and deeply cut leaves.

At the northern end of the lime avenue is the quarry pool—an old mine worked in the last century for the fossil fuel coprolite, and now a deep pool edged with willows. Beyond is Lode Mill, recently restored to working order—the flour is on sale to visitors.

Nearer to the house are more intimate enclosed gardens. A spectacular one is the herbaceous garden which was laid out in its present form in 1952. The garden is D-shaped, with long sweeping borders, 12ft deep, backed by tall beech hedges. Paved areas at regular intervals are set with seats flanked by tubs of clipped box. The borders are undoubtedly at their best in June and July, when numerous varieties of delphiniums, lupins, peonies, salvias, irises and achillea fill the enclosure with colour and scent. In the centre of the lawn is a statue of Father Time.

Beside the herbaceous garden is the Dahlia Garden with its long border, dating from 1952, running through a narrow corridor of beech hedges. In spring this garden is hazy with forget-me-nots. Dahlias flower in August—varieties include 'Sunset Boulevard', 'Arabian Knight' and 'Good Intent'. More statuary graces the dahlia garden: 18C stone griffins at the entrance and a marble figure of Apollino and a pair of bronze urns in a central bay.

West of the house are more enclosed gardens. In spring, do not miss the polygonal hyacinth garden with its formal beds, as intricately cut as a parterre, filled with 4000 blue and white hyacinths. These are replaced later in the year by red and yellow dahlias. Father Time stands in the centre, holding a sundial.

Just beyond the hyacinth garden is the narcissus garden, where formal beds, backed by yew hedges and planted with white and yellow spring flowers and silver foliage, surround a statue of Narcissus.

The western grounds are dominated by the very grand Coronation Avenue. Planted in 1937 to commemorate the coronation of King George VI and Queen Elizabeth, the avenue runs for about half a mile, its entrance flanked by a pair of lead sphinxes. It was originally planted with four rows of horse chestnuts and London planes on either side of a broad grassy walk, the intention being to remove either the chestnuts or the planes to leave a double avenue. The decision was made easier by a storm in 1968, which severely damaged many of the plane trees. The result is a majestic double avenue of chestnuts. A cross avenue, also of chestnuts, bisects the main avenue, with large marble urns at either end.

To the north is Temple Lawn, laid out in 1953 to celebrate the coronation of Queen Elizabeth II. The lawn stretches along part of the north western side of the garden, broken by island beds of trees and shrubs. In the centre is a circular, roofless temple with ten

Corinthian columns and surrounded by a yew hedge with a single entrance guarded by lead figures of a lion and lioness. In the middle of the temple is a marble copy of Bernini's David, signed G. Fossi, 1801.

Balancing on the other side of the Coronation Avenue, is Pilgrims Lawn. Completed in 1966, this was the last planting carried out by the 1st Lord Fairhaven. Island beds here feature tall conifers and trees and shrubs good for autumn colour and interest. In the middle of the lawn is a circle of incense cedars (*Calocedrus decurrens*) surrounded by a hedge of *Berberis* x *steriophylla*. On the north side is a stone statue of a pilgrim leaning on a staff—yet another item from Lord Fairhaven's vast art collection.

Anglesey Abbey is an outstanding garden and unique in conception; now as it comes to maturity, Lord Fairhaven's vision can be fully appreciated. Allow plenty of time for your visit if you intend to do justice to this spacious garden.

Cambridge College Gardens

Christ's College, Clare College, Corpus Christi College, Downing College, Emmanuel College, Gonville and Caius College, Jesus College, King's College, Magdalene College, Pembroke College, Peterhouse College, Queen's College, St Catharine's College, St John's College, Sidney Sussex College, Trinity College, Trinity Hall—all in the centre.

Newnham College, off Sidgwick Avenue, W of centre; Robinson College, off Grange Road (W side), W of centre; Selwyn College, off Grange Road (E side), W of centre.

Churchill, to the NW, off Storey's Way. Fitzwilliam, New Hall, St Edmund's House—to the NW, off Huntingdon Road and Madingley Road.

Girton College, to NW, follow Huntingdon Road; Homerton College, to SE, follow Hills Road; Wolfson College, to SW, follow Barton Road

The 2-acre Fellows Garden of **Clare College** (open Mon to Fri 2–4, closed weekends on Public Holidays and when conditions require, wheelchair access, no dogs, approach from Queen's Road or from city centre via Senate House Passage, Old Court and Clare Bridge) is perhaps the most impressive of the Cambridge college gardens. Created in 1946/7 by Fellows of the college and head gardener Walter Barlow, it is now owned by the Master and Fellows. It lies between the college and the River Cam; the Master's garden, to the north, is closed to the public.

The garden is skilfully divided into several smaller enclosures and perspective is cleverly managed throughout, as are contrasts between light and shade, gloom and bright colours. In the centre is the pool garden, with a four-sided lily pool and majestic cypresses; surrounded by yew hedges and old walls, this is used as a setting for performances of Shakespeare plays in May Week. The two old apple trees are a reminder of the site's former use as a kitchen garden and orchard.

Elsewhere are superb specimen trees including a dawn redwood (*Metasequoia glyptostroboides*), a swamp cypress (*Taxodium distichum*) and a Judas tree (*Cercis siliquastrum*). The smooth lawns are planted with colourful island beds and edged with bright

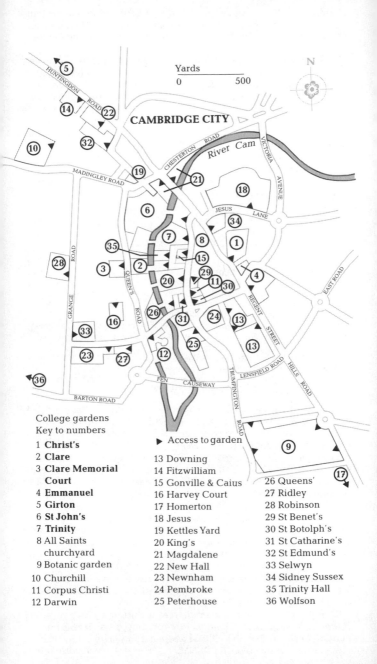

CAMBRIDGE CITY

Yards
0   500

N

HUNTINGDON ROAD

CHESTERTON ROAD

River Cam

VICTORIA AVENUE

MADINGLEY ROAD

JESUS LANE

GRANGE ROAD

QUEEN'S ROAD

EAST ROAD

REGENT STREET

LENSFIELD ROAD

TRUMPINGTON ROAD

HILLS ROAD

FEN CAUSEWAY

BARTON ROAD

College gardens
Key to numbers

▶ Access to garden

1 **Christ's**
2 **Clare**
3 **Clare Memorial
   Court**
4 **Emmanuel**
5 **Girton**
6 **St John's**
7 **Trinity**
8 All Saints
   churchyard
9 Botanic garden
10 Churchill
11 Corpus Christi
12 Darwin

13 Downing
14 Fitzwilliam
15 Gonville & Caius
16 Harvey Court
17 Homerton
18 Jesus
19 Kettles Yard
20 King's
21 Magdalene
22 New Hall
23 Newnham
24 Pembroke
25 Peterhouse

26 Queens'
27 Ridley
28 Robinson
29 St Benet's
30 St Botolph's
31 St Catharine's
32 St Edmund's
33 Selwyn
34 Sidney Sussex
35 Trinity Hall
36 Wolfson

borders. Himalayan poppies and primulas flourish in damp shady areas by the yew hedges. There is a yellow and blue garden, and a red border along the Cam. A yew tunnel leads to a scented garden, planted with stocks and nicotianas, viburnums and chimonanthus.

Cross Queen's Road to Clare Memorial Court, where you can see ancient and beautiful trees including a Japanese wing nut (pterocarya) and a locust tree (*Robinia pseudoacacia*). Statues by Henry Moore and Barbara Hepworth stand on the lawn; behind is the main court and a huge Pyrenees pine (*Pinus nigra cebennensis*).

Emmanuel College Garden (in the centre, off St Andrew's Street, car parks at Parker's Piece and Lion Yard, wheelchair access, no dogs) is also recommended. In New Court, to the left of the Front Court, is a charming herb garden designed by John Codrington and laid out in 1961. The box-edged beds, of triangular shape, are planted with a great variety of herbs, with coloured stones and shining pieces of coal for background.

In the Paddock is a long lily pool of ancient origins—it may have been the fish pond of a Dominican monastery, before that monastery's dissolution in 1539. It is now lushly planted, and furnished with an island. Another pool can be seen in Chapman's Garden—connected to the first by a channel leading under the buildings—and in the private Fellow's Garden (open once a year under the National Gardens Scheme) is a 17C swimming pool. The *Metasequoia glyptostroboides* planted by the pool in Chapman's Garden is one of the original six raised from seed sent to Cambridge Botanic Gardens from the Arnold Arboretum, USA. It was given to Emmanuel College and planted in 1949. Now at a height of around 90ft, it is probably one of the tallest in the country.

Emmanuel has a magnificent collection of trees, including a vast and ancient oriental plane in the Fellow's Garden, copper beeches, limes and tulip trees. Its herbaceous borders are some of the best in Cambridge.

Both **Christ's College** (St Andrew's Street) and **Trinity College** (Trinity Street) have interesting trees. An ancient mulberry grows on the western side of Christ's Fellows' Garden—one of 300 bought in 1608, on the order of James I, who wished to encourage the silk industry. To the right of the Great Gate at Trinity is a small lawn known as Newton's Lawn and formerly Sir Isaac Newton's garden. On the lawn stands a small apple tree, reputed to be a direct descendant of the tree at Woolsthorpe Manor, Newton's home near Grantham in Lincolnshire, which inspired the theory of gravity by dropping an apple.

The Wilderness at **St John's College** (St John's Street) was improved in the late 18C by Lancelot 'Capability' Brown: martagon or turk's cap lilies now flourish beneath the trees, as do plentiful spring flowers. The garden at **Girton College** (along the A604, about 1½ miles north-west of the town centre) owes much to Miss Elizabeth Welch, garden steward in the late 19C, who planted a yew walk and a honeysuckle walk. There is an orchard, with a unique collection of apple trees, including five original Blenheim Oranges.

Cambridge University Botanic Garden

ADDRESS AND TELEPHONE: University of Cambridge Botanic Garden, Cory Lodge, Bateman Street, Cambridge CB2 1JF. Tel. Cambridge (0223) 336265

OWNERS: University of Cambridge

DIRECTIONS: S of city centre. Entrances in Trumpington Road, Bateman Street and Hills Road. Public transport: 5 minutes' walk from BR station. Buses from city centre

OPENING TIMES: throughout the year, daily 8–6 or dusk if earlier.

ADMISSION: free on weekdays. Sun £1, children 50p

CAR PARKING: limited to streets around the garden. Coaches by arrangement with the Director

TOILETS: yes

REFRESHMENTS: light refreshments served from Gilmour building, May to September except Mon

SHOP: yes, in Gilmour building

DOGS: no

WHEELCHAIR ACCESS: yes. Toilets for the disabled: yes

PEAK MONTHS: peaks throughout the year (rock garden best in May or June)

NOTABLE FEATURES: splendid lake, stream and water garden; excellent rock garden; fine collections of trees and shrubs; various glasshouses; winter garden, chronological bed; scented garden

This garden, less than a mile from the city centre of Cambridge, belongs to the University of Cambridge. The present 40-acre site was acquired in 1831, a 5-acre garden having existed in the city centre since 1762. Primarily intended for botanical and horticultural education and research, the garden is also a peaceful haven and retreat from the noise of the city.

Chronological beds show a wide selection of plants in their order of introduction into Britain, and families of plants are grouped in systematic beds. There are fine collections of trees and shrubs, and for those interested in design, several different types of garden, including a winter garden, a scented garden and splendid rock gardens—all displaying a wide variety of plants.

There are several entrances into the garden from the surrounding roads but the grandest gate is on Trumpington Road. This gives access to the Main Walk, a long straight path leading through the garden to a raised circular pool and tiered fountain. The path is flanked on either side by an impressive array of large conifers. Spreading cedars such as the cedar of Lebanon (*Cedrus libani*) and an Atlantic cedar (*Cedrus atlantica*) contrast with the towering spires of Wellingtonias (*Sequoiadendron giganteum*) and other magnificent trees.

The stream, water and rock gardens lie to the north-west of the Main Walk, in a corner near the entrance. A 17C water course known as Hobson's Conduit runs along the western boundary of the garden, parallel to Trumpington Road, and supplies water for the lake. Among the waterside plants is *Lathraea clandestina*, a parasite which feeds on willow roots and bears large purple flowers in spring.

By the stream leading from Hobson's Conduit to the lake is a thicket of Caucasian wing-nuts (*Pterocarya fraxinifolia*); at the end of the lake is a woodland area. Among the trees here are the graceful *Tetracentron sinense* from China and a grove of pawpaw (*Asimina triloba*) from America. Ferns and Himalayan poppies grow beneath, in the peat-enriched soil, and primulas burst into colour in spring. The lake itself is very beautiful, with floating waterlilies and overhanging trees.

A high bank to the north shelters the water garden, home to many native wetland species. Particularly noteworthy is the great fen ragwort (*Senecio paludosus*), long believed to be extinct until it was rediscovered at a site about 15 miles away in 1972. Royal ferns (*Osmunda regalis*) grow to unusual height here, and you can also see great spearwort (*Ranunculus lingua*), with dark blue-green leaves and golden-yellow flowers about 2in. across. Beyond the water garden, on the lawns, are collections of willows and poplars.

The rock gardens are another great attraction, and full of interesting plants. Designed by R.W. Younger in 1951, they comprise two main areas. In the larger, limestone garden, plants are grouped according to the place of origin—North America, Europe, Asia, South Africa and Australasia.

The systematic beds, across the main walk from the lake, are an important educational exhibit and a source of plant material for teaching purposes. All 80 families are clearly labelled. The beds are informal in shape despite their orderly arrangement.

In 1964 work began to establish a new pinetum in the far south-western corner of the garden, and elsewhere you can see excellent examples of tree species hardy in this country—alders, birches, beeches, wild pears and crab apples. Plantings of maples, chestnuts, limes and ash line the Trumpington Road perimeter and a collection of oaks back the terrace garden near the glasshouses. Among varieties to be seen here are a magnificent common oak (*Quercus robur*), a sessile oak (*Quercus petraea*), the evergreen holm oak (*Quercus ilex*) and a splendid specimen of cork oak (*Quercus suber*).

To the north-east of the systematic beds a new area of woodland has been developed, as part of a memorial to Humphry Gilbert-Carter, director of the gardens 1921–50.

Conservation of plants is an important function of botanic gardens and at Cambridge a large area has been set aside for the cultivation and display of native British plants—some rarely seen nowadays in the wild. Several different habitats have been developed, including an artificial limestone mound. A collection of wetland plants has been donated by Wicken Fen Nature Reserve, north-east of Cambridge and a special conservation bed displays rare flowering plants and ferns native to eastern England. Here you can see bloody cranesbill (*Geranium sanguineum*) hardy and vigorous, and perennial flax (*Linum perenne*) with deep blue flowers on graceful arching stems.

Between November and April the winter garden is filled with

interesting ornamental plants. The brilliant crimson winter stems of Westonbirt dogwood (*Cornus alba* 'Sibirica') contrast to good effect with the yellow-green stems of *Cornus stolonifera* 'Flaviramea'. Many of the plants here flower in winter or very early spring—hellebores, various forms of heath (*Erica carnea*), fragrant white *Viburnum farreri* and bright yellow winter jasmine (*Jasminum nudiflorum*). In late winter the Chinese bush honeysuckle (*Lonicera fragrantissima*) adds its sweet scent to the air. Other fragrant plants can be found in the scented garden, which will be especially appreciated by blind or partially-sighted visitors.

Students and botanists, as well as general visitors, will be intrigued by the nearby chronological bed, displaying plants in the chronological order of their introduction into Britain, from medieval to modern times.

The glasshouse range consists of a long corridor with a number of houses leading from it so that heat and humidity can be carefully adjusted from place to place to suit the plants. There is a spectacular display of decorative shrubs and plants in the temperate house, particularly interesting in winter and spring, and floral displays in the conservatory, attractive throughout the year. An alpine house provides suitable conditions for temperate plants grown in pans plunged into sand beds. The central raised beds contain an excellent collection of saxifrages of known wild European origin.

For an exotic display of tropical plants visit the palm house and adjacent tropical houses. Tea, banana, rubber and other economic plants can all be seen here. There are several trees including figs and palms, and a jungle of smaller plants below. The range of glasshouses also includes a house containing plants from drier climates.

Peckover House

ADDRESS AND TELEPHONE: Peckover House, North Brink, Wisbech, Cambridgeshire, PE13 1JR. Tel. Wisbech (0945) 583463

OWNERS: The National Trust

DIRECTIONS: B1441 N bank of River Nene in centre of Wisbech. Public transport: coach link from Peterborough BR and Kings Lynn BR

OPENING TIMES: house and garden, 30 March to 27 October, Sat, Sun and BH Mon 2–5.30; garden only, 1 April to 23 October, Mon, Tues and Wed 2–5.30

ADMISSION: £2 (£1 on garden only days), children £1, NT members free. Party rates (applicable to groups of 15 or more, and by prior arrangement with the custodian, tel: 0945 583463) adults £1.50, children 75p. Private party visits can also be arranged

CAR PARKING: town car park within walking distance

TOILETS: yes

REFRESHMENTS: tea room

SHOP: no

DOGS: no

WHEELCHAIR ACCESS: by arrangement with custodian. Toilets for the disabled: no

PEAK MONTHS: no special peaks

NOTABLE FEATURES: Victorian garden; unusual trees; flower borders; orange trees under glass

Walking along the North Brink of the River Nene, close to the town centre of Wisbech, most people are quite unaware of the hidden garden behind the plain brick façade of Peckover House. For 150 years this was the home of the Peckovers, a Quaker family who, as successful bankers, contributed much to the history of Wisbech; at that time it was called Bank House. In 1943 the Hon. Miss Alexandrina Peckover, the last member of the family, gave the property to the National Trust.

Today, most visitors come to see the elegant house and its splendid interior, but the garden, which you reach by going through the house, also has many notable features.

While the house is Georgian, built in 1772, the garden is more Victorian in style. For a town garden it is quite large—about $2\frac{1}{2}$ acres. It is surrounded by high brick walls, which divide it into three main areas. The National Trust has maintained the garden sensitively, making a few sympathetic changes and additions to its general layout of lawns, curving paths, plantings of trees and shrubs and rich flower borders.

Immediately behind the house is a spotless lawn with a perimeter path of gravel leading under tall trees and through rich shrubberies of dark green laurels, hollies, yew and box. Mahonias, spotted laurels (*Aucuba japonica*) and variegated hollies also grow here. In the shady parts the ground is covered with hardy ferns and hostas.

From the steps of the house the Wilderness Walk leads through the shrubbery around the eastern side of the lawn passing a very tall maidenhair tree (*Ginkgo biloba*) and a tulip tree (*Liriodendron tulipifera*). Both these trees are now very old and reaching the end of their lives: the Trust has already planted replacements nearby. There is also a beautiful Japanese pagoda tree (*Sophora japonica*), which during late summer and autumn carries panicles of yellow pea-like flowers.

To the west of the main lawn is another lawn, set with informal beds. Here philadelphus and other shrubs flower above a ground covering of bergenias, alchemillas, vincas and a number of different hostas. There are two specimens of the Californian redwood (*Sequoia sempervirens*) and some splendid variegated hollies (*Ilex aquifolium* 'Argentea Marginata'), as well as a tall Chusan palm (*Trachycarpus fortunei*) and a young monkey puzzle (*Araucaria araucana*).

On its way back to the house, the perimeter path passes a rustic house with columns of solid tree trunks supporting the roof. This summerhouse was restored in the 1970s by the National Trust and now offers delightful views over the lawn to the shrubberies and trees. At the opposite end of the lawn is a series of ironwork arches clothed in roses and at the foot of the garden wall is a border

The ancient orange trees at Peckover House

designed on a repetitive pattern with plants chosen to provide colour and interest throughout the year.

Almost hidden away behind the shrubberies on the western edge of the lawn is a small rose garden where climbing roses, such as the eye-catching 'Paul's Scarlet', sprawl over arches. The central bed is of 'Margaret Merril', surrounded by beds of other roses and edged with lavender. Opposite the rose garden a border of bright flowers—sedums, chrysanthemums, fuchsias asters and others—runs along the bottom of a brick wall, which screens the next part of the garden from view.

The gateway at the top end brings you into the central compartment, an intimate, peaceful little garden enclosed on three sides by high brick walls and on the fourth by a yew hedge. Here is the second Victorian summerhouse—a white-painted shelter decorated with green lattice work. The summerhouse overlooks an oval lily pool edged with variegated thyme. The gravel walk around the pool is backed by pretty borders of peonies, hydrangeas and lilies (*Lilium henryi*). The latter are particularly attractive in summer, with beautiful orange reflexed flowers, spotted brown, and with dark orange anthers. The surrounding walls support a number of climbers including *Clematis montana rubens*, with rose pink flowers during June, and the old rambler rose 'François Juranville' which has pink flowers and a strong fragrance.

Beyond the topiary peacocks which ornament the yew hedge, a

gravel walk leads between glorious flower borders edged with pinks. The borders are mirror-images of each other, reflected across the walk. Short ornamental hedges divide the borders into bays, each bay containing plants grouped for colour. There are doronicums, euphorbias, daylilies, roses, perovskia, agapanthus, caryopteris and Michaelmas daisies. Honeysuckles, clematis and roses clothe the back walls and pairs of iron pillars flank the walk, each supporting a rose and a clematis.

The double borders end at an orangery, housing three old orange trees. These were moved here from Hagbeach Hall, Emneth, a hundred years ago and were then believed to be 200 years old. They still bear fruit regularly. Other conservatory plants, such as plumbago, fuchsias and begonias, give a colourful and exotic display.

Beyond the orangery, behind a golden privet hedge, are two smaller greenhouses, one housing a collection of tender ferns. The third main area of garden lies to the other side of the privet hedge. Originally this was the kitchen garden and was bisected by a drive. Now it is lawned and planted with specimen trees, borders of shrubs and herbaceous plants of flowers for cutting.

Among the trees here are a large beech and many fruit trees such as quince, a medlar, a Dartmouth crab apple and a black mulberry.

CHESHIRE

Arley Hall and Gardens

ADDRESS AND TELEPHONE: Arley Hall, near Northwich, Cheshire CW9 6NA. Tel. Arley (0565) 777353

OWNERS: The Hon. M.L.W. Flower and Mrs Flower

DIRECTIONS: 5 miles W of Knutsford. Signposted from M6 (exits 19 & 20) and M56 (exits 9 & 10), off the A50 at High Legh and off A559 near Great Budworth. Public transport: not reasonable

OPENING TIMES: April to first week of October, Tues to Sun. April, May, September and October 2–6. June, July and August 12–6. House from 2pm

ADMISSION: grounds, gardens and chapel £2.10, children under 17 90p, children under 8 free; Hall £1.20 extra for adults and 50p extra for children under 17, children under 8 free. Coach parties by arrangement (reductions and extended hours)

CAR PARKING: yes

TOILETS: yes

REFRESHMENTS: café

SHOP: yes, including plant sales

DOGS: on lead but not in the Hall

WHEELCHAIR ACCESS: yes. Toilets for the disabled: yes

PEAK SEASON: May to August

NOTABLE FEATURES: double herbaceous border; ilex avenue; enclosed gardens—flag garden; scented garden, herb garden, walled garden, wild garden and fish garden; rhododendron dell, pleached lime avenue and woodland garden

The Warburton family and their descendants have owned property at Arley in Cheshire since the 12C and built their first house here in 1469; a medieval tithe barn near the present house is all that remains from that time. Arley Hall is 19C, built in Jacobean style.

There have probably been gardens at Arley for several hundred years. The first records date from the 1740s, when Sir Peter and Lady Elizabeth Warburton lived here; they built walled gardens and established walks and shrubberies. However, much of the garden you see today is the work of Rowland and Mary Egerton-Warburton, who built the present Hall.

The Egerton-Warburtons were well travelled and had undoubtedly seen many gardens abroad when, in the 1830s and 1840s, they began laying out an English country garden within the framework of the older, 18C, brick walls. They created a series of intimate family gardens in the manner of enclosures or 'rooms'—a style later to be adapted and developed at Hidcote and Sissinghurst.

Successive generations of the family have each left their mark, and the result is a garden of some 12 acres, displaying a great variety of styles and designs. It was first opened to the public in 1960.

The main garden occupies a triangular shaped area to the south-west of the house and you can reach it via an avenue of pleached lime trees, which leads into a cobbled courtyard. The clock tower was built by Rowland Egerton-Warburton, above the gateway to his new house. On the right is the 15C tithe barn, and around the corner from this, a wrought iron gate leading into the first of the enclosed gardens. This is the Flag Garden, so named because of the flagstone paving which surrounds formal beds of floribunda roses edged with dwarf lavender. Old brick walls on two sides of the garden are clothed with climbing plants—honeysuckles, hydrangeas and ivies—and the flame creeper (*Tropaeolum speciosum*) spills out of yew hedges.

The Flag Garden was created in 1900 by Antoinette Egerton-Warburton. Nearby is Furlong Walk, a terraced walk of 220 yds which separates the garden from the parkland beyond; this replaced the earlier 18C drive. Now the terrace offers good views back towards the Hall and across the ha-ha to the parkland. When Rowland Egerton-Warburton went blind he had a taut wire stretched along the distance of the walk, with a bell at either end. By hooking his walking stick over the wire he could follow the walk to the end, and when the bell rang he turned back again.

Half-way along the Furlong Walk, a break in the shrub borders on the right marks the entrance to Arley's most important and impressive feature, the double herbaceous borders. About 90 yds long and ending with a brick and stucco alcove, these are among the oldest herbaceous borders in the country; they are clearly shown on a map of 1846. They now flank a wide grass walk. One border is backed by an old brick wall, the other by a yew hedge, and both are now divided into five bays by huge yew buttresses.

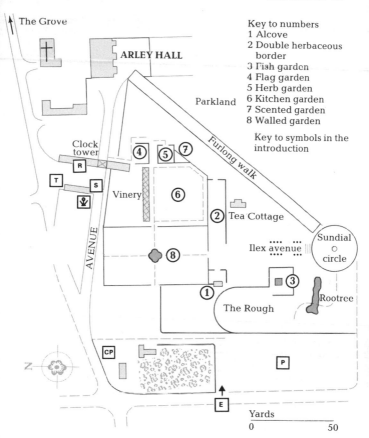

The Grove

ARLEY HALL

Parkland

Key to numbers
1 Alcove
2 Double herbaceous
   border
3 Fish garden
4 Flag garden
5 Herb garden
6 Kitchen garden
7 Scented garden
8 Walled garden

Key to symbols in the
introduction

Clock
tower

Furlong walk

Vinery

Tea Cottage

Ilex avenue

Sundial
circle

Rootree

The Rough

N

Yards
0   50

Many of the old plants have been kept and new ones added, to give a glorious display of colour in summer. The season begins with blue, mauve, yellow and white flowers—most attractive when viewed against the green yew hedge. As summer proceeds the borders explode into a riot of colour which lasts well into September. None of the plants here are labelled but in the alcove are several framed pictures identifying the flowers in sequence, month by month, as they appear.

An archway in the yew hedge leads southwards to a little half-timbered building called the tea cottage. In Victorian times this was used for garden tea-parties and would have been surrounded by a formal garden with beds of hybrid tea roses and topiary. However the hybrid teas did not do well on this site and the topiary was difficult to maintain, especially after neglect suffered in the war years.

In 1961 Viscountess Ashbrook developed the present lawned area, with sweeping beds of shrub and species roses underplanted with geraniums and other ground covering plants.

To the west of the tea house is the ilex avenue—an unusual avenue of clipped holm oaks (*Quercus ilex*). It was planted in the 1840s or 1850s, by Rowland and Mary Egerton-Warburton, who had probably seen something similar in the Mediterranean. Originally the seven pairs of trees which flank the grassed walk were clipped as cones but during the 1914–18 war they were left to their own devices, and afterwards re-trained as the giant cylinders you see today.

To the right of the avenue lies the fish garden. Once part of a sunken bowling green, this garden was created in 1930.

At the end of the ilex avenue, steps lead down to the sundial circle—a small lawn with a central sundial, ringed by borders of shrub roses, azaleas, philadelphus and other shrubs. A path to the west leads into an area known as the Rootree—formerly a rock garden and alpine dell established by Rowland and Mary Egerton-Warburton. Here too the war years left their mark—the garden ran wild, and in 1960 the whole area had to be redeveloped. Heavily shaded by mature trees, it is now planted with azaleas, rhododendrons, pieris and other woodland shrubs. The pool provides excellent conditions for ferns, primulas and other moisture-loving plants.

A rocky path above the pool leads to a semi-wild area, the Rough, where naturalised bulbs flower among shrubs under a canopy of tall trees. An archway in the opposite corner leads back to the herbaceous borders.

On the north side of the herbaceous borders are tall wrought iron gates draped with honeysuckle—the entrance to a large 18C walled garden. Until the 1939–45 war, the brick walls enclosed a typical kitchen garden with fruit trees against the wall, borders of herbs and flowers for cutting, and large vegetable plots. In 1946 the walled garden became a commercial market garden and in 1960 it was given its present design, mainly of lawns with shrub borders around the walls.

Two gravel paths divide the garden into quarters and where the paths cross is an ornate lily pond set around with four Dawyck beeches. The south-facing border at the far end contains tender shrubs and a collection of mixed red roses.

An archway in the wall to the east gives access to the second walled garden. This is still used as a kitchen garden for growing vegetables and flowers for family use. A greenhouse against the south-facing wall contains vines and figs.

A rose-bordered path leads through the kitchen garden and back towards the flag garden. Two small, intricate gardens can be seen in this area. The herb garden was made in 1969 by Lady Ashbrook and includes all her favourite herbs such as eau-de-cologne mint and bergamots, majorams and thymes, planted in a simple formal design. On the other side of the yew hedge is the Scented Garden. This small enclosed plot, established in 1977, is filled with aromatic shrubs and flowers.

Before leaving Arley, walk around the house to the north to view the most recently developed area of the garden, the Grove. Lady Ashbrook's son Michael has been busy here since the 1970s, clearing brambles and self-sown trees and planting rhododendrons, azaleas, magnolias, sorbus, malus, prunus, birches, oaks and acers, together with drifts of daffodils. This garden is informal, in contrast to the rest, and contributes to the immense variety of design and planting.

There is much to be enjoyed here, especially by those interested in garden history, and design. The planting is varied and the standard of maintenance very high. These gardens deservedly won the Christie's/Historic Houses Association Garden of the Year Award in 1987.

Capesthorne Hall

ADDRESS AND TELEPHONE: Capesthorne Hall, Macclesfield, Cheshire SK11 9JY. Tel. (0625) 861221

OWNERS: Mr and Mrs W. Bromley-Davenport

DIRECTIONS: entrance off the A34 Alderley Edge to Congleton Road. Public transport: Macclesfield BR to Chelford station

OPENING TIMES: April, Sun only 12–5; May, August and September, Wed, Sat and Sun 12–6; June and July, Tues, Wed, Thurs, Sat and Sun 12–6. Also Good Fri and all BH. Hall open same days as grounds but 2–4

ADMISSION: park, gardens, chapel £1.50, OAPs £1.25, children 50p; including the Hall £3, OAPs £2.50, children £1. Coaches parties by prior arrangement. Reductions for groups of 20 or more

CAR PARKING: yes

TOILETS: yes

REFRESHMENTS: café

SHOP: yes

DOGS: in park only

WHEELCHAIR ACCESS: yes. Toilets for the disabled: yes

PEAK SEASON: July and August to see herbaceous borders at best; otherwise no special peak

NOTABLE FEATURES: parkland, lakes, trees, herbaceous borders, woodland with rhododendron walks

Situated in the beautiful countryside of east Cheshire, Capesthorne Hall has been the home of the Bromley-Davenport family and their ancestors, the Capesthornes and Wards, since Domesday, when the family was responsible for keeping law and order in the King's forests of Macclesfield and Leek.

The magnificent Hall and its surrounding parkland are steeped in history. To the left of the long main drive, standing in pastureland, is a red-brick pillar capped with a stone ball finial. This commemorates the site of the first Hall, built at Capesthorne in the 15C and replaced in 1722 by the new Hall and chapel. A few grassy mounds show where the old Hall once stood and two ancient, false acacia trees (*Robinia pseudoacacia*) close by are said to be survivors from its gardens.

From the monument you get spectacular views of the Hall and the majestic five-arched Capesthorne Bridge, spanning one of the three man-made lakes in the park. In typical 18C English manner, the parkland is enhanced by bold groups and belts of trees. The light sandy soil here has proved excellent for the growing of oaks, limes, chestnuts, beeches, larches and pines, many of which have reached a considerable height.

The Hall forms an impressive centrepiece. Its oldest parts date from 1719 and were designed and constructed by Francis and William Smith of Warwickshire. The parkland is thought to have been laid out about the same time. Alterations and additions were made to the Hall in the 19C by Edward Blore, and, following a disastrous fire, the centre portion was rebuilt in 1861 to a design by Anthony Salvin.

The brick-built Hall is largely Jacobean in style but with a Victorian façade overlooking a large forecourt, enclosed by a low wall. The sundial in the centre of the forecourt shows the time in Peking, Babylon and Mexico, as well as Britain. Roses are trained along the walls of the forecourt and roses and honeysuckle soften the stone columns at the Hall entrance.

The main areas of garden at Capesthorne lie to the south and west of the Hall and can be reached by going through Edward Blore's Dutch gabled Tower Lodge. The principal lawned garden, overlooking a lake, was laid out in the 1960s to a design by Vernon Russell-Smith and replaced the former kitchen gardens. This lakeside garden features spectacular herbaceous borders. Irises, delphiniums, peonies, roses, potentillas and other plants put on a brilliant summer display in the top borders, backed by an old brick wall—once heated by internal flues to encourage the ripening of peaches and apricots. The borders divide half-way along, to reveal the Milanese Gates—elegant wrought iron gates dating from 1750 and depicting St Andrew holding his cross. They were transferred to Capesthorne in the middle of the last century, from Wootton Hall in Staffordshire.

From the gates, a broad path leads down to the lakeside, flanked by another pair of deep herbaceous borders. These are backed on either side by rows of acers and cherry trees (framing views of the lake) and filled with irises, lupins, phlox, dahlias, geraniums and old varieties of gallica and rugosa roses.

At the far end of the lakeside garden is a terrace, home of the peach house and vinery until the 1950s. Now it makes an excellent platform from which to view the lake, with Capesthorne Bridge in the distance. The back terrace wall is clothed with vines intertwined with clematis and roses, and below the terrace wall is a large bed of hybrid tea roses—a favourite of the late Sir Walter Bromley-Davenport—including 'Peace', 'Sunsilk', 'Fragrant Delight', 'Prima Ballerina' and 'Ernest H. Morse'.

Leaving the lakeside garden by the Milanese Gates, proceed to Capesthorne's chapel, set in a secluded garden. The path leads through an attractive iron gateway, under large old yew trees and through an avenue of clipped yews to the chapel door. A fine specimen of *Magnolia grandiflora* displays its beautiful cream flowers against the chancel wall in May. Vines and roses sprawl over the family vault. To the left of the chapel, exactly opposite the Milanese Gates, a double flight of stone steps leads up to the terrace and lawns lying to the west of the Hall.

A magnificent glass and iron conservatory once stood at the top of the steps between the chapel and the Hall. Built in the 19C by Sir Joseph Paxton, this was entirely devoted to tropical plants and fruit trees, but proved prohibitively expensive to heat and maintain, and was demolished in the 1920s. A tunnel gave access to the boiler room—you can see the entrance under the yew trees close to the flight of steps.

The west terrace stretches the full length of the Hall and features a broad gravel walk with a stone balustrade of unusual design, surmounted by a row of decorative stone vases. The retaining wall and balustrade supports a mass of climbing roses in many shades of pink.

From the terrace there are good views across the west lawn, which slopes down to a ha-ha, with parkland beyond. Nothing remains of the large parterre that once graced this lawn, although in a dry summer when the grass begins to brown, you can see the ghostly outlines of flower beds and paths.

On the northern edge of the lawn stand two holm oaks (*Quercus ilex*)—an unusual sight in the north of England—and close by a charming rose arbour has recently been constructed. The perimeter path skirts the edge of the lawn, with a clipped yew hedge on one side and a long line of American ornamental hawthorns (*Crataegus phaenopyrum*) on the other, and leads on to a grove of Lombardy poplars (*Populus nigra* 'Italica'). Fine specimens of the tree of heaven (*Ailanthus altissima*) and Caucasian wing-nut (*Pterocarya fraxinifolia*) also grow here. On the opposite side of the lawn another path, returning to the Hall, passes through an avenue of limes and maples—most of which are gifts from American visitors to the Bromley-Davenport family.

A guidebook *The Capesthorne Walks* outlines four possible exploratory routes around the estate, taking in the mill, lakes, parkland, gardens, woodland and the rhododendron walk, where purple *Rhododendron ponticum*, yellow *R. luteum* and others make a beautiful display in spring.

Chester Zoological Gardens

ADDRESS AND TELEPHONE: Chester Zoo, Chester CH2 1LH. Tel. Chester (0244) 380280

OWNERS: North of England Zoological Society

DIRECTIONS: on the outskirts of Chester, just N of the town centre. Signposted off the A41 ring road. Public transport: C40 bus from Chester Town Hall

OPENING TIMES: every day throughout the year, except Christmas Day, 10–dusk

ADMISSION: £4.60, children £2.30

CAR PARKING: yes

TOILETS: yes

REFRESHMENTS: café

SHOP: yes

DOGS: guide dogs only

WHEELCHAIR ACCESS: yes, wheelchairs for hire. Toilets for the disabled: yes

PEAK MONTHS: spring and summer

NOTABLE FEATURES: spring and summer bedding displays; rose garden; rock garden; butterfly garden; South American garden; displays of plants in animal and bird houses

The famous floral bedding displays at Chester Zoo rival the Blackpool Illuminations in colour and scale. Every autumn 80,000 spring-flowering plants—polyanthus, pansies, wallflowers, tulips, daisies and forget-me-nots and others—are planted out in borders and beds, filling every possible space with bright colour from March through to late May. These are replaced by 80,000 summer bedding plants, including geraniums, begonias, marigolds, calceolaria, verbena, heliotrope, Canna lilies and more than 100 varieties of fuchsias. Just 22 staff are employed to look after 110 acres of grounds, and all the bedding plants are grown in the zoo's own 2152 sq yd nursery.

These spectacular bedding displays are rivalled by excellent plantings of trees and shrubs throughout the grounds and in the animal enclosures. The bird house contains a fine selection of abutilons. The tropical house features—along with bright tropical birds—palm trees, rubber trees, banana plants, hibiscus, bougainvillaea and ferns. When in flower, orchids and poinsettias are brought in to add colour and interest.

A butterfly garden has been planted outside the tropical house, to encourage native butterfly species.

A garden trail takes in several garden areas. Close to the entrance is the Jubilee Garden, opened in 1977 to commemorate the Silver Jubilee of Queen Elizabeth II. The steep banks of the shady dell are clothed with rhododendrons, berberis, hypericums, potentillas, hydrangeas and fuchsias. The central pool of water is surrounded by hostas, gunnera and astilbes, and the impressive tall bronze fountain depicts Noah and the Four Winds.

Not far away, opposite the sealion pool, is the South American Garden—a huge island bed shaped like South America and planted with species and varieties of plants encountered by early explorers of Brazil, Argentina, Chile, Venezuela, Peru, Colombia and Equador. The striking Chilean orange ball tree (*Buddleia globosa*) is laden with orange-yellow pom-pom flowers in June, and the wire-stemmed *Pernettya mucronata* bears small white flowers in late spring/early summer, followed by dense clusters of marble-like berries. The common blue passion flower (*Passiflora caerulea*) is also a native of South America. Among the trees are the Roble beech (*Nothofagus obiqua*) and *Liquidambar styraciflua*.

Summer bedding in the South American garden includes calceolaria, nicotiana, mimulus and schizanthus along with well-known crop plants such as potatoes, tomatoes and maize. Scarlet-flowering runner beans are trained up bamboo canes.

Chester Zoo gardens were established and developed by Mrs Elizabeth Mottershead, wife of the zoo founder. In memory of Mrs

Mottershead's 40 years of continuous effort, a rock garden was created in 1968. This lies on the garden trail, in a tranquil spot beyond the Oakfield restaurant. A series of small pools is linked by a stream, which winds its way between boulders and under rustic bridges. Throughout spring and summer the stream margins are bright with small plants and flowers, especially primulas. Bold drifts of hostas flower in June and July.

The Memorial Garden is bounded by conifers, including a specimen of the dawn redwood (*Metasequoia glyptostroboides*). Shrubs such as *Berberis thunbergii atropurpurea* offer variations of leaf colour and form.

The Fountain Garden and the rose garden make a spectacular combination in the centre of the grounds. In the Fountain Garden, well tended lawns, bright with beds and borders of annuals, surround a circular pool and bronze fountain depicting a group of playful otters. In summer the pool is encircled by scarlet bedding begonias—a splendid sight, viewed with the rose garden beyond.

The rose garden is planted in formal Victorian style, with such well known roses as 'Fragrant Delight' and the deep crimson 'Frensham'. There are some fine colour combinations, including a bed of bright vermilion 'Trumpeter' matched with white standard 'Iceberg' roses.

Dunham Massey

ADDRESS AND TELEPHONE: Dunham Massey Hall, Altrincham, Cheshire WA14 4SJ. Tel. (061-941) 1025.

OWNERS: The National Trust

DIRECTIONS: 3 miles SW of Altrincham off the A56. Public transport: nearest BR station Altrincham. Buses from Altrincham and Warrington

OPENING TIMES: 30 March to 3 November, garden open daily 12–5.30 (except Sun and Bl Is 1–5.30). Park open all year round. House open except Fri

ADMISSION CHARGE: house and garden £3.50; garden only £1.50, children 50p. Family ticket £8.75. Park only £1 per car (NT members free). Coach parties welcome

CAR PARKING: yes (£1)

TOILETS: yes

REFRESHMENTS: restaurant (except Fri)

SHOP: yes

DOGS: in park only, on lead

WHEELCHAIR ACCESS: yes (special car parking by arrangement). Toilets for the disabled: yes

PEAK MONTHS: no special peaks

NOTABLE FEATURES: historical garden and deer park; moat; mount; parterre; fine trees and shrubs; woodland and stream gardens

A remarkable series of paintings in the house at Dunham Massey records the history and development of the gardens here in the 17C and 18C. In the Great Gallery, bird's-eye view paintings by Adriaen van Diest (1697) and John Harris (1751) clearly show the large moated house set in an impressive stretch of grounds.

The main structure of the 18C park has survived, with the 18C high brick wall surrounding the estate, the Elizabethan mill and the Tudor mount—despite some neglect earlier this century, when large areas of the formal gardens around the house were turned over to vegetable production.

During the 19C an informal pleasure ground with winding paths was developed to the east of the house, on the site of a walled kitchen garden. A number of trees survive from this period.

More significant changes were made early this century, when the Grey family laid out the parterre between the house and the moat, planted more trees and shrubs in and around the east lawn and created a water garden along the banks of the feeder stream. In 1976 the property passed into the hands of the National Trust, and since then much clearing, pruning and replanting has been done.

You approach the red-brick house from the north, crossing the moat via a small bridge. Avenues of newly planted lime trees radiate from the house, planted along the lines of the original triple avenue. Around 230 acres of parkland are open to the public, with a few areas protected as sanctuaries and grazing areas for the 150 fallow deer. The entrance to the garden lies to the east of the house.

The east front of the house looks out over a lawn with a mixed border screening the entrance path. In the border you can see the tall Japanese angelica tree (*Aralia elata*), with rhododendrons, buddleias and a mixture of hydrangeas. To the front is *Hypericum kouytchense* (*H. acmosepalum*)—a splendid semi-evergreen shrub.

Beyond the tall swamp cypress (*Taxodium distichum*) at the north-east corner of the house lies the entrance to the north parterre, laid out in 1905. Overlooking part of the moat and commanding a good view up the North Avenue, the parterre is bounded to the east and west by golden yew hedges. The intricate beds are planted in strong colours, particularly blues, purples and golds.

Beyond the yew hedge to the west is the mount, a relic from the much earlier Tudor garden. Once encircled by rings of clipped hedges and crowned by a gazebo, it is now grassed over, with laburnums and rhododendrons around its base.

An 18C orangery stands on the main lawn to the east, with shrub borders on either side. Myrtles and mandarin oranges are moved in here for protection during winter.

In front of the orangery, 3 acres of lawn are fringed with specimen trees. Behind is a canal, its banks well planted. Beyond a small bridge are groups of shrubs, richly coloured in autumn.

From here it is only a few yards to the North Avenue. In the centre of this avenue are the dogs' graves, and in the far north, beyond the ha-ha, an obelisk erected in the mid 18C by George Booth, the 2nd Earl of Warrington.

Beyond the birch woodland, a row of tall copper beeches marks the boundary of a long-lost rose garden. Close by, at the end of the canal, is the Well House, which once supplied fresh water to the house. To one side of the Well House is an arbour, restored using false acacia timber grown in the garden.

The woodland garden begins on the far side of the main lawn. Foxgloves and bluebells are being encouraged to grow here and many acers and rowans have been planted, together with a collection of late-flowering azaleas. A spring-fed stream, bordered with moisture-loving plants, runs over a series of low waterfalls, around the woodland boundary.

The National Trust has done a great deal of work at Dunham Massey, recreating a beautiful garden on an important historical site and providing, not only an area of green space close to the spreading city of Manchester, but also a garden of great variety and horticultural interest.

Hare Hill

- ADDRESS AND TELEPHONE: Hare Hill Gardens, Over Alderley, near Macclesfield, Cheshire SK10 4QB. Tel. (0625) 828981

  OWNERS: The National Trust

  DIRECTIONS: off B5087 between Alderley Edge and Prestbury. Public transport: Alderley Edge BR 2½ miles or Prestury BR 2½ miles. Buses from Macclesfield and Wimslow past Prestbury BR, then ¾-mile walk

  OPENING TIMES: 30 March to 27 October, Wed, Thurs, Sat, Sun and BH Mon 10–5.30; 20 May to 7 June, special daily opening for rhododendron season; 2 November to end of March, Sat and Sun 10–5.30. House not open

  ADMISSION: £1

  CAR PARKING: yes. Coaches by arrangement with the head gardener

  TOILETS: yes

  REFRESHMENTS: no

  SHOP: no

  DOGS: no

  WHEELCHAIR ACCESS: with assistance. Toilets for the disabled: yes

  PEAK SEASON: May and June for rhododendrons

  NOTABLE FEATURES: rhododendrons; walled garden; woodland and parkland; link path through to Alderley Edge

The gardens at Hare Hill extend to about 12 acres, and consist of three main areas—a rhododendron walk, a woodland garden with ponds, and a walled garden in a sheltered glade. The best time to visit is in late spring and early summer when the rhododendrons are in flower.

The gardens are thought to date from about 1820, when Hare Hill House was built, but the planting in and around the walled garden was established this century by Colonel Charles Douglas Fergusson Phillips Brocklehurst (1904–77) with advice from James

Russell. The Colonel died in 1977 and left the gardens to the National Trust in his will, in memory of his twin brother, and to mark his own long association with the Trust's country houses.

Since 1978 the Trust has developed the gardens further, especially the area around the walled garden, not as a period garden, but with plants popular today. The driveway runs through parkland to the car park, which is sheltered by tall sycamores and beech trees. A bank of rhododendrons at the entrance sets the scene for the rhododendron walk, which leads eastwards towards the walled garden. This walk skirts the edge of densely planted woodland. Groups of rhododendrons frame open views across the parkland.

The rhododendron walk also features a good collection of hollies, some of considerable height. A Himalayan musk rose scrambles through one holly, while another is almost smothered by *Clematis montana*, a tumbling cascade of soft pink flowers in late spring and summer. *Hydrangea petiolaris*, normally a strong-growing climber, grows horizontally across the ground and *Cornus canadensis*, the creeping dogwood, forms starry carpets of white flowers in summer. A few acers such as the coral bark maple (*Acer palmatum* 'Senkaki') provide interest later in the year and the National Trust plans to add more genera to extend the season in this part of the garden.

A suprising feature on one side of the walled garden is the eucryphias—surprising because they have grown and flowered here particularly well, despite being in a frost pocket. To the rear of the walled garden is the gardener's bothy and more plantings of rhododendrons along the paths, which from this point disappear into the woodland.

The design inside the walled garden has been kept simple, contrasting with the richness and density of planting around the outside walls. To the south are good views of the parkland, through ornate black and gold iron railings set up after the 1939–45 war.

Woodland lying to the north, beyond the bothy, is rich in chestnuts, beeches, sycamores and young oak trees, and is managed to encourage wild flowers. Bracken is being controlled to permit further planting of rhododendrons. Two rustic bridges cross ponds and streams. On its the way back to the rhododendron walk, the path passes the Dell—a grassy hollow sheltered by shrubs and trees, with a stone urn as a focal point and daffodils in spring. The pieris is spectacular in late spring, with yellow and mauve flowering rhododendrons either side. At the bottom of the slope is a good specimen of *Magnolia delavayi*, with parchment-coloured flowers in late May.

The tulip tree nearby is almost mature enough to flower—something to watch out for on a return visit.

Jodrell Bank Arboretum

ADDRESS AND TELEPHONE: Jodrell Bank Visitor Centre, Macclesfield, Cheshire SK11 9DL. Tel. Lower Withington (0477) 71571

OWNERS: University of Manchester

DIRECTIONS: off the A535 about 3 miles NW of Holmes Chapel. No public transport

OPENING TIMES: Easter to October, daily 10.30–5.30, November to Easter, weekends only 12–5. Science Centre open at same times as Arboretum.

ADMISSION: £3, OAPs £2, children £1.65, children under 5 free but not admitted to planetarium, family ticket £8. Reductions for coach parties

CAR PARKING: yes

TOILETS: yes, in Science Centre

REFRESHMENTS: café

SHOP: yes

DOGS: no

WHEELCHAIR ACCESS: flat site but can get waterlogged in wet weather. Hard pathways for trails lasting ½ hour and 1 hour. Toilets for the disabled: yes, in Science Centre

PEAK SEASON: spring blossom and autumn colours

NOTABLE FEATURES: Arboretum; malus and sorbus collections; rose and heather gardens; ponds; views of Pennine hills and radio telescope

Jodrell Bank is best known as the home of the world-famous Radio Telescope. The 35-acre arboretum is a relatively new attraction.

Before 1972 this university-owned site (which lies across the car park from the Science Centre) was open pasture. Sir William Mather and Professor Sir Bernard Lovell were jointly responsible for setting up the arboretum. With generous financial support from the Granada Foundation, several thousand varieties of trees and shrubs have been planted, including the National Council for the Conservation of Plants and Gardens' designated National Collections of flowering crab (malus) and rowans and whitebeams (sorbus). Fine collections of old-fashioned and shrub roses have also been established.

Much of the arboretum is laid out as woodland, with glades and large areas of open lawn set with heather and rose gardens and shrub beds. Long grassy rides—Lovell Way, Mather Way, Pennine View, Jodrell Way etc—cut through the tree plantings.

The first tree groups you encounter are birches and alders (betula and alnus species) just left of the entrance. There are good specimens of the white barked *Betula pendula*, the yellow *B. lutea* and the brown *B. nigra*. The alders include the handsome weeping grey alder (*Alnus incana* 'Pendula') a large mound of pendulous branches and grey-green leaves, and *Alnus glutinosa* 'Imperialis' with deeply and finely cut foliage. There is a small collection of mock orange or philadelphus, among the birches and alders.

There are good groups of dwarf mountain pines (*Pinus mugo*) and the native Scots pine (*Pinus sylvestris*) on the way to the heather garden; also a collection of berberis and fine specimens of the dawn redwood (*Metasequoia glyptostroboides*), the swamp cypress (*Taxodium distichum*) and the tulip tree (*Liriodendron tulipifera*).

Large island beds set into lawn contain the Heather Society's calluna collection of some 150 varieties, duplicating the collection at Harlow Carr in Yorkshire. Nearby is a group of potentillas—yellow, white and orange-red flowering varieties.

Eastwards, beyond the heather and rose gardens, the remainder of the tree park is more densely planted, with large numbers of fast-growing species such as birch, pine and larch. These act as nurse trees, providing shelter for some of the more delicate specimen trees, but will eventually be removed. The malus collection of around 100 species and varieties can be seen here and scattered throughout the park—their white, pink and carmine flowers make a spectacular sight in spring. There are also some 80 different members of the genus sorbus; the whitebeams (*Sorbus aria*) are especially striking.

Towards the eastern end of the Pennine View ride are several specimens of southern beech (nothofagus). Among these is *N. procera*, renowned for its rich autumn colours, and the smaller leaved *N. antarctica*. Limes grow nearby. The Crimean lime (*Tilia x euchlora*) attracts bees in large numbers; the flowers have a strongly narcotic effect which leaves them drowsy and can even kill them.

The tree park's five ponds are planted to encourage wildlife.

Lyme Park

ADDRESS AND TELEPHONE: Lyme Park, Disley, Stockport, Cheshire SK12 2NX. Tel. Disley (0663) 62023

OWNERS: The National Trust but administered by Stockport Metropolitan Borough Council

DIRECTIONS: 6½ miles SE of Stockport, off A6 just W of Disley. Public transport: buses from Stockport and Buxton to Disley, then 1½-mile walk from gates

OPENING TIMES: garden, all year daily, except 25 and 26 December 11–5 (summer) 11–4 (winter)

ADMISSION: park and garden £3 per car

CAR PARKING: yes

TOILETS: yes

REFRESHMENTS: café

SHOP: yes

DOGS: under control in park, on lead in garden

WHEELCHAIR ACCESS: to parts of the garden (telephone in advance). Toilets for the disabled: yes

PEAK MONTHS: no special peak

NOTABLE FEATURES: orangery; rose garden; Dutch garden; terraces; rhododendrons and shrubs in informal ravine/stream garden

From the A6 at Disley a long twisting driveway climbs up through the tree-studded parkland of Lyme Park. This estate has been famous since Tudor times for its breed of red deer, which once provided sport for the Legh family, its owners for 600 years (the National Trust took over in 1946). The view of the splendid Palladian style mansion is saved to the very last minute, as you round the final bend of the drive.

It is an unlikely place to find a garden. The estate covers some 1377 acres and in parts rises as high as 1200ft above sea level to the wild rugged moorland edge of the Peak District. The 15-acre garden itself lies at 800ft. Spring comes late, summer is short and the clouds frequently hang low. The rainfall is high, about 40in.

Despite the challenges of the climate, gardening has been practised at Lyme Park for several hundred years. Apples and other crops were grown here in the 17C. In the late 19C, the 1st Lord Newton began laying out steps and terraces, the sunken Dutch garden, and he built the orangery.

The garden lies to the south of the house, which is built around a square inner courtyard. Parts of the north front of the great mansion date back 400 years. Pass under the central archway of the house, cross the inner courtyard (its walls faced with a warm pink-coloured stone quarried on the estate), and go through the archway of the south front. A wide view opens up across the lawns to an informal garden pond, which is believed to date from the 17C, when it was probably rectangular in shape and came up as far as the Hall. To the east a series of wide stone steps and broad walks ascends Lord Newton's grassy terraces, a suitable starting place for your tour.

Accessible from the terraces and set back a little from the house is Lord Newton's glass-roofed orangery, a beautiful stone and glass building containing a splashing four-tiered fountain. Oranges are no longer grown here but a wide range of plants including figs, camellias and abutilons, provide colour and interest for much of the year.

Blazing formal displays of spring and summer bedding enhance the lawns either side of the orangery entrance, and wrought iron gates lead into a small rose garden, enclosed by walls and yew hedges, with stone steps leading up to a terrace and summerhouse. A splendid view can be had from the terrace over formal beds of roses, set in a symmetrical pattern around a small fountain. Further east, the herbaceous borders, colourful in summer flank a central walk and provide a contrast to the rugged moorland beyond.

Killtime Garden, an informally planted ravine, can be found across the lawns from the herbaceous borders. A gushing stream from the moorland enters this garden near an old stone bridge and races through the ravine to meet the garden pond lower down. This area is now a garden glade with woodland shrubs and moisture-loving plants providing a long season of interest on the steep banks of the stream, beneath a canopy of tall trees. Paths lead through the ravine to the water's edge. Several philadelphus add fragrance and later hydrangeas and hypericums bring colour to the ravine, followed by cotoneasters and mahonias in autumn and winter.

The pleasant wildness of the ravine area accentuates the formality of the Dutch garden, to be found past the garden pond, west of the house. Laid out by Lord Newton in the late 19C, this sunken garden was originally known as the Italian garden and featured an intricately shaped parterre, ornamented with vases and statues (replicas of the originals). Today, brightly coloured carpets of bedding surround a fountain.

The Vicary Gibbs Garden lies below the west front. Gibbs of Aldenham, Hertfordshire, a friend of the family, made a gift of choice trees and shrubs to Lyme Park, including the Algerian oak (*Quercus canariensis*), *Aesculus* x *hybrida* and *Cornus kousa*. These are complemented by other plants which were first raised at Aldenham, such as Malus 'Gibbs' Golden Gage' and Malus 'Aldenhamensis'.

Ness Gardens: University of Liverpool Botanic Gardens

ADDRESS AND TELEPHONE: University of Liverpool Botanic Gardens, Ness Gardens, Ness, Neston, South Wirral, Cheshire. Tel. (051 336) 7769/8733

OWNERS: University of Liverpool

DIRECTIONS: 9 miles NW of Chester. S off the A540 between Ness and Burton

OPENING TIMES: all year round except 25 December, daily March to October 9.30–dusk, November to February 9.30–4

ADMISSION: £2.50, OAPs and children £1.50, family ticket £6

CAR PARKING: yes. Coaches welcome

TOILETS: yes

REFRESHMENTS: restaurant

SHOP: plant sales area

DOGS: no

WHEELCHAIR ACCESS: yes, but limited. Toilets for the disabled: yes

PEAK SEASON: peaks from May through to October

NOTABLE FEATURES: many unusual plants; heather garden; collections of rhododendrons\azaleas; collection of roses laid out to show development of the modern rose; large rock garden; herbaceous borders; herb garden; water garden; collection of native species for conservation; many shrubs and trees first introduced by Forrest and Kingdon Ward

Ness Gardens are spread over some 50 acres of undulating land in the southern part of the Wirral peninsula, overlooking the Dee Estuary and with views to the Welsh hills. The gardens have a low average rainfall, about 30in. due to the 'rain shadow' created by these hills and cold air rolling down them lowers the temperatures, although frosts are generally fewer and less severe than those further inland.

The gardens were founded in 1898 by Arthur Kilpin Bulley, a successful cotton broker from Liverpool who took a keen interest in natural history and gardening. Appreciating the site's assets— the south-facing position and the variety of soils, including boulder

Key to numbers
1 Experimental area
2 Heather garden
3 Herb garden
4 Herbaceous section
5 Native plant
   collection
6 Pergola rose walk
7 Plant houses
8 Rhododendron border
9 Rock garden
10 Rose garden
11 Specimen shrubs
12 Terrace

Key to symbols in the
introduction

Stott Willow
collection →

Meadow

Water
garden

Spinney

NESTON ROAD

Pine
wood

Yards
0   200

clay or marl, sand and silt—Bulley decided to grow a wide range of hardy plants from all over the world. He arranged for business-men and missionaries to send seed from abroad, but the results were disappointing. In the words of his wife, Bulley ended up with 'the best international collection of dandelions'.

After seeking professional advice from the Regius Keeper of the Royal Botanic Garden at Edinburgh, Bulley financed George For-rest to collect plants in Western China in 1904 and 1910. F. Kingdon Ward's services were hired in 1911 and a year later R.E. Cooper was commissioned to collect in Bhutan. The new introductions were grown at Ness and Bulley founded the famous seed firm of Bees Ltd. He also opened his garden regularly to the public.

By the time Bulley died in 1942, the gardens were suffering from inevitable neglect due to the war. In 1948 his daughter, Miss Lois Bulley, gave the gardens to the University of Liverpool on the condition that a specified area should be kept open to the public. Since then the gardens have been restored, and in places replanted and developed.

Bulley's design and planting can still be seen in several areas. The surrounding shelter belts, for instance, contain poplars, holm oaks (*Quercus ilex*) and Scots pines (*Pinus sylvestris*) planted by Bulley to screen the garden from the fierce gales that lash off the Irish Sea.

Bulley's rock garden, although largely rebuilt, still lies in a valley sun trap to the south of the house. It is constructed of red sandstone, mostly excavated from within the gardens, and contains a wide variety of plants, including the orange-flowering *Primula bulley-ana*, complemented by the pink purple spikes of *Primula beesiana*. There are early flowering bulbs—snowdrops, crocus, and *Scilla tubergeniana*—followed in March by dwarf narcissus *Iris recticu-lata* and *Scilla sibirica*, and in May and June by a dazzling display of candelabra primulas.

Rhododendrons grow well at Ness and can be seen to very fine effect in the long serpentine border below the pine woodland in the eastern boundary of the garden. The best time to view this border is in April and early May, when you can see the scarlet flowers of rhododendron 'Elizabeth', purple *R. russatum* and pink *R. davidsonianum*. Here too is the pinkish *Rhododendron rox-ieanum*, which was raised from seed sent to this country from China by Forrest. Interest is provided later in the year by lilies and hydrangeas planted between the rhododendrons. A peat garden has been established in pine woodland behind the border.

Many people make annual visits to Ness Garden in mid May, to see the garden's outstanding azalea collection in flower. The main part of the azalea border was planted in 1900 but many newer varieties have been added since, extending the flowering season and range of colours. The azaleas are underplanted with bulbs, for interest in early spring, mid summer and autumn.

The heather garden comes into its own in late summer/early autumn when thousands of plants form a patchwork of colour on a steep west-facing hillside. Early flowering varieties like *Erica* x *veitchii* and *E. australis* are incorporated to provide colour by the end of April; in May *Erica tetralix* takes over, followed by the Connemara heath (*Daboecia cantabrica*). But undoubtedly the various coloured forms of Cornish heath (*Erica vagans*) make the greatest impact, together with the vast range of *Calluna vulgaris* cultivars. Ranging in flower colour from white and pale bluish-pink to deep purple and fiery red, many of the heathers also have bright foliage. *Calluna vulgaris* 'Robert Chapman', for instance, has young growth of gold which changes through bronze in autumn to copper in winter.

No botanic garden would be complete without a good collection of trees and shrubs. At Ness there are excellent collections of sorbus and magnolias and among the older plantings, you can see Forrest's original *Pieris formosa forrestii*. This beautiful specimen, with young leaves of flaming scarlet, was almost destroyed in the bad winter of 1962–63, but has since grown back.

Newer features at Ness include a terrace garden, excellent herbaceous borders and a rose garden where a good collection of roses—china, noisette, bourbon, floribunda, and others—are laid out to portray the development of the modern rose. The Ledsham herb garden was added in 1974. This features all the main culinary herbs. A laburnum arch stands on one side and a garden for the blind, with braille labelling, on the other.

Around the water garden grow endangered native species, all raised from seeds or cuttings taken from the wild. Among these are *Primula scotia, Gentiana verna, Saxifraga roseacea* and willows. Seeds from these plants have provided fresh stock for replanting in the wild as well as supplying the seed bank at Kew Gardens.

Tatton Park

ADDRESS AND TELEPHONE: Tatton Park, Knutsford, Cheshire, WA16 6QN. Tel. Knutsford (0565) 654822

OWNERS: The National Trust but administered by Cheshire County Council

DIRECTIONS: 3½ miles N of Knutsford. 4 miles S of Altrincham. Signposted from A556. Public transport: Knutsford BR. Buses from Manchester or Chester Sun only

OPENING TIMES: 29 March to 30 September, daily except Mon (open BH Mon) 12–4. Park, daily except Mon (open BH Mon)11–6. October to end March, daily except Mon 11–4. Mansion and Old Hall open at different times. Closed 25 December

ADMISSION: gardens £2, children £1.40p. Extra for farm and Old Hall. All-in-ticket £5, children £3.50. Family ticket £15. Parties welcome at reduced charges for 12 or more

CAR PARKING: yes, £1.70, including NT members

TOILETS: yes

REFRESHMENTS: café

SHOP: yes

DOGS: on lead in garden

WHEELCHAIR ACCESS: yes. Toilets for the disabled: yes

PEAK MONTHS: no special peak

NOTABLE FEATURES: Japanese garden; restored Italian garden; arboretum; rose garden; rhododendrons and azaleas; fernery

Tatton Park was the home of the Egerton family for 400 years until Maurice Egerton bequeathed it to the National Trust on his death in 1958.

Today the pleasure grounds at Tatton Park extend to 60 acres set in a large area of parkland landscaped by Humphry Repton at the end of the 18C. The work of six generations of the Egerton family can be seen here, displaying the changes in gardening fashions and ideas about garden design over the last 200 years. Elaborate formal gardens contrast with large areas of informal planting, and you will need to allow plenty of time to see everything that Tatton has to offer.

The beautiful stone and glass orangery, built in 1818, is one of the first things that you come to. It is still in use, and although it is closed to the public, you can see many of the orange trees and a selection of exotic climbers through the windows. Behind the orangery, a show house and a fernery, open to visitors, house a colourful collection of conservatory plants, and tall banks of ferns. The fernery was designed by Joseph Paxton in the mid 19C. Here you can see the giant fern (*Woodwardii radicans*), as well as New Zealand tree ferns and a kowhai (*Sophora tetraptera*) with fragrant yellow flowers in May and June. At the far end, water trickles into a pool, surrounded by mossy rocks. A creeping fig (*Ficus radicans*) almost completely covers the inside walls.

The outside walls support a variety of climbing plants. A long border, divided into bays by yew buttresses, displays shrubs, roses and herbaceous and annual plants. At the end of the walk another border overlooks a stretch of lawn planted with trees, and Lady Charlotte's fountain and arbour. In front of the small rose-covered trellis shelter is a graceful Brewer's weeping spruce (*Picea brewerana*) and a collection of magnolias. Either side of the tiered fountain are Yoshino cherries (*Prunus* x *yedoensis* 'Moerheimii').

The mixed borders end in topiary of monstrous proportions, and a gap in the yew hedge lets you through into a sunken, paved rose garden. Known as Her Ladyship's Garden this small walled area was laid out in 1913 in an intricate pattern of beds, with a small pool as a focal point. It is especially pretty in the summer when the Edwardian polyantha roses bloom and the pergola is covered with flowers.

To reach the Tower Garden, go through the gap in the wall behind the rose garden pool. The tall brick tower, dating from before 1750, dominates a small enclosed garden. In the centre is the unusual *Dacaisnea fargessi*, which bears small yellow flowers in spring and peculiar sticky blue pods in autumn. Elsewhere there are hostas and hydrangeas; and by a gateway near the tower, a specimen of the Kentucky Coffee Tree (*Gymnocladus dioica*), so called because the early settlers in North America used the seeds as a coffee substitute. It is a handsome slow-growing tree, with leaves tinted pink as they unfold, turning clear yellow in autumn.

Leaving the Tower Garden by this gateway, winding paths take you through woodland, where you can see rhododendrons and other shade-loving plants, beneath a canopy of sweet chestnuts. The glade of dawn redwoods (*Metasequoia glytostroboides*), was grown from some of the first seeds to be introduced into Britain in 1948. South of this is the Golden Brook and lake bordered by swamp cypress (*Taxodium distichum*) (which you can recognise by the knobbly 'knees' around the base of the trunk), and waterside plants such as *Gunnera manicata*. The water fowl here come from all over the world.

Close to the wooden bridge which spans the brook is a group of unusual twisted weeping mountain ashes (*Sorbus aucuparia* 'Pendula'), and across the bridge is another curiously twisted plant—the corkscrew hazel (*Corylus avellana contorta*).

The fine arboretum along the western boundary of the garden contains a good selection of broadleaved and conifer species, including a tall Wellingtonia (*Sequoiadendron giganteum*), the white or Weymouth pine (*Pinus strobus*) and the Chilean Incense cedar (*Austrocedrus chilensis*). The arboretum is beautiful in spring, with glades of bluebells, hybrid rhododendrons, forsythia and viburnums, crab apples and cherries. In summer look for the fragrant mock orange (philadelphus), lilacs and dogwoods. The maples colour magnificently in autumn, and the Persian ironwood (Parrotia persica) turns crimson and gold. There are plenty of conifers here too.

From the aboretum it is a short walk along the edge of the Golden Brook to the Japanese garden. This was the creation of the 3rd Baron Egerton, Alan de Tatton, who brought in Japanese workmen in 1910, to construct a rural landscape in miniature, full of streams and small islands. A thatched teahouse stands on a central island, and stone pagodas, lanterns and symbolic figures are carefully placed throughout. In one corner is a mossy mound capped with white stones representing a snow clad Mount Fuji. Across an arched bridge over the brook is a Shinto Temple, brought from Japan. Japanese maples (*Acer palmatum*), glades of bamboos, Kurume azaleas and dwarf conifers complete the theme.

A Grecian temple marks the edge of the gardens. It overlooks parkland and a lake formed by subsidence (which began in the 1920s and is still continuing). The temple stands at one end of the broad walk, a long avenue of beech trees planted 250 years ago, which formed the main driveway to the house until Humphry Repton created the longer curving drive used today. Many of the beech trees have had to be replaced, but the avenue still forms an attractive walk with plantings of rhododendrons and some unusual trees such as the thorny, large leaved castor oil tree (*Kalopanax pictus*).

Half-way along the broad walk is another novelty—an African style hut with a thatched roof of heather. It was constructed earlier this century by Maurice Egerton, perhaps to remind him of his frequent safaris in Africa. Beyond the hut he planted a dell with rhododendrons and azaleas—some of which he introduced to Britain himself. The mass display of colour in the dell is at its best in May and June.

A leech pool, now ornamented by a fountain and surrounded by Royal Fern (*Osmunda regalis*), and a small beech maze are among features to be found just off the broad walk. Closer to the house a wide expanse of lawn has been planted with lime trees, each commemorating a special family occasion.

From the south front of the house you get the best view of the spectacular Italian garden. Designed by Joseph Paxton in the mid 19C, it is laid out in a series of balustraded terraces and parterres, and decorated with fountains, vases and steps. In spring the intricately shaped beds, edged with clipped box, are bright with polyanthus and forget-me-nots, followed later by sea thrift, which forms a second row of edging, and pink dahlias.

Over the years the Italian garden has seen many changes and long periods of neglect. The present display is an accurate reconstruction of Paxton's design, and, although only completed in 1986, already has an air of maturity.

CORNWALL

Cotehele House

ADDRESS AND TELEPHONE: Cotehele House, St Dominick, near Saltash, Cornwall PL12 6TA. Tel. Liskeard (0579) 50434/51222

OWNERS: The National Trust

DIRECTIONS: reached by a maze of country lanes—14 miles from Plymouth via Tamar Bridge, 4 miles from Gunnislake, 8 miles SW of Tavistock, 6 miles from Calstock or 2 miles E of St Dominick. Can be reached by footpath from Calstock (1 mile) or by boat cruises from Plymouth. Public transport: Calstock BR then footpath (1 mile). Alternatively cruise with Plymouth Boat Cruises Ltd from Plymouth to Cotehele Quay

OPENING TIMES: all year, daily (house and restaurant closed Fri) 11–6 or dusk if earlier

ADMISSION: house, garden and mill £4.40; garden and mill only £2.20. Reductions for pre-booked parties; no party bookings on Sun or BH weekends. No unbooked parties accepted. Party organisers should obtain a copy of coach route from administrators as many of the lanes leading to Cotehele are too narrow for coaches

CAR PARKING: yes, by house and by quay

TOILETS: yes

REFRESHMENTS: restaurant

SHOP: yes

DOGS: no

WHEELCHAIR ACCESS: yes, but glen very steep. Toilets for the disabled: yes

PEAK SEASONS: spring and summer

NOTABLE FEATURES: terraces and formal garden; climbing plants and trees; wooded valley garden with medieval dovecot

Cotehele House stands high above the River Tamar, at the head of a spectacular, steep, wooded glen.

A romantic looking building, with its high gables, lancet windows and crenellated tower, Cotehele was built between 1485 and 1627 and was for centuries the home of the Edgcumbe family. In the late 16C Richard Edgcumbe built another house at Mount Edgcumbe on the Rame Peninsula, some 10 miles down river, and after this Cotehele was used mainly as a country retreat. The gardens are on different levels around the house and much of the present design dates from Victorian times.

The main driveway, from the south, passes beneath huge old sycamore trees, leading to the carriage turning circle in front of the house. Around the main entrance are bushy ceanothus—a haze of

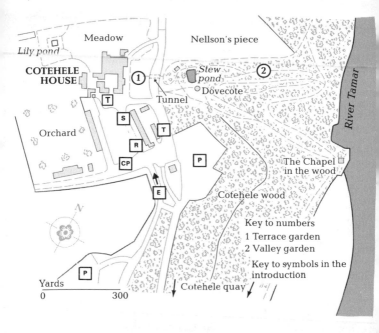

blue in May. A cobbled path to the left leads into a small courtyard known as Retainer's Court. The camellias here include *C.* x *williamsii* 'J.C. Williams', one of the very best hybrids, bearing glorious pink blossoms from winter onwards, and *C. saluenensis* 'Cornish Snow', with single white flowers, flushed pink on the reverse. *Myrtus communis* on the west wall bears white flowers in July and August, followed by purple-black berries, and *Hydrangea petiolaris* flowers creamy white in June.

Passing through an archway, you enter a meadow area, bright with daffodils in spring. An ornate white-painted gate gives access to the upper garden, formal in design, centring on a square lily pool with an island of pampas grasses. Medieval stone walls enclose this garden and provide support for ivies, jasmines and other climbers. Herbaceous plants and small shrubs flower in summer beneath the north wall.

The lawns surrounding the pool are planted with interesting trees, including a recently planted Judas tree (*Cercis siliquastrum*) and a young cork oak (*Quercus suber*). There is also a big tulip tree (*Liriodendron tulipifera*) and a golden ash (*Fraxinus excelsior* 'Jaspidea' or 'Aurea') with beautiful yellow leaves in autumn and shoots of golden-yellow particularly conspicuous in winter.

Two young specimens of the Tree of Heaven (*Ailanthus altissima*) stand on the lawns above the pool. On rising ground to the west another bright border, featuring fuchsias, kniphofias, alstroemerias, rudbeckias and hemerocallis, is set off to advantage against a dark yew hedge. Behind, in a nursery area, straight rows of larkspur, asters, dahlias and other flowers are grown for cutting.

The mood changes to the north of the house as you enter a region of meadowy banks and slopes informally planted with trees and shrubs and carpeted in spring with daffodils and bluebells. Near the house is a magnificent spreading copper beech (*Fagus sylvatica* 'Purpurea') and another tulip tree. There is also an ancient mulberry (*Morus nigra*) and a group of whitebeam (*Sorbus aria* 'Lutescens').

A path running through this meadow brings you to a little dell planted with acers—*Acer japonicum* 'Vitifolium', *A. palmatum* 'Dissectum Atropurpureum' and many more. Passing next through a grove of rhododendrons, you come to a high peaked archway, covered in white-flowering wisteria—the entrance to the Terrace Garden, below the east front.

This garden is simple in design with three terraces, dating from 1862, now divided between neat strips of lawn and long rose beds. The granite house walls, are clothed with a huge *Magnolia grandiflora*, a passion flower and several roses including the Macartney rose and two very attractive old hybrids—'Zephirine Drouhin' with clusters of cerise-pink, sweetly scented blooms, and climbing 'Souvenir de la Malmaison', with large, strongly fragrant, double flowers, creamy with rosy centres.

The walls surrounding the Terrace Garden are also well covered with climbers and shrubs, and the wall borders overflow with phlomis, senecio, euphorbias and others—the dark purple leaves of the smoke tree (*Cotinus coggygria*) make a particularly good contrast with the grey stone. Below two recently planted magnolias on the lowest lawn the ground falls away steeply, giving views into the Valley Garden, or Woodland Glen, above the river.

A flight of steps and a tunnel connect the Valley Garden with the terraces. Out in the sunlight again, a curving path leads past a large specimen of *Camellia japonica* 'Elegans' and on towards a thatched summerhouse, overlooking a stew pond. Long ago fish were kept here, ready for serving at table; now the pond is edged with the lush foliage of gunnera, hostas, ferns and white arums. Across the water stands a large medieval dovecot, shaped like a beehive.

Rhododendrons and azaleas fill the upper woodland with colour in spring; there are also some good camellias and magnolias, and a tall embothrium. *Hypericum calycinum*, the rose of Sharon, produces golden flowers in summer, followed by the showy heads of hydrangeas, and the acers turning to fiery colours in autumn. Zigzag paths lead down through the woodland, and a stream tumbles from top to bottom, its margins lost among primulas, ferns hostas and large-leaved *Gunnera manicata*.

Further into the glen there are dark, ferny walks beneath tall spruces, larches and hemlocks. Leaving the garden through a picket gate at the bottom of the valley, you may go on to explore the Chapel in the Wood and Cotehele Quay half a mile downstream.

At one time the quay would have been alive with the bustle of river traffic carrying coal, limestone, manufactured goods and agricultural produce. The introduction of the railway effectively signed its death sentence, and after the National Trust took it over in 1947 a great deal of restoration work was necessary. The Cotehele estate was the first to be given to the National Trust by the Inland Revenue, having been accepted by them in lieu of death duties, thus setting an important precedent.

Glendurgan

ADDRESS AND TELEPHONE: Glendurgan Gardens, Mawnan Smith, near Falmouth, Cornwall TR11 5JZ. Tel. Bodmin (0208) 74281

OWNERS: The National Trust

DIRECTIONS: 4 miles SW of Falmouth and ½ mile SW of Mawnan Smith on road to Helford Passage. Public transport: by bus from The Moor, Falmouth to Helford Passage

OPENING TIMES: March to end October, Tues to Sat and BH Mon (closed Good Fri) 10.30–5.30 (last admission 4.30). House not open

ADMISSION: £2, children £1. No reductions for coach parties, who must book in advance

CAR PARKING: yes

TOILETS: yes

REFRESHMENTS: no

SHOP: no

DOGS: no

WHEELCHAIR ACCESS: limited, there are some very steep slopes. Toilets for the disabled: yes

PEAK MONTHS: April to June

NOTABLE FEATURES: valley garden; exotic and tender trees and shrubs; views across valley; laurel maze; pond; walled garden

In 1762 George Croker Fox moved the family business which had originally been established in Fowey in the mid 17C to Falmouth. By 1789 his business had prospered and he built a house—Grove Hill—above the harbour and established a garden. The Fox family were Quakers and very keen gardeners; members of the family established gardens throughout the surrounding countryside, at Roskrow, Trebah, Rosehill, Tredrea, Penjerrick and Glendurgan. Alfred Fox planted Glendurgan in the 1820s and 1830s.

As ship agents, the Fox family were able to commission travellers to bring back plants from all over the world and they took full advantage of west Cornwall's mild climate, to raise plants from Asia, North and South America and Australia. Many of these exotic and tender plants can still be seen in Glendurgan, which is a deep, steep-sided valley garden, with profuse, lush growth slightly reminscent of a tropical forest. There are actually three valleys, converging into one, which runs down to the little village of Durgan on the Helford River.

Many of the trees at Glendurgan date from Alfred Fox's time: it was he who planned and planted the unusual laurel maze in 1833, and designed the curving drive to the house. Since then, successive generations of enthusiastic gardeners have maintained and added to the rich wealth of planting.

Having wandered down the drive, passing beneath an old Monterey pine, oaks, chestnuts and other trees, you reach the house and garden. Taking the path to the left of the lawn, after 100 yds or so at an intersection the left path will take you past some camellias while to the right there is a path across the valley. From here you get a fine view of the River Helford. It is a breath-taking sight combined with the contrasting form and habit of the trees and shrubs in the valley below. In early spring Lent lilies bloom, then primroses followed by bluebells and wild columbine. Camellias, rhododendrons, magnolias and cherries provide colour from March to June and later in summer hydrangeas and eucryphias flower throughout the valley.

On the lawn in front of the house is an aloe, with giant prickly leaves—a strange and spectacular sight. Close by is a Chinese dogwood (*Cornus Kousa*)—a fine shrub covered with white flowers in early June and later carrying strawberry-like fruits. Below are several impressive tulip trees (*Liriodendron tulipifera*), with gnarled old trunks, and many kinds of magnolia.

Winding paths—sometimes steep—lead down from the intersection past the tulip trees and a pond through the valley to the village of Durgan, once a fishing community with about 20 little cottages on the bank of the River Helford. If you walk along the upper paths you can look down through the tree tops to the stream far below. Whichever route you take there are many fine trees and shrubs to be seen, including metasequoia, cryptomeria, cedar, and fine rhododendrons such as the beautiful blue-flowered *Rhododendron augustinii*. One of the latest flowering rhododendrons at Glendurgan is *R. crassum*, which has sweetly scented flowers in July. There are several tender hybrids too, including the deep scarlet-flowering *R. barclayi* 'Helen Fox' and 'Beauty of Tremough' which displays large trusses of pink flowers against handsome foliage. Among the magnolias are *M. campbellii mollicomata*, two *M. soulangiana* 'Alba Superba', *M. x thompsoniana* and *M. x soulangiana* 'Lennei'.

In the area around the pool are some really magnificent trees. Overshadowing the pool, on its own little island, is a Deodar cedar (*Cedrus deodara*). Not far to the north is one of the tallest trees in the garden—a swamp cypress (*Taxodium distichum* 'Pendens') which turns to a rusty brown spire in autumn. To one side is a large spreading golden yew. *Magnolia delavayi* with its enormous leaves and the Chusan palm (*Trachycarpus fortunei*) with its fan-shaped leaves and fibrous trunk provide a tropical effect. From the poolside, there is an unusual view of the maze, 'in plan', laid out on the opposite slope, like a piece of tapestry.

Further down the valley from the pool the waving foliage of bamboos heralds a little dell with a stream. Nearby is conical *Thujopsis dolabrata*.

The main path continues down towards the village, passing the steep 'cattle rush' where the farm animals were driven for water, and two fine specimens of evergreen cleaster (*Elaeagnus x reflexa*). It is worthwhile descending to the bottom of the valley and leaving the garden for a moment to wander into the tiny village and enjoy the scene along the river front with its bobbing boats and strong smell of seaweed. It is widely believed that in ancient times Phoenicians put to port at Durgan to trade with the Cornish, this being the first shelter offered in the river and where loading and unloading would not have been affected by the state of the tide.

Returning to the garden again, you can join a cool ferny walk beneath trees to the western valley. Here the colours are more restricted—mainly yellows and blues—with bog arums and king cups along the stream, and hypericums further up the slope. Hydrangeas bloom blue and mauve in summer.

On a little plateau above the western valley, and overlooking the eastern valley, is the giant's stride—a stout pole with ropes attached to a revolving plate at the top from which bold children can swing out above the valley. From here a path takes you round the east slope of the valley and gives splendid views across the tips of the trees and over the maze. This is one of the finest prospects in the garden, looking down over the laurel bushes of the maze with a *Magnolia campbellii* in the foreground, *Michelia doltsopa* and *Cornus capitata* nearby. Beyond the maze are trees of all sizes, shapes and shades. There is a copper beech, a large weeping Mexican cypress (*Cupressus lusitanica* 'Glauca Pendula'), golden Monterey cypress (*Cupressus macrocarpa* 'Lutea'), the large spire of a swamp cypress (*Taxodium distichum* 'Pendens') and golden spikes of yew (*Taxus baccata* 'Aurea'). Around the pool and stream the huge leaves of gunnera contrast with the graceful foliage of the bamboos and tree ferns.

More splendid views into the valley are to be had closer to the house. Primroses and bluebells cover the banks and slopes in spring, followed in May and June by fragrant rhododendrons such as 'Lady Alice Fitzwilliam' and 'Tyermannii'. The latter is a tender hybrid with richly scented white flowers flushed with pale rose.

Glendurgan is a unique haven, off the beaten track; a hidden valley with exotic, colourful planting.

Lanhydrock

ADDRESS AND TELEPHONE: Lanhydrock, Bodmin, Cornwall PL30 5AD. Tel. Bodmin (0208) 73320

OWNERS: The National Trust

DIRECTIONS: signposted from A38 Bodmin to Liskeard road and from B3268 Bodmin to Lostwithiel road 2½ miles SE of Bodmin. Public transport: Bodmin Parkway BR then 1¾-mile walk via the original driveway

OPENING TIMES: house and garden, April to end October daily (house closed on Mon but open BHs) 11–6 but closing at 5 in October. Garden also open November to March, daily during daylight hours

ADMISSION: house and garden £4.20; gardens only £2.40

CAR PARKING: yes

TOILETS: yes

REFRESHMENTS: snack-bar and restaurant

SHOP: yes

DOGS: only in park on lead

WHEELCHAIR ACCESS: yes, but strong pusher needed for wheelchairs in places. Toilets for the disabled: yes

PEAK SEASON: April to June

NOTABLE FEATURES: formal garden with parterre; magnolias; rhododendrons and some rare trees and shrubs; woodland walks; fine views over valley of River Fowey; extensive parkland with avenue

Only 2½ miles from the south-western edge of Bodmin Moor, and more than 330ft above sea level, Lanhydrock is not favoured by the same mildness of climate as other National Trust gardens in Cornwall. It is, nevertheless, an exciting place, crowded with interesting plants and features.

Lanhydrock has a long history. John Robartes planted the sycamore avenue leading to the house in the mid 17C. Some of these ancient trees can still be seen in the 19C double avenue of beech trees.

At the end of this avenue is an ornate two-storey arched gatehouse of 1651, decorated with tall pinnacles. Beyond, in a formal setting, stands the large granite house, its lines softened by a covering of lichens and its wings enclosing a quiet forecourt. The house was first built in the 17C, but it was largely rebuilt after the fire of 1881. With the church tower close by and the Higher Garden and woodland rising above to the west, this is a romantic and peaceful scene.

The gardens at Lanhydrock are laid out in a more orderly fashion than most in Cornwall. A plan of 1694 shows a formal area of grass plots edged with flower beds to the north and east and a bowling green to the west. These lay within the confines of high walls which linked the gatehouse to the main house.

In the late 18C these walls were removed and the parkland was brought right up to the house. In 1857 the architect George Gilbert Scott designed the present formal gardens, surrounded by a low wall.

The formal garden to the east links the gatehouse to the main house via a series of low, grassed terraces. Here, 38 clipped fastigiate Irish yews serve to emphasise the vertical lines of the gatehouse and of the finials on the surrounding walls. Rose beds bring colour to the terrace lawns in summer. The urns, the work of Louis Ballin, goldsmith to Louis XIV, were brought to Lanhydrock from Queen Marie Antoinette's mansion in Paris.

Just north of the house is a parterre, created in 1930; its compartments, surrounded by low box hedges, are filled each year with spring and summer bedding. Above this is the Church Border, backed by a stone wall which shows off a rich planting of fuchsias, Agapanthus 'Headbourne Hybrids' and clematis.

Further north lies the croquet lawn, bordered by magnolias, rhododendrons and other shrubs. From here onwards the garden is much less formal, and with a wide range of plants, but not many tender species, owing to the climate. Frosts can still strike in May so the emphasis is on hardy hybrid rhododendrons rather than species. Near the croquet lawn you can see rhododendron 'Hugh Koster' and 'Pink Pearl'—both mid-season flowering.

The Church Path is flanked by tree and shrub borders. Here is *Magnolia virginiana*, the sweet bay or swamp bay, identifiable by its leaves which are glossy green above and blue-white beneath.

From June to September it bears small creamy-white fragrant flowers. Opposite is a group of azaleas. There is a good planting of camellias, including 'Lady Clare' and 'St Ewe'. More magnolias interplanted with rhododendrons and fronted by hydrangeas lie to the north.

The arched gateway marks the entrance to the Higher Garden, first laid out in the 1860s as a shrub garden but altered and extended in 1933. Magnolias are a particular feature at Lanhydrock and the first part of the Higher Garden is especially well blessed with them. Near the stream (known as Borlase's Stream) are *M. campbellii mollicomata* and *M. x veitchii*. Both are more than 60ft high and flower in March and April. Later in spring, *M. x soulangiana* 'Lennei' displays its enormous fleshy goblet-like flowers, rose-purple outside and a creamy soft purple inside.

In the nearby Magnolia Glade is a young *M. campbellii* 'Alba' and an interesting hybrid, 'Charles Coates'. The latter, raised at Kew, is a cross between *M. sieboldii* and *M. tripetala*, and in May and June has attractive fragrant creamy-white flowers with showy bright red stamens. In the autumn this part of the garden is brought to life by the crimson and gold foliage of a pendulous form of the Persian ironwood tree, *Parrotia persica* 'Pendula'.

Concealed behind the clipped yew hedge is the Herbaceous Circle, made up of four wedge-shaped beds. Two of these segments were created early this century by Lady Clifden, and the other two were laid out to complete the circle in 1972. The beds contain herbaceous plants for interest in late summer and early autumn.

Still more magnolias can be seen in garden around the thatched cottage. There is a very large *M. campbellii mollicomata*, planted in 1933, and a fine speciment of the cucumber tree (*M. acuminata*), whose fruits when young and green resemble cucumbers. The lawn in front of the cottage (last occupied in 1885, but kept open as a shelter for visitors) is dominated by grand *M. campbellii mollicomata*, while the cottage walls support *Chaenomeles japonica* and *Camellia reticulata* 'Captain Rawes'. The latter has large attractive semi-double rose pink flowers.

Behind the cottage is a long border planted with shrubs and hostas and beyond the well are several plants raised from seed collected by Roy Lancaster on his expedition to China in 1980–81. Among these are *Cornus macrophylla*, *Hypericum pseudohenryii* and species of berberis and cotoneaster.

Leaving the well, the Broad Path stretches back towards the house, flanked by rhododendrons such as 'Cynthia'—a hardy hybrid which carries magnificent trusses of wide funnel-shaped rose-coloured flowers in mid season—and sweetly fragrant *R. loderi* varieties. At the far end is *R. smithii*, noted for its attractive plum-coloured bark and scarlet flower trusses. From this point you can see across the garden to the parkland beyond.

To ascend to a greater height, take the path through the Magnolia Tunnel where *M. x soulangiana* 'Lennei' and 'Rustica Rubra' are trained over iron supports. The Angle Path then climbs gently up the hillside to the garden's highest point. There is a good deal to see on the way, including *M. hypoleuca*—a handsome tree with large fragrant creamy-white flowers in June—and elegant *Cornus kousa*, which also flowers in June. Quite close to the path is *Prunus serrula*, easily recognised by its beautiful shiny red-brown bark.

There are some good hardy hybrid rhododendrons, such as 'Mrs Charles E. Pearson', 'Unknown Warrior' and 'Queen Wilhelmina', while higher up the hill you can see the beautiful foliage of the brewer's weeping spruce (*Picea brewerana*).

In early spring the lily tree (*Magnolia denudata*) is delightful, with its fragrant pure-white cup-shaped flowers. Half-way along the path a planting of the lacecap Hydrangea 'Blue Wave' contributes colour in summer, and nearer the top of the rise are more trees and shrubs including *Osmarea burkwoodii (O. delavayi* x *P. decora*), rhododendron 'May Day', which has brilliant signal-red flowers in mid-season, *Pieris formosa forrestii*, the paper birch or canoe birch (*Betula papyrifera*)—a striking tree recognised by its white papery bark—and a Chinese persimmon (*Diospyros kaki*).

A level Top Walk follows the contours of the hill through groups of camellias, rhododendrons, azaleas and hydrangeas. From here there are magnificent panoramic views to the east, over the house and park to the valley of the River Fowey and to Caradon Hill at the south-east corner of Bodmin Moor.

The iron gates at the east end of the Top Walk lead to the Woodland Garden through which you can descend again to the house. On the way there are more hybrid rhododendrons: 'Alice', 'Mars' and 'Lady Eleanor Cathcart', to name but a few.

Mount Edgcumbe Gardens and Country Park

ADDRESS AND TELEPHONE: Mount Edgcumbe Country Park, Cremyll, Torpoint, Cornwall, PL10 1HZ. Tel. Plymouth (0752) 822236

OWNERS: Plymouth City Council and Cornwall County Council

DIRECTIONS: from Plymouth via Torpoint car ferry, then follow A374 to Antony then B3247 to Mount Edgcumbe. From Cornwall follow A38 to Trerulefoot roundabout, then A374 and B3247 to Crafthole, Millbrook and Mount Edgcumbe. Public transport: from Plymouth via Cremyll Ferry (pedestrian) at Admirals Hard, Durnford Street, to park entrance (½ hourly in summer, hourly in winter)

OPENING TIMES: daily all year round 8am to dusk. (House and Earl's Garden open Easter to October, Wed to Sun and BH 11–5.30. Tel. Country Park for more information)

ADMISSION: free, but there is a charge for the House and Earl's Garden when open. Coach parties by prior arrangement

CAR PARKING: yes

TOILETS: yes

REFRESHMENTS: restaurant

SHOP: yes, Cremyll Lodge entrance and house

DOGS: not allowed in house and Earl's Garden; on lead in formal gardens and park

WHEELCHAIR ACCESS: yes, two wheelchairs available. Toilets for the disabled: yes, in Orangery restaurant

PEAK MONTHS: April and May for camellias and rhododendrons. Bedding displays in summer in formal gardens

NOTABLE FEATURES: Grade I historic gardens and park; formal gardens showing French, Italian and English styles; National Collection of camellias; 18C landscaped park with follies; coastal walks and views; woodland, parkland

Situated in the east of Cornwall, just across Plymouth Sound, and covering 864 acres, Mount Edgcumbe Country Park is one of the most beautiful country parks in England. An 18C landscaped park, the first of its kind in Cornwall, it surrounds a fine house and historic formal gardens in French, English and Italian styles. Many visitors come to picnic and walk in the park or along the 7-mile strip of coastland and to enjoy the superb panoramic views.

Owned and maintained since 1971 by Plymouth City and Cornwall County Councils, the parkland and gardens are the result of centuries of work by the Edgcumbe family. The Rame Peninsula came into the family's ownership by marriage in 1479; in 1539, Henry VIII granted Piers Edgcumbe a royal licence to enclose part of the land as a deer park, and the house was begun in 1547 by Piers' son, Sir Richard Edgcumbe. The family moved here from Cotehele, some 10 miles up the Tamar.

Substantial tree planting was undertaken in the 17C and by 1729, according to a surviving estate plan, there were blocks of woodland crossed by straight avenues and rides. There was also a walled formal garden in a natural amphitheatre overlooking Drake's Island

The French garden at Mount Edgcumbe

and a Wilderness in the French style with serpentine walks and hedged alleys enclosing groves of trees.

In 1742, Sir Richard, 1st Baron Edgcumbe, retired from politics and began landscaping the park in the 'natural' manner fashionable in the 18C, planting woodland along the headland and constructing a range of follies. The formal gardens were swept away by his successor, George Edgcumbe, who planted many new exotic species. An Ionic temple, called Milton's temple, was constructed at the foot of the amphitheatre.

In 1779 French and Spanish fleets sailed into the Sound and threatened attack. To stop the woodland from being used as cover by possible invaders, the trees along the coast and in the Wilderness were felled—in acknowledgement of this sacrifice, George Edgcumbe was made 1st Earl of Mount Edgcumbe.

The formal gardens you can see today are planted on the former site of the Wilderness overlooking Plymouth Sound. Begun by George's wife, Lady Emma, and developed further by their successors—Richard, 2nd Earl of Mount Edgcumbe, and his wife, Lady Sophia—they now comprise three main areas, the Italian, French and English gardens, as well as a Summer Garden, rose garden and Fern Dell, all separated by hedges and shrubberies but connected by a maze of pathways.

From the entrance by the Cremyll Lodge Visitor Centre, follow a path between tall hedges to the Italian garden, with its vast orangery overlooking a lawn, gravel paths, colourful beds of annuals and a central marble fountain.

The orangery, dating from 1755, was designed by Thomas Pitt to house 25 orange trees brought back from Constantinople by Richard Edgcumbe—it is now used as a restaurant. Across the garden, is a small ornate terrace with stairways either side of an alcove housing a bust of the Italian poet Ariosto. A statue of Apollo stands on the terrace with figures of Bacchus to his left and Venus to his right.

The path continues from the orangery to an area of smooth lawns and trees. An impressive Wellingtonia stands close to a white pavilion—Thomson's Seat—built in the 1760s. On the pavilion wall is a quotation from *The Seasons* by James Thomson. From here you can look across the estuary to the city of Plymouth on the opposite hillside.

The path carries on along the coast to the Block House and an 18C battery, built to defend the mouth of the river. The three guns on top of the battery are all that remain of 21 cannons captured from the French during the Napoleonic Wars. The strange cube-shaped Block House was constructed in 1856 and you can climb the stairway to the roof for magnificent views across the river. Behind, in a little glade, is a small garden containing shrubs and a memorial to George Edgcumbe's friend, Timothy Brett.

The French garden lies beyond, enclosed by tall hedges. This garden dates from 1803 and features a parterre of intricate geometric beds defined by a weave of low box hedging and filled in summer with bedding plants in the colours of the French flag. In the centre is the delightful Shell Fountain, with large clam shells at each corner. This was Lady Sophia's favourite garden and after her death the Earl placed a memorial urn here.

Behind the conservatory is the Summer Garden, a small 20C herbaceous garden colourful in July and August with perennial plants set against a dense screen of Leyland Cypress. Trees of heaven (*Ailanthus altissima*) stand in the border.

Next to the French garden, and in complete contrast, is the English garden, laid out by Lady Emma Edgcumbe in the 1770s. The description 'English' refers to the design rather than the plants, for many distinctly non-English trees can be seen on the lawns, such as cork oaks (*Quercus suber*), palms and magnolias. To one side of the lawns, beneath very tall specimens of the Maidenhair Tree (*Ginkgo biloba*), is the entrance to the Fern Dell. This little hollow contains fewer ferns than originally intended, but the huge boulders and shade of oak trees help to create a cool and tranquil atmosphere on a hot summer's day. Various family pets are buried here.

On the opposite side of the English garden is the rose garden. In summer, pink and white Tea and Noisette roses bloom within an attractive design of low box hedges, underplanted with pink and white impatiens ('Busy Lizzie'). New formal garden areas are being developed, including an American and a New Zealand garden.

The Earl's Garden, which surrounds the house, is a terraced shrub garden, with lawns, statuary and summer houses. The 18C 'Shell Seat' has recently been restored, as have the Victorian flower beds beside the house.

The parkland is also well worth exploring, especially the amphitheatre with its camellias. The owner hopes eventually to grow more than 1000 varieties.

Further along the coast are some surviving 18C follies—temples, arches and a mock ruin.

The coastline stretches from Mount Edgcumbe to the southern end of Whitsand Bay, taking in Penlee Point and Rame Head, with pleasant woodland walks, rocky cliffs and sandy beaches along the way. The majority of footpaths are well defined with reasonable gradients.

During the winter of 1989/90 two severe storms devastated the Park; the sea wall facing Plymouth Sound was badly damaged and about 800 trees were felled. The storms also reduced many of the recently planted areas in the deer park to ruins. Luckily none of the formally planted areas were badly affected, but like the great storm of 1891, when it was reported that 2000 trees were blown down, Mount Edgcumbe is once again replanting so that the future generations will be able to enjoy the beautiful park.

Pencarrow House

ADDRESS AND TELEPHONE: Pencarrow House and Gardens, Bodmin, Cornwall. Tel. St Mabyn (020 884) 369

OWNERS: Molesworth-St Aubyn family

DIRECTIONS: 4 miles NW of Bodmin off A389 and B3266 at Washaway

OPENING TIMES: house Easter to 15 October, Sun to Thurs, April,

May and September 1.30–5; June, July and August 11–5.
Gardens daily during season until sundown

ADMISSION: gardens £1, children 50p. House extra. Reductions
for pre-booked parties of 20 or more

CAR PARKING: yes

TOILETS: yes

REFRESHMENTS: café

SHOP: craft centre

DOGS: yes

WHEELCHAIR ACCESS: in part, difficult in woodland. Toilets for
the disabled: yes

PEAK SEASONS: no special peak but rhododendrons in spring

NOTABLE FEATURES: collection of conifers, especially American
and Antipodean species, and of rhododendron species and
hybrids

The gardens at Pencarrow House are particularly recommended
to tree lovers. The splendid tree collection here was started in the
early 19C—the time of the great plant hunters—by Sir William
Molesworth Bt. Pencarrow makes a speciality of North and South
American tree species. David Douglas (1798–1834) contributed a
great many conifer seeds collected in North and South America
and the Cornishman William Lobb (1809–63) brought seed back
from South America and California. Rhododendron seed was sent
here from the Himalayas by Sir Joseph Hooker and Nathaniel
Wallich, Director of the Calcutta Gardens.

The site, a valley between the edge of Bodmin Moor and the town
of Wadebridge, proved favourable for the growing of conifers and
by the middle of the 19C Sir William had planted a very extensive
collection—almost every known conifer that would survive the
British climate. Several trees have now reached a considerable
height and width. Many have died or fallen however, and others
are past their best years. The present owner, Lt.-Col. J.A. Molesworth-St Aubyn, is carrying out an extensive programme of
clearing and replanting.

The Palladian house built in the 1760s by Robert Allanson of York,
is approached by a mile-long drive passing through mainly coniferous woodland. At the start of the driveway, turn and look back
across the road, where you can see the remains of an earlier
driveway, flanked by an avenue of monkey puzzles (*Araucaria
araucana*). The largest is over 70ft tall and they were all raised from
seed collected in Chile in 1844 by William Lobb.

A little way down the densely wooded main drive, the route cuts
through the grassy banks and mounds of an ancient British en-
campment, now overshadowed by giant trees. Along the drive are
many interesting specimens worth a closer look. The spruces
include a broad-girthed tiger-tail spruce (*Picea polita*) and a
Brewer's weeping spruce (*Picea breweriana*)—perhaps the most
beautiful of all spruces—with slender pendulous branchlets water.
Many pines can be seen, including a lovely young spreading-leaf
pine (*Pinus patula*) from Mexico and a fine specimen of the Crimean

pine (*Pinus nigra var caramanica*), distinctive with its vertical branches near the bole rising like organ pipes.

Silver firs are also well represented, the European form (*Abies alba*) doing particularly well. The Caucasian fir (*Abies nordmanniana*) and Noble fir (*Abies procera*) have both grown to handsome sizes and there are good specimens of *Cryptomeria japonica*, the Japanese cedar and both the Californian and Japanese nutmegs (*Torreya californica* and *T. nucifera*).

The Molesworth family has lived at Pencarrow since Elizabethan times, but the present house dates from 1776. On its walls are roses, wisterias and *Magnolia grandiflora*—all cut low, to show off the fine architecture. Two massive specimens of *Magnolia campbellii* can be found to the rear of the house, near the service area—beautiful in March, covered in water lily-like blooms.

A wall to the east, covered with climbing roses and shrubs, shelters a lawn planted with cultivars of the Hinoki cypress (*Chamaecyparis obtusa*)—some of them uncommon—the Roble beech (*Nothofagus obliqua*), a very large Monterey pine (*Pinus radiata*) and two splendid cedars.

The chief area of formal garden lies south of the house. A sunken garden laid out by Sir William has now been greatly simplified, leaving a large expanse of lawn with flights of steps and ornamental urns. A fountain, the central focal point, is flanked by clipped evergreens.

A rockery to the east of the lawns offers rather more excitement, if you can find it beneath the tall trees and overgrown shrubs. Its grey granite boulders, brought here by cart from Bodmin Moor, are now swamped with camellias, rhododendrons, azaleas and acers, against a background of dark conifers.

To reach what is perhaps the most interesting, and certainly the most sheltered area, follow the path leading behind the rockery and signposted 'To the American Garden'. This leads past a water garden, a grove of eucalyptus underplanted with brilliant azaleas and the Old Palm House which is now dramatic in controlled dereliction—two tall palm trees have burst through the timber slatted roof and the floor is hidden beneath a jungle of ferns and weeds. The path then runs along the edge of a lake, smothered with aquatic plants and flanked by blue hydrangeas.

Perhaps the most spectacular sight in the American garden is that of the magnificent 80ft *Cunninghamia lanceolata* with its tremendous girth, thought to be the largest in Britain. Here, too, are many fine young hybrid rhododendrons.

The trees and shrubs have been numbered and catalogued recently by Dr David Hunt from Kew Gardens.

Trebah Gardens

ADDRESS AND TELEPHONE: The Trebah Garden Trust, Mawnan Smith, Cornwall, TR11 5JZ. Tel. (0326) 250448

OWNERS: Major and Mrs Hibbert/The Trebah Garden Trust

DIRECTIONS: 3 miles SW of Falmouth. 1 mile SW of Mawnan

Smith. Signposted from Treliever Cross roundabout on A394. Public transport: regular bus service from Falmouth to garden entrance

OPENING TIMES: every day of the year 10.30–5 (last admission). House not open

ADMISSION: £2, children and disabled visitors £1. Reductions for booked parties. Guided tours available

CAR PARKING: yes. Coaches by prior arrangement

TOILETS: yes

REFRESHMENTS: in shop

SHOP: yes

DOGS: yes, on lead

WHEELCHAIR ACCESS: limited but worth visiting for views from top of ravine. Toilets for the disabled: no

PEAK MONTHS: spring for rhododendrons, summer for hydrangeas and Mediterranean plants but something to see all months

NOTABLE FEATURES: ravine garden with views of Helford Estuary; rhododendrons, tender shrubs and trees, aquatic and bog plants; unusual plants

The 25-acre garden of Trebah (pronounced Tree-ba), is planted in a ravine some 500 yds long, dropping by 200ft to the Helford Estuary and overlooked by a fine 18C house.

Like many other great gardens in this part of Cornwall, Trebah was created by a member of the Fox family. Charles Fox came to Trebah in 1826 and using the 18C house (built by the Nicholls, another old Cornish family) as servant quarters, built himself a second large mansion. This was destroyed by fire in 1948.

Having first established massive screens of maritime pines (*Pinus pinaster*), to shelter the ravine from strong coastal winds, Fox then set about planting the garden, using seeds and plants collected all over the world (the Fox family had shipping interests).

Fox followed a somewhat unusual method of garden design. Before planting a tree seedling his gardeners would first erect a tall scaffold tower, to give an impression of the tree when fully grown. Fox directed operations from a top window of the house, through a megaphone.

Standing on the top lawn, you can look down through the ravine. Hundreds of rhododendrons blossom in spring and early summer, together with a wide variety of shrubs, followed in mid and late summer by 2 acres of blue and white hydrangeas.

A network of paths—Petri's Path, Peter's Passage, Fox Path, Radiata Path and so on—leads down through the valley to a small private cove. A stream tumbles down the centre of the ravine, connecting a series of small pools and fringed by a lush water garden. Primulas, astilbes, irises, ligularias, ferns and bamboos can be seen here—and *Gunnera manicata* growing to extravagant proportions.

Many of the rhododendrons have also reached a remarkable size. The rhododendron valley, for instance, is dominated by three huge specimens of rhododendron 'Trebah Gem' planted in 1900 and now

Chusan palms flourish at Trebah. (Marian Nickig)

at least 45ft tall. Further down are two fine *R. Loderi* 'King George', with soft pink buds opening in May to large white fragrant blooms. Other strongly fragrant rhododendrons at Trebah include 'Lady Alice Fitzwilliam', *R. lindleyi* and *R. polyandrum*. Look out for the rare and tender *R. protistum* along the side of the Beach Path.

Numerous tender trees and shrubs thrive here, in the mild Cornish climate. A large Chilean laurel (*Laurelia serrata*) with bright green, strongly aromatic leaves dominates the Chilean Coomb.

Elegant *Cornus kousa* is a feature of many gardens, with its white bracts in June. At Trebah the more tender *Cornus capitata*, with sulphur-yellow bracts, also does well. Here too is the loquat (*Eriobotrya japonica*), a small tree with 'corrugated' leaves.

Magnolias are well represented, with fine specimens of *Magnolia* x *soulangiana*, *M. delavayi*, and the pink tulip tree (*M. campbellii*) whose pink flowers open early in goblet shapes and then spread like those of a water lily. There are also many eucalyptus, eucryphias, pieris and camellias. Tree ferns (*Dicksonia antarctica*, *D. squarrosa* and *Cyathea dealbata*) flourish here, and there are three exceptionally tall Chusan palms (*Trachycarpus fortunei*).

The exotic looking, but hardy Chinese fir (*Cunninghamia lanceolata*) can also be seen at Trebah, as can the pocket handkerchief or ghost tree (*Davidia involucrata*).

At the very bottom of the ravine, steps lead over the coastal footpath and onto the private beach of Polgwiddon—used to prepare for the D-Day attack on Normandy. Visitors to the garden may use the beach.

Visitors unwilling or unable to descend the steep paths may prefer to explore the camellia walk—or venture a little way down the ravine to the Koi Pool and waterfall, a recent construction, and along Petri's Path to take in the view across the valley.

The present owners, Tony and Eira Hibbert, bought the property in 1981 and have carried out a major clearance and restoration programme, besides developing the new water gardens and a new sunken garden at the entrance. The Hibberts have also established the Trebah Garden Charitable Trust to which the gardens and property have been conveyed to ensure that they can be enjoyed by the public for ever.

Temperatures of –15°C in January 1987 killed many mature and beautiful trees including the largest *Eucalyptus overta* in England, a 100-year-old *Rhododendron sinograndes* and the rare *Magnolia globosa sikkim*. In the gales of January 1990 Trebah lost 72 trees with a girth of 12ft or more.

Trelissick

ADDRESS AND TELEPHONE: Trelissick Garden, Feock, near Truro, Cornwall TR3 6QL. Tel. Truro (0872) 862090/865808

OWNERS: The National Trust

DIRECTIONS: 4 miles S of Truro, on the B3289 above the King Harry Ferry. Public transport: bus service twice daily (except Sun) from Truro (early afternoon). Western National 85 passing close Truro BR, tel. (0872) 40404

OPENING TIMES: March to end October, Mon to Sat 11–6 or sunset; Sun 1–6. Closes at 5 in March and October. House not open. Woodland walk is accessible throughout the year

ADMISSION: £2.50. No reductions for parties

CAR PARKING: yes, £1 for non-members, refundable on entry to garden

TOILETS: yes

REFRESHMENTS: yes (limited hours in November and December)

SHOP: yes

DOGS: in woodland and park only

WHEELCHAIR ACCESS: limited to upper part of garden: gravel paths. Toilets for the disabled: yes

PEAK MONTHS: April to August

NOTABLE FEATURES: rare shrubs and plants; extensive collection of hydrangeas; walks and views.

Trelissick stands high above the estuary of the River Fal on the Cornish coast, its 25 acres of garden surrounding the road that takes traffic down to the King Harry Ferry. There are magnificent views of the River Fal, the estuary and surrounding parkland. Fine trees fill this garden, along with lush underplantings of rhododendrons, camellias, magnolias and one of the largest collections of hydrangeas in the country.

Many tender species of shrubs do well in the mild climate here, but the garden has had its fair share of disastrous weather. The dry summer of 1976 seriously affected many plants, and then in January 1979 the temperature plummeted to a record low of 6°F (–14.5°C), causing much damage. In the following December a terrifying storm, with winds of 120mph, blew down several of the trees and damaged many more. But the garden has made a good recovery, although it received another battering in the gales of 1990.

The first house at Trelissick was built in 1750 by John Lawrence, a captain in the Cornish Militia during the Seven Years War. This was a modest residence, but in 1800 the estate was purchased by Ralph Allen Daniell, a tin mining magnate, who was then probably the richest man in Cornwall. Daniell contributed much to the estate but it was his son Thomas who made the most substantial alterations, and additions, laying out miles of carriage drives, winding through woodland and park, and engaging Frederick Robinson to redesign the house (in 1825).

However, he over-strained his finances and the property had to be sold—first to the Earl of Falmouth and then in 1844 to the Gilbert family. The Gilberts planted much of the present parkland and introduced some of the older exotics into the garden, besides adding to the mansion.

In 1937 the estate was inherited by Mrs Ida Copeland and her husband Ronald, who was managing director and later chairman of the Spode china factory. The Copelands were responsible for much of the garden we see today; over the next 20 years they planted a great many of the more tender species, taking advantage of well-established woodlands. In 1955, Mrs Copeland gave Trelissick to The National Trust.

Trelissick contains several separate and quite distinct gardens, two of the smallest being close by the entrance. There is a fig garden which, following the devastating frosts of 1979, has been replanted with the present collection of cultivars. Opposite is the small, walled parsley garden, once used for growing herbs for the house and now filled with climbers, tender shrubs and flowering plants—many fragrant and several unusual types.

More scented plants can be found at the entrance to the main garden, including heliotropes below the long brick wall of the kitchen garden (not open to the public). Across the walk a small, shady fern garden is almost hidden behind the dense branches of *Chamaecyparis pisifera* 'Squarrosa'.

East of the kitchen garden, a closely-mown lawn sweeps down to the road, dominated by a splendid Japanese cedar (*Cryptomeria japonica*) and surrounded by mixed borders of trees, shrubs and herbaceous plants. Soft colours fill the border beneath the kitchen garden wall; stronger colours are confined to the south-facing border near the lane.

You can reach another part of the garden by crossing a wooden bridge over the road. This area, rising to the north, is known as Carcadden, and was originally an orchard and nursery site, but after the National Trust acquired the property it was developed to its present form. Now large trees shelter camellias, rhododendrons, magnolias and flowering shrubs, which provide a succession of colour and interest from early spring. Deutzias give a good show in early summer and then the hydrangeas come into their own.

Trelissick has an extensive collection of hydrangeas, planted in groups or as single specimens throughout the garden. There are more than 130 different species and cultivars, ranging from the popular lace-caps and hortensias to some quite uncommon species. One of the most remarkable sights is *Hydrangea paniculata* 'Grandiflora'—a really showy shrub with large white blooms throughout the summer months—and one of the most unusual is hydrangea 'Ayesha', which has rather flattened dense heads of cup-shaped greyish florets.

Another exciting part of the garden is the dell—a shady area under a high canopy of mature trees. Tree ferns (*Dicksonia antarctica*) give an exotic touch, and lower down are large-leaved *Gunnera manicata*, hostas, rodgersias, astilbes, ferns and candelabra primulas. There are also many fine rhododendrons, here and throughout the garden.

On higher ground to the south is the hydrangea walk, with flowering cherries set here and there amid the hydrangeas. Further on, beneath large conifers, oaks and beeches, winding gravel paths meander through mature plantings of shrubs. Rhododendrons, azaleas, camellias and hydrangeas give colour here through much of the year.

The lime-free soil and the mild climate at Trelissick have encouraged many rhododendrons to grow luxuriantly, and the garden even has its own hybrids: 'Trelissick Port Wine' and 'Trelissick Salmon'. There are many other locally raised hybrids too, such as 'Glory of Penjerrick' and 'Trewithen Orange'. The latter was raised at Trewithen near St Austell and bears pendant trusses of deep orange flowers in early to mid season.

Red-flowering rhododendrons were a particular favourite of Mr Ronald Copeland. You can see fine specimens of such hybrids as 'May Day', 'Tally-Ho', 'Gwilt King', 'Fusilier' and the ever popular 'Elizabeth'—a small shrub which carries lovely dark red flowers in April. One of the most beautiful species of rhododendrons is *R. leucaspis*, one of the first to flower in February with large saucer-shaped flowers, creamy-white with rich brown anthers. Several *R.*

cinnabarinum bloom in May, while in April it is the turn of the deep blood red *R. thompsonii* and the shell-pink *R. williamsianum*.

Trelissick is principally a plantsperson's garden but its variety of features and location on the Fal near the King Harry Ferry makes it popular with other visitors. Many of the Cornish gardens are noted for their splendour in springtime but Trelissick also provides summer borders, brilliant displays of hydrangeas and bright-foliaged trees and shrubs in autumn. An additional feature is the pleasant woodland walk, which follows the estuary and circumnavigates both house and garden. This walk offers many fine vantage points from which to view the River Fal.

Trengwainton

ADDRESS AND TELEPHONE: Trengwainton Garden, near Penzance, Cornwall TR20 8RZ. Tel. Penzance (0736) 63021. Head gardener (0736) 63148

OWNERS: The National Trust

DIRECTIONS: 2 miles NW of Penzance on B3312. Public transport: Penzance BR 2 miles. Buses from Penzance BR to Madron then ¾ mile walk

OPENING TIMES: 1 April to 30 September, Wed to Sat and BH Mon 11–6; March and October 11–5. House not open

ADMISSION: £1.80, children 90p. Coach parties by prior arrangement

TOILETS: yes

REFRESHMENTS: no

SHOP: no

DOGS: yes, on lead

WHEELCHAIR ACCESS: yes. Toilets for the disabled: yes

PEAK SEASON: April to June

NOTABLE FEATURES: tender plants growing outdoors; walled gardens with many tender species; woodland garden with rhododendron collection

Nowhere else in mainland Cornwall will you find such a comprehensive and diverse collection of tender and exotic plants as that at Trengwainton. Situated at the south-west extremity of the county, only 2 miles from Penzance, Trengwainton enjoys a mild climate with very few frosts and an early start to spring. This permits outdoor displays of many plants from warmer parts of the world which, elsewhere in Britain, would normally have to be kept in heated greenhouses.

The garden began to take its present form in the early part of the 19C, when Sir Rose Price enlarged the house and made the driveway down to a new entrance lodge. Sir Rose was also responsible for the building of the series of walled gardens, with their unusual sloping beds, at the lower end of the drive, and for planting the surrounding woodland.

Towards the end of the 19C, the property was purchased by the Bolitho family. From 1925 onwards Lt.-Col. Edward Bolitho, later Sir Edward, gathered trees and shrubs from all over the world. He took shares in Kingdom Ward's plant hunting expedition to Assum and Burma (1927–28). The woodland and walled gardens created by Sir Rose Price proved ideal for the culture of species brought back from the expedition and under the auspices of Mr Creek, the talented head gardener, many of the plants were successfully propagated.

Today Trengwainton boasts a spectacular collection of rhododendrons and many extremely large specimens of magnolia, along with good plantings of hydrangeas and camellias. Primulas, lilies and other moisture-loving plants can be seen in the lush and colourful stream garden.

Many of the more tender plants are to be found in the five walled gardens on the north side of the drive, close to the entrance. The atmosphere here is intimate and the concentration of plants quite overwhelming. Arranged in a line from east to west, these gardens are connected by a path running down the south side below a 'Cornish hedge'—a stone wall hosting numerous plants, including ferns and fuchsias.

The first of the walled gardens is dominated by one of the finest trees at Trengwainton—a huge *Magnolia* x *veitchii*. This fast-growing hybrid of *M. campbellii* and *M. denudata* was planted in 1936 and is now huge. It is a marvellous sight in April when it bears numerous white flowers flushed with pink. Beyond the magnolia is a *Metasequoia glyptostroboides*, the Dawn Redwood, and a little further on, a native of Chile—*Embothrium coccineum lanceolatum* ('Norquino Valley' form), with scarlet flowers along its branches in spring. Elsewhere in this brick walled area is a fine cider gum (*Eucalyptus gunnii*), distinguished by its sage green-coloured sickle-shaped leaves and attractive smooth grey peeling bark. There is also a border of camellias.

The second enclosure has a large *Magnolia campbellii* near the entrance. Also known as the giant Himalayan pink tulip tree, it carries very large water lily-like pink flowers which first open in February and continue through March. In July and August colour is provided by the creamy-white fragrant flowers of *Stewartia sinensis*. Against the west wall is *Michelia doltsopa*, a semi-evergreen tree closely related to the magnolia.

Passing under the canopy of a *Styrax japonica*, a beautiful small tree with white flowers in June, you enter the third enclosure where there are fine specimens of *Magnolia mollicomata, M. sprengeri diva* and *M. cylindrica*. The latter not often seen, has elegant white flowers which appear before the leaves in April. A narrow border in this garden contains several tender rhododendrons. In the north wall is a door leading to part of the old kitchen garden, where the purpose and value of Sir Rose's raised vegetable beds, sloping towards the south to catch the sunshine, can be appreciated.

Creamy-white-flowering *Buddleia fallowiana* 'Alba' grows in the fourth enclosure, along with the slender conifer *Athrotaxis selaginoides*. There are many large fuchsias in the borders of this section and on the top wall is the common blue passion flower (*Passiflora caerulea*).

The last enclosure is the smallest. Its walls support many climbing plants including the climbing hydrangea (*H. petiolaris*). A rarity is the Chatham Island forget-me-not (*Myosotidium hortensia*) now also planted in groups along the woodland walks.

Outside the walled garden the broad sweep of the drive continues up towards the house, accompanied by the Stream Garden beneath trees to the left. The stream was confined to a culvert underground until the 1920s when Lt.-Col. Bolitho opened it up as an attractive feature. The present planting of moisture-loving plants was the work of Mr G. Hulbert, head gardener at Trengwainton from 1948 to 1959. In spring the banks are covered with colourful primulas, followed by arums, rodgersias and astilbes, and later kaffir lilies. Blue hydrangeas bloom in the woodland in late summer.

Across the drive is a grassy meadow. The large oak (*Quercus pendunculata*) here was planted in 1897 in honour of Queen Victoria's Diamond Jubilee. Nearer to the drive is a Bhutan pine (*Pinus wallichiana*) planted by the Queen Mother in 1962 and further up the meadow a young Mexican pine (*Pinus patula*) was planted by HRH Princess Anne in 1972.

Passing under a canopy of beech trees, many of which were destroyed in the storm of January 1990, the drive continues to the house. This area of the garden is spacious and open, with large lawns lying to the east and south of the granite-fronted building. From the terrace there are fine views of St Michael's Mount and Mount's Bay.

The south wall of the house supports *Clianthus puniceus*, New Zealand lobster's claw or parrot's bill, which has claw-like bright red flowers carried in pendulous heads in early summer. Here, too, is *Dendromecon rigidum* with bright yellow poppy-like flowers. Further along the wall, *Wisteria sinensis* blooms mauve in May.

Beyond the top lawn and beds of dwarf rhododendrons is the magnolia garden. Here are more of Trengwainton's outstanding magnolias, including a huge *M. Sargentiana robusta*—at its best in April, when it is covered in large rose-pink flowers. Another notable specimen is *M. delavayi*. This gives interest for much of the year with its large attractive leaves but in summer it is a magnificent sight, with enormous parchment-coloured flowers often measuring 10in. or more across.

The lawns around the house are bordered by azaleas, rhododendrons and still more magnolias. The tree in the middle of the top lawn is a Myrtle (*Myrtus luma*) and was planted in 1890.

A ha-ha marks the limits of the lower lawn and you can return through the woodland, beginning at the gap in the rhododendrons opposite the sundial. Here is a fine Japanese cedar (*Cryptomeria japonica* 'Elegans') and on the other side of the narrow path is a layer of the original *Rhododendron falconeri*. (The original was planted in the 1880s.)

Further on, near a well which once provided drinking water for the house, is a planting of camellias. Throughout the woodland there are rhododendrons and bluebells in spring.

Towards the lower end of the drive is an area of the woodland known as the Jubilee Garden. Here are blue and pink meconopsis, the Himalayan poppies, and a group of hypericum 'Rowallane'. Near the stream is a large *Rhododendron magnificum*, recognised by its dense trusses of bell-shaped purple-rose flowers in February and March. Close by is *R. macabeanum* which blooms in March and April with large trusses of bell-shaped flowers, pale yellow with a purple blotch. This part of the garden also shelters a number of impressive tree ferns (*Dicksonia antarctica*).

Trengwainton, is a garden of rare quality, worth seeking out among the country lanes above Penzance. The spring scenes are especially memorable, but the variety of plants and their impressive growth make it a rewarding experience at any time.

The garden lost more than 200 trees in the storm of 25 January 1990. Unfortunately a large number fell in the important shelter-belts. An extensive replanting scheme was begun in autumn 1990.

Trewithen

ADDRESS AND TELEPHONE: Trewithen House and Gardens, Grampound Road, near Truro, Cornwall. Tel. St Austell (0726) 882763/883794 and 882418

OWNER: Mr Michael Galsworthy

DIRECTIONS: on A390 between Probus and Grampound. 6 miles E of Truro. Public transport: BR stations Truro and St Austell, 6 miles. Buses from Truro or St Austell

OPENING TIMES: beginning of March to end September, Mon to Sat 2–4.30. Closed Sun. House open April to July and August, BH Mon, Mon and Tues afternoons only 2–4.30

ADMISSION: gardens, March to June £1.75, children £1; July to September £1.50, children £1. House £2.75

CAR PARKING: yes

TOILETS: yes

REFRESHMENTS: no, but picnic area

SHOP: yes (plants)

DOGS: on leads

WHEELCHAIR ACCESS: to much of gardens. Toilets for the disabled: yes

PEAK MONTHS: February to June for flowering shrubs and trees; September for autumn colours

NOTABLE FEATURES: choice shrub collection; many rare plants and trees, especially magnolias, camellias, rhododendrons in woodland setting; plants raised by the garden creator; formal walled garden. Famous for the main south lawn landscaped vista. The gardens are set in 150 acres of parkland

Trewithen is one of the finest gardens in Cornwall, excellently managed and notable for its marvellous plant collection.

The Cornish word Trewithen means 'the house in the spinney'. When George Johnstone inherited the estate in 1904, the handsome stone house was surrounded by a thick woodland of mature beech and other trees, set in an 18C landscaped park. Many of the trees had been planted in the 1740s by Thomas Hawkins, then owner of

Trewithen and a keen dendrologist. More were then planted by John Hawkins in 1820–40.

Johnstone devoted the rest of his life to creating a 28-acre garden, south of the house, using the existing mature trees as a framework. The trees, together with laurel windbreaks, sheltered and protected this almost level site, standing 250ft above sea level, from gales, and Johnstone was able to grow many tender trees and shrubs in the mild Cornish climate.

Many plants cultivated by Johnstone can still be seen in the garden today, including rare species from Asia, Australasia and America, mostly raised from seed collected in the wild by such celebrated plant hunters as Wilson, Forrest and Kingdon Ward. Rhododendrons and camellias are particularly well represented. Johnstone raised a number of hybrids himself including the beautiful deep orange-brown flowering 'Trewithen Orange' (raised from *R. concatenans* x 'Full House'), 'Alison Johnstone' (amber flushed pink, named after Johnstone's wife) and 'Jack Skilton' (named after his head gardener).

Johnstone also played an important part in the story of *Camellia* x *williamsii* 'Donation'. Colonel Stephenson Clarke raised 'Donation' at Borde Hill in Sussex and gave a cutting to Johnstone. The original plant then died, so subsequent propagation was done from the Trewithen specimen, enabling this handsome orchid pink camellia to populate gardens around the world.

Johnstone's main interest, however, lay in magnolias. In 1955 the Royal Horticultural Society published his authoritative work *Asiatic Magnolias in Cultivation*, and he planted every available variety of magnolia at Trewithen. One of the best of these is a tree of *Magnolia campbellii mollicomata*, which grows by the south lawn, in a glade just below the house.

This glade is perhaps the most admired part of the garden at Trewithen. Its broad lawn stretches southwards from the house for over 218 yds and its irregularly shaped sides are lined with a remarkable selection of trees and shrubs, many of them collectors' items and rare in cultivation. The glade was a direct result of a government order made during the 1914–18 war for the felling of 300 trees. This having been achieved, Johnstone planted the glade with banks of newly introduced exotic species, and his own hybrids.

The superb tree of *Magnolia campbellii mollicomata* dominates the first part of the glade (on the right as you look south). More than 65ft high, the tree is a stunning sight in early March, when it is covered with large pink water-lily like blooms. Close by is the pink tulip tree (*Magnolia campbellii*) with blooms of a deeper shade of pink, and large specimens of *M. liliiflora* and *M.* x *soulangiana*. About the same time as *M. c. mollicomata* flowers, the fragrant yellow racemes of *Corylopsis platypetala* also appear.

Further south are more magnolias including *M. kobus*, *M. dawsoniana* and *M. salicifolia*. A group of *Enkianthus chinensis* is particularly attractive in May, when it produces yellow and red bell-shaped flowers. *Stewartia koreana* and *S. monadelpha* are also noteworthy for their camellia-like flowers in summer and their brilliant tints in autumn.

Rehderodendron macrocarpum stands on the other side of the lawn. Introduced from China in 1934, this tree bears white bell-like flowers in May. Now 36ft high, it is one of only two mature specimens in Britain; the other is at Maidwell Hall in Northamptonshire. Also bordering on this lawn is a group of the rhododendron hybrid 'Alison Johnstone', the fire bush from Chile (*Embothrium coccineum* 'Longifolium') which turns scarlet from head to foot in May, acers such as the coral bark maple (*Acer palmatum* 'Senkaki') and more magnolias. At the end grows a tall specimen of *Nothofagus procera*.

Walking through the woodland east of the south lawn, you will be rewarded with views across the parkland. Flanking the path is an avenue of sycamore trees and a row of *Ginkgo biloba* and *Metasequoia glyptostroboides*.

The woodland garden, west of the lawned glade, is full of notable plants. Camellias play a strong role. Along with 'Donation' you may spot 'Trewithen Pink' and a camellia named after Johnstone's daughter, 'Elizabeth Johnstone' and also a splendid single pink named after the present owner's late wife 'Charlotte Galsworthy'.

The massive beech trees shade rhododendrons such as *R. macabeanum*, which came to Trewithen as a seedling, a gift from Sir Edward Bolitho of Trengwainton near Penzance, who received the seed from Kingdon Ward's 1927–28 expedition. The largest example at Trewithen is 20ft tall and has a spread of 34ft. It is particularly attractive in March and April, when weighed down by brilliant yellow trusses.

There are fine banks of *Pieris formosa forrestii*, scarlet in its young leaves, groups of eucryphia and more magnolias. *Magnolia sargentiana robusta* is worth watching out for, as is *Michelia doltsopa*—a tender member of the magnolia family with white heavily scented flowers in early spring.

In a corner to the south-west of the garden, primulas, rhododendrons and New Zealand tree ferns (*Dicksonia antarctica*) enjoy the moist, sheltered conditions offered by a former cock pit. These are best seen in May.

Visitors with energy and time can follow a path from the western boundary to a water garden in a quarry setting. Along the way you will pass the Coronation Planting, which includes *Magnolia sprengeri diva* and *Magnolia campbellii* x *Magnolia mollicomata* —a seedling raised at Kew Gardens.

The walled gardens, just west of the house, is the only formal part of garden at Trewithen. Beds of roses fill the centre of this sheltered enclosure, which was formerly used as a herb garden and drying area. Around the walls are borders of perennials, and the walls themselves are clothed in tender climbers. The bright red lobster's claw (*Clianthus puniceus*) from New Zealand reaches right to the top of the wall and in spring *Ceanothus arboreus* 'Trewithen Blue' shows its beautiful deep blue flowers.

The present owner, Michael Galsworthy, is George Johnstone's grandson. He keeps the garden fresh with appropriate new planting, guided by Michael Taylor, the head gardener, who holds the RHS Waley Medal for the care and cultivation of rhododendrons.

CUMBRIA

Acorn Bank

ADDRESS AND TELEPHONE: Acorn Bank Garden, Temple
Sowerby, near Penrith, Cumbria. Tel. Kirkby Thore (07683)
61893 (shop) 61281 (evenings and out of season)

OWNERS: The National Trust

DIRECTIONS: just N of Temple Sowerby, 6 miles E of Penrith on
A66. Public transport: Penrith BR. Infrequent buses from Penrith

OPENING TIMES: 29 March to 3 November, daily 10–6. House
open only by application to the Sue Ryder Foundation

ADMISSION: £1.20, children 60p. Reductions for pre-booked
parties

CAR PARKING: yes

TOILETS: yes

REFRESHMENTS: no

SHOP: yes

DOGS: in wild garden only

WHEELCHAIR ACCESS: to herb garden and herbaceous borders
only. Toilets for the disabled: yes

PEAK MONTHS: no peak season

NOTABLE FEATURES: herb garden; old orchard; herbaceous
borders; roses; wild garden

Acorn Bank lies in the Eden Valley, just north of Temple Sowerby,
on the fringe of the Pennines. The area has a high annual rainfall
(45in.) and although the location is generally cool, the garden—
some 2½ acres in size—is enclosed by high walls, which retain
warmth and provide a sheltered, tranquil climate, encouraging
spring flowers.

The site at Acorn Bank has a long history, dating from Domesday.
The nearby village of Temple Sowerby takes its name from the
Knights Templars who kept a religious house at Acorn Bank as
early as 1228. This was transferred to the Knights of the Hospital
of St John in 1323 and remained in their ownership until the
Dissolution of the Monasteries, when Henry VIII granted the estate
to Thomas Dalston. The name Acorn Bank is recorded in 1597 and
refers to the ancient oakwood at the rear of the house.

Dalston families lived at the Manor for the next two centuries and
it was probably during the mid 17C, that one of the Dalstons
enclosed the garden with brick-lined fruit walls. They were followed by the Boazman family. In 1930 the estate was bought by
Dorothy Una Ratcliffe, the Yorkshire dialect writer and traveller,
and her husband Captain Noel McGrigor Phillips. Una Ratcliffe
totally renovated the garden with the assistance of two gardeners
from Yorkshire. She also established an area of wild flowers on the
wooded bank behind the house, introduced ornamental ironwork

and statuary into the garden and planted trees in the park.

In 1950 Una Ratcliffe gave the Manor and 186 acres of park and woodlands along the Crowdundle Beck to the National Trust. Today the house is leased to the Sue Ryder Foundation, and is not open to the public. The gardens, are managed directly by the National Trust, and are open daily.

Wrought iron is used to excellent effect in this garden; especially worth noting are the front gates, leading to the forecourt. These gates were made in 1933 and now, in their recently restored state, it is easy to see why the design by A.W. Ellwood won first prize in a national ornamental ironwork competition.

In the forecourt stands a 17C sundial and by the front door an old climbing rose 'Gloire de Dijon' shows its buff yellow, sweet smelling flowers in the summer. The walls shelter jasmine, clematis, Virginia creeper, *Magnolia grandiflora* and *Indigofera heterantha* with elegant foliage and bright purplish rose flowers.

Around the stable gateway are borders with *Primula denticulata* and *P. auricula* as ground cover and by the garden wall *Aster* x *frikartii* 'Monarch', just right for a shady border.

Through the gateway to the right, between the walled garden (essentially an orchard) and the park, is the wonderful herb garden. Established in 1969, it now contains nearly 250 species and is one of the most comprehensive collections in the country, including not only culinary herbs but also herbs used for brewing, dyeing, perfumes, and medicinal purposes. This is entirely appropriate, since the Knights Templars and Hospitallers would almost certainly have grown large quantities of herbs.

Three long borders have been included in the herb garden to accommodate plants requiring differing aspects. The border at the foot of the brick-faced wall to the left is the sunniest of the three. This wall is in fact a 'hot' or heated wall. Clay pipes incorporated into it during the 18C were used to circulate warm air and thus prevent frost damage to the fruit trees. In the central border grow plants favouring partial shade; in the furthest border, plants for heavy shade. The herbs are neatly planted and identified and provide colour and fragrance for many weeks of the year.

There is a booklet that records most of the herbs by name and gives their uses, both culinary and medicinal. It makes interesting reading. For instance, did you know that the root of the yellow gentian *Gentiana lutea* was used in liquor distilling, that moonseed (*Menispermum canadense*) is beneficial for rhuematism and arthritis, that betony (*Betonica officinalis*) is a remedy for headaches and that the bark of the flowering dogwood (*Cornus florida*) can be used to make black ink?

The orchard (in the larger walled area) is surrounded by mixed borders beneath old brick and sandstone walls and bisected by a path lined with yew hedges and an avenue of *Prunus cerasus* 'Rhexii' with pure white, fully double flowers in May. All the apple trees here are late flowering, early ripening types, chosen to avoid the frosts. Old cooking apple trees such as 'Dumelow's Seedling' and the rare 'Scotch Bridget' can be seen along with some young trees of old varieties such as 'Keswick Codlin'. The perry pear 'Blakeney Red' also finds a home in the orchard along with the Nottingham medlar and Portuguese quince.

In spring the orchard floor is carpeted with flowers such as the white *Anemone nemorosa* 'Vestal' and the yellow wild tulip *Tulipa sylvestris*.

The walled garden borders are mixed and various. A narrow border by the north facing wall, nearest to the herb garden, accommodates shade-tolerant plants such as primulas. This wall provides support for the Morello cherry and several varieties of clematis. Colour is provided by berberis, hydrangeas and spiraea.

Astilbes and hostas are grouped in the cool, deep border beneath the top wall of the garden. Here, too, is the wax bell *Kirengeshoma palmata*—known for its waxy yellow flowers in the late summer. A magnificent specimen of the summer-flowering horse chestnut *Aesculus parviflora* produces its white flowers in July and August. Geums, campanulas, peonies and potentilla enjoy the sunshine under the south wall with the dense evergreen *Osmanthus* x *burkwoodii* which produces a mass of white flowers in the spring.

Further along, a gateway gives access to the oak-covered bank from which the estate takes its name. Una Ratcliffe set up a wild flower and bird reserve here in the 1930s. More than 60 varieties of narcissus can still be found here, including the small wild daffodil—the Lent lily.

Rose beds are laid out near the dovecote in the walled garden. Among the Rugosa roses is the uncommon 'Belle Poitevine'. Beyond the yew hedge are more specimen roses including the soft pink flowering threepenny-bit rose (*Rosa farreri* 'Persetosa').

White-flowering *Rosa fedtschenkoana*, pink *R. setipoda* and *R. moyesii* 'Fargessii' with its glowing, vivid carmine flowers, stand beside the steps to the sunken garden, with its circular pool and a wishing well surrounded drystone terrace walls with trailing rock plants. A pair of ornate wrought iron gates, said to have been brought from Verona by Una Ratcliffe, add grandeur to the setting.

Acorn Bank is especially beautiful in spring, when the wild garden above the Crowdundle Beck is in bloom and the orchard is filled with daffodils, wild tulips and anemones. It is also spectacular in summer, with its colourful borders and rose beds. And all the year round, it provides a peaceful, tranquil haven.

Dalemain

ADDRESS AND TELEPHONE: Dalemain, Penrith, Cumbria. Tel. Pooley Bridge (0768) 486450

OWNERS: Mr and Mrs Bryce McCosh

DIRECTIONS: on A592, 3 miles SW Penrith, Junction 40 of M6. Public transport: Penrith BR 3 miles

OPENING TIMES: Easter Sun to early October, daily except Fri and Sat 11.15–5. House also open

ADMISSION: house and garden £3, children £2; gardens only £2, children free. Family tickets are available. Coach parties welcome

CAR PARKING: yes

TOILETS: yes

REFRESHMENTS: bar lunches

SHOP: yes

DOGS: no

WHEELCHAIR ACCESS: limited in garden. Ground floor of house. Free entry. Toilets for the disabled: yes

PEAK MONTHS: peaks throughout the spring and summer

NOTABLE FEATURES: herbaceous borders; unusual plants; knot garden; wild garden

Both house and garden at Dalemain have evolved in accordance with needs and fashions since the Middle Ages. In Elizabethan times the house was considerably extended and in the mid 18C it was given an impressive pink stone façade. The park was landscaped during this latter period, in the style of Capability Brown. Some old walnut trees and Spanish chestnuts dating from this time can still be seen growing along the edge of the River Eamont.

The terraced walk begins around the corner of the house, past the front door. With its strong buttressed retaining wall, the terrace remains much the same as it was in the 1680s, when Sir Edward Hasell laid it out. The stone sundial was made for Sir Edward in 1688.

On the terrace wall and spilling over onto the gravel walk are several rambling roses, and below the house walls is a long deep herbaceous border.

The end of the terrace is marked by a large handsome Grecian fir (*Abies cephalonica*) in the shadow of which lies the knot garden. In Elizabethan times this knot garden would have been twice the size, but it was partly destroyed in the Victorian era, to make room for a vinehouse. Today the intricate symmetrical patterns of low box hedges, clustered round a central Travatine marble fountain, are filled with herbs, violas, antirrhinums and campanulas. The old Victorian vine border is now a mass of shrub roses, spiraeas and lilies.

From the knot garden the ground slopes gently upwards to the west, bounded on the north and west sides by an old brick wall. On one side of the gravel path is a narrow border and a lawn planted with old apple, plum and pear trees; on the other, is a deep border containing a collection of shrub roses. The roses are accompanied by a wealth of fine border plants—tree peonies, sedums, phlox, irises, meconopsis, rodgersias and many others. The wall supports a number of apple trees.

At the top of the garden is a Georgian summerhouse built into an alcove of the west wall.

The door in the west wall opens into Lobb's Wood, where a path meanders through beech and oak planting at the top of a steep bank overlooking the Dacre Beck. Still further along the west wall is a Tudor summerhouse with a pointed roof and mullioned windows, dating from before 1550.

A narrow, steep flight of stone steps leads down into the low garden. Here, sheltered by a high bank, is the wild garden started by Mrs McCosh's mother earlier this century and consisting mainly of a meadow area along the banks of the Dacre Beck. In spring the meadow is filled with drifts of daffodils, and flowering trees and shrubs and there is a fine bed of Himalayan blue poppies (*Meconopsis grandis* GS.600). An avenue of cherries lines the path to the beck and elsewhere there are ornamental maples, lilacs, forsythias and azaleas.

Throughout the gardens at Dalemain the vegetation is noticeably rich and lush—the result of a combination of knowledgeable gardening, long establishment and the lakeland climate.

Graythwaite Hall

ADDRESS AND TELEPHONE: Graythwaite Hall, Ulverston, Cumbria. Tel. Newby Bridge (0448) 31248

OWNERS: M.C.R. Sandys, Esq

DIRECTIONS: off A590 at Newby Bridge (4 miles)

OPENING TIMES: April to end of June or July, daily 10–6

ADMISSION: £2, children free. Parties by prior arrangement

CAR PARKING: yes

TOILETS: yes

REFRESHMENTS: no

SHOP: no

DOGS: no

WHEELCHAIR ACCESS: difficult. Toilets for the disabled: no

PEAK MONTHS: April, May and June

NOTABLE FEATURES: garden landscaped by Thomas Mawson; spring garden with rhododendrons; terraces; water garden; Dutch garden

Graythwaite, close to the western shore of Windermere, is another of the Lake District's splendid spring gardens. From the beginning of April to the end of June, with a peak in May, you can see a succession of rhododendrons, azaleas, camellias, flowering cherries, magnolias and spring flowers.

Graythwaite Hall was probably begun in the latter part of the 15C or early part of the 16C, and more building work was carried out later, particularly in the 18C. Its imposing, and rather misleading, Victorian appearance was brought about by re-facing in the last century.

At that time there were no views out from the Hall, for it was set in a hollow and surrounded by dense plantings of mature forest trees and huge overgrown shrubs. In 1889 Colonel T.M. Sandys, whose family had lived at Graythwaite since it was built, brought in a local nurseryman, Thomas Mawson (1866–1933) from Windermere, to landscape the gardens. This was Mawson's earliest and most important commission and was to mark the turning point in his career—following on this, he built up the largest international landscape design practice of its time.

Mawson worked at Graythwaite between 1889 and 1895, following the instructions he had received to landscape 6 acres of garden, using existing trees where practicable and introducing more shrubs. With considerable foresight, he made the garden as labour saving as possible.

His first task involved an incredible amount of earth-moving. The drive had to be levelled and many trees were removed. Then he altered the lie of the land to the south, creating views from the Hall over terraces to a lawn which slopes away to the south-west. Views were opened up to the parkland and countryside beyond. Cowsheds and barns were removed and replaced with Scots pines, Douglas firs and other trees. The stables to the east of the house were moved and a Dutch garden created in their place.

Subsequent generations of the Sandys family have added to the framework and expanded the plantings, but only a few minor changes have been made to the layout which remains as Mawson planned it, a satisfying combination of formal and informal elements.

Mawson's spacious terraces with their grand flights of stone steps survive unaltered. These are balustraded in pinkish St Bees sandstone, the same used for cladding the house. His formal terraced rose garden has been rearranged—now the beds radiate from a central sundial made by Dan Gibson. Above the rose garden is the Lady's Walk, another Mawson terrace.

One of the finest views in the garden is of the wide undulating lawn, sloping away to the south-west, framed by fine trees and a mixture of shrubs and set with large mounds of rhododendrons. To the east of the house a crenellated yew hedge continues the lines of the terraces. To the west a stream marks the boundary of the lawn and is richly planted with masses of shrubs and moisture-loving plants.

The stream was definitely landscaped by Mawson, who added bends and cascades and built a bridge. Some trees and shrubs here were established in Mawson's time, others have been planted since.

Like many other Lakeland gardens, Graythwaite has a good selection of rhododendrons. The acid soil, the high rainfall and the close proximity of the Gulf Stream create conditions ideal for the numerous species grown here. Many rhododendrons have been planted along the stream and more in the woodland beyond, including the beautiful *Rhododendron litiense* with wide bell-shaped flowers of soft yellow in May and *R. hemsleyanum* which carries large white trumpet-shaped flowers in May and June. There are also plantings of mahonia and bamboo.

More bamboos surround the pool into which the stream runs and there are rodgersias, primulas and other moisture-loving plants such as the umbrella plant (*Peltiphyllum peltatum*) which has large lobed and toothed leaves and in spring carries rounded bunches of white and pink flowers. Close by are two Douglas firs, 150ft high.

More recently Major Sandys has planted specie and hybrid rhododendrons in the woodland garden, including *Rhododendron anthopogon* and *R. Wardii*. The latter is a particularly beautiful species, with clear yellow flowers, blotched crimson.

Against a background of mature trees on the hillside to the west a path leads up to the dogs' cemetery, known as the happy hunting ground. Another path leads through a picket gate into a meadow of long grass and wild flowers below specimen trees.

A long circular walk skirts round the lawn, passing through plantings of red, pink and purple rhododendrons, and will eventually bring you to Mawson's Dutch garden which lies on the site of the old stables to the east of the house. This small garden, enclosed by clipped yew hedges, features geometric parterre beds of bright flowers, edged with low box hedging and surrounded by gravel. In the centre is an unusually tall sundial, also made by Dan Gibson. But most dramatic in this little area is the topiary work—two rows of yews clipped as spheres, the upper part of golden yew and the lower half of dark green yew.

Between the Dutch garden and the house are many more shrubs including dwarf rhododendrons such as *R. orbiculare* and *R. williamsianum* and viburnums, mahonias and buddleias. Several of the shrubs have been chosen for their fragrance—lilacs, for example, and scented *Magnolia sieboldii*—while others such as mahonias and acers contribute to the variety of leaf form.

No doubt the historical importance of the garden attracts many visitors to Graythwaite but many more come simply to enjoy the wonderful show of spring-flowering shrubs and the peaceful setting. The severe damage caused to the gardens by the gales of January and February 1990 has since been used as an opportunity to increase the variety of tree and shrub specimens.

Holehird Gardens

ADDRESS AND TELEPHONE: Holehird Gardens, Windermere, Cumbria. Enquiries should be addressed to: The Lakeland Horticultural Society, Hon. Secretary, Dr David Kinsman, Windy Hall, Crook Road, Windermere, Cumbria, LA23 3JA. Tel. (09662) 6238

OWNERS: the estate is held in trust and administered by Cumbria County Council. Part of gardens leased to Lakeland Horticultural Society

DIRECTIONS: off the A592 between the junction with the A591 and Troutbeck. 1½ miles N of Windermere. Public transport: Windermere BR 1½ miles, summer only

OPENING TIMES: all year round, daily 9–sunset

ADMISSION: free, but donations welcomed

CAR PARKING: yes

REFRESHMENTS: café

SHOP: no

DOGS: on a lead

WHEELCHAIR ACCESS: limited. Toilets for the disabled: no

PEAK MONTHS: peaks throughout the year

NOTABLE FEATURES: Lakeland Horticultural Society's garden with winter border, conifer collection, alpine garden and walled garden; fine trees and shrubs; terraced walk; pool and water garden; magnificent views

The Lakeland Horticultural Society was founded in 1969 by a group of enthusiastic gardeners wishing to promote horticulture in the Lake District. Today the society has more than 1300 members and leases part of the gardens at Holehird with the object of developing and maintaining a wide range of plants suited to the conditions of the area.

The gardens were once owned by the Manchester industrialist John Dunlop, but it was William Grimble Groves who in the early part of this century stocked the beds and borders with the results of plant collecting expeditions made to the Kansu province of China. In 1945, H. Leigh Groves gave the estate to the Westmorland County Council for 'the purpose of the better development of the health, education and social welfare services of the County'. The estate, currently administered by the Cumbria County Council, is still held in trust.

Sadly the gardens were neglected during and after the 1939–45 war; many plants were lost during this period and the gardens in general deteriorated and became overgrown. By 1971, when the Lakeland Horticultural Society acquired the lease for 2½ acres of the sloping ground to the east of the house, a great deal of restoration work was necessary. Much of the garden had to be cleared and replanted and the members have been busy planting ever since. In 1978 the society also took on the walled garden.

A good place to start a tour of the Lakeland Horticultural Society's garden is by the entrance to the society's offices and the service yard. From here the drive continues northwards; above is a large grassed slope covered with daffodils in April. On the opposite side, below the driveway, are two borders containing NCCPG collections of hydrangea and astilbe.

At the top of the drive, near the white gates which mark the garden boundary, is the winter border. This area has been planted with shrubs carefully selected for their colour and interest between November and April. Various types of *Erica carnea* flower from January onwards.

Among the winter-flowering shrubs are *Daphne mezereum* and rhododendron 'Praecox', the latter flowering rosy-purple in February and March. From December onwards *Hamamelis mollis* produces clusters of large sweetly scented golden-yellow flowers.

Higher up the grass slope is an island bed containing a collection of dwarf and slow-growing conifers in many tones and shades— sage-green *Juniperus recurva coxii*, steely blue *Juniperus horizontalis* 'Glauca' and the light yellow-green sprays of *Thuja orientalis* 'Aurea Nana'.

Further along the path, past two monkey puzzles (*Araucaria araucana*), is a mixed group of rugosa type roses and various azaleas. At the highest point of the path is a seat given in memory of a local plant collector, William Purdom. Several of the plants he introduced to Britain early this century are planted close by, including *Rhododendron purdomii, Potentilla fruticosa purdomii* and *Buddleia alternifolia*.

From here you can fully appreciate the superb lakeland setting. The views are breathtaking—Lake Windermere in the middle distance and beyond the rugged outlines of Crinkle Crags, Wetherlam and Coniston Old Man. On a clear day you can see Scafell.

Behind the path, close to the boundary wall, a few trees survive from the original garden. There is an elegant Antarctic beech (*Nothofagus antarctica*) and an umbrella pine (*Sciadopitys verticillata*) so named because the leaves appear in dense whorls like the spokes of an umbrella. Both trees are believed to have been planted around the turn of the century, as was the massive *Viburnum rhytidophyllum* further along the path.

Just before the steps is a young *Crinodendron hookeranum*, bearing crimson lanterns in May. Normally associated with milder locations, this crinodendron is protected under a tent throughout the winter months.

On the slope below is a heather garden where many forms of calluna and daboecia enjoy the lime-free soil and flower colourfully from June through to October.

Towards the southern edge of the lawn is a magnificent *Davidia involucrata* or pocket handkerchief tree. This specimen is now more than 50ft tall and every June is covered in flowers—the white bracts or 'handkerchiefs' are most noticeable. At the foot of the hill is the Lakeland Horticultural Society's alpine garden, where some favourite and a number of uncommon saxifrages, dianthus, phlox and lewisias thrive. Among the geraniums growing here is the attractive *Geranium sanguineum lancastrense* with dark green leaves forming a perfect background for the delightful flowers, salmon pink with a beautiful crimson veining. *Geranium renardii* also does particularly well at Holehird.

Past the Lakeland Horticultural Society's offices and near the car park is the walled garden, formerly the kitchen garden. The society took the garden on in 1978, after it had been neglected for many years. The first task was to dismantle the glasshouses and conservatories, which had deteriorated far beyond repair. The whole area then had to be replanned and planting began in 1981.

Today there is a central lawned area with island beds of shrubs. Beneath the walls are deep herbaceous borders and a collection of herbs has been started in one corner. New fruit trees are being trained against the garden wall.

Across the drive from the walled garden, the grounds around the house are still maintained by the estate's trustees. The house itself is leased to the Leonard Cheshire Foundation as a nursing home and although visitors are welcome to stroll in the gardens here they are asked not to wander too close to the house and to respect the privacy of the residents.

Just off the top drive, a pool and water garden form an attractive feature on the slope above the house. The pool is surrounded by bamboo and *Gunnera manicata*. As the stream descends the hillside, it almost disappears in a mass of lush marginal and semi-aquatic vegetation, including astilbes, meconopsis, irises and primulas.

Across the lawn, below the house, is the terraced garden where a flight of steps, clothed with ferns and other self-sown plants, leads down to a fountain. A natural rock outcrop on one side of the steps has been developed as a small alpine garden and in the cracks of the paving around the pool edge edelweiss (*leontopodium spp*) and alpine asters (*Aster alpinus*) grow. From here the view is splendid— over the meadow to Windermere and the magnificent hills beyond.

Below a retaining wall of lakeland stone lies the terrace border,

which holds a collection of shrubs including *Viburnum davidii,
Berberis wilsoniae, Daphne retusa* and *Cotoneaster adpressus.*
Climbing and rambling roses enjoy the shelter and support offered
by the wall. Two very old favourites here are 'Dorothy Perkins' and
'Excelsa', although for fragrance neither of these can match the
carmine pink flowering 'Zephirine Drouhin'.

Further along the border is a new collection of peonies and just
before the second viewpoint at the end of the terrace is a newly
planted fernery. Elsewhere in the garden the trustees are re-intro-
ducing many of the species of trees, shrubs and plants that were
lost from the garden during the war years.

Holehird's gardens are continually being developed and enriched with plants appropriate to the landscape and the climate
(the annual rainfall is 69in.); it is a splendid showcase for the
demonstration of gardening in the Lake District.

Holker Hall

ADDRESS AND TELEPHONE: Holker Hall, Cark-in-Cartmel,
Grange-over-Sands, Cumbria. Tel. (05395) 58328

OWNERS: Lord and Lady Cavendish

DIRECTIONS: 5 miles W of Grange-over-Sands on B5278. Public
transport: BR and buses to Cark-in-Cartmel, then 1 mile walk

OPENING TIMES: Easter to end October, daily except Sat, 10.30–6.
House closes 4.30

ADMISSION: gardens and grounds only £2.50, children £1.40

CAR PARKING: yes

TOILETS: yes

REFRESHMENT: yes

SHOP: yes

DOGS: on lead only

WHEELCHAIR ACCESS: yes. Toilets for the disabled: yes

PEAK MONTHS: spring and early summer

NOTABLE FEATURES: formal garden; woodland walk with many
unusual trees and shrubs, rhododendrons and magnolias; rose
garden

Lying between Morecombe Bay and the hills of the Lake District,
the gardens and park at Holker Hall feel some benefit from the
Gulf Stream.

The land on which Holker Hall now stands belonged to Cartmel
Priory at the time of the dissolution of the monasteries. In the 1550s
it was bought by the Prestons and it is believed that George Preston,
in 1604, built the first house on the site. But it was not until the
1720s that any interest was shown in establishing a garden. The
then owner, Sir Thomas Lowther, reconstructed much of the house
and laid out extensive formal gardens.

Sir Thomas married Lady Elizabeth Cavendish, a daughter of the

2nd Duke of Devonshire, and through this marriage Holker became the property of the Cavendish family.

The formal garden which Sir Thomas laid out around the house was swept away as the landscape movement gained popularity and replaced with 200 acres of 'natural' parkland. In the 19C the 7th Duke of Devonshire, with advice from Joseph Paxton, redesigned the garden. Alterations were made later by Thomas Mawson and generations of the Cavendish family have continued to be involved in the development of the garden over the decades.

Today, the result of 200 years of changes can be seen in the contrasting styles within the 22 acres of garden around the Hall.

The oldest part of the formal garden is by the main block of the Hall. Here paths lined with yew hedges divide the garden in four, the beds filled with geraniums, lupins, roses and peonies. A balustraded terrace gives fine views over the adjacent parkland.

A flight of steps leads down into the lower, larger formal garden, which has recently been redesigned. The garden is bounded by hornbeam hedges on the south and west sides, with marble busts set into 'alcoves'. The central walk is lined with Portuguese laurels and urns containing fuchsias and summer bedding. In the centre, where the paths meet, four box-edged beds each contain a weeping silver-leaved pear. The surrounding borders are filled with summer colour and scent from phlox, catmint, thymes, gypsophylla and germander.

The woodland garden has a fine collection of rhododendrons. The acid soil, mild climate and sheltered, well drained conditions are ideal for them. The rhododendron season begins with *R.* 'Nobleaum', which in mild spells in winter opens its brilliant rose-scarlet buds into wide funnels of rich rose-pink, flushed with white; it ends in late September when *R. auriculatum* displays its large white funnel-shaped, richly scented flowers.

The approach to the woodland garden is marked by a circular pool and a fountain which throws a jet of water high into the air. Around the pool a huge *Rhododendron arboreum*, believed to be over 100 years old and covered with crimson flowers, and a large cut-leaved beech (*Fagus sylvatica heterophylla*) shade the fountain and there are groups of eucryphias, kalmias, azaleas and a honeysuckle tree (*Lonicera maackii*).

From the pool a flight of steps leads up to a 17C Italian statue of Neptune. The Italianate cobbled steps, now flanked by evergreen oaks (*Quercus ilex*), are said to have been the suggestion of Sir Joseph Paxton. Also by the fountain is a large monkey puzzle (*Araucaria araucana*) which was grown from seed brought back from Chile by William Lobb in 1844. In the 1870s the tree had already reached a height of 30ft when a strong gale blew it down. It took seven shire horses to re-erect it and its roots were embedded in concrete.

On the parkland side of the fountain, the Japanese cherry walk shows its brilliance in spring, underplanted with tulips and irises. Beyond are groups of rhododendrons. specimens of the Indian bean tree (*Catalpa bignonioides*), the tulip tree (*Liriodendron tulipifera*), *Ginkgo biloba*, *Hoheria lyallii* from New Zealand and the rarely seen winter's bark (*Drimys winteri*).

In autumn there is glorious colour from *Acer pseudoplatanus*

'Prinz Handjery' and 'Brilliantissimum' and *Corcidiphyllum japonicum*.

In a large clearing is a gently sloping lawn with a sunken, paved rose garden. Designed by Thomas Mawson in 1912, the rose garden is planted with many fine old-fashioned and species roses such as damask, noisette and gallicas. It is reached by a curved pergola swathed in wisterias, honeysuckles, roses, clematis and vines. There are unusual plants here, like the Chinese climber *Schisandra grandiflora rubriflora* which has deep crimson flowers borne on drooping stalks during the late spring.

Surrounding the rose garden, old swamp cypresses are draped with climbing roses and honeysuckles and there is a collection of sorbus on the lawn.

The northern perimeter of the woodland garden is bounded by a wall which provides shelter for many tender shrubs. The evergreen *Carpenteria californica* produces large white flowers and golden anthers in July. Also along the wall are some marvellous specimens of magnolia.

The woodland walk leads back in the direction of the Hall, with attractive trees such as the pocket handkerchief tree (*Davidia involucrata*), *Cornus controversa*, *Stranvaesia davidiana* and the sorrel tree (*Oxydendrum arboreum*). These have reached magnificent heights, towering over the autumn-colouring shrubs.

Hutton-in-the-Forest

ADDRESS AND TELEPHONE: Hutton-in-the-Forest, near Penrith, Cumbria. Tel. Skelton (08534) 449

OWNERS: Lord Inglewood

DIRECTIONS: 3 miles from Exit 41 of the M6 on the B5305 (5 miles from Penrith)

OPENING TIMES: garden and forest walk open all year round 11–5, except Sat. House open end of May to end of September, Thurs, Fri, Sun and BH Sun and Mon 1–4

ADMISSION: house and garden £2.80, children £1; gardens only £1, children 50p. Coach parties by prior arrangement

CAR PARKING: yes

TOILETS: yes

REFRESHMENTS: café

SHOP: yes

DOGS: on lead

WHEELCHAIR ACCESS: limited. Toilets for the disabled: no

PEAK MONTHS: no special peaks

NOTABLE FEATURES: terraces with topiary; walled garden; woodland; parkland with ponds

Some scholars have linked Hutton with the medieval tale of Sir Gawain and the Green Knight, and the gardens still have a certain 'lost world' atmosphere, being in parts overgrown and wild. The landscape is richly wooded and the house sits protected by trees.

Hutton's pele tower, the oldest part of the house, was constructed by Thomas de Hoton or Hutton in the mid 14C. By 1670 when Daniel Fleming of Rydal visited Hutton the house was already quite large and he wrote that it 'was formerly a strong place having a high tower well moated with a drawbridge over it which was a good defense against the Scottish inroads'. The last of the Huttons had by then sold the estate to a Cockermouth family, the Fletchers.

According to Bishop Nicolson, who dined at Hutton with Sir Henry Fletcher in 1705, the house was neglected and overrun by rats, but the gardens were 'in a very good condition with several new plants from ye Indies, fair plantations of Fir, Beech, Elm, Lime Trees etc'.

When Sir Henry Fletcher died without an heir, the property passed to Henry Vane, who planted more than 50,000 trees. However, the greatest changes took place in the 19C, when William Sawrey Gilpin tackled the gardens and George Webster and Anthony Salvin restored much of the house.

Today the south side of the house overlooks a series of grassy terraces, with gravelled walks and massive sturdy topiary specimens at either end. Sir George Fletcher (1633–1700) was probably responsible for the original layout of these terraces, which were reconstructed in the 19C. The four lead statues were made by the Dutch sculptor Van Nost in about 1700. They can be seen in an engraving by Kipp (c 1750) surrounding a circular pool in a plantation to the west of the house, but the pool no longer exists.

Below the terraces to the south is the woodland low garden where huge rhododendrons blossom in late spring and early summer among overgrown dark yews. Here in 1870 Lady Vane, with the help of her neighbour Captain Markham and under the guidance of Anthony Salvin, laid out a formal rhododendron garden, its paths arranged in a geometric design like two interlocking stars. Recently, with the aid of the Countryside Commission, the paths have been cleared and replanting of the area has begun.

From the south terrace, looking beyond the woodland low garden, through trees, you can see the still water of the middle pond. The oldest of three ponds created from the streams which flow around the house, this dates from the 18C and was originally used for breeding fish. The two other ponds, one downstream near to the Penrith Road, and the other upstream, were constructed by Henry Vane in the second half of the 19C.

The 18C walled garden, to the north of the house, can be seen from the gallery inside the house: a rectangle divided into four smaller enclosures by yew hedges and linked by gravel paths. For several years it was used as a market garden but now it is intended to establish it as a formal garden to complement this side of the house. Fan and espalier fruit trees are being trained against the walls and borders have been planted with shrubs and herbaceous plants.

Views from the east side of the house take in the park, which is believed to date back to medieval times although the earliest record of its layout is a plan from the early 18C. The park was redesigned by William Sawrey Gilpin for Sir Francis Vane in the early 19C.

Once a year it is the setting for the Skelton Agricultural Show.

One of the most enchanting aspects of Hutton-in-the-Forest is the surrounding woodland. There are many fine trees to be seen here and a delightful woodland walk, with 17C dovecot, has been laid out through Grove Wood. There are several magnificent mature hardwoods: predominately oaks, beeches and lime trees. There is also a wide variety of conifers, planted by Sir Henry Vane in the 19C. Many of these are now very large.

Grove Wood contains a mixture of broadleaved trees and conifers planted this century to ensure replacements for the older trees. The intention is to maintain a mixture of hard and softwoods and a balance between native and introduced species.

The wildlife at Hutton is interesting and varied; it includes red squirrels, roe deer, hen harriers and kingfishers.

Levens Hall

ADDRESS AND TELEPHONE: Levens Hall, Kendal, Cumbria LA8 0PD. Tel. Sedgwick (05395) 60321

OWNER: C.H. Bagot Esq

DIRECTIONS: off the A6 5 miles S of Kendal at Levens Bridge. (Take exit 36 from M6, left at first junction.) Well signposted. Public transport: Oxenholme BR 4 miles. Buses from Kendal to Lancaster (hourly) stop outside

OPENING TIMES: Easter Sun to end September, Sun to Thurs 11–5. Closed Fri and Sat

ADMISSION: house and garden £3.25; gardens only £1.90

CAR PARKING: yes (not tarmac)

TOILETS: yes

REFRESHMENTS: café

SHOP: yes

DOGS: no

WHEELCHAIR ACCESS: yes to garden (has ramps) but not to house. Toilets for the disabled: yes

PEAK MONTHS: Easter to May; July and August

NOTABLE FEATURES: 17C topiary garden; park

Levens Hall is best known for its remarkable topiary display. Now, in full maturity, the massive specimens, some 20ft tall, add to the dramatic atmosphere of this 17C garden. The garden has unique historical significance, as it illustrates the changes that took place in garden design during the Stuart period.

The area surrounding the house is formal in style, being divided into many sections and filled with topiary specimens shaped out of yew and box. This formal area was originally linked in one design with an adjoining park. Created between 1692 and 1715, the design showed a leaning towards the natural landscape style that was to take over in the 18C introduced by William Kent and others. A plan

Levens Hall: best known for its remarkable topiary

kept in the house and dating from about 1730 shows that the layout
has hardly been altered since that date.

Levens Hall stands on the left bank of the River Kent, at the head
of the estuary where the land is fertile. In 1170 an estate on this
site was presented by William of Lancaster to his daughter and her
new husband Norman de Hieland (later de Redman). The de
Redman family built the pele tower and Hall, between 1250 and
1300. This grim, bleak, medieval shell was later turned into a
gentleman's residence and in 1690 Colonel James Grahme began
alterations to make it the largest and finest Elizabethan mansion
in Cumbria.

In 1692 he hired Monsieur Guillaume Beaumont, a gifted French
horticulturist, to lay out the gardens. Beaumont had trained under
André Le Nôtre at Versailles and came to Levens Hall after working
for James II at Hampton Court. The Duke of Hamilton, Sir Nicholas
Shireburn, Lord Weymouth, Sir Christopher Musgrave, Sir William
Bromley and Lord Preston were other notable names on Beaumont's

impressive list of clients, but he will be remembered above all for the fantastic topiary garden at Levens Hall.

Today we can see cones, circles, spirals, pyramids and other geometric shapes clipped in yew and dark green and gold box. They are massive specimens, often more than 20ft high. Many of the topiary 'characters' have their own names such as 'The Judge's Wig', and 'Queen Elizabeth and Her Maids of Honour'.

Below the topiary, and covering the entire garden are narrow paths and box-edged beds bursting with brightly coloured spring and summer flowers—forget-me-nots, wallflowers, primroses, begonias, geraniums, antirrhinums and many more.

More topiary was added in the 19C and 9 miles of box edging had to be replaced. Yet much of the original Stuart period topiary still exists.

Maintenance of this garden is, obviously, very labour intensive. Even with the aid of modern electric clippers, it takes two men six weeks to complete the hedge clipping. 'Bedding out' is another massive task.

To the back of the topiary garden, furthest from the Hall, a border runs along the length of the walls from the topiary garden through to the old orchard. The previous owner, Robin Bagot, planted this with climbers and shrubs such as clematis, philadelphus, ceanothus, and old fruit tree varieties.

Follow the border past the huge battlement-shaped yew hedge which divides the topiary garden from the orchard. More flowers can be seen in the orchard and beds of herbaceous plants line the grass walk to the enormous beech hedge, providing a succession of soft colours, particularly blues, throughout the summer months.

The beech hedges, planted by Beaumont, are now in their prime and stand an impressive 20ft tall. They form a circular enclosure around a carpet of grass. Another grass walk, lined with borders, leads out of this enclosure to one of the earliest sunken ha-has in England.

Unfortunately, the A6 now divides the Hall and formal garden from the park. Of the 15 deer parks which once existed in the Kendal area at the time of Elizabeth I, this is the only survivor, so it is well worth crossing the road, and carefully following the public footpaths.

The park extends across the valley and takes in the gorge of the river Kent. An avenue of oak trees, now it its prime, runs beside the river. The landscape movement had not really got underway when these oaks were planted, yet they have been positioned in lines and groups, complementing the beauty of the winding river in its valley. You may see the Norwegian and black fallow deer and the rare Bagot goat roaming through the park.

The unique landscape at Levens Hall has survived the trials of time, although at one point its future looked doubtful when the Ministry of Transport proposed driving a 4-lane link road through the east end of the park to join the M6 and the Kendal by-pass. Six years of battling by the devoted owner at that time, Robin Bagot, resulted in an alternative route being chosen. So the park remains intact and this 17C chapter in garden history remains alive to show that it has, as the Rev. William Gilpin once said: 'All that is best in Landscape and Design'.

Lingholm Gardens

ADDRESS AND TELEPHONE: Lingholm, Keswick, Cumbria CA12 5UA. Tel. (07687) 72003

OWNER: Viscount Rochdale

DIRECTIONS: off A66 for Portinscale, then 1 mile S towards Grange. Public transport: Mountain Goat Bus Service. Boat trips from Keswick land within ½ mile of gardens

OPENING TIMES: April to end October, daily 10–5. House not open

ADMISSION: £1.70 (accompanied children free). Coach parties by prior arrangement

CAR PARKING: yes

TOILETS: yes

REFRESHMENTS: café open 11–5 weekdays, 1–5 Sun

SHOP: plant centre

DOGS: no

WHEELCHAIR ACCESS: yes. Toilets for the disabled: yes

PEAK MONTHS: April, May and June

NOTABLE FEATURES: formal and woodland gardens; rhododendrons, azaleas, meconopsis, daffodils, primulas; specimen trees and shrubs

On the wooded western shore of Derwentwater is a fine Victorian mansion, Lingholm. The house was designed in the 1870s by Alfred Waterhouse for Colonel J.F. Greenall but towards the end of the 19C it was often used for summer lettings. The Potter family spent several seasons there, and it was the red squirrels in these woods that inspired Beatrix Potter to write *The Tales of Squirrel Nutkin*, published in 1903. *Peter Rabbit* may also have been composed at Lingholm, although Mr McGregor's plot, where Peter went in search of lettuces, appears to be based on Lingholm's neighbouring Fawe Park.

The house and garden certainly have the perfect setting, commanding fine views of the hills surrounding Derwentwater. The soil is acid and rather peaty, the rainfall high (65in.) and the hills and woodland offer excellent protection and shelter to a fine collection of rhododendrons.

The gardens began to develop early this century under Colonel George Kemp, who later became Lord Rochdale. Terraces and formal gardens were laid out and in 1927 a water garden was created to a design by Symons Jeune.

Unfortunately some of these features have proved too time consuming and costly to keep up, but the collections of trees, shrubs, rhododendrons, azaleas and woodland plants have continued to be developed over the years.

Many fine trees are set in the lawns between the car park and the house, notably Caucasian firs (*Abies nordmanniana*), a magnificent spreading blue cedar (*Cedrus atlantica glauca*), Wellingtonia (*Sequoiadendron giganteum*) and the iron tree or Persian ironwood (*Parrotia persica*). You can recognise the latter by its attractive flaking bark, and its clusters of crimson-stamened flowers, which emerge before the leaves.

The entrance to the garden is via the memorial garden—through the wrought iron gates and down the steps smothered in tiny violas, ferns and geraniums. Provision is made for wheelchairs to avoid these steps, rejoining the main route further on; some seats are also situated along the way. This little sunken garden contains a lily pool surrounded by borders of shrub roses, mixed herbaceous plants, small rhododendrons and primulas.

The route now leads on to the main terrace which is divided into sections by yew buttresses. The main section contains an important collection of dwarf rhododendrons from all around the northern hemisphere, both hybrids and rarer species, including the charming *R. Williamsianum* with bronze young growth and shell pink bell-shaped flowers in April and *R. fastigiatum*, a dense dome of small grey leaves with purple funnel-shaped flowers in April and May. The small postrate Tibetan alpine *R. radicans* is another delightful plant. It forms a low mound of creeping stems with tiny leaves and carries rose-purple flowers in May and June.

Two other sections are devoted to a wide selection of herbaceous plants suited to acid soils, such as meconopsis, geraniums, euphorbias and hostas. There are also long beds of roses on the opposite side of the terrace.

At the end of the terrace, the gardens open into a large lawned area, with drifts of daffodils in spring. Near to the house is a large cucumber tree (*Magnolia acuminata*), recognisable by its long oval-shaped leaves. The cup-shaped flowers are borne in May and June and are greenish yellow with blue markings. The common name refers to the fruit which is cucumber shaped, about 2in. long, and green when young but ripening to dark red. The path leading towards the woodland garden passes by Silver Hill Cottage and alongside a grassed bank planted with a wide variety of shrubs. There are several hollies such as *Ilex* x *altaclarensis* 'Hodginsii' and 'Golden King'—one of the best variegated hollies.

The woodland garden provides a home for Lingholm's main collection of rhododendrons. Many of the species and hybrid rhododendrons were planted between 1925 and 1935, but since 1946 some of the more recent hybrids have also been introduced.

The Lingholm rhododendron collection is very large and the looping walk through the woodland reveals some spectacular displays of colour in spring. Among the first to flower is *Rhododendron sutcheunense*—an outstanding large shrub which carries rosy pink flowers in February and March. *R. lutescens* also shows its primrose yellow flowers in February and continues through to April. A host of species and hybrids provide colour from March right through June with *R. auriculatum* in August and September.

Many of the plants have been selected for attractive stems or foliage, to add interest to the woodland beyond the main rhododendron flowering period. There is, for instance, *R. shilsonii* with its beautiful, metallic stems. When it flowers in March and April *R. shilsonii* is a mass of blood red bell-shaped flowers. *R. hodgsonii*, has exceptionally handsome foliage—the leaves are dark green above and grey/fawn below, and as long as 12in. *R. brevistylum* is also grown for its leaves which are green, shiny and aromatic.

Several of the rhododendrons are scented, such as *R. auriculatum*, which has white richly scented flowers borne later in the year, in July or August. *R. crassum* is also scented. *R. griffithianum* is magnificent, with its reddish-brown peeling bark and loose trusses of widely bell-shaped flowers, white and scented. Many other exceptionally beautiful rhododendrons can be seen here at Ling-holm—*R. discolor, R. fargesii, R. eximium, R. macabeanum, R. thomsonii*, and the ideal woodland species *R. augustinii*, with delightful blue flowers.

There are some quite unusual rhododendrons too, such as *R. coryphaeum* and *R. micranthum*. This latter is a very interesting and distinctive Chinese species—from May to July it has racemes of tiny bell-shaped flowers. Another striking species is *R. grierson-ianum* with its unusual long tapered flower buds, opening to brilliant scarlet flowers in June.

There are several other notable plants in the woodland garden— *Magnolia soulangiana, Eucryphia glutinosa* and *Amelanchier canadensis*, to name a few, and also two large specimens of European silver fir (*Abies alba*), one of which measured 144ft in 1983.

Throughout the woodland garden the vegetation has been kept as natural as possible to show the rhododendrons at their best and the identification and labelling of the plants is to a very high standard.

The gales of February 1990 damaged a number of important trees but the affected area has since been replanted.

There is much more to see at Lingholm than can be described here. The gardens are very large and the plant collection extensive. Allow plenty of time to explore this garden, especially if you are able to visit during the rhododendron season.

Muncaster Castle

ADDRESS AND TELEPHONE: Muncaster Castle, Ravenglass, Cumbria. Tel. Ravenglass (0229) 717614 or 717203

OWNERS: Mr and Mrs Patrick Gordon-Duff-Pennington

DIRECTIONS: 1 mile SE of Ravenglass on A595. Public transport: Ravenglass BR ¼ mile

OPENING TIMES: end March to end October, Tues to Sun: gardens 11–5; castle 1–4.30

ADMISSION: house and gardens £3.25, children £1.75; gardens and owl centre only £1.75, children £1.25. Coach parties by prior arrangement (reduced admission)

CAR PARKING: yes

TOILETS: yes

REFRESHMENTS: café

SHOP: yes

DOGS: on lead

WHEELCHAIR ACCESS: limited. Toilets for the disabled: yes

PEAK MONTHS: April/May

NOTABLE FEATURES: outstanding rhododendron collection; rare shrubs and woodland gardens

Muncaster Castle is set in countryside of great natural beauty and commands magnificent views over Eskdale to Scafell, the highest mountain in England. Its remoteness is almost a feature in itself.

Muncaster is built on the site of a Roman pele tower. It was built to provide protection against the raiders who frequently used the Cumbrian coast as a route into England. A medieval castle was built around the tower, which was added to in 1862–66 by Anthony Salvin.

The present owner's grandfather, Sir John Ramsden, inherited the estate in 1917, and imported a collection of rhododendrons from his other garden at Bulstrode, near Gerrards Cross in Buckinghamshire.

Sir John financed plant hunting expeditions by Ludlow, Sheriff and Kingdon Ward and many rhododendrons grown from seed collected on those expeditions were planted in the woodlands around the castle, to create what was then the largest collection of species rhododendrons in the country.

While at Muncaster (1917–58) Sir John also carried out much breeding work, and his programmes of crossing produced many new hybrids such as 'Joan Ramsden', 'Muncaster Bells', 'Muncaster Mist', 'Blue Haze' and 'Ember Glow'.

The woodland planted in the 1780s by John, Lord Muncaster, gives good shelter from winds, and the climate is generally mild—the Gulf Stream passes close by. Rhododendrons and many other interesting plants have flourished in these clement conditions, and the acid soil.

The collection of rhododendrons at Muncaster is still one of the finest in the country, as evidenced immediately by the sweeping driveway, planted on both sides with masses of rhododendrons and azaleas beneath a tall canopy of beech, pine and fir trees. This is a marvellous sight in May, when the display of colour and scent is at its best. Candelabra primulas and other small moisture-loving plants grow in the damp verges.

Many more rhododendrons can be seen in the woodland to the side of the drive, together with fine trees. Muncaster has at least 15 types of southern beech—*Nothofagus procera* and *N. betuloides* do particularly well. There are some very tall eucryphias, as well as magnolias, camellias and good specimens of *Pieris formosa forrestii*.

Other trees make the garden worth visiting out of the rhododendron season. The popular *Populus Wilsonii*, given to Sir John Ramsden by the Emperor of Japan, is interesting for its large attractive leaves, often more than 10in. in length, sea-green above and greyish beneath.

But it is the rhododendrons and azaleas that really steal the show here, growing as splendid single specimens or in dense groups. The large-leaved species are particularly at home, including the magnificent *R. macabeanum* with dark shiny green leaves, grey beneath, and carrying large trusses of purple-blotched pale yellow flowers in April. Another is *R. sinogrande*, with enormous shiny dark green leaves, up to 2ft 8in. long and 1ft wide. These also flower in April—huge trusses of creamy-white flowers with a crimson blotch.

The magnificent Himalayan *R. falconeri* saves its display of waxy creamy-yellow flowers until May. The soft pink blossoms of *R. Callimorphum* also look their best at this time, and *R. augustinii* flowers blue. *R. beanianum* is smothered in loose trusses of red waxy bell-shaped flowers from mid to late spring.

Even more spectacular than the drive and woodlands is the Ghyll, a sharp deep valley. In May this is ablaze with rhododendrons and azaleas, set among ornamental trees and shrubs, including green and purple-leaved acers, magnolias, camellias and, later, blue-flowered hydrangeas.

The formal walk of the long grass terrace is another outstanding feature. Looking over the very grand crenallated hedge of clipped box and yew, you get an excellent view down into Eskdale, with the River Esk glistening in the bottom of the valley and the Lakeland hills as a backdrop. To the rear of the terrace, shrub borders offer still more rhododendrons, along with tree heathers, pieris, weeping pear and other well-chosen trees and shrubs.

Since 1983, Phyllida Gordon-Duff-Pennington and her husband Patrick have been caring for the garden. Changes lie ahead—many of the woodland trees are reaching the end of their time and will need replacing and much propagation work is being done to re-stock the gardens with shrubs and to maintain the excellent collection of rhododendrons.

Rydal Mount

ADDRESS AND TELEPHONE: Rydal Mount, Ambleside, Cumbria. Tel. Ambleside (05394) 33002

OWNER: Mrs Mary Henderson (Wordsworth's great-great-granddaughter)

DIRECTIONS: off A591 1½ miles from Ambleside, 2½ miles from Grasmere. Public transport: Windermere BR. Buses from Windermere and Ambleside to Grasmere stop at Rydal Church. See Lake District National Park Visitor Centre at Brockhole (Tel. 096 62 6601) for details of special tours

OPENING TIMES: 1 March to 31 October, daily 10–5.30. 1 November to end February, daily excluding Tues 10–4. House is also open

ADMISSION: £2, children 80p, pre-booked parties £1.70

CAR PARKING: yes and for coaches

TOILETS: yes

REFRESHMENTS: no

SHOP: yes

DOGS: on lead

WHEELCHAIR ACCESS: very limited. Toilets for the disabled: no

PEAK MONTHS: July and August

NOTABLE FEATURES: terraces and summerhouse; water garden; ancient mound; views across Rydal Water and down Rothay Valley

Situated between Grasmere and Ambleside, Rydal Mount perches on the lower slopes of Nab Scar. It is a typical Lakeland setting, the house commanding a magnificent panoramic view down Rothay Valley to Ambleside and the head of Windermere. Nearby, to the west, lies Rydal Water, surrounded by the majestic Lakeland hills.

Rydal Mount's most famous inhabitant was William Wordsworth, who, had he not succeeded as a poet, would almost certainly have been a landscape gardener. Indeed, in a letter to a friend Wordsworth wrote of his three related callings as poet, landscape gardener and critic of works of art; and he designed not only the 4½ acres of garden at Rydal Mount but also the gardens of many of his friends and neighbours.

Wordsworth's gardening was a practical demonstration of his deep love of nature. He believed that a garden should be informal and harmonise with the surrounding countryside, with lawn, and trees carefully planted so as not to obscure the views—and he created just such a garden when he and his family moved to Rydal Mount in 1813. Despite some new planting, the garden remains virtually as the poet planned it.

Built in 1550 and enlarged in the 1750s, the house was known as Keens until a Liverpool family, the Norths, renamed it Rydal Mount. In 1812 the property was sold to Lady Diana le Fleming who let it in the following year to William Wordsworth, his wife Mary, sister Dorothy, sister-in-law Sara Hutchinson and his three children. It was to be Wordsworth's home until his death in 1850.

Most of the garden at Rydal Mount lies to the west of the house where the ground slopes steeply away. Here two terraces stretch out along the side of the fell. One of Wordsworth's first tasks was to improve the contours and planting of the Sloping Terrace, which had been made by previous owners.

Immediately below the Sloping Terrace and following its line is Isabella's Terrace (named after Isabella Fenwick, a family friend), which Wordsworth constructed on the level so as to make walking easier for the ladies.

You can reach the Sloping Terrace by way of stone steps near the corner of the house. William's brother Christopher tells us that in between the steps 'yellow flowering poppies and wild geraniums grew'.

Wordsworth planted Scots pines, birches and sycamores below the terrace—many of these are still growing. You can examine the fine foliage of a magnificent specimen of the fern-leaved or cut-leaved beech (*Fagus sylvatica* 'Heterophylla'), which seems to stretch out its branches to the fells. Beneath are rhododendrons and Wordsworth's favourite flowers—daffodils, bluebells and primroses. Ferns grow in the shade beneath the rough slate retaining walls of the terraces, and the walls themselves are clothed with mosses and ivies.

At the far end of the Sloping Terrace Wordsworth built a rustic summerhouse in local stone and timbers and with a pebbled floor:

here he often sat to compose poetry. His favourite walk stretched from the summerhouse to the Far Terrace, which reaches out to the fell and gives splendid views of Rydal Water shimmering at the foot of the hills. Of this walk he wrote:

> A Poet's hand first shaped it; and the steps
> Of that same Bard—repeated to and fro
> At morn, at noon, and under the moonlight skies
> Through the vicissitudes of many a year—
> Forbade the weeds to creep o'er its grey line.

The ground below the summerhouse falls away steeply—in spring this is one mass of bluebells. A series of small bubbling and cascading streams and pools forms the water garden: here grow foxgloves, bluebells, cowslips and other flowers which Wordsworth collected while on Lakeland rambles. Through the trees you can glimpse the fells and Rydal Water.

Below the water garden a raised croquet lawn is shaded by splendid mature copper beech, sycamore and yew trees. From here a winding path leads you to the Sloping Lawn and back to the house. The lawn is kidney shaped, narrowing towards the house, and is surrounded by maples, flowering shrubs, rhododendrons and old-fashioned azaleas.

A gate on the lower side of the lawn leads to Dora's Field— a small paddock on the steep slope between the garden and the main road. Wordsworth first bought the field with the intention of building a house on it, but later gave it to his daughter Dora. After her death he planted the paddock with 80,000 daffodils as a memorial to her. Today Dora's Field is under the protection of the National Trust and each spring it becomes a sea of golden flowers.

To the front of the house, beyond the gravel semicircular forecourt, wide steps lead down to the Mound. This is thought to have been used in the 9C as a look-out post and for beacon fires to warn of approaching enemies. The Mound was the Wordsworth's favourite place for afternoon tea and entertaining. Windermere is visible from here, and, on a clear day, the town of Bowness, some 7 miles away.

Both the house and garden at Rydal Mount are open to the public, thanks to Mrs Mary Henderson (née Wordsworth), great-great-granddaughter of the Poet, who acquired the property in 1970. It is worth noting that special events such as candlelit poetry readings are sometimes held at the house and that the garden is also part of a three-garden tour (organised by the Lake District National Park Visitor Centre, tel. 096 62 6601) which also takes in Rydal Hall and Brockhole on Windermere.

Further up the road, at Grasmere, you will find another of Wordsworth's homes—Dove Cottage. The Wordsworths lived here from 1799 to 1808. The poet stocked the garden with wild flowers, ferns and mosses and built a summerhouse overlooking the Water.

Although the garden at Dove Cottage was small, the Wordsworths were very fond of it, as evidenced by 'A Farewell' which William composed in July 1802 before setting out on a trip.

> Farewell, thou little Nook of mountain ground,
> Thou rocky corner in the lowest stair
> Of that magnificent temple which doth bound

One side of our whole vale with grandeur rare;
Sweet garden orchard, eminently fair,
The loveliest spot that man hath ever found,
Fairwell! we leave thee to Heaven's peaceful care,
Thee and the Cottage which thou dost surround.

A growing family caused Wordsworth to move first to Allan Bank and then to Rydal Mount.

Dove Cottage is owned by the Wordsworth Trust and is open daily.

Sizergh Castle

ADDRESS AND TELEPHONE: Sizergh Castle, near Kendal, Cumbria LA8 8AE. Tel. Sedgwick (053 95) 60070

OWNERS: The National Trust

DIRECTIONS: 3½ miles S of Kendal on A591. Public transport: Kendal BR 3½ miles, but not operational Sun, except May to September; Oxenholme BR 3 miles. Buses from Kendal to Lancaster drop at drive end

OPENING TIMES: 31 March to end October, Sun to Thurs 12.30–5.30 (castle open after 1.30)

ADMISSION: castle and garden £2.80, children £1.40; garden only £1.40, children 70p. Reductions for pre-booked parties of 15 or more visiting castle and garden

CAR PARKING: yes

TOILETS: yes

REFRESHMENTS: café open 1.30–5

SHOP: yes

DOGS: no

WHEELCHAIR ACCESS: yes, via main gravel paths. Toilets for the disabled: no

PEAK MONTHS: no special peak

NOTABLE FEATURES: rose garden; rock garden with collection of dwarf conifers and ferns; castle with pele tower

The strong defensive pele tower at Sizergh dates from about 1350, and the castle has retained many characteristics of a stronghold. Indeed, so dominant is the building that some parts of the garden seem overshadowed and threatened by it.

Many varied elements exist within the 14 acres of garden—rose, wild and rock gardens, lawns and a terrace, a lake and herbaceous borders. The original 17C approach to the castle was from the south-west through an avenue of beech trees, since replaced by limes and more recently by rowans (*Sorbus aucuparia* 'Beissneri') and now surrounded by a rose garden. Visitors not wishing to tour the castle will find themselves in this part of the garden first.

Among pollarded yews are island beds of roses and flowering trees and shrubs. Climbing up one of the yews is *Rosa longicuspis*, its white banana-scented flowers contrasting well with the dark yew foliage. Forsythias, buddleias and wall hydrangeas are also here, along with magnolias such as *M. x soulangiana* and *M. liliiflora (quinquepeta)* 'Nigra'. The roses and shrubs are underplanted with bulbs and herbaceous plants for added interest. There are eight different varieties of lily.

The old gate piers at the end of the rose garden date from the 17C and lead on to the main lawn below the pele tower. A series of low terraces in the enclosed area to the right of the gateway is all that remains of a Dutch garden constructed in 1926. Intricate flower beds would once have dominated the garden, which only survived 20 years before being abandoned to grass.

To the left of the gateway a steep walk rises above the lawn to a high terrace and wall. The wall is constructed of limestone faced with bricks, to retain warmth and encourage fruit trees to set and ripen their fruit. It provides shelter for a large collection of shrubs and climbers, many of which are semi-hardy.

Clinging to the tower and softening the hard, defensive lines of the castle is a densely spreading Boston Ivy (*Parthenocissus tricuspidata*)—this shows rich crimson and scarlet foliage in the autumn. From spring to mid summer the castle steps, descending to the terrace and lake, are clothed with the purple-pink flowers of *Erinus alpinus*, the fairy foxglove.

The lake may originally have been part of the castle's moat and was extended to its present size in 1926. It has a small island—just large enough to support a young weeping hornbeam. Across the lake to the north-east is the wild garden, a flowery meadow sloping down to the water's edge.

The Dutch garden, terrace and lake all formed part of a design made in 1926 for Lord Strickland. The construction was carried out by T.R. Hayes and Son of Ambleside, a notable local firm of nurserymen, as was the building of the rock garden. For the knowledgeable gardener, plant enthusiast and fern-lover, this will be the climax of the garden tour.

Lying to the north of the castle, the rock garden extends over nearly an acre. Local weathered Westmorland limestone has been used—arranged so naturally that you might assume the boulders and outcrops have always been there. An artificial stream passes between rocks, tumbling down small cascades and forming pools before eventually joining the lake.

The rock garden is set within a shallow dell and the surrounding trees give good protection to a wide range of plants. As well as rock plants there are bog plants and marginals.

Dwarf conifers were planted in the rock garden for decorative effect in 1926. Although they have retained their form, many of the dwarfs are now very large indeed. There is one prostrate blue form of the noble fir—now measuring more than 15ft across—and some species forms of dwarf cypresses, thujas, junipers and pines. In all there are 75 species of hardy conifer—many of them 'dwarfish'—in and around the rock garden and they form a good contrast to the green and copper foliage of the Japanese maples, especially in the autumn when the maples turn crimson and scarlet.

The rock garden also has an excellent collection of hardy ferns—some 120 species. There are several varieties of the royal fern, including the slender royal fern (*Osmunda regalis gracilis*) which reaches a height of 8ft each year. There are unusual polypodies, and many forms of dryopteris and blechnum. It is a pteridophilist's paradise.

DERBYSHIRE

Chatsworth

ADDRESS AND TELEPHONE: Chatsworth House Trust, Chatsworth, Bakewell, Derbyshire DE4 1PP. Tel. Baslow (0246) 582204

OWNERS: Chatsworth House Trust (Home of the Duke and Duchess of Devonshire)

DIRECTIONS: 8 miles N of Matlock, 2 miles S of Baslow on B6012. No public transport available

OPENING TIMES: late March to end October, daily 11–4.30. House also open

ADMISSION: garden only £2.25, children £1.10. Family ticket £6.25. Farmyard and adventure playground extra. Coach parties by prior arrangement (reductions)

CAR PARKING: yes

TOILETS: yes

REFRESHMENTS: restaurant

SHOP: yes

DOGS: on lead

WHEELCHAIR ACCESS: garden only. To most parts but the grounds are extensive, 2 wheelchairs available. Toilets for the disabled: yes

PEAK MONTHS: June

NOTABLE FEATURES: landscaped garden with cascade, canal pond and fountains; rock garden; azalea dell; woodland; conservatories and display house

The garden at Chatsworth has undergone many changes through the centuries, instigated by the best of gardeners and garden designers and resulting in a medley of interesting features. The 100-acre grounds are still being developed by the present Duke and Duchess of Devonshire, with new plantings and paths adding to the attractions.

The earliest reference to a garden at Chatsworth dates from a letter written by Bess of Hardwick in 1560 (she and her husband, Sir William Cavendish, built the first house there in 1552), but the garden only really began to take shape in 1690, with the engagement of George London and Henry Wise, who laid out great parterres to the west and south of the house. These were swept away in the 18C by Capability Brown, who also planted up the parkland and even altered the course of the River Derwent. Only

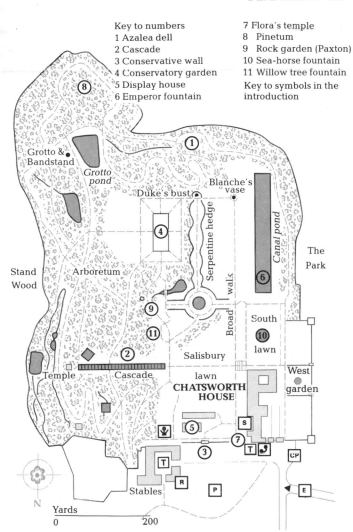

Key to numbers
1 Azalea dell
2 Cascade
3 Conservative wall
4 Conservatory garden
5 Display house
6 Emperor fountain

7 Flora's temple
8 Pinetum
9 Rock garden (Paxton)
10 Sea-horse fountain
11 Willow tree fountain
Key to symbols in the
introduction

the magnificent cascade, the sea-horse fountain and the canal pond were allowed to remain.

In the 19C, Joseph Paxton—gardener, engineer and architect—designed the Great Conservatory, a huge hot house which drew world-wide attention at the time. Paxton was also responsible for the enormous and somewhat unusual rock garden, the emperor fountain and the pinetum.

The entrance to the house is marked by an avenue of tulip trees (*Liriodendron tulipifera*). Outside the front door is a weeping ash (*Fraxinus excelsior* 'Pendula'), planted in 1830 by Paxton, surrounded by a circular lawn—here aconites, crocuses, snowdrops, hyacinths, narcissus, tulips and fritillaries provide interest and colour from January to June.

The garden entrance is near Flora's Temple; or you can go through the orangery, which links the house and garden. Flora's Temple used to be a bowling green house and was originally built a quarter of a mile away but was moved to its present site c 1760. It now heralds the start of the Broad Walk which, flanked by golden yews (*Taxus baccata* 'Aureomarginata') and green yews (*Taxus baccata* 'Fastigiata'), crosses the lawns, continues through an avenue of beeches and ends over a third of a mile away with Blanche's Vase silhouetted against the skyline. The colour scheme of the Broad Walk borders is mainly yellow, orange and red, with annuals, herbaceous plants and roses mingling in a mass of different shades in summer.

Paxton's 'Conservative Wall', a series of glass compartments, begins at Flora's Temple and ascends the hillside in steps for a length of 330ft. Figs, apricots and peaches find a suitable climate in the glass cases, along with many shrubs which prefer warmer conditions. In the central case two specimens of *Camellia reticulata* 'Captain Rawes', dating from 1850, are covered with carmine rose-pink flowers in March and April.

A large collection of camellias is also housed in the First Duke's Greenhouse; and the nearby display house provides three different climatic conditions, suiting a wide range of plants.

This display house, completed in 1970, is of outstanding design— its weight is suspended from the outside. It is the work of G.A. Pearce, who was also responsible for the plant houses at Edinburgh Botanic Garden. The tropical section houses the giant Amazonian water lily (*Victoria amazonica*)—brought by Paxton from Kew and first persuaded to flower at Chatsworth. Pawpaws and bananas also do well here. In the centre section the night-flowering cactus (*Selenicereus grandiflorus*) opens its flowers as night falls. In the third (temperate) section are more camellias, along with other plants such as the tender rhododendron 'Fragrantissimum'.

Beyond the display house are 3 acres of lawns created by Brown— once called the Great Slope but now known as the Salisbury Lawn. From the hillside above, the cascade glitters its way down huge steps to the lawn. Over 200 yds in length, the cascade was designed by Grillet in the mid 1690s. A cascade house or temple was built at the top in 1703. There are 24 groups of falls, with steps of varying widths providing different 'tunes'. The water comes from man-made reservoirs on a plateau above the hill, fed by miles of conduits, which drain water from the surrounding moorland.

From the cascade the water is piped underground to work the sea-horse fountain on the south lawn, then underground again to another fountain in the west garden before it falls into the River Derwent. Since the water is not recirculated there are times in dry summers when it has to be rationed.

Not far from the cascade, in a secluded dell surrounded by huge rocks, is another unusual water feature—the Willow Tree Fountain. The original willow tree was set in place in 1692 and has twice been replaced; this latest reproduction gives much the same effect as the other two, water spurting from its leafless copper branches.

The path leads on into Paxton's rockeries, a most unusual rock garden, very dramatically constructed with huge boulders piled one on top of another. A waterfall flows over one of the largest rocks, known as the Wellington Rock, and then tumbles through the narrow 'striad' into a pond. A wealth of plants enjoy the damp conditions created in this area, among them *Gunnera manicata* with its massive rhubarb-like foliage, and primulas such as *P. japonica* which flowers in early summer and *P. florindae* which provides colour in July and August. In May and June the rockeries are ablaze with azalea flowers and around the pond at the bottom red hot pokers (kniphofia) form a fiery prelude to the rampant climbing roses.

After meandering through the rock garden the path passes under a stone archway and into the old conservatory garden. Alas, only the stone base walls remain of Paxton's Great Conservatory. Ironically, Paxton's grandson was given the sad task of demolishing the conservatory, in 1920, following the years of wartime neglect.

The former (¾ acre) site of the conservatory, is now planted with flower beds and a maze (not open to the public because of previous damage caused to the hedges) and surrounding the whole is a terrace, separating the garden from the enclosing wooded hillsides.

The path continues through trees up to the grotto, designed by a Bakewell geologist, White Watson, in 1798. Above this, strangely, is a bandstand and both grotto and bandstand are reflected in the still waters of the grotto pond, an ancient fish pond. This secluded and (usually) tranquil area has become a haven for wildlife, especially for wild pheasants and water fowl.

At the far corner of the pond is a magnificent white or Weymouth pine (*Pinus strobus*) which at 121ft is one of the tallest in England. More grand trees can be found a little further south, in the pinetum. Many of the conifers planted here in 1829 by the 6th Duke were new introductions to Britain, and despite a disastrous gale in 1962 some of the original plantings can still be seen, including Wellingtonia, (*Sequoiadendron giganteum*), noble fir (*Abies procera*), beach pine (*Pinus contorta*), Oregon Douglas fir (*Pseudostuga menziesii*) and monkey puzzle (*Araucaria araucana*).

Returning to the house, you pass through the azalea dell and ravine. These are one solid mass of colour towards the end of late spring and the scent is incredible on a windless sunny day.

The path leads out onto lawns at the southern end of the Canal Pond —perhaps the most dominant feature at Chatsworth. The 314 yds of canal were dug in 1702 but it was not until 1843 that Paxton installed the Emperor Fountain. The huge jet of water was originally intended as a gesture of welcome to Tsar Nicholas (Emperor of Russia) but in the end the Tsar decided not to visit.

Not far to the east of the Canal Pond, across the Broad Walk, is the Serpentine Hedge, a wavy beech hedge planted in 1953. At the far end is a bronze head of the 6th Duke.

This garden cries out for exploration—but remember to take a comfortable pair of shoes.

Elvaston Castle

ADDRESS AND TELEPHONE: Elvaston Castle Country Park,
Thulston, Derby DE7 3EP. Tel. Derby (0332) 571342

OWNERS: Derbyshire County Council

DIRECTIONS: entrance off the B5010 between Thulston and
Borrowash. Approximately 4 miles SE of Derby and 4 miles NW
of junction 24 of M1. Road signs from A6 and A52. Public
transport: Derby BR. No reasonable bus service

OPENING TIMES: all the year round, daily 9–dusk. House
occasionally open for events

ADMISSION: car parking fee, daily Easter to 31 October and at
weekends the rest of the year

CAR PARKING: yes

TOILETS: yes

REFRESHMENTS: café open daily Easter to end of October and at
weekends the rest of the year

SHOP: yes (Easter to end October)

DOGS: must be 'under control'

PEAK MONTHS: no special peaks

NOTABLE FEATURES: formal parterre and Italian garden; old
English garden (walled) with herbaceous borders, rose garden
and herb garden; lake with ornamental rockwork; rhododendron
dell; fine trees and some unusual species

Within easy reach of most parts of Derbyshire, South Yorkshire, the
eastern edges of Staffordshire and the cities of Nottingham and
Leicester is Elvaston Castle Country Park—over 200 acres of beautiful wood and parkland, with gardens.

Elvaston is an estate in the grand manner and for centuries was
the home of the Stanhope family, the earls of Harrington. It suffered
a considerable period of neglect when in 1939 the present Earl left
to take up residence in Eire; the castle remained vacant until 1969
when it was acquired by Derbyshire County Council and carefully
restored.

Three aspects of the estate are now offered for the public to enjoy:
the castle and buildings (with information centre, countryside
museum, shop and café); semi-natural park and woodland; and
some particularly interesting gardens, consisting of formal gardens,
an old English garden, a rhododendron dell, lakeside features and
many fine trees.

The castle's present neo-Gothic appearance owes much to the
3rd Earl of Harrington, who engaged James Wyatt to remodel the
old manor. The 3rd Earl also invited Capability Brown to landscape
the grounds—a commission which Brown turned down because
'the place is so flat'.

The 4th Earl, Charles, appointed William Barron to lay out the
grounds in 1830. Barron was a very successful horticulturist. After
a three-year apprenticeship in his native Berwickshire he took
charge of the glasshouses at the Royal Botanic Garden in Edinburgh
before coming to Elvaston Castle where one of his first tasks was

to improve the drainage (constructing some drains over a mile in length). He also extended the kitchen garden and erected hot-houses.

Barron's knowledge of trees and their culture was unique and he quickly gained a reputation for moving large trees. By this means he produced a very comprehensive collection of conifers at Elvaston. It was here that the first Caucasian fir (*Abies nordmanniana*) was planted in England.

Barron laid out formal vistas, introduced topiary, created a lake with rockwork and planted trees. Gradually the pleasure grounds, non-existent in 1831, were formed and extended until by 1851 they covered nearly 80 acres.

The 4th Earl was succeeded by his brother, Colonel Leicester Stanhope, who was forced to cut the gardening staff from 90 to 8, and sold many of the more valuable trees from the collection. Despite this the gardens at Elvaston are still able to boast many unusual tree species and Derbyshire County Council hopes that in the future a tree trail can be developed, to introduce visitors to notable examples.

Credit must go the Derbyshire County Council for the excellent restoration work in the garden and for the exceptional way in which the estate has been organised as a country park. Even the huge car park is unobtrusive on the landscape, blocks of parking bays being separated and hidden by mass plantings of shrubs.

The walk to the castle and park centre is through mixed wood-land, bringing you into Elvaston Avenue. This broad grassed vista was planted by Barron to highlight the eastern front of the house. Barron took care to place evergreens on the outer edges of avenues and vistas, so the changing seasons make little impact on the view.

To the south of the great house is a formal parterre garden, intricately embroidered in dwarf box. The parterres themselves are not very old; the original garden had deteriorated so much through neglect that in 1970 the council completely replaced it.

A tall, thick dark yew hedge separates the parterre garden from the Italian garden, where crowds of flat-topped pillars and domes of dark and golden yew form a symmetrical pattern. Topiary of monstrous proportions forms the southern edge of this garden and around the perimeter stand the towering pines, monkey puzzle trees (*Araucaria araucana*) and cedars planted by Barron.

The Moorish temple just beyond the formal gardens to the south is all that remains of Barron's Alhambra garden—shown in an 1860 print as a series of raised lawns, with beds of heathers and other plants set in gravelled walks.

Close by is an avenue which leads to the Golden Gates. Tradition has it that these gates came from the Palace of Versailles, and although called 'golden' they have actually been painted blue since the 1850s.

A walk eastwards through woodland underplanted with masses of rhododendrons brings you to what used to be the estate's kitchen garden. Today it is open to the public as the Old English Garden, and has fine herbaceous borders, a rose garden and a herb garden laid out with blind people in mind.

The wall itself provides protection and support for a great many climbing plants. There is a wide variety of honeysuckles and clematis and near to the gateway is *Campsis grandiflora*—a beautiful oriental climber with drooping panicles of deep orange and red trumpet-shaped flowers in the late summer and early autumn. Here too is the blue passion flower (*Passiflora caerulea*) and *Jasminum* x *stephanense* which has clusters of fragrant pale pink flowers in June and July. The herbaceous borders are alive with colour in summer—the flowers include geraniums, verbascums, rudbeckias, geums, phlox and campanulas.

At the centre of the walled garden is a lawned area, bounded by flowering shrubs and with an island bed displaying heathers, spiraeas, dwarf rhododendrons, viburnums and mahonias. Towards the north-east corner of the walled garden a gentle slope leads into a paved area with raised beds of herbs. Again designed for blind people or those with restricted sight, this part of the garden features scented plants. Various types of mint, hyssop, thyme, lavender, sage and marjoram fill the air with an enticing mixture of scents on a sunny day.

The herb theme continues in the rose garden nearby, where the beds are edged with lavenders 'Hidcote' and 'Munstead'. In the centre is a display of 'Orange Sensation', a vivid vermilion colour with a rich sweet fragrance. The delightful pink and cream floribunda 'Pink Parfait' and that fine red rose 'Rob Roy' contribute to the colour in the garden while more perfume drifts across from the heavenly scented *Rosa rugosa* 'Blanc Double de Coubert'—an old shrub rose which carries large pure white semi-double flowers throughout the summer.

Leaving the Old English garden there is another opportunity to see more of William Barron's tree planting, on a walk through mixed mature woodland, leading to the lake on the other side of Elvaston Avenue. The 5-acre ornamental lake was created by Barron in 1839 and is possibly an extension of a smaller one. It was designed to link different features such as the rock archways, which frame views across the lake.

The rockwork, mainly gritstone and tufa, also owes its existence to Barron and although much is now missing, in its heyday it caused the Duke of Wellington to exclaim: 'The only *natural* artificial rock work I have ever seen!'.

Derbyshire County Council has devised a lakeside trail to take in the rock features, the water wheel and pump house, and the boat house. Between the lake and castle is a recently planted rhododendron garden—another example of the council's keenness, not only to preserve the estate, but to add and develop new features of interest.

Haddon Hall

ADDRESS AND TELEPHONE: Haddon Hall, Bakewell, Derbyshire DE4 1LA. Tel. Bakewell (0629) 812855

OWNERS: The Duke of Rutland

DIRECTIONS: 1½ miles SE of Bakewell on A6. Public transport:

Matlock BR 6½ miles. Buses from Matlock, Bakewell, Buxton, Belper, Chesterfield, Derby and Nottingham

OPENING TIMES: April to end September, Tues to Sun and BH Mon 11–6. Closed Sun in July and August. House is open

ADMISSION: £3, children £1.80. Coach parties by prior arrangement

CAR PARKING: yes

TOILETS: yes

REFRESHMENTS: yes

SHOP: yes

DOGS: no

WHEELCHAIR ACCESS: no; garden is a series of steep terraces with steps

PEAK MONTHS: June and July

NOTABLE FEATURES: terraces well planted with roses; collection of clematis; spring bulbs; 17C terraces; delphinium border; herbaceous borders

Haddon Hall lies only a few miles away from the grand mansion and estate of Chatsworth, yet in style, design and atmosphere they are worlds apart. Best known for its roses and spring bulbs, Haddon also attracts visitors by its tranquillity and intimacy.

The grey stone manor house is medieval—some parts date back to the 12C. Perched high on a limestone escarpment, it overlooks a beautiful valley and the meandering River Wye. Tradition has it that in the 1560s the heiress of the Hall, Dorothy Vernon, eloped with John Manners, son of the Earl of Rutland. The door through which Dorothy escaped, and the packhorse bridge she crossed to meet her lover, can still be seen today.

In the 18C Haddon was abandoned, the family preferring to reside at Belvoir Castle, and over the following two centuries it was almost completely neglected. In 1912, the 9th Duke of Rutland started restoring the Hall, clearing the garden of giant yews and sycamores and stripping the walls of ivy.

Admission to the garden is through the Hall itself, reached by a pleasant walk through meadows, across the river and uphill. Dorothy Vernon's door, on the east side of the building, leads out into the garden.

The garden is built on seven terraces, of which two are currently open to the public. The basic structure of walls, balustrading and steps is 17C, although the lower terraces may date from a century earlier.

From Dorothy Vernon's door, you step down onto the Bowling Green Terrace. Above the high retaining wall, clothed in purple aubrieta, is Dorothy Vernon's Walk—the path she took on the way to meet John Manners. In spring, the geometric formal beds are bright with daffodils, more than 60 varieties, in groups and clearly labelled. Spring bedding has a place here too, with polyanthus and wallflowers providing much of the colour. In summer the roses come into their own—the wall roses first and then by the end of June, beginning of July, the floribundas and hybrid teas.

The garden also has a collection of 40 or more varieties of clematis. Immediately to the right of the door, 'Mrs Cholmondely' shows large pale blue flowers from May to August, intertwined with the white and carmine double flowers of a Bourbon rose, 'Variegeta di Bologna'.

On the retaining wall rising above the Bowling Green Terrace is *Rosa primula*, the incense rose. The foliage and wood of this delightful shrub emit an incense-like perfume which drifts across the lawn on a still, warm summer's afternoon.

A wide flight of stone steps leads down from the Bowling Green Terrace to the Fountain Terrace below. An Albertine rose tumbles down the sides of the steps, its coppery buds opening into scented flowers of pink shaded with gold inner petals.

The rectangular fountain pool adds to the charming, romantic character of this lawned terrace and the rose beds here contain many favourites such as 'Wendy Cussons', 'King's Ransom' and 'Picture'. On the walls 'Mme Gregoire Staechelin' is a sight to behold, smothered with clear pink frilled flowers in June, but unfortunately only for a few weeks.

'Mme Alfred Carrière', a very old wall rose and a favourite in Victorian times, puts on a splendid display with double white blooms flushed pink. It flowers regularly through the summer and has a gorgeously sweet fragrance.

Under the house wall on the Fountain Terrace is a 'sixteenth century border'—designed to display plants native to this country or of 16C introduction. Here you can see sweet rocket (*Hesperis matronalis*), aquilegias, *Nigella hispanica*, love-lies-bleeding (*Amaranthus cordatus*) and *Gladiolus byzantinus*. A little further along is the delphinium border, containing at least 30 varieties of delphinium—a marvellous sight at the end of June.

A viewing point in the corner of the Fountain Terrace furthest away from the house gives magnificent views over the scenic Wye Valley. The retaining wall below is gradually being planted with all kinds of wall and rock plants to give a waterfall effect of flowers in springtime. Magnolias, buddleias and philadelphus enjoy a sheltered tranquil spot at the foot of the wall, together with a range of herbaceous plants.

The path along the side of the Hall passes the aviary, where hunting birds were once kept, and then continues downhill past the Chapel Bank, a grassy bank planted with wild flowers and native bulbs.

Hardwick Hall

ADDRESS AND TELEPHONE: Hardwick Hall, Doe Lea, Chesterfield, Derbyshire S44 5QJ. Tel. (0246) 850430

OWNERS: The National Trust

DIRECTIONS: 9½ miles SE of Chesterfield, 6½ miles W of Mansfield off A617 at Glapwell. Public transport: Chesterfield BR

9½ miles. Chesterfield to Nottingham bus, alight at Glapwell then a 2-mile walk

OPENING TIMES: 30 March to end October, daily 12–5.30; Hall Wed, Thurs, Sat, Sun and BH 12.30–5. Closed Good Fri

ADMISSION. Hall and gardens £4.50, under 17s £2.20, gardens only £1.80, under 17s 90p

CAR PARKING: yes

TOILETS: yes

REFRESHMENTS: yes, when Hall is open

SHOP: yes, when Hall is open

DOGS: on lead in Country Park, not in garden

WHEELCHAIR ACCESS: yes. Toilets for the disabled: yes

PEAK MONTHS: peaks throughout the season

NOTABLE FEATURES: herb garden; flower borders; orchards; collection of roses; views

The saying many of us learnt at school—'Hardwick Hall, more glass than wall'—does little to prepare the visitor for the sight of this impressive and very original building. The garden is also unusual.

Standing on the very top of a windswept hill, some 600ft above sea level, the Hall was built by Bess of Hardwick in the late 16C. Bess had lived in the manor house (now in ruins) to the south-west of the present Hall but four marriages helped her up the social ladder and improved her finances, enabling her first to extend the old manor house and then in 1591 (aged 70) to build Hardwick Hall.

Since its completion in 1597 the Hall, and indeed its contents, have changed very little. Although the Elizabethan garden has not survived, the stone walls surrounding the courtyards and gardens are as old as the Hall itself.

The present garden falls into three distinct sections and dates in part from the late Victorian times; considerable work was also done in the 1930s and after 1959, when the National Trust took over.

The entrance to both Hall and garden is by way of an Elizabethan gatehouse, which leads into the west courtyard. In Bess' time this would probably have been cobbled; today a central path leads between two large rectangular lawns to an entrance set in the towering west front of this most impressive Hall. 160-year-old Lebanon cedars stand either side of the gatehouse on the lawns, adding to the grandeur of the scene, although the north tree was severely damaged in the gales of January 1990 leaving only a 30ft stump.

The courtyard is enclosed by high stone walls decorated with ornate finials and with flower borders below. These borders are being replanted according to a late 19C design, with hot and dark colours. One already completed border, under the south wall, shows an excellent colour scheme of cool blues under the cedar, leading to pale yellows, then through stronger yellows into hot oranges, reds and finally purple.

Proceeding from the west courtyard to the south court, you arrive at the main part of the garden—a large area of simple design, divided into quarters by two hedged grasswalks—one of yew running north to south and one of hornbeam, from east to west. In the centre, the 'Rondel' where the alleys meet, statues and seats complete the formal design. The whole area is surrounded by broad walks and high stone walls.

A mixed south-facing border runs the length of the courtyard, beneath the main courtyard wall: this features soft colours, whites and silvers. Towards the centre is an old sea buckthorn (*Hippophae rhamnoides*), entangled with clematis 'Perle d'Azur', which displays light blue flowers between July and August.

The north-west corner consists simply of a large lawn, planted with trees and backed by the yew and hornbeam hedges on two sides. It is a romantic setting with specimen trees of Hungarian oak (*Quercus frainetto*), tulip tree (*Liriodendron tulipifera*), *Catalpa speciosa*, beech and magnolias set off against the dense yew hedge.

The other three quarters, as well as being backed by the alley hedges of yew and hornbeam, are enclosed by holly hedges. In the south-west quarter is the herb garden, redesigned and greatly enlarged by the National Trust in the 1960s. Culinary and medicinal herbs are planted in neat blocks and hops and other climbers trained up wooden tripods. Nearby is a nuttery with cobs, filberts and walnuts, and against the hornbeam hedge a cut flower border, housing the National Collection of *Scabiosa caucasica*. Lily-of-the-Valley 'Hardwick Giant' can also be seen in this corner. It is as large, perhaps larger, than Fortin's Giant, with a pale edge to its leaves.

The other two quarters are planted as orchards, one productive and one ornamental. Old varieties of apples, pears, plums, gages and damsons flourish and bear fruit in the productive orchard, which also has a border of old roses. The ornamental orchard features pears, including Jargonelle, and crab apples, such as *Malus hupehensis*; and spring flowers such as daffodils and late pheasant's eye narcissus, followed by wild flowers through the summer.

Beyond the orchards, to the south, is a mulberry walk, leading to the garden pavilion—used for picnics and also by the 6th Duke's orchestra as a smoking room.

Giant hogweed grows beneath the east boundary wall—a reminder of the original planting.

To reach the east garden, just step through the gate in the wall. Smooth lawns are broken only by the central pool which serves as a water reserve in cases of fire. The borders that line the courtyard walls have recently been replanted with hybrid musk roses. At the eastern end, a concealed ha-ha permits views over the parkland, and a magnificent double avenue of limes.

Kedleston Hall

ADDRESS AND TELEPHONE: Kedleston Hall, Derby DE6 4JN. Tel. Derby (0332) 842191

OWNERS: The National Trust

DIRECTIONS: 3 miles N of Derby signposted off A38. No public transport available

OPENING TIMES: 30 March to end October, Sat to Wed 11–6. Hall open 1–5.30 (last admission 5)

ADMISSION: house and garden £3.50, children £1.70

CAR PARKING: yes

TOILETS: yes

REFRESHMENTS: restaurant, open 12–5

SHOP: yes

DOGS: only in park on lead

WHEELCHAIR ACCESS: yes, but difficult in house— contact Administrator. Toilets for the disabled: yes

PEAK SEASON: spring for rhododendrons, autumn colours

NOTABLE FEATURES: magnificent lakes in parkland; rhododendrons; woodland walk; fine trees

Kedleston Hall is situated in pleasant countryside just 3 miles north of Derby. It is a grand mansion with 12 acres of garden set in 500 acres of parkland. Since the 12C it has been the home of the Curzon family, but in 1987 Viscount Scarsdale gave both the Hall and park to the National Trust.

There have been several houses here over the centuries. The medieval Hall was replaced in the early 18C and in 1721 the royal gardener Charles Bridgeman was called in to landscape the grounds. A plan dating from 1758 shows a traditional arrangement of house and church with a few houses and other village buildings. Bridgeman's formal gardens are shown around the house. To the north was a canal with circular and octagonal ponds, and vistas north. However, all Bridgeman's work was swept away when Nathaniel Curzon, later 1st Lord Scarsdale, inherited the property in 1758.

Nathaniel Curzon decided to rebuild the house completely, although it was less than 70 years old. He called in the architect Matthew Brettingham, but soon replaced him with James Paine. In 1759 he brought in an enthusiastic young architect—Robert Adam, then at the beginning of his career. Adam was initially engaged to design the landscapes, but by 1760 he had succeeded Paine as architect and supervised the imposing north front. Besides creating the magnificent interiors for which Kedleston is so well known, Adam also designed the pleasure grounds and park.

By an Act of Parliament, Lord Scarsdale was granted permission to re-route the road around the northern edge of the park and to move the entire village—cottages, malthouse, mill, forge, rectory and inn—to its present site about half a mile to the west. Only the medieval church was allowed to remain at the west end of the house. A map of 1764 clearly shows these transformations and includes new features in the park such as the Long Walk, the Sulphur Bath House and a hermitage.

In the park to the north of the Hall the small Cutler Brook was dammed with a series of six weirs, to create a river-like lake. Adam built the magnificent triple-arched bridge across the lake with a weir below. He also designed the fishing house on the bank.

The Long Walk was laid out to form a circuit of about 3 miles, starting off towards the west to take in the hermitage and then turning south and east through Priestwood and Vicarwood and returning north to the Hall front via the lake and weirs. Many ornamental trees and fragrant flowering shrubs were planted along the walk with openings left at intervals for views. By the 1920s the walk was thickly besieged by hollies and laurels and became known as the Dark Walk.

Strong evidence of Adam's layouts remains today. The willow-edged lake is truly magnificent, curving like a river across the parkland. Adam's splendid bridge carries the drive as it winds up towards the imposing north front of the Hall. The Long Walk still proves attractive to many visitors who want to spend an afternoon strolling through the park and mixed woodland.

Most of the garden, or pleasure ground, lies to the south. From the south front of the Hall, you look across closely mown lawn to the park and wood beyond the ha-ha.

The broad gravel walk leading westwards from the house marks the start of the Long Walk. It follows the line of the churchyard wall, where a shrub border is being developed. The walls of the old aviary and slaughter house, to the rear of the stable complex, now support vines, wisteria, climbing roses and hydrangeas. Two pergolas are draped with roses, clematis and honeysuckles. A sunken circular rose garden adds colour to the scene in summer, its beds cut into the lawn in front of a hexagonal temple-like summerhouse.

Mounds of rhododendrons add interest to the south-western edge of the pleasure grounds and an orangery is rather poorly positioned in a shady spot to the west.

The Long Walk continues westwards through woodland filled with wild flowers. About half a mile from the house, it passes the hermitage. This is in a ruined state but the Trust has plans for its restoration. Among the many trees along the walk are two massive variegated sycamores. Rhododendrons abound, together with a varied mixture of shrubs including hollies and philadelphus.

More interesting trees can be seen in the pleasure grounds, such as the magnificent fern-leaved beech (*Fagus sylvatica heterophylla*) near the orangery. Red and gold shades predominate in autumn.

There are many fine rhododendrons in the garden and grounds; among hybrids recently identified are the magnificent brilliant red Exbury hybrid 'Fusilier' and the rose-pink 'Mrs Furnivall'.

Drawn to Kedleston by the splendid house, many visitors are pleasantly surprised by the beauty of the park and pleasure grounds. Following restoration work by the National Trust, there could be even more to see in the future.

Lea Gardens

ADDRESS AND TELEPHONE: Lea Gardens, Lea, Matlock, Derbyshire DE4 5GH. Tel. Dethick (0629 534) 380

OWNERS: Jonathan and Jenny Tye

DIRECTIONS: 5 miles SE of Matlock off A6. Public transport: Whatstandwell BR (then 2¾-mile walk) or trains to Matlock and buses (fairly regularly) from Matlock to Lea village, then ½ mile walk

ADMISSION: £2, children 50p. Wheelchairs free

CAR PARKING: on road verge only

TOILETS: yes

REFRESHMENTS: home-made

SHOP: yes, and nursery

DOGS: on lead

WHEELCHAIR ACCESS: limited (gravel paths, strong pusher needed) but welcome. Toilets for the disabled: no

PEAK MONTHS: May and June for rhododendrons and azaleas

NOTABLE FEATURES: 4-acre spring garden including: collection of rhododendrons and azaleas, and rock garden with alpines and conifers

Particularly renowned for its colourful displays of rhododendrons and azaleas, beneath Scots pines and birch trees, Lea Gardens also has an impressive collection of other plants and shrubs. You don't have to be a rhododendron fanatic to enjoy this garden—but it helps!

Even before the garden opens to the public in March, the rhododendrons have begun their show, and the display continues to August, though May is perhaps the best month. Lea has produced an excellent guidebook, detailing a suggested route and highlighting many of the rhododendrons and azaleas along the way.

The gardens were started in 1935 by John Marsden-Smedley, local squire and manufacturer of fine woollen garments, who also planted much of the woodland around Lea village. Having tried planting rhododendrons on various sites, he discovered that they grew exceptionally well on the present site of Lea Gardens. Here were the added advantages of mature Scots pines, yews, silver birches, sycamores, chestnuts and oaks to provide the necessary shelter and ideal woodland conditions.

Originally an old quarry, the site still contained plenty of good stone and skilled craftsmen were called in to build drystone walls, platforms and pathways. Ash was brought from the furnaces of Marsden-Smedley's woollen mill and sand beds were topped up with soil from other parts of the estate. Then the plant collecting began.

Before Marsden-Smedley died, in 1959, a collection of 350 varieties of specie and hybrid rhododendrons and azaleas had been established in the 2-acre garden. Leading nurseries and rhododendron breeding centres of the time sent plants, including Bodnant,

Exbury and Knaphill; even delicate and semi-hardy specimens flourished in this sheltered quarry.

In 1959 Peter and Nancy Tye acquired the garden, and were joined by Joyce Colyer, who had been estate manager for John Marsden-Smedley, and who had an extensive knowledge of the garden and the collections. To complement the rhododendrons, Nancy Tye created alpine screes, and new areas of garden were developed for rock plants, ornamental shrubs and trees. In 1960 the gardens were opened to the public.

The present owners, Jonathan and Jenny Tye, have continued development work since their arrival in 1980. The garden now covers some 4 acres and contains around 550 different varieties of rhododendron and azaleas.

Clematis macropetala and *C. alpina* cover a stone archway at the entrance, framing a view over the alpine screes to the rhododendrons and azaleas beyond. Above is a canopy of Scots pine and birch trees, one of which supports *Clematis montana* 'Alba', a cascade of pale flowers in late spring (May).

Rocks of millstone grit and a local porous limestone stand here and there in the gravelled alpine screes. Dwarf conifers give height; other plants include saxifrage, phlox, aubrieta, double arabis and many varieties of dianthus. Spring colour is provided by miniature daffodils and specie tulips.

The suggested viewing route begins with rhododendrons 'Elizabeth' and 'Mrs G.W. Leak', by the collection of alpine troughs. From this upper level you get magnificent views across massed rhododendrons and azaleas, a blaze of colour in late spring.

On the first path is *Rhododendron 'Britannia'*—an old favourite amongst the hardy hybrids. A slow grower, forming a compact bush, this carries trusses of gloxinia-shaped flowers of a glowing crimson-scarlet colour in May. Further along is *R.* 'Naomi Pink Beauty', an Exbury hybrid, 15ft high and bearing satin pink, delightfully fragrant flowers.

R. 'Christmas Cheer' gives early colour to this part of the garden. Once forced for Christmas decorations, this old *R. caucasicum* hybrid produces white flowers, pink in bud.

Near to the shed at the end of the path is *R.* 'Loder's White' and *R. campylocarpum* with *R. stringillosum* below, and a little beyond is a *Eucryphia glutinosa*. The latter is covered in white flowers in July and August and goes on to display beautiful shades and tones of foliage in the autumn.

The zig-zag path now turns back towards the entrance. Tall *Magnolia sieboldii* overhangs the pretty, coppery-blotched, creamy white flowers of the azaleodendron 'Glory of Littleworth'. Further along is *R. Shilsonii* with its plum-coloured bark, metallic in appearance, and loose trusses of blood-red flowers opening in April.

R. 'Fabia' and *R.* 'Fabia Tangerine' add scarlet-orange and vermilion to the colour range in June while 'Vanessa' displays soft pink flowers, spotted carmine at the base.

R. Williamsianum hybrids begin the next path which leads past some splendid specimens, including *R. fulgens, R. orbiculare* and *R. thompsonii*, a well-known Himalayan species with attractive smooth, plum-coloured bark and intense blood-red flowers opening in April.

Next to a maidenhair tree (*Ginkgo biloba*)—is *R. campanulatum* and *R.* 'Hawk' an Exbury hybrid bearing mid-season flowers, apricot in bud, opening to sulphur yellow.

Further along are two large specimens of the hybrids *R.* 'Idealist' and *R.* 'Letty Edwards'. 'Idealist' is a particularly striking shrub when in flower, having large pale cream bell-shaped flowers with a dark red blotch in the base.

On path four of the suggested route, you pass under trees of *R. Loderi* 'Pink Diamond' and 'King George', and lower down, on path five, is *R. auriculatum*, which flowers very late, in mid summer, producing large trusses of richly scented white flowers. Over the boundary wall you can see a new planting of American hybrids. Back towards the house, a gateway leads into a different type of garden, planted with new hybrids. These are being studied for hardiness, quality and willingness to flower.

A collection of some 14 different forms of *Acer palmatum* can be found by the house, along with dwarf conifers and a small thyme lawn, while in front of the house are dwarf rhododendrons set among rocks and several forms of specie *R. yakushimanum*. To the left is a collection of kalmias.

Mr and Mrs Tye can usually be found in the garden and they are always happy to talk to visitors.

Melbourne Hall

ADDRESS AND TELEPHONE: Melbourne Hall, Melbourne, near Derby, Derbyshire DE7 1EN. Tel. (0332) 862502

OWNERS: Lord and Lady Ralph Kerr, Melbourne Hall Garden Charity

DIRECTIONS: 7 miles S of Derby off A514 between Derby and Ashby de la Zouch. Public transport: Derby BR 7 miles. Frequent buses from Derby to Melbourne Market Place, then 2 minute walk

OPENING TIMES: April to September, Wed, Sat, Sun and BH Mon 2–6. House only open during August; for details contact the curator

ADMISSION: £2, OAPs £1. Family ticket £5. Coach parties by arrangement with the Curator

CAR PARKING: limited

TOILETS: yes

REFRESHMENTS: café

SHOP: yes

DOGS: no

WHEELCHAIR ACCESS: special route. Toilets for the disabled: yes

NOTABLE FEATURES: early 18C design; birdcage arbour; statuary; terraces; Great Basin; vistas

Melbourne Hall is not only one of the very few remaining examples of a late 17C/early 18C 'Queen Anne style' formal garden, but

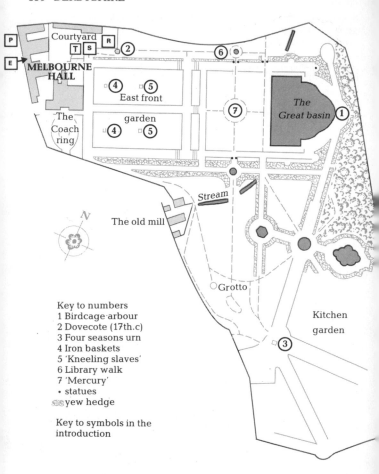

Key to numbers
1 Birdcage arbour
2 Dovecote (17th.c)
3 Four seasons urn
4 Iron baskets
5 'Kneeling slaves'
6 Library walk
7 'Mercury'
• statues
▨ yew hedge

Key to symbols in the
introduction

almost certainly the finest in the country. Most gardens of this period
and style were swept away or drastically altered in the 18C, with
the development of landscape gardening.

When Sir John Coke first settled at Melbourne in 1629 he
constructed a terrace, a kitchen garden and canal ponds, but little
more was done until the very end of the 17C, when Thomas Coke,
his great grandson, inherited the estate.

Thomas Coke had travelled much in France and Holland and had
studied architecture and garden design. He was greatly influenced
by André le Nôtre, head gardener to Louis XIV and creator of the
grand formal gardens of Versailles.

Coke consulted with the leading English garden designers at the
time, George London and Henry Wise, and William Cooke also had
a hand in the design. The result was a composition of formal,
geometric symmetry, with parterres, lawns, pools, fountains, stat-

uary and carefully aligned vistas. When Thomas Coke died Melbourne passed to his wife's family, who preferred to live most of the year in London. Perhaps mainly for this reason this French-style Derbyshire garden was left undisturbed by the changing fashions and fads of garden design. In 1906 Lord Walter Kerr and his wife Lady Cowper made Melbourne their home and began to restore the gardens without greatly altering Coke's original plan.

Entering the garden from the courtyard, take the Library Walk past the 17C dovecote (now the Muniment Room) and through a yew hedge into the East Front Garden. A series of symmetrically planned, rectangular terraced lawns, once embroidered with parterres, descends from the house to a formal lake known as the Great Basin.

On the first lawn beneath the house are two large iron baskets, overflowing with colourful bedding plants. A central path marks the garden's main axis, flanked either side by domes of clipped yew and by two statues known as the Kneeling Slaves. Steps lead down to the water.

Set back in four yew alcoves around the Great Basin are delightful lead statues of putti, designed by the Dutch artist Jan Van Nost. A statue of Mercury, the winged messenger of the gods, stands in front of the lake.

The Great Basin was designed by Coke to replace his great-grandfather's canal pools. Nearly as wide as the terraces, it is elaborately shaped and framed by splendid mature taxodiums. In springtime, daffodils line the water's edge.

Standing a little beyond the great basin is a an elaborate wrought iron arbour known as the Birdcage. Appropriately positioned on the central line down from the terraces, this is the masterpiece of the ironsmith Robert Bakewell who began work on the elegantly domed structure in 1706. Thomas Coke paid £120 for it.

A yew tunnel forms a boundary between the East Garden and mature woodland to the south. This is a sombre and mysterious place—the ancient yews lean inwards, their densely matted branches excluding the light. No one knows exactly when the yews were planted, but it may well have been before Thomas Coke inherited Melbourne.

A little over half-way down the Yew Tunnel, and in line with the statue of Mercury in the East Front Garden, the yews open out into a circle to surround a small pool and fountain. This circular pool is exactly matched on the northern side of the East Garden.

Following advice from London and Wise, the gardens to the south were laid out as a pattern of radiating *allées* flanked by beech and hornbeam hedges and backed by trees. Many of these hedges have since been replaced with yew, but the trees have continued to grow, resulting in a mature woodland with some splendid specimens.

The main axis of this part of the garden runs between the trees lying on the line from the Birdcage Arbour, and continues beyond three pools to the notable Four Seasons urn. This urn was designed by Jan Van Nost and presented by Queen Anne to Thomas Coke when he was her Vice Chamberlain.

Side avenues radiate off from this main axis, with major intersections marked by statues or by pools and fountains (fed by underground streams), which help arrest and focus the eye. On the western edge of the woodland lie the mill and the stream from which Melbourne takes its name—Mill on the Bourne. In spring the banks and margins of the stream are ablaze with colour.

Further along the path, past the mill, is a grotto—probably Victorian and built round a mineral water spring. The inscription reads:

> 'Rest weary stranger in this shady cave,
> And taste if languid of the mineral wave.'

DEVON

Bicton Park

ADDRESS AND TELEPHONE: East Budleigh, East Devon EX9 7DP. Tel. Colaton Raleigh (0395) 68465

OWNERS: Bicton Park Trust Co.

DIRECTIONS: leave M5 at exit 30, take A3052 to Newton Poppleford, then turn right on to A376 towards East Budleigh; or leave A30 for B3180, then left to Newton Poppleford and right to East Budleigh. Public transport: Devon General bus from Exmouth or Sidmouth

OPENING TIMES: March to October 10–6. House not open

ADMISSION : £3.75, children under 16 £2 (under 3 free); OAPs £3 (special golden days Wed and Thurs £2.50 plus discount on railway and restaurant). Family ticket £2.75 per person (minimum 1 paying child). Coach parties £3.50, OAPs £3.25, children £2.50. Re-entry tickets and season tickets available

CAR PARKING: yes

TOILETS: yes

REFRESHMENTS: café

SHOP: two gift shops

DOGS: on lead

WHEELCHAIR ACCESS: yes, to most of garden. Also carriage for wheelchairs on railway. BTA award for wheelchair accessibility. Toilets for the disabled: yes

PEAK MONTHS: May to September

NOTABLE FEATURES: formal early 18C gardens and temple; 19C palmhouse; American garden, Japanese garden; Hermitage garden; pinetum

Bicton's 60 acres contain an 18C Italian garden, with a temple and glasshouses of the period; a fine early 19C palmhouse; an American garden, Hermitage garden and pinetum, also dating from the 19C; a recently laid out Japanese garden, a bird garden, a 1½-mile 18in. gauge railway, a countryside museum and several modern attractions with little connection to any aspect of gardening.

The head gardener, Mr Bill Hearne, who has been at Bicton for 12 years and leads a team of 5 garden staff, combines a respect for the original design with a regard for the enjoyment of the many visitors to Bicton. Historical features have been preserved and new developments planned by and large in harmony with them. The popular attractions intrude very little on their peaceful setting.

Entering from the pleasantly grassed and hedged car parks, you find yourself approaching the oldest part of the garden. The path leads to the top terrace of the Italian garden, which was laid out in 1735, following plans drawn up by André le Nôtre, creator of Versailles, or possibly by one of his pupils.

Before going further, turn right to the palmhouse, an elegant structure of double—though not equal—domes. Each tiny glass pane is shell-shaped and convex, so that the rain runs down the central channels, avoiding the ironwork. When we visited, on a hot day in early June, the scent of the many bougainvilleas growing against the white walls was overpowering, and the sound, and occasionally the feel, of the water sprays, most welcome. Although not particularly large by the standards of the period, the house has an impressive variety of palms, tree ferns and bromeliads, intertwined by many tropical climbers. The path back to the Italian garden passes a well filled fuchsia house, featuring bush, standard and hanging varieties, and a geranium (pelargonium) house.

The original pillared temple at the top of the Italian garden now houses a small café and bar and there are seats on the top walk. From these vantage points you can look right down over the three grass terraces to the lake and fountain at the foot of the valley and up again towards an obelisk framed by woods on the opposite slope.

The high side walls of the terraced garden, built by French prisoners during the Napoleonic wars, are now clothed with Bull bay magnolias. Beneath are mixed, mainly herbaceous borders. Hot reds, yellows and oranges provide the colour theme for the upper terrace, changing to cool blues, whites and mauves on the lower levels nearer the lake. Some well established pairs of trees, such as the gold Hinoki cypresses (*Chamaecyparis obtusa* 'Aurea') on the upper lawns and the Himalayan cedars (*Cedrus deodara*) at either end of the lake, provide height and variety to the landscape, while formal summer bedding (preceded by tulips and other spring bulbs) brightens the sloping lawns. The original statues of the four seasons by the lake and the stone urns by the temple place the gardens firmly in their historical context.

After a visit to the orchid and temperate houses to the east of the temple, walk down to the American garden, passing the Shell House (which holds a sizeable collection of shells and fossils and a recording of the cries of seagulls) and a rockery, which was due for replanting when we visited. Above the vertical rocks is a Lucombe or saddle oak (*Quercus* x *hispanica* 'Lucombeana').

The American garden contains a tulip tree (*Liriodendron tulipifera*), a snowdrop tree (*Halesia carolina*) and a group of calico bushes or American laurels (*Kalmia latifolia*) with charming miniature pink goblets of flower. There are also specimens from other countries, including a pocket-handkerchief tree (*Davidia involucrata*), a tree of heaven (*Ailanthus altissima*) and *Podocarpus salignus* —all set on a sloping lawn. A narrow canal and a pergola with climbers lie to the west of this lawn and a pool with damp-loving plants at its foot. A small, very English church, tucked under the hill opposite, completes the international landscape.

You are now only a step from the Japanese garden, something of a triumph for Mr Hearne, who laid it out with the guidance of reference books and was rewarded by its receiving a Grade 2 listing. An effect of great peace and tranquillity has been achieved by simple, restrained design and planting: upright or flat stones set in beds of contrasting gravel, a single red acer, some surrounding azaleas and camellias; a border of delicate pink and orange oriental poppies; two small bridges, an arbour and a few pieces of statuary. The garden is enclosed by a bamboo fence of authentic design.

Walking up the valley (or taking the train) you come to the Wilson collection. This woodland, named for the plant collector E.H. Wilson, who travelled widely in America, China and Japan, suffered badly in the gales of January/February 1990, losing several large macrocarpus, though some tall spruces remain. The clearings are now planted, rather oddly, with tulips followed by summer bedding. The pinetum, where there was even more destruction, is being replanted with shrubs and a shelter belt, while a new pinetum is planned for a less exposed position, on the site of the old deer park. This will be carefully landscaped and provide look-out points over to Bicton agricultural college and back towards the formal gardens. The nearby avenue of trees is known as Yellow Peers (the hickory trees turn yellow in autumn). It forms the farthest boundary of the garden. From here there is a steep descent to the Hermitage, a summerhouse built for Lady Rolle in 1839, complete with a miniature lake fed by the stream that runs through the tiny valley. A Hermitage Garden has been laid out recently on the hillside, largely of contrasting conifers. Here a stream with waterfalls rushes down to a pool well filled with waterlilies. Nearby is the terminus for the train line.

Walking back towards the formal gardens, you pass the World of Fun for children, which has been attractively planted with shrubs and flowers. A World of Adventure further on, with recorded sound, seems more incongruous. The nearby bird garden, featuring colourful species from different parts of the world, appropriately complements the exotic specimens in the palmhouse above.

Further developments are planned, including a garden for blind and partially-sighted people, and a new 14-acre garden with a magnolia walk.

Castle Drogo

ADDRESS AND TELEPHONE: Drewsteignton, Devon EX6 6PB. Tel. Chagford (O647) 433306

OWNERS: The National Trust

DIRECTIONS: 4 miles S of A30 Exeter to Okehampton road via Crockernwell (cars only). Coaches must turn off A 382 Moretonhampstead to Whiddon Down road at Sandy Park. Public transport: Devon General bus 359 from Exeter (passing close Exeter Central BR. Tel. Totnes 0803 864161). Yeoford station 8 miles

OPENING TIMES: garden, April to end October daily 11–6

(October 11–5); last admission 30 minutes before closing. House closed on Fri

ADMISSION: house £3.80; garden and grounds only £1.60; pre-arranged parties £3

CAR PARKING: yes, special parking for disabled people

TOILETS: yes

REFRESHMENTS: yes, in castle. 11am–30 minutes before closing. Also tea hut in car park

SHOP: yes

DOGS: no

WHEELCHAIR ACCESS: reasonable access to most of garden, special parking and access by arrangement at shop. Toilets for the disabled: yes

PEAK MONTHS: end May (azaleas and flowering shrubs); July/August (herbaceous borders) July/September (roses)

NOTABLE FEATURES: outstanding setting overlooking the gorge of the river Teign; views of Dartmoor; Lutyens designed walled garden with terraces, herbaceous borders, rose beds and arbours; tree and shrub slopes; huge circular croquet lawn

'The house is the scene for acts of charity that should begin at home and covers hen-wise with wings of love all those about her that are dependent, weaker or smaller'. This quotation from Sir Edwin Lutyens is displayed above one of the entrances to Castle Drogo: but its tender imagery is startlingly at odds with the appearance of the castle.

From the first, Julius Drewe, the founder of Home and Colonial Stores, envisaged his country house as a fortress. He retired at the age of 33 and was willing to spend the then considerable sum of £60,000 on its building in an exposed area of Dartmoor. Although the original design put forward by Edwin Lutyens was modified, the castle, with its sheer grey walls and castellations, is more suggestive of baronial warfare than charity and protection.

For the design of the garden, Lutyens initially favoured formal beds near the castle entrance, with terraces on the south-east side of the gorge below the walls. Gertrude Jekyll was consulted, and drew up plans for planting on the south-facing terraces and wild planting along the approach road, but these schemes—the former being perhaps over-optimistic in view of the exposed position of the castle—all came to nothing. The only garden areas existing to the south of the castle are the small formal Chapel Garden, which was slow to establish owing to the buffetings of the wind. To the west, the rhododendron garden and shrubbery below the castle wall survive well. Lutyens finally designed a garden with borders and rose lawns north of the house in a more sheltered location and George Dillestone from Tunbridge Wells, who was known to Julius Drewe from his work at the family home in East Sussex, was called in to carry out the planting. You approach the castle gradually, descending through the main formal gardens, enclosed in their high yew hedges.

The entrance drive is flanked first by a pair of clipped yew hedges and then by clumps of evergreen oaks through which the moorland can be glimpsed. From the car park you follow a woodland path till you can see, through an arch of yew, a great circular croquet lawn, one acre in size, which can now be rented for mammoth games of croquet. Turning right by a pair of *Chamaecyparis lawsoniana* 'Kilmacurragh', walk down a sloping gravel path with raised shrub borders to either side.

Owing to destruction of many shrubs by the high winds, most of the shrub border planting dates from 1982. There are sizeable rhododendrons, prunus, acer, philadelphus and magnolia. The smoke bush (*Cotinus coggygria*) provides bright autumn colour, along with many of the acers and other shrubs.

The path leads down to a terrace from which you have a panoramic view of the splendid rectangular formal garden, with lawns and rose beds in the centre and the double herbaceous borders on the terraces above them. The whole area is surrounded by yew hedges, with woods to either side; and at each corner of the rectangle, tall blocks of yew conceal secluded arbours. These are one of the most original features of the garden, each arbour containing four standard *Parrotia persica* or Persian ironwoods, trained over arching steel supports and horizontal wires. The circular motif of the supports, taken from a design by Lutyens, and the graceful drooping habit of the parrotias combine to pleasing effect. These arbours are a recent addition; the parrotias replaced original plantings of weeping Camperdown elms which fell victim to Dutch elm disease.

The subtle design of the paths between the herbaceous borders is characteristic of Lutyens' work. He had just completed his work on New Delhi and the alternating semicircles and straight lines of the paths are taken from an Indian motif. The borders hold a traditional mixture of herbaceous plants. Spring borders are planted at the foot of the retaining walls.

The rose beds on the lawns, both square and rectangular, contain varieties of floribunda and hybrid tea bushes.

Leaving this garden you step down to the castle and a view over the side of the gorge. A path to the right of the courtyard leads you down into the rhododendron dell, where there are species and hybrid rhododendrons. Many smaller species are now being planted, to replace shrubs that have grown too large, and the sheltering pines are also being renewed.

Following the path at the foot of the wall you come to the Chapel Garden, planted on a small terrace right up against the castle, but nevertheless vulnerable to wind currents. This has recently been replanted.

As you turn the corner of the castle to rejoin the courtyard, you pass beneath an extensive planting of yew, covering an area that was once intended to be a wing of the castle but never completed.

This is a garden to enjoy in late spring and summer, with sunshine lighting up the granite castle, its gardens and the beauty of the surrounding moorland.

Coleton Fishacre

ADDRESS AND TELEPHONE: Coleton, Kingswear, Dartmouth, Devon TQ6 OEQ. Tel. Kingswear (O80 425) 466

OWNERS: The National Trust

DIRECTIONS: 2 miles from Kingswear, take Lower Ferry Road, turn off at tollhouse. Public transport: Devon General bus 22 Torquay to Kingswear (passing Paignton BR) alight ¾ mile SW of Hillhead, then 1½ miles. Paignton BR 8 miles; Kingswear (Dart Valley Rly) 2¼ miles by footpath, 2¾ miles by road

OPENING TIMES: April to end October, Wed to Fri and Sun 11–6. March, Sun 2–5. House not open

ADMISSION: £2, parties £1.50

CAR PARKING: yes

TOILETS: yes

REFRESHMENTS: no

SHOP: no, but some plants for sale

DOGS: no

WHEELCHAIR ACCESS: limited; steep slopes. Toilets for the disabled: no

PEAK MONTHS: April to October

NOTABLE FEATURES: formal gardens with Lutyens influence; unusual and rare plants; stream-fed valley with camellias, rhododendrons, specimen trees and shrubs from all over the world. 'Mediterranean' planting; views of sea and valley

The least spectacular approaches often reveal the most rewarding gardens, certainly the journey up from the lower Dartmouth Ferry gives little clue to the kind of experience that Coleton Fishacre offers. The Devon lanes, which have their own beauty, contain not a hint of the sub-tropical splendours, dramatic landscape and quality of design to be found here.

The attractive grey stone house and its gardens were designed for Rupert D'Oyly Carte in 1925 by Oswald Milne, a pupil of Edwin Lutyens, and constructed of stone taken from a quarry within the valley. Whether Milne sought Lutyens' advice, or simply followed his style is not known but the influence is unmistakable both on the terraces below the front elevation of the house and in the walled rill garden. Advice for the shelter-belt planting was sought from Edward White, the President of the Royal Institute of Landscape Architects. Lady Dorothy D'Oyly Carte herself carried out most of the planting, helped by a staff of six, and over many years constantly extended it, using specimens from many countries. The result was a garden of distinction whose development was only interrupted by Rupert D'Oyly Carte's death in 1947. The estate was then sold to Mr Rowland Smith, who maintained it as it was, but neglected necessary thinning and clearing. The present head gardener, David Mason, considers that this was in some ways a blessing, for when the National Trust acquired the garden in the the early 1980s it was, although badly in need of renovation, botanically the same as that envisaged by its creators. The Trust has subsequently renewed the original scheme, and is extending it in harmony with the original design.

From the first, Coleton Fishacre had many natural advantages, including a north-west to south-east-facing valley fed by springs and a stream that never dries up even in the hottest seasons. This, together with the presence of the sea and reasonably high rainfall, gives high humidity and creates a micro-climate where sub-tropical plants can flourish. The belt of Monterey pines and holm oaks, planted in 1926 at the beginning of the original venture, provides essential shelter from the sea winds. Acid Dartmouth shale permits the growing of many camellias and rhododendrons in the valley—a camellia known as the 'Madeira' hybrid and other specimens were brought home from a d'Oyly Carte voyage. The National Trust intends, as part of its future management plan for the garden, to remove some of the more ordinary shrubs and introduce species rhododendrons as well as other tender specimens such as acacias, unusual pittosporums, podocarpus, lyonothamnus, species leptospermums and correas.

You come first to the formal gardens: on the right of the path the Seemly Terrace, with the beautiful rill garden below, on your left, as you turn the corner of the house, the striking main terraces with the bowling green lawn beyond. These form the immediate surroundings of the house, but also link it to the valley beyond with its high wooded hillsides and deep winding watercourse.

The rill garden, a triangular walled area sloping to the south-west, echoes Lutyens' work at Hestercombe. A stone channel bisects the lawns and fills the garden with the constant sound of running, falling water. Herbaceous planting in the lawn beds on either side of the rill rise high at the centre and fall away to ground cover at the edge, and the two longer walls of the triangle provide shelter for many climbers and for mixed shrub and plant borders. As you stand at the lowest point of the triangle, where the water flows away to feed the valley stream and its ponds, you can look back to the source of the water, a pool flanked with arum lilies and overhung by two vast wisterias and a cestrum on the south-east-facing wall. The two side walls, stepped downwards and converging at the point where you stand, lend an intense perspective to the garden they enclose.

The four central beds, two rectangles and two freer, though exactly reflecting designs, are planted mainly in soft pastels, with the occasional burst of warmth from an orange mimulus or a red abutilon, and include the pink shades of *Canna iridiflora* and a ginger lily (*Hedychium coccineum* 'Tara'), sprays of pale pink thalictrum and heads of brighter pink *Verbena* x *hybrida* 'Sissinghurst'. Among the blue shades are delphiniums, monkshood and veronica, and there are many silver-leaved plants. *Dicentra oregana*, *Sphaeralcea fendleri*, verbenas and diascias are used as ground cover.

Under the shady north-east-facing wall the yellow tubular flowers of *Erythronium dens-canis* 'Charmer' contrast with the deep red leaves of heucheras. Here too you can see the red tubular flowers of tender *Mitraria coccinea* from Chile, and the deep red pendant clusters of *Berberidopsis corallina*, as well as *Cestrum newellii*, again red flowered. On the opposite, west-facing wall more tender and unusual plants flourish: *Hibbertia aspera* with potentilla-like yellow flowers, *Araujia sericofera*, the 'cruel plant' which traps the probosces of visiting moths, and the grey-leaved, lilac-flowered Australian mint bush, *Prostanthera rotundifolia*. Here too you can see the flowers of the pineapple guava from America, *Feijoa sellowiana*, whose distinctive red and white petals and boss of crimson stamens are succeeded by green egg-shaped fruits.

Just beyond the far wall of the rill garden is a border containing part of the National Collection of *Agapanthus africanus*, the African lily, as well as some of the garden's large range of olearias; while on the wall the tender climber *Maurandia erubescens*, a distant cousin of the homely snapdragon, shows its pink trumpets. Nearby is the sweet-scented, white-flowered *Carpenteria californica* and an Australian climber, *Kennedya macrophylla*, recently introduced, with yellow-eyed, scarlet pear-shaped flowers. A rare small plant against one pillar, *Billardiera longiflora*, produces unusual blue-black fruits. Although these areas are full of plants that are perhaps of most interest to specialists, they provide an effective and harmonious display.

The Seemly Terrace above the rill garden has a double border of shrubs and plants on either side of a paved path and a Lutyens-style seat from which to enjoy them. Partially tender shrubs here include a variegated coprosma, 'Beaton's Gold', from New Zealand and *Acacia pravissima*, with interesting sculptured leaves. At the far end of the terrace grows a cut-leaved beech, *Fagus sylvatica* 'Asplenifolia', and overhanging the rill garden below is *Taxus baccata* 'Dovestoniana', the Westfelton yew.

The planting on the house terraces makes a bold contrast to the delicate charm of the rill garden. Part of its effect derives from the restrained and elegant background of the grey stone house, on which many climbers hang: *Trachelospermum jasminoides*, the star jasmine, which clambers on the chimney and its relative *Mandevilla suaveolens*, the Chilean jasmine; sweet-smelling *Holboellia latiflora*; a Banksian rose (*Rosa banksiae lutea*); *Chimonanthus praecox*, the wintersweet, and *Solanum jasminoides* 'Alba', a white-flowered potato ribe. Wall shrubs include *Lagerstroemia indica*, with wavy trusses of flower, and *Fremontodendron californicum*.

Beneath the house are ranged three terraces, also in grey stone, and again echoing the work of Edwin Lutyens—this time with a domed pool set in the wall between the upper and lower terrace—and a double rectangular lily pool at lawn level, fed by a stream emerging through intricate brickwork, and planted with pink water lilies. The two most spectacular plants on the terraces when we visited in July were a vast specimen of *Leptospermum scoparium*, the New Zealand tree heath, or tea tree, growing from the centre terrace but displaying its pink flowers above the top level, and an enormous clump of *Beschorneria yuccoides* at the foot of the terraces, its fleshy coral spikes toppling over the lawn near a clump of *Geranium maderense*. Delicate mauve wand flowers (*Dierama pulcherrimum*) alternate on the top terrace with clumps of pale mauve lavender and on the central terrace with bushes of the darker lavender 'Munstead'; while the palest of pink fuchsias (*F. magellanica molinae*) spring self-seeded from the walls themselves. This quiet effect is enlivened by orange watsonias (*Watsonia beatricis*) near the domed pool and the salvias *S. involucrata* 'Hadspen' and *S. gesnerifolia*, with bright blue, *S. cacaliifolia*. Six vases, similar to original designs used by Lady Dorothy, are planted with *Astelia nervosa* and *Lotus berthelotii*. The hot colourings and spiky shapes throughout the terrace plantings are purposely in direct contrast to the softer and paler shades of the rill beds.

From the terrace you can either walk down to the upper pool, and then down the centre of the valley, or, as we did, cross to the bowling green, the last formal area. The raised bed above the Wellington wall is filled at the back with foliage plants, such as the green, grey and purple-leaved *Brachyglottis repanda* 'Purpurea' and *Buddleia farreri* and scented plants towards the front (*Rosmarinus officinalis* 'Prostratus' and *Lavandula stoechas*). From here you join a path flanked by tender, white-flowering *Myrtus apiculata*, ceanothus, cistus and echiums, with steep woods rising to your left and the wooded valley below on your right.

This leads you to the gazebo—no quiet look-out over cultivated lawns and flowers, but an eagle's nest perched above the quarry, with a view of the sea and the Blackstone rocks. It also gives a bird's eye view over the tops of trees and shrubs, including in spring the bright red flowers of Chilean flame trees (*Embothrium coccineum*) and rhododendrons, camellias and magnolias. In late summer a great ailanthus bears bright red berries and hydrangeas flower bright blue in the acid soil. From here you can continue round to your left to another viewpoint over a steep grassy hillside out to the grey islet of the Mewstone.

Alternatively you can leave the gazebo by a gravel path, leading past several deep purple magnolias and delicate Japanese cedars to the second pool, where a grove of rhododendrons overhangs the water. Following the stream you will come across clearings filled with the pale green or wine-coloured bracts of cornus, the delicate foliage of mimosa, and clumps of black-stemmed or variegated bamboo. The luxuriant growth of this secluded valley under tall trees, the sound of the stream and the wind in the pines above combine to create a sense of wildness and isolation—quite distinct from the civilised and cultivated area around the house.

To accommodate the South Devon coastal path, the garden, which used to reach to the cliffs, has now been bounded at the bottom of the valley by a fence, though you can leave it temporarily by the gate to reach the cove where the D'Oyly Carte yacht used to be moored. At this far point of the garden, under a Mexican pine and near several New Zealand ferns (*Dicksonia antarctica*) there are new plantings of hydrangea and camellia. A third pool is planned, with plantings of candelabra primulas, ferns and nothofagus species, which will provide an effective climax at the garden's lowest point.

The journey back on the far side of the stream takes you past a Kashmir cypress up high paths, unless you prefer to follow the path by the stream. From here you can look down on the fine tulip tree on the slope in front of the house, as well as the dawn redwood and swamp cypress by the stream. You can also see a bright planting of blue hydrangea, purple iris and yellow mimulus by the upper pond before rejoining the entrance path and leaving the garden.

Dartington Hall

ADDRESS AND TELEPHONE: The Dartington Hall Trust, Elmhirst Centre, Dartington Hall, Totnes, Devon TQ9 6JE. Tel. Totnes (0803) 862271

OWNERS: The Dartington Hall Trust

DIRECTIONS: take the Totnes/Buckfastleigh turn-off from the A38 (Exeter to Plymouth) just after the two Ashburton turn-offs and turn left towards Totnes. Follow this road until you reach the Dartington Parish Church, about 4 miles from the turn off, on your left-hand side, turn left and follow this road right up to the Hall. Public transport: there is very little transport in this area although Totnes can be reached by train or bus; local transport is intermittent

OPENING TIMES: daily throughout the year, 10.30–5

ADMISSION: no admission charge but visitors are requested to contribute at least £1.50 per head. Coach parties not encouraged and by appointment only

CAR PARKING: yes

TOILETS: yes

REFRESHMENTS: no

SHOP: no

DOGS: no dogs allowed in gardens

WHEELCHAIR ACCESS: to certain parts of the gardens. Concessions for allowing cars to be driven into the gardens to allow easy access can be arranged. Toilets for the disabled: yes

PEAK MONTHS: July/August

NOTABLE FEATURES: 25-acre landscape gardens, contributions by major garden designers; tiltyard; herbaceous border; trees and shrubs; rhododendrons and camellias; garden statuary

The Dartington Hall estate or campus contains a wide range of educational establishments: the Dartington Centre, Schumacher College and Dartington College of Arts. It is a private estate and a place of study for hundreds of people; visitors are requested to respect this fact.

The gardens surround a 14C Hall built by John Holand, Duke of Exeter and half-brother to Richard II. The site has been occupied continuously for over a thousand years, since pre-Saxon times. The oldest part of the present Hall is the building to the right of the main gate, which dates from the late 13C and now contains the College of Arts library. On the other side of the entrance is a 14C barn, now converted into a theatre.

During the late 14C and early 15C, John Holand laid out the Hall in an enclosed double quadrangle, covering about an acre. A blue leaflet obtainable from the reception office and the garden shop gives details of this medieval building and its subsequent history. The Holand family owned Dartington manor for less than a century, after which it was forfeited to the Crown, leased to various tenants and eventually bought by the Champernowne family. The fortunes of this family steadily declined, and over the centuries the Hall fell into ruins.

Dorothy and Leonard Elmhirst bought the Dartington Hall estate in 1925 and proceeded to restore the buildings, at the same time redesigning and replanting the gardens. William Weir, an authority on medieval architecture, supervised the building's restoration over more than 10 years and professional consultants helped to develop the gardens—most notably Beatrix Farrand, the American garden designer, and (after the 1939–45 war) Percy Cane, a British landscape designer.

Dorothy Elmhirst aimed to free the form of the garden from its accumulated overlay of shrubberies, flowerbeds and weeds, using the contours of the land 'to intensify the natural effects of height, depth and distance' (*The Gardens at Dartington Hall*, booklet on sale in office and garden shop). Great trees planted by the Champernowne family were cleared of undergrowth and vistas opened up, giving views through the garden and linking it with the surrounding countryside. The tiltyard, south-west of the Hall, was one of the first areas to be cleared, and for a time became an open-air theatre. Mrs Farrand tackled the courtyard and created walks through the rest of the garden. Percy Cane made the Glade, to the south above the tiltyard, cleared High Meadow and planted the azalea dell. The garden gradually developed into a much more open landscape, with separate and distinct areas linked by paths and vistas. It continues to grow and develop, under the guiding eye of the present gardens superintendent, Graham Gammin.

Dartington Hall gardens today make a peaceful setting for the College of Arts; the atmosphere is relaxed and welcoming to visitors. The first area you come to is the courtyard, surrounded on all four sides by medieval buildings; on the far side are the Great Hall and kitchens. An enormous swamp cypress (*Taxodium distichum*) stands on the lawn not far from the entrance gate, with flowering cherries (*Prunus yedoensis*) nearby. The grey stone walls support numerous climbing plants and wall shrubs above planted borders. Silver foliage plants including artemisia and rosemary flourish in a sunny south-facing Mediterranean border, interspersed with spring-flowering viburnums.

Adjoining the courtyard, to the south-west, is a wide lawn with fine trees, both mature and newly planted—cedars, beeches and oaks including a splendid Turkey oak (*Quercus cerris*). The ground beneath this tall and spreading tree is carpeted in spring with white, lilac and purple crocus (*C. vernus*). Beyond this lawn to the south, is a deep border of shrub and specie roses, above the tennis courts. To the west is a border of wild roses under cherry trees, and nearby a lead urn marks the head of a short flight of steps leading down to the tiltyard area.

The tiltyard may or may not have been used as a tournament ground in the 14C. Dorothy Elmhirst restored it in the 1920s, intending it to be used as an outdoor theatre, and her creation has been preserved; a vast amphitheatre with ancient grass terraces ascending the hillside on three sides above a central lawn.

A row of 18C Irish yews known as the Twelve Apostles initially screens the tiltyard from the Sunny Border and path above. This border is perhaps the most beautiful, certainly the best known at Dartington, planted mainly with blue, yellow and silver-grey biennials, perennials and shrubs, beneath old stone walls. It was redesigned in 1985 by the landscape architect Preben Jacobsen. The planting plan is repeated at every second pillar. Behind the wall is a private garden, the Elizabethan bowling green.

Standing at the head of a long flight of steps on the north side, you can see right through the tiltyard to Valley Fields beyond. Majestic Spanish chestnuts, more than 400 years old, overlook the western side; further down are four 18C London planes, and on a lower terrace a 100-year-old Monterey pine (*Pinus radiata*). Beyond all these, on the top terrace to the south-west, is a stone figure of a reclining woman, by Henry Moore.

Leaving the tiltyard by a path directly above the main steps, to the north, you enter the azalea dell. This area is beautiful in both spring and autumn, with Japanese maples and cherries, as well as sweet-scented, brilliantly coloured azaleas—Mollis, Ghent, Kurumes and Exbury hybrids. There is a small pool, with a damp garden below, and higher up a fountain (dry when we visited) made from an old cider press. The granite swans were carved by Willi Soukop in 1949. *Elaeagnus umbellata* 'Parvifolia', overhanging the fountain, bears fragrant yellow flowers in May and June and small rounded orange fruits in autumn. Above the path are *Acer griseum*, with peeling bark, and a pocket handkerchief tree (*Davidia involucrata vilmoriniana*).

The guidebook details various walks through the woodland above—a rhododendron walk (the lower path), a camellia walk (the middle path) and a spring walk (the highest path). Several magnolias of considerable size and beauty can be seen on the lower level—*M. delavayi*, which flowers in darkness, but can also be caught at 8am in high summer, *M. campbellii* and *M. x veitchii*.

Five paths converge to the west, under a chestnut tree; nearby are an 18C lead statue of Flora and the hydrangea walk. Climbing the steps, you reach High Meadow, planted with trees good for autumn colour, including stewartias and a katsura (*Cercidiphyllum japonicum*). Walking south and crossing the upper drive, you arrive in the Glade, and from here can look down the hillside to the Henry Moore figure. There is a neo-classical temple surrounded by *Laburnum x watereri* 'Vossii', sumachs, a liquidambar and a wide variety of other trees and shrubs.

Descending the Glade, you arrive at the top of the Heath Bank, and a flight of steps designed by Percy Cane, planted on either side with winter-flowering heaths such as *Erica carnea* and with magnolias. The steps descend to the top of Valley Field. Follow the half-circular stone path to join another path below the peat garden. This leads on, to your right, to the glasshouses and plant centre; or back past the tiltyard to the Great Lawn, with the Hall and exit beyond.

The Garden House

ADDRESS AND TELEPHONE: Buckland Monachorum, near Yelverton, Devon. Tel. 0822 854769

OWNERS: The Fortescue Garden Trust

DIRECTIONS: 5 miles N of Plymouth, clearly signed off the A386 Plymouth–Tavistock road. Public transport: bus 84 from Plymouth, change at Yelverton for the local Hopper service, which brings you to the garden entrance

OPENING TIMES: every day, April to September, 10–5. House open for teas and occasional exhibitions

ADMISSION: £1.50, children 50p

CAR PARKING: yes. Coach parties by appointment

TOILETS: yes

REFRESHMENTS: teas in house

SHOP: plant sales

DOGS: no

WHEELCHAIR ACCESS: no. Toilets for the disabled: no

PEAK MONTHS: May to August, especially third week in May and third week in August

NOTABLE FEATURES: wide range of plants, including many unusual species; romantic 2-acre cottage garden

This beautiful west country garden is planted on a hillside to the west of Dartmoor, about 450ft above sea level, in a valley running down to the River Tavy. It contains around 8000 plants, including unusual and rare specimens, many of which are offered for sale in the adjoining nursery. Around 80 per cent of the nursery's plant business is to garden visitors.

Records of a vicarage in the lower part of the walled garden stretch back more than 600 years, to 1305. The Abbot of Buckland Abbey moved here at the time of the Dissolution of the Monasteries by Henry VIII, changing his cloth to become the Vicar of Buckland Monachorum. The old tower with spiral staircase in the walled garden dates from this time—originally it was the entrance to the abbot/vicar's fine three-storeyed house. In 1826 the old vicarage was pulled down and a new house built higher up the slope.

Lionel Fortescue, a retired Eton Classics master, and his wife bought the house and 7 acres of land, including the 2-acre walled garden, in 1945, and immediately set about planting the shelter-belts of Leyland cypress which protect the garden from north-west and north-east winds. Another early task was to thatch the large barn, opposite the main grass path from the tower. The Fortescues made the gardens and lawns in front of the house and planted an avenue of prunus 'Tai Haku' along the entrance drive, together with other trees and shrubs.

The walled garden needed a great deal of preliminary labour. Over two years, many tonnes of stone were removed from the soil and land drains cleared and repaired. The Fortescues were for-tunate in being able to command the services of four prisoners of war from a nearby camp—these were replaced after a year by European voluntary workers. The soil was enriched with leaf-mould, bracken, farmyard manure, peat and shoddy. Then the planting began. Keith Wiley, now the garden manager, has written of the care given in those early years to arrangement and grouping, particularly of colours. ('The Garden House, Buckland Mona-chorum', *The Garden*, April 1985.) Mr Fortescue was ruthless in disposing of any plant, however rare and beautiful, that did not accord with his tastes and standards, and a lot of time was spent moving plants about in wheelbarrows from place to place—'The result of all this has been a healthy, beautifully colour-co-ordinated garden full of the very best forms of plants.'

Keith and Ros Wiley came to work at The Garden House in 1978, and now manage the garden for the Fortescue Garden Trust. They have greatly extended the range of plants, concentrating particu-larly on filling up gaps in the bottom terraces of the walled garden, around the tower and barn, and extending the flowering period in this area. The soil here is now very rich, ideal for moisture-loving plants. It is mainly alkaline (pH 7 to 8) having been limed for vegetables; whereas the top terrace is acid (pH 5), suitable for lime-haters such as rhododendrons, camellias and pieris.

Entering the walled garden from the plant sales area, you are faced with perhaps the best, certainly the most often photographed view—a narrow smooth grassy path, stretching into the distance, with deeply planted borders on either side. To the right, some way along the path, is the thatched barn, and beyond this, to the left, the tower. The planting is breathtaking, a profusion of soft and bright colours, punctuated at irregular intervals by softly rounded conifers, blue and green. Wand flowers (*Dierama pumilum*) sus-pend their carmine pink bells from slender grassy stalks. Visiting in July, when the colour is at its height, we saw pale blue *Cam-panula lactiflora*, red and white astilbes, bright yellow hemerocallis, white mallow, pale pink lavatera 'Barnsley', mauve meadow rue (*Thalictrum dipterocarum*), the single yellow rose 'Golden Wings' and the single crimson 'Dortmund'. Many of the roses are old and their names lost or unknown. Moneywort or creeping jenny (*Lysimachia nummularia* 'Aurea') flowers bright yellow at ground level.

Hostas, rheums, rodgersias, astilbes and thalictrums can be found in plenty at this lower level, flourishing in the damp rich soil. Erythroniums flower in spring, including the very beautiful pink *E. revolutum johnstonii*; also wood anemones, crocuses including *Crocus tomasinianus* and drifts of *Chionodoxa sardensis* and *C. gigantea* under magnolias and corylopsis.

A narrow flight of steps descends to your right through shallow terraced beds into a little dell, where an old wooden seat is overhung by *Magnolia virginiana, Rosa rubrifolia* and sweet-scented philadelphus. This wildish area is given structure by two small hedges of variegated box and two *Chamaecyparis lawsoni-ana* 'Aurea Densa'.

Imaginative and skilfully shaped hedges, of various genera, can be found throughout the garden. Conifers and other trees and shrubs are grouped for foliage colour and contrast—on the first level you can see red and pink berberis, purple cotinus, gold ribes, silver willow, *Cornus controversa* 'Variegata' and silver-variegated *C. alternifolia* 'Argentea', acers and many others. Planting is often in twins and pairs, and many delightful partnerships have been formed, whether by accident or design—deep blue *Clematis integrifolia* 'Hendersonii' growing through *Viburnum tomentosum*, *Malva moschata* 'Alba' with *Selinum tenuifolium*.

A magnificent Japanese wisteria (*W. multijuga*) hangs over the entrance gate and *Magnolia grandiflora* 'Goliath' covers the near wall of the thatched barn. Climb half-way up the old tower to reach the second terrace level—or climb to the top for a bird's eye view of the garden. The main lawn is situated on this second level, and at the far end, an unusual round stone seat, constructed like a battlement or lookout. At the entrance to the lawn, note a pair of silver shrubby willows, either side of the path, underplanted with purple cranesbill.

An alpine area to the east features numerous small plants, such as the delightful, profusely flowering rhodohypoxis, geraniums, silver-leaved plants and many unusual specimens. Climbing higher, you reach a gold corner around a seat, planted with golden ferns, golden grasses and *Acer palmatum* 'Katsura', bright yellow/orange in spring—and above, on the very top terrace, is a splendid collection of rhododendrons, including dwarf specimens such as shell pink *R. cephalanthum crebreflorum*, here growing unusually large. Here too is a fine specimen of *Magnolia salicifolia*, over 30ft high, and nearby is magnolia 'Leonard Messel'.

The Wileys plan to extend and develop the garden upwards and outwards, but always, says Ros Wiley, 'keeping the feeling of it being somebody's private garden'. Around 10,000 visitors come every year, but more are needed, since the garden relies on plant sales for income.

Killerton

ADDRESS AND TELEPHONE: Killerton, Broadclyst, Exeter, Devon EX5 3LE. Tel. Exeter (0392) 881345

OWNERS: The National Trust

DIRECTIONS: on W side of Exeter to Cullompton road (B3181, formerly A38) entrance off B3185, from M5 northbound, exit 29 via Broadclyst and B3181 Exeter to Cullompton road. Public transport: Devon General bus 54/A from Exeter (passing close Exeter Central), alight Killerton Turn, ¾ mile; 55/A/B Exeter to Tiverton (passing close Exeter Central BR), alight Silverton, 2½ miles (tel. Exeter 0392 56231). Pinhoe railway station, not Sun, 4½ miles; Whimple, not Sun, 6 miles; Exeter Central and St David's, both 7 miles

OPENING TIMES: park and garden, all year during daylight hours

ADMISSION: house and garden £3.60; garden only £2.20 (winter rate £1). Pre-booked parties £2.80—organisers please book visits and arrange meals beforehand with administrator

CAR PARKING: yes

TOILETS: yes

REFRESHMENTS: tea room and restaurant

SHOP: yes, plant sales area

DOGS: in park only

WHEELCHAIR ACCESS: lower levels of garden accessible, but gravel paths and grass. Motorised buggy with driver available for tour of higher levels. Toilets for the disabled: yes

NOTABLE FEATURES: 15 acres of hillside garden; magnificent 150-year-old arboretum with rare trees and shrubs; borders; spring flowers and rhododendrons; 19C chapel

This 15-acre garden arboretum is planted on a south-west-facing hillside above Killerton House and set in 7000 acres of park, forest and farmland. Killerton was the home of the Aclands, one of Devon's oldest landowning families, for nearly four centuries, until the estate was given to the National Trust in 1944.

The parkland was first laid out by Sir Thomas Acland, 7th Baronet, and his agent, the young Scotsman John Veitch, in the 1770s. The son of an Edinburgh nurseryman, Veitch had travelled south at the age of ten to seek his fortune. When Sir Thomas invited him to Killerton, to establish 500 acres of parkland, he was just 19 but already gaining a reputation as an outstanding nurseryman and horticulturist.

In the 23 years between Sir Thomas's death and the arrival at Killerton of the 10th Baronet, 'Great Sir Thomas', Veitch acted as agent for the estates and started his own nursery at Budlake. By the time the 10th Baronet arrived, with his wife Lydia, plans had already been made for a section of the park to be enclosed as a pleasure ground. In 1808, Veitch planted the beech walk, the sweet chestnuts and the two tulip trees in the chapel grounds. Lydia was familiar with Stourhead, home of her half-brother, Richard Colt Hoare, as well as her father's Mitcham Grove in Surrey, and she may well have contributed planting ideas. Detailed letters from Veitch to Sir Thomas survive, recording work in progress.

In 1832, with his son James, Veitch moved his nursery to 25 acres of land at Mount Radford in Exeter. (It was James Veitch Junior, grandson of John Veitch, who started the famous Veitch nursery in Chelsea, London.) The Veitch family maintained a close association with Killerton and supplied the garden with trees and shrubs. In the 60 years following John Veitch's death in 1839, the Veitch firm sent more than 20 plant collectors on expeditions all over the world—they introduced a great range of new plants and trees to Britain, many of which were first established at Killerton. The first seeds of *Sequoiadendron giganteum*, the Wellingtonia, were planted at Killerton in the 1860s. Lobb also introduced the fire bush (*Embothrium coccineum*), the Chilean holly (*Desfontainia spinosa*), *Berberis darwinii*, *Escallonia macrantha* and many others. John Gould Veitch brought back species including *Acer palmatum*, *Cryptomeria japonica* 'Elegans' and *Magnolia heptapeta* 'Nigra'. E.H. Wilson introduced the pocket handkerchief tree (*Davidia involucrata*), *Magnolia wilsonii* and others.

Around 1900, William Robinson was asked to give his advice on the garden: following his visit the terrace garden was constructed, separating the south side of the garden from the house. John Coutts, later curator of Kew Gardens, was then the head gardener, and greatly disliked the terrace wall, he held that it 'spoilt the park, starting as it does nowhere and ending nowhere'. Coutts planted many newly introduced magnolias, azaleas and rhododendrons among the sequoias at the top of the slope. This is now known as Lady Gertrude's Glade (Gertrude, wife of the 12th Baronet, Sir Charles, was a great admirer of Gertrude Jekyll and William Robinson). Coutts also widened the paths at Killerton, cleared the old quarry of cherry laurel and replanted it as a rock garden, and introduced hardy cyclamen throughout the garden.

The mixed borders of perennials and annuals in the terrace garden are best seen in mid to late summer, although flowering continues through autumn. Height and structure are provided by *Cephalaria gigantea*, buddleia, tree peonies, shrub roses and centaurea. The colour scheme is finely planned—plenty of soft silver- and grey-leaved plants highlighted by bright splashes of colour (lythrum 'Brightness', potentilla 'Miss Willmott' etc). You can view these excellent borders from the grass slopes above, or at close hand from the terrace path. The two large urns are made of Coade stone, a tough weather-resistant artificial stone manufactured in the early 19C by the firm of Coade and Seely in Lambeth.

Another much narrower border against the house wall features a collection of semi-tender perennial plants and many excellent foliage plants, backed by *Fremontodendron californicum*, eccremocarpus and *Solanum jasminoides* 'Abba'.

Beyond the borders is a ha-ha, separating the garden from parkland, and above it is the steeply rising lawned hillside, planted with groups of hybrid rhododendrons and mature trees such as *Quercus* x *hispanica* 'Lucombeana', the Lucombe oak, the black mulberry (*Morus nigra*) and the weeping silver lime (*Tilia petiolaris*). To the west is a granite cross, a memorial to the 10th Baronet, and sitting on the seat nearby you can enjoy the wonderful view westwards to the hills of Dartmoor. The trees are well labelled and include an umbrella pine (*Sciadopitys verticillata*) and a Monterey pine (*Pinus radiata*).

Not far away is the bear's hut, a curious little 19C building where a black bear was once kept as a family pet. Part of the floor is lined with deer's knuckle bones—not for the squeamish. Behind this hut is a Victorian rock garden, planted in a shady quarry by John Coutts and containing a variety of alpines and sun-loving small plants.

A mature beech walk runs from west to east, some way above the lawn, and is a good place to begin your exploration of the woodland. At the start of the walk are two ancient sweet chestnuts, dating from the 1780s and now overgrown with *Hydrangea petiolaris*. Not far distant are several cork oaks (*Quercus suber*). Numerous beautiful and interesting trees can be seen below and above—vast Californian redwoods, Japanese maples, magnolias, embothriums, halesias and liquidambars. The Chilean Fire Bush (*Embothrium coccineum*) produces its orange-scarlet flowers in May and June, and the Chinese yellow wood (*Cladrastis sinensis*) bears pink-tinged white fragrant flowers in July. The hillside is ablaze with colour in autumn, when the leaves turn, and the autumn cyclamen (*Cyclamen hederifolium*) flower under the trees and shrubs. Spring brings drifts of *C. coum* and *C. repandum*, and daffodils including 'Parkinson's early straw-coloured bastard daffodil'.

More trees are to be seen in the grounds of the chapel, to the east—sweet chestnuts and walnuts, two enormous tulip trees, Chusan palms, a Chinese fir, red-barked *Arbutus* x *andrachnoides* and others. The chapel is open to visitors, and its interior is peaceful and cool.

Knightshayes Garden

ADDRESS: Bolham, Tiverton, Devon EX16 7RQ. Tel. Tiverton (O884) 254665 or 253264

OWNERS: The National Trust and Knightshayes Garden Trust

DIRECTIONS: 2 miles N of Tiverton, turn right off Tiverton to Bampton road (A396) at Bolham. 7 miles Junction 27 M5. Public transport: Devon General bus 373/4 from Tiverton Parkway BR (tel. Barnstaple 0271 45444) Devon General 55/A/B Exeter to Tiverton (passing close Exeter Central BR), tel. Exeter (0392) 56231. On all alight Tiverton 1¾ miles. Tiverton Parkway station 8 miles

OPENING TIMES: 29 March to end October, garden daily 11–6 (October 11–5). Last admission 30 minutes before closing

ADMISSION: house and garden £4; garden and grounds only £2.20. Pre-booked parties £3; organisers should book visits and make arrangements for meals beforehand with administrator. Visitor reception and information tel. Tiverton (0884) 257381

CAR PARKING: yes and parking for disabled people near house

TOILETS: yes (baby changing facilities in women's WC)

REFRESHMENTS: café

SHOP: NT shop and plant sales

DOGS: in park only, on lead

WHEELCHAIR ACCESS: yes, garden route avoiding steps; wheelchairs available. Toilets for the disabled: yes

PEAK MONTHS: April to October

NOTABLE FEATURES: formal gardens around house; spring flowers; rhododendrons and azaleas in spring; specimen trees; 'garden in the wood'; autumn colour. Scented plants for blind and partially sighted people

Knightshayes Court, with its large elaborate house, extensive grounds and luxuriant gardens appears the embodiment of continuity and permanence; it is quite surprising to discover that although the house (the work of William Burges) dates from 1870, the greater part of the garden has been created since 1945. The framework was established by Edward Kemp of Birkenhead at the time the house was built, but Sir John and Lady Heathcoat Amory were responsible for the planning and planting of the last 40 years. They took good advice—from Graham Thomas over a number of years for the Paved Garden in particular, from Lanning Roper for the Pool Garden and from Sir Eric Savill and Norman Hadden for their masterpiece, the Garden in the Wood—but they themselves were the prime movers of the whole enterprise.

The entrance drive to Knightshayes takes you to car parks partly concealed by the woods that protect the house from the north. The entrance to house and gardens lies through the former stables, now converted into a National Trust restaurant, shop and plant sales area. From here a wide path between grassed and wooded slopes brings you round the north-west side of the house to the conservatory, built in 1963 to house tender and free-flowering plants.

When we visited in July there were plenty of free-flowering plants in evidence: abutilons 'Golden Fleece' and 'Canary Bird' produce unusually large yellow bells, in contrast to the deep red of abutilon 'Nabob'. Generous pots of lilies are interspersed with tender foliage plants, and the orange Chilean glory flower (*Eccremocarpus scaber*) scrambles up a pillar. A vigorous morning glory (ipomoea) makes a blue sky of trumpet flowers above a carpet of semi-tender plants.

The conservatory stands at the western end of the top terrace and from here you can walk along the south-facing house border and also enjoy the view over the terraces to the countryside beyond. As the main part of the gardens lies to the east of the house, the southward link with fields and pastures is very strong. Growing against the house is a fine *Magnolia grandiflora* 'Exmouth', which produces its cream globes of flower in summer; a crimson flowering quince *Chaenomeles* x *superba* 'Rowallane', *Solanum crispum* 'Alba', the white flowered potato vine, and a vast Himalayan musk rose with creamy-white flowers (*R. brunonii*), entwined with the cerise clematis *C. viticella* 'Abundance'. The tender aromatic honey flower (*Melianthus major*), which only grows in well protected places, displays its glaucous toothed leaflets beside the path, and pale blue flowered *Teucrium fruticans*, another tender specimen, grows against the wall. The house border also holds spring and autumn bulbs.

At the eastern end of the terrace, a herbaceous border has been planted in front of the service wing: pinks, mauves and whites are predominant from May into the summer, including an unusual mauve sage, *Salvia sclarea* 'Turkestanica' and delicate mauve dieramas, or wand flowers. Some replanting took place in 1990 to create a more formal design of clipped yew in a quartet of three-quarter trefoils. Low dianthus, artemesia and veronica have been included in the foreground, while behind are massed plantings of colourful argyranthemum, osteorpermum and salvia.

The grassed terrace below runs between an interesting engraved stone seat to the east and a lead cistern, flanked by obelisks of yew, to the west; stone eagles and urns decorate the steep grass banks. The terrace below this holds a border of roses, with cistus, lavenders and other sun-loving plants and extends at its eastern end into a wide bed containing old-fashioned shrub roses and herbaceous geraniums in delicate shades. On the bottom terrace, where garden merges into parkland, the old rose garden has been replaced by a fountain and a design of paving stones interspersed with nepeta, to the east of which stands a cedar of Lebanon.

Leaving the top terrace by a short upward flight of steps you come to the garden 'rooms'. On your right, a yew hedge encloses a lawned area with a copy of a Borghese vase under the trees. Along this hedge canters Sir Ian Heathcoat Amory's topiary hunt—a green fox forever eluding green hounds. To your left are raised beds of alpine plants and dwarf shrubs, through which you can step up into the paved garden. There is much silver here—a great lead cistern filled with a colourful array of foliage and flower; silver leaved plants and small geranium interspersed with grey paving-stones, and four charming lead figures of children representing the seasons. Flanking the cistern are two standard wisterias, whose mauve blossoms fill the air with scent in spring.

The next garden room, once a bowling green, has been transformed into a water garden of great simplicity. Lawns surround a circular pool with lilies: the deep red nymphaea 'Escarboucle', the white 'Gladstoniana' and the yellow 'Moorei', with a single silver weeping pear (*Pyrus salicifolia* 'Pendula') reflected in the water. The spectacular leaves of *Acer pseudoplatanus* 'Brilliantissimum', turning during the season from shrimp pink to yellow and to green, are visible beyond the yew hedge.

Leaving the garden rooms you arrive at the edge of the Garden in the Wood: a woodland carefully thinned so as not to lose the predominance of the trees but letting in sufficient light for beds of shrubs and shade-loving plants. Its name expresses exactly what it is: a woodland enriched with plants, not a wood subordinated to the demands of a garden or a garden overshadowed by trees. Looking upwards you see the shelter of beech, oak, birch, larch, and pine; wandering through the maze of grassed paths you pass in spring drifts of snowdrops and daffodils and innumerable rhododendrons and azaleas. The latter are mainly in pastel shades, but with space allowed for occasional bolder reds and purples. These are complemented by the blossoms of other shrubs, including numerous magnolias which have come to maturity during the last forty years. All are underplanted with crocus, anemone, narcissus, trilliums or cyclamen according to season. There are hellebores and hostas, ivies and euphorbias, but also, and more surprisingly, such sun-lovers as New Zealand phormiums and silver-foliaged plants. Moreover as Penelope Hobhouse observes in *The National Trust: a Book of Gardening*, climbing roses, species clematis and honeysuckle, as well as rhododendrons and azaleas, have found here conditions approximating to their natural habitats, with their roots in cool shade and their heads reaching upwards to the light. They benefit, as she points out, from the combination of a 'south-sloping site, allowing free frost drainage and the rich lime-free soil'.

Because of the proliferation of the planting it is not always easy to identify the particular areas mentioned in the garden guide, but you can make your own voyage of discovery among the beds and grass walks, aided by occasional signs to the main areas.

Early on, we noticed a bed with *Magnolia* x *soulangiana* sheltering two smaller shrubs—an elegant Japanese angelica tree (*Aralia elata* 'Aureo-variegata') and a holly green leaved *Osmanthus delavayi*. Earlier in the year Lent lilies had bloomed; in July astilbes were showing feathery heads of white and pink. The climbing rose *R. polyantha* 'Grandiflora' twines its creamy white blossoms through the dark needles of a pine tree and nearby is a paper bark maple (*Acer griseum*), with cinnamon coloured peeling bark. Even sun-loving buddleias and prunus manage to blossom in these areas.

At the top of the wood is an open lawn surrounded by trees and planted with young birch, acer and a cut-leaved alder. Just below this is the glade, where lawns, open to the sky, slope down from a stone seat, decorated with griffons and a lion head and shaded by a group of larches. The lower border here contains sages, hostas, meconopsis and euphorbias and nearby a sloping circular lawn is bordered by mounds of low growing dissected acers in shades of red and green. A weeping Huon pine (*Dacrydium franklinii*) from Tasmania shows its dark green scale like leaves to good effect near silver grasses, spiky phormiums and a silver variegated co-toneaster. At the lower rim of the grass circle a gold acer and a spreading golden yew provides bright contrast with a group of Douglas firs.

Moving east you come to Sir John's Wood, predominantly com-posed of tall slender larches and dark evergreens, and Michael's Wood (named for the head gardener of the last 25 years, Michael Hickson) where there are further groups of acer and pools of dapple-leaved autumn flowering cyclamen. Among the rich variety of shrubs and other plants here are a graceful *Cornus controversa* 'Variegata', and clethra, a late summer shrub with scented cream flowers.

Below the Garden in the Wood proper is an extension to the south garden, established initially to accommodate large rhododendrons. It now includes a collection of southern beech, nothofagus, and many dogwoods, including *Cornus kousa chinensis* with its attrac-tive cream bracts and *C. nuttallii*, the Pacific dogwood. Japanese cherries add colour in spring. There are Atlantic cedars and a graceful Himalayan cedar (*Cedrus deodara*), among many other interesting and distinctive trees.

Three other features remain to the north and west of the house. The first, a walled garden, is not open to the public but is clearly visible across the little valley. It was well known as a kitchen garden in Victorian times and now contains a nursery for other National Trust gardens and for plant sales. The second is a fine stand of Douglas firs to the east of the kitchen garden, planted in the 1870s and now of a considerable height. In the western valley lies the Amorys' final venture: a former American garden transformed into a planting of willows and old-fashioned scented azaleas around a dell pool. This forms a link with the fields beyond. One of the many pleasures of Knightshayes is that its exotic conservatory, Mediter-ranean style planting, formal enclosed gardens and wonderfully enhanced woodlands seem completely at home in the countryside of East Devon.

Marwood Hill Gardens

ADDRESS AND TELEPHONE: Marwood Hill, Barnstaple, North Devon. Tel. Barnstaple (0271) 42528

OWNERS: Dr J.A. Smart

DIRECTIONS: 4 miles N of Barnstaple on B3230, turn W at Muddiford (cars only). Signs on A361 Barnstaple to Braunton road (coaches). No public transport available

OPENING TIMES: daily (except Christmas Day) dawn to dusk. House not open

ADMISSION: £1, children 10p

CAR PARKING: in lay-by on back road, which adjoins main road

TOILETS: yes

REFRESHMENTS: teas in church room, Suns and BH (or by prior arrangement for parties)

SHOP: plant sales area

DOGS: on lead only

WHEELCHAIR ACCESS: no. Toilets for the disabled: no

PEAK MONTHS: April to August

NOTABLE FEATURES: camellias; Australian plants; rhododendrons; trees and shrubs; lakes; rock and heather gardens; bog garden

Marwood Hill Gardens are entirely the creation of Dr James Smart, who moved here in 1949 and began to clear the walled garden and surrounding areas. In the early 1960s, Dr Smart bought pasture land to the south and east, across the valley, and set about re-planting the slopes with trees and shrubs. A stream in the bottom of the valley, flowing from east to west, was dammed in 1969 and a lower dam added eight years later, creating three big ponds or lakes.

The garden now contains a planted quarry, double shrub and herbaceous borders, an alpine scree and many other areas of interest. Marwood Hill holds a National Collection of astilbes, now over 140, and these can be seen in the magnificent bog garden. It also has a National Collection of Japanese irises (*Iris encata*). Camellias feature strongly at Marwood, as do rhododendrons, azaleas and magnolias—the soil on the far side of lakes is acid. Dr Smart also takes a special interest in Australian plants.

You enter at the top of the garden, from a back road. Directly below are the double herbaceous borders and an arched pergola with many different wisterias and beyond these the house, with silver birches on the front lawn. Alternatively, by turning right you can visit the walled garden and plant sales area, with camellia house, a small pool and waterfall; and further east, scented rhodo-dendrons and azaleas, with the hebe bed and Australian plants below. All these areas lie close at hand, on the very upper slopes. Below are the lakes and bog garden, and grassy slopes planted with trees and shrubs.

Visiting in late spring, you may see *Exochorda* x *macrantha*, with arching branches and long heads of paper-white flowers, *E.* 'The Bride' and *Magnolia stellata* 'Water Lily'. Both these are situated to the west, not far from the shelter belt of larches, where you may also see an unusual clipped hedge of camellia 'Donation'. In the grassy areas above the middle lake are rhododendron 'Coronation Day' with very large fragrant flowers, mottled rose with a crimson blotch; rhododendron 'Alpine Glow', with widely funnel-shaped flowers of delicate pink; lilac-pink *Magnolia* x *loebneri* 'Leonard Messel'; and pieris 'Forest Flame'and 'Firecrest'. Here too is the rare bumble bee plant (*Maddenia involucrata*) from China, with flowers resembling bees.

The double herbaceous border provides a modest display of colour in summer. Nearby there is a bed of peonies and tree peonies. *Prunus tenella* 'Firehills' flourishes in a bed with *Cornus kousa*.

West of the walled garden and plant sales area is an interesting collection of Australian plants, including leptospermum and callistemon, flourishing despite their exposed position. A collection of hebes can be seen a little way up the slope, overhung by *Magnolia sargentiana*; and in mid summer a brilliant display of *Eryngium giganteum* 'Miss Willmott's Ghost', below *Hydrangea villosa*.

Alpines too numerous to list fill a raised scree bed below the walled garden. Below this bed you can see eucryphias, magnolias and cornus.

The lower garden and lakes can be reached by two main routes; down the slope, past walled terracing, or by the steps below the rose garden. Rich and varied planting can be seen around the lakesides and by the dams—one huge bed of spreading rock plants and dwarf bulbs, one of prostrate conifers and one of heathers; and south of the first lake, a bed of hostas and moisture-loving plants. Three graceful slim poplars make a striking group above the heather bed; nearby is the fossil tree *Metasequoia glyptostroboides*. Other trees include prunus, *Cedrus atlantica glauca*, eucalyptus and the snowdrop tree (*Styrax japonica*). The statue of a mother and two children, on the island, is by the Australian sculptor John Robinson.

The small quarry garden, to the west, is planted with dwarf conifers and shade-loving flowers—dog's tooth violets (erythroniums) for the spring, dwarf cyclamen for autumn.

A fine collection of trees, shrubs and rhododendrons is situated on the far side of the lake, including *Eucalyptus simmondsii*, magnolias, large-leaved Himalayan rhododendrons and pieris. Beyond the eucalyptus collection, south-west of the second dam, are collections of sorbus, betula and malus.

The western part of the garden has been developed since 1977; it includes the splendid bog garden and many young trees and shrubs. At the far end of the third lake, across a little stone bridge, is a scented arbour, overgrown with honeysuckle and jasmine; and beyond this the folly, and three small groups of *Betula jacquemontii*, below the shelter belt.

Overbecks Garden

ADDRESS AND TELEPHONE: Sharpitor, Salcombe, Devon TQ8 8LW. Tel. Salcome (054 884) 2893

OWNERS: The National Trust

DIRECTIONS: 1½ miles SW of Salcombe, signposted from Malborough and Salcombe. Public transport: Tally Ho! bus 606 from Kingsbridge (tel. Kingsbridge 0548 3081) with connections from Plymouth and Dartmouth, alight Salcombe, then 1½ miles

OPENING TIMES: garden, daily 10–8 or sunset if earlier. Museum within house, daily 12–4.30

ADMISSION: garden only £1.80 (no reductions)

CAR PARKING: small car park with charge refundable on admission. Suitable for small 24 seater coaches only. Tel. to check

TOILETS: yes

REFRESHMENTS: yes and picnics allowed on top terrace

SHOP: yes

DOGS: no

WHEELCHAIR ACCESS: yes, wheelchair available. Toilets for the disabled: yes, with help

PEAK MONTHS: March through to autumn

NOTABLE FEATURES: rare plants, shrubs and trees suitable for sub-tropical climate, spectacular view over Salcombe estuary

Perched high above the mouth of the Salcombe estuary, and reached by narrow roads winding up the hillside, Overbecks is well worth the effort required to reach it. One of the few gardens in the country with a sheltered 'micro-climate' which enables tender trees and shrubs to flourish, its planting is being constantly extended and improved under the guidance of its head gardener, Mr Tony Murdoch, and the National Trust. Their aim is to develop a Mediterranean type garden with foliage and flower contrast.

As the garden guide points out, Overbecks is a 20C creation. In 1901 the basic design of steep south-west-facing terraces was laid out by Edric Hopkins and later extended by Mr G.M. Vereker and his wife, who also planted most of the mature trees and shrubs, many of which are tender. Mr Otto Overbeck, who bought the property in 1928, continued to increase the range of planting. A peculiarity of the garden, as far as the West Country is concerned, is that its soil has a high lime content (pH 7.5), unsuitable for the rhododendrons and camellias which flourish in many gardens throughout the region. This deficiency is more than made up by the quality of the lime tolerant plants which grow here.

The 'Mediterranean' atmosphere is set as soon as you enter the garden and find yourself descending steps between an avenue of *Trachycarpus fortunei*, the Chusan palm named for Robert Fortune, the explorer who discovered them. Looking over the wall to your left you will find a line of *Crinodendron hookeranum*, which produce their hanging crimson lantern-shaped flowers in early summer. Deep red clumps of New Zealand flax (*Phormium tenax*) add to the exotic atmosphere.

Passing the front of the house, where there is a small National Trust shop, you find the main lawn in front of you, while to your left a remarkable view of the estuary opens out. On the stone walls of the terrace and in front of the conservatory, glazed pots have been planted with agaves—accustomed to flourish in Salcombe gardens in the past. In the conservatory are orange and lemon trees, begonias and pelargoniums and a beautiful passion flower, *Passi-*

Overbecks is a Mediterranean type garden, perched high above the mouth of the Salcombe estuary

flora antioquiensis from Colombia, whose pendant, rose red flowers reveal a violet centre.

Leaving the conservatory on the right a golden border has been created; golden-leaved hops are covering the wall and, below, various golden-leaved plants have been used to brighten up a dark corner.

The borders of the lawn are sheltered by steep rocky walls and by the woods above. Here grow some spectacular specimens: *Beschorneria yuccoides* from Mexico with blue-green sword-shaped leaves and spikes of red flowers on pink, fleshy stems; huge blue heads of echium, the viper's bugloss, grown to fantastic size and self-seeding; bright clumps of orange or red watsonias from South Africa, contrasting with their compatriot, the graceful mauve angel's fishing rod or wand flower (*Dierama pulcherrimum*). There are blue agapanthus and white arum lilies, and in the shade, *Matteuccia struthiopteris*, the ostrich feather fern. Backing the Museum border, introducing an almost incongruously English note, are two climbing roses—the pale pink 'Anemone' and the silky-white, gold-stamened *R. laevigata* 'Cooperi', intertwined with the wine-red *Clematis viticella* 'Abundance'. At the front of this bed we noticed a cream viola set against the black mondo grass *Ophiopogon planiscapus* 'Nigrescens'.

Two outstanding trees grow on the south-east bank above the lawn: the unusual *Euonymus fimbriatus*, whose young red leaves turn to a striking gold-green by summer, and a very tender camphor tree, *Cinnamomum camphora*, with aromatic, shiny dark green leaves tinged with burgundy. In a recent hard winter this tree died right back, but new shoots are now emerging from the base. A larger specimen can be found above the Statue Garden.

On the path to the Belvedere, above the lawn, we noticed silvery *Convolvulus cneorum* growing near a deep red phormium and the twisting climber *Actinidia kolomikta* whose green leaves are dappled with pale pink. Nearby two silver hebes show to advantage against phormium 'Dazzler' and a cream and green yucca contrasts with a dark purple *Aeonium arboreum* 'Atropurpureum' and Overbecks' own fuchsia, 'Sharpitor', which has the palest of pink flowers and variegated foliage. The bright blue flowers of *felicia* stand out against the pale yellow osteospermum 'Buttermilk'. Red and green bushes of pittosporum from New Zealand grow near bright orange gazanias, and in a raised stone bed the French lavender (*Lavandula stoechas*) shows its deep purple flowers and bracts. *Fascicularia pitcairniifolia*, a rarity from the Pitcairn islands, was recovering from previous hard winters at the time we visited.

The Belvedere, a small look-out point above the lawn, provides another spectacular view over the estuary and garden. Here grow more tender flowering shrubs: the yellow Moroccan broom (*Cytisus battandieri*), an acacia, and yellow-flowered, silver-foliaged senecio spilling over the bank. From here you can cross the path to the Rock Dell, where a number of sub-tropical flowers and shrubs flourish: among them dark red cannas, the aromatic honey flower (*Melianthus major*) and the yellow argyreanthemum 'Jamaica Primrose', while a wisteria clambers over a palm in the shrub border. Many shades of spiky yucca and phormium grow here, as well as more Chusan palms, with their hairy trunks and fans of sword-shaped leaves. The top terrace of all has been recently grassed and provided with seats for a picnic area, with a bird's eye view of the garden and the estuary.

The only formal area is the Statue Garden, its herbaceous beds and borders centred by a statue of a young girl with a nest of birds. Here the yellow flowers of the ginger lily (*Hedychium gardnerianum*) fill the air with scent and the South African pineapple lily (*Eucomis punctata*) shows dense heads of pale green flower. The dark red bells of the purple bellvine, (*Rhodochiton atrosanguineum*) grow among the more usual herbaceous plants, of which there are many striking groupings, such as that of pale green *Cephalaria gigantea* near the lime green flowers of *Nicotiana langsdorfii* contrasting with blue and red salvias. There are clumps of pink and mauve alstroemeria 'Ligtu hybrids', spikes of yellow and orange knitophia and red bell-heads of penstemon. Above this mass of colour stands a dark, shimmering camphor tree.

Further on is a small 'secret garden', where you can sit on a white seat under a cherry tree or look down over a balustrade on a small orchard of exotic fruits, including the Japanese banana tree (*Musa basjoo*). A loquat (*Eriobotrya japonica*) produces orange and yellow fruits by the wall in autumn and a pink American pillar rose scrambles above.

One of the treasures of the garden is the 40ft *Magnolia campbellii*, which was planted in 1901 and whose pink flowers are visible from far up the estuary in March. This stands on the lowest terrace, where the woods are being cleared for new plantings of pittosporum and griselinia and an unusually large-flowered perpetual sweet pea scrambles over supports in a border. The path then leads you back to below the house, where on the walls below the lantern trees grows the climber *Holboellia latifolia*, with porcelain-coloured, scented flowers. A small but interesting plant here is the winged pea (*Lotus berthelotii*) with silver foliage and red pea flowers. Great clumps of the perennial poppy *Romneya coulteri*, white splashed gold, grow from the bank, and the slopes below the path are covered in late summer with pink and white hydrangeas. Bluebells flourish in spring under the shelter of a golden and a green macrocarpus and new plantings of blue agapanthus and golden knifophia are being established. Further on in the woods, under the shelter of beech trees, there are varieties of cornus, including *C. capitata* whose sulphur-yellow bracts are followed by crimson, strawberry-like fruits. Returning from the woods, you will find yourself back near the entrance lawn, enabling you to take a final look at the marvellous estuary view which is an integral part of this unusual and rewarding garden.

RHS Garden, Rosemoor

ADDRESS AND TELEPHONE: Great Torrington, Devon EX38 7EG. Tel. (0805) 24067

OWNERS: The Royal Horticultural Society

DIRECTIONS: 1 mile SE of Great Torrington on B3220 to Exeter. Public transport: BR to Barnstaple, then by bus

OPENING TIMES: daily 10–5 (6 in summer)

ADMISSION: £1.75, children 50p, parties of 20 or more £1.50. RHS members free

CAR PARKING: yes

TOILETS: yes

REFRESHMENTS: yes

SHOP: yes and plant sales

DOGS: yes, on lead

WHEELCHAIR ACCESS: yes. Toilets for the disabled: yes

PEAK MONTHS: March to October

NOTABLE FEATURES: 30-year-old, 8-acre garden designed and created by Lady Anne Palmer with specimen trees, shrubs and plants from many parts of the world. New Royal Horticultural Society garden for the West Country, opened in spring 1990, with rose gardens, herbaceous borders and a visitor centre, developing over 15 years to include demonstration gardens, water gardens, an alpine lawn and fruit and vegetable gardens

A visit to Rosemoor offers the rare opportunity to witness the making of a new Royal Horticultural Society Garden. This unusual and exciting venture has been made possible by Lady Anne Palmer's gift to the RHS of her house and present garden, together with 32 acres of pasture land to the south and west. Visitors can watch the new garden develop in its sheltered meadow setting, and take the opportunity to visit Lady Anne's original creation—a mature but still developing garden, laid out over the last 30 years and filled with trees, shrubs and plants from Europe, the United States, South America, Australia and New Zealand, Japan and Papua New Guinea.

Lady Anne's garden will remain the jewel in the crown of the whole design, according to Maj.-Gen. Jeremy Rougier, the Director of Rosemoor and instrumental, with Christopher Bailes the Curator, in planning the new developments. Its 8 acres, which include an arboretum, surround Rosemoor House on three sides and along the upper south-west slope of the Torridge valley, protected by a shelter belt of trees.

The soil is a retentive silty loam over clay, with a pH of 5.5. The attractively illustrated garden guide defines five main areas: the lawns below the main drive, planted with specimen trees and shrubs and terminating at the large pond; a woodland garden and trail below the lawns, running parallel to the road; an area of divided gardens above the main drive (kitchen garden, stone garden and temple, croquet lawn and tennis court); a woodland garden above these; and a developing arboretum, lying furthest from the house to the south along the valley slope. These lawned areas merge into one another and are not always easy to identify; however, many trees and plants are listed in the guide and there is a rolling programme of labelling in progress.

Entering from the old parking area along the drive, look ahead and to your right over the main lawn to the pond. Walking over this lawn you pass beds combining tree, shrub and flower planting. One of the first has a basic structure of conifers including a form of the Japanese nutmeg tree, *Torreya nucifera* 'Spreadeagle'. These are offset by spiky variegated New Zealand phormiums, feathery *Filipendula ulmaria* 'Variegata' and a spurge (*Euphorbia mellifera*).

This green, gold and yellow bed contrasts with its further neighbour, which is planted mainly in silver and soft colours, though a gold *Acer negundo* forms the centrepiece. Other lawn beds, here and above the main drive, provide plenty of interest and variety.

At the far point of the lawn, a large oak dominates a heather bed containing many winter and spring flowering ericas with callunas for late summer and autumn. Near the pool are oaks, willows, a black gum (*Nyssa sylvatica*), a tree of heaven (*Ailanthus altissima*) and a swamp cypress (*Taxodium distichum*). The twisted branches of the contorted hazel (*Corylus avellana* 'Contorta') stand out boldly in winter. The water's edge is crowded with many moisture-loving plants.

Turning back towards the house past a large copper beech, and a shady bed with hostas, you come to the lower woodland area. The first bed contains small rhododendrons sheltered by magnolia 'Maryland', itself sited beneath a large birch (*Betula nigra*) with attractive, peeling bark.

Nearby, the rare Californian bayberry (*Myrica californica*), is protected by the unusual crimson-flowered *Magnolia sprengeri*. Within this woodland are many dogwoods, a large *Magnolia campbellii*, a graceful autumn-colouring ironwood (*Parrotia persica*) and the spectacular *Stewartia pseudocamellia*; also azaleas, camellias and rhododendrons, acers and ilex, the latter a particular interest of Lady Anne's.

The house itself shelters some tender and sun-loving plants, including two raphiolepsis, *R. umbellata* and *R. indica*.

Keeping the house to your left and climbing up the slope you pass on your right a hedge of pink-flowering *Rosa foliolosa*. Another collection of sun-lovers can be seen on south-west and west-facing walls: callistemons, a bright red cestrum and others. Nearby are raised beds and a scree bed for small alkaline loving plants, many from New Zealand.

The woods above provide more familiar plantings, including hollies (part of the National Collection of ilex). From here, walk down into the Stone Garden, a garden 'room' housing a temple and statuary and stocked with a rich mixture of conifers. Sitting in the temple, you can see in early summer the beautiful flowers of the tree peony *P. suffruticosa* 'Rock's variety'. There is a bed of Pacific Coast irises, flowering in late spring and early summer and a mixture of *Dierama pulcherrimum*, the angel's fishing rod, flowering later in the season.

Nearby are the croquet lawn and tennis court, both now given over to planting: the former has a border of shrubs, shrub roses and rhododendron species around a central lawn. Note the delicate winter hazel, *Corylopsis willmottiae* 'Spring Purple'. There are also several specimens of the Chilean fire bush (*Embothrium coccineum*). The nearby tennis court is gravelled, with beds of spreading conifers, spiky yuccas and phormiums.

Beyond to the east is the most recent area of the 30-year-old garden—a still developing arboretum. An underpass links Lady Anne Palmer's garden with the new one and a visitor centre containing a restaurant, shop and plant centre.

The new areas of the RHS garden follow the contours of the fields and use natural features, such as the existing stream. Two large rose gardens, each 430ft square, are already providing a memorable display. The shrub rose garden contains 400 roses of 130 varieties, the new rose garden 1500 roses of 60 varieties. In addition, the first 218 yds of what will eventually be a 436 yd long herbaceous border has been opened, together with extensive and varied beds around the new visitor centre.

The two bottom squares in the square are planted as colour theme gardens. The whole field is to be hedged with yew and there will eventually be a water feature in the centre, visible over the hedges.

In later seasons, demonstration gardens will be provided, as at Wisley, and there will be alpine beds, water gardens, fruit and vegetable gardens and trial grounds. The full development is expected to take 15 years, and during that time the present number of 4 garden staff will be increased to 20.

This ambitious project will absorb a considerable amount of RHS funding over the coming years, but should in future provide a notable horticultural resource for the West Country, and a rewarding place to visit.

DORSET

Abbotsbury Sub-Tropical Gardens

ADDRESS AND TELEPHONE: The Strangways Estates, Abbotsbury, Weymouth, Dorset. Tel. Abbotsbury (0305) 871387

OWNERS: Ilchester Estates

DIRECTIONS: 9 miles NW of Weymouth. From the B3157 Weymouth to Bridport road, turn off 200 yds W of Abbotsbury village, at foot of hill

OPENING TIMES: March to October, daily 10–6. 4 November to 4 March 10–4, closed Mon

ADMISSION: £2.40, OAPs £2, children 60p. For party rates tel. (0305) 871387

CAR PARKING: yes

TOILETS: yes

REFRESHMENTS: yes

SHOP: no

DOGS: yes

WHEELCHAIR ACCESS: partial. Toilets for the disabled: no

PEAK MONTHS: March to May, August and September

NOTABLE FEATURES: rare plants and trees

Situated right on the Dorset coast, on the sunny coastal strip between Portland and West Bay, and protected by thick windbreaks of *Quercus ilex*, Abbotsbury shelters an enormous number and range of plants, including many tender Mediterranean species, and wonderful trees.

The sea nearby acts as a permanent heat reservoir, radiating warmth throughout winter (owing to the steeply shelving structure of the Chesil Bank, it hardly recedes at all at low tide). The only danger is of severe wind chill from the north.

Both coniferous and broadleaved trees grow here to exceptional height, obviously enjoying the shelter and mild climate, and tended by regular teams of tree surgeons. Here are the world record English oak (140ft), and British record Caucasian wing nut (120ft) and the tallest Monterey Cypress in the northern hemisphere. Close planting keeps all the trees slim and shapely, with long straight boles. The average-sized visitor may feel somewhat disorientated—Abbotsbury is more like the land of Brobdingnag than an English garden.

Unlikely as it may seem, Abbotsbury was once a walled garden—started in 1765, by the Countess of Ilchester, near Abbotsbury Castle. The castle no longer exists: the garden soon outgrew its walls, extended by the 2nd Countess and her son William Fox-Strangways, the 4th Earl. Fox-Strangways, a famous botanist, imported plants from the Caucasus, the Himalayas, China, Japan and South America, and his successors followed his example, so by the end of the 19C there was a considerable collection.

The garden was largely neglected in wartime and grew wild, but was reclaimed from the 1960s onwards by Lady Teresa Agnew, her husband Lord Galway and their head gardener, John Hussey. John Kelly, the present curator, has extended the woodland garden from 17 to 20 acres and new plantings are being made from China, Nepal and Mexico, with the help of Roy Lancaster, plant hunter and garden writer.

Handsome peafowl do guard duty along the walls and roost near the tea rooms. Children should enjoy seeing these, and the tea garden budgerigars. Having crossed the tea area, you are next confronted by a vast and beautiful Caucasian wing-nut (*Pterocarya fraxinifolia*), with diamond-patterned bark like a complicated weaving. Behind is a forest of camellias, some dating from the 18C, when camellias were first introduced to Britain.

Next on your right comes the entrance to the Victorian garden, where Chusan palms tower above gold *Robinia pseudoacacia* 'Frisia' and cornus 'Ormonde', a rare hybrid between *C. nuttalli* and *C. florida*. The palms are now the tallest in Britain, at 40ft: in Victorian times they were about 6ft. Osmanthus and pittosporum have also grown to an extraordinary size. Rare *O. yunnanensis* (near the arch entrance to the west lawn) is breathtaking in early spring, with creamy-white, sweetly scented flowers. The lawn centres on a circular bed of shrub roses, a popular Victorian feature—here among other species are *R. centifolia* 'Chapeau de Napoleon', which bears globular heavy-scented pink flowers, and the damask double-white 'Madame Hardy'.

On the west lawn, a semicircle of cannons threatens a large conservatory, erected in 1985 to house the National Reference Collections of salvia and eucalyptus. The cannons stood on Butler's Cliff, overlooking the sea, until about 1760, defending Lyme Bay.

Walking up onto West Hill, past a protective windbreak of evergreen oak, you can see in mid spring the creamy-white flowers of *Magnolia* x *veitchii* 'Isca', 70ft high, which has grown here since the beginning of the century. A brilliant contrast is provided by the bell-shaped flowers of *Rhododendron arboreum* 'Blood Red'. Rhododendrons flourish throughout the gardens, mainly *R. arboreum* and *R. fortunei*, enjoying the acid soil. Limestone covers most of central and west Dorset, but Abbotsbury is based on a fault. A bamboo screen gives additional protection against wind and marks the garden's former boundary.

You now enter the 1984 extension, where new plantings are being made. One area called 'China' contains specimens brought from China by Roy Lancaster—some as yet unnamed. A Secret Walk begins at the bamboo ride, invisible from other parts of the garden. The late summer visitor will be pleasantly surprised by the spectacular white flowers of the tall hybrid rhododendron 'Polar Bear'. *R.* 'Fragrantissimum', a greenhouse rhododendron, grows outside all winter, as does *R. latoucheae*, only recently introduced to cultivation.

Busby's Ground, in the woodland valley, is planted with rhododendrons, hydrangeas and various tender species. It is named after the gardener who worked here in the early 1980s, reclaiming the land from invasive sycamore. Visiting in spring, we saw a row of callistemon, struggling back to life after the cold winter, near a mass of vibrant blue hydrangeas. Medieval strip lynchets (farming terraces) can still be seen on the higher slopes.

The valley trees are extraordinarily tall, slender and graceful, with long straight boles. Many of the oaks are over 120ft. The ginkgos (80–85ft) include a few females—thought to be very rare in Britain, although numbers are difficult to estimate, as ginkgos conceal their sex until they are 80 years old. Near the lower valley walk, a Himalayan musk rose rises 90ft up a towering Scots pine. Lacecap hydrangeas are massed along the stream. Crossing the wooden bridge, you can see *Gunnera manicata*, besides clumps of bamboo and thickly planted primulas and astilbes.

In this central valley area are the tallest Caucasian wing nut in Britain and a lofty dawn redwood. Climbing coronation walk and the upper valley walk, you can inspect at close quarters the soaring trunks of Monterey pines and cypresses.

Yellow *Magnolia delavayi* blooms freely in August, a sizeable tree: not far away is *M. campbellii*, which produces very big rose pink blossoms in spring. Planted in 1864, this specimen delayed blooming until 1900. Another can be seen further down the slope, near a cinnamon-barked myrtle and a parrotia. Near the top of the wood, we saw a dark red *Cotinus coggygria* strikingly partnered by *Cornus controversa* 'Variegata'; nearby is a silver and white bed.

You emerge from the wood onto a wide grassy slope, crowned by a dazzlingly bright herbaceous border in the shape of a Prince of Wales feather. A bold mix of perennials is linked by blue and white delphiniums and white trailing standard roses—'Sanders White Rambler', one of Gertrude Jekyll's favourites. Look out for the tiny twinspur *Diascia cordifolia* 'Ruby Field', the only hybrid in the genus, bred by John Kelly.

At the edge of the lawn, *Rosa filipes* scrambles over trees, 50ft high and 50ft wide, like a great waterfall in flower; and nearby is the rare and graceful tree *Phellodendron japonicum*. Doubling back down the long rose border, you pass *Myrtus apiculata* from Chile and *Styrax hemsleyana* with rounded leaves and pure white pendulous flowers in early summer. *Lonicera maackii* 'Podocarpa' is normally a bush—here an enormous tree. The rose beds contain many very lovely old-fashioned roses, best seen in June.

Finally we found two rectangular lily pools, in a clearing on high ground, filled with fish and pink water lilies: it seemed an odd place to put a water garden. These ponds were built in 1896, for irrigation.

Cranborne Manor Gardens

ADDRESS AND TELEPHONE: Cranborne Manor Garden Centre, Cranborne, Wimborne, Dorset. Tel. Cranborne (072 54) 248

OWNERS: Viscount and Viscountess Cranborne

DIRECTIONS: on B3078 10 miles N of Wimborne

OPENING TIMES: April to September, 9–5 every Wed. House not open

ADMISSION: £2.50, OAPs £2, children under 16 50p. Coach parties by prior arrangement only

CAR PARKING: yes

TOILETS: yes

REFRESHMENTS: café open Wed and Sun 10–5

SHOP: garden centre and gift shop open March to December, Tues to Sat 9–5, Sun 10–5 closed Mon. January and February, Tues to Sat 9–5.

DOGS: no

WHEELCHAIR ACCESS: to most of garden. Toilets for the disabled: no

PEAK MONTHS: April to July

NOTABLE FEATURES: formal gardens laid out by Mounten Jennings and John Tradescant; knot, green and herb gardens designed by present Marchioness of Salisbury; white, river and kitchen gardens; fine trees and meadow lawns

An English garden is a hard thing to define, especially since, over the centuries, styles have been borrowed and plants introduced from all over the world. Nevertheless, certain gardens have a peculiarly 'English' feel to them and of these, Cranborne Manor is a distinguished example.

Cranborne village, though not particularly far from main roads and towns, feels deep in the countryside. The splendid beeches to the south and west of the manor link countryside with house, as do the meadows that surround and, by invitation, infiltrate the gardens themselves. The Jacobean manor, constructed out of local stone on the ruins of a former hunting lodge, provides a background in harmony with the surrounding countryside, and the gardens, both formal and landscape, in turn complement the house—a fact that says much for the skill of the garden designers, from Mounten Jennings and John Tradescent in the 17C to members of the present family and gardening staff.

Entering through the walled garden centre and nursery, you join the main entrance drive, flanked by a double avenue of mature beeches, the inner row green, the outer copper. The path leads through an archway between two brick gatehouses into the rectangular, walled south court, with a full view of the south front with its elegant portico of mellow grey stone. The court itself, once a parterre, is now stone flagged, partly cobbled and its central sundial is set in lavender, with surrounding orbs of box.

Herbaceous borders to either side are planted in cool, subtle colours. When we visited, arching shrub roses and clumps of peonies, both in pale pink, were coming into flower, interspersed with sheaths of pale blue and white iris and dark spikes of yucca. Clumps of pink dianthus and mauve lavender spilled over on to the stone paths. This relaxed, appropriately chosen planting sets the tone for the gardens as a whole.

Leaving the court in the direction of the west lawn, you come to a knot garden, recently designed by the Marchioness of Salisbury. A central topiary piece is surrounded by lavender and santolina, while the outer beds of box, divided into diamonds, are filled with plants familiar in the 16C and 17C: sweet rocket, yellow day lilies, poppies, pink and blue linaria, clumps of *Lavandula stoechas* or French lavender.

The west lawn beyond, framed in beech woods, leads you to the Mount Garden, laid out by John Tradescant in the reign of James I. The mount commands a view of the nearby fields; you can also look back from here to the west front of the manor, with its lichened grey slate roof and five red brick chimneys, set cornerwise to the compass. Surrounding the mount are beds of lavender interspersed with lilies, separated by tall, solid drum shapes of yew. The outer herbaceous beds in part repeat the south court's cool colour themes, with white foxgloves and light blue delphiniums, pale peonies and roses, punctuated by tall silver cardoons and grey *Phlomis fruticosa*, the Jerusalem sage. There are also splashes of bolder colour: vivid dark delphiniums and salvia, clumps of bright red poppies and the acid green flowers of *Euphorbia characias wulfenii*.

From the Mount Garden you can step into a bowling *allée*, a feature of the period. Before you walk along it, look back across the mount and its flower beds to a hedged meadow garden and the woods beyond.

The *allée* is narrow, and 17C bowlers must have needed a good eye to keep the bowls from disappearing under its yew hedges. At the far end, you can turn left down a grassed path to the little river which provides the garden's northern boundary, first passing the statue of a countryman, framed in yew. A herbaceous border runs the length of the path on your right, while beyond the gate are crab apple orchards set in tall grass, never mown before July, to encourage the many wild flowers. Spring bulbs flourish here before the grass grows high.

The Crane is a winter-bourne, drying up even in wet summers. It is stone-lined, with small pools and cascades. A paved path, furnished with tall shrubs, leads westwards along its northern bank, and at the hedge you can cross by a charming arched stone bridge to a clipped grass strip by the meadow.

Returning towards the manor and turning left past the statue of the countryman you find yourself in the north court, standing on the balustraded terrace, under a pillared porch. This bears the coat of arms of the 2nd Earl of Salisbury (1647) and was originally the only entrance to the house. Looking out beyond the grey stone balustrade, the eye follows the central path of the White Garden below to an avenue of poplars and planes reaching out into the meadows. The avenue was originally of Cornish elms, which died of Dutch elm disease in the 1970s. Though lacking the grandeur of the elms, the poplars have their own grace, their leaves shimmering against the slope of the opposite hill.

White wisteria, roses and clematis clamber along the balustrade, and in the garden below, two central rows of apple trees are underplanted with white dianthus, including the old garden favourite 'Mrs. Sinkins'. The lawns to either side are bordered with white shrub roses and peonies, philadelphus and *Crambe cordifolia*, the plumes of *Aruncus sylvester* with their tiny starry flowers, white rosemary and potentilla, silver variegated grasses and silver artemisia, including *A. ludoviciana* with its handsome cut leaves. Clumps of blue miscanthus, blue-green and white-edged hostas set off the pale background of flower and foliage. When we visited, in a dry summer, a welcome light rain was falling and a string quartet was playing snatches of music from the steps of the porch.

To the east, the kitchen garden provides complete and homely contrast. Neat rows of vegetables—potatoes, peas, beans—with lines of sweet williams and other flowers for cutting, stretch out in front of a low stable building. In the centre of the garden is an apple tunnel, through which you emerge to sun-baked beds of pinks and iris under a sheltering north wall.

On the eastern lawn, the last of the gardens surrounding the manor, there is an ancient, spreading evergreen oak (*Quercus ilex*), said to have been planted by Tradescant himself. To reach this, you take the cobbled pergola walk, under roses and wisteria, emerging to a little avenue of pleached limes, which guides you back towards the original entrance, and beyond it to the remaining three enclosed gardens.

The first of these is a Green Garden, designed by the Marchioness of Salisbury. It is enclosed in yew, with the statue of a huntsman set in the western hedge, and a row of slim junipers ahead of you as you enter. At their feet, enclosed in box, are plantings of 'non-flowering' green herbs and other ground cover plants valued for their foliage.

The yew hedge to the south, 15ft high and 10ft thick continues along the next two garden rooms—punctuated with 'windows' so that you are always conscious of the surrounding fields. The chalk wall in the Chalk Wall Garden is furnished with a variety of shrubs, including a red-stamened, white petalled magnolia and two sturdy, purple-flowered Judas trees.

The herb garden at the end has a peculiar charm. White-flowered climbing roses are trained flat against its south-facing wall, and in the beds below are clumps of mauve-flowered allium, green and white apple mint, golden marjoram and purple, blue-flowering sage. Small shrub roses are interspersed among the herbs in the central beds, edged with mounds of silver santolina, and a small hedge of single white roses runs along under the windows of yew. Apart from its visual pleasures, this is a particularly rewarding garden for blind or partially sighted people.

The tea room lies outside the herb garden and beyond it the garden centre, which specialises in old-fashioned roses, clematis, herbaceous and unusual plants and box and yew hedging.

Highbury

ADDRESS AND TELEPHONE: Woodside Road, West Moors, Dorset BH22 0LY. Tel. Ferndown (0202) 874372

OWNERS: Mr and Mrs Stanley Cherry

DIRECTIONS: off B3072 Bournemouth to Verwood road (last road at N end of village), 8 miles N of Bournemouth, 6 miles NE of Wimborne. Public transport: buses, but limited at weekends

OPENING TIMES: Sun and BH 2–6, 1st Sun in April until 1st Sun in September, inclusive; parties at other times by appointment. House not open

ADMISSION: 65p, OAPs and parties 45p, children 25p.

CAR PARKING: no

TOILETS: yes

REFRESHMENTS: no, but tea and light refreshments in the orchard from 3pm

SHOP: plants for sale

DOGS: no

WHEELCHAIR ACCESS: yes. Toilets for the disabled: no

PEAK MONTHS: a year-round garden, most colourful in May and June

NOTABLE FEATURES: great quantity of rare and unusual plants, trees and shrubs

This half-acre garden in a residential area near Bournemouth is crammed with interesting specimens and collections—dwarf conifers, grey and silver-leaved and variegated plants, herbs, ferns, grasses, heathers and herbaceous plants, along with many rare and unusual shrubs and trees. There are now over 700 shrubs, planned for year-round and foliage interest. Mr Stanley Cherry, who with his wife Janet has owned and developed the garden since 1966, admits cheerfully that 'we're about three times overplanted according to the rules'—but though experts might disapprove, the plants are obviously happy and very well cared for.

The garden suffered badly in the storms of November 1989 and January 1990; a number of trees required surgery, others now lean at angles and one of a pair of 40ft golden chamaecyparis was lost. Reconstruction is underway.

You are likely to meet both Mr and Mrs Cherry either at the gate or in the garden itself, and they are very willing to answer questions. Labelling is comprehensive—Dymo tape on white plastic labels—and arrows helpfully indicate the best route round. All kinds of free leaflets and catalogues are available from the information centre—a small summerhouse on the lawn—including details of other local gardens, weather reports and extensive newspaper correspondence on the building of the Burma to Siam railway.

Immediately above the entrance gate to your right is *Laburnocytisus Adamii*, a cross between a laburnum and *Cytisus purpureus*, purple broom. This is quite a botanical curiosity nowadays, though it was more common at the beginning of the century. In May it produces yellow and sometimes pink laburnum flowers and purple broom blossoms, all together at the top of the tree. In the left border is a weeping berberis (*B. thunbergii* 'Aurea') and a variegated holly. Against the house front is a tall pineapple or Moroccan broom (*Cytisus battandieri*) above more berberis and cotoneaster.

The two limestone statues on either side of the front door—one a Toby jug replica, the other a decently clothed Adam, taken from a woodcut in a Victorian Bible—were made in 1939 by a stonemason in Buckinghamshire.

Right of the door is a group of conifers—perhaps rather unwisely situated so near to the house—*Juniperus chinensis* 'Kaizuka' mixing attractively with *Chamaecyparis pisifera* 'Boulevard', a tall cone of *Thuja occidentalis* 'Rhinegold', *Juniperus chinensis* 'Ob-longa', offering two shades of foliage, and spreading *Juniperus* x *media* 'Pfitzeriana'. Bright tigridias (peacock tiger flowers) also flourish in this protected spot—their delicate flowers last only a day.

From a seat near the path you can admire stone urns planted with lavender and *Glechoma hederacea* 'Variegata' or step across to explore beds of gold and silver-leaved plants.

An impressive bed of fastigiate conifers borders the lawn. These were planted in 1976 as an experiment to discover which conifers sold by local nurserymen were truly 'dwarf' and which merely slow-growing. The race is on between bright green *Chamaecyparis lawsoniana* 'Erecta', *C. l. 'Columnaris Glauca', C. l.* 'Allumii', *Juniperus communis* 'Hibernica' and *Cupressus chinensis* 'Stricta', among others. At their feet, not competing, are various spreading and small bush conifers, including the attractive *Juniperus squa-mata* 'Blue Star'.

Passing to your right a large flagpole (the Scottish flag is raised on celebratory occasions) and a graceful birch (*Betula albo-sinensis*, planted in 1980), follow the arrows round past shrub beds to the main lawn. Here by the small pool is *Decaisnea fargesii*, the blue bean tree, which produces seed cases like blue broad beans. The pool itself is crammed with aquatic plants, including three varieties of water lily, and well hedged in with box, forsythia and self-seeded *Cotoneaster simonsii*—along with a stone trough containing dwarf conifers and alpines. The total effect is far from restful: this is 'water gardening' at its most intense.

Highbury has an impressive collection of ferns, inconspicuous beneath a towering golden privet, but worth searching for and well labelled when eventually discovered. Especially fascinating are the cristate or crested ferns, with divisions like fingers at the leaf ends—a deformity highly valued by the Victorians.

The lower part of the garden is rather cluttered up with statues, including a Venus, a David and an unnerving skull. The trees and shrubs are more interesting: *Acer platanoides* (the Norway maple), *Ginkgo biloba* and *Rhus glabra* 'Laciniata' frame a large circular heather bed. *Trochadendron aralioides*, greatly prized by flower arrangers, displays its little green umbrellas near the statue of a sleepy Buddha.

The paved garden comes next, surrounded by a thick shrubbery of specimen trees and shrubs, large and small. *Eucalyptus ni-phophila*, the alpine snow gum; *Cercidyphyllum japonicum* with its striking heart-shaped leaves; *Choisya ternata*, the Mexican orange blossom; and far too many others to mention. Look out for *Illicium anicatum*, the strong-smelling and very slow-growing aniseed tree, below *Itea ilicifolia* with its long catkins in July. Also *Colletia cruciata*, an unusual spiny shrub, shaped like an anchor, and the very rare *Lycestaria crocothyrsos*, collected by Kingdon Ward from Assam in 1929, which has yellow flowers and green gooseberry-like fruits.

Many small plants and shrubs enjoy the shelter and shade here, along with a collection of dwarf spring bulbs, planted in memory of family members, pets and friends. One border is devoted to herbs—soapwort, tansy, sweet bergamot, sweet Cicely, Solomon's seal and lovage, to name but a few—and this leads down to a narrow box-edged bed of 16C and 17C plants, including two charming specimens of hedgehog holly (*Ilex aquifolia*), the first holly to be cultivated in England.

Follow the path on to the enclosed lower garden, near the plant sales area. Here are conifers, heathers, more shade-loving plants and many lovely grasses—angel's fishing rod (*Dierama pulcherrima*), blue grass (*Festuca glauca*), squirrel tail grass (*Mordeum jubatum*), quaking grass (*Briza media*). A cunninghamia or Chinese fir stands in this garden, a relation of the monkey puzzle, turning red in winter. You should also find *Paliurus spina-christi*, the crown of thorns shrub, with its seed heads like little hats, silver-leaved symphoricarpus 'Highbury Silver', a garden original, and plentiful berberis, including white-stemmed *B. dictophylla*.

The plant sales shed is overhung by an enormous *Salix fragilis* or crack willow. Take this opportunity of buying *Chamaecyparis lawsoniana* 'Highbury Gold', propagated from a chance sport on a tree in the garden. The path leads onwards under large trees planted in 1910 to the Mountbatten memorial garden, a small orchard and a shelter bed for growing plants of doubtful hardiness. The greenhouse contains rare plants and interesting succulents, including a collection of lithops (living stones) from South Africa.

You can drink tea under the trees and chat with Mr or Mrs Cherry; their knowledge, enthusiasm and kindness make any visit to Highbury a memorable and very pleasant experience.

Ivy Cottage

ADDRESS AND TELEPHONE: Ivy Cottage, Aller Lane, Ansty, Dorchester, Dorset, DT2 7PX. Tel. Milton Abbas (0258) 880053

OWNERS: Anne and Alan Stevens

DIRECTIONS: 12 miles N of Dorchester. A354 from Puddletown to Blandford; after Blue Vinney Inn take first left signed Dewlish/Cheslebourne, through Cheslebourne to Ansty then first right before Fox Inn. No public transport available

OPENING TIMES: every Thurs beginning April to end October 10–5, also certain Sun (see National Gardens Scheme Book for Sunday openings). House not open

ADMISSION: £1, children 20p. Coach parties by prior arrangement

CAR PARKING: no

TOILETS: yes

REFRESHMENTS: teas on Sun only

SHOP: plant sales

DOGS: no

WHEELCHAIR ACCESS: no, the garden slopes steeply and the bridges are narrow. Toilets for the disabled: no

PEAK MONTHS: all year round

NOTABLE FEATURES: unusual perennials; moisture-loving plants; specimen trees and shrubs; spring bulbs; raised alpine beds

This 1½-acre garden will delight anyone interested in unusual perennials and moisture-loving plants: it also has many interesting trees and is good for spring bulbs. It is now largely managed and maintained by Anne and Alan Stevens; they laid it out together in the early 1960s and have been opening it to the public since 1980.

Lying 400ft above sea level, the garden is vulnerable to cold north-east winds and frost, but is shielded by a poplar windbreak, with conifers, holly and yew to the north. No tender plants can be grown here, and even half-hardy specimens must be taken indoors in winter. The main lawn area is on a south-west-facing slope, with the cottage at the top.

Standing by the cottage, not far from the garden entrance, you can appreciate not only the artistry of the rich flower border to your left, leading in great sweeps and curves down to the lower garden, and the island bed to your right, but also the trees—silvery poplars and willows offset by conifers. The hedge behind the border is an intriguing mix of yew, beech, privet, hawthorn, hazel, sycamore, holly, ash, lonicera, field maple and no doubt many more—the whole providing both shelter and winter interest.

A narrow stream runs through the garden, crossed by small plank bridges. The garden has a number of natural springs, which keep the soil damp, and Mrs Stevens has taken the opportunity to plant plenty of moisture-lovers. At the end of May, the asiatic primulas are at their best—Mrs Stevens has over 40 varieties, and they self-seed all over the place, thriving in the rich moist soil. She also has the National Reference Collections of lobelias and trollius.

Many small and medium-sized specimen trees grace the lower part of the garden, such as *Liquidambar styraciflua*, the sweet gum, *Davidia involucrata* (not yet old enough to display its 'paper hand-kerchiefs') and several malus, including *M. floribunda* with a clematis growing through it. Beyond is a vegetable plot, laid out simply but attractively. Further up, by the house, are various conifers.

Mrs Stevens is usually on hand to discuss plants and planting with visitors.

COUNTY DURHAM

Bowes Museum

ADDRESS AND TELEPHONE: The Bowes Museum, Barnard Castle, County Durham, DL12 8NP. Tel. Teesdale (0833) 690606

OWNERS: administered by Durham County Council

DIRECTIONS: located in town of Barnard Castle 12 miles along the A66 from Scotch Corner. Signposted through town. Public transport: buses from Darlington, Richmond, Bishop Auckland and Upper Teesdale. Darlington BR 17 miles

OPENING TIMES: all year round (except the week leading to

Christmas and 1 January), daily 10 5.30, Sun 2–5 (note March, April and October the museum closes at 5 and from November to February closes at 4)

ADMISSION: free. Coach parties by prior arrangement

CAR PARKING: yes

TOILETS: yes

REFRESHMENTS: café open April to September

SHOP: yes

DOGS: on lead in grounds

WHEELCHAIR ACCESS: yes, but strong pusher needed for wheelchairs or descend from terrace via sloping driveway. Toilets for the disabled: yes

PEAK SEASON: parterre best with spring and summer bedding

NOTABLE FEATURES: French style parterre; great variety of trees

The Bowes Museum was founded by Josephine Bowes (1825–74), the French wife of John Bowes (1811–85), the last of an old County Durham family. Both husband and wife were keen collectors of art. In 1862 Mrs Bowes sold the Château Dubarry at Louveciennes and used the proceeds to buy land at Barnard Castle for the museum. Pockets of land were purchased from five different owners between 1864 and 1870, amounting in all to about 20 acres, and by 1869 Mrs Bowes had laid the foundation stone for the museum building, which was designed by Jules Pellechet.

Mrs Bowes died in 1874, two years before the museum roof was completed, but in her will she set out detailed instructions for the museum, arranging for the appointment and function of a management committee, specifying opening hours and even making provision for fire precautions and insurance. It is not clear exactly what she had in mind for the grounds, except that the landscape should be a formal framework for the museum building.

After the death of his wife, John Bowes lost much of his enthusiasm for the project but continued to oversee the construction of the building, the landscaping of the grounds and the transportation of the collection from France. Financial problems caused by fluctuations of his coal investments delayed the official opening until seven years after his death. The museum was finally opened to the public in 1892 and received nearly 63,000 visitors in the first year.

It was, and remains, an impressive sight. Tonnes of earth had been excavated to create the high terrace on which the museum stands, looking out across the valley to the distant Pennines. A parterre was laid out below, in the French manner with raised beds and gravel walks. The basic layout remains the same today, but the beds have been altered. Fleurs-de-lis—for the kings and queens of France—and shell-like scallops now form the basis of the pattern, picked out with 1600 yds of low box hedging and filled with tulips and forget-me-nots in spring and 8000 geraniums in summer; conical shaped yews mark each corner. The pattern also incorporates coloured gravels and is repeated either side of the elliptical pool. This design was introduced in 1982/3; at the same time, three fountains were installed in the pool.

The parterre makes a stunning sight when viewed from the balustraded terrace. To appreciate its scale at ground level, climb down one of the zig-zag flights of steps. A herbaceous border lies immediately below the wall. The fountain head in the centre is a replica of a bronze mask believed to have been made in the 17C for the water gardens at St Cloud near Paris. The original mask can be seen in the museum, along with the architect's plans and drawings for the building, terrace and entrance gates.

Some of the excess spoil from the excavation work which created the terrace was spread to either side of the parterre to make curving grassy banks and mounds which rise towards the terrace, forming an amphitheatre around the parterre.

The rest of the grounds are more informal in character. John Bowes was interested in trees and planted a great variety. A double row of lime trees was established around part of the perimeter—these are now mature and have attained a magnificent size.

South-west of the parterre, partly hidden by a large monkey puzzle tree (*Araucaria araucana*) and a mound topped with silver birches, rowans and pines, is the Roman Catholic chapel of St Mary. Below a crucifix on the rear wall is the grave of John and Josephine Bowes, whose remains were reburied here when the chapel was completed in 1928.

The grand wrought iron entrance gates, with a lodge either side, lie on the central axis of the museum building and parterre and were made by J.W. Singer and Sons of Frome, Somerset, in 1907. Beyond each lodge (now the museum's Archaeology Department) are war memorials, the one to the west commemorating soldiers of the Durham Light Infantry and to the east the servicemen of Barnard Castle, who died in the 1914–18 and 1939–45 wars. Stone artefacts under the lime trees, behind the East Lodge, include masonry from Piercebridge Roman Fort and a cup and ring stone from Greta Bridge.

The flat lawn with borders of roses and shrubs lying due east of the museum marks the first site of the Catholic chapel. Begun in 1875, it rose to window height and was then demolished, partly for financial reasons and partly because of access problems. This area is now a picnic site and beyond lie a bowling green and tennis courts. Although run by local clubs, these may be used by non-members—apply for day tickets at the museum reception.

A thick barrier of shrubs beneath trees conceals the boundary wall. Celandines and bluebells bloom here in spring. Another part of the grounds worth a visit is the grassy mound close to the car park north-west of the museum. A brick path, with grass growing through the cracks, winds to the top of the mound, where there is a lawn, and statues representing leaders of Church and State through history. These statues were removed from the Houses of Parliament during renovation work in the 1970s and acquired by the musuem.

In 1981 and 1982 some 69 specimen trees were planted throughout the grounds to extend interest and ensure continuity. There are common varieties such as field maples (*Acer campestre*), English yew (*Taxus baccata*), horse chestnuts (*Aesculus hippocastanum*) and common beech (*Fagus sylvatica*), as well as more decorative ones such as Raywood ash (*Fraxinus oxycarpa* 'Raywood') which turns plum purple in autumn and the weeping silver lime (*Tilia petiolaris*), one of the most beautiful of all weeping trees. The conifers include a young Wellingtonia (*Sequoiadendron giganteum*) and Douglas fir (*Pseudotsuga menziesii*).

The gardening staff regularly prepare a large number of tubs and troughs of indoor plants—the superb evergreen *Nerium oleander* with large white blooms, *Ficus benjamina*, agapanthus, and others—to decorate rooms and galleries within the museum building.

Raby Castle

ADDRESS AND TELEPHONE: Raby Castle, Staindrop, near Darlington, County Durham DL2 3AH. Tel. (0833) 60202

OWNER: The Rt. Hon. Lord Barnard

DIRECTIONS: 1 mile N of Staindrop on the A688 Barnard Castle to Bishop Auckland road. Public transport: United/UK Transport service 8 Bishop Auckland to Barnard Castle, every 2 hours 10–4 (on Sun irregular service)

OPENING TIMES: Easter to end of September; May and June, Wed and Sun; July, August and September, daily except Sat; BH, Sat, Sun, Mon and Tues. Park and gardens 11–5.30; castle 1–5. No admission after 4.30

ADMISSION: castle and gardens £2.25, OAPs £1.75, children £1.20; gardens and coach house only 80p, OAPs/children 60p

CAR PARKING: yes

TOILETS: yes

REFRESHMENTS: café

SHOP: yes

DOGS: not in garden, on lead in park

WHEELCHAIR ACCESS: yes. Although there are steps within the walled garden there are alternative routes suitable for wheelchair users. Toilets for the disabled: yes

PEAK SEASON: herbaceous borders best June, July and August

NOTABLE FEATURES: walled garden containing individual gardens; ancient yew hedges and fig tree; herbaceous borders; shrub beds; roses; climbing plants

Raby Castle makes an immediately striking impression, glimpsed from the A688—an imposing structure, set on rising ground, with battlemented walls and square crenellated towers. Although it looks like a fortress, it was intended more as a strongly defended residence.

The Nevills built Raby castle in the 14C and occupied it until 1569, when, following the failure of the Rising of the North, it was delivered into the hands of the Crown. Sir Henry Vane the Elder bought it in 1626 and it remains in his family's possession—the present owner is the 11th Lord Barnard.

Over the centuries the castle has been subjected to several

*The walled gardens at Raby Castle cover five acres
and lie on a south-facing slope. (Neil Jinkerson.
Jarrold Colour Publications)*

schemes of renovation and improvement and the land around it
has also altered considerably. By the end of the 18C the moat had
been drained, stables and outbuildings constructed and two large
ponds created. Thomas White, a pupil of Capability Brown, was
called in by the 2nd Lord Barnard during the 1740s, to landscape
the park.

Further planting of the parkland has been carried out by the 10th
Lord Barnard, a keen forester—today more than 30 types of tree
can be seen in clumps and plantations on land grazed by sheep,
red and fallow deer and a herd of Longhorn cattle.

Thomas White was also responsible for designing the complex
of walled gardens, on a south-facing slope some distance to the
north of the castle. The original walled garden at Raby was much
larger than the present enclosed 5 acres. Many alterations and
developments have been made over the centuries, and especially
during the last 10 or 15 years, but several original features have
been retained in the current layout of lawns, flower beds and
herbaceous borders.

The walls were built in the 18C from locally handmade bricks
and incorporated an internal flue system to provide heat for the
cultivation and ripening of sub-tropical fruit. Today the apricots
have been replaced by apples and the peaches by pears, but a very
old fig tree survives on the south terrace, overlooking the park.
Believed to have been brought from Italy by William Harry, Lord
Barnard, c 1786, this white Ischia fig now completely fills a 60ft
long house, constructed around it in 1899.

The south terrace and the Raby Fig are reached by a gateway in
the centre of the lower wall, which features a fine wrought iron
gate a little older than the walls themselves. Bearing the monogram

of Christopher, the 1st Lord Barnard, this gate was designed by James Gibbs in the early part of the 18C and was originally hung at Shipbourne Church, near the Vane family seat of Fairlawn in Kent. In the latter part of the last century the church underwent repairs and the gate was given to the 9th Lord Barnard by Fairlawn's owner, Mr Cazalet.

Stretching up the slope from this gate is an enormous double yew hedge, which pre-dates the walled garden by several centuries and which, according to tradition, was planted by the first owners of the castle to provide wood for bows. Now the huge lumpy hedges form boundaries within the walled garden.

Until recently, the large garden compartment to the far west served as a kitchen garden and nursery; now mostly laid to lawn, it awaits development. The remaining fruit, vegetables and flowers for cutting have been confined to one side and apples, pears and roses are trained along the brick walls. Growing against the lower wall is the Raby redcurrant, developed by a head gardener here in the 19C and now more than 120 years old. For colour this garden has borders of shrubs and herbaceous plants and watching over the scene is an unusual Gothic-style gardeners' cottage, designed by the architect James Paine in the 18C.

The next three sections of the walled garden are divided into long narrow compartments by the ancient yew hedges and brick walls. At the top of the first is an ornate conservatory—a replica of an earlier one—with vine and jasmine covered pergolas to either side. Two raised plant beds are designed especially for disabled or blind visitors and filled with plants unusual to touch or of pleasant scent. In front of the conservatory is a sloping lawn, planted with beds of roses around a statue. A beech hedge screens off another garden at the foot of the slope, where curving beds and borders of informal design display heathers and low-growing conifers.

The central walled garden section between the mammoth yew hedges, features a pink/purple and silver border at the top end, overlooking a rose lawn. Beds of yellow, pink, red, peach and white roses lead the eye down the slope to a large circular basin pool. Waterlilies open on the pool in summer, and in the centre is a statue on a small rockery island. Beyond the basin, the path is flanked by lavender and hypericum, and runs down to a gateway leading to the south terrace.

A summerhouse is set against the upper wall of the next compartment, to the east. The white Japanese Chippendale seat inside was made according to a design drawn by James Paine, recently discovered in the castle archives. A drawing for a gazebo has also been recovered.

Around the summerhouse are splendid borders of shrubs and herbaceous plants, while in front is a formal rose garden arranged around a square, with a standard 'Albertine' rose for a centrepiece. Lower down the slope, young yew hedges create four geometrically shaped enclosures—each with a variegated maple in the centre.

The final garden, the East Garden, is much larger and like the West Garden, largely laid to lawn. The most interesting feature here is the summer border running along the top, below the wall. Designed by the dowager Lady Barnard, the present Lord Barnard's mother, this contains mainly old varieties of plants. Blue and yellow predominate, with shrubs such as *Buddleia alternifolia*, and herbaceous perennials such as the bright yellow *Baptisia tintoria* and spiky flowered *Asphodeline lutea*.

The walls of the East Garden support a great number of shrubs and climbers, including buddleias, clematis and the 'Wedding Day' rose—a vigorous climber characterised by its red thorns and its richly perfumed blooms, which are deep yellow in bud and open to a creamy white before turning pinkish. The expanse of sloping lawn is broken by just two trees—the purple-leaved *Malus purpurea* and a fine tulip tree (*Liriodendron tulipifera*), easily recognised by its oddly shaped leaves and mass of golden foliage in autumn. More trees may be planted here in the future.

ESSEX

Beth Chatto Gardens

ADDRESS AND TELEPHONE: White Barn House, Elmstead Market, Colchester, Essex CO7 7DB. Tel. (0206) 822007

OWNER: Mrs Beth Chatto

DIRECTIONS: 5 miles from Colchester, ¼ mile E of Elmstead Market, on the A133. Public transport: BR to Colchester, then taxi (7 miles)

OPENING TIMES: 1 March to 31 October, Mon to Sat 9–5. November to February, Mon to Fri 9–4. Closed Sun and BH and for 2 weeks over Christmas and New Year. House not open

ADMISSION: £1, children free. Coach parties by prior arrangement

CAR PARKING: yes

TOILETS: yes

REFRESHMENTS: no

SHOP: nursery

DOGS: no

WHEELCHAIR ACCESS: yes. Toilets for the disabled: no

PEAK MONTHS: May to September

NOTABLE FEATURES: distinctive quality of planting

Most gardens reflect their creators' preference and taste; only a few set an original style. Beth Chatto's garden at Elmstead Market is one of the latter kind and few people who visit it, or who have seen her displays at Chelsea over the last ten years, can mistake its quality. Mrs Chatto is one of this century's most creative and influential gardeners.

Beth Chatto herself gives a clue to her methods in her book *The Dry Garden* when she writes: 'In deciding what to plant I first select each plant, tree or shrub for its shape and character, not for the colour of its flowers', adding 'Colour schemes often seem to make themselves'. While other gardeners may also follow this method, nowhere is it practised more effectively. The outstanding impression of the Beth Chatto gardens (for there are many gardens in one) is of respect and enthusiasm for the whole plant, not just the flower.

Few of the more usual garden hybrids or cultivars—delphiniums, carnations, chrysanthemums or hybrid tea roses—are to be seen here. Colour, of which there is a great deal, though not of the bedding-out variety, is constantly enhanced by structure: the juxtaposition of spike and curving mound, of feathery spray and bold shiny leaf, of spreading plant under fastigiate column. Here the delicate shades of a minute flower ('the sort of thing we used to throw on the bonfire to burn' as one contemptuous visitor to Chelsea was overheard to say) is preferred to more showy blossoms, especially to those whose leaves and habit do not 'earn their keep'.

The gardens, laid out in what was in 1960 'a small depression' and is now a shallow valley, take advantage of what less tenacious gardeners might find a handicap: the dry windy climate of East Anglia, where the rainfall averages 20in. a year. Beds of plants that will tolerate drought have been laid out, both in sun and shade, and the enriching of the soil with organic matter and mulches is so successful that no watering is ever carried out after the initial planting period, however scorching the summer.

The driest ground—on the slopes leading to the house and in the beds on its south side—is reserved for Mediterranean plants that love to bake in the heat; in complete contrast, the wetland at the bottom of the valley, where a small stream has been used to create four large ponds, nurtures lush displays of bog and water plants.

As you enter the garden proper, you come first to these water gardens, set between sloping grass walks. The first pool is dominated by a large oak—one of an original group which preceded the garden proper—a swamp cypress (*Taxodium distichum*) and a weeping willow (*Salix* x *chrysocoma*). In the beds beneath and on the fringes of the pool grow some striking tall plants: a clear green *Angelica archangelica* with its great heads of flowers like cow parsley and *Rodgersia podophylla* x 'Rotlaub' with triangular bronze leaves and feathery panicles. The flat pale pink heads of *Peltiphyllum peltatum* set on red hairy stems arrive in early spring, to be followed by huge scalloped leaves. There are mounds of ornamental grass (green and white miscanthus) dwarf bright yellow trollius, bold *Iris versicolor* and *Iris laevigata* and delicate *Houttuynia cordata* 'Flore Pleno', whose bright red stems carry glaucous heart-shaped leaves and double cones of white flowers.

By the waterside here and around the succeeding ponds grow two varieties of the bog arum—yellow-flowered *Lysichiton americanus* from California, and its relative, the white *Lysichiton camtschatcensis* from Japan (in this garden, the paddle-shaped leaves grow to enormous size). Also in the giant class—the giant of them all—is *Gunnera manicata*.

On a more modest scale, there are plantings of red, mauve and pink candelabra primulas; of *Myosotis scorpioides* 'Mermaid', the water forget-me-not, and *Pontederia cordata*, the blue pickerel weed. Growing away from the water's edge, but enjoying the damp, are many astilbes: *A. taquetii* 'Superba', with pink flowers on red stems, and *A. chinensis* 'Pumila'. These delicate plants are underpinned by the broad shapely leaves of hostas—notably blue-green

H. sieboldiana and the handsome glaucous yellow-edged *Hosta sieboldiana* 'Frances Williams'.

A beautiful white cherry, prunus 'Tai Haku', marks the third pond, with a tall conical dawn redwood (*Metasequoia glyptostroboides*) and a sweet gum (*Liquidambar styraciflua*), brilliant-leaved in autumn. Under the prunus are plantings of asters: *A. ericoides* in prostrate form, *A. cordifolius* 'Silver Spray' and *A. tradescantii*, producing tiny sprays of white flowers. There is the splendid green and white-leaved *Symphytum* x *uplandicum* 'Variegatum' (variegated comfrey), and *Astrantia major* 'Sunningdale's Variety'. This, one of the loveliest of variegated plants, has creamy yellow leaves splashed with two shades of green, which dim slightly when it produces its greeny-white, purple-centred stars of flower, but regain variegation later.

At this point the water narrows to a stream, forming the canal bed, which is shaded by an English oak and a pin oak (*Quercus palustris*); great bushes of *Viburnum plicatum* 'Mariesii', whose layered branches are loaded in spring with flat heads of white flower; and a red acer. This is the thickest and most lush planting in the garden: iris, ferns, and, unusually, spiked heads of *Phormium tenax*, the New Zealand flax, flourish in the damp; there are marsh marigolds, both single and double, rushes and different shades of pink knotweed (polygonum). We also saw the graceful golden meadowsweet (*Filipendula ulmaria* 'Aurea') and a *Senecio smithii*; not the usual silver variety, but one with enormous blue-green leaves and heads of white daisies held separate and high.

As an extension of the canal bed, and a full stop to the water gardens before the stream drops into the reservoir, a pool has been created around a swamp cypress. Here, among others, grow plants of tall *Kirengeshoma palmata*, whose tall stems bear waxy yellow flowers in autumn, which droop gracefully from red stems over light green lobed leaves.

One of the great pleasures of the Chatto gardens is the presence of completely different garden areas, lying side by side. From damp you step to dry—in this case to a bed of sun-loving plants, which grow, as the short but informative garden guide tells you, on retentive silt. This island bed, or rather the western side of it, faces the ponds, while the eastern, shady side gives home to rhododendrons and myriads of bulbs in the spring. We saw some memorable plant associations: under pale pink prunus, dark red *Berberis thunbergii* and blue-green hostas beside the heart-shaped evergreen leaves of *Epimedium perralderianum*; a dark black fritillary waving above brilliant blue ajuga, pink-flowered saxifrage and gold-edged hosta; blue ajuga showing again to brilliant effect under orange-red *Euphorbia griffithii* 'Fireglow'; the splendid ribbed leaves of the white helleborine (*Veratrum album*) near a white *Paeonia emodi*. Used in different plant combinations were clumps of Bowles golden grass, blue-black *Geranium punctatum variegatum*, clumps of mauve and white viola 'Milkmaid' and, a constant refrain, *Alchemilla mollis*, its rain-sheltering leaves framing bright lime-green flower sprays. At the point of the bed is the amazing *Rheum alexandrae*, a pillar of neatly folded yellow bracts, aging to red and concealing tiny red flowers.

A particular problem for any gardener is growing on clay, and at the south end of the small valley, Mrs Chatto has tackled the problem of a shady clay bank. This was created, as she describes in *The Damp Garden*, by depositing field soil on top of 'sticky, plasticine like clay', and by terracing the resulting bank with logs, to create three levels. After top dressing, the bank was then planted with balsam poplar (*Populus trichocarpa* x *balsamea*), a golden poplar (*Populus* x *serotina* 'Aurea') and a silver willow, together with spruces and hollies, both plain and variegated.

Flourishing beneath these trees in May we saw the charming single yellow peony *Paeonia mlokosewitschii*; the white three-petalled flowers of trillium; a dark purple species clematis, 'Pamela Jackman', growing through a viburnum; the contrasting shapes of neat Solomon's seal and its cousin, feathery *Smilacina racemosa*. There were dark blue aquilegias, dark red bergenias, and a red campion, commonly found in the hedgerows but looking entirely at home here.

Under a well-established paulownia, with purple foxglove-like flowers, we found recent plantings of shade tolerant plants: purple *Viola gracilis* and the yellow mountain pansy, *V. lutea*; lithospermum 'Heavenly Blue' mingling with mauve heather; a flood of mauve thyme *Thymus longicaulis* and a very low-growing gold potentilla, *P. tabernaemontani* 'Goldrauschi'. In the background are pale pink cow parsley, foxgloves and Solomon's seal; and three varieties of tiarella: *T. cordifolia* with white flowers and bright green leaves; the pink buds of *T. wherryi*; and the lime green flowers of *T. breweri*. Bright golden grass (*Millium effusum* 'Aureum') lightens the shade.

The path here turns back towards the house and you climb up past the heat loving plants: *Sedum rosea, Ballota pseudodictamnus* and the fleshy *Euphorbia myrsinities*. There are clumps of pale pink thrift, tall alliums and variegated rue, pale spikes of *Iris pallida*, pink cistus spilling over the path and the tubular yellow flowers between grey-green leaves of *Onosma albo-roseum*. There are thymes, sage and lavender and the lovely viola 'Bowles Black'.

Passing the house, you come to raised beds made from concrete blocks, with red ragstone (the only local stone) used for the plants to grow over. Here the predominant impression is of contrasting greys, silvers, mauves, whites and yellows—a flood of silver-white *Cerastium columnae* mingling with feathery *Artemisia discolor*, almost identically matched in colour; a striking dark red sempervivum; three contrasting thymes, lemon-scented *T.* x *citriodorus* 'Silver Queen', *T. doerfleri* with lavender-pink flowers, and *T.* 'Golden Carpet'.

Here too are the pale green rosettes of *Raoulia hookeri* from New Zealand; French lavender (*L. stoechas*); hairy-leaved, yellow *Phlomis fruticans*, woolly silver ballota and glowing brightly, the acid yellow flowers of *Euphorbia polychroma* and great clumps of *Euphorbia characias wulfenii*. Above all this stand graceful shrubs small trees and shrubs: the pineapple broom (*Cytisus battandieri*) from North Africa; the Mount Etna broom (*Genista aetnensis*); grey-leaved *Buddleia fallowiana* and a selection of smaller conifers providing a sculptured backdrop.

The most recent extension to the garden is a collection of island beds near the reservoir (a small lake, adjoining the property). These beds are built a round single trees or groups of shrubs: *Eucalyptus gunnii*, silver cornus, willow and birch and dark green, gold and silver conifers including a Himalayan cedar (*Cedrus deodara*). There are contrasting shrubs and sub-shrubs, herbaceous plants and bulbs. It is a relaxing and informal place to wander at the end of your garden tour, which has probably stretched your mind and demanded your constant attention.

A last pleasure: along the entrance drive are two long borders leading to some separate beds near the house. Here, where you park, you can also picnic on the grass or just sit and enjoy a selection of shrubs and plants that reflects those in the enclosed garden and demonstrates once more Mrs Chatto's vast knowledge of her subject and highly individual style.

Hyde Hall

ADDRESS AND TELEPHONE: Hyde Hall Garden, Rettendon, Chelmsford, Essex. Tel. Chelmsford (0245) 400256

OWNERS: Hyde Hall Garden Trust

DIRECTIONS: in Rettendon, off the A130 Chelmsford to Southend road. Public transport: not easy, hourly bus service between Chelmsford and Southend then 1 mile walk

OPENING TIMES: 29 March to 30 October, Sun, Wed and BH 11–6. Also other times by appointment. House not open

ADMISSION: £1.50, OAPs £1, children free. Coach parties: horticultural and other societies are welcomed

CAR PARKING: yes

TOILETS: yes

REFRESHMENTS: no

SHOP: no

DOGS: yes, on lead

WHEELCHAIR ACCESS: yes, two invalid chairs available. Toilets for the disabled: yes

PEAK MONTHS: April to September

NOTABLE FEATURES: many

The top of a windy hill in Essex is not the most predictable location for a garden; and even after you have turned out of Buckhatch Lane and are climbing the hill by a winding cinder road, it is some time before you glimpse flowering trees and Austrian pines near the car park. Stepping into the garden itself is like entering a different world.

It is now over 30 years since Dr and Mrs Robinson came to farm at Hyde Hall. As the garden grew and developed, they eventually retired from farming, but the old farm buildings remain and the orchard slope to the north of the estate (which now houses most of the National Collection of malus or flowering cherries), is still known as the Pig Park. Wandering through this area in early spring,

Hyde Hall: Diascia rigescens on a windy Essex hillside. (Harry Smith)

when it is alight with blossom—the wine-red flowers of M. 'Profusion' and the white flowers of the spreading bush M. *sargentii*, among many others—it is hard to visualise pigs rooting around.

This large informal slope is also planted with garryas, many varieties of camellia, and magnolias (mainly M. x *soulangiana*). There are also herbaceous plants and shrub roses— many different varieties of *Rosa moyesii*, a single bush of the hybrid perpetual R. 'Reine des Violettes', growing flat as a carpet, and the rampant white climber R. *filipes* 'Kiftsgate', disciplined over supporting hoops in a circular bed.

Exploring further along behind the house, you will find a kitchen garden and a planting of slow-growing conifers and shrubs; nearby a statue of Hermione is surrounded by shade-loving ferns, hellebores and hydrangeas. The tea yard is incorporated within the farm buildings, and centres on a golden catalpa.

The most intensive and spectacular planting, however, lies to the south and south-east of the house. In early summer, *Fremontodendron californicum* displays its bright yellow cup flowers on the first outhouse wall, along with ceanothus 'Puget Blue', a pink climbing rose, a star jasmine (trachellospermum), a variegated ivy, an Australian tea tree (leptospermum), with pink and white flowers, and *Arbutus menziesii* with peeling cinnamon-coloured bark and orange-red strawberry-like fruits later in the season. This prolific planting is characteristic of the Robinsons' style and bears witness to their enormous enjoyment of plants and shrubs, which flourish in response.

Two more ceanothus grow against the front of the house—*C. arboreus* 'Trewithin Blue', and a small *C. gloriosus*—also two pittosporums, green and white 'Irene Paterson', another fremontodendron and a white wisteria draped over the porch.

Between the house and the top pond is a planting of brightly coloured pansies, forget-me-nots, species tulips, bellis and arabis, under a flowering cherry. This dazzling medley of colours is matched by the nearby border of red and yellow wallflowers and tulips, backing a long bed of hybrid tea and half standard roses.

The great top pond stretches nearly the whole width of the garden. This is a former farm pond, now cleared out and deepened, planted with waterlilies and bordered by shrubs and flowers. Fish—some of quite alarming size—glide in the still depths.

West of the pond is an alpine bed and a paved area furnished with planted stone pots and two stone seats. Mounds of bright yellow alyssum, silver sedum, woolly-leaved ballota and miniature aquilegia overspill the dry-brick walls, and the damp waterside verges are planted with feathery astilbe, hostas, primulas and trollius.

From here, you can look down the full length of the water. The northern side is bordered by fastigiate yews, a clear blue rosemary (not yet identified), *Daphne tangutica* with white, purple-splashed flowers, three junipers (*Juniperus communis* 'Compressa'), yellow potentilla, deep blue gentians and many others.

Passing under a graceful specimen of *Eleagnus angustifolia* 'Caspica', with silver willow-like leaves, you come to the far end of the pond and a brick-edged bed, overhung by a swamp cypress (*Taxodium distichum*) and two tall willows. Great sections of tree trunk have been filled with house leeks (sempervivums) for decorative effect. Among the surrounding hellebores, phlox and variegated grasses, you can see the fascinating purple fingers of *Lathraea clandestina*, a parasite which flourishes on willow roots.

Nearby is a bright gold bed, most of its colour provided by shrub foliage: a very elegant weeping beech (*Fagus sylvatica* 'Aurea Pendula'), gold philadelphus (*P. coronarius* 'Aureus'), golden elder (*Sambucus canadensis* 'Aurea') and a gold holly. There are two varieties of elaeagnus, variegated green and gold, and the invaluable bush honeysuckle, *Lonicera nitida* 'Baggesons Gold'. At a lower level grow gold box and berberis, a gold spiraea, yellow-flowered *Kerria japonica* and yellow almond-scented gorse.

The soil at Hyde Hall is mostly alkaline, so to grow rhododendrons and pieris, plenty of peat and humus had to be dug in. Now they flourish in the woodland garden, north of the pond. Here, and in the nearby Jubilee Garden, more than 30 trees were lost in the hurricanes of October 1987 and January 1990. Here grow less hardy plants and flowering shrubs, with a carpet of *Cyclamen cilicium* in autumn.

The main trees in the woodland are a *Eucalyptus gunnii* (a 10ft shoot from the original tree, planted in 1963), *Magnolia obovata* and a weeping spruce (*Picea breweriana*). Magnolia 'Lennei' flowers purple against an attractive grouping of pale mauve and pale yellow rhododendrons. Here too are bright green and pale variegated acers; tree peonies and the variegated cornus *C. alba* 'Elegantissima', underplanted with Solomon's seal, white trillium and many shades of hosta.

Windbreaks were a first necessity if any of the planting was to survive, and the rose beds to the east are backed with leyland cypresses and laurel. The first long stretch is devoted to old roses—albas, damasks, bourbons and many gallicas—'Tuscany', the maroon old velvet rose; 'Camaieux', white splashed crimson; *R. officinalis*, the apothecary's rose, light crimson; cerise pink 'Belle de Crécy'. Pale pink foxtail lilies (*Eremurus robustus*) have grown and spread by themselves.

Continuing round the edge of the lawn, you come to the modern roses and the Rope Walk—here climbers have been trained along ropes, over beds of hybrid teas, a splendid sight in summer. The nearby iris and herbaceous beds, have been deliberately planned for colour, starting with reds and pinks, and moving through purples and lilacs to blues and whites, oranges and reds, with peony beds in the centre. These beds are at their best in high summer.

In the southern area you can also find the lower pond, fed by a narrow stream which descends through a planting of small conifers, past an alpine scree; here we saw geraniums, species tulips, ajuga, iris and violas; and the dwarf *Salix* x *moorei*. A twisted Pekin willow (*Salix matsudana* 'Caradoc') can be found nearby and not far away is a whole bed of willows, cut back every year for their new yellow, green and silver stems in winter. Winter interest is well provided for with three beds devoted to heathers and conifers, such as *Chamaecyparis obtusa* 'Chaboyadori' with its interesting scooped foliage, low-growing *C. obtusa* 'Nana' and spiny *Pinus nigra* 'Nana'.

Hyde Hall holds the National Collection of viburnums and many can be found in this area: among them *V. opulus*, known as the guelder rose, *V. plicatum tomentosum* with layered branches, and *V. betulifolium* with profuse bright red fruits in autumn. There are also acers, philadelphus, weigelas, golden yews and many more.

On your way out through the farmyard, visit the excellent cool greenhouse, where the climber *Kennedia macrophylla* displays its flame-coloured pea flowers; and *Clianthus puniceus*, the glory pea, its red claws. Nearby are a small alpine house, a conservatory and a warm house.

Dr and Mrs Robinson are generous with their information and assistance when possible, and it is a generous garden, enormously varied and still in the process of development.

GLOUCESTERSHIRE

Barnsley House

ADDRESS AND TELEPHONE: Barnsley House, Cirencester, Gloucestershire GL7 5EE. Tel. Bibury (0285 74) 281

OWNER: Rosemary Verey

DIRECTIONS: on the B4425, 4 miles NE of Cirencester in the village of Barnsley. No public transport available

OPENING TIMES: Mon, Wed, Thurs and Sat 10–6, also two NGS days in May and June 2–6. Other days and parties by appointment. House not open

ADMISSION: £2, OAPs £1, children free. (No charge December to February.) Conducted tour of garden by Mrs Verey (pre-booked parties only): £25 plus VAT

CAR PARKING: yes

TOILETS: yes

REFRESHMENTS: no

SHOP: plants for sale

DOGS: no

WHEELCHAIR ACCESS: vegetable garden not accessible. Toilets for the disabled: no

PEAK MONTHS: all year

NOTABLE FEATURES: decorative vegetable garden; knot garden; herb garden; spring bulbs; herbaceous borders; laburnum walk; autumn colour

Rosemary Verey began to design and plant this garden in 1939, when she and her husband David moved into Barnsley House. It is about 3 miles from Bibury, renowned as the prettiest village in the Cotswolds, 4 miles from Cirencester, where all the Roman roads meet.

Built in 1697 from honey-coloured Cotswold stone, Barnsley House is perfectly matched and complemented by its 4-acre garden; a rare partnership achieved by combining an imaginative, structured layout with softly muted flower colour and bold foliage effect. Mrs Verey emphasises that in a sense 'everything has just happened'—that the garden has been 'tightly planned but also allowed to change and develop'. Whether by chance or the guidance of the gardener however, the result is an ideal balance between interest and repose, excitement and tranquillity.

The north-west front of the house, suddenly revealed after a rather abrupt entrance from the B4425, immediately awakes anticipation, appearing like a hanging tapestry above a neat row of dark *Chamaecyparis lawsoniana* 'Ellwoodii', a flight of steps, a stone dog and sheep on pillars and a sloping lawn, bright with daffodils in spring.

Close to the house, a box hedge is clipped in attractive flowing shapes like pillow lava, under laurel and pyracantha; to the west of the front door, the Chinese Virginia creeper (*Parthenocissus henryana*) spreads its veined leaves, dark red in autumn. A wide lawn lies south-west of the house, a generous sweep of grass bordered by mature trees. In the far corner stands an 18C summerhouse; while in a secluded spot among trees, including the variegated poplar *P. candicans* 'Aurora', a purple sycamore, a whitebeam and the glaucous foliage of *Cedrus atlantica* 'Glauca', stands the statue of an Edwardian lady, net-veiled and hatted.

Formal structures and planting styles throughout the garden hark back to earlier centuries. A charming knot garden is laid out on gravel near the west wall of the house on the lines of the parterres so popular in Italy, France and England in the 16C and 17C. Two squares offer different designs, twisted like Celtic strapwork: the first in two shades of box, the second in box and shiny-leaved *Teucrium chamaedrys*, with a central boss of *Phillyrea angustifolia*, a great favourite in the 16C. Mrs Verey suggests the last as it could be a suitable substitute for box, though it is now seldom used and difficult to obtain. Double topiary orbs of clipped variegated holly stand at the four corners of the knot garden and a small sundial, planted round with purple violas, marks the centre.

A herb garden runs down the east side of the south lawn; here again, Mrs Verey has used low box hedges, this time in large diamond shapes, filled and surrounded with herbs cultivated since early times for use in cooking and medicine. We saw hyssop, rue, chives, camomile, wormwood, sorrel (*Rumex acetosa*, good for salads and soups) yellow marjoram and oregano, grey-leaved *Camphorita balsamita*, which has a very delightful and distinctive smell, and meadowsweet (*Filipendula hexapetala*, a common wild plant with medicinal powers). Mrs Verey recommends planting naturally tall herbs together (fennel, lovage, rosemary) and low herbs next to the edging (chives, thyme, parsley, dwarf hyssop, wall germander, winter savory and alpine strawberries). Box edging gives good protection, though it may take goodness and moisture from the soil; this can be prevented by cutting the roots back close to the plant each spring.

One of Mrs Verey's preferences in garden design is for the main axis of the house to be continued out through the door into the garden. Here, opposite the drawing-room door on the south-east front, a wide path of irregular Cotswold stone has been laid through the centre of the south lawn, offering a vista through to the lower garden. The path is attractively overgrown with spreading clumps of pink, purple, mauve and white rock roses and geraniums: two bordering rows of dark Irish yew, cone-shaped, stand single file on either side. This is a path for looking down, not walking on; it is pleasant to see plants taking precedence. Mrs Verey says she just threw the seeds down to see what happened, a characteristically modest disclaimer, for though spontaneity is encouraged, clear bounds have been established and are rigorously preserved.

Scented plants are grown near the house: west of the drawing-room door an early Dutch honeysuckle, red and yellow, reaches to the first-floor window, rising above *Euonymus fortunei* 'Silver Queen', and on the opposite side of the door the lilac-flowered shrub honeysuckle, *Lonicera syringantha*, puts out its pale sweet-smelling flowers near a dark-leaved myrtle. Wisteria, grown as a shrub, adds to the scented border. The astonishing red succulent *Eaonium arboreum* 'Atropurpureum' adds a touch of drama to the nearby sitting-out area. Ranged in front of the house are four pots for summer planting—two with standard fuchsias, two with *Lippia citriodora*, whose crushed leaves yield a strong distinctive lemon smell.

The flower borders which sweep round the front lawn are full of interest throughout the year, beginning with crocuses in early spring. In her book *Classic Garden Design* (1984) Mrs Verey describes how she plants small *Iris reticulata* in corners of borders, puts crocuses, scillas and pushkianas down the middle, so that their foliage is hidden by the leaves of emerging herbaceous plants, and colonises them under deciduous shrubs. She also favours small drifts of daffodils and recommends planting these through hardy geraniums and tough plants such as *Campanula glomerata*.

Mrs Verey avoids bright flower shades but makes ample use of striking gold foliage: in the east border, *Lonicera nitida* 'Baggesen's Gold' contrasts with a variegated elder and to the south bed a splendid spreading gold juniper sets off dark red tree peonies on one side and delicate blue aquilegia, underplanted with silver *Stachys byzantina*, on the other. In the west border the bright gold of two *Philadelphus coronaria* 'Aureus' is set off by the subtly shaded *Populus alba* 'Richardii', with its young silver leaves and mature gold growth.

Grey artemisias in the border near the south front frame many small delicate flowers planted there for close inspection. We noted in June yellow asphodel, primulas, small dark violas, the spikes of later-flowering blue perovskia and woolly yellow-flowered Phlomis russeliana. Tall blue polemonium grows everywhere, self-seeding throughout the garden: Mrs Verey's son brought the original seeds back from Israel. These borders are richly planted and would repay a visit in all seasons.

In the 1960s the Vereys were offered a small 18C temple from nearby Fairford Park. David Verey had this transported and rebuilt in the south-east corner of the garden, where it overlooks a lily pond, surrounded by moisture-loving plants: iris, primulas, marsh marigolds and mimulas. Sitting in the peaceful space of the temple area, you can look out between two sentinel cypresses and a pair of elegant iron gates down a long vista to the west, culminating in a wall fountain.

You reach the lower garden through an entrance in the south wall, passing between two rustic stone figures bearing fruit and flowers. The route to the potager is not suitable for disabled visitors, as it involves a small flight of steps and the crossing of a ditch by a plank path.

Mrs Verey's 'potager', or decorative vegetable garden, is a stunning and unforgettable sight, in quite a different aesthetic class from the average British vegetable patch. She was inspired by the Château de Villandry vegetable garden, itself a modern reconstruction of 16C gardens, based on engravings by du Cerceau; and also by features at Versailles. Narrow brick paths run between the beds, dividing them into many different shapes. The paths themselves are intricately patterned. The beds are most beautifully planted, with, for example, red and green varieties of salad bowl lettuce, sweet peas trained in a cross of St Andrew, adjacent rows of standard gooseberries and onions, goblet-shaped apple trees underplanted with variegated strawberries. A stone pot, surrounded by blue-grey cabbages and a ring of lavender, marks the centre. Small sitting arbours have been constructed on either side of the garden, one shaded by a vine and the other by the brilliant golden hop, *Humulus lupulus aureus*. Near the vine, Victorian plums grown on dwarf rooting stock have their branches trained strictly downwards, to economise on space. The garden is surrounded by trellis and typical Cotswold drystone walling—the flat, slate-like stones packed in close layers.

Several fine trees stand just outside the potager—a tall silver birch, a dawn redwood and a an unusually shaped, spreading ginkgo. Turning to the left as you return to the main garden, you will find a small avenue of pleached limes, reminiscent of Hidcote's 'stilt garden' but serving quite a different purpose: where the stilt garden creates an enclosed space, this small avenue leads you onwards to enter a laburnum tunnel. On the right side, two rows of limes converge, cunningly straightening out the angle of the south wall, aligning the avenue with the main garden. In late May and early June the laburnum walk is thick with yellow racemes of blossom, underplanted with masses of mauve allium globes. Clouds of blue forget-me-not and silvery-leaved artemisia grow in the adjoining bed.

'As no man be very miserable that is master of a garden here, so will no man ever be happy who is not sure of a garden hereafter …where the first Adam fell, the second rose.' This quotation from John Evelyn is inscribed on a tablet set on a small pillar at the end of the laburnum walk; a present from Mrs Verey to her husband on his 60th birthday in 1973. Like all the garden's statues, it was made by the sculptor Simon Verity; nearby is the ingenious and fetching frog and sheep fountain visible from the temple—four fat frogs spouting water at two affectionate sheep carved on a tablet of spangled Purbeck stone. Grouped around the fountain are peonies and many foliage plants—ivies, giant hogweed, fatsias and ferns.

Walking back along the line of the laburnums and limes, savour a last display of gold leaves: a young robinia, a golden elm and privet and *Spiraea japonica* 'Goldflame', contrasting with purple maple and cotinus.

From here the way leads past a long hedge of *Rosa rugosa*, with bright green leaves and purplish flowers, on to the wide west entrance lawn.

Hidcote Manor Garden

ADDRESS AND TELEPHONE: Hidcote Manor Garden, near Chipping Campden, Gloucestershire GL55 6LR. Tel. Mickleton (0386) 438333

OWNERS: The National Trust

DIRECTIONS: 4 miles NE of Chipping Campden. Turn E to Hidcote Bartrim at the junction of B4081 and B4632 (originally A46). Public transport: Honeybourne BR 4½ miles. Bus from Stratford-upon-Avon (passing close to Stratford-upon-Avon BR): alight at Mickleton then walk 1 mile

OPENING TIMES: 30 March to end October, daily except Tues and Fri 11–8, no entry after 7pm, or 1 hour before sunset if earlier. House not open

ADMISSION: £3.80. Family ticket £10.40. Parties of 15 or more by prior arrangement: Hidcote gets very crowded at peak times

CAR PARKING: yes, free coach and car park 100 yds

TOILETS: yes

REFRESHMENTS: café/restaurant

SHOP: yes, and plant sales area

DOGS: no

WHEELCHAIR ACCESS: to part of the garden only. Toilets for the disabled: yes, in forecourt

NOTABLE FEATURES: series of small gardens; remarkable design; rare shrubs and trees; herbaceous borders

One of the most famous and highly admired of English gardens, Hidcote often gets badly overcrowded especially on fine Sundays and Bank Holidays. Come prepared to queue, not only at the entrance, but also along many of the garden paths. The gardeners are well skilled in traffic control, and at protecting sensitive areas from damage in wet weather, appearing as if from nowhere armed with boards and wire screens, foiling any attempts at shortcuts.

The garden is intricately divided, to form a series of small 'garden rooms' or compartments, referred to somewhat vaguely by Vita Sackville-West as 'a series of cottage gardens' but very different from each other in character and intention. The Old Garden with its deeply planted borders is very much in the style of a huge cottage garden, but most of the 'rooms' focus on just one idea or feature, one colour or species of plant. Hence their names—the White Garden, the Fuchsia Garden, the Red Borders, the Stilt Garden, and so on. Leading off from these are a number of vistas and avenues, framing long and beautiful perspectives. No wonder so many people bring their cameras, for Hidcote seems made to be photographed.

Laurence Johnston created Hidcote in the early part of this century. Born in Paris, of American parents, he grew up in France and became a British subject in 1900. When he first acquired Hidcote (a gift from his mother) it was bare farmland, planted only with a clump of beech trees and one fine cedar. Between 1907 and 1914 he planned and laid out the garden, along strong formal lines: probably he was influenced by his observation of traditional French gardens and he may have trained as an architect. Single-minded and resolute by nature, he went on plant-hunting expeditions to discover ever more beautiful and rarer specimens—to South Africa in 1927 with Major Collingwood (Cherry) Ingram and in 1931 to Yunnan in China, with George Forrest. He fought in the Boer War and the 1914–18 war and was twice wounded. In 1948 he moved back to France and to his other garden near Mentone, giving Hidcote to the National Trust.

The garden is an astonishing and original creation, the achievement of a man with great imagination and vision. Many of Johnston's ideas may have lost some of their first impact, having been so much taken up, copied and adapted: but some features still remain unmistakably 'Hidcote'. The magnificent clipped hedges, for instance, with their mixed and swirling colours—the tapestried hedge of green and variegated holly, yew, box and copper beech above the fuchsia garden, the handsome copper

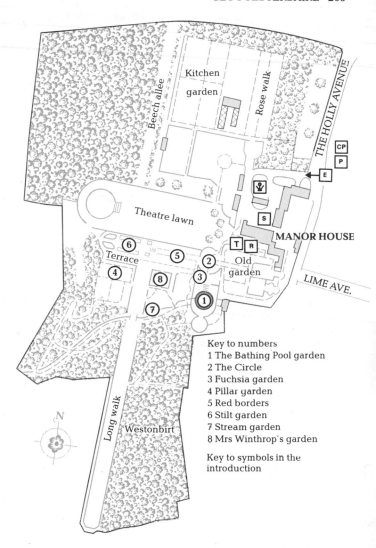

Kitchen garden

Beech allée

Rose walk

THE HOLLY AVENUE

CP
P
E

S

MANOR HOUSE

Theatre lawn

T R

6
5
2
Old garden

Terrace

4
8
3

7
1

LIME AVE.

N

Long walk

Westonbirt

Key to numbers
1 The Bathing Pool garden
2 The Circle
3 Fuchsia garden
4 Pillar garden
5 Red borders
6 Stilt garden
7 Stream garden
8 Mrs Winthrop's garden

Key to symbols in the introduction

beech and hornbeam hedge intricately interwoven round the Circle. There are many other examples. Vita Sackville-West likened one hedge to 'a green and black tartan' and she noted with pleasure how different textures of leaf had been combined—'the "flatness" of Yew contrasted with the inter-planted shine of Holly'. Equally striking are the single-species hedges, sharply clipped and geometrically exact—the tall yew hedges surrounding the Theatre Lawn, or the long rectangular hedges of hornbeam either side of the Long Walk. Vita Sackville-West compared the copper beech hedges evocatively to 'an Isfahan carpet, with their depths of rose-madder and violet, and the tips of young growth as sanguine as a garnet seen against the light'.

The garden's main axis runs from the ancient Cedar of Lebanon (*Cedrus libani*) overlooking the Old Garden, through the cottage borders, the Circle and the red borders into the stilt garden. Running parallel on the north side is the Theatre Lawn, a long flat stretch of grass, bordered by yew hedges, the setting for an open-air theatre every July. There is a raised circular 'stage' at the far end, also surrounded by yew hedges and crowned by a 200-year-old beech tree: its stone steps are flanked on either side by stone baskets of fruit and flowers.

Step through a narrow gap in the tall hedge and you will find yourself in the Stilt Garden. This is Looking Glass Land, a sharply defined area of acute perspectives and boundaries. Double alleys of pleached hornbeams are joined at each end to form solid boxes, open to the sky and with slim naked trunks connecting them to the ground. Standing inside is an unsettling experience, like having your head cut off.

Wrought iron gates and holm oaks at the top of the Stilt Garden frame a magnificent view over the Gloucestershire countryside. Sheep are kept from invading the garden by a concealed ha-ha, but their loud bleating can often be heard.

The Long Walk leads off in a south-westerly direction from the other end of the Stilt Garden. It is certainly long and makes an impressive vista, framed through the doorway of a delicate gazebo (one of a pair painted and decorated by Major Johnston). Smooth-lawned and bordered by sharply clipped hornbeam hedges, the Long Walk swoops down to the furthest southern boundary of the garden. It is crossed by a running stream, artfully concealed beneath a dip in the ground.

Walk down the nearby steps and you will find yourself between the magnificent red borders. Here red-leaved or red-flowered plants, some of great size, are boldly planted in deep borders and offset by plenty of green foliage. In early summer we saw dark red prunus, *P. cerasifera* 'Atropurpurea' and *P. spinosa* 'Purpurea', planted opposite each other; ornamental rhubarb sporting pinky red sprays of flowers on soaring stems above carmine leaves; the bronze/purple leaves of canna 'Le Roi Humbert'; purple-leaved cordylines; and red hemerocallis 'Kwanso Flore Pleno'.

The flower 'borders' in front of the house are referred to collectively as the Old Garden. In these deep, wide beds, the planting is of extraordinary intensity and abundance, like cottage garden planting but on a much larger scale. The effect of haphazard, careless luxuriance is deceptive: careful attention has been paid to colour groupings and gradations, following the principles of artist and plantswoman Gertrude Jekyll. The central borders are largely restricted to pinks and mauves—a double pink, silver-leaved thalictrum; campanula 'Hidcote Amethyst', a rosy purple hibiscus (*H. syriacus* 'Ardens'), white potentillas—all set off by big sprays of *Rosa rubrifolia* and clumps of irises. Among the early-flowering shrubs are deutzia and weigela; showy phlox and campanulas take the lead in July. Blowsy pink peonies bow to the ground, too heavy for their own stems.

The north border is mainly blue and white—pure white *Clematis flammula*, the grey-blue clematis 'Perle d'Azur' (vigorous and prolific from mid summer), *Abutilon vitifolium*, blue and white with delicate hanging bells and white philadelphus 'Belle Etoile', sweetly scented. The yellow climbing rose 'Laurence Johnston', raised in France 1923, makes an eye-catching contrast.

The south border includes several rhododendrons, growing on lime-free soil, introduced at planning stage many years ago. *Magnolia sinensis* shows its pendant white flowers, *Rosa californica* 'Plena' its semi-double dark pink blooms. A striking group of blue poppies (*Meconopsis sheldonii* 'Branklyn') flourishes in a shady place and climbing hydrangeas scramble over walls, including the magnificent *H. petiolaris*.

The White Garden, adjoining, was between seasons when we visited and being sterilised; but judging from a photograph it can look very striking, with its plump topiary birds and abundance of white roses in June. Vita Sackville-West mentions the stunning effect of scarlet *Tropaeolum speciosum* (Scotch flame flower) trailing over the yew and box hedges—'more amazingly brilliant in that place full of shadows, than ever it had appeared on the whitewashed cottage in Scotland'.

Return to the Circle and turn south for one of Hidcote's most arresting views: through the fuchsia garden and across the bathing pool garden to an enclosed plain circle of lawn. Hidcote's wonderful topiary and clipped hedges show here to their very best advantage—an archway of mingled copper beech and evergreens, two sizeable crested birds standing sentry on stout pedestals and finally a plain rectangular doorway cut into a solid yew façade, shaped like a house front. The reverse view is equally effective, from circle back to Circle.

Hidcote's fuchsia garden displays these lovely plants to good advantage in simple low box-edged beds, two circles surrounded by quartered squares.

The bathing pool garden is mostly taken up by an enormous round pool; despite its name, it is not intended for bathing, but the stone surrounds are ideal for sitting on. *Magnolia x soulangiana* and the yellow blooms of *Rosa* 'Fruhlingsgold' lighten the tall yew hedges and there are several large clumps of *Carex pendula*, the great drooping sedge, which loves moist soil.

Stepping through a side 'door' in the hedge, you enter quite a different world—the lushly planted jungle-like Stream Garden. Many specimens here have reached quite an astonishing height— vast *Lysichiton americanus* (bog arum), like outrageously overgrown spinach; *Peltiphyllum peltatum*, a saxifrage with huge circular lobed and toothed leaves; enormous *Rodgersia pinnata* 'Superba' with its bronze pinnate leaves and long panicles of bright pink flowers. *Gunnera manicata* (Brazilian rhubarb) always makes an awesome display and in July and August you are not likely to miss *Cardiocrinum giganteum*, the giant lily.

A great many of the trees, shrubs and herbaceous plants in the Stream Garden come from China, Tibet and Japan—graceful overhanging magnolias, camellias, rhododendrons and plentiful hydrangeas. *Aesculus indica*, the pink-flowered Indian horse chestnut, stands at the end of the stream; nearby is *Cercidiphyllum japonicum*, with its fallen leaves in autumn smelling like jam.

Westonbirt comes next, a wilder and more open area, planted for autumn colour. Here are many beautiful acers—*A. griseum* with its flaking and peeling bark, *A. pseudoplatanus* 'Brilliantissimum' with shrimp-pink leaves in spring—also sorbus, betula and prunus. Burnet roses grow in large tangled prickly bushes, blossoming in May and June. There are several bamboos, including an imposing clump of Chilean *Chusquea culeou*. Beyond all this stretches the open country, a peaceful view over fields and sheep-covered hills.

Retrace your steps to the formal enclosures and visit Mrs Winthrop's garden. This was designed for Major Johnston's mother, who must have been very fond of yellow and blue. A yellow-leaved hop (*Humulus lupulus* 'Aureus') appears strikingly against a copper beech hedge. Other true yellows are provided by *Lilium szovitzianum* and the beautiful single peony *Paeonia mlokosewitschii*. Mauve violas are set against golden lysimachia. The gold of *Lonicera nitida* 'Baggeson's Gold' and the acid green of *Euphorbia polychroma* contrast with the blue-green leaves of *Thalictrum speciosissimum*, which also produces acid-green flowers. *Alchemilla mollis*, lady's mantle, grows freely everywhere. The garden is structured round a central brick circle, incorporating a semicircle of steps. In summer there should also be large pots of aloe and cordylin. Two Chusan palms (*Trachycarpus fortunei*) provide added structural interest. The hedges are beech, hornbeam and lime. A seat in this garden seemed a curious omission.

The Terrace Garden is not far away, just below the pleached hornbeams in the Stilt Garden and planted on two levels, supported by drystone walls. Here in the full sun grow alpines and other small, fine-leaved plants, a medley of whites, pinks, greys, silvers and greens. Dianthus, including *D.* 'Hidcote', are mainly responsible for the intoxicating smell: also a big pineapple-scented broom, *Cytisus battandieri*, silver leaved and yellow flowered.

The Pillar Garden below is full of splendid peonies—'Souvenir de Madame Cornu', rich apricot stained with pink like the dawn sky; 'Madame Louis Henry', like diluted wine; yellow 'L'Esperance'. In the lower beds, pink peonies bloom with purple allium and lilac, after spring-flowering magnolias and the fastigiate prunus 'Ama-no-gawa' and followed by old French roses.

The kitchen garden lies to the far north, now used as a nursery. Just adjacent is the old rose border, filled with old French roses of the 19C and species. *Robinia* x *ambigua* 'Decaisneana', a pink-flowered false acacia, grows at the top, underplanted with viburnum. Dark obelisks of yew lead down the border to another long bed, crossing at right angles and planted mainly in white and silver. There are seats here.

Six Portuguese laurels (*Prunus lusitanica*, very like box) line your approach to the pine garden: they look in rather better shape than the central feature, a Scots pine. Under the pine grow purple-red and orange dwarf perennial wallflowers (erysimum or treacle mustard), rock roses and white bladder campion. We also saw an apricot quince (chaenomeles) and silver *Hebe pageii*. On the slab garden behind stands a Chinese coffin tree (*Juniperus coxii*—its wood is used by the Chinese for coffin making) and a fascinating berberis, *B. temolaica*, with glaucous stems aging to purple and deciduous glaucous leaves. Old mossy stone troughs and sinks are planted with rather sickly-looking alpines. There is a rectangular pond, planted behind with roses, including white and purple rugosas, *R. rubrifolia, Rosa sericea* 'Heather Muir', named for the owner and gardener of nearby Kiftsgate. This whole area is pleasantly relaxed and informal..

Hidcote is indisputably an admirable, a remarkable achievement, and a highly conscious one. You are unlikely ever to forget it.

Kiftsgate Court

ADDRESS AND TELEPHONE: Kiftsgate Court Gardens, near Chipping Campden, Gloucestershire, GL55 6LN. Tel. Mickleton (0386) 438777

OWNER: Mrs Anne Chambers

DIRECTIONS: off the A46, 3 miles NE of Chipping Campden. Turn E to Hidcote Bartrim at junction of B4081 and A46. Public transport: Honeybourne BR 4½ miles away. Bus from Stratford-upon-Avon (passing close to Stratford-upon-Avon BR): alight at Mickleton then walk 1 mile

OPENING TIMES: 1 April to 30 September, Sun, Wed and Thurs, 2–6, also BH Mon. House not open

ADMISSION: £2.20, children 80p

CAR PARKING: yes

TOILETS: yes

REFRESHMENTS: tea room open from May to August

SHOP: plants for sale

DOGS: no

WHEELCHAIR ACCESS: not very good. Toilets for the disabled: no

PEAK MONTHS: June and July

Kiftsgate lies just across the road from Hidcote; it is rare to find two great gardens so close. Their relationship has always been happy and fruitful. Heather Muir, who developed Kiftsgate gardens from 1920 onwards, was a lifelong friend of Laurence Johnston, owner and creator of Hidcote, and Kiftsgate benefited from Major Johnston's plant hunting expeditions to Japan and China.

Kiftsgate is more rambling, less obviously 'designed' than Hidcote. Hidcote is an ingenious garden, a showpiece. Kiftsgate makes less effort, is less famous and not so crowded in the peak season.

The garden has considerable natural advantages: situated high in the Cotswold hills, above the Vale of Evesham, it commands sweeping dramatic views over the countryside. It is built on a very steep slope, with a zig-zag path leading down from the top borders to the lower garden and swimming pool.

A bluebell wood lies to the south. Scotch firs, radiate pines and limes tower on each side of the house and vast limes border the front drive.

The house is late Victorian with a Georgian front and high

portico—originally part of nearby Mickleton Manor. From the terrace you can see across the Evesham Valley to the Malvern Hills. Rosa 'Fruhlingsgold' stands guard over the precipice, abundant in June. In the Wide Border, purples and pinks recur. Among the shrub roses is *R. Wilmottiae*, sporting small mauve-pink flowers on arching stems. *Brunnera macrophylla* 'Variegata' produces clouds of minute blue flowers like forget-me-nots in May and June, against big heart-shaped cream and green leaves, and *Perovskia atriplicifolia* follows in August with panicles of purple-blue flowers. There are some bold and striking colour contrasts in the yellow border. Beyond the hedge lies the rose border; but before doubling back, take a look to your left, through an arch of *Sorbus aria* (whitebeam) into a tiny enclosure devoted to ferns and ornamental grasses.

By far the most impressive feature of the rose border is *R. filipes* 'Kiftsgate'. When last measured, this astonishing white rose was 80ft by 90ft by 50ft high; this now seems a moderate estimate. Many other lovely old shrub roses grow in this garden, along with pale pink and white deutzias. The beds are edged with *Rosa versicolor*, striped pink and white.

Walk under an arch of copper beech and through the bridge garden to the white or sunken garden. The wide beds are full of white flowering shrubs, designed to provide a continuous display. Among the white roses is *R. sericea* 'Heather Muir', a single white early flowering shrub with fern-like foliage, growing up to 12ft high.

The north border is an unexpected treasure of gold and silver blooming on a steep north-facing bank, held together by heavy clay soil. You can descend the steep hillside to the lower garden by a zig-zag path and steps made of staddle stones—once used for supporting barns, to keep rats from the grain. Tall Scots pines surround a paved circle with seats.

Sezincote

ADDRESS: Sezincote, Moreton-in-Marsh, Gloucestershire

OWNERS: Mr and Mrs D. Peake

DIRECTIONS: take the A44 from Moreton-in-Marsh towards Evesham and after 1½ miles the lodge gates are on the left. Not very well signposted. No public transport available

OPENING TIMES: Thurs, Fri and BH Mon 2–6, or dusk if earlier. Closed December. House open Thurs and Fri May to September, 2.30–6

ADMISSION: garden £2, children £1 (under 5 free). House £3

CAR PARKING: yes. Coaches by appointment

TOILETS: yes

REFRESHMENTS: no

SHOP: no

DOGS: no

WHEELCHAIR ACCESS: not suitable: sloping valley, steep paths.

Toilets for the disabled: no

PEAK MONTHS: May, July and October

NOTABLE FEATURES: magnificent variety of trees, water garden and Indian garden

The Prince Regent paid a short visit to Sezincote in 1806 and was much impressed with its splendid 'Moghul' architecture; shortly afterwards he reconstructed Brighton Pavilion to incorporate the Indian style.

Sezincote was built by Samuel Pepys Cockerell, Surveyor to the East India Company, for his brother Charles. Cockerell planned the house with Thomas Daniell, the artist, who had just returned from a 10-year stay in India. It was Daniell who designed the bridge over the Snake Pool, decorated with kneeling Brahmin bulls and lotus flowers, and the temple to Surya, the Hindu sun god, which stands above the Thornery or water garden, north of the house. Humphry Repton was consulted over the planning and layout of the park and garden, but the exact extent of his contribution is not known. The view from the house is of a typically English 18C landscape, sweeping across the Evenlode valley into the Cotswold hills, with the lake curving round like a long river.

Although much of the planting has been done this century, mainly by Lady Kleinwort and Graham Thomas, a superb framework already existed. Most importantly, there was a great variety of mature trees. The name Sezincote is actually a corruption of Cheisnecote, 'the hillside of the oaks', and paintings of the Thornery by Thomas Daniell show that it was originally a kind of arboretum.

The Thornery is practically the first thing you see, having paid your money and walked up a path to the bridge. Looking uphill to your right you can see the shrine, above the top pool, and to your left is the three-headed snake and Snake Pool. Four enormous Lebanon cedars (*Cedrus libani*), nearly two centuries old, grow near the Rock Pool, below which lies the Island Pool, backed by a belt of rhododendrons.

Before exploring the Thornery more closely, follow the path along to the house, a splendid sight with its blue onion domes and mixed Hindu and Muslim detail. The Lebanon cedars stand some way below, underhung with pink cherries in spring.

The Indian garden was laid out in 1965 by Lady Kleinwort. Modelled on the traditional 'Paradise Garden', it is full of symbolic meanings, not immediately obvious, but made clearer by the guidebook: for instance, the crossing of the four canals symbolises the meeting of humanity and God. Rows of thin Irish yews stand on either side of the long paths.

An enormous copper beech towers above the orangery entrance, matched by another to the left of the lawn and echoed in colour by a purple-red smoke bush (*Cotinus coggygria* 'Notcutt's Variety') near the steps. Dark yews and beeches line the far bank, underplanted for contrast with light coloured shrubs and trees: prostrate golden yews, a silver willow, a robinia.

The orangery is an impressive and beautiful structure, curving its long length around the lawn, with all its arched white-framed

*Sezincote: the bridge over the Snake Pool is deco-
rated with kneeling Brahmin bulls*

windows thrown open on sunny days. It was full of flies on the day
we visited, making the atmosphere inside rather sinister. The
octagonal pavilion at the southern end was once used as an aviary
for tropical birds. Tender shrubs and climbers are trained all along
the inside wall—the double and very big early-flowering yellow
Banksian rose joins heavily scented *Jasminum polyanthum* above
an arch, *Abutilon megapotamicum* from Brazil and *Abutilon* x
milleri display their eye-catching pendant flowers. Ferns are grown
in a mirrored recess at the far end.

Neat fuchsia plants stand in white metal boxes on either side of
the orangery steps, with small palms at top and bottom. *Cotoneaster
dammeri* covers a low retaining wall. The overall effect is very
colonial, restrained and civilised. Follow the path to your right up
the hillside: here the planting gets wilder. A big hedge of golden
philadelphus tumbles above *Viburnum plicata* 'Mariesii' with its
plates of white flowers and a dark green prostrate yew, rearing up
like a wave. We searched a long time for the ruined grotto, very
well concealed under the hillside, behind a yew and a deutzia and
not really worth the effort.

Walk back towards the Thornery over the north lawn, past
another long hedge of *Cotoneaster dammeri*, and a pretty variegated holly. The path curves upwards under another splendid
copper beech, past some maples and through a meadow area. Here
is a rare specimen of *Betula ermanii*, along with other fine trees.

The Thornery or water garden is perhaps the most beautiful part
of Sezincote. For a detailed description of the many trees and

shrubs, the visitor is referred to *A Walk with Graham Thomas*, a yellow leaflet included in the guidebook.

Above the temple to Surya, an enormous yew has almost vanished under the extraordinarily rampant *Rosa filipes* 'Kiftsgate' and 'Paul's Himalayan Musk'. The pool is surrounded by raised beds, with shallow steps leading up to the temple and statue of Surya. A small *Rosa rubrifolia* near the temple complements *Cotinus coggygria* 'Atropurpurea'.

Particularly noticeable higher up the banks is a very healthy big specimen of *Lonicera korolkowii*. Bright rock roses (helianthemum) tumble over the borders. This lovely place is an apt setting for Surya, the beaming sun god, who presides over functions of the intellect. The water is appropriately crystal clear, and the pale grey mud is matched by plentiful grey foliage and white flowers in the surrounding planting.

The stream continues eastwards, spreading occasionally into small pools and planted lushly with primulas, irises, lilies, hostas, astilbes, veratrum and *Lysichitum americanum*: also tree peonies and roses. A great clump of Chinese bamboo stands near the Indian bridge, and plentiful hydrangeas grow close by. Walk under the bridge, by way of the stepping stones, and then follow the path on down, past the Snake Pool and Rock Pool towards the cedar grove. The streamside planting includes rare hydrangeas and some very striking trees. Left of the great Island Pool, *Phormium tenax* 'Purpureum' (New Zealand flax) sports its spiky leaves among masses of damp-loving plants and near two weeping pears (*Pyrus salicifolia* 'Pendula'). Yellow irises and clumps of yellow day lilies (hemerocallis) grow under a contorted willow (*Salix matsudana* 'Tortuosa'). A wooden bridge spans the water, beyond an island smothered in juniper and osmanthus. We saw a snake swimming here in the late afternoon sunlight.

Take time to look at the trees—cherries and witch-hazels, plentiful acers and smoke bushes. A great weeping hornbeam hangs over the path—part the leaves to see its knotting and twisting trunk and snaking branches. *Cercidiphyllum japonicum* is also very striking, a tall multi-stem tree with roundish leaves and purple crocus-like flowers.

Snowshill Manor

ADDRESS AND TELEPHONE: Snowshill Manor, near Broadway, Gloucestershire WR12 7JU. Tel. Broadway (0386) 852410

OWNERS: The National Trust

DIRECTIONS: near Broadway, 3 miles S of W end of Broadway, 4 miles W of junction of A44 and A424. Public transport: hard to reach by public transport. Moreton-in-Marsh station, 7 miles. Bus: Castleways BR, Evesham to Broadway, then 3 miles

OPENING TIMES: Easter Sat, Sun and Mon 11–1 and 2–6; April and October, Sat and Sun 11–1 and 2–5, May to end September, Wed to Sun and BH Mon 11–1 and 2–6. House also open

ADMISSION: £3.50, family ticket £9.60. Coach parties by written

appointment, Wed to Fri only. No concession for pre-booked
parties. School parties accepted by prior arrangement, Wed to Fri
mornings only

CAR PARKING: yes, 250 yds from manor entrance

TOILETS: yes

REFRESHMENTS: no

SHOP: yes

DOGS: no

WHEELCHAIR ACCESS: not good. Toilets for the disabled: no

Built and terraced on the Cotswold hillside, this garden looks out
over some very beautiful countryside. In this idyllic, restful, typically English country setting, the garden and museum strike a
disquieting note.

The planting is not very original, but succeeds in parts. Left of
the terraced garden is a very pretty double flower border, bright in
June with red oriental poppies (*Papaver orientalis*) and the smaller
yellow Welsh poppies. The left border is backed by yellow potentillas, strung along a wooden fence. Espalier fruit trees—figs, pears
and apples—a potato vine and other flowering climbers are trained
along the wall.

Behind the wall and directly below the manor house is a series
of terraces—Armillary Court, a shrubbery and the Well Garden
with kitchen gardens beyond. These were designed by M.H. Baillie
Scott, commissioned by the architect Charles Wade, who bought
Snowshill in 1919 and lived here until his death in 1956. Wade
seems to have been an extraordinary man, an obsessive 'collector'
of items of craftsmanship—suits of armour, bicycles, toys, musical
instruments, Chinese laquer cabinets, an Egyptian vase, a wooden
cat, clocks, traps, religious statues and much else. He converted
Snowshill from a derelict farm into a home for his collection, using
the house for display and living in a small cottage, called the Priest's
House. Like the manor house and cottage, the garden is stuffed
with *objets d'art*, many semi-religious. A decorative gold armillary
provides a focal point in the main courtyard, where eight big shaped
yews lean ponderously towards the sun and old roses grow up the
lichen-covered wall.

Descending further steps into the Well Court, note a blue astro-
logical clock and a shrine to the Virgin above a formal lily pool.
Wade was very fond of blue—several seats and all the doors,
windows and gates of the house and farm buildings are painted in
'Wade Blue'. He also loved blue and mauve plants, which go well
with the Cotswold stone, though less well with 'Wade Blue'.

A spring rising under the house has been diverted into a number
of small basins, fed by trickle fountains, and pools. A pink shrub
rose grows over an old well head.

Two former cow byres now house old farm machinery and a
miniature village. Behind one is a shady grove of towering white
guelder roses (*Viburnum opulus*), with damp-loving hostas,
gunnera and ferns growing below. Climbing the steps, overhung
by two small weeping cherries, you emerge near the shrubbery.
This has been developed since Wade's time, but still seems overgrown and gloomy. It would have appealed perhaps to Tennyson

and indeed the whole garden has a distinctly Victorian atmosphere. Its main beauties are the grassy terraces, the soaring grey stone walls of the manor and the high surrounding hills.

HAMPSHIRE

Exbury Gardens

ADDRESS AND TELEPHONE: Exbury, near Southampton, Hampshire SO4 1AZ. Tel. Fawley (0703) 891203

OWNERS: Exbury Gardens Ltd (Chairman, Edmund de Rothschild)

DIRECTIONS: from London, take the M3, A33, M27, M271 (Exit 3), A35, A326, B3054. Public transport: enquire for seasonal service; nearest bus route 2½ miles away

OPENING TIMES: early March to early July and early September to mid October 10–5.30. House not open

ADMISSION: £3, OAPs and children £2.50, under 12 free. Party rate £2.50. Reduced rates early and late season; 50p extra BH weekends and May weekends. Organisers of parties should write or telephone for details

CAR PARKING: yes

TOILETS: yes

REFRESHMENTS: café

SHOP: yes

DOGS: yes, on lead

WHEELCHAIR ACCESS: much of the garden is accessible by wheelchair, though not all paths suitable. Wheelchairs available. Toilets for the disabled: yes

PEAK MONTHS: May and early June

NOTABLE FEATURES: rhododendrons and azaleas

Exbury lies just north of the Solent, near Southampton, bounded by the New Forest and the Beaulieu river. This peaceful 250-acre wooded garden, created out of traditional New Forest Land c 1919, is home to more than 2000 species and hybrid rhododendrons, along with many other acid-loving plants and trees.

Lionel de Rothschild, the garden's founder, was an enthusiastic collector and skilled hybridiser, especially of rhododendrons. In search of new species, he sponsored expeditions to the Himalayas, Burma, China and Japan, financing such famous plant hunters as Frank Kingdon-Ward, George Forest and Joseph Rock. In all, he created more than 1200 new hybrids in his laboratories, including the world-famous Exbury strain of deciduous azaleas.

Exbury was landscaped and planted in the inter-war years. Lionel de Rothschild employed over 150 men; they dug deep wells and laid miles of piping for irrigation and even constructed a private railway network, mainly for transporting rocks to the rock garden. Rare trees and shrubs were planted and countless rhododendrons, many of which still survive today, now more than 50 years old. The garden was fully established by 1935 and included 2 acres of glasshouses, devoted to orchids, Rothschild's second passion.

During the 1939–45 war, the house and grounds were taken over by the Navy. The glasshouses were used for growing vegetables and the garden became overgrown. It took until the 1960s to restore Exbury to something like its former glory. The gardens were first opened to the public in the 1950s on an occasional basis and by the early 1970s visitor numbers exceeded 50,000 a year—now they exceed 120,000.

Late April, May and early June are the peak flowering time; depending on the season, you should see wonderful displays of rhododendrons and azaleas. These will mostly be over by mid June, but the garden is a delightful place to walk all year round, with its winding woodland paths and views across swamp and marsh to the Beaulieu River and the Solent. It is perhaps especially lovely in early spring, when the magnolias and camellias give promise of the riches to come.

The garden falls into three main areas—Home Wood, Yard Wood and Witcher's Wood. A winter garden lies to the south, beyond the pond area and camellia walk. The rock garden and water gardens can be found to the north, and a wide daffodil meadow to the west, with a rose garden and heather gardens situated towards the centre. Tea rooms, toilets and a large plant centre and shop are all situated by the main entrance, to the east.

Exbury House, an impressive neo-Georgian structure, was greatly extended and improved when Lionel de Rothschild bought the estate, and is now the home of Edmund de Rothschild—the present chairman of Exbury Gardens Ltd—and his family. Surrounded by wide lawns, cypresses, and cedars of Lebanon, it makes an excellent starting point from which to explore the garden.

Follow the main path southwards into Home Wood, through Scots pines and native oak. This area is well stocked with hybrids, including *R.* 'Janet', dropping its large, white, red-throated flowers all over the path in mid April. Nearby is *R.* 'Rothenburg', a rich, deep, creamy-yellow. We also noted a wonderful planting of yellow rhododendrons—'Cowslip', 'Yellow Curlew' and 'Moonshine'. The Bridal Walk, adjacent to the main path, features red and white rhododendrons amd white evergreen azaleas—a simple but stunning combination. The guide brochure (written by Alan Toogood) gives a useful picture-list of Exbury's award-winning plants, but unfortunately not all the rhododendrons are labelled.

In the heart of Home Wood are three ponds, linked by a chain of small oval pools. This pleasant valley area has been excellently designed for the comfort of visitors, with open glades and seats. The top pond is sheltered by bamboos (with viburnum and *Hydrangea acuminata* behind) and surrounded by plentiful hostas, primulas, leucojum and narcissi. *Taxodium distichum*, the swamp cypress, dominates a small island—this is also brightened in May by *R.* 'Purple Emperor' and an orange species azalea. The small connecting pools are overhung by graceful Japanese maples. The excellent *R.* 'Carita' can be found close by, a cross between *R.* 'Naomi' and *R. campylocarpum*.

Near the middle pond is a wonderful collection of deciduous

azaleas, strongly scented and a dazzling mixture of brilliantly clashing colours. The parentage of Exbury hybrids includes Ghent and Mollis azaleas. Camellias also feature here.

The camellia walk runs between the winter garden and the top pond. Here you can see, among others, *C.* 'Donation', with clear pink veining on large pink flowers, *C.* 'Alba Simplex', white with yellow stamens, and the double 'Augusto Pinto', with complex many-petalled grey-pink flowers. In mid April we saw delicate corylopsis underplanted with primroses—a very effective partnership. Follow the main path southwards through the winter garden to the new river walk.

A broad meadow stretches between Home Wood and Witcher's Wood, filled with daffodils in spring, and commanding another excellent view of the river. A number of young trees have been planted here in recent years, including golden conifers. The Elizabeth de Rothschild commemorative rose garden is situated nearby, a rectangle enclosed within yew hedges. The beds are planted with hybrid tea roses, floribundas and climbers—a selection of old favourites such as 'Golden Showers', 'Whiskey Mac' and 'Rosemary Rose'. A well-weathered gazebo, with classical stone pillars, supports an aged knotty wisteria and climbing roses.

Witcher's Wood is very pleasant, filled with rhododendrons and tall pines. Dark red *R.* 'Gaul' blooms early in a glade of pieris. Another glade is planted with varieties of sorbus, including 'Joseph Rock' and *S. discolor*, interspersed with small new rhododendrons. The guidebook lists a number of unusual specimen trees, such as Brewer's Weeping Spruce (*Picea breweriana*) and *Cryptomeria japonica* 'Elegans', the Japanese cedar. You cannot fail to notice the prickly Devil's club tree (*Oplopanax horridus*), near the dwarf conifer and heather plantations. This striking tree bears greeny-white flowers in panicles, followed by scarlet fruits. A short walk from here in a small hollow on the north edge of the main lawn is the recently restored iris garden.

Lovers' Lane, the main path in this area, is flanked by many-coloured specimens of the Solent strain of deciduous azaleas. The Lady Chamberlain Walk, a semicircle to the south, features the Exbury hybrid 'Lady Chamberlain', with its distinctive long tubular orange-salmon flowers.

Yard Wood begins near the balustraded stone bridge over Gilbury Lane. *Magnolia* x *veitchii* shows its pale pink globe-shaped flowers, on the south side of the bridge, beyond two fastigiate Dawyke beeches and low-branching *R.* 'Naomi'. Further along the drive is clear yellow *R. litiense*, from the Yunnan; and dark crimson *R.* 'Bibiani' stands by the crossroads. Turn left here for Jubilee Pond and the cascades, or continue round a bed in the road to Azalea Drive, breathtaking in late May and early June; in late autumn the range of maples is striking.

The rock garden should on no account be missed, for it is an extraordinary achievement. Covering 2 acres, it took Lionel de Rothschild and his many helpers four years to build. Huge sandstone blocks (transported from Sussex by rail) framed the basic structure for an adventurous and very beautiful garden, which now holds a huge collection of alpine rhododendrons and conifers, along with pieris, brooms, skimmias and many other shrubs and flowering plants. The remains of a *Pinus radiata* windbreak still clings to the rising ground to the east but unfortunately the belt was badly damaged by the gales of October 1987. The lavender-blue rhododendron 'Blue Diamond' was blooming all over the rocks when we visited in April.

The water garden, below, is a marshy area with winding streams. Here grow candelabra primulas and *Gunnera manicata*.

Finally, follow Jubilee Hill down to Jubilee Pond, set in a peaceful valley protected by huge pines and fed by three cascading streams. This wide valley is planted with bamboos (the garden holds 14 varieties), Japanese maples and the original strains of the Knap Hill and Exbury deciduous azaleas. As well as an interesting collection of hydrangeas from Switzerland this area is also notable for the bank of late-flowering rhododendrons planted in the mid 1980s and now fully established.

Greatham Mill

ADDRESS AND TELEPHONE: Greatham, near Liss, Hampshire. Tel. Blackmoor (042 07) 219

OWNERS: Mr and Mrs Pumphrey

DIRECTIONS: from A325, at Greatham turn on to B3006 towards Alton; after 600 yds turn left into 'No through road' lane to garden. Public transport: Liss railway station 3 miles; buses very infrequent

OPENING TIMES: mid April to end of September every Sun and BH 2–6. Other days by appointment only. House not open

ADMISSION: £1, children free

CAR PARKING: yes

TOILETS: yes

REFRESHMENTS: no

SHOP: plant sales

DOGS: no

WHEELCHAIR ACCESS: partial. Toilets for the disabled: no

PEAK MONTHS: May to August

NOTABLE FEATURES: originality and variety of planting; rare plants and shrubs; damp-loving plants in stream setting; small new arboretum

Mrs Frances Pumphrey rejects any suggestion that she sat down and planned her garden systematically on paper. In her contribution to *The New Englishwoman's Garden*, she relates how she stood at her bedroom window looking down over the triangular site of her proposed front garden and meditated on its potential. Without further thought, she embarked on the necessary clean sweep of old fruit trees, Michaelmas daisies and golden rod. She then set about creating the garden—visible as soon as you arrive at the foot of the entrance drive in front of the old mill.

As Mrs Pumphrey herself emphasises, there were certain natural advantages in the valley landscape: the front triangle of ground is bounded by the River Rother and the tail race from the old mill stream and there is a beautiful old wall between it and the front courtyard. An additional bonus is the long frontage of the mill house, with its deep pink brick and white windows, which provides a perfect backdrop to the masses of flower colour in the beds and borders. On the practical side, the former field proved to be wonderfully fertile.

All these advantages have been used to the full. As you come through the front garden gate, you can see in the damp ditch to your left, in late summer, the bold yellow and orange daisy flowers of ligularias and the yellow trumpets of hemerocallis; earlier in the year there are primulas and iris. At the top of the bank are the graceful wands of angel's fishing rod (*Dierama pulcherrimum*) and clumps of the distinctive blue grass (*Festuca glauca*). On the right is an island bed, largely of herbaceous plantings, where we saw the bulbous heads of mauve carduums and delicate pale pink flowers of a tree mallow, lavatera 'Barnsley'. The far corner of the bed was awash with mauve—bold panicles of phlox, starry inflorescences of thalictrum and sprays of the 'everlasting' statice.

On the left is a shrub border, bright with *Elaeagnus pungens* 'Maculata', whose size Mrs Pumphrey now somewhat regrets, grouped with a buddleia and a variegated cornus. Further on, shade-loving plants and dwarf shrubs are protected by trees rooted in the river verges below. A striking group of *Daphne collina*, with its dark green foliage, is set against a gold-leaved currant, and the multi-coloured leaves of *Tovara virginiana* 'Painter's Palette'. Scrambling along the courtyard wall, still vigorous in a dry, late summer, was the prolific blue clematis 'Perle d'Azur'.

With the encouragement and support of her husband and aided by the skills of her gardener, Jim Collins, Mrs Pumphrey then turned her attention to the field behind the mill, once again bordered by the River Rother. As you walk across the courtyard towards it, you are treated to a variety of plants in pots, notably a large collection of bush, standard and hanging fuchsias. The south-east-facing front of the house is clad with many climbers, including a wisteria and a fremontodendron, and in the house border is a dianella, or flax lily, whose insignificant blue flowers yield to bright, china-blue berries in August.

The erstwhile field through the little white gate has been transformed over the years into a series of interconnecting garden areas, terraced or divided by groups of trees. Directly behind the house, having passed on your left a flourishing herb garden, is a bank of coral, wine and green berberis, edged with dark green bergenias. Opposite, a bright lime green *Robinia pseudoacacia* 'Frisia' is invaded by the grey-green leaves of *Macleaya cordata*, the plume poppy and a gold shrub honeysuckle, *Lonicera nitida* 'Baggeson's gold'. Nearby, the curious coiling stems of the annual horned poppy, *Glaucium luteum*, which bears yellow flowers all summer, are displayed in a raised bed, which also housed white agapanthus, gold variegated comfrey, yellow nicotiana and mauve violas. Distinctive plant associations can be found everywhere, some composed of familiar material: in a rose bed further on are red

'Frensham', white 'Iceberg' and 'Pink Parfait' with an edging of pink diascias; on a raised terrace nearby is a splendid row of the giant tobacco plant *Nicotiana sylvestris* with its sweet, white scented trumpets and enormous leaves.

Mrs Pumphrey prefers that particular plants should not be mentioned, on the very reasonable grounds that gardens change and develop. But whatever the future changes in this garden, there will always be both striking and subtle plantings to enjoy. There are also many unusual shrubs and trees: in the centre of a rock bed furnished with conifers of every size and habit, we noticed the rare elm *Ulmus* x *elegantissima* 'Jacqueline Hillier', with dark green double-toothed leaves.

A group of alders, their roots set deep in the spillway from the leat, marks The Dell, a miniature valley housing a deep and spacious damp garden. Here there is room for many of Mrs Pumphrey's favourites, including primulas and marsh marigolds (*Caltha palustris*) in spring, with astilbes and ligularias for later in the year. Climbing the opposite bank you arrive at what must, geographically speaking, be Mrs Pumphrey's final venture, as it is divided from the field beyond by a stout fence. A miniature arboretum is being developed here and we saw many beautiful young specimens, among them magnolias (*M. stellata* and *M.* x *loebneri* 'Leonard Messel'), a variegated tulip tree (*Liriodendron tulipifera*) 'Aureomarginatum'), the honey locust (*Gleditsia triancanthos* 'Sunburst') and the curious bladder senna (*Colutea* x *media*), a shrub with seedpods resembling tiny pink sickle-shaped balloons. In a dry summer, all these and many others were vigorous and healthy; partly, no doubt, owing to the local water supply, but also to the constant care and attention which all plants in this garden receive.

Walking back to the mill, you cross the former tennis court, the last area of family garden to be surrendered. Here tall sun-loving plants bask on a terrace above a dry stone retaining wall and we were again impressed by the range and interest of the plantings and their incorporation into a natural and harmonious whole. Greatham Mill now has a nursery shop, where young plants raised from garden stock can be bought.

Hillier Gardens and Arboretum

ADDRESS AND TELEPHONE: The Curator, The Hillier Gardens and Arboretum, Jermyns Lane, Ampfield, near Romsey, Hampshire SO51 OQA. Tel. (0794) 68787

OWNERS: Hampshire County Council

DIRECTIONS: between the Hampshire villages of Ampfield and Braishfield, 3 miles NE of Romsey and 9 miles SW of Winchester. ¾ mile W of the A31 along Jermyns Lane. The gardens are signposted from the A31 Winchester to Romsey road and the A3057 Stockbridge to Romsey road. Public transport: regular bus service (Hampshire bus 66) from Winchester to Romsey: alight in Jermyns Lane, 20 minutes' walk to entrance

OPENING TIMES: Mon to Fri 10.30–5, all year round (March to second Sun in November, weekends and BH 10.30–6)

ADMISSION: free on weekdays. Weekends and BH £1.80, OAPs £1.40, children 50p; friends tickets £7.50, reductions for large parties. Parties by prior arrangement, please contact the Curator

CAR PARKING: yes

TOILETS: yes

REFRESHMENTS: teas in house weekends only April to October

SHOP: yes

DOGS: no

WHEELCHAIR ACCESS: most parts accessible. Toilets for the disabled: yes

PEAK MONTHS: May and October

NOTABLE FEATURES: spring-flowering trees and shrubs including rhododendrons, azaleas, magnolias and camellias. Spectacular autumn colours, at their best in October

This beautiful and wide-ranging garden and arboretum was established over about 20 years, from 1953, by Sir Harold Hillier, the well-known plantsman. Initially centred on Jermyns House, Sir Harold's family home, it spread rapidly outwards to cover the whole estate, about 100 acres. Sir Harold's main concern was to develop a collection of plants, especially trees, shrubs and hardy woody plants from all over the world, and this garden is of considerable botanical interest. It now contains perhaps the best hardy woody plant collection in the northern hemisphere, covering over 10,000 different species and varieties—in all, around 36,000 plants. Conservation is an important aspect, many of the plants here are very rare in the wild, some on the verge of extinction.

In 1978, Sir Harold gave the garden to Hampshire County Council, who now hold it in trust. It has since been extended to 160 acres and a number of new areas laid out, some specifically designed for educational purposes—an education officer has been appointed. School parties often visit and there are several plant trails. A number of booklets and current interest sheets are available at the entrance.

The garden contains nine National Collections of plants—carpinus (hornbeams), cornus (dogwoods or cornels), corylus (hazels and filberts), cotoneasters, ligustrum (privets), lithocarpus (evergreen trees, mostly natives of south and east Asia), photinia (large Asiatic shrubs or small trees), pinus (pines) and quercus (oaks).

The car park and entrance lie to the west, at a considerable distance from Jermyns House, on the eastern boundary. Starting your tour in Acer Valley, above the picnic area, you can see a wonderful collection of maples, brilliantly coloured in autumn. The effect was stunning when we visited, on a sunny October day—they are also fluorescent in fog! They range from decorative dwarf Japanese species, such as *A. palmatum* and *A. japonicum*, to the large timber trees of North America—*A. rubrum, A. macrophyllum* and others. For colour, few can match *A. rubrum* 'Schlesingeri', a rich deep scarlet in autumn, but you should also look out for *A. circinatum* x *japonicum* 'Aconitifolium', a lovely mix of butter

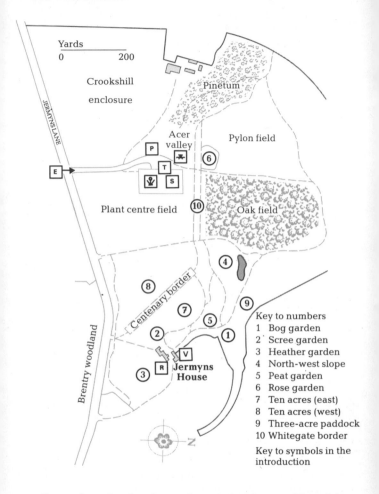

Yards
0   200

Crookshill
enclosure

Pinetum

Acer
valley

Pylon field

Plant centre field

Oak field

Centenary border

Brentry woodland

Jermyns
House

Key to numbers
1 Bog garden
2 Scree garden
3 Heather garden
4 North-west slope
5 Peat garden
6 Rose garden
7 Ten acres (east)
8 Ten acres (west)
9 Three-acre paddock
10 Whitegate border

Key to symbols in the
introduction

yellow and coral-red and green leaves. *A. palmatum* 'Heptalobum
Elegans' has delicate feathery leaves, green turning yellow tinged
with red, and *A. palmatum* 'Rufescens' turns a glorious burnt
yellow. The snake-bark maples have distinctively vertical markings or 'striations' on their trunk and branches, and characteristic
clutches of winged seeds—one example here is *A. davidii* 'George
Forrest', with large green leaves and green markings.

A broad grassy path leads through this small valley, above a
gently sloping bank, planted with maples, and descending to a
narrow stream, almost hidden from view. On the other side, just
above the picnic area, is a collection of azaleas. (The garden soil is
generally acidic, with the pH ranging between 5.1 and 6.7, although the type of soil varies from light Bagshot sand through silty
loam to London clay.)

At the bottom of Acer Valley, look out for *Sassafras albidum*—an aromatic tree from the Eastern USA, deciduous and broadly conical shaped, with attractively coloured autumn leaves. On the slope above is the 15-acre pinetum, one of the garden's older areas—it was planted in the 1960s. Many of the conifers here have reached maturity and will soon need thinning—Harold Hillier concentrated on planting as many different specimens as possible, and often neglected to give individual trees enough root space. One of the most unusual species to be found here is the aptly named bristle-cone pine (*Pinus aristata*). This tree is native to the mountains of the south-western United States (Colorado, Arizona and New Mexico) and specimens up to 2000 years old have been recorded. It is slow-growing and very resistant to disease. There are many other species of pine, along with firs, spruces and Lawson cypresses.

Retracing your steps through Acer Valley, you can see on your left a collection of spindle trees (euonymus spp). *Euonymus alatus* is very beautiful in autumn; it can be recognised by the broad corky wings on its shoots. Other strikingly coloured specimens are *E. hamiltonianus var. sieboldianus* 'Red Elf' and *E. h. s.* 'Coral Chief'.

You now cross over to the Whitegate border—this was in process of renovation and replanning when we visited. Harold Hillier always paid more attention to the garden areas around the house, so the areas near the car park tend to be fairly rough and ready. The Whitegate border hosts a collection of shrubs and trees of general garden interest—deutzias, philadelphus, hydrangeas and others. Two tulip trees (*Liriodendron tulipifera*) stand at the top, and a catalpa—this blew out of the ground in the gales of October 1987, and had to be replanted, but has survived well. Nearby is ceanothus 'Autumnal Blue', an exceptionally hardy, evergreen hybrid, flowering dark blue in late summer and autumn. Further along is *Viburnum globosum* 'Jermyns Globe', a hybrid raised at Hillier's West Hill Nursery in Winchester. *V. carlesii* forms and *V. x carlcephalum* also flower here in spring, and a selection of shrubby potentillas provides colour from late spring through to autumn. At the far end of this border is another spectacular spindle tree, *Euonymus europaeus* 'Red Cascade', with rosy red fruits, and just beyond the path, *E. hamiltonianus var. maackii* (pink fruits with orange seeds).

Descending north-west slope, you get a wonderful view of the pond with its backdrop of trees on rising ground beyond. The many different species here mix and blend harmoniously and colour to spectacular effect in autumn. Deciduous species—maples, birches, sorbus and taxodiums—stand out against dark green conifers. You should easily spot *Eucalyptus dalrympleana*, with its slender white trunk and branches—planted in 1959, this is now one of the tallest trees in the gardens. North-west slope itself is planted with collections of cotoneasters, hollies (fenced off to protect the berries from Roe deer) and slow-growing conifers.

The pond is planted with a very wide range of aquatic and marginal species, both native and exotic, and carefully grouped with an eye to colour and form. Huge-leaved *Gunnera manicata* grows here, and plentiful bamboo and cortaderia (tall with waving plumes) and ornamental miscanthus. Among the trees are swamp cypresses, the Kilmarnock willow (*Salix caprea* 'Kilmarnock') and the columnar, tawny-coloured *Taxodium ascendens* 'Nutans'. On the lawn above the pond, a lovely small specimen of *Ginkgo biloba* 'Fastigiata', bright yellow in autumn, is set strikingly against dark red *Acer platanoides* 'Crimson King'.

Following the path around and below the pond, you get a closer view of many interesting and beautiful trees, including *Prunus serrula* with satiny dark red bark, and an unusual cut-leaved alder, *Alnus glutinosa* 'Imperialis'. Further north is an eye-catching group of *Hippophae rhamnoides*, the sea buckthorn, with silver willow-like leaves and bright orange-yellow berries in autumn. The path then continues below Three Acre Paddock. You pass *Acer pensyl-vanicum*, a small snake-bark maple from eastern North America, with three-lobed leaves turning bright yellow in autumn and then several dogwoods—*Cornus florida* 'Spring Song' with deep rose red bracts, *C. florida* 'Apple Blossom' with apple-blossom pink bracts and *C.* 'Eddie's White Wonder', which bears plentiful large white flower heads in spring.

The Japanese angelica tree (*Aralia elata*) grows to the right of the path, recognisable by its huge leaves, heads of creamy-white flowers with a sickly scent and vicious thorns on the young branches. To the left are some unusual oaks, including the Armenian oak (*Quercus pontica*) with rich yellow autumn colour and the rare Daimyo oak (*Quercus dentata*, from Japan, Korea and China), with very large, broadly lobed leaves. Another more size-able tree here with very conspicuous leaves is *Populus violascens*, from China.

Continuing past the bog garden, you arrive at the foot of the magnificent peat garden, with its undulating low peat-block walls, supporting beds up a steep slope. Dwarf rhododendrons thrive here, and many acid moorland plants from China, along with other ornamental lime-hating species, members of the Ericaceae family—gaultheria, cassiope (natives of the northern arctic and mountain areas) and pieris.

You now enter Ten Acres, one of the first areas to be established by Harold Hillier, and now divided into two areas, east and west, by the long Centenary border. It contains a wide-ranging collection of trees and shrubs—in all, more than 2000 species and cultivars. Both eastern and western areas are planted for year-round interest. The eastern part has a fine collection of witch-hazels (hamamelis), which blossom in winter even in deep snow and fill the air with miraculous fragrance—the gardens usually hold a special winter weekend opening at this time of year. The Chinese witch-hazel (*Hamamelis mollis*) is the most popular, with its clusters of large, broad-petalled, sweet-smelling, yellow flowers from December to March and yellow autumn colour. *H. m.* 'Pallida' is one of the best varieties, with sulphur yellow flowers and strong but delicate scent; another is *H. m.* 'Goldcrest', with large golden flowers, claret red at the base and orange in bud. This flowers in February or March; *H. m.* 'Pallida' is often much earlier. *Hamamelis* x *intermedia* varieties are a cross between *H. japonica* and *H. mollis*; these have medium to large flowers, not strongly scented, with folded and crimped petals. You can see 'Ruby Glow' and 'Diane', both with coppery red flowers and rich autumn colour. Ozark witch-hazel (*H.*

vernalis) has plentiful small flowers, in shades of yellow, pale orange, copper and red, heavily scented, and for beautiful autumn colours. *H. v.* 'Sandra' is especially striking.

Further along the path you can see a number of unusual hollies, including one with a very strange name—*Ilex fargesii, subsp. fargesii, var. fargesii*—and *Ilex pernyi* with small triangular spined leaves.

Dogwoods (cornus) flower in this eastern area from May to July and sorbus provide interest in late summer, joined by *Nyssa* species in autumn. The sorrel tree (*Oxydendrum arboreum*) bears long drooping heads of pure white flowers in July and August, and the leaves turn red and yellow in autumn.

The 754ft double Centenary border runs diagonally across Ten Acres, from north-east to south-west. Made in 1964, to commemorate 100 years of Hillier nurseries, it holds an enormous range of shrubs, sub-shrubs and herbaceous plants, backed by hollies, yews and junipers, box and large-leaved shrubby yews (cephalotaxus). The border comes into full flower in summer and autumn, with spiraeas, hypericums, olearias and others followed by a splendid display of hardy fuchsias. Daphnes provide scent and colour in winter and spring.

Ten Acres West is especially good for magnolias, followed by hydrangeas in summer and early autumn. Below here is the spring walk, running parallel with Jermyns Lane and planted with many rhododendrons, pieris and camellias. Visiting in March and April you can see a wonderful display of camellias in full bloom, covering about 492ft on the western side. The Japanese *Camellia sasanqua* produces small fragrant blossoms in winter and early spring: most varieties are white, but 'Crimson King' flowers bright red. Mahonias grow here too, and ornamental trees including cherries. Not far off is Brentry Woodland which is only open to visitors in the spring when the rhododendrons are in bloom.

Jermyns House is open for teas at weekends. The scree garden below features alpine plants and slow-growing conifers: Magnolia Avenue runs from north-west to south-east and beyond this to the east are beds of prostrate and slow-growing conifers and a heather garden.

Jenkyn Place

ADDRESS AND TELEPHONE: Bentley, Hampshire GU10 5LU. Tel. Bentley (0420) 23118

OWNER: Patricia Coke

DIRECTIONS: 4 miles SW of Farnham on A31; turn N in Bentley marked with Heritage signs. Public transport: Waterloo BR to Bentley (1 mile)

OPENING TIMES: mid April to mid September, Thurs to Sun and BH Mon 2–6. House not open

ADMISSION: £1.50; children 5–15 years 75p. Coach parties by prior arrangement

CAR PARKING yes

TOILETS: yes

REFRESHMENTS: no

SHOP: no

DOGS: no

WHEELCHAIR ACCESS: yes. Toilets for the disabled: no

PEAK MONTHS: June and July

NOTABLE FEATURES: many, including rare shrubs and trees, double herbaceous borders, rose garden

Jenkyn Place is a garden of distinction, or a series of small gardens, beautifully designed and planted by Gerald and Patricia Coke, with a wide selection of trees, shrubs and plants. Although it looks enormous from the garden plan provided at the entrance, it is in fact no more than 6½–7 acres. It is planted on a slope, with low hedges separating the formal areas and vistas both crosswise and lengthwise.

The entrance, into a shady forecourt, reveals nothing of the pleasures to come, but you pass immediately from this into the small light Dutch garden, bounded to the north and east by white stone walls, to the west by the old dairy, now a garden room, and to the south by arches leading on to a stone terrace. In the centre stands a boy-with-fish fountain, surrounded by *Daphne collina*, which fills the garden with scent from its mauve flowers in May. Four 18C square lead tubs are planted with pelargoniums and datura. Sun-loving shrubs and climbers flourish on the entrance wall—passion flower (*Passiflora caerulea*), hibiscus, cistus and tree peonies. The beautiful single peony *P. mlokosewitschii* provides both lemon flowers in May and red and black seeds in open pods in winter. On the west-facing wall grow dark red clematis 'Niobe', a myrtle, *Leptospermum lonigerum* 'Silver Sheen' and pink *Clematis texensis* 'Duchess of Albany', underplanted with cistus and campanulas and other low-growing plants. Walking through to the terrace you pass a large bush of sharp-spined *Colletia armata* 'Rosea', smothered with pink blossom from late September.

The small paved terrace provides the first of many views through the garden, this time over the the end of the herbaceous border. The terrace itself is well planted with alpines in troughs and boasts an enormous rosemary bush and a golden bay (*Laurus nobilis* 'Aurea'). The yellow climbing rose 'Gloire de Dijon' can be seen on the dairy wall, to the right.

Turn back through the Dutch garden, passing a fig tree and roses climbing over the dairy, and walk through the archway. Steps on your right lead up to a long, rectangular rose garden. From the circular seat in this sunny garden (sited under a lion head set in the wall) you can see down the full length of the lawn, which frames four long beds, each containing three varieties of hybrid tea roses, and a central, shallow pond, with fountain. Pink, white and red water lilies fill the pond in summer. There are also beds of shrub roses—one of rugosas, including 'Sarah van Fleet', a semi-double pink with gold stamens and another bed of damask roses such as

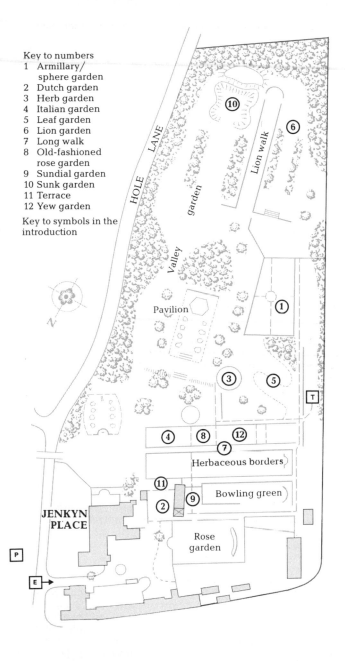

Key to numbers
1 Armillary/
   sphere garden
2 Dutch garden
3 Herb garden
4 Italian garden
5 Leaf garden
6 Lion garden
7 Long walk
8 Old-fashioned
   rose garden
9 Sundial garden
10 Sunk garden
11 Terrace
12 Yew garden

Key to symbols in the
introduction

HOLE LANE

Valley garden

Lion walk

Pavilion

Herbaceous borders

Bowling green

JENKYN PLACE

Rose garden

'Hebe's Lip' (petals white, tipped red). Many other bush and climbing roses decorate the walls.

There are bonus plantings here, as throughout Jenkyn Place: one wall shrub is *Caesalpinia japonica*, with racemes of yellow flowers in June. Nearby are the evergreen *Rosa bracteata*, and the Japanese medlar or loquat (*Eriobotrya japonica*), with heavily scented white flowers in summer.

Emerging from the light and airy space of the rose garden, you can either walk along past the bowling green, enclosed with yew hedges, and see the planting of magnolias and other shrubs, or descend into the sundial garden, filled with pots of pelargoniums in summer. Here two large stone pots flank the entrance to the garden room/old dairy. There is also a raised bed of agapanthus, the South African lily, edged with acaena, the New Zealand burr.

The wide herbaceous borders, below, are a major feature, planted exclusively for high summer. A yew hedge stands to the north and a thorn hedge to the south. As in each garden area, various ornaments have been chosen with care to enhance and complement the planting. A stone seat at the west end of this garden, backed by yew, provides a good viewing point. The plants spill over onto stone paths, running either side of the central grass walk. Two 18C statues of children stand against the thorn hedge, and two more flank the exit from the sundial garden.

The border provides a splendid variety of form and colour; there are many specialities, such as the collection of penstemons, including the distinctive pink/purple 'Sour Grapes'. Among the centaureas (relatives of knapweed) are *C. dealbata*, the perennial cornflower with pink blooms, and *C. macrocephala*, yellow-headed. Day lilies, delphiniums, phlox, poppies, peonies and many other familiar favourites flourish alongside more unusual plants, such as a graceful red South African bugle lily (*Watsonia beatricis*) and a dark red scabious, (*Knautia macedonica*). An enormous specimen of *Photinia serrulata*, with pink-red shoots and bright red leaves in autumn, stands at the house end of the border, near wrought iron gates.

The Long Walk, a grassy path, runs parallel to the borders on the other side of the thorn hedge, backed by the rock border, a favourite feature of Mr and Mrs Coke. The thorn hedge usefully sucks all moisture from the soil, providing the ideal dry environment for rock plants. The rock border holds a wide variety of small plants and bulbs, which flourish happily down its considerable length.

From the Long Walk you can step down into three small gardens. The first and most distinctive, is the Italian garden, which while lacking any peculiarly Italian feature, is given a slightly Mediterranean feel by some Irish yews, and the blue and green colour scheme. In the centre is a beautiful 18C lead tank, decorated with flying birds and filled and surrounded by lavender and rosemary.

Paved beds at the top are attractively planted with two kinds of blue iris, light and dark blue, grouped around two specimens of *Magnolia grandiflora* 'Exmouth', evergreen with creamy white flowers. To the left is a bed of dwarf conifers, of varied shape and form, underplanted with ivy. A bush of winter sweet (*Chimonanthus praecox*) flourishes against the wall, displaying its yellowish, purple-centred flowers in winter and early spring.

Next to the Italian garden is a small area devoted to old-fashioned roses and further on again there is a yew garden. This was once the kitchen garden, and is still in process of development. Golden dwarf pines (*Pinus mugo* 'Ophir') stand in pots either side of a marble seat, and two specimens of feather or needle grass (*Stipa gigantea*) give a fountain effect at the top of the steps. There are new plantings of silver and golden yews. Bush clover (*Lespedeza thunbergii*) produces purple, drooping, pea-like flowers in late summer and autumn, in contrast to the powder-blue flowers of *Caryopteris* x *clandonensis*, planted nearby.

Continue your gradual descent through borders of peonies, to the leaf garden. Of all the garden areas, this will give most enjoyment to plant-lovers and specialists. Planted on two levels, it provides constant interest throughout the year. In the upper garden, we noted the graceful Russian olive (*Elaeagnus angustifolia* 'Caspica'), with willow-like, silvery leaves and scented yellow flowers, growing near *Cornus florida* 'Tricolor', with creamy white leaves, flushed pink. *Philadelphus coronarius* 'Aureus' provides bright yellow foliage and *Stranvaesia davidiana* 'Pallette' an arresting mixture of cream, green and pink. There are many others, which it would be tedious to list, but which are a constant surprise and pleasure as you walk around.

There are herbaceous plants, too, in a wide bed backed by a hornbeam hedge: these include interesting forms of euphorbia, hellebore and pulmonaria and the unusual variegated ground elder, which is non-invasive, unlike the more common form. The bed also accommodates a number of small trees, including the snakebark maple *Acer davidii* 'George Forrest', and gold and silver variegated cornus.

Berberis, sorbaria and acer feature in the lower leaf garden, providing brilliant colour with leaves or berries in autumn. There is also a bed devoted entirely to cistus and hebe.

Near the leaf garden is a circular herb garden with a white marble Bacchus which has become the 'logo' for the garden—it appeared one year on the cover of the National Gardens Scheme guide.

One last formal area claims attention: the Armillary Sphere Garden. The circle of grass around the sphere is divided into four quarters, separated from each other by a herringbone brick path, edged with flagstones. In the centre of each quarter stands a single specimen tree, each as yet young (the white mulberry *Morus alba*, the medlar *Mespilus germanica* 'Nottingham', the persimmon *Diospyrus lotus* and *Prunus serrula*). Once again an elegant seat has been provided. A lilac hedge, a pleached lime hedge and a dwarf hedge of hedgehog holly (ilex 'Ferox') provide interest at the boundaries.

Descend via the Lion Walk (dominated by a copy of Canova's sleeping lion in St Peter's in Rome) to the Lion Garden; the stone lions here are English 18C. This spacious grassy area is planted with specimen shrubs, among which we noted golden *Sambucus racemosa* 'Plumosa Aurea'; pale green *Syringa pokinensis* and large-flowered *Lonicera myrtilis*, with purple and orange seeds. On a rise above the sunk garden sprawls a giant *Lonicera mackei* 'Podocarpa', which covers the whole mound with enormous twisting snake-like branches. This is a relative of honeysuckle.

Returning northwards through the valley garden, you can see the house properly for the first time, at the head of the valley. A wooded area to the east is filled with wild flowers in spring—celandines, primroses, anemones, wild daffodils and bluebells. Among many specimen trees in this area are the unusual *Liriodendron tulipifera* 'Aureomarginatum', with distinctive, four-lobed, yellow-edged leaves; and the hardy, trifoliate orange (*Poncirus trifoliata*), which bears yellow-orange fruits. There are many more interesting trees in this very pleasant, informal area.

By the end of your first visit to this notable garden, you may be suffering from horticultural indigestion; the best remedy is to make a number of visits. Overall management of the garden has now passed to a Trust, chaired by John Coke, the eldest son of the present owner, and this arrangement should ensure that the garden remains open to the public for many years.

Mottisfont Abbey Garden

ADDRESS AND TELEPHONE: The Head Gardener, The White House, Hatt Lane, Mottisfont, near Romsey, Hampshire S051 0LJ. Tel. Lockerley (0794) 41220/40757

OWNERS: The National Trust

DIRECTIONS: 4½ miles NW of Romsey, ¾ mile W of A3057. Public transport: Dunbridge BR ¾ mile

OPENING TIMES: April to end September, daily except Fri and Sat 2–6, last admission 5. Evening openings of the rose garden during rose season, telephone for details

ADMISSION: £2. Coach parties should book in advance (no reductions)

CAR PARKING: yes

TOILETS: yes

REFRESHMENTS: tea rooms in nearby village

SHOP: yes

DOGS: in car park only

WHEELCHAIR ACCESS: recently improved. Special parking area adjacent to walled garden (enquire at admission kiosk on arrival). Toilets for the disabled: yes

PEAK MONTHS: June and July

NOTABLE FEATURES: rose garden; ancient spring; fine trees; river

Mottisfont is perhaps most famous for its walled rose garden, containing the National Trust's collection of historic roses, but it has many other attractions—magnificent trees, an ancient spring, a parterre. Bounded to the east by the swirling River Test, to the north and south by broad water meadows, it is a beautiful and peaceful place to spend a quiet afternoon.

Mottisfont Abbey was founded in 1201 by the Priory of the Holy Trinity, and consecrated in 1224. It was badly struck by the Black

*Mottisfont's walled rose garden contains the
National Trust's collection of historic roses*

Death: two priors died in succession and the monks became very poor. Finally the priory was suppressed by the Reformation in 1536. Mottisfont then passed into the hands of William Lord Sandys (see The Vyne).

Many of the trees are very old: one oak dates from medieval times. The gigantic London plane, towering on the south lawn near the river, is probably at least 250 years old. In fact it is two trees, melded together. The double trunk measures more than 40ft round and the branches extend over an area of at least 1500 sq yds. More enormous planes grow along the riverside, also beeches and cedars, walnuts and sycamores. A big semicircle of trees—planes, beeches and willows—surrounds the abbey. Cedars of Lebanon flank the main drive, and Spanish chestnuts (*Castanea sativa*), with their great fluted and twisted trunks.

Under the south front is an intriguing parterre, laid out by Norah Lindsay for Mr and Mrs Gilbert Russell in 1938. Edged with box and lavender, it is filled with seasonal bedding plants. The scent is heavenly on summer evenings, wafting under the house windows. *Magnolia grandiflora*, wisteria and ceanothus clothe the walls.

The rose garden lies some distance away to the north-west. Designed by the Graham Thomas, gardens consultant to the National Trust, it contains his very impressive collection of moss roses, centifolias, damasks, gallicas, rugosas (of Japanese origin) and China roses.

Various lovely climbers cover the outside walls of the entrance yard—pink escallonia, honeysuckle, the semi-evergreen jasmine *J. humile* and yellow-flowering *Clematis rehderana*. Inside the yard are toilets and a National Trust shop, where you can buy a very useful key plan to the rose garden, listing the roses both alphabetically and by bed.

The rose garden is divided into four main areas, each containing rose beds and borders and edged with dwarf box hedges. Paths meet and cross at a small pool and fountain, surrounded by Irish yews. To extend the season, herbaceous borders have been planted, set with rambling roses on poles. The walls are covered in climbing roses, and long narrow beds run beneath.

Fruit trees grow all through the garden, with roses scrambling through them. Other recurrent themes are groups of white foxgloves, clumps of yellow *Phlomis russeliana* and standard hibiscus. Dianthus (pinks) too are scattered everywhere, in every shade of pink and in pure white, drowning the roses with their pervasive scent.

The planting of the herbaceous borders is rich and varied. Pale yellow scabious and aruncus have grown to enormous size. *Stachys olympica* displays its soft, tall grey spikes and tiny mauve flowers in June and July. Purple sage, in full blue flower, sets off pink geraniums with a background of silver-leaved *Centaurea dealbata* 'John Coutts'.

Every visitor will find his or her own favourites among the roses. In early July we admired the climbers 'Lady Hillingdon', a yellow tea rose with apricot buds, dating from 1910; 'Rambling Rector', a rambler with abundant small double white flowers; and the deep pink, peony-shaped 'Constance Spry', bred by David Austin in 1961.

There are some strikingly odd looking roses, notably 'Roger Lambelin', a hybrid perpetual with crinkled petals, deep red and white. 'Leda', a painted damask dating from before 1838, has dark red buds opening to white flowers, tinged with dark red round the edges, as if touched up with a paintbrush.

Two fruit trees are smothered in the rampant single pink *Rosa complicata*. Rose arches span the paths and ramblers are trained over tall wooden frames: we saw 'Goldfinch' and 'Violette', both multifloras, with clusters of delicate flowers.

'Rosa Mundi', the pink and white striped Gallica, edges one bed. Gallicas are perhaps the oldest of roses, believed to date from 1000 BC. Nearby is 'Duc de Guiche', an 1835 Gallica, with fine dark pink enfoldings.

R. 'Complicata' from the 20C takes up a huge amount of tree and ground space with its tangly growth habit and single pink flowers. Below grows the lovely Bourbon 'Souvenir de St Anne's', blush pink fading to white.

Beyond the north wall lies a smaller garden of more recent origin. Designed and planted to provide a contrast to the main garden, it contains the latest additions to the Trust's National Collection of historic rose varieties. The bright pink moss rose 'Goethe' has scented foliage reminiscent of sweetbriar, and the low growing 'James Veitch' is a subtle combination of crimson and mauve. The paths of this triangular-shaped garden are edged with dwarf lavender 'Hidcote'. Stepping stones have been set across the larger beds to allow access to the centre of the garden, where a pergola of pink and purple rambler roses provides welcome shade on a sunny day.

The underplantings are rich and varied, mainly in hues of grey and soft green. Artemisias abound—at least five varieties—while the mauve flowers of the perennial wallflower, 'Bowles Variety', contrast with the tall delicate spikes of the pale pink toadflax

'Canon Went'. A further door gives access to the main grounds, where, in the shadow of an enormous oak tree, you can look across the recently established park to the hills and meadows beyond.

The beech circle, not far from the rose garden, was planted to replace an older circle. Nearby is the underground ice house, a primitive and dank form of refrigerator. On a terrace above the main lawn is a pleached lime walk, shady and green in summer, which leads to a sunken octagonal court near the house. All along the terrace stand 19C urns, decorated with classical figures; below grow plentiful fuchsias, white hydrangeas and yuccas. The lines and proportions of the avenue are graceful and pleasing and there is a lovely prospect across the lawns to the river and woods beyond.

Before you go, take a look at Mottisfont's famous spring, 50 yds south-west of the house. Water surges up deep and clear, as it has done for many centuries, in a wide chalk bowl surrounded by a flint wall and buttercups, then flowing away over steps and slopes to join the surging river.

Spinners

ADDRESS AND TELEPHONE: Spinners, School Lane, Boldre, Lymington, Hampshire. Tel. (0590) 673347

OWNERS: Mr and Mrs P.G.G. Chappell

DIRECTIONS: from A337 Brockenhurst to Lymington, turn E for Boldre and Pinney (not road to Boldre church); cross Boldre Bridge; just before Pilley village, turn right into School Lane. Public transport: not really feasible

OPENING TIMES: mid/late April to 1 September, daily 9–6, winter 8–5 or dusk. Other times by appointment. Nursery 8–6 all year round. House not open

ADMISSION: adults £1, children under 5 free. Coach parties on application

CAR PARKING: no

TOILETS: 1 in house

REFRESHMENTS: no

SHOP: nursery with wide variety of hardy plants, trees and shrubs

DOGS: no

WHEELCHAIR ACCESS: no. Toilets for the disabled: no

PEAK MONTHS: April to June

NOTABLE FEATURES: unusual and rare plants, rhododendrons and azaleas.

This woodland garden, on the edge of the New Forest, is a showcase for Peter Chappell's excellent and deservedly famous nursery. Although small (just over 2 acres), it is crammed full of interesting, beautiful and rare plants, especially shade-loving herbaceous plants and bulbs.

Planted on a steep slope, rising to the east, the garden is partly sheltered by a canopy of oak woodland, but also includes an open area and sloping lawn to the west, below the house. The woodland area is crossed by narrow winding paths, opening into pleasant glades. Hazels and other small trees which tended to darken the wood have been removed, along with the New Forest ash trees, which are liable to disease and shallow-rooting; only some holly remains as a windbreak.

Mr Chappell bought the land and started to clear and plant the garden in 1960, and opened it to the public in 1971. Five years later, he gave up his job as a schoolmaster, to devote himself full-time to the garden and nursery, in partnership with his wife. Almost immediately, they were hit by disaster—the great drought of 1976—but the garden survived. Peter Chappell now has a partner, Mark Fillan, who travels widely to collect seeds.

Rhododendrons and azaleas grow throughout the woodland, although by no means dominating the scene. A splendid specimen of *R. Loderi* 'King George' displays dark pink upright buds in spring and large, pale pink, scented flowers, fading to white; nearby is *R. davidsonianum*, one of the Triflorum series, with soft pink flowers in April and May. There are several compact Japanese and Formosan rhododendrons, with attractive foliage. Camellias are also a feature, especially the Williamsii hybrids; also magnolias, pieris and both lacecap and mophead hydrangeas. *Cornus kousa* displays creamy-white, lance-shaped bracts in late spring and early summer, and the leaves turn attractive colours in autumn. Other cornus species and varieties can be seen in the lower garden, and a very large selection is stocked in the nursery.

Japanese maples are everywhere, notably bright pink *A. palmatum* 'Chisio Improved' and *A. palmatum* 'Red Pygmy'. The nursery list gives dozens more, with evocative and colourful names —'Burgundy Lace', 'Bloodgood', 'Butterfly', 'Crimson Queen', 'Garnet'.

The woodland floor is thickly carpeted with flowers in spring—violets, periwinkles, erythroniums, dicentra, epimediums and anemones, to name just a few—and bloodroot, named for its bright red sap, with white anemone-like flowers. Lungwort (pulmonaria) also flowers early, making excellent ground cover.

Later come the herbaceous plants, including many varieties of hosta and some lilies. Euphorbias make a showy display—bright *E. epithymoides*, with heads of green-yellow bracts, *E. griffithii* 'Fireglow', with bright green leaves and brick-red bracts and *E. griffithii* 'Dixter', burnt orange.

In the first clearing, directly below the steep woodland slope, we saw white *Dicentra eximia* 'Alba', fringed bleeding heart, with blue-green leaves, set against a yellow-leaved berberis. Nearby are plantings of *Trillium grandiflorum* and *T. g.* 'Flore Pleno', a double form. Plentiful hellebores (*Helleborus orientalis*) also grow in this area, and many varieties of pulmonaria. Cranesbills, or true geraniums, are another garden speciality. In the nursery you can buy 'Mrs Kendall Clark', with pearl grey flowers *G. macrorrhizum* 'Ingwersen's Variety', excellent for ground cover, with light pink flowers, and *Geranium renardii* with white flowers veined lilac, among many others. Tall ostrich ferns and primulas flourish in a large boggy area, below a holly thicket.

Following the narrow stone path that runs round behind the house, you will find peonies and tree peonies, day lilies, more euphorbias and plentiful lady's smock. The tree with orange/yellow bark is *Acer pensylvanicum* 'Erythrocladum'—the young shoots in winter are red-pink, with pale striations.

Before descending to the sales area proper, take the little path leading to the right. Here you will find many varieties of erythronium, with delicate six-petalled flowers, pointed and reflexed, including *E. revolutum* 'White Beauty', a white form of the American trout lily, with a yellow centre and heavily mottled leaves; also the very beautiful creamy-yellow *E. oregonum* and *E. tuolumnense* 'Pagoda', with large yellow flowers.

Note also a small specimen of *Rhododendron roxieanum oreonastes*, with glossy strap-shaped narrow leaves and bell-shaped creamy flowers; and the beautiful, equally slow-growing *Menziesia ciliicalyx* 'Lasiophylla', with small mauve buds and delicate pitcher-shaped flowers.

Just south of the nursery is an open grassy area, with herbaceous and shrub beds and specimen trees set in the lawn. Two outstanding magnolias flower here—*Magnolia* x *loebneri* 'Leonard Messel', with lilac-pink flowers, deeper in bud, and white-flowered 'Merrill'. Further up, by the garage, is a pool, surrounded by skunk cabbages (*Lysichiton americanus*) and variegated irises.

The nursery offers many treasures, so don't miss this opportunity to look round (there is no mail order service). The prices are not high, compared to those of London nurseries and garden centres. Mr Chappell takes money and gives advice at the garage.

The Vyne

ADDRESS AND TELEPHONE: The Vyne, Sherborne St John, Basingstoke, Hampshire RG26 5DX. Tel. Basingstoke (0256) 881337

OWNERS: The National Trust

DIRECTIONS: N of Basingstoke, off the A340. Well signposted. Public transport: BR to Basingstoke, then bus to Sherborne St John, 1–1½ mile walk. (Very limited request stop bus service operates from Basingstoke)

OPENING TIMES: Good Fri 29 March to end October, daily except Mon and Fri 12.30–5.30; open BH Mon (closed on following Tues). House open

ADMISSION: house and garden £3.40; garden £1.70, children under 17 half price, under 5 free. Party rate for house and garden £2.20. Coach parties must book

CAR PARKING: yes

TOILETS: yes

REFRESHMENTS: café

SHOP: yes

DOGS: no

WHEELCHAIR ACCESS: yes, and wheelchairs available. Toilets for the disabled: no

NOTABLE FEATURES: lake, woodland walk, wild area

The Vyne was built during Henry VIII's reign, some time between 1500 and 1520, by William Sandys, the King's Lord Chamberlain. Henry stayed here at least three times, once with Anne Boleyn. Although altered through the centuries, The Vyne retains much of its original character. The building is long and low, E-shaped, and the warm pink and red brickwork, diamond-patterned, dates from the early 16C.

Perhaps The Vyne's main attraction is its peaceful old-English atmosphere. No garden survives from Tudor times, but neither have any great changes been made. After the Civil War, William, the 6th Lord Sandys, sold The Vyne and retired to Mottisfont Abbey; it was bought by Chaloner Chute, Speaker of Richard Cromwell's parliament. John Chute landscaped the grounds after a style but rather half-heartedly, between 1755 and 1776. He enlarged the lake and set up a Chinese Gothic bridge. Fields and orchards were allowed to remain. The lawns north and west of the house were described in a 1776 survey as the 'Pleasure Garden' and the field on the far side of the lake as the 'old pheasant ground'.

The wide north lawn leads from the house down to the lake, overlooked by a majestic portico; this is the earliest English example of a classical portico being attached to a country house and they look quite natural together. The architect was almost certainly John Webb, who studied under Inigo Jones, and he may also have designed the domed red brick garden house.

Fine trees add distinction and grace to the prospect—spreading cedars, a group of pines and white willows. A lime colonnade leads off at an angle on the east side, a soaring mass of green in June. Stretches of grass near the water have been left to grow long and wild; the rest of the lawn is well mown, but daisies are allowed to invade, giving a pleasantly rural feeling. A much larger wild area lies to the west, beginning under the cedars and planted with walnuts, maples, *Viburnum plicatum tomentosum* 'Mariesii' and great thickets of purple and yellow shrub roses. There is a lakeside walk which takes you westwards, through fields. The Chinese Gothic bridge was a ruin when we visited, sticking out of the water at angles of distress, but there are plans to restore it.

The herbaceous border, on the west front, is a recent planting along traditional lines, backed by a thick yew hedge and seen to good advantage from the oak gallery on the first floor of the house. Grey thalictrum grows near bright *Euphorbia polychroma*, grey sedum against the vibrant green of *Alchemilla mollis*. Clumps of tall perennials have been planted in traditional style nearest the hedge—*Lysimachia clethroides* with its lance-shaped leaves and arching racemes of starry grey-white flowers and the mauve-flowered spikes of acanthus, or bear's breeches, whose leaves appear in Classical architecture. There are many beautiful peonies, of varying colours. Medium-sized herbaceous plants grow in front—yellow and orange day lilies, delicate blue polemonium and blue-leaved *Hosta sieboldii*, to name but a few. The bed is edged with low growers such as purple *Sedum maximum atropurpureum* and silver-leaved dianthus.

The public entrance to the house is here, on the west front; the path leading up to the door is lined with beds of the early hybrid tea rose *Gruss an Aachen*, which has delicate, deep-cupped pearly pink flowers, turning to white. The peach-yellow climber rose 'Gloire de Dijon' shows to advantage against the red brick. Two tent-shaped structures support claret vines on either side of the door and there is a small grey stone sundial, planted around with lavender.

The entrance drive, to the south, curves past an enormous oak and shaggy limes. Stone eagles spread their wings on pillars by the main door: a gift to John Chute from his friend Horace Walpole. The Chute family emblem, a mailed hand holding a broken sword, is mounted on another pillar further to the east and repeated on the weather vane. *Romneya coulteri*, the perennial white poppy, blossoms in the borders here, along with golden feverfew and geraniums. Follow the path round to the pleasant tea rooms, with sitting-out area, and toilets at the back.

The Vyne is an enormously peaceful and relaxing place to visit, catering not so much for the garden specialist as for those who appreciate country pleasures, fresh air and harmonious, hospitable surroundings. Look around the house too, if you have time.

HEREFORD AND WORCESTER

Abbey Dore Court Garden

ADDRESS AND TELEPHONE: Abbey Dore Court, near Hereford, HR2 0AD. Tel. Golden Valley (0981) 240419

OWNER: Mrs Charis Ward

DIRECTIONS: 14 miles SW of Hereford. 3 miles off the A465 (signposted). Mid-way between Hereford and Abergavenny. No public transport available

OPENING TIMES: 3rd Sat in March to 3rd Sun in October, daily except Wed 11–6. House not open

ADMISSION: £1.25, children 50p. Coach parties by prior arrangement

CAR PARKING: yes

TOILETS: yes

REFRESHMENTS: café

SHOP: yes and nursery

DOGS: no

WHEELCHAIR ACCESS: yes. Toilets for the disabled: yes

PEAK MONTHS: late May, June and early July

NOTABLE FEATURES: walled garden; herbaceous borders; riverside walk; pool and rock garden; fern border; circular herb garden

When Mrs Charis Ward arrived at Abbey Dore Court in the summer of 1967 she had little thought of opening a garden to the public. At that time, the place was a wilderness. There were remnants of a Victorian garden around the house—mainly two large Wellingtonias on the lawn to the south-east, an old kitchen garden of which two walls survived and a very overgrown riverside walk. From these unpromising beginnings, after a great deal of hard work, a beautiful garden has arisen.

The north section of the walled garden has been developed into a herbaceous garden, rich with interesting and unusual plants. There are many types of geranium, poppy, dianthus and campanula. Euphorbias make an important contribution to the display, along with a fine collection of sedums. Trees and shrubs lend structure.

Behind the orchard wall, facing south, is a long raised border. Not an inch of space is wasted here. To list individual species would be an endless task, and indeed the border is best viewed as one mass planting.

A path between the two handsome Wellingtonias (*Sequoiadendron giganteum*) leads to the lower lawn, which is informal in shape and surrounded by a wealth of trees, shrubs and hardy perennial plants. In the west corner is a circular herb garden, laid out in 1976, and behind this a collection of shrub roses. Close by are *Acer palmatum* 'Senkaki', the coral bark maple and *Osmaronia cerasiformis*, the Oso berry. Across the lawn is a border of white foxgloves, irises and soft pink peonies, with a selection of shrubs. A gold border is planted along the lawn's southern edge, with a fern border nearby.

Beyond the lower lawn, at the southernmost point of the garden, Mrs Ward has laid out a formal garden. A long straight path flanked at the start by a pair of young willow-leaved pear trees (*Pyrus salicifolia*), runs the length of the garden, with deep borders on either side. A framework of trees and shrubs has been planted including *Acer pseudoplatanus* 'Brilliantissimum' and *Acer platanoides* 'Goldsworth Purple'. Several willows, and a fine selection of cornus and viburnum give added structure to the borders.

Returning towards the house, you can take a very pleasant walk beneath the trees along the river bank. In springtime, daffodils, tulips, primulas and hellebores flower beneath the Scots pines. In summer the walk is green with ferns and hostas and there is a collection of euphorbias.

Across the bridge lies Stephen's Meadow, once part of the land belonging to the Cistercian Order that founded Dore. Mrs Ward decided to garden in the meadow in 1980 and dug a pool, creating a rock garden with the surplus soil. At least 20 varieties of willow can now be seen along the south bank of the pool.

Berrington Hall

ADDRESS AND TELEPHONE: Berrington Hall, near Leominster, Herefordshire HR6 0DW. Tel. (0568) 615721

OWNERS: The National Trust

DIRECTIONS: 3 miles N of Leominster, 7 miles S of Ludlow off A49. Public transport: Leominster BR 4 miles. Buses from Birmingham to Hereford stop at Luston then 2 mile walk

OPENING TIMES: 30 March end April, Sat and Sun 1.30–5.30. May to end September, Wed to Sun (open BH Mon) 1.30–5.30. October, Sat and Sun 1.30–4.30. (Note grounds open 12.30, house opens 1.30)

ADMISSION: house £2.70; grounds only £1. Coach parties by arrangement. Reduction for 15 or more

CAR PARKING: yes

TOILETS: yes

REFRESHMENTS: tea room

SHOP: yes

DOGS: no

WHEELCHAIR ACCESS: to grounds only (not tea room). Toilets for the disabled: yes

PEAK MONTHS: no special peak

NOTABLE FEATURES: many rare and unusual trees, shrubs and plants

Berrington Hall was designed in the 1770s by Henry Holland for Thomas Harley and built in brick, faced with local red sandstone brought to the site on specially constructed tramways from quarries to the north. Today the large rectangular sandstone mansion has a warm and tranquil air, as do the surrounding garden and parkland.

Capability Brown, Holland's father-in-law, was responsible for the layout of the graceful parkland and its 14-acre lake, and it was probably he who chose the position for the house with its panoramic views over the countryside towards the Black Mountains. For once there were no earlier formal gardens for Brown to sweep away, instead he was able to start this landscaping project from scratch, and the parkland remains largely untouched today.

The gardens owe much to the present Lord Cawley. Although not as varied in layout as many of the gardens in this part of the country, they hold many interesting and rare plants, shrubs and trees, set in a quiet and peaceful location.

As you walk up the driveway towards the mansion, you can see a wealth of beautiful and unusual trees and shrubs in the crowded borders flanking the drive, such as winter sweet (*Chimonanthus praecox*), which from November has very fragrant waxy pale yellow flowers with purplish inner petals, and the Syrian hibiscus (*Hibiscus syriacus*). A young tulip tree (*Liriodendron tulipifera*) and an Indian bean tree (*Catalpa bignonioides*) add to the variety of leaf forms and there are several maidenhair trees (*Ginkgo biloba*), beautifully coloured in autumn. Also magnolias and mountain ash, the twinberry (*Lonicera involucrata*) with its small yellow flowers and bright red bracts visible in June, and the white Persian lilac (*Syringa* x *persica* 'Alba').

Nearer to the Hall is the double gorse (*Ulex europaeus plenus*)—a very fine shrub with golden yellow flowers in April and May almost covering the whole bush. Here, too, is *Paeonia lutea ludlowii*—a splendid variety with large golden disc-like flowers in June.

The rarest of the plants at Berrington Hall is to be found on the sunny outside wall of the old kitchen garden. It is *Thladiantha Oliveri* (a member of the Cucurbitaceae family), a vigorous climber with heart-shaped leaves. Among the roses enjoying the shelter and support offered by the wall are 'Mme Gregoire Staechelin'—a marvellous sight when in flower, bearing large heavily scented blooms with delightful frilled pink petals—and the yellow Banksian rose (*Rosa banksiae* 'Lutea') which has double yellow rosette-like flowers. Here too is the Macartney rose (*Rosa bracteata*) with rambling stems clothed in prickles and brown down and lemon-scented flowers, white with beautiful golden yellow anthers.

The Glasnevin form of *Solanum crispum* is trained against the wall. It flowers throughout the summer with slightly fragrant rich purple-blue and yellow potato-like blossoms. Close by is the extremely floriferous *Abutilon* x *suntense*—a lovely deep violet flowering form.

A section of pergola joining the kitchen garden wall is clothed with a double row of wisteria, with its long racemes of mauve pea-like flowers. In autumn small bright yellow 'ragwort' heads of *Senecio scandens* flower on the wall behind. Another vigorous climber found on the wall is the *Campsis* x *tagliabuana* 'Madame Galen', which carries panicles of salmon red flowers in late summer, and there are also several clematis such as *Clematis armandii* and *C. orientalis*. The uncommon *Crinodendron patagua* grows below the wall, bearing its white cup-shaped flowers in late summer.

You can enjoy a short walk between herbaceous borders in the kitchen garden, reached through the centrally positioned wrought iron gates. Most of the area within the walls is currently being replanned—projects include the setting up of a historic apple collection. A plantation of over 40 varieties of pre-1900 apple varieties associated with the Hereford and Worcester area has been planted, and ancient pear varieties will be trained along the walls.

Another walled enclosure, adjacent to the kitchen garden, was once used as the drying ground, where laundry could be hung on clothes lines out of sight of the house. This area is now a camellia garden. Along with a number of young camellias, at their best in early spring, you can see the attractive *Jasminum officinale* 'Aureum'—the golden-leaved variety of the common white jasmine. In a corner is *Clerodendrum bungei*—a dark-stemmed shrub with unpleasant smelling heart-shaped leaves. In late summer it carries rosy-red, fragrant flowers.

Salvia microphylla (*Salvia grahamii*) has been re-introduced to Berrington in recent years. Tender but easy to propagate, it is a very good shrub for under a wall, blooming over a very long period, with bright red flowers fading to magenta-purple.

Along the western boundary there is a small wooded garden, where many shrubs thrive in the shelter offered by the mixed woodland planting. Here you can see the beauty bush (*Kolkwitzia amabilis*)—a lovely graceful shrub which in May and June becomes a mass of bell-shaped pink and yellow flowers—as well as deutzias and philadelphus.

At one end of the woodland, the planting opens into a glade, lined with a semicircle of hydrangeas, and with fine views through the trees to the surrounding countryside. In the other direction, a pleasant rhododendron and azalea walk leads towards the house.

As the woodland begins to open into the front lawn, you pass a specimen of *Sambucus nigra* 'Laciniata', the cut-leaved variety of the common elder. Berrington has a good collection of hollies and in this part of the garden you can see *Ilex aquifolium* 'Golden King' and 'Silver Milkmaid'.

The ha-ha has been restored in front of the house, to improve the view over the surrounding countryside and the lake with its herons and many ducks. In autumn the front lawn is sometimes brightened by the white spikes of autumn lady's tresses.

Bredon Springs

ADDRESS AND TELEPHONE: Bredon Springs Garden, Paris, Ashton-under-Hill, near Evesham, Worcester WR11 6SZ. Tel. Evesham (0386) 881328

OWNERS: Mr Ron Sidwell

DIRECTIONS: Bredon Springs is in the hamlet of Paris above and behind Ashton-under-Hill. 6 miles from Evesham turn off A435 (Evesham to Cheltenham road) to Ashton-under-Hill (½ mile). Turn right at T-junction and take first left (Bakers Lane). Follow farm track over two cattle grids. Park on small car park (12 cars). Alternatively park in village by church. Walk through churchyard into field beyond, alongside large pool (with tall wire fence) and diagonally across second field to enter Bredon Springs by bottom gate. No public transport available

OPENING TIMES: April to end of October, Wed, Thurs, Sat and Sun also BH Mon and following Tues 10–dusk. House not open

ADMISSION: 75p (to National Gardens Scheme), children free. Coach parties by prior-arrangement. Leave coach in village and take footpath

CAR PARKING: very limited, see above

TOILETS: yes

REFRESHMENTS: no

SHOP: no

DOGS: welcome

WHEELCHAIR ACCESS: no. Toilets for the disabled: no

PEAK MONTHS: most of year but especially mid summer

NOTABLE FEATURES: an unusual wild garden in a natural setting; large plant collection, many unusual plants

Bredon Springs perches on the lower south-east-facing slope of Bredon Hill, at a height of 250–300ft. It is situated above and behind Ashton-under-Hill parish church in the ancient hamlet of Paris, which dates back to about the 12C. As the name Bredon Springs suggests, an abundant supply of deep water springs from the rocks here.

Access has not improved much through the centuries, and the journey to Paris is still something of an adventure. However, if you are searching for the unusual then your journey to this garden will be worth while.

The present owner, Mr Ronald Sidwell, came to Bredon Springs in 1948 and has been very active in the garden here ever since. In 1951 and 1974 he bought more land to create the present garden of about 1¾ acres. When he arrived, Mr Sidwell found the land planted with fruit trees. Many were old, and due to poor drainage many more were dead. A few of the very best trees were retained and over the years Mr Sidwell created a really original garden.

Although some visitors might perceive this garden as an untidy jungle, it is in fact a true wild garden. Plants are allowed to seed and cross-breed freely, and are left to grow wherever they germinate. Foxgloves, mulleins and spurges do this rather well. Elsewhere, 'man-made' plantings are planned and grouped to look as natural as possible.

Botanically-minded visitors will be particularly interested in the large plant collection here. At first Mr Sidwell aimed to display as many plant families as possible, but later concentrated on geographical origins. Now he has plants from many different countries, and showing many different characteristics of growth.

But it is not just the selection of plants or their arrangement that makes this garden so unique. It is an 'ecological garden' as much as a wild garden; for Mr Sidwell the birds and other wildlife are as important as the plants. With this attitude, he has developed a gardening style that could become popular in the 21C. Dense shrubs have been planted with birds in mind—indeed about 20 different species of birds nest in the garden each year. Many plants provide them with food, either berries or seeds. The birds keep the aphids and slugs in check. All forms of life are tolerated in this garden, and control measures only taken in very extreme cases. As Mr Sidwell says: 'better an odd molehill here and there than a strychnine-poisoned dog'.

There has been no attempt, either, to alter the nature of the soil anywhere in the garden. Mostly it is alkaline, although in the northern corner the pH registers neutral. In the southern corner calcareous tufa is to be found at a depth of 3ft, and at 18in. deep the soil is 20 per cent calcium carbonate. Plants have been chosen to suit these conditions, although some plants that are normally recognised as acid-lovers—candelabra primulas, *Iris kaempferi* and several magnolias—do very well here.

The entrance to the garden from the track lies above the cottage, through the top entrance gateway, set in an informal hedge of *Thuja occidentalis*. Then a steep flight of steps leads down through a mixed planting of trees and large shrubs, and masses of daffodils in spring. One of the old fruit trees—pear 'Pitmaston Duchess'—remains by the side of the cottage. It still bears some fruit.

In front of the cottage is an area of lawn bounded by mixed beds of shrubs and unstaked herbaceous plants. Down the slope a little to the south is the Old Bog Garden. *Gunnera manicata* is particularly successful in the deep moist soil here, its large almost clumsy leaves contrasting with the fronds of ferns and the narrow blades of irises. There is quite a good collection of irises here.

Extremely good fuchsias grow throughout the garden, including 'Mrs Churchill' which has been outside for several years; also campions, phlox and some very nice dieramas and foxgloves. The lovely lavatera 'Bredon Springs' with pentagonal flowers, can be found near the cottage.

A grand oak tree (*Quercus robur*) dominates the southern edge of the lawn and nearby flourishes *Nerine bowdenii* ('Fenwicks Variety' is a particularly good type and grows like a weed). There is also a collection of hellebores (*H. orientalis* types); a lovely specimen of *Clerodendrum bungei* which has fragrant rosy-red flowers in August and September; and some very good strains of candelabra primula in many different colours—mostly natural hybrids between *P. bulleyana* and *P. burmanica*.

The south-eastern boundary is dense with trees and shrubs, and bulbs and ground cover add variety. This part of the garden Mr Sidwell fondly calls his 'Birds Nest Country'—the dense planting provides cover for the wildlife. In one part is a small pool and in the eastern corner, in the shade cast by the arching branches of a beautiful *Salix* x *chrysocoma* and another English oak (*Quercus robur*), is one of the springs that keep the soil here so moist and after which the cottage is named. It flows fast as it emerges—about 8 gallons per minute. At Easter the daffodils put on a marvellous display.

There is much more to see along the winding paths—a *Magnolia wilsonii*, for instance, and a very large specimen of *Viburnum* x *bodnantense*. Feverfew is allowed to seed wherever it chooses and so are the inulas, which provide food for the goldfinches.

Burford House

ADDRESS AND TELEPHONE: Burford House Gardens, Tenbury Wells, Hereford and Worcester (nursery in Shropshire). Tel. Tenbury Wells (0584) 810777

OWNERS: Treasures of Tenbury Ltd

DIRECTIONS: on A456 about ½ mile W of Tenbury Wells. Ludlow, 7 miles

OPENING TIMES: Easter to end October, Mon to Sat 11–5, Sun 2–5. House not open

ADMISSION: £1.95, children 80p. Coach parties by prior arrangement; reductions for parties of more than 25

CAR PARKING: yes

TOILETS: yes

REFRESHMENTS: café with home-cooked food

SHOP: yes and plant centre

DOGS: no

WHEELCHAIR ACCESS: yes. Toilets for the disabled: no

PEAK SEASON: May and June

NOTABLE FEATURES: many interesting and unusual plants

Less than a mile to the west of Tenbury Wells stands Burford House, a handsome, austere red-brick Georgian house built in 1726 for William Bowles, proprietor of the Vauxhall Glass Works in London and MP for Bewdley, Worcestershire, on the site of Burford Castle, which dates back to Saxon times. The garden is highly original and famed for its extensive range of plants.

The Treasure family purchased the property in 1954 and John Treasure at once set about creating a modern garden, in keeping with the house and in a style that would easily accommodate a wide variety of plants.

When the Treasures arrived at Burford, the 4-acre site, bounded by the River Teme to the south-west, contained only a few relics of past planting—a large Wellingtonia, a blue Spanish fir (*Abies pinsapo* 'Glauca'), a copper beech, Scots pines and a few trees on the boundary.

John Treasure began by making a series of irregular shaped beds in the extensive lawns behind the house. Today the area of garden to the south of the house shows the island bed system at its best: planted thoughtfully and with flair and originality. To achieve the effects he wanted, John Treasure mixed shrubs and roses with herbaceous plants, bedding plants, climbers and even grasses. One particular border at the far end of the south garden always attracts attention. Based on a scheme of reds and maroons, it includes such diverse plants as *Berberis thunbergii* 'Rose Glow', *Cotinus coggygria* 'Royal purple', the red-flowered potentilla 'Gibsons Scarlet', red and purple penstamons, *Sedum maximum atropupureum*, *Salvia superba*, crocosmia 'Lucifer', the dark maroon *Clematis viticella* 'Royal Velours', dahlias and deep blue aconitum.

Another technique used to great effect by John Treasure is that of the 'dipping line', where plants are arranged according to their height, with the tallest at each end of the bed rather than in the middle or grouped at the back. This means that you can often see right across the centre of the bed to the next grass walk or stretch of lawn.

However, Burford is not all free-flowing irregular lines. In a corner of the south garden is a circular pool surrounded by paving and ornamented by slim columns of *Chamaecyparis* 'Witzeliana', while to the front of the house a long rectangular canal pool serves both to set off and to reflect the straight lines of the house. This canal, with its sparkling fountain and small water lilies, is set centrally in a large lawn.

Water plays an important role in these gardens. The River Teme, which marks the south-western edge of the garden, flows at too low a level to contribute much to the landscape, but it does provide an inexhaustible supply of water. This is pump-fed to streams and ponds in the garden and even feeds the fountain in the canal pool.

The stream gardens host rich, dense plantings of moisture-loving and aquatic plants: a large planting of *Gunnera manicata* is grouped for effect with astilbes, primulas and irises along the banks of winding streams.

Conifers appear as single specimens, in groups or as screening. There many forms of Lawson's cypress: *Chamaecyparis lawsoniana* 'Allumii' with large soft flattish sprays of blue-grey foliage, *C.l.* 'Kilmacurragh' noted for its dark green foliage, and *C.l.* 'Wisselii', its fern-like sprays of blue-grey contrasting with the golden yellow of *C.l.* 'Lutea'.

Clematis appear in great numbers throughout the garden, trained against walls and also pegged to the ground, and twisting through trees and shrubs.

Hergest Croft Gardens

ADDRESS AND TELEPHONE: Hergest Croft, Kington, Herefordshire. Tel. Kington (0544) 230160

OWNERS: W.L. and R.A. Banks

DIRECTIONS: ½ mile from A44 on western edge of Kington. Hereford 20 miles. Gardens well signposted from Kington. Public transport: Hereford BR 20 miles. Buses to Kington

OPENING TIMES: 29 March to 27 October, daily 1.30–6.30. House not open

ADMISSION: £1.60, children 80p. Reductions for booked parties of more than 20

CAR PARKING: yes

TOILETS: yes

REFRESHMENTS: teas

SHOP: yes gifts and rare plants

DOGS: on lead

WHEELCHAIR ACCESS: limited. Toilets for the disabled: no

PEAK MONTHS: May and early June for rhododendrons and azaleas otherwise no special peak

NOTABLE FEATURES: fine collection of trees and shrubs; National Collections of maples, birches, zelkovas; azalea garden; woodland garden with rhododendrons; herbaceous borders; rare species

Spectacular is the only suitable word to describe the 50-acre gardens at Hergest Croft. The varied planting includes fine collections of trees and shrubs from all over the temperate world, making this a garden for all seasons.

William Hartland Banks, a banker by profession but also a keen gardener and photographer, and his wife Dorothy began building Hergest Croft in open fields in 1896. Little of the present garden layout existed at that time, only a line of beech, oak and hornbeam to the east and a sycamore a little way from the house. Influenced by the writings of William Robinson and Gertrude Jekyll, W.H. Banks planted, planned, altered and extended the gardens for more than 30 years, until his death in 1930.

Today the garden is tended by William and Dorothy's son, Dick, and their grandson Lawrence. Besides many and varied trees, there are exotic shrubs, roses, rhododendrons, unusual ferns and many of the more old-fashioned herbaceous plants. The National Collections of birch, maple and zelkova are also held here.

The entrance to the garden is heralded by *Acer micranthum—*

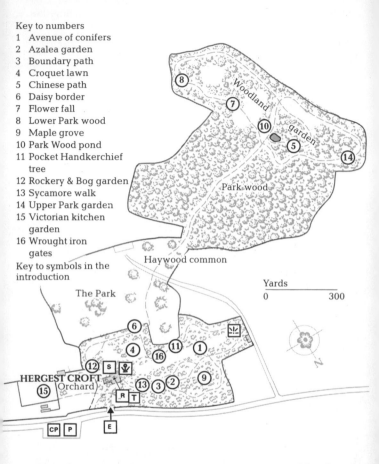

Key to numbers
1 Avenue of conifers
2 Azalea garden
3 Boundary path
4 Croquet lawn
5 Chinese path
6 Daisy border
7 Flower fall
8 Lower Park wood
9 Maple grove
10 Park Wood pond
11 Pocket Handkerchief
   tree
12 Rockery & Bog garden
13 Sycamore walk
14 Upper Park garden
15 Victorian kitchen
   garden
16 Wrought iron
   gates
Key to symbols in the
introduction

collected by Lawrence Banks in Japan—and a raised border of
gentians, foxgloves, geraniums and other flowering plants runs
along the path; but the real horticultural adventure begins on the
other side of the house.

From the verandah the lawn stretches away to the south, edged
with fine specimens of the weeping beech (*Fagus sylvatica*
'Pendula') and fern-leaved beech (*Fagus sylvatica heterophylla*),
and several maples including the coral bark maple (*Acer palmatum*
'Senkaki').

The sycamore walk, bordered by many interesting shrubs, roses
and tree peonies takes you past the umbrella pine (*Sciadopitys
verticillata*), its leaves fused together very like the spokes of an
umbrella. A magnificent sycamore tree stands at the end of the
path. Brace and cable hold some of the branches firm without
distracting from the stateliness of this splendid tree, which was
growing here before Hergest Croft was built.

The path makes a long sweeping curve left, by a border of mahonias, hydrangeas, berberis and other shrubs. On the opposite side is *Eucryphia glutinosa*—a mass of large white flowers in August. On the right a gate leads into the azalea garden. Towards the end of May this gently sloping hillside is bright with pink, yellow, orange and red azaleas. Here, too, are many noteworthy trees. Amongst the birches are large-leaved *Betula maximowicziana*, and *Betula jacquemontii* with dazzling white stems. Two chance seedlings are betula 'Hergest' and betula 'Haywood', the latter having extremely attractive bronze-coloured bark. There are also firs, larches, pines, walnuts, zelkovas and acers.

Before returning to the main garden, the path passes under a magnificent pocket handkerchief tree (*Davidia involucrata*). Beyond the tree are rhododendrons, including *Rhododendron Loderi* 'King George', and 'Loder's White', spectacular in May.

The wrought iron gates leading back into the main garden were made for the Wembley Exhibition in 1924, and from here the boundary walk continues round the inner garden, passing the croquet lawn on the left. The lawn is enclosed by tall yew hedges and flanking the entrance are two ginkgos. Further along, *Prunus maackii* shows off its shiny red-brown bark.

It is a ¾-mile walk to the Woodland Garden in Park Wood—which lies on the other side of a hidden valley—and sensible walking shoes are a good idea; but the effort is well rewarded, especially in May and early June when the rhododendrons put on a sensational display. Rhododendrons crowd around the pool, follow the stream and paths and tumble down the hillside.

Among the taller specimens is *Rhododendron calophytum*—one of the best of the Chinese species, with white to pink wide bell flowers blotched with maroon. *R. insigne* has leathery leaves with a metallic lustre and large trusses of soft pink flowers spotted with maroon.

Now retrace your steps back through the oak and beech woodland, across the park and through the wrought iron gates. Inside the main garden again, a grassed walk leads past borders of fragrant viburnums, philadelphus and free-flowering *Exochorda giraldii*. The emphasis here is on white flowers.

To the east, beyond the mulberry, is the old rockery and bog garden. Today it contains several not-so-miniature conifers, a few maples, some shrubs and ferns.

Cross the orchard to find the Victorian kitchen garden, with its rows of fruit and vegetables and flowers. Colourful herbaceous borders and rose beds can be seen near the tennis court.

How Caple Court

ADDRESS AND TELEPHONE: How Caple Court, How Caple, Hereford. Tel. How Caple (098 986) 626

OWNERS: Mr and Mrs P.L. Lee

DIRECTIONS: off B4224 at How Caple, 9 miles S Hereford. No public transport available

OPENING TIMES: Mon to Sat 9.30–4.30. Sun (May to 30 September only) 10–5

ADMISSION: £2, children £1. Coach parties by prior arrangement

CAR PARKING: yes

TOILETS: yes

REFRESHMENTS: tea room on Sun and BH

SHOP: plant nursery and retail fabric shop

DOGS: on lead

WHEELCHAIR ACCESS: limited. Toilets for the disabled: no

PEAK MONTHS: May, June and early July. October for autumn colours

NOTABLE FEATURES: many fine trees and shrubs; sunken Florentine water garden (under reconstruction); terrace gardens; plant nursery

The gardens at How Caple Court are still relatively unknown, having only been open to the public for a few seasons. Currently access is granted to about 11 acres of this garden, which is set on high ground above the River Wye, with excellent views towards the Forest of Dean and the Welsh mountains.

The manor dates back to Domesday and in the early 13C was given to the Caple family, who lived here for more than 450 years, until the last quarter of the 17C. The manor then passed to the Gregory family. Sir William Gregory, who was Speaker of the House of Commons, was responsible for major rebuilding work to both house and church. The terraces may also date from this period.

The Gregory family stayed at How Caple Court until 1781, and the manor then changed hands several times before its purchase in 1898, by the Lee family.

The gardens were laid out in Edwardian times, most of the developments being carried out by Lennox B. Lee, grandfather of the present owner. An extensive restoration and replanting programme is now underway and various features have emerged from a tangle of undergrowth, or have been carefully reconstructed, such as the cascading waterfall and a sunken Florentine water garden. In Lennox B. Lee's design, a number of water features linked the Florentine garden back to the house via the series of terraces.

Today, the best approach to the garden is along the driveway, which can be reached from the north-west corner of the courtyard. From the drive there are good views over a low wall of Herefordshire sandstone down to the dell garden. On the opposite side of the drive, the stone walls of an old barn support honeysuckles, wisteria and a large fig (*Ficus carica*).

A long border lines the eastern edge of the drive as it curves towards the gates and the entrance to the dell garden. Informally planted with a wide selection of shrubs, this border offers a range of coloured and variegated foliage, and flowers over a long period. The rich reddish-purple foliage of *Berberis thunbergii* 'Atropurpurea' contrasts with the golden yellow and green leaves of *Elaeagnus pungens* 'Dicksonii'. Mexican orange blossom (*Choisya ternata*) can be found here, along with *Deutzia* x *rosea* and weigela

'Abel Carrière'—a particularly fine cultivar with large bright rose-pink flowers. There are several shrub roses too, and at the end of the drive the beauty bush (*Kolkwitzia amabilis*). Throughout May and June, the drooping branches of this graceful shrub are covered in masses of soft pink bell-shaped flowers with yellow throats.

A low metal gate leads from the drive into the dell garden where a large area of lawn slopes to the south. An old cider press has been made into a feature, set into the lawn and surrounded by a planting of *Viburnum davidii*. The ground rises towards the east and beneath the high retaining wall of the driveway is a mixed border of mature shrubs. Shrub roses and potentillas bloom here in June and July, followed by buddleias.

On the opposite side of the lawn is a stand of mature trees—oaks, sweet chestnuts and beech—underplanted with a selection of rhododendrons, roses and buddleias. Half-way along is a massive tulip tree (*Liriodendron tulipfera*)—a beautiful tree recognisable by its odd four-lobed leaves, which turn orange and butter yellow in autumn. In June and July this tree bears a mass of tulip-shaped flowers, greenish-yellow outside with orange markings inside.

At the bottom of the dell the lawn opens into a level area—the old tennis court. On the slope to the side of the tennis pavilion and below the house is a herbaceous area with several unusual and interesting plants. Designed and laid out by Alan Bloom of Bressingham Gardens in Norfolk, this provides colour throughout the summer months.

Below the wall, on the other side of the pavilion, is a further collection of shrub roses and buddleias such as *B.* 'Lochinch' (*B. davidii* x *B. tallowiana*) which has fragrant blue-violet flowers with an orange eye.

Steps lead from the tennis court to a lower lawn, where the main feature is an almost circular pool surrounded by a newly restored stone pillar and timber rail pergola-like structure which hopefully in the future will once again support rambling roses. This pool once supplied water to the Florentine garden (now under reconstruction) and was itself fed by the cascade and waterfalls of the rock garden, high on a slope to the east.

On the western boundary is mature mixed woodland, borderd by a roughly mown area. Here are several mature specimens of *Acer palmatum* richly tinted in autumn. Here too are the remnants of the Sunken Florentine Water Garden, at present still partially hidden by brambles. Paved with local stone, the garden has two canals which meet in the centre, where a fountain once played. The remains of four circular stone raised beds can clearly be seen—these would have been bedded out with bright summer flowers. Surrounding the garden, close to the retaining walls, are the pillars of a ruined pergola. Yews that had spread and grown to a massive 20ft have now been hacked back into rough columns. All around lie broken urns and statues. Once reconstruction has been completed and the water again flows down the canals and the fountain plays between bright flower beds, this part of the garden should look very beautiful.

In order to complete the garden tour, retrace your steps to the garden pool and climb the grass bank to the wrought iron gates in the high wall. This way leads to the terraces, which command magnificent views over the Herefordshire countryside.

The terraces are linked by a central stairway of steep stone steps. On the first level is a rectangular sunken paved garden with a central lily pond surrounded by columns of yew and planted around the outside with roses. More roses grow on the retaining wall.

A summerhouse is strategically positioned at the west end of the second terrace, commanding a view down to the circular pool and rock garden below. The third terrace is paved, with formal rose beds. The next level is softer to the eye, lawned and with three rectangular stone lily pools. The retaining wall on this level is smothered with rambling roses and honeysuckles.

Close by the terraces is a delightful medieval church, dating back to the 13C and containing many interesting features including a recently restored 16C diptych from southern Germany. From the terraces the way out is past the house, across the croquet lawn which is surrounded by deep rich herbaceous borders, and through the stable building back into the courtyard.

The small nursery area in the courtyard has many unusual old roses and herbaceous plants for sale.

Spetchley Park

ADDRESS AND TELEPHONE: Spetchley Park, Spetchley, near Worcester. Tel. (090 565) 213/224

OWNER: R.J. Berkeley, Esq

DIRECTIONS: 3 miles E of Worcester on A422

OPENING TIMES: April to end September, Mon to Fri 11–5, Sun 2–5, Sat closed. House not open

ADMISSION: £1.70, children 90p

CAR PARKING: small. Coach parties by prior arrangement

TOILETS: yes

REFRESHMENTS: tea room on Sun and BH Mon

SHOP: plant sales

DOGS: no

WHEELCHAIR ACCESS: yes. Toilets for the disabled: no

PEAK MONTHS: April to June, but also all summer

NOTABLE FEATURES: splendid borders around walled garden; trees and shrubs; rose lawn

The Berkeley family has been at Spetchley since 1605, when Rowland Berkeley purchased the estate. At that time there was a moated Tudor house on the site but, despite the Berkeleys being Royalists, the house was burnt to the ground by Scottish Presbyterians prior to the battle of Worcester in 1651. The present imposing Palladian style mansion dates from 1811 and was constructed in Bath stone to a design by John Tasker.

The gardens lie mostly to the east of the house, while to the south large sweeping lawns descend to the large garden pool or lake.

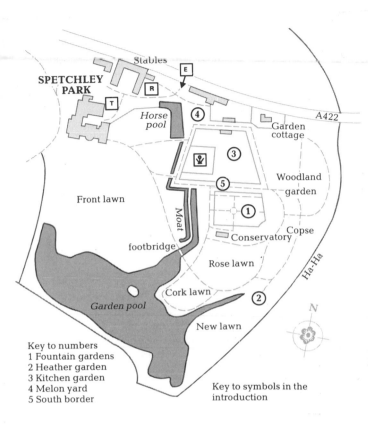

SPETCHLEY PARK

Stables

Horse pool

Garden cottage

A422

Woodland garden

Front lawn

Moat

Copse

Conservatory

footbridge

Rose lawn

Ha-Ha

Cork lawn

Garden pool

N

New lawn

Key to numbers
1 Fountain gardens
2 Heather garden
3 Kitchen garden
4 Melon yard
5 South border

Key to symbols in the
introduction

Beyond is a deer park, little altered since the 17C except for the
removal of a diseased elm avenue.

Over the past two centuries, the gardens have been altered and
extended by two successive generations of the Berkeley family.
Rose Berkeley, with the help of her sister Ellen Willmott, introduced
many interesting and beautiful plants at the beginning of this
century. After Rose's death in 1922 Captain Rob Berkeley continued
work in the grounds, followed by his son John, the present owner.

You enter the garden through the melon yard, where numerous
tender plants enjoy the shelter and protection of the old high brick
walls. Here in July, *Cytisus battandieri* displays its cone-shaped
clusters of pineapple-scented, yellow flowers against greyish
leaves. The vigorous climber *Campsis* x *tagliabuana* 'Madame
Galen' with its salmon-red flowers in late summer also does well
against the wall and the extremely fragrant *Trachelospermum
jasminoides* carries lovely white flowers in July and August.

The melon yard provides a home for olives (*Olea europaea*) and
the double pomegranate (*Punica granatum* 'Flore Pleno') which
has showy orange-red flowers. Tubs of *Agapanthus umbellatus* add

further to the warm Mediterranean atmosphere of this enclosure.

To the south of the melon yard is a much larger walled garden, once the kitchen garden. Part of this area is now used for plant sales while elsewhere there are good specimens of *Paulownia tomentosa*, the fragrant white-flowering *Osmanthus delavayi*, *Viburnum macrocephalum* which gives spectacular displays in May with its heavy trusses of white flowers, and that striking climbing plant *Actinidia kolomikta* with heart-shaped leaves, variegated green, white and pink.

Surrounding the kitchen garden walls are magnificent borders, crowded with many kinds of plants. The west border is home for a large *Hydrangea sargentiana* and across the path a group of *Rosa rubrifolia* with attractive purplish foliage. Potentillas, kniphofia, phlox, nicotiana, geraniums and hostas help to fill the west border and in spring there are jonquils (*Narcissus jonquilla*).

The east border is particularly noteworthy in May when the lilacs are in flower and the north border for its magnolias and splendid cut-leaved walnut (*Juglans regia* 'Lacinata'). The south border is a marvellous mixture of shrubs and herbaceous plants. Peonies, irises, mulleins, geraniums and roses fight for attention in summer and in autumn colour is provided by a magnificent maidenhair tree (*Ginkgo biloba*).

In the centre of the south border is an alcove built of Bath stone. This faces the fountain garden, which is divided into four, with a central fountain. These separate garden areas, surrounded by yew hedges, contain, in all, 36 beds, divided by paved paths. Originally each bed featured a different botanical family, but this plan has been abandoned and now each garden is a jungle of trees and shrubs. However, some lovely specimens are to be found here. There is a large *Acer griseum* with attractive peeling bark, some particularly good magnolias such as *Magnolia kobus, M. mollicomata* and *M. Wilsonii*. The honey locust (*Gleditsia triancanthos*), threepenny bit rose (*rosa farreri persetosa*) and the slender Serbian spruce (*Picea omorika*) can also be seen here, and *Corylopsis Willmottiae*, one of the many plants named after Rose Berkeley's famous sister Ellen Willmott.

Beyond the fountain garden to the south lies the rose lawn where 17 beds, mostly of hybrid tea roses, are a central feature. Many favourites appear here—'Peace', 'King's Ransome', 'Ernest H, Morse', 'Papa Meilland', 'Just Joey' and 'Whiskey Mac', to name a few.

A conservatory overlooks the rose lawn. Towering above this is a fine cut-leaved beech (*Fagus sylvatica heterophylla*) and inside, the wall supports *Plumbago auriculata* (formerly *P. capensis*) which produces clusters of blue flowers throughout the summer. Outside grows *Berberis montana*—not often seen—and a *Wisteria floribunda* 'Macrobotrys' which in June displays its huge 2ft long racemes of yellow flowers tinged with purple. Close by is an old beech tree, covered in a hybrid vine called 'Spetchley'. All around are fine looking cedars dating from the 18C plantings.

The western edge of the rose lawn is bounded by part of the moat which remains from the days of the earlier Tudor house. The moat joins the garden pool just below the bridge and water lilies flower colourfully all summer long. Across the path from the rose lawn is the Cork Lawn which takes its name from a gnarled cork oak (*Quercus suber*), and here too is a magnificent *Quercus x hispanica* 'Lucombeana'—the Lucombe Oak—a hybrid between the cork oak and the Turkey oak.

South-east from the Cork Lawn, across a narrow canal overhung by swamp cypresses (*Taxodium distichum*), is the new lawn. This was planted by Captain Rob Berkeley after the 1939–45 war and all the trees and shrubs were chosen specifically for their spring and autumn attractions. There are several sorbus and malus species, good specimens of *parrotia persica*—noted for its crimson and gold autumn shades—and *Salix matsudana* 'Tortuosa', the twisted form of Pekin Willow. A splendid dawn redwood (*Metasequoia glyptostroboides*), with attractive shaggy, orange-brown bark, can also be found here, and *Nyssa aquatica*, particularly noteworthy for its rich autumn colours. By the heather bed grows a fine *Quercus coccinea* 'Splendens', or scarlet oak, which also puts on a remarkable display in autumn.

Going northwards from the new lawn, you can walk through the copse, where towering pines form a windbreak to protect the rest of the garden. In spring primulas, rhododendrons and azaleas bring colour to the copse, despite the alkaline soil. In autumn it is the turn of *Acer palmatum* and *A. japonicum*, along with the golden rain-tree (*Koelreuteria paniculata*) and *Cornus kousa*.

A walk through the woodland garden—planted with magnolias, rhododendrons and hydrangeas—brings you back to the kitchen garden. The garden lost a few important trees in the gales of winter 1990.

Stone House Cottage Gardens

ADDRESS AND TELEPHONE: Hon. Miss Louisa Arbuthnott, Stone House Cottage Gardens and Nursery, Stone, near Kidderminster, Worcestershire. Tel. Kidderminster (0562) 69902

OWNERS: Major and the Hon. Mrs Arbuthnott

DIRECTIONS: 2 miles SE of Kidderminster on the Kidderminster to Bromsgrove Road (A448). Driveway next to church in Stone. Public transport: trains to Kidderminster then taxi (2 miles)

OPENING TIMES: March to end of October Wed, Thurs, Fri, Sat 10–6. Also Sun in May and June 2–6. House not open

ADMISSION: £1, children free. Coach parties by appointment, evening visits can be arranged

CAR PARKING: yes

TOILETS: yes

REFRESHMENTS: no

SHOP: excellent plant nursery

DOGS: no

WHEELCHAIR ACCESS: yes. Toilets for the disabled: no

PEAK MONTHS: peaks throughout the year

NOTABLE FEATURES: collection of unusual and rare plants; many climbers; unique design for a small garden

Stone House Cottage Gardens are not quite an acre in size but contain an amazing collection of trees, shrubs herbaceous and climbing plants, many of them unusual or rare. It is the work of Major James Arbuthnott and his wife Louisa, who over the last ten years or so have turned this one-time kitchen garden into a plants-person's paradise.

It is an unusual walled garden, wedge shaped rather than rectangular and not completely walled in. The southern boundary is hedged with a mixture of species, and windows cut into the hedge frame views across the countryside to the distant Malvern Hills.

The Arbuthnotts began by trying to give an impression of size. The illusion has been partly created by dividing the garden into a number of separate enclosures, radiating off a main axis between the entrance and the house. A bold geometry underlies the design, with a repeated theme of radiating and crossing axes. At many points you have a choice of three views or three routes, and the whole area is cleverly broken up by hedges and shrubs to give a constant sense of surprise and adventure.

All the various parts are relatively enclosed but there are interlocking vistas, so you can look through one into the next. There are yellow and white gardens, a sheltered enclosed garden, a shady area, one for early plants, herbaceous borders, raised beds for smaller items, and lawns with shrubs and small trees, and the surrounding walls are clothed with many climbing plants.

Around 2000 plants jostle for space in the garden and along the walls. The Arbuthnotts' selection methods are very simple—if they don't like a plant, they don't grow it. Plants are propagated and sold in the adjacent nursery—the garden and nursery are conceived very much as one entity.

The originality and creativeness of the hard landscaping owes much to Major Arbuthnott's unique building works. At various points around the walls he has constructed towers and look-out points of novel design, adding to the garden's interest, variety and amusement. Built onto the ridge of one wall near to the house is a Venetian arched tower, complete with machine gun, a polite reminder that there is no need to take your own cuttings—plants are for sale in the nursery.

The garden entrance is through a recently constructed round tower, another example of the Major's building skills. In a shady corner behind the tower is an attractive water feature on two levels, surrounded by a small courtyard garden. Sit down for a while on the wall seat with its tiled shelter and enjoy the planting of astilbes, hostas, meconopsis and Solomon's seal. On the walls are clematis and honeysuckles.

From the tower you have a choice of three routes across the garden. The central grassed path, the main axis of the design, leads towards the house through a straight corridor of yew hedges. Under a clematis arch to your right you will find a path running below a wisteria-draped wall to a small lawned area of trees and shrubs. Most visitors, however, start off along the path to the left, under an archway of *Clematis alpina* 'Francis Rivis' and clematis alpina

'Willy' mixed with the climbing rose 'Veilchenblau', and follow the southern boundary through an informal area planted with interesting shrubs. From this route you get the 'window' views through the hedge to the surrounding countryside and the Malvern Hills.

Elaeagnus angustifolia 'Caspica' is one of the most striking shrubs here, especially in June when it is covered in small yellow flowers. It has a stunning smell. Other shrubs include *Exochorda* x *macrantha* 'The Bride' with arching branches and *Stewartia sinensis*, coloured rich crimson in autumn. Through a break in the yew hedge on the right you get a glimpse through to the garden lying on the other side of the main axis, and further along are two *Buddleia alternifolia*, one of the ordinary form and the other the silver-leaved 'Argentea'. Across the path is a slender Antarctic beech (*Nothofagus antarctica*).

At the far end of the walk, in a shady corner by a shelter built into the wall, is a group of foliage plants that prefer not to be in full sun. Silver-leaved philadelphus, variegated sambucus and the slender golden-leaved *Ribes sanguineum* 'Brocklebankii' do well here.

The wall running towards the house has a border below it, just wide enough to take climbers and shrubs, with smaller items to the front. Along the wall, dividing the border into bays, are buttresses of pittosporum. All kinds of shrubs grow in the bays—winter's bark (*Drimys winteri*), *Ceanothus arboreus* 'Trewithen Blue', *Buddleia fallowiana* 'Alba', a selection of potentillas, a large *Azara dentata* and *Azara macrophylla* 'Variegata' with pretty cream variegated leaves. Clothing the wall there are clematis, honeysuckles, roses including 'Mermaid' and some lovely specimens of *Trachelospermum jasminoides* 'Wilsonii' and 'Variegatum'. The latter is a pretty plant with fragrant flowers of white and leaves splashed with cream.

In front of the border is a bed containing many early flowering subjects, and walking a little way up the yew corridor, you come to the enclosed garden. Here, in the shelter of the surrounding hedges, grows the alpine mint bush (*Prostanthera cuneata*) from Australia, with mint-scented leaves and white flowers.

Around the house are raised beds of geometric shape, containing many small, pretty and unusual plants, including some alpines. There are various types of erodium, penstemon, thyme, dianthus, geraniums and many more.

Nearby are double herbaceous borders where salvias, phlox, lavatera, campanulas, agapanthus, sedums, roses and others jostle for position, giving a brilliant display in summer. The yellow and white garden, on the other hand, is much more selective in colour. White, cream and yellow flowers mix with silver foliage to give a soft and charming effect.

The long brick wall stretching from the house back to the entrance supports a wide range of climbing shrubs. There are several clematis, including *C. calycina*, the large-flowered pale blue 'Mrs Cholmondeley' and the double, scented 'Duchess of Edinburgh'. Among the roses are 'Lady Hillingdon', 'Cooper's Burmese', 'Fortune's Double' and the shell-pink-flowering 'New Dawn'.

Further along is a massive wisteria and a pergola supporting roses entwined with clematis. A striking combination is the blood-red flowering rose 'Parkdirektor Riggers' and the pink clematis 'Duchess of Albany'.

The path leads on, across another lawned area dotted with carefully selected trees and shrubs, and returning to the towered entrance.

There can be no doubt that Stone House Cottage Garden is a wonderfully original and artistically designed garden, an adventure in store for any keen gardener or plant enthusiast.

HERTFORDSHIRE

The Gardens of the Rose

ADDRESS AND TELEPHONE: Chiswell Green, St Albans, Hertfordshire. Tel. (0727) 50461

OWNERS: The Royal National Rose Society

DIRECTIONS: on the outskirts of St Albans, 18 miles from London. Easy access from the M1 and M25 motorways and the A1(M). Well signposted. Public transport: regular Green Line coaches (including departures from the Green Line Coach Station, Victoria) and local bus services. Frequent BR services via St Albans City station on the London St Pancras to Bedford line and via Watford Junction on the London Euston to Birmingham Line. Underground by Bakerloo line to Watford Junction

OPENING TIMES: mid June to mid October, Mon to Sat 9–5. Sun and August BH 10–6

ADMISSION: £2.20; accompanied children under 16 free; Royal National Society members and one guest free; registered disabled persons £1.50; parties (20 or more) £1.70, for every 20 persons at party rate, 2 additional free entrances will be allowed, plus free refreshment for coach driver

CAR PARKING: yes

TOILETS: yes

REFRESHMENTS: café

SHOP: yes

DOGS: on lead only

WHEELCHAIR ACCESS: yes. Toilets for the disabled: yes

PEAK MONTHS: June to August

NOTABLE FEATURES: over 30,000 roses: species, hybrids, different varieties. The British Rose Festival, a major display of cut roses, is held in the gardens early each July

In 1959, the Royal National Rose Society moved from cramped accommodation in central London to its present headquarters at Chiswell Green, acquiring with the purchase of Bone Hill not only a large house for administrative offices, but 8 (later increased to 12) acres of ground for gardens and trial grounds. The Society has just embarked on an ambitious scheme whereby the gardens will be extended to some 60 acres by the year 2000. It is intended that it will become an all-season garden with national and international collections of roses and all sorts of other plants.

From the time of its foundation in 1876, the Society was active in breeding roses, and particularly in developing the larger and brighter hybrid which culminated in the modern hybrid teas and floribundas. Its present displays, however, also include examples of all the early rose families as well as modern climbers, ground cover and miniature roses. As the rose, in one form or another, is many people's favourite flower, and it has entered the language as a symbol of beauty and sweetness, such a collection cannot fail to attract an enormous number of visitors and give a great deal of pleasure.

However, the popularity of the rose and its historical and literary associations do not necessarily make the task of maintaining the National Rose Society Collection a bed of roses. As the years pass, the number of varieties that pass through the trial grounds increases and not all can be included in the garden. Combining a living encyclopaedia of roses with an effective layout poses another problem, and to add to these difficulties, the soil in the garden is what the Society's guide describes as 'a thinnish layer of loam overlying a gravelly subsoil' which must constantly be improved by adding organic matter as well as supplying the correct feeding for the roses. Fortunately, the Society has tackled these problems with verve and dedication, and all visitors, except the most exacting, will find something to please them.

The gardens consist mainly of a series of rose beds, framed by extensive, well-kept lawns. These are punctuated by plantings of vertical conifers, some of considerable size, and golden orbs of yew, which were retained from the existing garden at Bone Hill, and provide essential variation in a flat landscape. To these have been added other features, including the Henry Edland pavilion (named after the secretary of the Society at the time of the move from London to St Albans) an extensive pergola, centring on a lily pond, and a series of small model gardens.

When you enter from the car park you immediately find yourself in the Rope Walk, where a vivid collection of climbers is displayed. They are planted in no observable combination of colours, though at the Catenerary, a circular pergola, *R. longicuspis*, a species climber with masses of white flowers, associates agreeably with others of its kind. Against the dark green of the conifers near the house, and on the house itself, other vigorous climbers such as the cream multiflora 'Rambling Rector' and the rambler *R. filipes* 'Kiftsgate' are shown to spectacular advantage.

Leading from the front of the house to the pool and pergola is the Princess Mary Walk, where favourite hybrid teas and floribundas from past years are displayed. We noted several oustanding varieties: the floribunda 'Amber Queen', a prizewinner from 1984, which combines an attractive, pale full bloom with dark foliage; the pale pink 'English Miss' another floribunda, cupped and sweetly scented; and 'Arthur Bell' a large semi-double floribunda which changes shade spectacularly through the season—bright yellow in bud, mid-yellow in full bloom and aging to cream. Unusually for a yellow rose, this is very fragrant. In the Trials Award-Winner's Border, near the entrance, each variety has been limited to three specimens, to save space and provide the enthusiast with an unusually wide selection.

Climbers have been combined with clematis on the brick pergola near the pond, and this generally shows both to advantage. The white, gold-stamened multiflora 'Seagull' supports dark purple clematis 'Gipsy Queen'; white clematis 'Marie Boisselot' associates nicely with the purplish cerise rose 'John Cabot'; clematis 'Ascotiensis', bright blue with green stamens, offsets the yellow rose 'Lawrence Johnston', named after the creator of Hidcote. There are many such combinations, underplanted with miniature dianthus and other low growing plants. The central pool, encircled by the dwarf polyantha rose 'The Fairy', makes a charming focal point.

Nearby we saw a successful combination of roses used both as standards and bushes: crimson/scarlet 'National Trust' (HT); another hybrid tea, the salmon-pink 'Paul Shirville' and HT 'Pink Favourite'. A pity that these outstanding varieties are almost lacking in scent.

A chevron of rose beds leads up to the Henry Edland Pavilion. The gaudy purple-red floribunda 'News' catches the eye first, but there are also cooler shades, including that of the single violet 'Escapade' and the outstanding 'Iceberg', which has proved its value over thirty years, and is deservedly repeated as a climber on the pavilion itself.

For those tired of phalanxes of blooms (the modern bush has little in the way of grace to commend it) the Society has put together some beds of 'curiosities'—'Nearest to Black', 'The first Hybrid Tea' and a rose ('Bonica' by Meilland) that can be satisfactorily cut with mechanical shears. Ground cover roses are displayed on a tiered bed.

Visitors who prefer old-fashioned roses will find plenty of them in this southern area of the garden, in several adjoining beds. Their generous arched bushes have been combined with other shrubs and with garden flowers to provide an attractive display. We saw some outstanding associations: in a bed of hybrid perpetuals, notably light crimson 'Ulrich Brunner' and crimson 'Prince Camille de Rohan', dark, pale and mid blue delphiniums were set against *Gleditsia triacanthos* 'Sunburst' and *Lonicera nitida* 'Baggeson's Gold' and underplanted with lavender. *R.* 'Souvenir du Dr Jamain' another crimson, was associated with a philadelphus, mauve foxgloves and purple violas. These complementary plantings, which might with advantage be extended into the modern rose beds, give an added beauty to the rose, rather than detracting from it.

At the northern end of the lawns, in the garden named after the Society's patron, the Queen Mother, are the early rose families (gallicas, albas, centifolias, damasks, portlands), grouped in separate beds, each with a notice giving their history and origin. Few are repeat flowering, portlands being a notable exception, but all attract by their subtle and gentle colouring (white, cream, crimson, maroon, and pink). Here you can find *R. gallica* 'Officinalis', the Red Rose of Lancaster, otherwise known as the Apothecaries' Rose; *R. gallica versicolor*, crimson striped pink, dating from before the 16C; the outstanding damask 'Hebe's Lip', a creamy-white tinged with red; and the original portland rose, a light crimson, dating perhaps from 2000 years ago. The Society has recently undertaken the first stages of underplanting with a variety of suitable companion plants.

In complete contrast are the individual small neat gardens at the western end of the garden, beyond the house. Five 'model' areas have been created, complete with paving, trellises and garden ornaments to simulate domestic gardens. Here again, the roses, whether ancient or modern, appear to best advantage when associated with clematis and other garden shrubs and plants; particularly happy is the combination of roses with the sun-loving silver foliaged plants—artemisia, helichrysum, lavender, thyme, and the silver weeping pear (*Pyrus salicifolia* 'Pendula'). The double violet clematis 'Countess of Lovelace' also showed up particularly well against a pale pink climbing rose.

Nearby is a sunken garden full of every conceivable shade of miniature rose. Developed in the distant past from a deviant China rose, these have since been crossed with many other roses to widen their colour range. Appropriately, they are associated here with rock plants. A standard form of the delicate pearl-pink ground-cover rose 'Nozomi' stands in the centre of a bed containing a miniature sedum, arabis and dwarf campanulas.

As you leave the garden, take a look at roses in the trial grounds, some of which may perhaps one day replace our current favourites.

Whatever your personal tastes, the existence of these gardens provides an unusual opportunity to view a very wide range of roses, recognising old favourites and discovering new. The presence of so many marvellous blooms together in one place gives great pleasure, which the occasional failing in originality of design or planting cannot seriously dampen.

Hatfield House

ADDRESS AND TELEPHONE: the Curator, Hatfield House, Hatfield, Hertfordshire AL9 5NQ. Tel. Hatfield (0707) 262823

OWNER: The Marquess of Salisbury

DIRECTIONS: 21 miles N of London on Great North Road (A1000). 2 miles from A1(M) (signposted). 8 miles from M1 and 7 miles from the M25. Public transport: entrance directly opposite BR station in Hatfield. 25 minutes from King's Cross or Finsbury Park: trains every 30 minutes. Green Line and local bus services

OPENING TIMES: 25 March to second Sun in October. Park open 10.30–8 daily except Good Fri. West Gardens 11–6 daily except Good Fri. East Gardens 2–5 Mon only, except BH Mon. House open weekdays, from 12 noon except Mon and Good Fri (guided tours only, last tour 4.15 pm); Sun 1.30–5 (no guided tours, guides in each room). Also open Easter, May Day, Spring and August BH Mon, 11–5. Parties of 20 or more must book in advance

ADMISSION: house, park and gardens £3.90, OAPs £3, children £2.70; park, gardens and exhibition only £2.15, children £1.10. Reductions for pre-booked parties

CAR PARKING: yes

TOILETS: yes

REFRESHMENTS: café

SHOP: gift shop and garden shop

DOGS: not in house or gardens but allowed in the park

WHEELCHAIR ACCESS: to privy and scented gardens, view over knot garden; access to some of the Wilderness. Gravel paths may cause difficulty in the lime walk. Toilets for the disabled: yes

PEAK MONTHS: April to October: particularly spring and summer in formal gardens, spring and autumn in Wilderness

NOTABLE FEATURES: knot garden, privy and scented gardens; Wilderness

The gardens at Hatfield House have the advantage of two splendid backdrops, the house itself and the Old Palace, built by the Bishop of Ely in 1492. The Palace was later annexed by Henry VIII, and later the young Elizabeth was confined here during the reign of her sister Mary. Although it was partly demolished by the 1st Earl of Salisbury, the remaining wing—the Great Hall—is still marvellously preserved and provides the setting for a remarkable present day re-creation of a 16C knot garden.

Entry to the gardens is directly from the north court of Hatfield House, and you pass through a low wrought iron gate, to the right of which are pale pink flowering cherries in the spring, and to the left a shady border planted with *Phillyrea latifolia* and yew. From here you can easily reach the Old Palace, by crossing a grassed area where a huge horse chestnut (*Aesculus hippocastanum*) with surrounding seat, overshadows four classical statues.

As you approach the deep red brick façade of the Old Palace, you discover the knot garden—actually seven separate knots and a foot maze—lying below you. It was the custom in Tudor times to site a knot garden or parterre so it could be viewed from above, either from banks or from mount. The present high banks are ideal for the purpose, having been constructed in the 19C to enclose a rose garden.

The knot garden itself was planted by the present Marchioness of Salisbury in the early 1980s, following original Italian designs. The outer hedges are of clipped hawthorn, with hawthorn standards; they incorporate seats, over which honeysuckle and other climbers are trained. The knots themselves are made of box (*Buxus sempervirens*) with small box cones set at their corners. They are filled according to the English tradition, not with the neat bedding favoured in France but with a profusion of spring bulbs followed by flowering plants and shrubs, all known to have been used in the 15C, 16C or 17C.

Groups of crown imperials (*Fritillaria imperialis*) and small species tulips, patches of mauve and white anemone and tiny purple violets bloom here in the spring beside the pale green flowers of Lent lilies (*Helleborus foetidus*) and groups of 'spring snowflakes' (*Leucojum vernum*). There is spring blossom too, from two flowering cherries (*Prunus cerasifera*) and four sweet almonds (*Prunus dulcis*). In the summer shrub roses abound, including *R.* x *alba maxima*, white flushed pink, contrasting with delphiniums and pinks (Robert Cecil's favourite flower).

Near the central fountain of this garden—a boy with fish—is the foot maze, with ankle high hedges and four tiny wooden gates. With its twists and turns and final, central goal, it is supposed to represent the Christian life. You can only enter the knot garden if you join a guided tour, but the view from the banks alone is rewarding.

You now move away from the Old Palace and into the gardens backed by Hatfield House, the mansion which Robert Cecil, the first Marquess of Salisbury, built for himself in 1607–11. Cecil was intensely interested in gardens and employed the French designer Salman de Caux to design *allées*, avenues, walks, fountains and pools and a 'Great Water Parterre' (for a fuller description, see the detailed garden guide by the Marchioness of Salisbury). Also included was a banqueting area, where family and guests could eat informal alfresco meals while enjoying the delights of the gardens (including 24 gilded lions and artifical fish in the pools). Sadly, these elaborate designs fell into disrepair during the 18C, when the fashion for landscape led to the park being extended up to the house. This agreed with the tastes of the 1st Lady Salisbury, who rode until she was in her nineties.

Cecil also sent his head gardener, John Tradescant the elder, on expeditions abroad to bring back trees, plants and seeds. Tradescant continued to be employed by the 2nd Earl of Salisbury, and introduced at Hatfield the great double anemone (*Anemone grassensis*) from Italy, which the present Marchioness hopes to re-introduce from French seed.

With the renewed fashion for more formal gardens, the 2nd Marquess, as keen a gardener as the first, attempted to restore Hatfield to its Jacobean glory by building terraces, a parterre and a maze, as well as a vast conservatory. This second formal garden also fell into disrepair apart from the privy garden, which had been established at the end of the 19C. It was later redesigned by Lady Gwendolen Cecil with island beds and a central lily pool. It has now been renewed and replanted by the present Marchioness.

An undulating yew hedge borders the privy garden, with yew terminals surrounding Italian stone seats. One mulberry tree, out of four planted by James I, remains to form a link with the distant past. There is a surrounding square walk of pleached limes, which provides shade in summer and gives access to the knot garden, the privy garden, the scented garden and the Wilderness. In the planted border in the lime walk we noticed an unusual celandine with bronze foliage, *C.* 'Brazen Hussy', providing striking contrast with the bright green and maroon leaves of an *Epimedium rubrum*.

In spring the island beds of the privy garden are filled with tulips, wallflowers and polyanthus, contrasting with the acid green of *Euphorbia amygdaloides* as well as the paler green of hellebores. Bright daisy flowers of *Bellis perennis* and hebe 'Hagley Pink' flourish at the edges of the beds. Later a variety of peonies come into flower, including the single yellow *P. mlokosewitschii*, as well as the white and cream lupin 'Noble Maiden', followed by the pink, mauve and red bell flowers of penstemons. Poppies, foxgloves and numerous other herbaceous plants fill the beds to overflowing.

Giving height at the centre of the beds are old shrub roses, such as the species *Rosa glauca* with its tiny pink flowers and purple foliage. There are also some 40 of the modern 'English Roses', which retain the old rose flower formations and habit but have the advantage of perpetual flowering. Tall herbaceous perennials include *Eremurus himalaicus*, a fringed fox-tail lily, and *Cimicifuga racemosa* 'Purpurea', whose white wands of flower top most other plants. The planting throughout is both selective and profuse.

From this delightful place you step down into the scented garden, also designed by Lady Salisbury. Some of the paved walks are centred with camomile (which needs replanting every spring after the wear and tear of the previous year). In spring, as we entered, delicious scents from the briar hedge and from a nearby *Daphne odora* 'Marginata' were filling the air. There is a lavender walk, a thyme path and a central herb garden, with sundial, where the smaller herbs grow between semicircles of paving. The outer beds are edged with Munstead lavender and filled with old fashioned roses chosen particularly for their strong scent.

On the south-facing wall a sweet-smelling wisteria overhangs a seat and around the garden there are varieties of philadelphus, the scented mock orange. The white flowers of the wintersweet (*Chimonanthus praecox*) and lemon-yellow flowers of *Mahonia japonica* provide fragrance in early spring.

Large stone dishes are filled with geraniums in summer and on the north side of the garden there is a raised border with shrubs where the dark purple *Viola cornuta* flourishes in the shade. Approaching the gate in the south wall you pass a silver-leaved *Elaeagnus commutata* and lines of silver-leaved Guernsey stock, both of which smell sweetly in summer.

This gate marks the end of the formal gardens and the entry to the Wilderness—not a truly wild area but one designed according to the 17C and 18C fashion for informal plantations with winding paths. At Hatfield the Wilderness was created in the 19C and consists of a long rectangular woodland, filled with a combination of native trees and more exotic specimens. It is relaxing to wander here in spring among drifts of bluebells or enjoy the foliage colour in autumn.

There is a distinctive urn, with two-tailed mermaids, near the edge of the Wilderness and nearby an enormous Spanish chestnut, which may have been planted by John Tradescant. In this area four copper beeches were lost in the gales of autumn 1987, and both here and throughout the Wilderness there is new planting including two new young golden-leaved elms. There are also groups of young silver birch and plantings of white-flowered *Amelanchier canadensis*, which has star-shaped white flowers in spring and bright leaves in autumn. Visiting in spring we saw not only rhododendrons in flower, some of considerable size, but camellias and magnolias, underplanted with with crocuses, lilies of the valley and many wild flowers. The many cherries and crab apples provide blossom in spring and some also colour brilliantly in the autumn.

A monkey puzzle tree (*Araucaria araucana*) towers among pines, and there is also a Californian big tree (*Sequoiadendron giganteum*). The beech and oak throughout the Wilderness have grown to great height and provide a pleasant light canopy for the rhododendrons.

The west gardens, which incorporate all the areas described above, could occupy anyone's attention for a day. On Monday afternoons only, the east gardens are open, and could absorb another day. (One ticket will admit to both gardens.) In the East Gardens you will find a parterre, maze, mount and pool gardens, an orchard and kitchen garden, a new pond and a wild garden. The maze is not open to the public.

Hatfield has been fortunate in its owners, many of whom have been skilled garden designers. The present Lady Salisbury is continuing the tradition, with gardens that reflect the history of both palace and house.

HUMBERSIDE

Burton Agnes Hall

ADDRESS AND TELEPHONE: Burton Agnes Hall, Driffield, North Humberside, YO25 0ND. Tel. (0262 89) 324

OWNERS: Burton Agnes Hall Preservation Trust Ltd

DIRECTIONS: 6 miles E of Driffield, 6 miles W of Bridlington, on A166. Public transport: Driffield BR or Bridlington BR 6 miles. Throughout summer there are regular bus services from Driffield, Bridlington, Scarborough, Hull, York and Leeds. Bus stop 200 yds

OPENING TIMES: Easter to end of October, daily 11–5. House open

ADMISSION: hall and gardens, £2.25, OAPs and children £1.75. Gardens only £1. Coach parties by prior arrangement. Reductions for parties of 30 or more

CAR PARKING: yes

TOILETS: yes

REFRESHMENTS: café

SHOP: yes

DOGS: no

WHEELCHAIR ACCESS: yes, also to first floor of Hall. Toilets for the disabled: yes

PEAK SEASON: no special peak but kitchen garden best June to August

NOTABLE FEATURES: formal garden; woodland garden; kitchen garden with flower borders; Elizabethan Hall

Burton Agnes Hall is a beautiful Elizabethan mansion, designed by Robert Smythson in 1598–1610. It houses one of the largest private collections of French Impressionist and modern paintings in the north of England. The Hall is approached via a handsome early Jacobean gatehouse (c 1610), which leads into a large forecourt.

The forecourt was once part of formal gardens but these were swept away by Lancelot 'Capability' Brown in the 18C. Long lines of yews neatly clipped into ball shapes now flank the drive on its way to the south front of the mellowed red-brick Hall.

To the east side of the Hall, an expanse of lawn is studded with rows of clipped yew domes and bronze statues. In the centre is a long ornamental pool. A fountain and screen terminate the vista and tall dark yews provide a backdrop. Further east an obelisk and circular ironwork temple stand before the ha-ha, with farmland beyond.

A dense woodland screen forms a boundary along the northern side of the formal garden and is planted with a mixture of flowering shrubs. An avenue or ride gives a view through to the countryside: meandering paths lead off on either side, beneath mature beech, oak and sycamore trees.

The large walled garden, to the east of the forecourt, has been recently redeveloped. Along the north and east walls over 60 varieties of clematis are planted, with a narrow border of 50 varieties of hardy geranium and 25 of violas.

A maze is laid out in the north-east corner, enclosing a thyme garden of 35 varieties and raised bog garden. Next to this is a 'jungle' garden surrounded by a bamboo hedge and including 16 varieties of bamboo. South of this is the campanula garden—150 varieties from large border to rockery and alpine types

Elsham Hall Country Park

ADDRESS AND TELEPHONE: Elsham Country Park, near Brigg, South Humberside DN20 0QZ. Tel. (0652) 688698

OWNERS: Captain and Mrs Elwes

DIRECTIONS: 8 miles S of the Humber Bridge. Signposted from A15 Humber Bridge Road, and from M180 motorway. Entrance is on the B1206 Brigg to Barton-on-Humber road. Public transport: limited bus service. Barnet railway station 3 miles, Elsham 1½ miles

OPENING TIMES: Easter to mid September, daily 11–5; mid September to Easter Sun and BH 11–4. Closed Good Fri and Boxing Day. House not open

ADMISSION: £2.50, children £2 (reductions in winter). Reductions for parties of more than 20

CAR PARKING: yes

TOILETS: yes

REFRESHMENTS: restaurant and café (tel. 0652 688698)

SHOP: yes

DOGS: no

PEAK SEASON: May to August

NOTABLE FEATURES: wild butterfly garden; young arboretum; lakes; wild flowers; spring blossom and bulbs; natural history quiz and trails

A new style of gardening has developed in recent years, prompted by the urgent need to compensate in some way, however small, for our destruction of the countryside and heedless ill-treatment of the environment. At Elsham Hall, the emphasis is on conservation and protection of wild plants (especially native species) and animals. To visitors in search of neat, well-manicured lawns or formal landscapes, the park and grounds may appear overgrown and neglected; but the mature woodlands, informal lakes and abundant vegetation cannot fail to attract and please conservationists and 'wild gardeners'.

The estate belongs to Captain and Mrs Elwes, who opened the park to the public in 1970. It has already won a number of prestigious awards, including the 1975 Conservation Award from the Royal Institute of Chartered Surveyors in conjunction with *The Times*; the 1983 Henley Award; and the 1984 Civic Trust Award for a contribution to the quality and appearance of the environment. In 1987 it gained a commendation in the Ford European Conservation Awards. There is much to be learned by coming here.

The trout lake lies at a short distance from the park entrance, beyond huge yew trees. This is the largest, although not the only area of water at Elsham—elsewhere in the grounds are a carp pond, where you can feed the fish (up to 25lbs in weight), and a duck pond, recently constructed in a woodland clearing. Mallards, Canada and snow geese, coots and other water fowl swim on the lake; and on its western shore is Elsham's nearest approach to a 'garden' in the traditional sense. A low brick wall at the water's edge is clothed with roses, and a broad grass walk follows the line of the bank. Fruit trees, a fig and a pyracantha, are trained against an old kitchen garden wall, on the other side of the walk. Self-heal (*Prunella vulgaris*) is allowed to spread freely through the grass here; and across the water, the woodland is fringed with meadow sweet (*Filipendula ulmaria*), purple loosestrife (*Lythrum salicaria*) and rose-bay willow herb (*Chamaenerion angustifolium*).

Little remains of the old kitchen garden. The enclosure is now largely devoted to small animals, with rabbit runs and pens for goats and poultry and muntjak deer. A few ancient cordons survive, relics of the old fruit and vegetable garden. A maze is planned.

The wild butterfly garden is sited in a woodland glade; a large raised wooden walkway passes over the site so that visitors will not disturb the breeding cycle of the insects or damage any of the plant life. More than 50 species of trees, shrubs, plants and grasses have been established in and around this garden, host plants for butterflies, bees, dragonflies and moths. Wild honeysuckle (*Lonicera periclymenum*), roses and ivies swamp the timber stilts of the walkway, and the floor of the glade is covered in a tangled mixture of wild and garden flowers. Buttercups grow everywhere, and speedwell and forget-me-nots flower in hazy blue drifts in late spring and early summer. Herb Robert (*Geranium robertianum*) can be seen for much of the summer as can the flowers of the wild strawberry (*Fragaria vesca*).

Among the taller plants are delphiniums, golden rod (*Solidago virgaurea*), hollyhocks, foxgloves, irises and spiky teasels. There are plenty of buddleias—orange and white varieties as well as purple. Rose bay and hairy willow-herbs (*Epilobium angustifolium* and *E. parviflorum*), ragwort, sedums, honesty and feverfew (*Chrysanthemum parthenium*) flourish between large-leaved butter-burr(*Petasites hybrides*) and Michaelmas daisies provide colour in September and October.

Many different kinds of butterfly can be seen here, particularly in September. Regular visitors include meadow browns, common blues, brimstones, painted ladies, red admirals and small tortoise-shells. New plant species are introduced from time to time and invasive species such as buttercups and ground elder are kept under control. Nettles are cut back in sequence so that there are always both young and old plants.

Fruiting and berrying trees and shrubs have been planted throughout the grounds, to attract a wide range of birds. In the woods, you can see mountain ashes or rowans (*Sorbus aucuparia*), mahonias, hollies, laurels, hawthorns, several varieties of prunus and the occasional rose or hypericum, beneath oak, beech and sycamore trees. Nettles, violets, dog mercury and star of Bethlehem cover the woodland floor.

Unusual and exotic birds—particularly birds of prey—are to be found in the aviaries of the bird garden, which is situated in a glade behind the kitchen garden, surrounded by a tangled thicket of hazel and other trees and shrubs. There is a resident falconer who gives daily displays in the season.

Part of Monk's Wood, on the eastern shore of the trout lake, has been cleared of diseased elm trees and replanted with an interesting collection of trees—around 85 species, mainly native to Britain. It will be 10, perhaps 20, years before this arboretum reaches maturity. Conifers grow at the northern end and broad-leaved species to the south. The trees have also been grouped according to similarities of leaf form. The arboretum floor is covered with snowdrops, aconites, scillas and daffodils in spring; further plantings are planned, to extend the flowering season into summer.

Nature trails are laid out throughout the gardens, parklands and woodland and visitors are challenged to attempt a wildlife quiz. Details of guided nature walks with the park warden are available from the park shop and special events are often organised, such as butterfly days in July.

The Georgian estate yard has been converted into a craft centre. There are plans for a 400-seat opera house.

Sewerby Hall, Park and Zoo

ADDRESS AND TELEPHONE: Sewerby Hall, Bridlington, Humberside. Tel. (0262) 677874; Sewerby Park (0262) 673769

OWNERS: East Yorkshire Borough Council

DIRECTIONS: at Sewerby, 2 miles NE of Bridlington, on B1255. Public transport: Bridlington BR 2 miles. Scenic ride on Sewerby trains from the N promenade at Bridlington along clifftop to Sewerby Park entrance gates. Buses from Bridlington

OPENING TIMES: park and zoo daily, all year round, 9 to dusk. Sewerby Hall Art Gallery and Museum, Good Fri to last Sun in September, Mon to Fri and Sun 10–6, Sat 1.30–6

ADMISSION: free in winter. From spring to mid September £1.20,

OAPs £1, children 60p (concessions granted to pre-booked parties)

CAR PARKING: Good Fri to 1 October up to 4 hrs 50p; over 4 hrs £1; coaches £1.50

TOILETS: yes

REFRESHMENTS: café

SHOP: yes

DOGS: only on lead

WHEELCHAIR ACCESS: yes. Toilets for the disabled: yes

PEAK SEASON: June to September

NOTABLE FEATURES: splendid formal garden with monkey puzzle avenue; Old English garden; garden for the blind; rose garden; bedding displays; fine trees and shrubs

Sewerby Hall stands on the clifftop overlooking Bridlington Bay and is a popular attraction with both local residents and holiday-makers. The Hall and park were first opened to the public on 1 June 1936. Besides recreational facilities—including golf, putting and bowling greens, a children's playground, zoo and aviary—it boasts 50 acres of well-kept gardens and woodland, displaying a wide range of hardy and tender trees, shrubs and plants, which survive despite the harsh North Sea gales.

The early Georgian mansion, with white stucco and yellow stone walls, was built by Mr John Greame in 1714–20, with additions in 1808, on the site of a medieval manor house. This grand building now houses art exhibitions, archaeological displays, a collection of trophies and mementoes commemorating the historic flights of the famous Yorkshire airwoman, Amy Johnson, and an Education Wing.

The scheme of the grounds around the house is largely Victorian, the layout and much of the tree planting having been done by Mr Yarburgh, who owned the property from 1841. In front of the house is a lawn bounded by balustrading supporting statues of Ceres and Flora. On the lawn grows a splendid copper beech and the chimera (grafted hybrid) +*Laburnocytisus adamii* (*Laburnum anagyroides* +*Cytisus purpureus*). This small tree displays a pretty but somewhat confusing arrangement of flowers. Some branches bear the yellow flowers of laburnum, some the dense clusters of purple-flowered broom, while others carry intermediate flowers of a coppery-pink shade.

North of the house is a large formal garden featuring rectangular lawns with an unusual avenue of six massive monkey puzzle trees (*Araucaria araucana*) flanking a central broad walk. Younger specimens have been planted to replace those already lost to old age or gales. Two splendid specimens of weeping beech (*Fagus sylvatica* 'Pendula') also grace the lawns.

In spring the lawns are bright with formal beds of bulbs and in summer a sub-tropical atmosphere is created by the effective use of annuals—bedding pelargoniums, begonias and lobelia—around standard fuchsias, the dwarf fan palm (*Chamaerops humilis*), *Fatsia japonica*, abutilons and tall yuccas.

The planting becomes more abundant and vibrant towards the

The Old English garden at Sewerby Hall

north end of the garden, where the central walk ends at the foot of a terrace. Stone steps lead up to the terrace which provides good views over the formal garden and itself has lawns, formal planting and a temple-like summerhouse.

The formal garden is surrounded by trees but the planting bordering the western side is more open, giving views through to the parkland. The ornamental trees include a maidenhair tree (*Ginkgo biloba*), dawn redwood (*Metasequoia glyptostroboides*), hollies and a golden Irish yew. A small rocky outcrop with annuals adds colour to a planting of junipers and heathers.

A shelter belt of trees forms the eastern boundary; snowdrops flower here in February, followed by daffodils, violets, anemones and summer wild flowers. A narrow path passes through the trees to the walled garden.

Formerly the kitchen garden, this high-walled enclosure is now planted for a succession of flowers throughout the year. A wrought iron gate gives access to a small paved courtyard centring on a wishing well. Through an archway beyond is the Old English garden. Here are topiary domes, pyramids and cones; worked yew hedges, neat gravel paths and intricately shaped box-edged beds filled with colourful herbaceous and seasonal plants. In the centre is a fish pond watched over by a statue fountain of St. Louis.

Below the sheltering walls are borders rich with climbing plants, shrubs and flowers. Here grows the Mexican orange blossom (*Choisya ternata*) which carries its sweetly-scented white flowers throughout late spring and early summer, several varieties of cistus, buddleia and jasmine, winter's bark (*Drimys winteri*), variegated ivies and the New Zealand daisy bush (*Olearia* x *haastii*)—a hardy shrub which is smothered in fragrant white flowers in July and August. Ornamental grasses, lilies, peonies, delphiniums and other flowers fill out the borders in summer.

Near the entrance is a small area set aside as a garden for blind and partially sighted visitors. Enclosed by beech hedges, this garden consists of raised beds of aromatic plants—spearmint (*Mentha spicata*), thyme (*Thymus vulgaris*), blue fescue (*Festuca ovina glauca*), Dutch lavender (*Lavandula angustifolia* 'Vera') and others—all labelled with braille plaques.

Several greenhouses stand against the northern wall of the Old English garden. One features geraniums, fuchsias and conservatory plants, another orchids belonging to Alan Mather Orchids, a commercial business, and grown in climatically controlled compartments.

Beyond the west wall lies a second walled garden, the rose garden. Crazy paving and gravel paths surround geometrically shaped beds of roses edged with low box. Each bed contains a single variety—'Superstar', 'She', 'Violet Carson', 'Telstar', 'Evelyn Fison' and many more—creating a rich and vibrant pattern of colours.

A statue of 'Pandora' at the centre of the garden is surrounded by arches of climbing roses, pink, yellow and white. A summerhouse to one side is partially covered with wisteria and around the enclosing walls are climbing roses and borders of flowering shrubs and herbaceous perennials.

A gateway to the south leads into a narrow walk between shrubs. Along this sunny aspect grows the moderately hardy *Pittosporum tenuifolium* with dark red flowers in spring and several varieties of viburnum, olearia, buddleia and cistus. There is a fine range of foliage shapes and colours—variegated hollies, golden yews, mahonia, red-leaved berberis and bright green figs.

The gardens at Sewerby Hall are kept in immaculate condition by East Yorkshire Borough Council.

Stewart's Burnby Hall Gardens

ADDRESS AND TELEPHONE: Stewart's Burnby Hall Gardens and Museum, Pocklington, East Yorkshire. For information: Secretary to the Trustees, Mr H. Clarkson, Oakdene, Percy Road, Pocklington, East Yorkshire. Tel. (0759) 302315 or Resident Warden, Mr R. Hodgson (0759) 302068

OWNERS: Stewart's Burnby Hall Gardens and Museum Trust

DIRECTIONS: at Pocklington, 14 miles E of York. Access from The Balk, off the Hull road, B1247

OPENING TIMES: daily, Easter to mid October 10–6

ADMISSION: £1.50, OAPs £1, children 50p. Reductions for pre-booked parties of more than 20

CAR PARKING: yes

TOILETS: yes

REFRESHMENTS: café, open Easter to 22 May weekends and BH only, 22 May to mid October, daily 10–5

SHOP: yes (plants)

DOGS: guide dogs only

WHEELCHAIR ACCESS: yes to most parts of the garden. Toilets for the disabled: yes

PEAK SEASON: June to September

NOTABLE FEATURES: lakes, large water lily collection, National Collection of hardy water lilies, other aquatic plants; rock garden; rose garden; trees and shrubs

The gardens at Burnby Hall, Pocklington, are a mecca for devotees of the genus Nymphaea; the two lakes are home to over 60 varieties of hardy water lily—5000 plants—forming one of the largest collections in Europe. From June to the end of September the water lilies blossom in white, cream, yellow, pink, red and crimson; peak season is July, when there are literally thousands of flowers. In 1989 the Water Lily Society recognised the garden as a National Collection.

At the beginning of this century the site was nothing more than ploughed fields. In 1904, Major Percy Marlborough Stewart began to construct the Upper Water, lining the entire floor of the lake with concrete, his intention being to stock it with trout. In 1920 the Upper Water was extended to its present size, covering 1½ acres, measuring approximately 600ft by 200ft at its widest point and holding 3 million gallons of water.

Major Stewart constructed the Lower Water in 1910 in a similar manner; this lake covers ½ acre, its dimensions being 330ft by 90ft and its capacity 1 million gallons. By 1935, Major Stewart's interests had turned from trout to water lilies. He built brick walled soil beds on the lake floors, stocking them with some 90 different species and varieties of water lily. Not all proved hardy in this north-eastern location.

Looking out today over the lily-filled lakes, you may spot the canary yellow blooms of 'Moorei', the pure white of 'Gladstoniana', the rich rose pink 'René Gerard', carmine red 'James Brydon', deep crimson 'Escarboucle' and dark ruby red 'William Falconer'. There are far too many to list here and the sight of their flowering in July defies description.

The depth of water in which the lilies grow varies from 6in. for miniature varieties to 4ft for the more vigorous types. A wide range of coarse and ornamental fish swim among the leaves, including rudd, roach, koi carp, golden orfe and shubunkin.

Although man-made, both lakes look entirely natural, being informal in shape and edged with reeds and water-loving marginal plants. There are borders of hostas, numerous ornamental grasses and rushes and many species of primula as well as irises and others such as the water forget-me-not (Myosotis palustris) and water plantain (Alisma plantago-aquatica).

The Upper Water lies at a level 10ft above the Lower Water, the two being connected by a cascading stream which runs through a well established rock garden constructed of large boulders. Gravel paths weaving around the rocks follow the course of the stream.

Stewart's Burnby Hall Gardens: for devotees of the genus Nymphaea. (Ward Lock Ltd)

The lawns around the lakes are planted with a variety of trees and shrubs. There are lilacs and laburnums, a dawn redwood (*Metasequoia glyptostroboides*) and swamp cypress (*Taxodium distichum*), a maidenhair tree (*Ginkgo biloba*), Japanese maples (*Acer palmatum*) and around 20 varieties of hollies. The trees and tall shrubs in borders and island beds are interplanted with spiraeas, potentillas, brooms and berberis and there is a planting of rhododendrons. Bedding plants are added in summer for colour.

Many of the trees and shrubs were planted by Major Stewart, who maintained an interest in the garden until his death in 1962, aged 90. New plantings are now introduced every year, funded by subscriptions from Friends of the garden.

The walled garden, close to the rock garden, was transformed in 1982 into a formal rose garden with long beds set into the lawn to display 1100 rose bushes in 17 varieties.

Among the floribundas here is the popular 'Arthur Bell', with large fragrant golden yellow blooms which stand up well to the rain, as do the vivid scarlet petals of 'Evelyn Fison', one of the best red floribundas. 'Glenfiddich' is a new floribunda with golden amber flowers.

There are hybrid tea roses too, such as 'Doris Tysterman' an English bred rose introduced in 1975 and a good bedding variety;

its shapely tangerine-coloured blooms are produced well into the autumn. More recent is 'Silver Jubilee', free flowering with salmon-pink blooms. 'Blessings', with fragrant coral pink flowers, is another excellent bedding variety.

The long timber pergola, supporting young climbing roses, clematis, wisterias and other climbers, was set up in 1988; at the same time, herbaceous borders were established below the walls. Both features should look splendid in a few years.

Two raised beds, recently built next to the rose garden, contain scented plants, to give pleasure to blind and partially sighted visitors. The Stewart's Burnby Hall Gardens and Museum Trust is responsible for new ideas and ongoing maintenance. The purpose-built museum houses sporting and other trophies collected by Major Stewart on his travels around the world.

ISLES OF SCILLY

Abbey Gardens

ADDRESS AND TELEPHONE: Abbey Gardens, Tresco, Isles of Scilly. Tel. (0720) 22849

OWNER: R.A. Dorrien-Smith, Esq

DIRECTIONS: sail from Penzance with Isles of Scilly Steamship Company (tel. 0736 66485). Fly by British Airways helicopter from Penzance Heliport (tel. 0736 63871). Fly by Skybus from Land's End with Isles of Scilly Skybus Ltd (tel. 0736 787017)

OPENING TIMES: daily throughout the year, 10–4. House not open

ADMISSION: £2.50. Parties by prior arrangement

CAR PARKING: no

TOILETS: yes

REFRESHMENTS: café

SHOP: yes

DOGS: no

WHEELCHAIR ACCESS: yes. Toilets for the disabled: no

PEAK MONTHS: March to September

NOTABLE FEATURES: collections of sub-tropical plants grown outdoors; exhibition of ships' figureheads salvaged off Scillies

Lying in the Atlantic Ocean, some 30 miles off the coast of Cornwall, and bathed by the Gulf Stream, Tresco is the second largest of the islands (750 acres) in the Scillies group. The 14-acre Abbey Gardens are home to a magnificent collection of sub-tropical plants including many rare species.

Winter temperatures rarely fall below 10°C, although there has been the odd exception, notably in January 1987 when sub-zero temperatures and freezing winds caused havoc on a scale previously thought impossible. But the wind is a constant enemy. Over the centuries, gales and storms have sent hundreds of ships floundering onto the rocks and the Abbey Gardens owe their survival to the foresight of the founder, Augustus Smith (ancestor of the present owner), who planted extensive shelter belts.

A Hertfordshire man by birth, Smith acquired the leasehold of all the Isles of Scilly in 1834 and set about building himself a granite house in the middle of Tresco, close to the ruins of a Benedictine Priory. The island was then barren and windswept. Smith began by barricading the garden from strong winds with shelter belts of conifers—particularly the recently introduced Monterey cypress (*Cupressus macrocarpa*) and the Monterey pine (*Pinus radiata*), both of which stand up well to gales. He also planted tall hedges of holm oak (*Quercus ilex*). Along the south-facing slope near to his house he cut out three long terraces—the Long Walk, Middle and Top Terraces—with high retaining granite walls. He then established a sub-tropical garden, with plants from Kew and seeds from all over the world. Today there are more than 3000 species, with a special emphasis on plants from the Southern hemisphere—Australia, New Zealand, Central and Southern America, South Africa and the Canary Islands.

Space limits us to a brief description of the most spectacular parts of the garden, and some particularly memorable plants. Continual efforts are made to keep species well labelled and visitors are advised to buy a copy of the guidebook, where many of the plants are described in detail.

There are numerous tall date palms from the Canary Islands, a small grove of the magnificent orange-barked *Myrtus luma* from Chile, acacias, eucalyptus and several forms of metrosideros—the Pohutakawa or New Zealand Christmas Tree. Especially noteworthy is a gigantic specimen of *Metrosideros tomentosa*. At 80ft tall, this is thought to be the largest in the world and has a profusion of aerial roots. In summer it is covered with rich crimson flowers. Some of the smaller plants are equally eye-catching—spiky-leaved agaves and aloes can be seen at almost every turn and there are excellent collections of banksia and protea species.

One of the most photographed parts of the garden is the area around the old priory ruins. The ancient walls and archways of St Nicholas' Priory are now alive with plants, providing support for both climbers and wall succulents. Here *Solanum jasminoides*, honeysuckles and the wonderful blue-flowering *Convolvulus mauretanicus* drape over the ruins while succulent rosettes of aeonium species and the pretty Mexican daisy (*Erigeron mucronatus*) spill out from the cracks in the walls. Banana trees flourish here, and there are beds filled with pelargoniums and agapanthus.

Not far away from the abbey, in the shelter of a huge holm oak (*Quercus ilex*) hedge, is a splendid rockery excavated into the 40ft cliff below the house. Throughout spring and summer the rockery is bright with aeoniums and mesembryanthemums, and spiky-leaved Mexican agaves.

The middle terrace, cutting across the garden from east to west, is very Mediterranean and includes a rock mass, known as Mexico, covered with the waxy, greeny-turquoise flowers of Chilean *Puya alpestris*. Aloes and other plants from Cape Province of South Africa feature on the overhanging cliff.

Further along a stone built summerhouse has acquired a 'roof' of Burmese honeysuckle (*Lonicera hildebrandiana*). This is a delightful and fragrant resting place from which to admire the many sub-tropical species on the terrace.

From the top terrace there are splendid views across the garden and over the Tresco Channel. A wooden ship's figurehead of the sea god Neptune presides over a grand flight of steps leading from the top terrace, down to the lowest point of the garden where it joins the Lighthouse Walk—named after the 17C cresset of St Agnes light.

Another area not to be missed is the aptly named Valhalla—the resting place of heroes. Here in an open-sided building is an exhibition of ships' figureheads—all wrecked on the Scillies during the last 300 years.

To ensure your trip is memorable for the right reasons, some planning is needed. Many people opt for a day trip, booking a crossing from Penzance to St Mary's on the Scillonian, which is operated by the Isles of Scilly Steamship Company. Sailing time is about 2 hours and you get magnificent views of the Cornish coastline and the Scillies themselves as the ship weaves between the islands to dock at St Mary's.

About half an hour before landing, depending on tides and weather, the Captain announces the arrangements for those passengers travelling to Tresco. Tickets for the launch from St Mary's to Tresco and for entrance to the gardens are then sold on board ship.

The Tresco launch leaves five minutes after the Scillonian has docked and will land you at one of two sites on the island—Carn Near, which is about ½ mile from the garden or New Grimsby, which is a 1¼-mile walk away. Day visitors should note that you land at one site and leave from the other. There are several hotels on Tresco and more on St Mary's.

For those who prefer to fly, British Airways operates a helicopter service from Penzance heliport, the helicopter lands right outside the garden gate. There is also a regular skybus service from Land's End Aerodrome to St Mary's.

The pure air and bright light of the Scillies can lead to serious sunburn, and photographers should make allowances for the high light intensity.

ISLE OF WIGHT

Ventnor Botanic Garden

ADDRESS AND TELEPHONE: Undercliff Drive, Ventnor, Isle of Wight PO38 1UL. Tel. (0983) 855397

OWNERS: South Wight Borough Council

DIRECTIONS: Hovercraft, vehicle or passenger ferry from Portsmouth, A0355 to Ventnor; passenger or vehicle ferry from Southampton, A3020 to Ventnor; passenger and vehicle ferry from Lymington, A0354/A3020/A0355 to Ventnor. Public transport: Southern Vectis bus from Yarmouth, Cowes, Fishbourne or Ryde. (Tel. 0983 522456 for details)

OPENING TIMES: 24 hours a day. Temperate house open 10–5

ADMISSION: garden free but 50p for temperate house (children 20p)

CAR PARKING: yes. Coach parties welcome

TOILETS: yes

REFRESHMENTS: café

SHOP: yes

DOGS: on lead

WHEELCHAIR ACCESS: to most of garden. Toilets for the disabled: yes

PEAK MONTHS: May to September

NOTABLE FEATURES: temperate house, Mediterranean and sub-tropical planting; wild meadow

For a small area—some 25 by 12 miles—the Isle of Wight is blessed with an unusually valuable resource: the 22-acre Botanic Garden on the Undercliff at Ventnor. Here, close beside the sea, enclosed by the downs and the hillside, tender and sub-tropical species flourish as if in their natural habitat. The protected site, together with the clear light of the south coast, gives Ventnor the kind of climatic conditions enjoyed by gardens in sheltered parts of the West Country and the Scillies. Of course, like others of its kind, Ventnor has connections beyond its immediate neighbourhood, maintaining links with botanic gardens throughout the world. It also has a flourishing Friends Society, with membership drawn not only from the island, but from much farther afield.

Ventnor is a very new botanic garden, begun in the late 1960s and opened in 1972. Its temperate house, designed by the Borough Architect to conserve heat and constructed in aluminium and steel, was only planted in 1987, yet the plants are already at an impressive height. This attractive glasshouse, sited below the southerly road from Ventnor and above the long shallow valley which contains the rest of the garden, already bears comparison with houses established elsewhere for a far longer time. It makes a good starting point for the visitor.

Two things—apart from the plants—catch your attention on entry: one is the marvellous natural light, the other the constant accompaniment of classical and baroque music: both, according to the curator, Simon Goodenough, contributing to the amazing speed of plant growth. Another favourable factor may be the fertile sandy loam in the beds, brought from areas of the island being cleared for building.

The plants are arranged in geographical groups—Australia, South Africa, the Canary Islands, New Zealand and South America—and selected for their texture, form and shape as well as for conservation purposes: 20 per cent are from species on the verge of extinction. As well as trees and shrubs, there are groups of perennials, and any gaps are filled by annuals in season. The nursery holds a collection of 70 South African pelargoniums, 18–20 of which are on display in the house, all grown from seed and all documented.

In the Australasian section there are many varieties of acacia, including the tall, silver *A. podalyriifolia* from Queensland and the willow-leaved *A. cuthbertsonii*. There are scarlet bottlebrushes (callistemons) and tall, blue-leaved eucalyptus. In the Canary Islands bed we noticed an attractive limonium, or sea lavender, which bears blue flowers. The New Zealand bed contains a number of pittosporums and clumps of bright, sword-leaved phormiums or New Zealand flax. Many delicate herbaceous and annual plants flower in the South African bed, along with a selection of pelargoniums, and several bold, showy strelitzias, called the bird of paradise flower because of the distinctive shape of their flower heads. *Brugmansia (Datura) insignis* from South America displays its pale, peach-coloured trumpets, and further on are two spectacular passionflowers from South America—*Passiflora edulis*, the purple granadilla, and *P. quadrangularis*, the giant granadilla, which derives its Latin name from its angled stems. Its flowers are outstanding: violet, banded white and deep purple. You leave the glasshouse past a last burst of colour: a bed of gold foliage, above which a collection of brilliant bougainvilleas climbs to the roof.

The garden has a policy of arranging school visits to the temperate house, and children, under supervision, are encouraged to touch the plants on the grounds that familiarity will breed respect, rather than contempt. It is worth stopping to look at the raised beds just outside the temperate house, built under a YTS scheme and planted by disabled people for people who are blind and partially sighted. The plants are tactile, like the tiny mats of *Raoulia australis*, or aromatic, like *Dianthus alpinus*, or surprising, like the exploding cucumber (*Ecbalium elaterium*), which squirts its seed at the unwary.

From the temperate house, you walk down to the main garden valley: the near, landward slope is laid out with lawn, terrace beds and borders, the far side is a grass slope well furnished with trees. When the garden here was replanted, a sample of soil was sent away to be analysed and subsequently returned with the recommendation that, as it was useless for horticulture, it should be used only for building on. With the help of compost, this verdict has been completely overturned. The majority of the soil is alkaline, although at the east end of the garden, a more acid area enables camellias and magnolias to flourish.

To your right as you come down the steps lies a walled garden which once belonged to the old hospital. Against the stone wall is a collection of hebes—pink, cerise, blue and purple. There are other tender plants: oleanders, daturas and the brilliant red New Zealand lobster claw (*Clianthus puniceus*). Trees on the grass nearby include *Firmiana simplex*, the Chinese parasol tree, with smooth grey bark and handsome lobed leaves. There is a special *Magnolia grandiflora* named for Charles Dickens, who lived for some time on the Isle of Wight.

To the left, past a low hedge of Portuguese laurel, a paved terrace interspersed with garden beds leads you eastwards, towards lily pool and tavern garden. As you walk along you will find many Mediterranean plants—cistus and lavenders and the Mount Etna broom (*Genista aetnensis*). The aromatic honey flower (*Melianthus major*) sprawls over the wall, displaying its toothed glaucous leaves. A handsome fan palm from the Mediterranean grows happily in the open and osteospermum 'Whirlygig', shows its attractive daisy flowers. A bed of dark grey gravel displays silver artemisias, sedum, diascias and a gold erysimum 'Bowles Hybrid'. Below the far end of the terrace is a culinary garden, which the café chef is encouraged to make use of.

The area in front of the café contains an oval lily pool and fountain, surrounded by a topiary hedge and rose arbor. These are currently being redesigned.

The great gale of October 1987 devastated the eastern end of the garden, tearing trees out of the slope below the car park. Although the devastation is still apparent, new planting is also very much in evidence. The area is being resurrected as a Victorian garden, where the remaining magnolias and camellias and a group of windmill palms (*Trachycarpus fortunei*) are being supplemented by tall blue echiums and bright red and yellow cannas. Other sub-tropical planting is gradually filling the beds: strelitzias, yuccas, cordylines and the striking *Beschorneria yuccoides*, which produces bright red flowers on coral stems above a blue-grey rosette of leaves. There is a sizeable collection of phormiums—perhaps reflecting the fact that this garden is twinned with that of the Timaru City Council in New Zealand—and a group of *Hebe cupressoides*, which is now endangered in that country. An interesting feature is a group of plants (*Pseudopanax*) with polymorphic leaves, that is, young leaves entirely different from those produced on maturity. The garden holds the National Collection of *Pseudopanax*. A terrace with seats has been built on the south-facing slope below the car park.

Nearby, where there was once a rather gloomy wooded area, new beds are being laid out with a combination of shrubs and herbaceous plants, both perennials and annuals. Along the seaward slope of the valley, as you return westwards, is a variety of specimen trees, mostly recent plantings, including conifers of contrasting form and habit.

At the top of this seaward slope, a path cuts through to the sea, giving a long view of Ventnor and the coast. The slope down to the cliffs has been divided, with the top area mown close, and the lower stretch left as a hay meadow. Wild flowers, including bee orchids, have seeded themselves and more seed is being brought from other wild areas in the island to supplement what has grown naturally.

Returning across the garden and climbing up the opposite slope towards car park and gift shop, you come to a medicinal garden, which includes plants used for healing by the Maoris, Native Americans and the Australian Aboriginals, as well as more tender plants from Africa and India, which are taken inside in winter.

New features like this are part of an overall programme of growth and diversification. Young people have been involved in projects where possible: YTS workers, to whom gardens originally meant little, still return to see the features they helped to construct. Its exposed location means that Ventnor depends crucially on the goodwill and integrity of the visiting public for its continued survival. Open 24 hours a day, with no boundary fence, it necessarily

relies on the honesty of visitors and walkers to protect its contents—
a trust which has so far been little abused. With its strong links to
the community and innovative programme of development, Ventnor promises much for the future and is already well worth the
journey to the Isle of Wight.

KENT

Goodnestone Park

ADDRESS AND TELEPHONE: Canterbury, Kent CT3 1QF. Tel.
(0304) 840218

OWNERS: The Lord and Lady FitzWalter

DIRECTIONS: S of the B2046 between the A2 and Wingham

OPENING TIMES: mid April to 7 July; 28 July to September,
weekdays, including BH, 11–5; also Sun 2–6. House not open

ADMISSION: £1.50, OAPs £1.30, children under 12 20p, visitors in
wheelchairs £1. Coach parties welcome

CAR PARKING: yes

TOILETS: yes

REFRESHMENTS: Sun only and not in April

SHOP: no

DOGS: no

WHEELCHAIR ACCESS: yes. Toilets for the disabled: yes

NOTABLE FEATURES: old roses; walled garden; woodland area
and rock garden; terraces

Goodnestone Park (pronounced 'Gunston') lies 15 miles south-east
of Canterbury, surrounded by extensive parkland and farmland.
The FitzWalter family home for over 250 years, it has a connection
with Jane Austen—her eldest brother Edward married Elizabeth,
a daughter of Sir Brook Bridges (3rd Bt), an ancestor of the present
owner, and Jane later conducted a regular, affectionate correspondence with their daughter Fanny.

The 15-acre garden divides roughly into three parts: formal
terraced lawns to east and west, a woodland garden at the top
and—the main and finest feature—a huge walled garden, filled
with old-fashioned roses. The soil is mainly chalk, but acid in the
woodland.

Like many great gardens, Goodnestone was neglected during
the war, when it was requisitioned as a prisoner-of-war camp; very
little was done between 1936 and 1955 and the woodland area was
left untouched until the early 1970s. Together with her head
gardener, John Wellard, Lady FitzWalter worked gradually to clear,
reclaim and replant it. (More than 30 years on, John Wellard is still
at Goodnestone: a skilled propagator, he produces hundreds of
plants every year, for the garden and plant centre.)

Old roses are a feature throughout the garden. Huge bushes of white 'Nevada' and yellow 'Maigold' alternate along the terrace; while 'Fantin Latour', 'Tuscany' and others can be found in a long bed further south. The spacious terraced lawns were designed in the 1840s and have hardly been changed since, except for the planting of mixed borders and ornamental trees. The eastern terraces overlook an open stretch of parkland, separated from the garden by a sunken brick wall. On the western side, an impressive series of wide stone steps breaks the smooth, soft lines of the terraces, harmonising in scale with the huge Doric portico, a Georgian addition to the house.

The eastern and western sides are divided by a sunny border, backed by a yew hedge. The huge sweet chestnut is probably as old as the house (built in 1704). A new avenue of young limes (*Tilia platyphyllos*), 100 yds long, strikes off to the west, following the line of a vista shown on an 18C map of the park: this was planted in celebration of three happily coinciding family events, a marriage, a coming of age and Lord FitzWalter's 70th birthday.

The woodland garden lies some way above the lawns. Emily FitzWalter, the present Lord FitzWalter's aunt, laid out a rockery (of York stone) and pool area here in the 1920s, and much of her original planting survives.

Not far away, below spring borders and a rose border, lies the spendid 18C walled garden. Covering roughly 4 acres, this is divided by crossing walls into three rectangles. The village church tower provides a focal point at the far end, exactly in line with the long central vista. Old roses and clematis grow in wonderful variety and abundance throughout, accompanied by many other excellent flowering shrubs and perennials.

The furthest section was redesigned towards the end of the 1980s, with fruit and vegetable beds backing the long central borders. On the end wall is an ancient wisteria, planted by Emily FitzWalter and flanked by ceanothus and climbing roses.

In the central section is a pair of late summer borders, edged with box. Silver weeping pears (*Pyrus salicifolia* 'Pendula') are planted in a line down the lawn, running parallel to a long path, spanned by rose arches. At the end of the path is a white ornamental seat, backed by white rugosa roses There is a gold corner opposite.

A very old specimen of sweetly scented *Abelia triflora*, also planted by Emily FitzWalter, hangs over one of the entrance gates, its fragrance harmonising in late summer with the strong lemony scent of an enormous free-standing *Magnolia grandiflora*, near the greenhouses.

Great Comp

ADDRESS AND TELEPHONE: Borough Green, near Sevenoaks, Kent. TN15 8QS. Tel. (0732) 882669

OWNERS: Mr and Mrs R. Cameron and the Great Comp Charitable Trust

DIRECTIONS: between Maidstone and Sevenoaks: take the A25 or A20, turning S onto the B2016 at Wrotham Heath and then

½ mile W at first crossroads. Public transport: Borough Green station 1½ miles

OPENING TIMES: 1 April to 31 October, daily 11–6; season ticket holders admitted in winter. House not open

ADMISSION: £2, children £1. Coach parties by appointment

CAR PARKING: yes

TOILETS: yes

REFRESHMENTS: tea room open Sun afternoons

SHOP: garden guide and plant sales

DOGS: no

WHEELCHAIR ACCESS: partial. Toilets for the disabled: no

PEAK MONTHS: year-round interest

NOTABLE FEATURES: conifers, heathers and herbaceous perennials

This beautiful 7-acre garden surrounding an early 17C house is owned by Mr and Mrs R. Cameron, who bought the original 4½-acre plot in 1957, adding extra land in 1962 and 1975. Together they redesigned and almost completely replanted it (retaining some mature trees, walls and paths from a former scheme) and maintained it until the early 1980s, when the Great Comp Charitable Trust was set up. Most of the work was done from 1970 onwards, after Mr Cameron had retired.

The garden is planned for year-round interest in a series of grass walks and lawn areas, flanked by woodland, shrub beds and borders. The main axis runs from the house north-west through a forecourt, lawn and terrace. On the other side it bisects a square raised lawn, continuing south-east in a wide walk between specimen trees and grouped heather beds. Conifers and heathers are a feature of the garden, combined with well-established herbaceous planting.

Entering on the north side, from the car park, and having paid your entrance money at the small summerhouse, you come out onto the wide front lawn, sloping up towards the top terrace. A splendid group of brilliantly coloured conifers can be seen opposite, near the forecourt. Viburnums dominate the left-hand shrub and herbaceous plant bed, backed by trees including a rowan with bright orange berries. Two ginkgos stand either side of the top path; nearby is *Sorbus torminalis*, the chequer tree or wild service tree.

The borders here are planted in what Mr Cameron describes as 'elevated cottage style': although you would probably find pink and mauve phlox and mauve and white violas in a cottage garden, you might be surprised to see elegant *Dierama pulcherrimum* (angel's fishing rod) with its purple-pink trumpet flowers suspended from slender stems; or a striking double crocosmia; or big spiky yucca and phormium.

Shallow paving steps lead up to the terrace (the Camerons laid all the paving themselves). Various berberis make a brilliant display under the balustrade, including yellow *B. thunbergii* 'Aurea', *B.t.* 'Rose Glow' with mottled rose shoots turning purple, and blue-green *B. temolaica*. Close by is a herb bed of gold sage, variegated thyme and variegated rue, overhung by fuchsia and abelia.

The top path, running parallel to Comp Lane, was planted in the 1970s, with borders to the right and left. The rich planting here includes Exbury azaleas grown from seed, hydrangea 'Blue Wave', *Styrax japonica*, clethras, *Hamamelis japonica* 'Arborea' (Japanese witch-hazel) and many magnolias. In all, the garden boasts over 50 magnolias (about 30 different varieties). A middle path curves up from the main front lawn: again thickly bordered with shrubs and trees including *Acer capillipes*, the snake-bark maple.

The area just beyond here, to the east, was planted in the 1960s. An enormous silver birch, *Betula pendula*, stands in your path: continue round it to view *Cercidiphyllum japonicum* with its round leaves, *Pinus sylvestris* 'Aurea' (turning yellow in winter) and a red oak (*Quercus rubra*). Mr Cameron recommends *Nothofagus obliqua*, a beech from Chile, as a woodland tree, as it is very fast growing—perhaps it may be the forest tree of the future—and it provides good shelter for rhododendrons. *Rhododendron falconeri* shows its large dark leaves to striking effect in a clearing, with *Cornus florida rubra*, the American dogwood. Further down is a fine dawn redwood *Metasequoia glyptostroboides*, discovered in China in 1941.

One great delight of Great Comp is the number of long vistas, giving a sense of spaciousness and relief from enclosure. One stretches eastwards from the summerhouse to the miniature 'Place d'Etoile', which centres on a Doulton Urn, and offers a choice of six surrounding paths. Following either of the middle paths, you should soon reach the lion summerhouse, tastefully converted from an old outside privy, backed by tall limes, and set in the centre of an impressive rock garden which, however, has no rocks.

The 'ruins' in this area were built to design by the Camerons, starting with stones from the edging of previous borders in 1976 and adding gradual extensions. Mr Cameron points out how with a bit of imagination you can build your own fake antiquities. Various conifers add to the picturesque effect. Sun-loving heathers and rock plants grow beneath the walls, and climbers tumble over them, including *Parthenocissus henryana* with its dark wine-red leaves and tendrils.

Continuing onwards to the main cross path, note in front of you a handsome specimen of the Chinese rowan *Sorbus hupehensis*, with attractive pink berries. The area about here was replanted from 1977 onwards, with many kinds of conifer and heather beds. *Erica arborea* 'Alpina' burgeons at the corner (the roots of this plant are still used to make briar pipes). There are many varieties of calluna or Scots heather, flowering in summer and autumn: also winter-blooming *Erica carnea* and its derivatives, and the pink and white Cornish heath, *Erica vagans*. Walking away from here, we saw *Magnolia* x *loebneri* 'Leonard Messel', which produces pink starry flowers in spring.

Having reached the garden's extreme south-eastern perimeter, a long straight path reaching from the vine urn to the temple, you should soon locate the main vista up to the house. Winter heathers grow to your left (blooming from February to May) and summer heathers on the right (flowering in August and September). All these are about 20 years old. Trees and shrubs in this area include the American smoke bush (*Cotinus americanus*) in the middle distance and some very striking groupings of conifers.

This lower garden area was mainly planted in 1962. We also admired *Quercus palustris*, the American pin oak, with its slender drooping branches. Here too is *Pinus muricata*, the picturesque Bishop pine from California, which keeps its cones for up to 40 years (these have held on for 20 years so far!); and several specimens of *Abies grandis*, the giant fir from western North America.

Near the Chilstone temple, erected in 1973, is silver *Pyrus salicifolia* 'Pendula', and nearby stands *Chamaecyparis nootkatense* 'Pendula', the weeping Nootka cypress, backed by *Campanula lactiflora*.

More mature pines border the path, and a tulip tree is strikingly complemented by a variety of Norway maple. Left of the central opening, note *Magnolia* x *veitchii*, beautiful in spring with its pink and white flowers. Underneath grow shade- and damp-loving plants: among them, hostas, ferns, irises, lysimachia and grasses, and a bright pink-red polygonum.

The big curving heather bed just below the Square contains some lovely conifers, all 25 years old or more, including shapely *Picea albertiana* 'Conica', two dwarf cypresses and a golden yew. Near the steps of the Square, you can see the Californian redwood *Sequoia sempervirens* 'Cantab', claimed by Mr Cameron to be the finest specimen in existence. The stump of a 19-year-old eucalyptus lost in the storm of 1990 stands on the lawn. A herbaceous border runs round the inside of the Square, colourful and cheering with tall coral-feathered plume poppies, pale yellow heads of achillea 'Moonshine', pink achillea 'Cerise Queen' and white achillea 'The Pearl'; pink gypsophila 'Rosy Veil' and pink sedum; euonymus 'Silver Queen' next to a yucca with white bells; buddleia, bergenias and a variety of dahlias.

Before leaving you may want to book tickets for one of the classical concerts held regularly at Great Comp, below wooden rafters in the converted old stables. Nearby is a fine and too rarely seen plant, *Berberis valdiviana*, with saffron yellow drooping flowers borne in racemes and large leathery leaves.

Hever Castle

ADDRESS AND TELEPHONE: Hever, near Edenbridge, Kent TN8 7NG. Tel. Edenbridge (O732) 865224

OWNERS: Broadland Properties Ltd, Edenbridge, Kent

DIRECTIONS: signposted from M25 Junction 6, from Edenbridge and from A21 Sevenoaks turnoff. Public transport: by train (Uckfield service) from London Victoria hourly. Taxis available at Edenbridge. 1 mile walk from Edenbridge to Hever

OPENING TIMES: mid March to beginning November daily. Gardens open 11–5 (castle opens 12 noon)

ADMISSION: castle and gardens £4.40, OAPs £4, children £2.20; gardens only £3, OAPs £2.60, children 5–16 £1.80. Reductions for parties (minimum 15) and student groups

CAR PARKING: yes

TOILETS: yes near car park and restaurant

REFRESHMENTS: café and refreshment tent

SHOP: yes, souvenirs and guidebooks

DOGS: on lead only

WHEELCHAIR ACCESS: yes. Toilets for the disabled: yes

PEAK MONTHS: April through to October

NOTABLE FEATURES: the 30-acre gardens contain a maze, herb garden, topiary garden, Italian garden, walled rose garden, rhododendron and spring gardens, wood and lakeside walks

Hever Castle and gardens have a singular history. In 1462 Anne Boleyn's grandfather built a manor house at Hever around the existing 13C moated gatehouse. The manor was Anne's childhood home and later the scene of much of her courtship by Henry VIII. After Anne's execution, the castle reverted to the Crown, and later Henry gave it to his divorced 4th wife, Anne of Cleves. After 17 years the royal connection was severed and the castle (although never fully fortified it has a drawbridge, turrets and a moat) passed into the hands of a series of families, among whom were the Waldegraves and the Meade Waldos. None of the owners or tenants appear to have developed the estate to any extent, although Captain and Mrs Sebright, in 1900, commissioned Joseph Cheal & Son, Kentish nurserymen, to lay out gardens in the immediate vicinity of the castle.

In 1903, however, the situation changed dramatically. Waldorf Astor, an American millionaire, bought and restored the castle, adding a 'Tudor Village', designed by Frank Loughborough Pearson, to house his guests and servants. Astor retained Joseph Cheal and Loughborough Pearson to design an ambitious series of gardens, covering some 30 acres and stretching eastwards from the castle, culminating in a new 35-acre lake. This involved completely reconstructing the landscape by excavating the lake and moving vast quantities of soil and rock on specially constructed railways. Mature trees were transplanted and Scots pines brought from Ashdown forest, 12 miles away. This ambitious and, on its own terms, completely successful project ensured that the gardens at Hever today are an entirely 20C creation, even though they draw much of their inspiration from earlier times.

In laying out the gardens immediately around the castle, Waldorf Astor was careful to incorporate only designs that would have been current at the time when the Boleyns (or Bullens) lived there—though he did not always make the same proviso for plants and shrubs. Having crossed the outer moat from the nearby car park, you step on to a topiary lawn, where an odd assortment of squat yew doves and peacocks, tables, chairs and corkscrews sit on the smooth grass slopes above the moat. To the left lies Anne Boleyn's orchard, filled with cherries and crab apples and drifts of daffodils and narcissi in spring. Across the orchard, the faintly Disneyesque roofs and chimneys of the Tudor Village (now a conference centre) cluster round the castle. The yellow stone walls of the castle itself are adorned with shrubs and climbers: near the drawbridge a yellow *Fremontodendron californicum* and a white wisteria were flowering in May, near the dark red leaves of summer-flowering canna. Many more shrubs and climbers for this area are listed in the detailed garden guide.

Beyond the drawbridge is the entrance to a vast square maze, 80ft by 80ft. On a fine Sunday in August, cries of puzzled visitors rose above the clipped yew hedges. Opposite this handsome feature lies Anne Boleyn's garden, said to be laid out and planted in Tudor style. Certainly the herbs, contained in two yew 'rooms' would probably have all been familiar in Anne Boleyn's time— thymes, sages, chives, lavender, angelica, lovage and fennel. A double herm stands at a turn in the path, gazing simultaneously in two directions. Beyond the herb garden lies a paved fountain garden, with bushes of 'Ballerina roses' in pale pink and with four weeping standard roses at the corners.

Standing in the Fountain Garden looking through into the chess garden you will see an elegant gold astrolabe, which dates from the reign of a later Queen Anne. Beyond is the Chess Garden in golden yew, based on 16C designs of chess pieces in the British Museum. From here you can easily enter the moatside walk, shaded by a pergola hung with laburnum, wisteria, clematis and roses. There is a pleasant view across to the extensive chestnut avenue on the far shore.

The 'Tudor' area ends here, and you progress to the Italian gardens, passing the newly established Winter Garden along the far side of the moat extension. The bank is lined with cotoneaster, *Acer greiseum*, rosemary and weeping willows. Waldorf Astor was not only a millionaire and garden enthusiast, but an avid collector of classical statuary, a taste that he was well placed to indulge while he was American Minister in Rome. When he acquired Hever, he had his collection of statues, busts, urns, well heads and sarcophagi shipped over from Italy. For these he laid out his Italian gardens, consisting of a half-moon pond, three large enclosed lawns with fountains and pools, a sunken garden, a Pergola Walk with a grotto for water-loving plants, a spectacular loggia and terrace overlooking the lake and—perhaps the most striking—a Pompeiian Walk running the length of the garden, some 220 yds long. Here he displayed his collection against a specially constructed background of stone walls and terraces, planted lavishly with trees, shrubs and flowering plants.

The half-moon pond, which you encounter first, has the virtue of simplicity. The pool is set in paving, with a statue of Venus with Cupid at her feet at the centre of the curved edge, backed by a clipped yew hedge. On your right, to the south of the pool, is the Cascade Garden, a generous outpouring of water over rock, surrounded by banks filled in with every conceivable colour of rhododendron and azalea, with Japanese acers. From here you turn into the Pergola Walk, a cool place on a hot day; climbers form a canopy overhead and cover the supporting stone pillars. There is a constant sound of water, both from fountains on the central lawns and from the grotto to your right, where ferns, hostas, primulas and many other damp-loving plants flourish.

At the central point of this walk you can enter the sunken garden. Here you may sit peacefully, listening to the miniature Silenus fountain. In the raised beds to either side of the pool are silver-leaved, white and yellow plants.

Walking along the northern Pompeiian wall, you can appreciate the extent and variety of Waldorf Astor's collection. The wall is divided into a series of bays, each housing several exhibits framed by judiciously contrived ruins. The planting is lavish, well maintained and in most cases very successful—the fifth bay contains a *Magnolia* x *soulangiana* spreading its purple-pink tulip-shaped flowers against the wall, a red *Acer palmatum dissectum*, a yellow honeysuckle, and a yellow *Fremontodendron californicum*. The plants frame a collection of statuary which includes an ornate table with caryatids and a small statue of a hermaphrodite.

Further on there are fig trees, bright blue ceanothus, wisterias, vines, red and yellow abutilon, mecopotanum and several examples of the valuable climbing single red rose 'Parkdirektor Riggers'. The busts of Roman dignatories from long ago gaze calmly, gravely or mournfully down on this vigorous plant life. Occasionally the bedding over-reaches itself and detracts from the centuries-old grey and white stone columns or funerary altars, but most of the planting is interesting and harmonious.

Having walked the length of this unique display, you come to the loggia, which commands a splendid view of the lake. In springtime the shores of the lake are covered in daffodils. The vast nymph fountain here is early 20C.

At this point you may be glad to know that you are near the restaurant, but there are still two more walled gardens to see—one a rose garden, with beds of well-established modern roses such as 'Amber Queen', 'Iceberg', 'Silver Jubilee', and climbing roses on the walls and pillars. A sacrifical altar also appears here, as well as two rampant lions, and two ancient columns are engulfed by laburnum. It is rare to find such distinguished plant supports. Leading back from the rose garden is a rocky enclosure for blue plants. The rocks are massive and high (brought from Chiddingstone Causeway). We noticed a ceanothus set high above our heads against a wall, and *Lithospermum diffusum* 'Heavenly Blue' cascading over a rock face. There are also blue rhododendrons, hydrangeas, pansies, blue polyanthus, hyacinths, forget-me-nots, ageratum, blue salvias and aquilegias with blue periwinkles providing ground cover.

From these last formal areas, or from the nearby restaurant, you can easily walk on to the lakeside, a favourite place for picnics. Here is a fine specimen of *Lirodendron magnoliaceae*.

You are now at the farthest part of the gardens and can return by a pleasant wooded walk, again attributed to Anne Boleyn—though she might have been startled to encounter the lake. Here you will pass some interesting specimen trees: a group of the graceful *Parrotia persica* which turns varied and subtle colours in autumn, an umbrella pine (*Pinus pinea*) sheltering a hillock above the restaurant, copper hazels and copper beeches and a tulip tree (*Liriodendron tulipifera*). Near the turning to the Sisters' Pool lawn (commemorating Anne and her sister Mary) a swamp cypress (*Taxodium distichum*) contrasts with a blue-grey Atlantic cedar (*Cedrus atlantica glauca*). There are many different species of pine and broad-leaved native trees, mostly of tremendous height.

Two more areas remain, apart from the Sisters' Pool lawn, which has a varied shrub border and a dahlia bed for autumn: a double border of well-established rhododendrons leading up the hillside from the Spring Garden, and the Spring Garden itself, which offers magnolias, flowering cherries and various groups of trees, including cut-leaved limes (*Tilia platyphyllos* 'Laciniata') and two Indian bean trees. This garden and the slopes below it command a panoramic view over the castle and formal gardens.

Leeds Castle

ADDRESS AND TELEPHONE: Leeds Castle, Maidstone, Kent ME17 1PL. Tel. Maidstone (0622) 765400

OWNERS: Leeds Castle Foundation

DIRECTIONS: 4 miles E of Maidstone at the Junction of the A20 and M20 London to Folkestone road. Public transport: 10 minutes from Bearsted BR. Combined admission and coach or rail tickets are available—enquire at London Travel Centres

OPENING TIMES: 1 April to 31 October, daily, 11–5, November to March, Sat and Sun only 11–4

ADMISSION: castle and grounds £5.60; grounds only £4.10, OAPs and students £3.10, children (5–15 years) £2.40 Family ticket £11.40. Coach parties, groups and school parties welcome. Private parties by appointment for guided tours

CAR PARKING: yes

RESTAURANT: café and restaurant

SHOP: yes

DOGS: no

WHEELCHAIR ACCESS: limited; transport through the grounds can be arranged; groups must pre-book. Toilets for the disabled: yes

This beautiful fairytale castle is set on two islands in the middle of a huge lake and surrounded by 500 acres of parkland and woods. Named after Led, chief minister of Ethelbert IV, King of Kent, in AD 857, and once a Norman stronghold, it was given to Eleanor of Castile as a dower by her husband Edward I. After her death he gave it to Margaret of France, his second wife. It became by tradition a Queen's castle. Henry VIII was perhaps its most famous owner and responsible for converting it from a fortress into a royal palace; on his death, it passed into private ownership. It was restored in the 1930s by Lady Baillie.

Well advertised and marketed, Leeds Castle is deservedly popular with the British public and tourists: the annual total of visitors is around 500,000. There are many pleasant walks, especially through the woodland and around the lakes. The main garden area is the Culpeper Garden, to the south-east.

A wide stretch of land south of the castle was flooded in 1982 to restore the Great Water—a lovely 6-acre vista and a home for wildlife, bordered in the far distance by poplars, Scots pines and beeches. A medieval sluice in the dyke near the 13C gate tower is still occasionally used to drain and refill the lake. In spring, the lakeside is covered with daffodils. The waterfowl are many and varied, including black swans and rare types of geese—the collection was started by Lady Baillie, who also commissioned Stephane Boudin and Russell Page to build a delightful Duckery.

The Culpeper Garden lies just beyond the restaurant area, on a southern slope, and below the old estate buildings. For hundreds of years this was a kitchen garden, until transformed in 1980 by Russell Page. This small and awkwardly shaped plot of land has been ingeniously laid out, with irregularly shaped beds divided by red brick and grass paths and edged with low box hedges (some dating back to early this century). You must spend some time in this garden to do it justice: it is impossible to get an overall view, as the plants are deliberately encouraged to grow very high in the centre of each bed. The style is 'cottage garden', profuse and colourful. The flowers are chosen to mix and blend and for year-round colour, and underplanted with bulbs. Against the walls grow 100-year-old pears, roses and clematis.

Continue along the Top Walk to the magnificent new aviaries, designed by Vernon Gibberd in metal and glass and housing rare and endangered species native to Australasia, Africa and South America. Nearby are 13 old-fashioned greenhouses, dating from 1928, where plants are grown for sale and for decorating the castle. One house contains around 90 different varieties of fuchsia, grown as standards and bushes and in hanging baskets. Most varieties are available from the shop during July and August. Another house features fan-trained peaches—seen at their best in flower in February and March.

The castle vineyard was replanted in 1980 with Mueller Thurgau and Seyual Blanc vines. You can sample the wine in the restaurant. The original vineyard, planted in 1086, belonged to Bishop Odo of Bayeux, and was recorded in the Domesday Book.

The yew maze was very young at the time of our visit. When fully grown it should be an impressive affair, with its central observation tower (made of yellow Kentish ragstone excavated from the site). A grotto lies below, designed and created by Simon Verity and Diana Reynell, with a crazy tunnel connecting two underground chambers.

Penshurst Place

ADDRESS AND TELEPHONE: The Comptroller, Penshurst Place, Tonbridge, Kent TN11 8DG. Tel. (0892) 870307

OWNERS: Viscount de L'Isle

DIRECTIONS: 7 miles W of Tonbridge on B21276. Turn W A26. Public transport: bus 231 from Tunbridge Wells

OPENING TIMES: April to beginning October, daily excluding Mon but including BH Mon 12.30–6. House open

ADMISSION: house and grounds £3.50, OAPs £3, children £1.75; grounds only £2.50, OAPs £2, children £1.20.

CAR PARKING: yes

TOILETS: yes

REFRESHMENTS: café

SHOP: yes

DOGS: no, except guide dogs

WHEELCHAIR ACCESS: yes to gardens but not to house. Toilets for the disabled: no

PEAK MONTHS: succession of displays throughout the open season

NOTABLE FEATURES: Italian garden; yew hedges; garden enclosures

Penshurst has been owned by the Sidney family since 1552 and was the home of Sir Philip Sidney (1554–86), the poet, soldier and diplomat. The stately manor house was built in the 14C by Sir John de Pulteney, a rich merchant and banker, whose successor, Sir John Devereux, surrounded it with defensive towers and walls.

A garden has existed here since at least the middle of the 14C, but formal gardens on a large scale were first laid out in the reign of Queen Elizabeth I. Sir Henry Sidney organised a massive earth-moving operation to the south and built walls and terraces in order to make a plat or flat area of ground 360ft by 300ft—originally the ground sloped in a south-easterly direction from the house to the Medway river in the valley. Here he created a typical 16C formal garden in box and gravel.

Family fortunes declining in the 18C and 19C, both garden and house fell into neglect. The garden's ancient walls and terraces were left unscathed by 18C landscape gardeners and survived into Victorian times, when the 2nd Lord de L'Isle and Dudley (1828–1898), the present owner's grandfather, devised the basic garden scheme you see today. He planted the tall yew hedges for which Penshurst is now famous—in total length they cover nearly a mile—and created a number of separate small gardens within hedged enclosures. On the site of the former Elizabethan garden, Lord de L'Isle laid out a magnificent parterre or Italian garden, with two hedged gardens to the east separated by a broad alley. The remaining 6 acres were planted as a kitchen garden.

The present Lord and Lady de L'Isle came to live at Penshurst in 1945. The garden had again been neglected during the war years and was overgrown with grass and weeds. It has since been completely restored and replanted, and new garden areas created, within the established structure of hedges and ancient walls.

The magnificent double herbaceous border is the first thing you see on entering the garden from the visitor's car park. Backed by yew hedges and overhung by carefully pruned apple trees, these borders form a dividing line between the former flower garden and the kitchen garden area. Just inside the entrance, tucked into the wall corners, are two splendid specimens of *Viburnum plicatum* 'Mariesii', laden with white blossom in late spring and early summer.

The borders are planted to give a continuous and brightly varying display of colour through the spring and summer months, with plantings of flag irises, coreopsis, *Anemone japonica*, achillea, asters, peonies, poppies, anchusa, hemerocallis, yuccas, lilies, astilbes, delphiniums, geraniums and many other perennials.

The old flower gardens, to your left beyond the hedge, are now known as the rose garden and the Spring and Autumn Garden. The first is planted with four square beds of 'King Arthur' roses, edged with red berberis, and 'Elizabeth of Glamis' in keyhole beds of lavender surrounding 17C polyhedron sundials. Each facet of these ingenious garden ornaments is a separate dial. The standard roses are 'Iceberg', 'Etoile de Holland', 'Mischief', 'Double Delight' and 'Elizabeth of Glamis' and the ground cover is *Stachys lanata*. The skilfully pruned apples trees (Newton's Wonder) are accompanied by two tall Williams pears.

In the Spring and Autumn Garden are rows of Kent cobnuts pruned into goblets, backed again by apple trees. These are underplanted with daffodils, myosotis and tulips for spring interest and hardy fuchsias for summer, through which grow spire lilies (*Galtonia candicans*) in late summer and early autumn.

Between these two gardens is the Middle Walk, a double shrub border designed by Lanning Roper, in strong colours including plenty of red and yellow. Senecio, cotoneaster, cotinus (smoke trees), phlomis and crambe flourish here and roses including *R. rubrifolia* and *R.* 'Frau Dagmar Hastrup'. The 'window' in the end hedge is matched by a 'squint' window in the house, which looks down from the solar to the Great Hall. Glancing to the west, you get a fine view of the church above the Italian garden.

Another border can be found beyond the Spring and Autumn Garden, also designed by Lanning Roper and planted in Lord de L'Isle's family colours; gold (yellow), silver and blue.

The great Italian garden or parterre centres on an oval fountain, surrounded by four panels of box-edged beds. The beds have been replanted in recent years with 'Elizabeth Arden' roses replacing old diseased stock in the beds. Yellow 'Jewel of Spring' tulips come up between the roses in spring. The surrounding terrace walls are clad with 'New Dawn' and 'Queen Elizabeth' roses. An exceptionally tall and spindly ginkgo, rather awkwardly placed, towers above the outworks of the house on the terrace above.

The Tudor Terrace to the east is planted with red acers. Having walked down this terrace, you reach another window, set in the southern boundary wall and overlooking the countryside.

Retrace your steps to the visitors' entrance and beyond this into the apple orchard, carpeted with daffodils in spring. A border of peonies, more than 100 yds long, runs parallel to the south garden wall, where there are groups of lilac (syringa 'Bellicent') and roses 'Bonica' and 'Rosy Cushion'.

Further on, past two rose-covered pergolas, is the Nut Garden, a plantation of Kentish cobnuts, with four avenues of crab apples converging to a square pergola. Primroses, miniature daffodils, bluebells, tulips and cowslips blossom in spring in the long grass beneath the nut trees, and the pergola is covered with wisteria, honeysuckle and climbing roses. The central feature is a wooden pavilion covered with *Vitis coignetiae* and crowned by a replica of Sir Philip Sidney's helmet (the original is in the house).

Half-way down the kitchen garden, Lord de L'Isle's grandfather created an axis running the whole length of the garden (about 280 yds) with high yew hedges on either side. Besides directing the eye towards the house and the parish church in the distance, this originally served to screen the vegetable beds. The golden yew globes date from around the same time.

Some way down the yew alley is Diana's Bath, a lily pond within a rectangle of yew hedges, artfully concealed from immediate view. This is a pleasant place to rest and watch the fish swimming—wires are stretched over the water surface to deter the predatory grey heron. Water hyacinths flower in the pond from spring through to autumn.

Just south of Diana's Bath is a lovely small garden, designed by John Codrington and known as the Grey Garden. The plants here are mainly grey, white and silver and include artemisia, dianthus, 'Iceberg' roses, Kent roses in four beds, clematis 'Madame le Coultrie' and the willow-leaved pear (*Pyrus salicifolia*).

To the east is the Theatre Garden, once the drying ground for household laundry and now landscaped to provide a grass-covered stage and auditorium. Yellow tulips grow here in spring and a variety of lacecap hydrangeas flower from summer to autumn—*H. villosa, H. paniculata*, 'Blue Wave' and 'Bluebird'. Next door is the magnolia garden, where a sunken area is planted with magnolias including *M. x soulangiana* 'Nigra', 'Rubra' and 'Alba'. Golden Irish yews stand on the terrace above.

The Flag Garden, a rectangular area to the north-west of the former kitchen garden, is the most recent area of development. This has been laid out in a Union Jack design, with lavender 'Hidcote', roses 'Lili Marlene' and 'Snowline' and red and white tulips in spring—all contained within a rectangle of pleached limes. At the south end is a viewing mound, planted around with 'Rosy Cushion' roses, which also overlooks two pheons in box.

The 18C lime avenue, which you can see beyond the garden wall to the north, lost 14 trees in the great storm of October 1987, but still provides a delightful walk. You can reach this, and the surrounding parkland, through a gate in the north-west corner of the Flag Garden, or by another entrance nearer the house. The parkland features a lake and medieval fishponds now in process of restoration; also an adventure playground and farm museum.

Scotney Castle

ADDRESS AND TELEPHONE: Lamberhurst, Tunbridge Wells, Kent TN3 8JN. Tel. Lamberhurst (0892) 890651

OWNERS: The National Trust

DIRECTIONS: 1 mile S of Lamberhurst on A21. Public transport: BR to Wadhurst, 5½ miles away. Bus Maidstone and District 256 Tunbridge Wells to Wadhurst, passing Tunbridge Wells BR, alight Lamberhurst Green 1 mile away

OPENING TIMES: 30 March to 10 November, Wed to Fri 11–6; Sat, Sun and BH Mon 2–6 or sunset if earlier. Last admission 30 minutes before closing. Old Castle open May to 25 August, same times as garden

ADMISSION: Wed to Fri £2, children £1; Sat, Sun BH Mon £2.80, children £1.40. Pre-booked parties £1.60, children £1. (No party reduction on Sat, Sun or BH Mon)

CAR PARKING: yes

TOILETS: yes

REFRESHMENTS: not at garden but picnicking in car park area

SHOP: NT shop open until a week before Christmas

DOGS: not in garden

WHEELCHAIR ACCESS: partly accessible to wheelchairs but very steep in places. Toilets for the disabled: no

PEAK MONTHS: April/June, September/October

NOTABLE FEATURES: picturesque castle with moat and lakes; herb garden; shrub and herbaceous plantings on slope of valley; mature specimen trees; ice house; view from top of valley; walk by river to mineral spring

There has been a manor house in the valley at Scotney at least since the 12C, when Lambert de Scoteni held it under the Barony of Leeds Castle. In the 14C Roger de Ashburnham inherited the estate through his mother and fortified the house, adding a gate house and four towers. Only one of the towers is still intact, though the foundations of the other three and the angle piers of the gatehouse remain. The old moat was replaced with a lake, which remains as an ornamental and integral part of the landscape today.

From the 15C to the early 17C Scotney was the home of the Darell family, who added a new east range to the castle, the red brick wall of which still remains. One of the Darell family, the second Thomas, was a Roman Catholic who sheltered priests and established Scotney as a house set apart from the life of local society, a pattern which continued until the beginning of the 18C.

In 1778 Scotney passed to the Hussey family from Staffordshire who were probably attracted by the local iron-smelting industry. Edward Hussey, the third of that name to own the castle, decided when quite young to build a new house and redesign the castle and garden in the Picturesque style. This is described by the contemporary garden writer Sir Uvedale Price as 'the use of studying pictures for the purpose of improving real landscape'. William Sawrey Gilpin, an artist and landscape gardener, advised on the design of the garden and the site for the new house at the top of the valley. The stone was to be quarried out of the hillside below, providing a dramatic vista from the new house to the old. The house, a solid Elizabethan-style building designed by Anthony Salvin, was completed in 1843 from the quarried stone.

The old castle and its lake remain as the focal point of the garden, as Gilpin intended. On first entering the estate turn sharp left and take the path to the Bastion, a balustraded terrace at the top of the valley. The old castle's Ashburnham tower and 17C red brick addition appear far away below between the trees. Glance behind you to see at the head of its lawn, Edward Hussey's Elizabethan-style Victorian home.

The bastion is sited immediately above the north face of the quarry, and from it you can look down in April over the white starry flowers of *Magnolia stellata* and the snowy mespilus (*Amelanchier canadensis*). Later in the spring you can enjoy the sight of purple and mauve *Rhododendron ponticum* and brighter shades of azaleas. Retracing your steps towards the entrance, you will find a steep path leading down into the quarry. Here acers, buddleias and shrub roses as well as spring-flowering shrubs, perch among enormous rocks, while jasmine, honeysuckle and other climbers scramble up the quarry sides. On the north side of the quarry, just below the Bastion, an oak tree clings tenaciously by its roots to the quarry face.

Taking the opposite path out of the quarry, you emerge on the upper walk of the garden, which leads you gradually downhill, giving a view over the fields to the left. Conifers, copper beech and other trees form a barrier between fields and garden; there are groups of shrubs and some herbaceous plants, which flourish in their shelter. In August we saw *Abutilon* x *hybridum* 'Canary Bird' with yellow bells borne in profusion. From time to time the castle emerges into view again on the right, just as intended, yielding a series of effectively contrived 'pictures' and keeping you conscious of your goal.

At the eastern point of the garden, where the path bends sharply to the right before the final descent to the castle, is a well preserved ice-house. This, unusually, has a conical thatched roof and a wooden door and could pass for a minute cottage. Emerging on to the circumference path of the moat, you can walk around between lake and river (the River Bewl), viewing the changing aspects of the marvellous castle reflected in its surrounding water.

The first prospect is over the inner castle ruins, where a play was being performed when we visited. This is followed by the soft red walls of the 17C addition, juxtaposed with the yellow and grey stone of the Ashburnham Tower. From close quarters Scotney, having been presented most skilfully as the focal point of a Picturesque and Romantic landscape, possesses an endearing and domestic quality.

Alders, hornbeam, and willow, as well as rhododendrons, separate the path from the river and the fields beyond. As you approach the island (actually an isthmus) you come in sight of a bronze 'Three piece reclining figure' given by Henry Moore in memory of Christopher Hussey. On the island there are specimen trees, among them a swamp cypress (*Taxodium distichum*) and the Persian ironwood (*Parrotia persica*), as well as shrub roses and yew. At the water's edge grow clumps of royal fern and iris. A small, low boat house lies half hidden in trees among the rushes, its wide mouth open to the water.

The castle can also be explored close to, giving a reverse view over the lake. As you enter by the old gate house, you come to a circular herb garden, designed by Lanning Roper for Mrs Hussey. An old well head marks the centre.

A vigorous wisteria scrambles up the landward castle walls, and inside, a large bush of *Viburnum tomentosum* has established itself, as well as clumps of phlox and a bushy honeysuckle. Step outside the 17C walls to see the peaceful lake, the waterlilies and the waterfowl.

After leaving the castle, climb up the south-facing lawns to the heather bed and shrub and herbaceous plantings. In one bed in late summer, the pale mauve spikes of *Acanthus mollis* and stiff poker heads of a yellow kniphofia rose above the grey-green leaves and violet blue flowers of the Russian sage (*Perovskia atriplicifolia*), pink sedum and a yellow potentilla.

On the way out towards the car park, you can also look westwards down the valley, where sheep graze.

Sissinghurst Castle Gardens

ADDRESS AND TELEPHONE: Sissinghurst Castle Garden, near Cranbrook, Kent TN17 2AB. Tel. Cranbrook (0580) 712850

OWNERS: The National Trust

DIRECTIONS: 2 miles NE of Cranbrook, 1 mile E of Sissinghurst village (A262). Public transport: Maidstone & District bus 4/5 Maidstone to Hastings (passing Staplehurst BR), alight Sissinghurst, then 1½ miles (tel. Maidstone 0622 690577). Staplehurst station 5½ miles

OPENING TIMES: Good Fri to 13 October, Tues to Fri 1–6.30; Sat, Sun and Good Fri 10–6.30. Closed Mon, including BH. Last admission 6pm. The garden may be overcrowded at around 3pm; visitors may be asked to wait. Part of house open

ADMISSION: Tues to Sat £4, children £2; Sun £4.50. Reductions for pre-booked parties on weekdays

CAR PARKING: yes. Coaches by appointment only

TOILETS: yes

REFRESHMENTS: café

SHOP: yes

DOGS: no

WHEELCHAIR ACCESS: admission restricted to two chairs at any one time because of narrow and uneven paths. Disabled visitors may be set down at garden entrance. Plan of recommended wheelchair route available. Toilets for the disabled: yes

PEAK MONTHS: July/August

NOTABLE FEATURES: many

Sissinghurst is perhaps the most popular of English gardens (and liable to serious overcrowding, notably on Sunday afternoons). Its most outstanding features are well-known—the White Garden, breathtaking in summer, the Spring Garden and lime walk, the orchard—and they seem to grow more beautiful by the year. But perhaps most visitors are drawn by something beyond mere excellence of design and planting—by a 'spirit of place', a still living and breathing history. All gardens link past to present, but the story of Sissinghurst is more than commonly interesting and romantic.

Originally a magnificent Tudor and Elizabethan mansion, Sissinghurst housed French prisoners-of-war between 1756 and 1763. By this time, it was already in ruins, as was the surrounding park, and it deteriorated rapidly: by 1800, much of what remained had

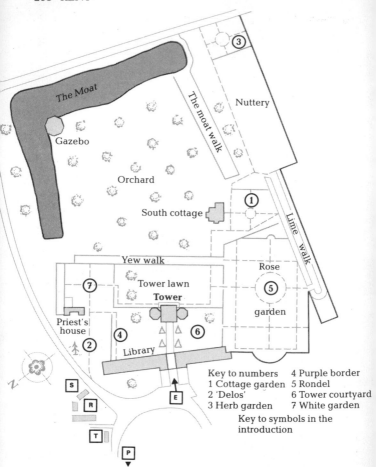

The Moat

Gazebo

The moat walk

Nuttery

Orchard

South cottage

Lime walk

Yew walk

Rose

Tower lawn

Tower

⑤

garden

Priest's house

⑦

④

②

⑥

Library

S

R

E

T

P

Key to numbers
1 Cottage garden
2 'Delos'
3 Herb garden

4 Purple border
5 Rondel
6 Tower courtyard
7 White garden

Key to symbols in the introduction

to be pulled down. From 1796 to 1855, Sissinghurst served as the parish workhouse; and then it was owned or leased by farmers.

When Vita Sackville-West, the novelist, poet, biographer and gardening writer, first saw Sissinghurst in 1930, the building was uninhabitable and the 6-acre garden hidden beneath heaps of rubbish and a tangle of weeds. She immediately fell in love with it. The place, she wrote, 'caught instantly at my heart and my imagination … I saw what might be made of it.' (*Journal of the Horticultural Society*, Vol. LXXVIII, November 1953). At least the soil was workable—'a top-spit of decently friable loam with a clay bottom, if we were so unwise as to turn up the sub-soil two spits deep'—and the pink brick Tudor walls were still standing, a good basic structural element for the garden to be, along with the old moat and a small nut plantation.

It took Vita—with her husband Harold Nicolson and two young

sons, Ben and Nigel—three years just to clear away the rubbish. Harold Nicolson then designed the garden, he and Vita having agreed on 'a combination of long axial walks, running north and south, east and west, and the more intimate surprise of small geometrical gardens opening off them, rather as the rooms of an enormous house would open off the arterial corridors'.

Harold Nicolson's design was severely linear and classical. By adding new walls and planting hedges, he created a number of separate garden areas, linked by vistas. His layout, which has been preserved, is precise but never oppressive: Sissinghurst is a very open garden (unlike Hidcote) and retains a strong connection with the surrounding fields and countryside.

Vita's planting, within this strictly formal design, was informal, exuberant and free. She encouraged plants to spill over onto the paths and allowed wildflowers to set seed. The White Garden in summer is perhaps the finest example of her art: a marvellous profusion of flowers, mainly white, amidst grey, silver and green foliage. She had a keen eye for colour and mixing of shades—Nigel Nicolson has rightly called her 'a painter in flowers'—and took care to plan and time her effects.

Although Sissinghurst looks most splendid in summer, it is also very beautiful in spring. Several areas feature spring flowers—the orchard, the lime walk, Delos. Vita intended various garden areas to flower in succession through the season, lying fallow when past their peak. Only three areas—the purple border, the herb garden and the cottage garden—provide interest from early spring right through to late autumn.

The tower courtyard, described by Vita Sackville-West as 'not rectangular but coffin-shaped', lies just beyond a long range of Tudor buildings, through a huge arch. Four stout Irish yews, underplanted with violets in spring, flank the central path, which continues to the Elizabethan tower. Rosemary 'Sissinghurst Blue' can be seen on either side of the tower arch.

The pink-red Tudor brick makes an excellent backing for climbing plants—the red rose 'Allen Chandler', by the entrance arch, and the flowering quince *Chaenomeles* x *superba* 'Knap Hill Scarlet', blooming profusely in spring. There is above a raised trough of blue columbines (*Aquilegia glandulosa*), and further along another quince, *Chaenomeles speciosa* 'Sanguinea Plena'.

Magnolia grandiflora reaches to the eaves, a strong vase shape, complemented by a well-trained ceanothus. The Chilean potato tree (*Solanum crispum*) displays corymbs of blue-purple flowers in mid summer, against glossy dark leaves, and a big bush of *Osmanthus delavayi* produces clusters of fragrant white flowers in spring, under the diamond-paned windows.

The library wall, to the north, is similarly planted, again with the deep crimson rose 'Allen Chandler' and chaenomeles 'Knap Hill Scarlet'. A raised stone trough holds trailing *Euphorbia myrsinites*, with blue-grey, sharp-tipped leaves and greenish-yellow bracts.

Not far away, under a south-west-facing wall, is the purple border, planted with annuals, perennials, shrubs and bulbs in subtle shades of purple, mauve and blue. In summer, this border is a mass of soft and blending colours: only *Rosa moyesii* stands out, bright scarlet. Clematis and vines grow behind.

The north-facing wall divides the rose garden from the tower courtyard. Two magnificent specimens of the very hardy climbing hydrangea *H. petiolaris*, join above the archway, and in summer their delicate white flowerheads swamp the wall and cascade over into the rose garden. *Viburnum plicatum tomentosum* 'Mariesii' is trained up the wall nearby, with aquilegias growing below.

The rose garden is divided into square box-edged beds, with a circular lawn, the Rondel, surrounded by yew hedges, in the centre. Vita Sackville-West loved old-fashioned roses—damasks, musks, centifolias, gallicas, bourbons—and planted them in random fashion, interspersed with a wide mixture of other shrubs, perennials and bulbs. In late April, we saw red stems of young peonies underplanted with pale star-flowers (*Ipheion uniflorum*) and the lovely magenta tulip 'Maytime' boldly combined with deep blue pansies. Deep lavender *Clematis macropetala* and mauve *Clematis montana* 'Ruby' twine round the stone walls of the entrance passage, flowering from late spring to summer. There are lilies, foxtail lilies (eremurus) and daylilies (hemerocallis)—and lots of irises. In summer, much of the foliage planting is subdued in colour—grey, grey-green and silver—an excellent background to the soft, bright colours of the old roses.

The roses are trained over hoops and supports, or allowed to grow free or ramble up trees. In June and July they blossom in full glory, filling the air with intoxicating scent—the blush-pink centifolia 'Fantin Latour', bearing double flowers in clusters; 'Charles de Mills', one of the best gallicas, with maroon flowers fading to dense purple; gallica 'Gloire de Dijon' with flattish, double flowers, irregularly quartered, orange fading to yellow-white; 'Camaieux', pale pink splashed with purplish-crimson; and many others.

Roses flourish everywhere at Sissinghurst, loving the heavy clay soil—*Rosa longicuspis*, the creamy-white climbing rose in the White Garden, clothing the central structure; 'Mme Alfred Carriere', another vigorous white climber, against the south cottage walls and a long fence of *Rosa eglanteria* behind the cottage. Vita decided early on to plant roses 'recklessly'—along with figs and vines—holding that Sissinghurst was 'a romantic place and it must be romantically treated'. Though distinctively English and Kentish, she thought Sissinghurst also had 'something foreign about it; a Norman manor-house, perhaps; a faint echo of something more southern'.

The lime walk, or spring garden, lies on the far side of the rose garden, beyond the Rondel. Harold Nicolson had charge of this area, and did all the planting. In spring, the long side borders are filled with flowers—grape hyacinths, narcissi, leucojum, tulips in all different colours, fritillaries (including tall crown imperials), anemones and many others. An avenue of pleached broad-leaved limes (*Tilia platyphyllos*) runs the length of the walk. After a brief three-week period of glory, the beds are left fallow; but clematis flowers at bulb time in one of the large Tuscan pots and impatiens has been planted in the other pots for summer flowering.

Turn left through an opening in the hedge for the cottage garden—once part of the south wing. Vita and Harold slept here, and he wrote his books in the ground-floor room overlooking the garden. The colour scheme is warm, featuring yellows, oranges, reds and golds. *Euphorbia sikkimensis* makes a striking impression, with its red leaf veins and young shoots; also *Euphorbia griffithii* 'Dixter', with red bracts. There are plentiful yellow and red wall-flowers, tulips and polyanthus, yellow trollius and poppies (*Papaver orientale* 'Sungold'), golden-yellow tree peonies (*Paeonia delavayii* and *Paeonia lutea ludlowii*) and yellow-green *Hosta fortunei* 'Aurea'.

Here, too, is a wide variety of shrubs and small trees—including yellow broom in the centre of one bed, *Fremontodendron* 'Californian Glory' against the cottage, and handsome *Elaeagnus pungens* 'Maculata', its shiny green leaves splashed with gold. *Magnolia kobus* fills one corner, bearing fragrant white flowers from mid to late spring, and underhung by mahonia; across the garden a false acacia (*Robinia pseudoacacia* 'Bessoniana') is underplanted with lilies-of-the valley and green and cream *Hosta undulata*. A magnificent twisting quince grows on the other side of the cottage.

The moat walk (originally the third arm of the moat, and still flanked on one side by the old moat wall, now blooming with wallflowers) begins just below the cottage garden. The nuttery lies to your right, beyond a bank planted with deciduous azaleas, and the orchard to your left. Don't miss the delightful herb garden, beyond the nuttery, surrounded by yew hedges.

The moat itself comes into view right at the end of the moat walk, overhung by huge oak trees, with the countryside beyond. Kingcups and irises grow by the water. Watch your step here, especially after rain—the paving stones can be slippery!

The orchard stretches down to the water, breathtakingly lovely in spring, lit with daffodils and flowering cherry and apple trees. This was the site of the original medieval manor house—explaining why the moat is now so strangely situated, far from any buildings. The gazebo was put up by Ben and Nigel Nicolson in memory of their father. *Rosa gallica* 'Sissinghurst Castle' grows here, a very ancient variety, rediscovered in 1930; Vita also used to grow climbing roses up the apple trees.

In startling contrast to this open, wildish area with its natural planting is the yew walk, bordering tower lawn and the White Garden—a long, narrow, claustrophobic alley, enclosed by high yew hedges. This makes a very strong division between formal and informal garden areas, changing the 'mood' abruptly. Turn left near the northern end for the White Garden.

The White Garden needs little introduction, having been described so often and so well in print, especially by Vita Sackville-West herself. The neat, intricately patterned box-edged beds were designed by Harold, a perfect framework for Vita's extraordinary planting. Nearly all the flowers here are white or grey. Tall white lilies, galtonia, delphiniums and speedwell seem to aspire towards the magnificent central white rose, rising out of clouds of silvery and grey-green foliage. The beds are full of treasures—*Pulmonaria officinalis* 'Sissinghurst White', peony 'Ivory Jewel'. This is definitely a summer garden, although a few plants flower in spring—the white sprays of *Spiraea* x *arguta*, and *Magnolia rustica rubra* and M. *lobbii*. The latter two, a disconcerting shade of pink, were planted before the idea of a white garden was conceived. A slender lead statue of a virgin (a replica of a wooden statue in the library) stands beside a silver-grey weeping *Pyrus salicifolia* 'Pendula', replaced after the 1987 gales blew down the original large tree. White wisteria (*W. venusta*) covers the wall behind the pergola.

For a new angle on the White Garden—indeed the whole garden—climb the four-storey Elizabethan tower, and look down from above. It is fascinating to see the whole garden with its many divisions—like a magnificently rich tapestry at the height of summer.

LANCASHIRE

Hoghton Tower

ADDRESS AND TELEPHONE: Hoghton Tower Preservation Trust, Hoghton Tower, near Preston, Lancashire PR5 0SH. Tel. (025 485) 2986

OWNERS: Hoghton Tower Preservation Trust

DIRECTIONS: on A675, Blackburn Old Road, midway between Blackburn and Preston. M6 exit 28; M61 exit 8

OPENING TIMES: Easter to end October, Sun and BH, also Sat in July and August 2–5

ADMISSION: house and garden £2.50, children £1. Coach parties by prior arrangement

CAR PARKING: yes

TOILETS: yes

REFRESHMENTS: café

SHOP: yes

DOGS: on lead

WHEELCHAIR ACCESS: difficult because of steps and gravel paths. Toilets for the disabled: no

PEAK MONTHS: April to June

NOTABLE FEATURES: rose garden; herbaceous and mixed borders; fine views over surrounding countryside

Hoghton Tower, the seat of Sir Bernard de Hoghton, enjoys extensive and dramatic views. The dark and mysterious looking fortified mansion sits comfortably on the summit of a steep outcrop some 650ft above sea level and commands views as far as the Welsh and Lakeland mountains, the Ribble Estuary and Irish Sea. On a clear day, you can see the Isle of Man.

The present house was built by Thomas Hoghton in the 16C. It is built around two courtyards, in the style of the late medieval period, with the lower courtyard surrounding the well house, kitchens, servants' quarters and stables, the upper comprising domestic quarters and Great Hall. Until the Civil War a central tower separated the two courtyards, but this was blown up during the occupation by the Roundheads. The house has been altered, rebuilt and superbly renovated over the centuries.

The approach to Hoghton Tower is stately. A long avenue of trees and colourful rhododendrons flanks the straight driveway as it majestically ascends the ¾ mile to the castellated gatehouse and mansion, surrounded by terraced walks.

The native woodland is lit in spring with daffodils, followed by rhododendrons. There are also three walled gardens. One of these, known as the Ramparts because of its raised grassed sentry walks, offers magnificent views westwards. It is a small garden designed around a central lawn with a large herb-filled urn. Surrounding the lawn, below the walls, are mixed borders containing dwarf conifers, small variegated privets and berberis, bright yellow potentillas and colourful herbaceous plants.

The rose garden, also enclosed by old walls, has for its centrepiece a three-tiered fountain set in lawn and edged with ivy. Down one side is an avenue of yews clipped into cubes; in contrast, the border beneath the house wall is bright with a mixture of hydrangeas and herbaceous plants with roses, honeysuckles and jasmines climbing the wall behind.

The third walled garden is known as the Wilderness. The largest of the three, it lies directly behind the house and consists mainly of lawn, surrounded by rough gravel paths, with borders of well chosen herbaceous plants and shrubs.

LEICESTERSHIRE

Belgrave Hall

ADDRESS AND TELEPHONE: Belgrave Hall, Church Road, Belgrave, Leicester. Tel. Leicester (0533) 669413

OWNERS: Leicestershire County Council, Museums, Arts and Records Service

DIRECTIONS: in Church Road, Belgrave. Just off the A6 2 miles N of Leicester

OPENING TIMES: all year round Mon to Sat 10–5.30, Sun 2–5. House open as a museum of life in the 18C and 19C

ADMISSION: free. Coach parties by prior arrangement

CAR PARKING: limited but not usually a problem

TOILETS: yes

REFRESHMENTS: no

SHOP: no

DOGS: no

WHEELCHAIR ACCESS: yes. Toilets for the disabled: yes

PEAK SEASON: throughout the year

NOTABLE FEATURES: formal garden; herbaceous borders; botanic garden; woodland garden; rock and water garden; glasshouses

Belgrave Hall is located in Church Road, Belgrave (now a suburb of Leicester) just off the A6 about 2 miles north of the city centre. On one side of the road is Belgrave House and Belgrave Gardens— now a public park and not to be confused with the Hall.

Belgrave Hall is the modest brick Queen Anne house opposite the park. Thought to have been built between 1709 and 1713, it is now owned by Leicestershire County Council Museums, Arts and Records Services and has been furnished in the style of the 18C and 19C. Exhibitions of harnesses, coaches and agricultural implements can be seen in the stable block.

From the front of the house there is no indication of the wealth of plants in the walled gardens beyond and you must go through the museum to reach this botanical paradise, where more than 6000 species of plants are displayed in just 1½ acres. The variety of gardens in this small area is also impressive, each surrounded by brick walls: a formal garden, a kitchen garden with herbaceous borders, the monument garden, a botanic garden, a small woodland garden and a rock and water garden.

The first garden you find on emerging from the museum is the formal garden immediately behind the house. In spring this rectangular enclosure is filled with bright colours—red and yellow tulips, dark red wall flowers, yellow polyanthus and blue pansies. These are replaced later in the year by brilliant displays of summer bedding. Borders below the walls display more bedding, along with interesting shrubs and climbing plants. The massive *Wisteria sinensis* on one wall is said to be over a hundred years old and in May still carries fragrant mauve hanging heads 8in. to 1ft long. Elsewhere around the walls of this garden you can see the cape figwort (*Phygelius capensis*) with fuschia-like flowers of coral red, *Akebia quinata* and *Hydrangea quercifolia*. There is also a coral plant (*Bereridopsis corallina*)—a beautiful evergreen shrub with deep crimson flowers in late summer. Honeysuckles twine along the walls. Among the clematis is the charming *Clematis rehderana* with soft yellow flowers smelling of cowslips, as well as *C. chrysocoma* and a small *C. macropetala*.

A central path divides the formal garden symmetrically into two and makes a vista through the archway, flanked by stone eagles, into and through the next garden, ending with the monument in the furthest garden. The second enclosure is home to two magnificent mulberry trees at least 200 years old.

The path continues between a pair of long herbaceous borders. This was probably the kitchen garden in earlier days but now contains peonies, euphorbias and a wide selection of colourful herbaceous plants along with some shrubs. *Ceratostigma willmottianum*, a small shrub here, bears rich blue flowers from late summer through to autumn, and there are specimens of *Abutilon vitifolium*, *Dipelta floribunda* and a delightful *Raphiolepis umbellata*.

Some new features have been recently completed in this area. Rose walks, behind the herbaceous borders, have been planted with Victorian and Edwardian roses underplanted with *Lilium regale*. A new bed near the entrance to the monument garden is planted with tree peonies. Near the entrance to the glasshouse yard a small fernery has been established.

Through the gateway to the right of the herbaceous borders lies the botanic garden, small but extremely interesting. Among the plant families represented is Oleaceae, its members including common white jasmine (*Jasminum officinale*) and the pretty small-leaved *Syringa microphylla*. London pride (*Saxifraga umbrosa* belongs to the Saxifragaceae, the maidenhair tree (*Ginkgo biloba*) to the Ginkgoaceae, and among the Caprifoliaceae are the beauty bush (*Kolkwitzia amabilis*), the snowberry (*Symphoricarpos albus*), *Viburnum tinus* and *Lonicera pileata*.

Further on, wood anemones (*Anemone nemorosa*), black snake-root (*Cimicifuga racemosa*), alpine columbine (*Aquilegia alpina*), larkspur (*Delphinium elatum*), love-in-a-mist (*Nigella damascena*), globe flowers (*Trollius europaeus*) and a selection of hellebores give some idea of the variety of plants in the Ranunculaceae family. Bamboos can be seen in the Gramineae bed, a range of poppies represent Papaveraceae and different kinds of brooms, gorses and vetches feature under Leguminosae. In all, this small botanical garden is an excellent educational feature, providing a good basic guide to plant identification.

An alpine house separates the botanic garden from the woodland garden near the house. This latter contains beds of heathers and heaths, and below a canopy of trees, rhododendrons, azaleas and shade-loving plants. Along one wall is a huge chaenomeles with beautiful scarlet flowers in spring. Next to it is *Kerria japonica*, with bright buttercup yellow flowers, and further along *Chaenomeles cathayensis* bears white flowers flushed with pink.

Beneath the trees at the farthest end of the woodland garden the ground is covered with the sprawling growth of lesser periwinkle (*Vinca minor*) which produces blue flowers continuously from April to June. Among the shrubs here are *Ligustrum delavayanum*, *Sycopsis sinensis* and the witch-hazel (*Hamamelis virginiana*), which produces small yellow flowers from September to November. The viburnums include *V. rhytidophyllum*—a mass of creamy white flowers in May—and *V. farreri* (*fragrans*) which bears sweetly scented white flowers in November and through the winter.

Two of the most striking rhododendrons are *R. racemosum* and *R. williamsianum*, the latter a charming shrub with bell-shaped pink flowers in April. Shade is provided by a wide range of trees, including some large yews, the field maple (*Acer campestre*) and several sorbus and prunus species. Towards the edge of the woodland is a snowdrop tree (*Halesia carolina*)—beautiful in spring, when it is draped with clusters of white bell-shaped flowers.

Retrace your steps through the botanic garden and herbaceous borders and you come to the monument garden where yews and shrubs provide a good background for a large monument to Edward Holdsworth. Originally this was sited at the now demolished Gopsall Hall, East Leicestershire, housed in a small temple crowned with a statue. Both monument and statue were brought to Belgrave under the museum's auspices and the statue now stands near the house.

An archway to the left of the monument gives access to the water and rock garden, an area still under development. Pools linked by water courses form the central feature of this garden, filled with and surrounded by aquatic and moisture-loving plants. Small plants occupy the cracks and crevices of the surrounding rock work and a collection of acers is being planted along rocky terraces. A small geranium house in this garden features a selection of pelargoniums; nearer to the stables there are temperate, tropical, orchid and cacti houses.

There is an incredible variety of planting and diversity of species to be seen in these 1½ acres of garden. Work continues to increase the selection of period plants and the garden's educational aspects are being strengthened. A tour of the museum and the gardens makes a very interesting day out—and one that children may well enjoy too.

University of Leicester Botanic Garden

ADDRESS AND TELEPHONE: University of Leicester Botanic Garden, Council of the University of Leicester, Beaumont Hall, Stoughton Drive South, Oadby, Leicester. Tel. (0533) 717725

OWNERS: University of Leicester

DIRECTIONS: 3 miles SE of city centre at Oadby, off A6 by racecourse. Public transport: Leicester BR 3 miles. Buses from Leicester

OPENING TIMES: Mon to Fri 10–4.30 (3.30 on Fri)

ADMISSION: free. Coach parties by prior arrangement

CAR PARKING: limited (on road)

TOILETS: yes

REFRESHMENTS: no

SHOP: no

DOGS: no

WHEELCHAIR ACCESS: to most parts of garden. Toilets for the disabled: no

PEAK MONTHS: May to October

NOTABLE FEATURES: rose garden; sandstone and limestone rock gardens; heather garden; sunken garden with parterre; meadow and arboretum; National Collection in conjunction with the NCCPG of hardy fuchsia, aubretia and skimmia

After the bustle and noise of Leicester's city centre, arriving at the University's botanic garden is like entering a peaceful oasis.

The botanic garden has occupied its present site, at Oadby, on the outskirts of Leicester, since 1947. At first it was planned around three large mansions—Beaumont, Southmeade and Hastings—then in 1964 another house, The Knoll, was purchased and the four areas, covering in all about 16 acres, were integrated into one large and remarkably diverse design.

Today the four mansions are student halls of residence. Dating from the turn of the century, the red brick and Tudor-style timbered houses lend an atmosphere of long establishment to this relatively

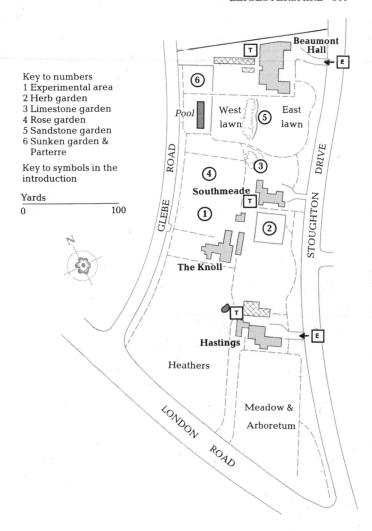

Key to numbers
1 Experimental area
2 Herb garden
3 Limestone garden
4 Rose garden
5 Sandstone garden
6 Sunken garden & Parterre

Key to symbols in the introduction

Yards
0   100

young garden. The original flagstone terraces and wide lawns have been retained.

Many of the trees planted when the houses were built have now reached maturity and add stability as well as interest to the garden. The most northerly part of the garden, around Beaumont Hall, is certainly the most exciting and impressive. Throughout the summer and into the autumn the delightfully fragrant creamy-white flowers of *Magnolia grandiflora* blossom against the house wall. Below the terrace, hebes and genista overlook a fine lawn and *Euonymous alatus* shows off its beautiful tones in autumn.

Bounded by shrub borders, the east lawn is ablaze in May with

*Cacti and succulents on display at the University
of Leicester Botanic Garden*

rhododendrons, azaleas and pieris; high above tower mature trees including Norway maple (*Acer platanoides*) and a magnificent spreading blue cedar (*Cedrus atlantica* 'Glauca').

A sandstone garden lies between the east and west lawns. A narrow stream trickling down from Beaumont, passes through sandstone rocks and ravines and under huge sandstone slabs. The banks are planted with primulas, ferns, hellebores and hostas, with prostrate junipers for groundcover. A collection of acers forms the structural backbone and provides a spectrum of changing colours—*Acer japonicum* 'Aureum', with its soft yellow foliage, the deeply cut leaves of *Acer japonicum* 'Aconitifolium', turning ruby red in autumn.

Across the west lawn, in the most northern corner of the site, is the sunken garden. Here is an intricate parterre, edged with box and filled with spring bedding plants (replaced later in the year by pelargoniums). Red brick paths weaving around and between the beds and the banks of the sunken garden are edged with grey and silver-leaved plants such as santolina and lavender. The surrounding and sheltering yew hedge creates a secluded suntrap: it is tempting to linger here.

Some way south of the sunken garden is a pergola clothed with vines and clematis, such as *Clematis tangutica* with yellow flowers followed by masses of silky seed heads. A long rectangular lily pool runs southwards from the pergola, its lines softened by plantings of marginal aquatics in recesses along both sides. Two rows of free-standing pillars run parallel to the pool on either side of the lawn: linked by ropes and draped with roses, they act as huge 'curtains', enclosing and protecting this secluded area.

A limestone rock garden links Beaumont and Southmeade—a series of rocky paths planted round with saxifrage and other alpine plants.

To the west lies the rose garden, composed of staid rectangular beds surrounded by lawn. This traces the development of roses to modern times. In summer the air is filled with the rich perfume of masses of shrub roses. Colours range from the pure white of *Rosa damascena* 'Mme Hardy' with its very large flowers, to the deep crimson and purple of *R. gallica* 'Charles de Mills'. The hybrid perpetual rose 'Gloire de Ducher' is outstanding with its large, velvety and very fragrant dark crimson flowers, shaded maroon. 'Frau Karl Druschki' is a really beautiful white rose but lacks a scent.

One of the most highly-scented roses in the garden is the salmon-cerise coloured hybrid tea 'Hector Deane'. All the best-known hybrid teas are to be found here—'Peace', 'King's Ransom', 'Super-star'—and there is also a collection of climbing roses. The fenced area next to the rose garden contains experimental plots and nearby, on the western boundary, is a good collection of hollies.

The heather garden lies to the south-west, past Hastings House, on a gently sloping site. Here, silver birches hang gracefully above colourful islands of callunas, ericas and daboecias. From its grand terrace, Hastings House looks over a fine lawn, overshadowed by cedars. Below is a meadow full of British grass species and wild flowers. The arboretum in the lower corner features a number of interesting trees, notably the unique and very strangely shaped *Sequoiadendron giganteum* 'Pendulum' a short distance from the path.

Your return route to Beaumont lies through a herb garden to the front of Southmeade House.

LINCOLNSHIRE

Belton House

ADDRESS AND TELEPHONE: Belton House, Belton, near
Grantham, Lincolnshire NG32 2LS. Tel. Grantham (0476) 66116

OWNERS: The National Trust

DIRECTIONS: 3 miles NE of Grantham on A607 Grantham to
Lincoln road. Public transport: Grantham BR 3 miles. Buses from
Grantham, Lincoln and Sleaford

OPENING TIMES: 30 March to end October, Wed to Sun and BH
Mon 11–5.30 (house open 1–5.30)

ADMISSION: £3.50. Parties at reduced rates by arrangement

CAR PARKING: yes

TOILETS: yes

REFRESHMENTS: café

SHOP: yes

DOGS: on lead in park only

WHEELCHAIR ACCESS: yes (for house make arrangements) Toilets
for the disabled: yes

PEAK MONTHS: no special peaks

NOTABLE FEATURES: formal gardens with orangery; parkland and
woodland walks; remains of 18C Wilderness garden; adventure
playground

Belton House is a fine Restoration house set in 600 acres of
tree-studded parkland. It was built by Sir John Brownlow between
1685 and 1688. The design was for a long time attributed to Wren,
but is now credited to William Winde.

The first gardens at Belton were laid out in 1700 in the formal
French manner fashionable at that time; they can be seen in an
engraving by Hendrik Hulsbergh for Colen Campbell's Vitruvius
Britannicus (1717) and in a later 'bird's-eye-view' by Thomas
Badeslade (c 1750). To the east of the house, four rectangular groves
of trees were divided into symmetrical patterns by walks centring
on *rondpoints*. Elaborate parterres lay to the north of the house and
to the south was a courtyard with lawns, paved paths and statuary.
A kitchen garden and orchards lay to the west.

Sir John's nephew, Lord Tyrconnel, introduced several new elements into the garden when he inherited Belton. He extended the
main lines of the garden to the south and east by planting two long
avenues of trees, and he created the Wilderness, complete with
Gothic ruin and cascade, to the west. His most striking legacy,
however, is the unusual arched tower which stands on rising ground
at the far end of the east avenue.

Known as the Bellmount, or 'Belle Mount', the tower originally
consisted of a very tall narrow-span arch, probably flanked by a
wing of lower arches on either side, the main arch supporting a
single room or observatory, reached via a spiral staircase. In the

late 18C, on the advice of Philip Yorke of Erddig, the 1st Baron Brownlow's brother-in-law, the wings were removed to leave the principal arch standing alone—a curious sight, it was nicknamed by the family 'Lord Brownlow's breeches'. The tower fell derelict in the present century, but the National Trust has recently completed the first phase of restoration.

The landscape gardener William Emes proposed that the park should be made more 'natural', in the manner of a Capability Brown landscape, and lakes introduced, but none of this work was carried out, although the formal gardens around the house were removed, leaving the house sitting in rolling parkland.

A century later, formal gardens were back in fashion, and the Dutch garden and Italian garden were laid out to the north of the house. The Dutch garden was planted in the 1870s in an attempt to recreate some of the formal spendour of the earlier gardens. Very elaborate in Victorian times, it is now maintained as a simple parterre planted with bedding and roses. From the steps of the terrace a broad central gravel walk leads down through the garden, flanked by a regiment of alternating columns and domes of clipped yew. An 18C sundial at the end of this main axis depicts the figure of Time attended by a cherub. This statue is recognisable to the south of the house in Badeslade's engraving of the grounds c 1750.

To either side of the central walk an intricate weave of narrow gravel paths is cut into the lawns, alongside beds of bright annuals. Standard roses lend height to the scheme, and vases, urns and statuary contribute to the serene atmosphere.

The Italian garden lies beyond and is larger and more formal than the Dutch garden. It was laid out about 1811 and overlaid around 1880. It contains the beautiful orangery designed by Sir Jeffry Wyatville in 1820. In the centre of the garden is a round pool with a high splashing fountain, surrounded by four grass plots edged with bedding and roses and bisected by gravel paths. A raised walk along the edges of the garden gives good views of the layout, with its ring of vases and urns filled with flowers. Domes of clipped box and columns of yew enhance the formal design.

Beyond a yew hedge to one side of the orangery is the parish church of St Peter and St Paul and facing the orangery at the opposite end is a wall fountain and screen, known as the 'exedra', brought from another part of the gardens in 1921.

The orangery, a fine stone and glass structure, is set amid borders of annual planting and shrubs on a terrace which gives good views across the garden, and glimpses of the house between magnificent tall cedar trees. The atmosphere inside the orangery is cool and refreshing—it contains a rectangular pool and fountain, together with beautiful camellias, climbing plants and terracotta tubs of lilies.

From the front of the orangery a perimeter path leads eastwards, skirting around the edge of the pleasure grounds, where several acres of lawn are planted with a variety of trees and shrubs. There are trees of every shape and colour here—spreading oaks, tall upright limes, pendulous birches and a cedar of Lebanon.

Further along the path, an attractive 18C stone temple overlooks a still rectangular canal. The canal seems strangely out of place, surrounded by such informality of planting. It once marked the boundary of the elaborately patterned tree groves at the east end of the house. The curious mound of earth to the rear of the temple is an old ice house.

Further along the path, you reach an area of light woodland, filled with wildflowers in spring. In the darkest part of the wood are a few rhododendrons.

The circular woodland walk leads back to the house, via the eastern avenues. There are some fine trees in the remaining parkland, but to complete the tour of the garden, cross the main drive to the west of the house, to the Wilderness Garden. Here, along the side of the River Witham, Lord Tyrconnel constructed a ruined grotto and cascades.

A massive timber and log adventure playground in nearby woodland has, sadly, interfered with the setting and upkeep of the ruin and cascades, and a long stretch of the River Witham, complete with ruin, has been fenced off for safety. It is possible to see the outline of the Gothic ruin through the plantings of yew, bamboo and other vegetation.

Doddington Hall

ADDRESS AND TELEPHONE: Doddington Hall, Doddington, Lincoln LN6 4RU. Tel. (0522) 694 308

OWNER: Antony Jarvis, Esq

DIRECTIONS: 5 miles W of Lincoln, in Doddington village on the B1190. Signposted off A46 Lincoln bypass. Public transport: Lincoln BR 5 miles. Buses from Lincoln

OPENING TIMES: May to end September, Wed and Sun 2–6; also BH Mon and Easter Mon. Parties of more than 20 at other times by arrangement. Hall also open

ADMISSION: house and gardens £3; gardens only £1.50; children half price

CAR PARKING: yes and for coaches

TOILETS: yes

REFRESHMENTS: restaurant opens 12 noon

SHOP: yes

DOGS: on leads

WHEELCHAIR ACCESS: yes. Toilets for the disabled: in Hall, on request

PEAK MONTHS: May to July

NOTABLE FEATURES: Elizabethan-style garden (walled) with knot garden; flower borders; wild garden with rhododendrons and shrubs

Doddington Hall is a splendid late Elizabethan house set in quiet picturesque Lincolnshire countryside. The three-storey brick house, symmetrical in design, with Ancaster stone quoins, is made even more dramatic by three roof turrets with lead cupolas rising some 20ft above the parapet.

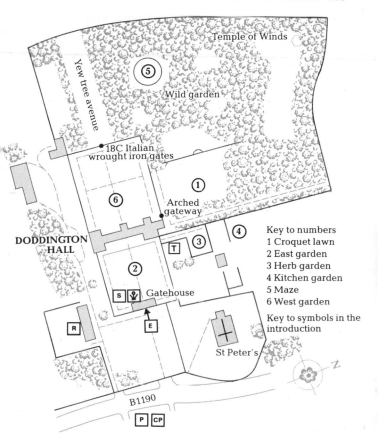

The exterior has changed very little since 1600, when Robert Smythson finished building the house for Thomas Tailor, the Registrar to the Bishop of Lincoln. Much of the garden layout exists within the pattern of old brick walls to be seen in Kip's drawing of 1707, although the gardens themselves have changed considerably, especially over the last 90 years.

The approach lies through a curious three-gabled Tudor brick gatehouse, giving access to the formal East Garden. This walled courtyard was once nearly roofed over by four huge cedars of Lebanon, which have since been cleared. Instead there is a formal layout of gravel paths, box edging, topiary and trained cherry trees, with tubs of flowers by the front steps. The whole courtyard was recently re-designed to set off the formal approach to the Hall and will incorporate four topiary unicorns, the family crest.

Through an arched gateway is the West Garden—the most formal and intricate of the gardens at Doddington. Here in 1900, within the warm sunny shelter of the old walls, an Elizabethan-style garden was re-created to a design by Kew Gardens and Country

Life. It consists of a knot garden and borders, and is at its best in late June and early July.

The knot garden is terraced into two halves. Curves and swirls of clipped box hedges surround beds of roses and irises near the house, and displays of roses and bedding are set in the lawns. The surrounding borders, edged with small pinks, overflow with shrubs, herbaceous plants and spring bulbs—their colours chosen to harmonise with the brick and stonework of the hall and enclosing walls. Soft shades of pink, mauve, magenta, blue and white mingle with silver and grey foliage, and in summer the air is filled with the sweet scent of shrub roses. In the border by the garden cottage is a small pocket handkerchief tree (*Davidia involucrata*), while the south-east corner is dominated by a splendid *Magnolia sieboldii* which bears fragrant white flowers from May to August.

Beyond the elaborate 18C Italian wrought iron gates in the west wall is a sombre alley of Irish yews. This alley leads down the main axis of the garden from the house and continues into an avenue of broad-leaved limes (*Tilia platyphyllos*), which stretches away across the fields.

Beyond the northern boundary of the avenue are the informal orchard and wild garden. The 4-acre wild garden is at its best in May, with a beautiful display of rhododendrons, spring shrubs and bulbs. Many of the trees and shrubs in this tranquil part of the garden were planted by the present owner's parents. Some of the rhododendrons were collected by a relative who went on Kingdon Ward's last plant expedition to Asia in the 1930s. Flowering currants, viburnums, cornus and many shrub roses can be found growing in the long grass, amid wild flowers. The two huge clumps of yew trees are believed to be older than the Hall; and certainly many of them date from Tudor times.

In a clearing beside the yew trees is a turf and gravel maze, laid out in 1986 in an intriguing pattern. An avenue of twisted catalpa trees leads on to a stout specimen of the rare hybrid cork or Lucombe oak which is grafted onto the stem of a wild cork oak. Its characteristic corky bark and greyish leaves make it easily recognisable. Nearby is a thicket of rhododendrons and, in a small glade, winter flowering shrubs such as witch-hazel and *Viburnum fragrans*, sheltered by clumps of bamboo.

In the furthest corner of the wild garden is the eight-sided Temple of the Winds. Although it looks like a relic from an earlier 18C landscape garden, the temple has a fibreglass roof, and was constructed in the 1960s. There is a good view from the temple across the surrounding countryside and back across a flowery meadow to the wild garden.

The east boundary of the wild garden is formed by the high brick wall of the kitchen garden, covered for its 80-yd length by climbing roses and shrubs. Below it a wide gravel path, overshadowed by an avenue of cherry trees, leads on towards the croquet lawn, enclosed in a pleached hornbeam hedge, at the northern end of the Hall. From this lawn you can also see three immense sweet chestnut trees. Believed to have been planted by the Elizabethans, these gnarled old trees are now in a state of collapse, but still produce crops of nuts.

From the croquet lawn, you can return to the house via a door in the kitchen garden wall, passing through a small herb garden on the way. Here, in an enclosure of holly hedges, a number of traditional varieties of herbs are preserved as a reminder of Doddington Hall's long history.

Springfields Gardens

ADDRESS AND TELEPHONE: Springfields Gardens, Springfields Horticultural Society Ltd, Camelgate, Spalding, Lincolnshire. Tel. Spalding (0775) 724843

OWNERS: Springfields Horticultural Society Ltd

DIRECTIONS: 1 mile E of Spalding town centre, off A151, clearly signposted. Public transport: Spalding BR (change at Peterborough for Spalding)

OPENING TIMES: April to September, daily 10–6

ADMISSION: £2 except for special events. Children under 16 free. Coach parties by prior arrangement

CAR PARKING: yes

TOILETS: yes

REFRESHMENTS: café

SHOP: yes both gifts and plants

DOGS: no, except guide dogs

WHEELCHAIR ACCESS: excellent. Toilets for the disabled: yes

PEAK MONTHS: April to mid May for bulbs and spring flowers. July to September for roses and summer bedding displays

NOTABLE FEATURES: magnificent displays of bulbs and bedding for colour; spring flowering trees and shrubs

NOTE: a parade is held each year, usually one day in May, when large floats decorated with tulip heads tour round the town and then park at the gardens

Lincolnshire's Fenland bears a distinct resemblance to parts of the Netherlands. Around the old market town of Spalding much of the flat open countryside lies just above sea level. The land is drained by a network of dykes and many of the older houses have clearly been constructed on Dutch lines. There is a long history of trading between the Netherlands and this part of England.

Bulbs have been grown on a commercial basis in south Lincolnshire for more than a hundred years and in the 1950s and 60s tulips so dominated the district that the vast fields around Spalding became known as Tulipland. Since then the acreage of tulips produced in the area has declined drastically, but a living catalogue of flowers thrives at Springfields Gardens on the edge of Spalding.

The construction of Springfields Gardens began in 1964 as an initiative by a branch of the National Farmers' Union. The idea was to create a showcase garden for the bulb industry, just as the Dutch had done several years earlier with the Keukenhof gardens near Lisse.

The garden layout, noticeably more continental than English in character, was the work of a Dutch designer, Carl van Empelen, who was known for his work in Europe. Trees and shrubs had to be planted in order to shelter the garden from cruel east winds, a lake was excavated and thousands of bulbs—all supplied by the British bulb industry—were planted ready for the opening in spring 1966.

Today Springfields Gardens is one of Britain's premier show gardens. Every April to mid May the beds and borders are filled with sheets of tulips, narcissi and hyacinths. It is a unique spectacle, a festival of colour.

Springfields Gardens is basically rectangular with a shelter belt to the east. Within the 25 acres there are formal and informal gardens and woodland. Thousands of bulbs are planted into the formal beds each year, but there is also a wide variety of spring flowering trees and shrubs, as well as herbaceous borders and good selection of climbing plants.

The garden was specifically laid out with large numbers of visitors in mind. Extra wide paths mean that even on a busy day there is plenty of room for everyone to walk safely without damaging the plants. Springfields is also well suited to the disabled visitor—all the paths, except the woodland walk, are paved, and the flatness of the landscape makes it ideal for wheelchair users.

Spring is naturally the busiest time at Springfields Gardens. From April to mid May thousands of visitors—not just gardeners—flock to see the brightly coloured displays. The formal beds cut into the large lawns, the beds in the paved walks and the glasshouses are filled with hundreds of varieties of tulips. Among the early tulips is 'Orange Nassau', a bright orange-red flower shaded with mahogany, while 'Apricot Beauty' and the pure white 'Diana' show their excellence for bedding. The Darwin hybrids always make a glorious display with colours varying from the sulphur yellow of 'Jewel of Spring' to the carmine-scarlet of 'Red Matador'.

The water lily shaped flowers of *Tulipa koeffmanniana* are retained in the Koeffmanniana hybrids such as 'Shakespeare' which is carmine-red on the outside but inside is salmon flushed scarlet with a golden yellow base.

The lily-flowered tulips are much admired for their pointed petals and graceful slim-waisted flowers. The rose-pink 'China Pink' is an example of this type of tulip, as is 'Aladdin' which has particularly beautiful crimson flowers edged with gold. Large-flowered tulips can be recognised early by the leaves which are often wavy and generally striped or mottled purplish-brown. There are parrot tulips and fringed tulips, too, such as 'Burgundy Lace' which is a rich wine red.

Hyacinths fill the air with their strong sweet fragrance. Colours vary from the white of 'Carnegie' and the primrose yellow of 'City of Haarlem' to the shell pink of 'Lady Derby', the deep rose of 'Pink Pearl' and the rich blue of 'Blue Jacket'. There are also masses of narcissi with varieties like 'Golden Harvest', 'St. Keverne', 'Texas', 'Golden Ducat' and 'Ice Follies' offering many different shades of yellow from light lemon through to coppery orange.

Throughout spring the blossom of cherries and apples adds further to the interest and the profusion of colour. Among the many shrubs in the garden, the bridal wreath (*Spiraea* x *arguta*) puts on a most impressive display with clusters of pure white flowers along its branches.

The rose and bedding plant industries have contributed a great deal to Springfields. In 1976 the British Association of Rose Breeders donated some 7500 rose bushes to the garden in order to establish a summer season and since 1982 bedding plants have also been introduced. Springfields is now open from April through to September and has become famous for both spring and summer mass colour displays of a very high standard.

Over the years the number of roses has gradually increased to exceed 12,000. There are both old and new varieties. One of the most popular bedding roses is 'Just Joey', with fragrant blooms of coppery-orange and ruffled petals, flowering well into the autumn. 'Typhoon' is also an excellent bedding type—a compact bush bearing large open scented blooms of copper and pink, tinged with yellow at the base.

Floribunda roses are well represented and colour is provided throughout the season by 'City of Belfast' which shows off its small velvety orange-scarlet flowers against attractive glossy foliage.

In July and August come the bedding displays, involving intensive planting of around 200,000 bedding plants—pansies, geraniums, dahlias, salvias, impatiens and marigolds and many others.

Springfields Gardens is a pioneering force in the horticultural world. There are trials of both bulbs and bedding plants, to examine flowering time, depth of planting and to evaluate new varieties. The latest varieties of bedding plants are on show each summer, and in the glasshouse there is a large display of hanging baskets.

Other features include a woodland with naturalised daffodils, a million gallon artificial lake, one of the largest sundials in the country, a maze and an excellent bulb and plant shop.

LONDON AND GREATER LONDON

Capel Manor

ADDRESS AND TELEPHONE: Capel Manor Horticultural and Environmental Centre, Bullsmoor Lane, Enfield, Middlesex. Tel. (0992) 763849

OWNERS: London Borough of Enfield

DIRECTIONS: 12 miles N of London, close to junction 25 of the M25/A10. Public transport: ½ mile from Turkey Street BR or by bus from Enfield, Waltham Cross and surrounding area

OPENING TIMES: weekdays all year round, except Christmas Day, Boxing Day and New Year's Day, 10–4.30. Weekends between April and October, 10–5.30 (Farm 1–5.30). Also special open weekends: check times with college. House not open

ADMISSION: £1.25, concessions 60p. Farm £1.50. Pre-booked guided tours available for groups

CAR PARKING: yes

TOILETS: yes

REFRESHMENTS: no but picnics encouraged

SHOP: plants for sale

DOGS: yes, on lead

WHEELCHAIR ACCESS: yes. Toilets for the disabled: yes

PEAK MONTHS: May, June and July: September, October and November

NOTABLE FEATURES: garden for disabled, trials garden and many others. Capel Manor Educational Farm 1 mile away

Capel Manor's 30 acres of landscaped gardens are within easy travelling distance (by car or rail) from north London and the perfect place for a day out from the city. It is also situated conveniently close to Crews Hill's 'Golden Mile' of garden centres.

Capel Manor College runs an impressive range of horticultural training and education courses, mainly on a day-release basis, and also operates an 'open learning' scheme. The gardens are designed especially for student practice, study and observation: but members of the general public are made very welcome, throughout the year and on special open weekends. The students themselves are remarkably courteous, helpful and ready to answer questions. Credit for their enthusiasm must go to the lecturers and administrative staff, not least to Capel Manor's dynamic principal, Dr Steve Dowbiggin.

Originally part of the estate belonging to Theobalds Palace (a principle residence of James I), Capel Manor has existed since the 12C. The present house was built in 1750, and a few trees from this period are still alive and growing. Sadly, the 1987 gale brought down the magnificent copper beech, planted in the 1770s (one of the original 12 brought into this country from Germany). A survivor of both the 1987 and 1990 gales is a rare *Zelkova carpinifolia*, the second tallest in the country. A ha-ha, built in the 19C, marks the original boundary of the site, following the line of a wall built by James I to enclose Theobalds Estate.

Today the gardens are divided for study and visiting purposes into a number of distinct small areas—the walled garden, theme gardens, historic garden, trials garden and so on. Many of the 5000 plants are labelled.

A shady woodland walk leads from the back of the house round the western side of the garden, planted with rhododendrons, camellias, azaleas, trilliums and primulas. A brilliant collection of Ghent azaleas, mainly yellow, stands in a clearing near the lawn. These plants, with their unusually heavy scent, were very popular in the 1920s, but went out of fashion. The Capel Manor azaleas owe their survival to neglect—overgrown during the 1930s, they were rediscovered along with the rest of the garden in 1968. Capel Manor's previous owner, Lt.-Col. Medcalf, died in 1958 and it was 10 years before the Capel Manor Institute of Horticulture and Field Studies took over the grounds. Frances Perry, the well-known gardening writer, played an important part in setting up the college and restoring the gardens; the college library is named after her.

Designed by David Stephens and Adrian Pyatt, the garden for the disabled was built by community programme volunteers, and is looked after by the Wednesday Club, a group of disabled students. Raised brick borders and easily accessible narrow flowerbeds contain brilliant examples of what any amateur gardener might achieve. A raised brick-built watercourse winds through the centre of the garden, divided into four sections of varying heights. From top to bottom it includes a rockery and waterfall, top pool, stream, bog garden and lower pool. There are five intermediate waterfalls. Combined with the different wall heights, this gives the garden many changes of level, without any steps or sharp inclines.

Leading on from this garden is the Hodgkinson garden for the visually impaired. This garden (sponsored by B&Q) was a silver gilt medal-winner at the Chelsea Flower Show in 1987; afterwards it was transported back to Capel Manor. There is a combination of paving materials—brick, metal and wood—besides water features and thoughtfully grouped scented plants. The college runs courses in horticultural therapy.

On the conifer bank are *Juniperus communis*, chamaecyparis and *Picea glauca albertiana* 'Conica', one of the best and most attractively shaped of rockery conifers. Ground cover is varied and colourful.

Just north of this garden lie three small theme gardens—the White Garden, the Architectural Garden and the Foliage Garden. College staff refer to this as the 'Sackville-West area', since the plant forms and associations are similar to those at Sissinghurst. The Architectural Garden, composed of species that lend variety of shapes, is worth visiting even out of season. The White Garden consists mainly of white and silvery-leaved plants—*Stachys lanata* 'Silver Carpet', senecio 'White Diamond', artemisia 'Lambrook Silver' and *Dicentra eximia* 'Alba', with its heads of drooping white and pink flowers above deeply serated foliage. There is also plenty of green and some boldly placed yellow poppies.

The Foliage Garden displays striking contrasts of shape, colour and height. There is a big *Cistus ladanifer* (the gum cistus) and two yuccas. Yellow hypericum and golden marjoram are offset by a spectrum of greens.

A rectangular Historic Garden is laid out near the main lawn, surrounded by shaped hedges of dark yew and guarded by two stone lions. It is planted in various 17C styles, with a knot garden, a Garden of Delight and a collection of medicinal herbs. All the plants are contemporary with Parkinson and Culpeper. The central feature is an iron well-head, restored by the borough architect. The wrought iron patterns match those of the wood carving and plaster mouldings in Capel Manor House.

On the site of the original copper beech tree, close to the Historic Garden, is the newly planted Italianate maze, a labyrinth holly, based on the design of William Nesfield, 1851, for the Great Exhibition. The four graceful statues overlook the central fountain.

A short walk further north brings you to the rock and water garden, a pleasant place to sit and relax. Constructed in 1978 from 150 tons of Macclesfield sandstone, it was designed by Peter

Robinson, one-time principal of Capel Manor. New outcrops of rock are added now and then for students to practice on. The planting is intensive—spreading conifers, a big specimen of *Hebe rakaiensis*, sweet-smelling yellow broom and lots of dwarf irises, notably blue/mauve 'Austrian Sky'. Goldfish and valuable Koi carp fill the pond.

Trials gardens cover 5 acres to the far north, a joint venture between Capel Manor and *Gardening* from *Which?* magazine. Here plants and equipment from different nurseries and manufacturers are rigorously tested and compared. This area is open to the public, but 'trials in progress' beds are not labelled.

Returning south towards the house you pass the modern Courtyard Garden, which demonstrates the use of paving and brick, with stone columns, a barbecue area and a semicircular pool with intertwining herons. Nearby is the Lovers' Garden.

Strolling on through the Victorian garden you can take a left turn towards the latest development at Capel Manor. This is the National Gardening Centre, which features several different gardens sponsored by industry.

Turning westwards, you pass the new lake development with its medley of aquatic plants.

It is well worth visiting the small alpine house, near the walled garden, a greenhouse surrounded by planted stone troughs. Some of the alpines are grown on tufa, redeposited limestone, which looks like a stone sponge. Inside the glasshouse are some old-style auriculas, including 'The General', which dates from the 1600s. There are saxifrages, lithospermum and a very rare specimen of *Stenomesson aurantiaecum*, collected in 1983 from the Andes. Like amaryllis, this produces its flowers before it comes into leaf. Note also *Polylepsis australis*, a rosaceous tree which will survive up to 13,000 feet above sea level.

A tropical display house has been built inside the walled garden. In cold weather this is very popular with visitors. It contains tropical and subtropical plants, including economic crops such as coffee, sugar cane, banana, ginger and cotton. A recent addition is the huge artificial interior landscape incorporating epiphytic plants and a waterfall.

The walled garden was the only part of the grounds cultivated between 1958 and 1968, when it was used to grow vegetables. Now it is packed with shrubs, climbers and herbaceous plants. Roses are planted chronologically, beginning with the oldest kinds, the gallicas, albas and damasks, and leading through the centifolia, moss, china and bourbons up to modern floribundas.

The long herbaceous border along the south wall follows the ideas and colour principles of Gertrude Jekyll. Two converging wooden pergolas support various climbers, including *Actinidia kolomikta*, with its distinctive heart-shaped leaves, looking as if someone has dipped them in whitewash. More fine climbers can be seen along the walls.

A weather vane overlooks the walled garden from the stables: crowned by a gold-plated horse, commemorating one of Lt.-Col. Medcalf's prize Clydesdales, this is so heavy that it will only turn in gale-force winds.

A trust fund has been established at Capel Manor with the aim of establishing it as the Horticultural Heritage Centre—a national showpiece with international appeal.

Chelsea Physic Garden

ADDRESS AND TELEPHONE: 66 Royal Hospital Road, London SW3. Tel. (071) 352 5646

OWNERS: Trustees of the Chelsea Physic Garden

DIRECTIONS: the garden lies in the angle between Royal Hospital Road and the Chelsea Embankment. Public transport: Sloane Square tube station: walk S down Lower Sloane Street, then turn right along the Royal Hospital Road. Bus 239 (Victoria to Putney) runs down Royal Hospital Road from Mon to Sat

OPENING TIMES: 17 March to 20 October, Wed and Sun 2–5, also Chelsea Flower Show week (21 to 24 May) 12–5

ADMISSION: £2, students with cards and children £1

CAR PARKING: no

TOILETS: yes

REFRESHMENTS: teas on Sun

SHOP: yes, plant sales and cards etc

DOGS: no

WHEELCHAIR ACCESS: yes. Toilets for the disabled: no

PEAK MONTHS: May and June

NOTABLE FEATURES: many rare plants, including the largest outdoor olive tree in Britain; a herb garden with culinary and medicinal plants; botanical orders beds; the oldest rock garden in Europe (1772); a historical walk

When the Chelsea Physic Garden was first established, Chelsea was just a small riverside suburb, surrounded by open fields. Now it lies in one of the busiest parts of London, bounded to the north by Royal Hospital Road, to the south by the Chelsea Embankment and the Thames, and to the east by Swan Walk. Despite this, it is a remarkably quiet, tranquil and private place, surrounded by its high 17C walls and sheltered by trees.

Chelsea was one of the very earliest botanic gardens, founded in 1673, 50 years after Oxford and about a century before Kew. It was set up by the Worshipful Society of Apothecaries of London, for the purpose of medical and scientific research.

In its long history, the garden has suffered several periods of neglect and financial crises. Dr Hans Sloane, a wealthy physician, was one of its earliest benefactors: having bought the Manor of Chelsea in 1712, he saved the garden from serious decline 10 years later by leasing it to the Apothecaries 'in perpetuity' for £5 a year—on condition it should be maintained as a physic garden. You can see a statue of Sir Hans in the middle of the garden, a copy of the original by Rysbrack, now in the British Museum.

Sir Hans also suggested Philip Miller as the new Gardener (in 1722). Over the following 50 years, under Miller's care, Chelsea became the finest botanic garden in the world: and Miller himself

The Chelsea Physic Garden: about a hundred plant families are displayed in botanical order

developed into a very great botanical horticulturist. His famous *Gardeners Dictionary* is still worth consulting today, and it was highly praised by Linnaeus. He and Miller met in 1736, when Linnaeus was visiting Britain: at first they did not get on very well, but eventually Miller adopted the Linnaean system of plant classification in the 7th and 8th editions of his Dictionary.

During this period, Miller was constantly in touch with other leading botanists and receiving seeds of new species from abroad, so he was responsible for introducing many plants into Britain, especially from North and South America, and notably the Madagascar periwinkle, *Catharanthus roseus*, which contains alkaloids now used to treat cancer. Chelsea also sent seeds abroad, helping to establish new crops in other countries—cotton in Georgia, for instance.

Miller's successors continued his work, so a great many of the garden's 5000 species come from gardens abroad. At first transport posed many problems, with plants more often than not arriving dead, until the development of Wardian Cases—miniature travelling greenhouses—in the 19C; their inventor, Dr Ward, was closely associated with the Chelsea Physic Garden.

In 1899, following on another financial crisis, the garden passed into the hands of the Trustees of the London Parochial Charities. In 1983 it was handed over to a new body of independent trustees, and opened to the public for the first time.

18C illustrations of the garden feature a great formal canal, surrounded by four *Cedrus libani* (cedars of Lebanon), introduced in 1683 from Leiden in Holland by John Watts, then gardener in charge. These have now gone, but around 100 notable specimen trees remain. Most striking of all is *Koelreuteria paniculata*, the golden rain tree, with its knobbly trunk and intricately twisted branches. Beside the herb garden stands a 30ft-high *Olea europaea*, the biggest olive tree in Britain, accompanied by *Quercus suber*, the cork oak and *Quercus coccifera*, the Kermes oak, near the glasshouses. Sadly, despite its sheltered position the garden has lost many trees in the last few years—30 blew down in the gale of October 1987, including a holm oak planted before 1751 and many other old and rare specimens.

Rectilinear display beds cover a large part of the garden, their plain and simple style harking back to the monastery gardens of the early medieval period. About a hundred plant families are displayed in beds in neat botanical order, starting with buttercups, Ranunculaceae (Dicotyledons) and ending with grasses, Gramineae (Monocotyledons). Most of the plants are herbaceous.

A big square herb garden lies to the north-east, planted with herbs used in cooking and medicine (including homoeopathic medicine), dyeing and perfumery through the ages and in our own times. Like the Apothecaries of 300 years ago, Chelsea's curator and gardeners work to maintain a reference collection of medicinal and culinary herbs and also provide facilities for research.

Feverfew is now being investigated for its possible power to cure migraine, a project undertaken in co-operation with researchers at King's College, London. The Natural History Museum also has beds here and plant samples are currently supplied to Glaxo Group Research. Physic garden beds can be turned over quickly to a new research 'tenant', but Chelsea gardeners continue to pursue their own special projects on cistus (sunroses), narcissus (daffodils) and salvia (sages) species. More research and historical material can be found in the glasshouses, along the north wall.

The rock garden (near Sir Hans Sloane's statue) is the earliest example of its kind ever seen in England—curiously it now qualifies as a listed building. It was built by William Forsyth in the late 18C, using 40 tons of old stone from the Tower of London, flints, chalk, and Icelandic lava brought back from Iceland by Sir Joseph Banks. The result is interesting but ugly.

South American, Australasian, Chinese and Californian plants are represented in special areas, including many tender species, which survive very well here. More lovely shrubs and small trees can be seen in the woodland garden, underplanted with winter and early spring flowers—snowdrops, cyclamen and hellebores. Chelsea holds the National Reference Collection of cistus, and a collection of hardy hypericums.

All these and many other delights are being reorganised into a historical walk.

Chiswick House Gardens

ADDRESS AND TELEPHONE: Chiswick House Grounds, Chiswick, London W4. Tel. (081) 995 5390

OWNERS: grounds managed by London Borough of Hounslow, The Civic Centre, Lampton Road, Hounslow, TW3 4DN. Tel. (081) 570 7728. English Heritage has responsibility for the house

DIRECTIONS: A4, A316. Public transport: Underground Turnham Green; BR Chiswick; buses E3, 290

OPENING TIMES: all year, daily, 7.30am to dusk. House open mid March to mid October 9.30–6.30 and mid October to mid March 9.30–4

ADMISSION: free to grounds

CAR PARKING: yes and for coach parties

TOILETS: yes

REFRESHMENTS: café

SHOP: yes, in house

DOGS: yes, but a 'clean up after your dog scheme' in operation

WHEELCHAIR ACCESS: yes, to grounds and ground floor of house. Toilets for the disabled: yes adjacent to café

PEAK MONTHS: May to September

NOTABLE FEATURES: cedars, Lucombe oak; statues and Ionic temple; Italian gardens

An impressive and ambitious 8-year restoration plan has been devised by Hounslow Council for Chiswick House grounds: they are certainly in dire need of repair and replanting. Many of the statues are broken or badly weathered, paths are worn, many trees have been lost through disease and the storms of recent years, shrubberies have reverted to scrub and the Wilderness is almost impenetrable. The council aims to restore these historic grounds to something like their former glory, preserving their 'unique flavour and interest' for garden historians and the general public alike.

The gardens were very well-known in the 18C and 19C and referred to in most books on garden landscaping. They were first laid out between 1718 and 1735 by Richard Boyle, the 3rd Earl of Burlington, a great patron of the arts and friend of artists and writers, such as the poet Alexander Pope. Lord Burlington himself was responsible for introducing the Palladian style of architecture into England.

A very formal, grand and geometrical style of landscape gardening had been popular since the Restoration in 1660: long straight avenues, canals and fountains were much favoured. Burlington's first layout was of this kind, including for instance a huge *patte d'oie* or goosefoot of three avenues radiating outwards from a central point.

Around this time, however, there was a move towards Nature, or an idealised conception of nature, drawn largely from the Italian countryside and inspired by Renaissance paintings. William Kent, a leading exponent of the 'natural style', was given a free hand at Chiswick and made many changes, introducing kinks and bends into the artificial river, creating a Wilderness with winding sinuous paths and placing small temples, grottoes and statues at strategic points.

Kent's first project was an exedra (an 'outdoor seat'), a semicircular hedge of clipped yew with seating and niches for classical statuary. The cascade, designed by Kent himself, was completed in 1738 and put at the head of the canal. Unfortunately it never worked properly (even after Lord Burlington had paid £181 2s 10d in 1746 for a new horse engine) and today it seems to be completely defunct. The north lawn also dates from this time, although few of the original trees are still standing.

Kent made graceful concessions to Lord Burlington's former scheme, planting *allées* along the radiating lines of the goosefoot. He also made two further *pattes d'oie* on the other side of the river, mirror images of each other, sharing one common avenue (only one of these remains).

Further important changes were made in the 1780s and 1790s by the 5th Duke of Devonshire (Burlington's grandson) and his landscape gardener Samuel Lapidge—these included much new planting and a new ride from the house to the cascade and along the terrace. American deer were introduced into the grounds at this period: they were notoriously savage and bad-tempered.

The 6th Duke, another keen gardener, built the conservatory in 1812 (it has been rebuilt several times since). The Italian garden, directly below, was added in 1814: by this time, Kent's influence was fading, and formal flower gardens were beginning to creep back into Britain. The 6th Duke's landscape gardener was the renowned Lewis Kennedy, a gardener of considerable enterprise, who also helped to bring avenues back into fashion—Duke's Avenue (now the approach from Turnham Green) was his work. Kennedy also introduced standard roses into Britain from France.

Entering from Park Road, you will soon come across the beautiful Classic Bridge, built in 1788 and decorated with urns and gilded cherubs. Make your way from here down the bank of the artificial river (2000ft long and 60ft wide) to the cascade at the far end. By the riverside grow Lombardy poplars and willows, ash, beech, chestnut and swamp cypress. The villa lies north of the cascade, unmistakable with its Palladian architecture and obelisk-shaped chimneys. Alexander Pope described it as 'the finest thing this glorious sun has shined upon'; Lord Harvey, less easy to impress, damned it as 'too small to inhabit and too large to hang on a watch-chain'.

The main *patte d'oie* begins just west of the villa, leading down through the main lawn to the exedra. Cedars of Lebanon and cypresses stand majestically either side with holm oaks, acer and a catalpa (Indian bean tree). This area is plentifully furnished with stone lions, sphinxes and urns and the exedra is lined with Classical statues, said to have come from Hadrian's villa at Tivoli.

Just south of the exedra, you will find the orange tree garden amphitheatre, with its great central obelisk, rising out of a central small pool. Theatrical performances are often held here on warm summer nights, with audiences picnicking on the steep grassy slopes. The orange trees of Lord Burlington's time have now been replaced by orange and lemon trees, brought into the garden each summer. An Ionic temple stands at the back: this was probably designed by Lord Burlington himself. 'Lilly's tomb', a monument to a pet greyhound, can be found above, by the railings.

Another obelisk stands on the garden's southern perimeter, the central feature of Kent's remaining *patte d'oie,* its plinth incorporating a second century Roman tombstone. 18C garden landscapes were stuffed full of such 'mementos mori', in accordance with current artistic taste: it was an age preoccupied by gloom and the classical era.

The fine conservatory or camellia house behind the villa, backed by the intricate Italian garden laid out below, is closed for restoration.

Books and catalogues are on sale just inside the house. Particularly recommended are Hounslow Council's cheerful yellow leaflets, setting out the Nature Trail, the Historical Trail and the three trails for people with disabilities—the Duke's Trail, the Tree Trail and the Park Trail. The latter is perhaps most comprehensive.

Greenwich Park

ADDRESS AND TELEPHONE: Department of the Environment, Superintendent's Office, Blackheath Gate, Blackheath, London SE3. Tel. (081) 858 2608

OWNERS: Department of the Environment

DIRECTIONS: at junction of A206, A2211 and A200. Public transport: ¼ mile E of Greenwich station. May also be reached by boat down the River Thames

OPENING TIMES: open daily, throughout the year, dawn to dusk. National Maritime Museum open to public at set times (entrance charge levied)

ADMISSION: none, but entrance fee to the National Maritime Museum

CAR PARKING: yes, near Observatory

TOILETS: yes

REFRESHMENTS: café. With prior notice will cater for coach parties. Also tennis courts, and concerts every Sun from May to the end of August

DOGS: yes, and on lead in café, flower gardens and children's playground

WHEELCHAIR ACCESS: yes. Toilets for the disabled: yes

Greenwich is the oldest of the Royal Parks and one of the most impressive, with its windswept heights, excellent views over the river and city and fine buildings. It covers 185 acres, stretching from Greenwich Pier in the north-west to Blackheath in the south. The Royal Observatory was housed here until 1948, when the murky London smog forced its exile to Herstmonceux in Sussex.

The name Greenwich derives from the Saxon Grenawic, the green village. Once a fishing village on the Thames, Greenwich was presented to the abbots of St Peter of Ghent in AD 914 by Elstrudis, daughter of King Alfred. The land was confiscated in 1414 by Henry V and after his death it came into the hands of Humphrey, Duke of Gloucester. Gloucester enclosed the park, in 1433, and built a house here, called Bella Court; the estate was renamed Pleasaunce by Margaret of Anjou, Queen of Henry VI, and the name was latinised to Placentia by the Tudors. Gloucester's boundary fence of wooden palings was replaced with a brick wall by James I.

In the middle of the park, about 218 yds from Flamsteed House, you will find Queen Elizabeth's Oak, an ancient ivy-covered tree guarded by railings. Queen Elizabeth I is said to have taken refreshment here, inside the hollow trunk, and later it was used as a lock-up for offenders against park rules. Thought to have been planted towards the end of the 12C, the oak died over a hundred years ago, but the ivy flourishes, full of nesting and twittering birds.

According to another legend, Anne Boleyn and Henry VIII once danced around the trunk. Henry VIII was born in the palace of Placentia, as were all his legitimate children—Mary, Elizabeth and Edward. Greenwich was Elizabeth's favourite home, despite the muddy streets—it was here that Sir Walter Raleigh gallantly flung down his cloak for her to walk on.

The Queen's House (reopened after restoration in summer 1990) was designed by Inigo Jones for Anne of Denmark, wife of James I. The first example seen in England of the pure Palladian style, it is reputed to have inspired the presidential White House in Washington. The house was completed in the reign of Charles I, who gave it to his wife, Henrietta Maria. Charles II demolished the palace of Placentia and commissioned Sir Christopher Wren to build the Royal Observatory, Flamsteed House.

Flamsteed House, designed by Wren 'for the Observator's habitation and a little for Pompe', now provides an excellent focal point, with its decorative brickwork and tall windows, set on steeply rising ground above The Avenue. Its pink time-ball, said to be visible for miles, rises to the top of a short staff every day at 12.55pm and falls at precisely 1pm.

A new palace was designed by John Webb, a pupil of Inigo Jones, but only one wing of this was completed before Charles ran out of money. Sir Christopher Wren produced a second design, during the reign of William and Mary, for a building in two identical parts on either side of an open courtyard, and this was used as a naval hospital until 1873, when it became the Royal Naval College.

William IV opened Greenwich Park to the public, in the early 19C, and in 1937 the Queen's House became the central part of the National Maritime Museum.

Starting at St Mary's Gate, to the north-west, and walking south-east up The Avenue, you get an excellent view over wide open stretches of green parkland, crossed by paths, to Observatory Hill on the left; and to the right, another hill crowned with tumuli or ancient graves, probably dating from Roman times. The steep slopes of Observatory Hill are planted with narcissi and other bulbs and an impressive variety of shrubs and trees, including many ericaceous plants.

Rounding the hill, you enter Blackheath Avenue, stretching from Wolfe's statue to Blackheath Gate and bordered all the way by horse chestnut trees. Great Cross Avenue runs from this central point eastwards to join Bower Avenue, bordered by sweet chestnuts. André Le Nôtre, landscape gardener to Louis XIV of France, is thought to have planned these paths in the reign of Charles II, although he never visited Greenwich.

Just beyond the statue of General Wolfe—commemorating his 1759 victory at Quebec—is a terrace commanding a wonderful view over the northern side of the park, the Queen's House and the Royal Naval College; and beyond these, the Cutty Sark, St Paul's Cathedral, Tower Bridge and the curving River Thames.

Flamsteed House is now a museum, housing a collection of astronomical instruments, clocks and chronometers. Nearby are the Old Royal Observatory, Greenwich planetarium and the domed Altazimuth pavilion. The tea house is well situated across the avenue, so you can pause here for a rest and light refreshment before inspecting the 24-hour clock and the Greenwich meridian line for Longitude 0. The meridian line is ever popular with tourists; here if so inclined you can stand with one foot in the western hemisphere and one in the eastern.

Blackheath Avenue is joined further south by a narrow path leading from the Ranger's House, near the park's south-west corner. Dating from the early 18C and once the home of Lord Chesterfield, this now houses the Suffolk Collection of Tudor portraits. The rose garden is stocked with bright hybrid teas and floribundas, including a Round Table bed, featuring roses connected by name with the legend of King Arthur—'Guinever', 'Excalibur', 'Merlin', and so on.

A little further south is an area covered by flagstones, known as Queen Caroline's sunken bath; this was once a part of Montagu House, home of Caroline of Brunswick, Queen of George IV. The house was demolished in the early 19C.

A 13-acre Wilderness occupies the park's south-eastern corner. This is closed to the public, but you can often see deer wandering close to the fence. Greenwich Park was originally stocked with fallow deer by Margaret of Anjou, Henry VI's formidable warrior Queen.

Colourful and well planned gardens extend to the north and west, encompassing a lake, heather garden, huge circular flower beds, a variety of shrubs and many rare trees. Entering from the western side, you soon encounter an ancient sweet chestnut (*Castanea sativa*) planted between 1662 and 1664 and still alive. The gardens also have liquidambars, ginkgos, a variety of cedars and pines and one or two paperbark silver birches. Bright Japanese azaleas flourish in island beds. The small lake, home to a surprising variety of waterfowl, is overhung by willows, weeping beeches and swamp cypresses.

Further north, on a hill above Lovers' Walk, are the remains of a Roman building; and nearby, to the west, Queen Elizabeth's oak. A boating pond and playground occupy the north-east corner, near the National Maritime Museum. Older children may prefer to look over the Cutty Sark, the famous 19C tea clipper and wool clipper, now in dry dock near Greenwich Pier.

Greenwich lost 250 trees in the great storm of October 1987, including *Euvodia hupatensis*, a rare Chinese tree, one of two in the country, old sweet chestnuts and oaks, ailanthus, and one or two weeping willows by the pond. A further 25 trees were lost in the gales of January 1990—craetagus, ilex, oaks and limes.

Ham House

ADDRESS AND TELEPHONE: Ham House, Ham, Richmond, Surrey TW10 7RS. Tel. (081) 940 1950

OWNERS: managed by The National Trust

DIRECTIONS: on S bank of Thames, W of A307, at Petersham. Public transport: bus from Ealing Broadway, Chessington, Richmond. Richmond BR

OPENING TIMES: garden all year daily except Mon 11–5.30. Closed Good Fri, 4 May, 24–26 December and 1 January. House open

ADMISSION: house £2, pre-booked adult parties £1.

CAR PARKING: yes, 400 yds

REFRESHMENTS: café

SHOP: yes

DOGS: no

WHEELCHAIR ACCESS: yes, disabled visitors may park near entrance. Toilets for the disabled: yes

NOTABLE FEATURES: restored 17C garden

Set among meadows just below Ham Common and beside the river, Ham House must have been the ideal place to raise a family in the 17C: peaceful, away from the main bustle of London, spacious and beautiful but modest and unpretentious. It has the feel of a home well loved and cared for. Built in 1610 for Sir Thomas Vavascour, Knight Marshall of James I, it was acquired in 1637 by William Murray, Earl of Dysart and handed on to his daughter Elizabeth, who numbered Oliver Cromwell among her lovers.

The house was originally a Jacobean H-shape, but like the gardens it has been much altered. Elizabeth herself made many

*The principle or cherry garden at Ham House has
been restored to its 17C appearance*

improvements and introductions, drawing on the rich purse of her
second husband, John Maitland, Duke of Lauderdale and High
Commissioner for Scotland.

A shady walk running parallel to the river leads to the magnificent
north entrance, a wide court centring on a statue of a reclining river
god. The entrance gates, blue and gilt, were designed by the
architect William Bruce, one of Elizabeth's Scottish cousins, and
erected in 1671. The stone was brought by water from Longannet
Quarry near the Firth of Forth. The south and east gates date from
a few years later. The court was restyled in about 1800, the forecourt
wall dismantled and 16 busts of Roman emperors and ladies
transferred to niches on the front of the house; 22 remain in their
original positions. The river god was introduced around this time:
like the pineapples along the railings he is made from Coade stone,
an artificial stone invented in 1769. Coade's 1784 catalogue lists 'A
river God, 9 feet high, with an Urn through which a stream of water
may be carried 100gns'. Portuguese laurels stand either side of the
house steps, and topiary yew cones front a low terrace.

In 1975 the National Trust undertook to restore the south and east
gardens to something like their original 17C appearance and to
stock them with plants typical of 17C gardens. Following a 1671
plan, the Principal or cherry garden was laid out in big diamonds
and triangles, edged by box (*Buxus sempervirens* 'Suffruticosa'),

set about with cones and filled with santolina or lavender. The simplicity and exactitude of the design allows wide gravel paths to run right through without interruption. The combination of greys and greens is very lovely, framed by the bright gravel and enhanced on hot sunny days by the occasional blue dragonfly. The garden is surrounded by yew hedges, clipped on three sides but growing tall and feathery to the south. An alley of pleached hornbeams runs along the west side, by the house—also very pleasant to look at, with its weathered red brick, white facings, rectangular windows and tall chimneys. Another alley lies to the east and cherries are trained along both the side walls.

Eight enormous grass squares stretch out below the terrace on the south front, striking in their plainness and symmetry. They would originally have been decorated, during the summer months, with tubs and pots of plants. This part of the garden gives a feeling of great spaciousness, of space ordered and controlled. Strong lines and bold design take precedence: plants and trees are not valued so much for themselves as for their contribution to the whole picture. A central axis runs from the house down through the squares and the Wilderness beyond to the south gate, continuing beyond that in a formal avenue leading to Ham Common. The overthrow of the south gates carries the motto 'Nemo me impune lacessit' (No man can harm me unpunished)—perhaps a deterrent to intruders.

Fruit trees are trained along the east and west wall, including several splendid figs, plum 'White Magnum Bonum' from the early 16C, plum 'Fotheringham' (1665) and apple 'James Grieves'. Below the terrace on the south front runs a long herb border: here are many kinds of sages, including *Salvia icterina* from the 17C, with a mottled light and mid-green leaf. Vines hang above, and small ferns sprout from the brickwork.

The Wilderness is an area of grassy walks, radiating out through two circles, bounded by hornbeam hedges and field maples. It is far from a wilderness in the modern sense. Paths are mown through long grasses and wild flowers. In the central clearing are reproductions of 17C garden chairs and the small summerhouses in the hedged enclosures nearby are replicas of those shown in a 1739 engraving.

The walled garden to the east was formerly a kitchen garden, with an orangery at the top; now it is lawned, with long rose borders running between the old (partly 17C) walls, and the orangery has been converted to a pleasant tea room. The roses are modern hybrid teas and floribundas, a jumble of bright colours in June. In the middle of the lawn stands a huge oak, the oldest tree in the grounds. A venerable specimen of Christ's Thorn (*Paliurus spina-christi*) is well supported on all sides and protected by railings near the tea room; nearby is a Judas tree (*Cercis siliquastrum*), damaged in the storm of October 1987 but still surviving (a young Judas tree has been planted nearby). Behind the orangery lies the stable block, dating from the 17C, but now in private hands, and the ice house, built about 1800 but covered in concrete in the 1939–45 war, when it was used as an air raid shelter.

A statue of Bacchus, with one hand broken off, is the main attraction of the ilex or holly walk below the rose garden. A mason's bill for July and August 1672 included the item 'ffor 1 Pedestall for ye figure Bacchus £6'.

It would be a pity to leave without looking round Ham House itself, with its very beautiful rooms and long gallery. Or in sunny weather, you might picnic by the riverside, watching the pleasure steamers, rowing boats and intrepid swimmers. Marble Hill House is just across the river.

Hampton Court

ADDRESS AND TELEPHONE: Hampton Court, East Molesey, Surrey KT8 9AU. Tel. (081) 977 1328

OWNERS: Department of the Environment

DIRECTIONS: on A308 at junction with A309. Public transport: Hampton Court BR or bus 131 from Wimbledon station

OPENING TIMES: daily, throughout the year. Palace open 9.30–6 (each day and including weekends; during winter 4.30)

ADMISSION: gardens free

CAR PARKING: yes

TOILETS: yes

REFRESHMENTS: café

SHOP: yes

DOGS: yes, on a lead

WHEELCHAIR ACCESS: yes. Toilets for the disabled: yes

PEAK MONTHS: April to September

NOTABLE FEATURES: many, including the maze and the famous Hampton Court vine

Lying in a loop of the Thames and bounded on the north by Bushy Park in Middlesex, Hampton Court is easy to reach from central London, especially by river: one of the many attractions it held for Henry VIII.

Cardinal Wolsey may well have regretted creating such a 'desirable property'. His vain attempt to keep the King's favour, by offering him free use of the palace and gardens, predictably backfired: Henry assumed full ownership in 1525.

In the 16C, Hampton Court was reputed to be 'more like unto a paradise than any earthly habitation'. Opened to the public by Queen Victoria in 1838, along with Bushy Park, it remains very popular with both tourists and local people. The maze, near the Lion Gate, is perhaps its most famous feature, along with the gigantic Black Hambro vine, but there is much pleasure to be gained simply from walking around, meditating on Hampton Court's eventful history and the changes its gardens have seen through generations.

On the east front stands the magnificent Fountain Garden, where a distinct shortage of fountains is more than compensated for by the trees. Cone-shaped yews—'black pyramids', Virginia Woolf called them—are reputed to form the initials W and M, for William and Mary, but the point may be missed at ground level.

These yews, originally intended as slender obelisks, begin the *patte d'oie* (goosefoot), a bold scheme established by Charles II after his restoration in 1660 and based on the ideas of André Mollet, mentor of André Le Nôtre, who was landscape gardener to Louis XIV. The goosefoot extends through the garden's giant semicircle, bounded by a small canal and 17C wrought iron gates, into three great avenues of limes in Home Park and Hampton Court Park, and the central Long Water.

The lime tree semicircle surrounding the Fountain Garden reached maturity at around the time Napoleon retreated from Russia. By 1986, only 25 of these original trees remained, all rotten or hollow, and the other limes were a haphazard mixture of ages and species. All 201 limes have now been felled and replaced: the trees alone cost £45,000.

It is tempting to follow the goosefoot out through the garden gates and down the banks of the Long Water, but best curb this impulse: the canal was aptly named and the walk soon loses its appeal. Choose instead the Broad Walk along the east front, impressive for its well stocked and labelled flower borders.

The Broad Walk was laid out in 1699 by George London and Henry Wise, chief gardeners to William of Orange, for the then considerable cost of £600. At the far northern end, by the Kingston Road, take a look at the putti on the gateposts, charming stone cherubs by John Nost. At the southern end begins the Great Terrace along the Thames.

William and Mary spent several months every year at Hampton Court, devoting much time and thoughtful attention to both palace and gardens. They employed Sir Christopher Wren as architect, who at first wanted to rebuild the entire palace, but had to accept a compromise, allowing much of the Tudor part to remain.

The Fountain Garden at this time deserved its name, boasting 13 fountains—a graceful compliment perhaps to the French gardens at Versailles. Queen Anne later reduced the number to five and George II cut it down to one. William also filled the garden with lacy beds of box 'scrollwork': Anne, who disliked the smell of box and the Dutch fashion for it, replaced these with grass and gravel. As Daniel Defoe pointed out in 1724, the scrollwork was 'not only very costly at first making but was also very expensive in keeping constantly clipped', and Anne was determined on economy.

Queen Mary introduced tropical plants from Virginia and the Canary Islands, and planted orange trees. She was very interested in propagation. Incidentally, she also introduced goldfish to England. She and William were devoted to one another: distraught after her early death at the age of 32, he dropped all work on Hampton Court for three years, but later adopted it as his chief administrative centre.

The south front was dominated in Henry VIII's time by a riverside mount, crowned with a gazebo, giving a fine view over the Thames, and led up to by a spiral 'cockleshell walk'. This garden, the Privy Garden, was then stuffed with sundials—16 of them—and with heraldic models of the King's Beasts—lions and leopards, dragons and unicorns, harts and antelopes. Henry also planted Queen

Anne's Bower nearby, an alley of arched hornbeams on a terrace, named for Anne Boleyn. The hornbeams were later replaced by pleached wych elms and the alley re-titled Queen Mary's Bower.

Queen Elizabeth liked Hampton Court, despite having been confined there as a princess by her half-sister Mary. She was responsible for the knot garden, below the windows of the south front. Intertwining low hedges of dwarf box form patterns filled with bright small flowers—once pinks, sweet william and candy-tuft, now begonia, lobelias and heliotropes.

William and Mary remodelled the Privy Garden as a parterre. Nowadays, shrubs and other plants are allowed more freedom: this is a pleasant secluded place to walk, probably appreciated by Hampton Court's Grace and Favour residents, in the mornings before the gates open.

Originally the Diana Fountain stood here, later removed to a large circular pond in Bushy Park's Chestnut Avenue. This splendid fountain, by Francesco Fanelli, is in fact being wrongly named—the bronze statue on top is of Arethusa.

A magnificent wrought iron screen, by the 17C craftsman Jean Tijou, has fortunately been restored to the southern (Thames) end of the Privy Garden, rescued in 1902 from the Victoria and Albert Museum.

At this end of the Privy Garden once lay the water gallery, built by Henry VIII and delighted in by a succession of queens. After Queen Mary's death, prompted perhaps by painful memories, William had the gallery demolished. Mouldings by Grinling Gibbons went to furnish a small outdoor banqueting house, which still stands. William also razed Henry's riverside mount to the ground: and wanting a better view of the Thames, he ordered the Privy Garden to be lowered by 10ft.

Just past the Privy Garden lie two exquisite sunk gardens, jewel-like in summer with their bright rectangular borders. Visitors are not allowed to enter, but may peer at the first garden through screens of lime and wisteria, at the second through pollarded hornbeam. They give a very special sense of calm and stillness, of beauty preserved through centuries. A lead statue of Venus stands at the far end of the larger garden, in a yew arbour; the smaller garden contains a single-jet fountain.

Passing Queen Anne's orangery on your right, follow the path along to the Great Vine. This knotty monster with its apparently fossilised lower trunk is still very much alive after more than 200 years, filling a large greenhouse and requiring the attentions of a full-time woman keeper. Its roots are said by legend to reach down into the Thames: certainly they extend freely outside the vinery, where they are kept tenderly manured. The vine measures 78in. around the base and at the time of going to press, its longest branch is 114ft. It bears at least 500 bunches of grapes each year, which are sold off to the public, and are delicious!

Near the Lion Gate on the north side stands Hampton Court's famous maze, a good place to lose the children. Planted in 1714, at the end of Queen Anne's reign, the hedges were originally horn-beam, now reinforced with privet and yew. Desperate people have been known to try and break through. It is quite easy to reach the middle of this maze, but just about impossible to find the exit:

fortunately at closing time the mazekeeper climbs up on a platform and shouts instructions. In the Middle Ages, mazes were built to symbolise the wanderings of the soul through earthly life towards God, and maze journeys were set as penances, not offered as pleasures. A point worth keeping in mind!

Also on the north side lies the Wilderness, which in William and Mary's time was planted as a symmetrical formal garden of clipped evergreens. Now much wilder, it is particularly lovely in very early spring, first with clumps of snowdrops and then with hundreds of crocuses, dwarf irises and daffodils. Later in the year, the yellow arches of the laburnum walk come into blossom.

Henry VIII's Tiltyard, on the west side, is now mainly occupied by an enormous rose garden, heavenly in summer and enhanced by a number of thoughtfully placed wooded benches. Here you may sit and rest, and drink the intoxicatingly scented air: or for more substantial refreshment, try the cafeteria.

Isabella Plantation (Richmond Park) and Waterhouse Woodland Gardens (Bushy Park)

ADDRESS AND TELEPHONE: Superintendent's Office, Department of the Environment, Richmond Park, Richmond Upon Thames, Surrey TW10 5HS. Tel. (081) 948 3209 and Bushy Park, Middlesex. Tel. (081) 979 1586

OWNERS: The Crown, managed on behalf of the Crown by the Department of Environment

DIRECTIONS: Isabella Plantation, Richmond Hill (B321) or Star and Garter Hill (B321) to Richmond Gate; Ham Gate Avenue (B352) to Ham Gate; Queens Road Kingston (B351) to Kingston Gate; from A3, A308 to Robin Hood Gate. Waterhouse Woodland Gardens: off A308 or B358. Gardens situated in centre of park. Public transport: Isabella Plantation by train, Norbiton BR 1½ miles, Kingston BR 2 miles, Richmond BR and LT 2½ miles. Buses to Richmond, Ham, Kingston. Waterhouse Woodland Gardens, Hampton Court BR or Teddington BR. Buses to Hampton Hill, Teddington, Hampton Court

OPENING TIMES: Isabella plantation open same hours as Richmond Park, usually 7am to dusk. Waterhouse Woodland Gardens 9am to dusk

ADMISSION: free

CAR PARKING: yes, within reasonable walking distance. Private hire coaches may have access to Isabella on weekdays only. Advance application must be made in writing to Superintendent's Office, D.O.E., Richmond Park, Richmond upon Thames, Surrey TW10 5HS

TOILETS: limited facilities in Isabella during summer season, near Broomfield Hill entrance. None in Waterhouse

REFRESHMENTS: two cafés in Richmond Park, none in Bushy Park

SHOP: no

DOGS: yes, on lead in Isabella; no dogs allowed in Waterhouse

WHEELCHAIR ACCESS: yes

PEAK MONTHS: April, May, June, September, October

NOTABLE FEATURES: azaleas, rhododendrons, water plants, unusual plants, trees

These two exceptional woodland gardens blaze like bright jewels in their wild and lovely parkland settings—the **Isabella Plantation** is in Richmond Park, once a royal hunting ground, and the Waterhouse Woodland Gardens in Bushy Park, near Hampton Court.

The Isabella is an immensely popular garden for weekend walks throughout the year, but especially in spring and summer. Visit out of season to avoid the crowds. The very early *Camellia* x *Williamsii* 'J.C. Williams', originally raised in Cornwall, may be opening its blush-pink flowers by Christmas Day; winter-flowering *Erica carnea* tinges the heather garden mauve in January. Camellias and early rhododendrons are well underway before Easter, and in spring the woodland floor is lit with sweet-scented narcissi, followed by bluebells.

From late April until mid June the plantation is one mass of bright colours: bring your camera, for the effects are truly astonishing, particularly around Thomson's Pond (to the north) and the Still Pond (to the south) and along the stream which runs right through the centre of the plantation, from Broomfield Hill down to Peg's Pond. The Kurume evergreen azaleas are particularly dazzling, their foliage almost completely concealed under wide blankets of blossom: reds, purples, salmons and yellows jumbled gaudily together in a magnificent patchwork effect. Nevertheless some visitors may turn with relief to the more restrained presentation of the deciduous species, with their sweetly scented flowers of yellow, salmon and orange interspersed with fresh green leaves.

Deciduous *Rhododendron luteum* grows freely here, unmistakable with its powerfully scented, yellow flowers: and so does *R. ponticum*, the very common purple rhododendron, introduced to Britain in 1763, which blossoms in June and July.

A collection of unnamed hybrids from Exbury Gardens in Hampshire may be found near the Ham Gate exit; and specimens of dwarf *R. yakushimanum* (pink in May, turning white) are displayed in a special circular bed near Thomson's Pond. Wally Miller, the Isabella's former head gardener, bred hybrid *R. yakushimanum* x 'Glakmour', which grows close by the central stream.

The streamside planting is very intensive, almost concealing the water in late spring—besides the many azaleas, you will see kingcups (*Caltha palustris* 'Flore pleno'), rushes, gracefully uncurling ferns, heathers, dark bergenias and day lilies. Children love running over the little bridges and along the narrow paths, but they should be guarded near the three ponds. The waterbirds are another great attraction—mallard ducks with their babies, moorhens, kingfishers and the occasional heron.

Thomson's Pond, to the north, is named after George Thomson, superintendent of Richmond Park from 1951 to 1971. The Isabella Plantation was largely his creation: he developed the waterside planting and diverted the original stream into two side tributaries.

The pond is set on a lawned slope, surrounded by a distinctive selection of small shrubs and trees. *Halesia carolina*, the snowdrop tree, with its upward-curving branches and drooping sprays of white bells, followed by winged fruits, stands near *Nyssa sylvatica*, a weeping black gum with vivid autumn colour.

The Isabella is well wooded with oaks, beeches, silver birch and conifers, along with swamp cypresses (*Taxodium distichum*), a 'paper handkerchief tree' (*Davidia involucrata*), a tulip tree (*Liriodendron tulipifera*) and a dawn redwood (*Metasequoia glyptostroboides*). A peculiar couple can be seen near the Still Pond—an ancient knotty low-branching beech either embracing or attempting to swallow a slim and upright oak. Nearby a vast tree stump has been converted into a bird table.

Bushy Park's **Waterhouse Woodland Gardens** have some advantages over the Isabella: they are not so well known and seem wilder and their planting less crowded. They are also much bigger (70 acres, as compared to the Isabella's 42 acres). There are two separate enclosures, within reasonably easy walking distance from any of the park entrances—Hampton Hill High Street to the west, Teddington, Kingston or the Chestnut Avenue leading down from Hampton Court.

The Longford River runs through the plantation: a tributary of the Colne, this was channelled off towards Hampton Court in 1638 by Charles I. Deeper, stronger and more vigorous than the Isabella's stream, it rushes and swirls through the woodland, pouring over waterfalls, extending long fingers across the lawns and spreading into large, still lakes. Rhododendrons grow high and wild in the first enclosure, nearly meeting across the paths. In the deep woodland, they tumble in great untidy banks along the streams and between trees: you can understand how excited 19C explorers must have been, when they first came across these astonishing plants growing wild in China, the Himalayas and Japan.

Purple *Rhododendron ponticum* grows everywhere, thriving in shade, as well as many more distinctive varieties, of all heights and colours. Golden *R. luteum* fills the air with scent and there are plenty of other azaleas, both deciduous and evergreen, as well as a grove of camellias, a welcome sight flowering profusely from late winter to early spring.

Besides many magnificent oaks, you will see pines and other conifers, beeches, planes, swamp cypresses and tulip trees. The raised pond is surrounded by chestnuts and overhanging willows and a fine specimen of *Metasequoia glyptostroboides*, the dawn redwood. Several handsome specimen trees, including spruces, stand on the lawn above the heath garden, along with some bold groupings of chamaecyparis.

The planting is lush in some places, but surprisingly sparse in others. Several of the long river outlets are now overgrown with grasses and overhung by trees. In a wild area near the dividing gate grow gigantic and very nasty looking *Gunnera manicata*, from South Brazil: don't touch them, as they may give you a rash.

Elsewhere are some stunning examples of streamside planting. In undulating beds along one stream grow rhododendrons, azaleas, heathers, candelabra primulas and hostas. Prunus 'Shirotae', the Mount Fuji cherry, spreads its canopy of blossom above. A pieris displays its tiny white bells and gently flaming leaves, orange-red on green.

The second enclosure, which runs up to Bushy Park's Chestnut Avenue, is rather different in character, simpler and more open, with paths winding around wide lakes. Several imposing *Taxodium distichum*, American swamp cypresses related to the English yew, grow along the waterside, distinguished by their 'knees' or pneumatophores—breathing roots which grow up rather than down. Some taxodiums have no knees, but seem to survive perfectly well without them.

A number of Big Cone Pines, *Pinus coulteri*, planted in 1963, have now grown to considerable size, spectacular with their twisting, snaking branches and grey-green needles. Facing them in the small pinetum is a row of *Pinus strobus*, the Weymouth Pine, another rapidly growing species, but more hardy than *P. coulteri*; and nearby a group of familiar *Pinus sylvestris*, the Scots pine.

In the Waterhouse, as in the Isabella, the planting is complemented by innumerable ducks, geese, moorhens and many other waterfowl, which line the water's edge, swim and roost peacefully on the islands.

Unfortunately the gales of 1987 and 1990 caused a considerable amount of damage to both gardens, but this is being used as an opportunity for new planting and for developing new features.

Kew Gardens

ADDRESS AND TELEPHONE: Royal Botanic Gardens, Kew, Richmond, Surrey TW9 3AB. Tel. (081) 940 1171

OWNERS: Royal Botanic Gardens, Kew.

DIRECTIONS: on A307 (Kew Road), main gate S of Kew Bridge. Public transport: Kew Bridge BR and Kew Gardens BR and Underground District Line. Buses 65 and 27 (also 7 on summer Sun). River steamers run from Westminster to Kew Pier, near Kew Bridge, during the summer months. (Westminster Pier. Tel. 071 930 2062, Kew Pier. Tel. 081 940 3891)

OPENING TIMES: daily 9.30am, except Christmas Day and New Year's Day. Closing times vary from 4pm to 6.30pm on weekdays and 4pm to 8pm on Sun and Public Holidays, depending on the time of sunset. Glasshouses open 10am, museums and Marianne North Gallery 9.30am, closing times vary. Kew Palace and Queen's Cottage open April to September; administered separately by the Department of the Environment

ADMISSION: £3 (no reduction for parties), OAPs and students £1.50, children 5–16 years £1. Advance payment is available for parties of 20 and over, applications to the public relations section. Season tickets (valid until the end of each calendar year) £5. Wheelchairs £1 (admits occupant and attendant). Parties of children and adults receiving full-time education (including teachers and lecturers) are admitted free except on Sat, Sun and BH. Apply for vouchers to the Information and Exhibitions Department. Guided tours available, tel. (081) 940 1171, ext. 4615

CAR PARKING: limited space for cars around Kew Green, close to main gate, or in the car park near the Brentford gate, reached via Ferry Lane off Kew Green

TOILETS: yes

REFRESHMENTS: restaurant and Kew Pavilion Bakery

SHOP: yes, in the orangery

DOGS: guide dogs only

WHEELCHAIR ACCESS: yes. Only electric wheelchairs of the kind permitted on the footways under the Chronically Sick and Disabled Persons Act, 1970, will be admitted to the Gardens. Wheelchairs can be hired at the main gate; book in advance from the Constabulary, tel. (081) 940 1171. Limited parking space for disabled badge holders near main gate. Toilets for the disabled: yes

PEAK MONTHS: year-round interest

NOTABLE FEATURES: many

Kew Gardens has a world-wide reputation as a botanic garden, a centre of study and plant conservation. While it is impossible here to do justice to the whole garden, whose 300 acres contain over 60,000 species, we have tried to describe the main areas and features of interest.

Augusta, widow of Frederick, Prince of Wales, and mother of George III, established the first botanic garden here in 1759, on 9 acres of land south of the Orangery, with the help of her head gardener William Aiton and botanical adviser Lord Bute. Sir William Chambers, co-founder of the Royal Academy, designed a number of ornate garden buildings, at her request, some of which survive, including the famous Pagoda.

George III inherited his grandfather's Richmond estate in 1760 and the adjoining Kew estate in 1772. The two properties were eventually joined. Sir Joseph Banks, who became unofficial horticultural director in George III's reign, introduced many new species from foreign parts and under his leadership the botanic garden became famous. Further land was added after 1841, when the garden was handed over to the state. Sir William Hooker, the first director, set up the Economic Botany Museum, the herbarium and the library; he was succeeded by his son, Sir Joseph Hooker. The Jodrell Laboratory was founded in 1876.

Since April 1984, the gardens have been administered by an independent board of trustees and are part-funded by direct grant from the Ministry of Agriculture, Fisheries and Food.

The Princess of Wales Conservatory. 'Conservatory' is an apt and accurate word to describe the most recent glasshouse in the gardens, planned from the early 1970s and opened by the Princess of Wales in 1987. Located about 220 yds north-east of the Palm House, it serves the dual purpose of conserving rare and threatened species, and informing visitors about plant life in widely differing temperature zones of the world. Its distinctive appearance—a cluster of shallow glass tents combined in one roof—and its considerable area—5370 sq.yds—catch the eye immediately. Its surroundings are attractively landscaped to tone in with nearby

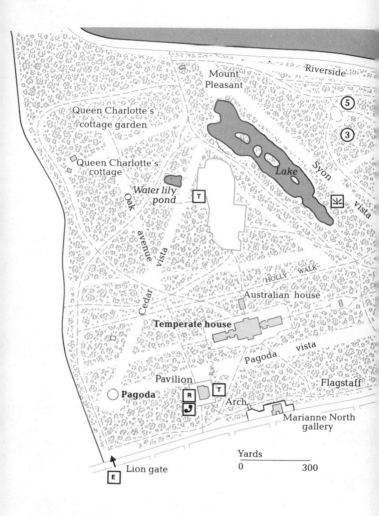

garden features, and include a miniature cascade emerging from the north side.

The conservatory has been designed to maximise winter light through its low-angle glass roof and to reduce bright summer sunshine from the east and west. It is constructed of glass, aluminium, steel and concrete. Being set mainly below ground level with a low volume in relation to its ground area it is economical on fuel and the temperature in each separate zone can be carefully controlled by computer.

The south entrance brings you immediately into the large dry tropical zone, typical of Africa and South America, where the fantastic shapes of cactus, yucca, agave and aloe spring from the

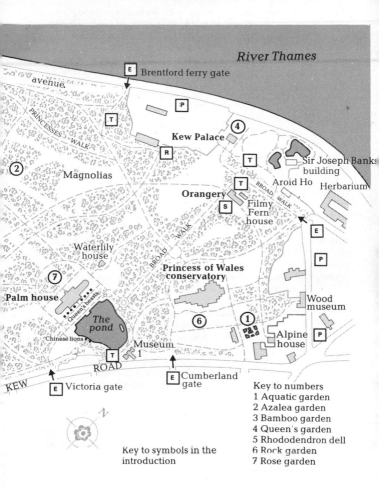

River Thames

E Brentford ferry gate

Kew Palace ④

② Magnolias

PRINCESSES WALK

avenue

Orangery

Waterlily house

Sir Joseph Banks building

Aroid Ho

Herbarium

BROAD WALK

Filmy Fern house

BROAD WALK

Princess of Wales conservatory

⑦ Palm house

Queen's beasts

The pond

Chinese lions

Museum 1

⑥

①

Alpine house

Wood museum

KEW

E Victoria gate

ROAD

E Cumberland gate

N

Key to symbols in the introduction

Key to numbers
1 Aquatic garden
2 Azalea garden
3 Bamboo garden
4 Queen's garden
5 Rhododendron dell
6 Rock garden
7 Rose garden

sand—an extraordinary display of growth from the arid ground. The toothed succulent leaves of agave, from South America, wither as its flower develops, leaving it to propagate by seed. Nearby tower the 'giant clubs' of *Cereus hildmannianus* and *C. jamacaru* from Brazil, set against a group of round 'golden barrel cacti' (*Echinocactus grusonii*) from Mexico, cosier in shape but with the same wicked spines. There is a collection of lithops (living stones) which mimic the pebbles they lie on; contrasting sharply with the vivid red flowers of *Euphorbia milii* and *Euphorbia splendens* nearby. This is one of the largest displays in the planthouse and leads on, either by a low or a high level door, into the contrasting 'wet tropics', whose average annual rainfall is 100in.

This rainforest area is laid out with beds interspersed by water-falls, pools and lush vegetation. Pillars have been provided to display the epiphytes—ferns, brilliant-flowered bromeliads and orchids—which flourish in the branches of the tall trees but take no nourishment from them. The central pool contains, among other water plants, the spectacular giant waterlily (*Victoria amazonica*) whose seeds are raised each year in December and January for planting out in April, and whose ribbed leaves achieve 6½ft or more across by July and can support a small child. Here can also be found the carnivorous pitcher plants (nepenthes) from south-east Asia and the amazing two-leaved *Welwitschia mirabilis* which may live for 2000 years in the Namib desert of South-West Africa. Nearby, enormous fish swim in a pond and can be seen through windows in a below water level walkway.

The small 'cloud forest' area which leads off at one corner, demonstrates how low temperatures and dense humidity at alti-tudes of 3280 yds produce stunted trees with knobbly, cork-like bark. These trees also are hung with ferns and bromeliads.

It seems ungenerous to draw attention to any shortcomings of the conservatory, which provides a unique resource not only for this country but for the rest of the world. However, we were conscious, even in this central wet tropical area, with its great variety and diversity of plant forms, of the extremely functional construction and low ceiling, which precludes any sense of grandeur. The contrast with the elegant interiors of the older glasshouses is marked. Within these limits, the utmost ingenuity has been used to provide variety and create some sense of height by the use of different levels, flights of steps, and viewing points. Other zonal areas nearby include temperate and tropical ferns, 70 per cent of which come from tropical areas and 30 per cent from temperate zones. There are ferns of all shapes and dimensions: tree-size, hanging, waist high or prostrate; with foliage ranging from sculp-tured to feathery. Ferns hang from high rock faces amid cascades of water, and edge the pools below. Perhaps the most curious is the 'stag's horn' fern (*Platycerium wandae*) in the tropical section which has both erect and hanging 'antlers' of green. Nearby are the temperate and tropical orchid collections—the latter representing 80 per cent of the world's 20,000 species—between them displaying a bright colour range of these perfect, somewhat unreal sprays of blossom.

Among the temperate orchids, the cypripediums are outstand-ingly beautiful, and the ophrys, which resemble bees in order to attract them, the most ingenious. A floral display of more common, though no less beautiful plants forms an entrance/exit porch to the north.

The **Alpine House** stands nearby, close to the rock and aquatic gardens. It is only a few years older than the conservatory, having been opened in 1981 and forms a compact pyramid, set appro-priately on a sandstone rock garden and surrounded by a moat. Three flights of graceful ventilating windows in the roof automat-ically regulate the temperature.

Inside are further banks of sandstone rock garden, brilliant in spring with alpines planted among the rocks and pots of flowers inserted to provide greater variety. Among the latter we saw the spectacular red, yellow and green hanging tubular clusters of *Lachenalia aloides*. There are many coloured cyclamen in the beds as well as yellow -flowering helichrysum and white allium.

In the south-east corner a waterfall and a pool encourage the growth of damp-loving, vivid flowering specimens, such as the heliotrope coloured *Pleione bulbocodioides* 'Versailles', a relative of the orchid, and varieties of erythronium, or dog's tooth violet, as well as diminutive primulas.

Alpine plants, as an information display in the corner of the glasshouse explains, flourish between the limit of tree vegetation and the zone of permanent snow cover. Alpine plants lie dormant beneath the snow in the winter, and even in summer must be content with poor soils, high winds and low temperatures, so they are generally small, with tufted or creeping habits. In the equatorial mountains of Africa and South America, however, cold nights and hot days produce gigantic forms.

A central refrigerated raised bed in the centre of the house is divided into two sections, one providing arctic conditions. Here a miniature *Primula stricta* had ventured into bloom, with *Artemisia borealis* and *Saxifragia oppositifolia*. By comparison, the woolly-leaved espeletias in the montane section seem enormous and the bright orange *Calceolaria darwinii* spectacular. This modest sized greenhouse is well worth a visit, even for the non-specialist.

Further displays of ferns may be found in the small Filmy Fern House behind the orangery. The Aroid House, closed for restoration until 1993, was built by John Nash in 1825 and transported from Buckingham Palace to Kew in 1836 at the request of William IV.

Many exotic waterlilies and other tropical plants including colourful climbers, are to be found in the Waterlily House, sited beside the Palm House. This also has its domestic side, showing the growth of rice and the loofah (*Luffa cylindrica*).

The Temperate House containing a large collection of tender woody plants from sub-tropical and warm temperate zones, lies within easy walking distance of the Victoria and Lion Gates (Kew Road), not far from the pavilion restaurant. Designed by Decimus Burton and constructed between 1860 and 1898, it covers an area of 5836 sq yds, about twice that of the Palm House. It incorporates two octagons, on either side of the main centre block and giving access to the north and south wings. The Australian House, built in 1952, lies behind the main block.

By the 1970s, the Temperate House was in a bad state of repair and the heating system was giving a lot of problems. After a full structural survey, it was obvious that large-scale renewal and some re-designing would be necessary. The original roof form and glazing pattern were restored at this time, together with Burton's decorative cornice. Narrower glazing bars were chosen, as the plants had suffered considerably from low light transmission, and semi-automatic ventilators installed. The heating system was considerably improved and a new layout introduced, with garden features including sculptures placed on diagonal vistas. Work on the building was completed in the autumn of 1980, and replanting took another year.

The collection is now arranged in geographical order. In the south wing, which catches the sun, you can see plants from Africa and the Mediterranean. These include strelitzias or crane flowers, with striking inflorescences—the boat-shaped spathes crested with upright flowers resemble the heads of African cranes. Huge *Strelitzia nicolai* is especially striking, with its horizontal leaf veins and sheaths of flowers. You can also see the bird of paradise flower, *Strelitzia reginae*, named for Queen Charlotte of the house of Mecklenburg Strelitz. On hot days, some species roll up their leaves to prevent moisture loss, notably *Strelitzia parviflora* 'Juncea'.

Strange forms of asparagus grow here too—*Asparagus virgatus* from tropical and South Africa, with delicate foliage and tiny green flowers, and tall *Asparagus macowanii* from South Africa and Natal, with its little bunches of narrow needle-like leaves.

The south octagon is kept cool, to house winter-flowering Cape (South African) ericas or heaths—these were very popular in England from the late 18C to the early 19C. Some of the 600 species here can be seen, many collected by Francis Masson, a gardener from Kew in the 18C. Cape proteas nearby display their huge cups of tiny flowers surrounded by bright-coloured bracts.

The main block is a magnificent tangled jungle of evergreen trees and shrubs, shot through by towering palms. For a bird's eye view from the top of the glasshouse, climb one of the elegant spiral staircases to the top gallery. In the centre and now reaching the roof is the Chilean wine palm (*Jubaea chilensis*); raised in 1846 from seed collected in Chile, this is now probably the largest greenhouse plant in existence. The palm *Washingtonia robusta* displays its viciously thorned stems and graceful fans of leaves. On the north side is a female date palm; the pinnate leaves of this tree are used in the Canary islands to make baskets and matting. Among the araucarias (relatives of the monkey puzzle) are *Araucaria cunninghamii*, the hoop pine, and *Araucaria bidwillii*, the Bunya Bunya pine. Here too is *Dicksonia antarctica*, the Australian tree fern, from the ravines of south and eastern Australia. There is a collection of fuchsias, from Central and South America, including *Fuchsia splendens* from Mexico and *Fuchsia boliviana* from South America—strikingly unlike modern garden hybrids. One area is devoted to a display of endangered plants from isolated oceanic islands—reflecting the important role Kew plays in plant conservation. Another area features economic plants, such as cumin, guava, tree tomato and olive, and a fragrant citrus walk.

In the north octagon are plants from New Zealand and Tasmania; the very odd *Pandanus forsteri*, apparently standing on its roots; towering *Metrosideros excelsior*, a member of the myrtle family; and New Zealand fuchsias.

The north wing, cool and moist, with a well-stocked carp pool, features Himalayan plants and montane rhododendrons from the mountains of tropical Malaysia, Indonesia and New Guinea, as well as plants from all over south-east Asia, China and Japan.

The Australian House lies to the rear of the Temperate House, backed by the holly walk. Built in 1952, it was the first aluminium house at Kew. Featured here is a collection of banksias (Australian honeysuckles)—woody plants ranging from tall trees to shrubs and small bushes. These are very drought tolerant and even take advantage of bush fires to germinate: the intense heat splits open their cone-like fruits, releasing the winged seeds. Here too are eucalyptus—a selection from the 600 species—callistemons and Australian acacias. The Moreton Bay chestnut or black bean (*Castanospermum australe*) grows here and this tree has medicinal powers which may prove important in the fight against AIDS—an alkaloid present in its leaves and seeds has been proved to reduce the infectivity of the HIV virus.

The magnificent **Palm House**, a vision of white-painted metal and sparkling glass, is now open after an £8 million restoration. It lies about 160 yds from the Victoria Gate, overlooking the pond and backed by the rose garden.

For the purposes of restoration, the original collection of tropical plants—palms, cycads and economic plants such as bananas and rubber plants—was reduced to essentials before being moved to the Aroid House and a specially built temporary palm house. A large pit was dug in the temporary house, to accommodate the taller palms. Fortunately very few plants died in the moving process, but Kew's only specimen of the ivory nut palm was lost.

Originally built in 1848 from wrought iron and glass, the Palm House has been renewed using much of the original ironwork, some recast iron and some stainless steel, and repainted and entirely reglazed. The traditional cast-iron heating pipes have been with retained, but with some modifications and additions, including soil-warming cables. The palms, cycads and tropical woody plants will be replanted into beds, to give them more space—previously they were grown in large terracotta and teak pots. A new marine area in the basement will display a collection of marine plants and will recreate a tropical coral reef.

In front of the Palm House are the Queen's beasts—much photographed and well loved, these are replicas of 16C heraldic emblems carved in 1953 for Elizabeth II's coronation. A statue of Hercules, in the centre of the palm house pond, by F.J. Bosio, was presented to Kew by the Queen in 1962. The pond is surrounded by swamp cypresses and weeping willows; on the south side is a pair of Guardian Chinese Lions.

Now more than 200 years old, the **Pagoda** was designed by Sir William Chambers and built in just 6 months, from 1761 to 1762. The mid 18C fashion for chinoiserie resulted in many fantastic and strange constructions, but the pagoda was an unusually accurate imitation of a Chinese Building. Ten storeys high, it is thought to have been decorated with dragons of iron and coloured glass, with bells in their mouths.

Although both bricks and timber are still in good condition, the Pagoda is closed to the public. It makes an excellent focal point to the south-east, not far from Lion Gate.

Kew is renowned for its wonderful **trees**, which include collections of birch (south of the Tea Bar); poplar and willow (between Brentford Ferry Gate and Princess Walk; oak (from Mount Pleasant north-east along River Side Avenue; alder, ash and conifers.

In the great storm of October 1987, Kew lost 800 trees. Several important groups were devastated, such as ash, hickory and a collection of *Celtis* species. On the whole, as Mark Flanagan has noted ('The damage caused by the hurricane force winds to the trees at the Royal Botanic Gardens, Kew', *Arboricultural Journal* 12: (3) 181–188), losses were greatest among species with big dome-shaped crowns, such as oaks, ash, limes and ailanthus. Individual trees are still mourned, such as the 200-year-old Turkey oak near the palm house pond, the black walnut adjacent to the orangery, and *Zelkova carpinifolia* in front of the herbarium, one of the very first introduced into cultivation; along with many botanical rarities. However, almost all of these have now been replaced, often with trees propagated from those which were destroyed in the 1987 gale.

The Rhododendron Dell and Lake. Many visitors to Kew come less for detailed botanical study than to enjoy wandering and picnicking among the trees and lawns. Favourite areas to visit in spring include the group of magnolias half-way between Kew Palace (the elegant Dutch House) and the lake, the nearby azaleas and the long rhododendron dell, where you can see a wide selection of all sizes and colours in something like their natural hillside habitat. We noticed in early April the bright red rhododendron 'J.G. Millais' and the miniature pink *R. primuliflorum cephalanthoides*.

The honking of geese as you near the end of the dell indicates the lake to your left, and branching off past the bamboo garden you can see, from the lake's north-east tip, the palm house, standing newly white and shining at the end of an avenue of trees. The lake itself is man-made, excavated in 1856–61 and enlarged in 1871 to 4½ acres. The gravel was used to landscape the gardens, and this landscaping adds greatly to the charm of a very flat terrain.

Many varieties of alder, spruce, birch and willow fringe the shores of the lake as well as the dawn redwood (*Metasequoia glyptostroboides*) and the Californian big tree (*Sequoiadendron giganteum*). Swamp cypresses (*Taxodium distichum*) provide shelter on the islands for the many wildfowl. There are notices asking visitors not to feed the birds, which are regularly fed (and bread thrown into the water is thought to have been responsible for an outbreak of botulism which greatly depleted the bird population). You can see geese, swans, mallards, coot and many others on the water, or waddling and dabbling at its edges. At the end of the lake there are two more splendid views—one along to the pagoda and the other over the tow path and the damp verges on the far side of the Thames to Syon House, crowned with a stone lion.

The Queen's Garden—tucked neatly between the river and Kew Palace, on the north-west side of the gardens—is laid out and planted in formal 17C style. Box-edged beds containing lavender, rosemary, tree southernwood (*Artemisia arborescens*) and heuchera 'Palace Purple' surround a Venetian well-head with a modern decorative top of wrought iron. To one side of this central parterre section, an avenue of pleached hornbeams leads down to the mount, crowned with a gilded rotunda and commanding a fine view of the River Thames. On the other side is a sunken garden, planted with sweet-smelling and medicinal herbs—accompanied by fascinating quotations from the old herbals.

Queen Charlotte's Cottage Grounds. Best seen in May when covered in bluebells, these woodland gardens were given to the nation in 1898 by Queen Victoria, to mark her Diamond Jubilee a year earlier. They cover about 40 acres to the south-west. An extra charge is made for looking round the 'cottage' which is still a royal palace and not owned by Kew. Elaborately furnished but never intended to be lived in, it was used as a picnic place by Queen Charlotte, wife of George III, and their family.

In accordance with Queen Victoria's own expressed wishes, the grounds are kept in a 'beautiful and natural'—or at least semi-natural—condition. Many kinds of birds and other wildlife can be seen here.

The Marianne North Gallery. This modest building houses 848 brilliantly coloured paintings, mainly of plants and flowers from all over the world, and shown in their natural habitats—the life's work of Marianne North, intrepid Victorian traveller and artist. It lies on the west side of the gardens, not far from Chambers' ruined arch. Marianne North herself gave both the paintings and the building (designed by her friend James Fergusson) to Kew.

A little way further north is the Flagstaff, 225ft high and made from a single trunk of Douglas fir (*Pseudotsuga menziesii*). The third to be erected here since 1861, it was presented by the Government and Forestry Industry of British Columbia.

Sir Joseph Banks Building. Opened in March, 1990, this single storey building, of striking design, houses Kew's economic botany reference collections and library, besides exhibitions and living plant displays. The building is partially covered with terraced roof gardens, with a curved glass roof covering the concourse. Much of it is recessed below ground level; the surrounding soil provides insulation, one of a number of energy conserving design features. The 7½-acre site includes two large lakes, linked by a cascade.

The Museum of Garden History
(The Tradescant Garden)

ADDRESS AND TELEPHONE: Museum of Garden History, St Mary-at-Lambeth, next to Lambeth Palace, Lambeth Palace Road, London SE1 7JU. Tel. (071) 261 1891. All enquiries other than membership to: The Chairman, Mrs John Nicholson, 74 Coleherne Court, Old Brompton Road, London SW5 0EF. Tel. (071) 373 4030, between 6am and 9am if possible, or after 6pm

OWNERS: The Tradescant Trust

DIRECTIONS: off Lambeth Palace Road. Public transport: bus (alight Lambeth Palace) 3, 44, 76, 77, 159, 170, 510, 507. Underground: Lambeth North ½ mile, Vauxhall ⅝ mile, Westminster ⅝ mile. BR: Waterloo/Victoria, use bus 507, Vauxhall ⅝ mile

OPENING TIMES: Mon to Fri 11–3, Sun 10.30–5. Closed Sat.
Groups and other times by appointment. The Museum closes
from the second Sun in December to the first Sun in March

ADMISSION: free but donation requested

CAR PARKING: no

REFRESHMENTS: yes

SHOP: yes, gift shop and plant sales

DOGS: no

WHEELCHAIR ACCESS: yes, possible. Toilets for the disabled: no

PEAK MONTHS: May, June, July

NOTABLE FEATURES: exhibitions, displays of historic garden tools,
objects relating to garden history. In the garden, tombs of the
Tradescants and of Admiral Bligh of the 'Bounty'

Opened in 1983, the tiny Tradescant Garden forms part of the
museum, housed in the former church of St-Mary-at-Lambeth, next
door to Lambeth Palace. The Tradescant Trust was formed in 1977,
to save the church from demolition and restore it for use as the
Museum of Garden History, a centre for garden-related lectures
and exhibitions.

The two John Tradescants, father and son, were 17C gardeners
and plant hunters, responsible for the introduction to England of a
great number of plants and trees. They travelled throughout Europe
and North America and on early voyages to North Africa and
Russia. John Tradescant the elder (1577–1637) brought the black
mulberry back from France, as well as vines and roses. From North
America he introduced the spiderwort (*Tradescantia virginiana*),
the Virginia creeper (*Parthenocissus quinquefolia*) and the stag's
horn sumach (*Rhus typhina*), among many others. He was gardener
in turn to Robert Cecil, 1st Earl of Salisbury, Lord Wotton, George
Villiers, Duke of Buckingham and Charles I.

John Tradescant the younger (1608–62) visited Virginia three
times and introduced from North America such plants as the tulip
tree (*Liriodendron tulipifera*), *Aquilegia canadensis, Yucca fila-
mentosa*, the swamp cypress (*Taxodium distichum*) and the
American cowslip (*Dodecatheon meadia*).

The Tradescants collected curiosities of many kinds—anything
that was 'strange and rare'—and displayed them in their house at
Lambeth, nicknamed the Ark. The *Musaeum Tradescantianum*, the
first ever museum catalogue, was published in 1656, and the
Tradescant Trust owns John Evelyn's copy of this first edition.
Following the death of the younger John Tradescant in 1662, the
museum collection passed into the hands of Elias Ashmole and
became the basis for the Ashmolean Museum at Oxford. John
Tradescant the elder also developed his own garden at Lambeth,
where he propagated the seeds, plants and trees brought back from
his travels.

The Tradescant tomb can be seen in the north-west corner of the
graveyard at St-Mary-at-Lambeth: both Tradescants are interred
here, along with Jane and Hester Tradescant, and the youngest
John Tradescant, who died in 1652, aged 19. Nearby is the tomb
of another local resident, Captain Bligh of the *Bounty*.

The churchyard is now planted as a 17C garden, with plants the Tradescants grew, or would have been familiar with. In the central knot garden are old roses such as the pure pink centifolia rose *R.* 'De Meaux', red and white *R. gallica* 'Versicolor' and fragrant pink *Rosa gallica* 'Officinalis', along with peonies, geraniums, teucrium, daphnes, irises, lavender, violas, pulmonaria and many others. In and around the tombs are small trees such as *Sorbus domestica*, *Robinia pseudoacacia* and *Rhus typhina*; also a variety of plants, such as *Hyssopus officinalis*, London pride (*Saxifraga umbrosa*), *Rosa damascena* 'Quatre Saisons', *Lychnis coronaria*, dianthus 'Sops in Wine', *Coronilla valentina, Artemisia absinthium* (wormwood), and *Rosa virginiana*.

The garden is maintained entirely by voluntary helpers, as are the garden history displays inside the museum.

Regent's Park

ADDRESS AND TELEPHONE: The Store Yard, Inner Circle, Regent's Park, London NW1 4NR. Tel. (071) 486 7905

OWNERS: Part of the Crown Estate, managed by the Department of Environment

DIRECTIONS: within the Outer Circle off Marylebone Road, Park Road, Prince Albert Road, Albany Street. Public transport: nearest underground stations are Baker Street, Regent's Park, Great Portland Street

OPENING TIMES: daily throughout year

ADMISSION: free

CAR PARKING: yes, from 11am

TOILETS: yes

REFRESHMENTS: café

SHOP: no

DOGS: yes but not in garden areas, except guide-dogs

WHEELCHAIR ACCESS: yes. Toilets for the disabled: yes

PEAK MONTHS: spring/summer/autumn

NOTABLE FEATURES: rose garden

Regent's Park was once a royal hunting ground, enclosed by Henry VIII and then known as Marylebone or Marybone Park. The land was let to noblemen by Charles II—large areas having already been given away by Charles I to his supporters—and by the 19C it was mainly private farmland.

John Nash, architect to the Prince Regent, was commissioned by the Prince in 1811 to lay out and design Regent's Park. Nash bordered the 671 acres of parkland with terraces of tall houses, built in neo-classical or Palladian style. He also planned to build 56 villas within the park, but these were reduced to eight, due to financial problems and disagreements; and other building projects were abandoned or later demolished. The terraces were badly damaged in the 1939–45 war, but, thanks to the efforts of the Crown Estate Commissioners, the Nash façades were preserved.

Nash designed the park itself in a roughly circular shape, with two circular roads, one inside the other. The much smaller inner circle contains the main garden area, Queen Mary's garden, which incorporates the rose garden and the famous open air theatre.

The Broad Walk, for pedestrians, runs from the Zoological Gardens in the north, straight through the park to the south side. The Regent's College lies south-west of the inner circle, by the boating lake. There is another small lake in the Queen Mary's garden.

Queen Mary's garden was formerly the site of the Royal Botanic Society, which leased this area from 1840 to 1932. The rose garden was originally planted with rose varieties donated by the British Rose Growers' Association, but the collection is constantly updated and new varieties added. There are now 30–40,000 roses. The rose garden tea room is a striking apparition, with its multitude of pointed domes and green and white striped deckchairs.

Old-fashioned and modern shrub roses can be seen by the small lake, set back from the waterside, overhung by cherry trees and interplanted with orange and white lilies. North of the lake, climbing roses are grown on wooden structures and through trees, and climbers and ramblers swing on ropes between supports. These surround a circular rose garden, featuring a mixture of hybrid teas and floribundas, with shrub roses grown in beds behind.

The small lake is overhung by willows, swamp cypress and tall redwoods and frequented by a variety of waterfowl. The island can be reached by a high-arched wooden bridge and is covered with rockery plants and alpines, together with a collection of tree heaths and various conifers.

Overlooking the lake is a hill planted with evergreen and acid-loving shrubs, such as mahonias and azaleas. A path leads steeply up the hill to a paved oval platform beneath shady trees and above the cascading waterfall. There is a herbaceous bank beyond the public lavatories and bright planting near the bronze mermaid fountain (given by the Constance Fund in 1950), including a great variety of standard, bush and bedding fuchsias. This fountain is approached by an avenue of ornamental cherries.

A little way north of the rose garden is St John's Lodge, one of Nash's eight original villas. Here, a circle of pleached limes surrounds beds of roses. There is also a long border of scented flowering herbaceous plants and shrubs.

Regent's Park has many other attractions, including the boating lake and the children's boating pond, the open air theatre and the bandstand. The zoological gardens lie to the north, and behind this is Primrose Hill.

Syon Park

ADDRESS AND TELEPHONE: Syon Park, Brentford, Middlesex. Tel. (081) 560 0881

OWNERS: The Duke of Northumberland

DIRECTIONS: from central London, A4 to Gillette Corner, turn left into A310, beyond first traffic lights signposted left. Public transport: BR Waterloo to Kew Bridge, then bus 237 or 267 to Brent Lea stop

OPENING TIMES: 10–6, 7 days a week all year round. House also open

ADMISSION: £1.50, OAPs and children £1, school parties 50p per head. Coach parties welcome

CAR PARKING: yes

TOILETS: yes

REFRESHMENTS: café

SHOP: yes, garden centre, National Trust, whole foods, arts centre

DOGS: no, except in outer park

WHEELCHAIR ACCESS: yes. Toilets for the disabled: yes

PEAK MONTHS: April to October

NOTABLE FEATURES: lakes by Capability Brown, mature specimen trees, Victorian conservatory with tender plants. Butterfly house (separate entrance fee)

Syon Park has a long and varied history, much of which is of horticultural interest. In 1539 Syon monastery, home of the English Bridgettines, was dissolved by Henry VIII, and after his death it was granted to the Lord Protector, the Duke of Somerset. Somerset built himself a fine Tudor mansion, much of which is incorporated into the present Syon House, and under his auspices the first botanical garden in England was created by Dr William Turner, who wrote his treatise on 'Names of Herbes' at Syon in 1548. Some of the first mulberry trees to be imported into England were planted at Syon during this period.

Towards the end of the 16C the estate was leased from Queen Elizabeth I by Henry Percy, the 9th Earl of Northumberland, who improved the estate and acquired extra land. The 10th Earl introduced many rare plants into the garden, earning Syon a widespread horticultural reputation. However, it was left to Sir Hugh Smithson, created first Duke of Northumberland in 1766, to carry out the landscaping of the estate which is still its main feature. Between 1767 and 1773 Northumberland employed Lancelot ('Capability') Brown to redesign the grounds, creating a 'natural' landscape of two lakes, one in the outer park and one near the house. Brown also planted the surrounding slopes with fine specimen trees, both native and foreign, many of which still remain. He created a new botanic garden and laid out a large lawn with a Doric column bearing a statue of Flora, goddess of flowers.

Between 1820 and 1827, the 3rd Duke commissioned Charles Fowler to design the Great Conservatory, which has recently been completely renovated, and the Riding School, now used as the garden centre. More rare trees were added by Richard Forrest, and by the middle of the 19C the main features of Syon Park as it remains today had been established.

The visitor coming by car or coach approaches from the south-west, passing one of Capability Brown's lakes on the left and Syon

House, with its distinctive stone lion, on the right. There is also a pedestrian entrance from Brent Lea, to the north.

The present entrance to the grounds brings you in by the Great Conservatory, where there are a group of demonstration gardens for elderly or disabled people. These are mostly raised beds planted with roses, alpines, conifers or bedding plants, one even incorporating a small pool. The entry to the aquarium is nearby.

The conservatory was re-opened after a complete renovation in 1988. With its graceful dome, 65ft high at the centre, and delicate cast iron tracery, the conservatory forms a splendid focal point for the gardens near the house and lake. The area under the dome and the two curving side wings together measure 382ft. In the central and surrounding beds there are many bright blue-flowered hydrangeas, as well as red showy callistemons—bottle-brush shrubs—and the fern-like *Acacia dealbata.* Windmill palms (*Trachycarpus fortunei*) grow well in the humid atmosphere.

The west wing of the conservatory, which contains many varieties of hanging fuchsia, as well as climbing plants, leads to a damp fernery and rock garden; the east wing, filled with bright geraniums, terminates in a dry hot area for cacti and succulents.

The formal garden on the south side below a terrace is being replanted as a memorial garden to the late 10th Duke of Northumberland. At the farthest point of the lawns there is a pool with a statue of Mercury and a rock bank, mainly planted with conifers. A large *Magnolia grandiflora* was producing its creamy heads of flower when we were there.

Leaving the conservatory you cross an area of grass and shrubbery where some of Capability Brown's original plantings can still be seen: notably a golden rain tree (*Koelreuteria paniculata*) and a swamp cypress (*Taxodium distichum*), planted in 1760. We also passed banks of rhododendron, which are preceded in the spring by drifts of daffodils. Among the hydrangeas, we noticed a *Parrotia persica* or Persian ironwood, with its graceful horizontal habit and bright autumn colour. We also passed a belt of trees and shrubs with attractive foliage contrast: a variegated and a red acer, a purple corylus, gold conifers and a gold *Robinia pseudoacacia* 'Frisia'.

The peaceful, curving lake, a quarter of a mile long was made from the Duke of Northumberland's river. A large plantation of *Gunnera manicata* with knobbly, giant's club heads of flower and enormous hairy leaves stands by the water's edge. Not far on there are more swamp cypresses, this time with a full complement of 'pneumatophores' (air breathing roots) sticking up through the soil and emerging like sea serpents from the water. There are silver weeping willows and a recumbent catalpa, or Indian bean tree, whose branches break the surface of the lake. Clumps of bamboo and groups of yellow and purple iris clothe the water's edge, near shade-loving hostas. In late summer, day lilies produce a succession of bright red or yellow trumpets.

On the north side of the lake we saw a variegated tulip tree (*Liriodendron tulipifera* 'Aureomarginatum') and nearby a golden catalpa (*Catalpa bignonioides* 'Aurea'), making a striking contrast with the blue-green of *Cedrus atlantica glauca*. We noticed *Cedrela sinensis*, with handsome large leaves, a sweet gum *Liquidambar styraciflua* and many fine old sweet chestnuts and vast yew trees, possibly part of the original plantings. Throughout the lakeside, beech, copper beech, pines and maples are interspersed with more unusual specimens.

Following the lakeside, you come to Flora's lawn, which when we visited it was not at its best. It is likely that this garden will be re-landscaped in future years.

Beyond the lawn a graceful small bridge crosses the lake, its balustrade entwined by *Actinidia chinensis*, the Chinese gooseberry. At the head of the lake, the river flows beneath a pleasing grouping of shrubs, and although this is the far point of the park, a protective screen of trees behind prevents any reminder of the city from intruding. The nearby lawns are criss-crossed by sloping paths interspersed with shrubs and heather beds have been established near the farthest boundary. If you make your return journey on the south side of the lake you will catch an occasional glimpse of the River Thames, with Kew Gardens on the far side. There are more trees of interest here before you regain the head of the lake near the conservatory.

The rose garden, entered through a turnstile in the wall to the west of the house, consists mainly of beds of hybrid tea or floribunda roses centred by standard bushes. Older shrub and species roses are much less well represented and when we were there few climbers were left on the pergola. In the spring, crocuses, daffodils and other bulbs flower under oaks and cedars planted by Capability Brown when he modified the terraces laid out by the Protector Duke of Somerset.

Syon estate is a thriving enterprise, with garden centre, restaurants, butterfly house and a series of events and exhibitions, but its chief distinction remains its 18C landscape, 19C conservatory and fine house. It is a unique resource in a busy area of west London.

GREATER MANCHESTER

Fletcher Moss Gardens

ADDRESS AND TELEPHONE: Fletcher Moss Gardens, Wilmslow, Didsbury, Manchester. Tel. (061) 434 1877

OWNERS: City of Manchester

DIRECTIONS: 4½ miles S of city centre on Wilmslow Road (A5145). Public transport: East Didsbury BR ½ mile. Buses from city centre

OPENING TIMES: all year round, daily, dawn to dusk. House not open

ADMISSION: free. Coach parties welcome

CAR PARK: small one off Millgate Lane (off Wilmslow Road)

TOILETS: yes

REFRESHMENTS: café

SHOP: no

DOGS: no

WHEELCHAIR ACCESS: no. Toilets for the disabled: yes

PEAK SEASON: May to July

NOTABLE FEATURES: rock garden; heather garden; young arboretum and wild flower meadow

Fletcher Moss parks and gardens are situated on the Wilmslow Road in the suburb of Didsbury, south of the city, and were given to the City by the late Alderman Fletcher Moss between 1914 and 1919. Playing fields take up most of the 21 acres but there is also a large rock garden, colourful in early summer. The rock garden is built on a steep bank, facing south, and is so well sheltered that peaches have been known to grow there.

Just inside the entrance, overlooking the garden, stands an alpine house. This was donated by Major Ralph Raffles and contains alpines and dwarf conifers in pots plunged into sand benches.

The rock garden is also well stocked with alpines and contains the largest hardy dwarf plant collection in the city's parks, besides conifers planted between massive boulders.

Paths and steps descending the bank bring you close to groups of ericas, saxifragas, violas, dianthus, phlox and others. A stream with waterfalls runs through the garden, lined with primulas, ferns and hostas; more marginal and aquatic plants surround a pool below. Trees include a weeping ash (*Fagus sylvatica* 'Pendula') and a tulip tree (*Liriodendron tulipifera*). The plants are well-arranged for colour, height and form.

A small arboretum is being established beyond the grass tennis courts, with sorbus, malus, prunus and others gradually merging into the more mature planting around the recreation lawns. Another recent venture has been the planting of a wild flower meadow east of the bowling green.

Heaton Park

ADDRESS AND TELEPHONE: Heaton Park, Manchester M25 5SW. Tel. (061) 798 0107

OWNERS: City of Manchester

DIRECTIONS: 3½ miles N of city centre, close to M66. Entrances off Middleton Road, Sheepfoot Lane and Bury Old Road. Public transport: Heaton Park BR on W side of park. Buses from city

OPENING TIMES: all year round, daily, dawn to dusk. House open and usually has exhibitions. Farm centre: Tues to Fri 10.30–3.30, weekends 1–4. Tram museum: most weekends, May to October

ADMISSION: free

CAR PARKING: several around park. Coach parties welcome

TOILETS: yes

REFRESHMENTS café

SHOP: no

DOGS: yes

WHEELCHAIR ACCESS: yes. Toilets for the disabled. yes

PEAK SEASON: peaks throughout the year

NOTABLE FEATURES: 600 acres of park landscaped by William
Emes, horticultural centre with demonstration gardens, azalea
dell, rose garden, bedding schemes

Heaton Park at the foot of the Pennines, to the north of Manchester,
covers 600 acres. The park and Hall were bought by the city in
1902 and now offer many attractions—sporting, fishing and recreational facilities, boating, children's play areas, farm centre with
hatchery, pets corner, tea rooms and a tram museum, as well as
several well planted garden areas.

Heaton Hall, extensively rebuilt from 1772 onwards for the 1st
Earl of Wilton, is surrounded by parkland landscaped by William
Emes, a pupil of Capability Brown, with later improvements made
by John Webb, a follower of Humphry Repton.

Around the Hall are lawns with colourful bedding—red geraniums, blue and white lobelia, scarlet salvias and orange marigolds—
centring on a Victorian fountain which once stood in Albert Square.
This fountain looks odd against the Hall, and may in the near future
be moved. Rose beds and more vibrant spring and summer bedding
schemes can be seen outside the Hall's recently restored orangery.
To the east, standing on the highest ground in the park, is a domed
temple dating from the William Emes landscaping period, about
1770. A valley with a lake and massive plantings of the invasive
purple *Rhododendron ponticum* lie between this folly and the
municipal golf course further east.

There are several garden areas on the opposite, western, side of
the Hall. The first is a terraced rose garden with colourful beds of
mainly hybrid tea roses set into lawns in a formal design. Walls
surround the garden on three sides and a line of conifers marks the
site of old vineries and glasshouses.

Close by is a grotto and a bed of azaleas. The dell, which lies at
the other end of a narrow dark tunnel, is filled with azaleas—May
is the best time to visit. Beech and oak trees surround and shelter
the area.

An ongoing project at Heaton Park is the development of a
horticultural centre within the walls of the old kitchen garden.
Already shrub borders have been established, and all the plants
are clearly labelled.

Several small individual gardens have been laid out within the
walled garden, to give visitors new design ideas. One of the best
is the low maintenance garden, planned around a patio with
railway sleepers highlighting a pool. Other gardens include an
alpine garden, an Old English cottage garden, and a wild flower
garden, which is at its best in June. Later it is hoped to establish a
garden for children and winter and town gardens. The large
glasshouses in the centre of the walled garden are used to grow
plants and flowers for civic functions.

Wythenshawe Park

ADDRESS AND TELEPHONE: Wythenshawe Park, Northenden, Greater Manchester. Tel. (061) 945 1768

OWNERS: City of Manchester

DIRECTIONS: off Wythenshawe Road B5167, 5 miles S of city. Public transport: Gatley BR 1 mile. Buses from city centre

OPENING TIMES: all year round, daily, dawn to dusk. House also open

ADMISSION: free. Coach parties welcome and guided tours available

CAR PARK: yes

TOILETS: yes

SHOP: no

DOGS: no

WHEELCHAIR ACCESS: yes. Toilets for the disabled: yes

PEAK SEASON: peaks throughout the year

NOTABLE FEATURES: 232-acre park with interesting trees and shrubs; walled garden; rose garden; rock garden; Charles Darrah cactus collection; glasshouses and tropical house

Given to the City of Manchester in 1926 by Lord and Lady Simon of Wythenshawe, this park has been described as one of the most beautiful in the country.

Among trees and shrubs on the estate are good specimens of the swamp cypress (*Taxodium distichum*), the maidenhair tree (*Ginkgo biloba*) and dawn redwood (*Metasequoia glyptostroboides*). Rhododendrons grow well here and there is a large collection. Other features include an excellent rock garden, rose garden and glasshouses with tropical display and cactus collection.

MERSEYSIDE

Croxteth Country Park

ADDRESS AND TELEPHONE: Croxteth Country Park, Croxteth Hall Lane, Liverpool L12 0HB. Tel. (051) 228 5311

OWNERS: Liverpool City Council

DIRECTIONS: entrance off Muirhead Avenue. Well signposted from M57. Travel W on A580 East Lancs Road, turn left into Lower House Lane, leading to Muirhead Road. Public transport: buses F8, 18 or 92 to car park entrance; 12, 13 or 102 to Princes Drive; 61 to West Derby

OPENING TIMES: park open daily throughout the year. Hall, farm and walled garden open Easter to end September, daily 11–5.

ADMISSION: park free, walled garden 50p, separate charge for Hall and Farm. Pre-arranged bookings preferred for coaches

CAR PARKING: yes

TOILETS: yes

REFRESHMENTS: café

SHOP: yes

DOGS: under control in park only

WHEELCHAIR ACCESS: yes, flat ground, no steps, but paths liable to be muddy in wet weather. Toilets for the disabled: yes

PEAK SEASON: no special peaks

NOTABLE FEATURES: attractive parkland and pleasure grounds; vegetable garden; herbaceous borders; herb garden; glasshouses; rare and unusual plants

Driving towards Croxteth Country Park, through the urban sprawl of the outskirts of Liverpool, it is hard to believe that in Victorian and Edwardian times this was the site of a great country estate extending over several thousand acres. Today only 530 acres remain—the Hall, gardens, farm, woodlands and some parkland.

For more than four centuries, Croxteth was the home of the Molyneux family, later the Earls of Sefton. The first Hall was completed by the end of the 16C—its Elizabethan architecture can be seen at the rear of the present Hall.

In 1702, the 4th Viscount built the most attractive part of the Hall, the Queen Anne Wing, which stands on a terrace and is richly embellished with decorative stonework. The grand west front was added by the 6th Earl in 1902.

Pleasure grounds and a walled garden were developed during the 18C and 19C.

In 1973 the Hall and park passed into public ownership, at the wish of the 7th Earl's widow, the late Countess of Sefton. By then the estate had shrunk to its present size by the sale of land for housing developments, and the Hall itself had been badly damaged by fire in 1952. Croxteth is now a country park, a centre for leisure, education and conservation of the environment.

The Hall is nearly in the centre of the park, set in a cultivated landscape of ornamental ponds, lawns, fine specimen trees and rhododendrons. The walled garden, just north of the Hall, was developed during the first half of the 19C and covers about 2 acres. While its principal function was to supply the Hall with fresh fruit, vegetables, cut flowers and pot plants, it was also kept as a showpiece, a place for guests to visit. In its heyday, it was maintained by a large staff of gardeners.

There are stories of how in Victorian times, Croxteth gardeners competed with those on neighbouring estates to provide the earliest supplies of choice produce, especially fruit, for the master's table. Croxteth often triumphed in this friendly rivalry, partly due to the system of heated flues within the walls, allowing tender and exotic fruits, such as figs and apricots to be grown and ripened outside.

The walled garden is now once again a horticultural showpiece, laid out to display techniques of vegetable and fruit growing, as well as flowers and herbs. It is the regular meeting place for a local Garden Society and a Young Growers' Club (for children).

The approach to the walled garden lies through a formal rose garden, a Victorian design of round and rectangular beds planted with modern varieties. Climbing roses on a rustic archway represent a Victorian 'Joke' feature where the distance between the upright poles decreases with distance and so creates an effect of perspective.

You enter the walled garden through one end of an impressive 150ft long lean-to greenhouse. The garden is divided by intersecting gravel paths into unequal sections for the cultivation of different crops. Several of these paths are lined with apple and pear trees, trained into a variety of shapes—open bush, goblet, single and double espalier, fans and cordons. Some of the trees are more than 120 years old.

One of the first sections you encounter is an area of formal beds, some surrounded by low box hedging, others by Victorian tile edging, but all filled with colourful bedding displays. Adjacent is the rose lawn, replanted in 1983 with modern varieties of hybrid tea and floribunda roses, in ten rectangular beds.

The herb garden is edged with box and features popular herbs such as rosemary, thyme, sage, bay, garlic and chives, as well as lesser known ones, such as henbane, tansy and marshmallow. Nearby are rows of apples and pears, named so that visitors can compare the merits of different varieties.

One large plot is devoted to the cultivation of a wide range of soft fruits, another displays vegetables on a three-course rotation, while another is laid out to plant collections, notably hardy fuchsias—a National Collection. A small plot featuring 'yesterday's vegetables' is arranged as a vegetable seed sanctuary in conjunction with Henry Doubleday Research Association. This is part of the campaign to save traditional vegetables facing the threat of extinction. Some of the old and rare varieties of runner beans include 'Painted Lady', 'Daniel's Defiance' and 'The Czar'. A variety of pea 'Commander' represents a 6ft tall type popular 100 years ago when pea sticking was the universal practice. Many other rare and uncommon vegetables are also grown.

A range of glasshouses and sheds is tucked away from sight behind a break in the north-west corner of the wall. These superseded the flue walls for the growing of early crops. The Forcing Pit House, a building of low construction with an abundance of heating pipes, was also used for plant propagation and the early forcing of vegetables followed by roof crops of cucumbers and melons; the latter may be seen during the summer months.

The teak house is a glasshouse constructed of highly durable teak wood and dates from about 1905. Its orientation is east to west, making it ideal for plant propagation and the early raising of flowers in pots.

The taller display house was once used solely to grow carnations for the last earl's buttonhole. This house now contains pot plant collections and displays and demonstrations. Behind is a mushroom shed, with a permanent display of the methods of mushrooms growing on one side and occasional 'live' cropping on the other.

Visitors who prefer flowers and shrubs should explore the borders below the garden walls, especially the one beneath the west or flue wall. This Victorian-style border is filled with bright annuals and perennials—petunias, marigolds, rudbeckias and fuchsias—and a wide range of shrubs including orange-flowering *Buddleia* x *wey-erana* and showy *Hydrangea paniculata* 'Grandiflora'.

The sunny south-facing border was used for growing early salad crops in the last century. It now displays unusual herbaceous and shrubby plants, such as the royal lily (*Lilium regale*), the Japanese anemone (*Anemone japonica*) and *Spiraea* x *bumalda* 'Goldflame'.

The third border running along the northern boundary of the garden, features hardy perennials fashionable at the turn of the century. Among these are delphiniums, lupins, peonies and red hot pokers (kniphofias) arranged in a repeat pattern popular in the 19C. The Morello cherry also grows well against the wall here.

WEST MIDLANDS

Birmingham Botanical Gardens and Glasshouses

ADDRESS AND TELEPHONE: The Birmingham Botanical Gardens, Westbourne Road, Edgbaston, Birmingham, B15 3TR. Tel. (021) 454 1860

OWNERS: Birmingham Botanical and Horticultural Society

DIRECTIONS: off the inner ring road and A456 at Five Ways then via Calthorpe Road and Westbourne Road (well signposted). Public transport: Birmingham New Street BR 1¼ miles. West Midland buses: 3, 10, 21, 22, 23, 29

OPENING TIMES: all year, daily except Christmas Day 9 8 or dusk, whichever is earlier (Sun from 10)

ADMISSION: £2.40 (Sun £2.70), children, students, disabled visitors, OAPs £1.20. Family ticket £6.50 (Sun £7). Reduced rates for parties if booked in advance

CAR PARKING: yes

TOILETS: yes

REFRESHMENTS: yes

SHOP: yes, both gifts and plants

DOGS: no

WHEELCHAIR ACCESS: yes. Toilets for the disabled: yes

PEAK MONTHS: throughout the year

NOTABLE FEATURES: tropical, palm and cacti houses; orangery; bog, rose, rock and disabled gardens; many plants of interest; many fine trees

The gardens here date from 1831 when the Birmingham Botanical and Horticultural Society, established two years earlier, decided to create a garden to display a wide range of plants from all over the world. John Claudius Loudon (1783–1843), a well known architect and designer of the time, was commissioned to design and plant the 17 acres of gardens, and these have continued to be developed ever since.

A new and impressive conservatory-style entrance has recently been completed to bring visitors into a grand ticket hall with aviary and picture gallery, but the garden tour really begins in the adjoining lily or tropical house, first opened in 1854. Here, in the humid steamy atmosphere, is a jungle of tropical plants.

Greeting you at the entrance is a dwarf Cavendish variety of banana (*Musa cavendishii*) and flanking the doorway is the Banyan tree (*Ficus benghalensis*) and the Bo-Tree or Peepal tree (*Ficus religiosa*), in the shade of which Buddha is said to have rested. Overhead are tropical climbers, such as *Thunbergia grandiflora*, twisting their way up to the roof, and showing off their vivid coloured flowers.

The central feature of the tropical house is a lily pool, some 24ft in diameter, planted with an imaginative selection of water lilies and other aquatics, such as the floating water hyacinth (*Eichhornia speciosa*) and water lettuce or tropical duckweed (*Pistia stratiotes*). Rice grows at the edges of the pool and all around is the lush vegetation of the Cassava or tapioca plant (*Manihot utilissima*), guava (*Psedium guajava*), Swiss cheese plant (*monstera*), sugar cane (*Sacchrum officinarum*), cordylines and crotons. There is also an excellent display of bromeliads.

After the heat and humidity of the tropical house, the cooler atmosphere of the adjacent palm house is very welcome. Again there is a wealth of interesting plant life. The fern collection in this house includes a splendid specimen of the stags horn fern (platycerium) and there are several hundred orchids. Towards the centre of the house is the very rare Latham's tree fern. William Latham was curator of the gardens in 1872 and he successfully crossed *Dicksonia antarctica* with *Dicksonia arborescens* to produce what is believed to be the only hybrid tree fern in existence. It was named *Dicksonia* x *Lathamii* in his honour.

Elsewhere in the palm house are small collections of cyclads and insect-catching plants including sarrecinia and dionaea species.

Next to the palm house is an orangery. Here, in the central beds, there are fruiting citrus bushes including the sweet orange (*Citrus sinensis*), grapefruit (*Citrus paradisi*) and a tall slender tree of the giant lemon (*Citrus limonia ponderosa*). Benches around this house support a colourful display of conservatory plants—pelargoniums, fuchsias, coleus and tradescantias.

The final glasshouse contains a good display of large cacti and succulents planted into a bed. Smaller species and a collection of pebble plants (lithops) are kept behind a wire cage.

The terrace outside the glasshouses faces south-east, providing not only fine views across the garden but also a sunny sheltered spot for more tender plants such as *Abutilon megapotamicum*, which produces its red and yellow pendulous lantern-like flowers throughout the summer. Also in summer, cacti and succulents are planted out into a terrace bed and there are excellent formal bedding displays.

A particularly fine sloping lawn below the terrace forms a natural amphitheatre—the 'stage' being a grand old Victorian bandstand, planted round with bright bedding displays in summer. The weeping form of the willow-leaved pear (*Pyrus salicifolia* 'Pendula') makes a large dome of silvery foliage in summer, to one side of the lawn and later in the year acers show their rich autumn colours. Near the terrace is a fine *Paulownia tormentosa* or foxglove tree. This handsome ornamental flowering tree has large leaves and, in a warm May, mauve foxglove-like flowers.

On the north-east perimeter of the lawn, close by a splendid copper beech, is a model garden of special interest to disabled people, with raised dark brick beds containing a variety of small shrubs, herbaceous plants and alpines. Beyond the woodland walk are three small plots laid out as examples of domestic gardens, giving further ideas and hopefully inspiration to visitors.

Nearby is the Dr E.H. Wilson Border. This border displays species introduced to Britain from China by the plant collector Ernest Henry Wilson, who trained as a gardener in these botanical gardens between 1893 and 1897. Among the shrubs in the border are *Maacki chinensis*, which has white peak-like flowers in July and August, the sweetly scented autumn flowering *Osmanthus armatus*, and the Chinese witch-hazel (*Hamamelis mollis*). Several rhododendrons were also introduced by Wilson, for example *Rhododendron davidsonianum*, *R. lutescens* and the outstanding *R. sutcheunense* which carries pink and rose bell-shaped flowers in February and March.

Beyond this China border is an azalea walk—at its best in May and early June when the dense shrubs are a mass of pink, yellow, orange and red flowers and a rich sweet perfume fills the air. There is a rhododendron collection too.

No botanical garden would be complete without a selection of bog plants and alpines. The bog garden here is dominated by the huge rhubarb leaves of *Gunnera manicata* but there are also ferns, astilbes, irises, spurges and a selection of primulas.

The rock garden was constructed in 1895, using millstone grit boulders from Yorkshire. A stream flows down the garden into a pool, below which is a mass of water lilies, marsh marigolds and marginal plants. In the crevices of rocks and on screes are many alpine plants: campanulas, gentians, dianthus and alpine phlox.

Near the rock garden is a pendulous form of Lawson cypress (*Chamaecyparis lawsoniana* 'Pendula') and a large spreading pocket handkerchief tree (*Davidia involucrata*). Above the West Lawn stands a magnificent group of pines —mostly Austrian (*Pinus nigra*), Scots (*P. sylvestris*) and the Himalayan or Bhutan pine (*P. wallichiana*). Below is a long, well planted herbaceous border.

Rose lovers should make their way to the north-west perimeter where a delightful rose garden has been created. A rectangular lawn is surrounded by beds of hybrid teas and floribundas—'Mullard Jubilee', 'Silver Jubilee', 'Just Joey' and 'Southampton' to mention but a few. In a border by the wall there are both old and modern shrub roses and at the lower end of the garden is a pergola draped with magnificent climbing roses such as 'Etoile de Hollande', which has richly fragrant flowers of velvet red. The popular yellow climbing rose 'Golden Showers' may also be seen here as may 'Handel', 'Zephirine Drouhin', 'Danse du Feu' and the old favourite, 'Albertine'.

Behind the children's playground, around an old cottage, believed to have been designed by Lutyens, a traditional cottage garden is being created. Adjacent to this area an extensive herb garden has been planted.

Birmingham Botanical Gardens certainly has a lot to offer visitors. To occupy the children there is an adventure playground, an outdoor aviary and a rabbitry, and on most summer Sunday afternoons a band plays from the bandstand.

NORFOLK

Blickling Hall

ADDRESS AND TELEPHONE: The Administrator, Blickling Hall, Norwich, NR11 6NF. Tel. Aylsham (0263) 733084

OWNERS: The National Trust

DIRECTIONS: on the B1354, 1½ miles mile NW of Aylsham, which is on the A140, 15 miles N of Norwich and 10 miles S of Cromer. Signposted off the A140 and from Aylsham. Public transport: North Walsham station 8 miles

OPENING TIMES: 30 March to 27 October, daily except Mon and Thurs but open BH Mon 12–5. Open daily July and August 12–5. House open 1–5

ADMISSION: house and garden £4.50; garden only £2. Coach parties by prior arrangement

CAR PARKING: yes

TOILETS: yes

REFRESHMENTS: café

SHOP: yes

DOGS: in park and picnic areas only, on lead

WHEELCHAIR ACCESS: yes. Toilets for the disabled: yes

PEAK MONTHS: July and August

NOTABLE FEATURES: yew hedges, herbaceous borders

The garden of Blickling Hall makes its presence felt as soon as you catch sight of the Hall's splendid Jacobean south front: red brick with white turrets and a central clock tower. Stretching out towards you are two spectacular yew hedges, continuing the lines of the two service wings. These are emphasised by their backing of pollarded limes, which stand out brightly above the dark evergreen.

As you approach the front courtyard, and pass under the east hedge, you can see how the yews have been shaped: their branches have been supported to slope gradually downwards from the planting bank to the level of the front courtyard. This gives the hedges themselves the appearance of two sloping green banks, tightly clipped and gently undulating. Their date of origin is uncertain, but they may have been planted as long ago as the late 17C. Their survival in such good condition is attributed to the lack of heavy snowfalls in Norfolk but must also be due to continuous care.

In the front courtyard you will find wisteria, vines and the Blickling pear tree trained against the west wall. Summer-flowering *Magnolia grandiflora* grows on the the south wall, by the main entrance to the house, and a magnificent rosemary flourishes by the bridge to the front door. Shade-loving hostas, hellebores and ferns and hydrangeas fill the moat garden. Having walked through the east wing, which houses tea and information rooms, you arrive at the east front and the impressive formal garden.

The east garden seems to have been an important feature of Blickling since Jacobean times; but it has changed a good deal during the years, only taking its present shape in the late 19C, when the existing lawn was excavated to form a parterre. A brick wall and side banks protect this area from winds. A photograph from the 1920s shows the parterre as laid out by Lady Lothian—a rather confusing mix of small beds and topiary. In the 1930s it was redesigned by Norah Lindsay, who had worked at Hidcote with Lawrence Johnston, and contributed to the design of many gardens of the period.

The only features of the former garden retained by Mrs Lindsay were the central 17C fountain, 16 yew 'acorns' and four abstract yew topiary shapes which have been likened to grand pianos. Mrs Lindsay simplified the many small beds into four large rectangles of herbaceous planting, surrounded by rose borders. Rows of conifers in the temple walk were replaced with azaleas and rhododendrons.

The four herbaceous beds are planted in pairs according to a carefully planned colour scheme, each pair sharing many of the same plants, placed in varying associations. They are supplemented by a south-facing border.

Having climbed the steps at the back of the parterre, guarded by herms and sphinxes, you start the walk to the temple—flanked in spring by red rhododendrons and azaleas in every shade of yellow, orange, coral and red, backed by beeches, copper beeches and dark yews. The temple itself may have been designed by William Kent and was probably moved to its present location during the 1830s. From here, avenues of Turkey oak and lime should lead away to the park, but sadly these were largely destroyed in the gales of October 1987 (the gardens lost 200 trees). However, much replanting has since been carried out.

The limes at the end of the north lawn are happily still standing, as is the Turkey oak near the lake. On the way down to the lake, note the beautiful group of 300-year-old oriental planes, their twisting and peeling branches sprawling over the grass. Underplanted with bluebells, these stand on a raised area known as the bastion. In the wood behind is a shaggy stone statue of the Dog of Alcibiades, belligerent but touching, acquired for the estate for £7 in 1876.

A meadow area by the west front is flooded with daffodils in spring, and later with lady's smock (*Cardamine pratensis*). Spring-flowering magnolias can also be found here: M. *tripetala*, the American umbrella tree, with white purple-flushed flowers, and M. *obovata*, with creamy white, red-stamened blossom. The shell fountain was out of order when we visited.

Turning back above the parterre, passing beds of peonies, we went in search of the orangery, at the end of a path to the south-east. Built in the late 18C, this was formerly heated for tender plants, but now houses more hardy specimens: camellias, palms, ferns, fuchsias and ivies. Jasmine and honeysuckle grow against outside south-facing wall. None of the plants appeared to be flourishing: possibly they would do better in the light and open air. The orangery also houses a statue of Hercules, and some 19C majolica plaques after the style of Lucia della Robbia.

The secret garden is more worth visiting. Planted by Norah Lindsay in 1936, it contains an attractive range of shrubs including philadelphus, cornus, and hydrangeas well as the Nepal laburnum (piptanthus), New Zealand flax (*Phormium tenax*) and an under-planting of lilies.

You are also free to wander through the park, enjoying views of the lake and the many splendid trees. Here too you can see the 18C Gothic Tower, the mausoleum for Lord Buckinghamshire and his two countesses and the icehouse (still in use in the 1930s).

Bressingham

ADDRESS AND TELEPHONE: Bressingham Steam Museum and Gardens, Bressingham, Diss, Norfolk IP22 2AB. Tel. Diss (0379 88) 382 and 386

OWNER: Alan Bloom

DIRECTIONS: 2½ miles W of Diss on A1066 Thetford to Diss Road. Public transport: Intercity to Diss every hour from London (Liverpool St) and Norwich

OPENING TIMES: 31 March to 31 October, 10–5. House not open

ADMISSION: £3, children £2; £2.50, children £1.50 on non-Steam days. Coach parties welcome

CAR PARKING: yes

TOILETS: yes

REFRESHMENTS: restaurant

SHOP: yes, plants and souvenirs

WHEELCHAIR ACCESS: yes. Toilets for the disabled: yes

DOGS: no, except guide dogs

PEAK MONTHS: June to September

NOTABLE FEATURES: hardy perennials, conifers and heathers

Best known as a nursery and garden centre, specialising in hardy perennials and conifers, Bressingham also attracts garden lovers and steam engine enthusiasts. Dating from the late 1950s, Alan Bloom's 6-acre display garden is stocked with a very wide variety of hardy herbaceous plants, 5000 in all, including many rare and uncommon types—Alan Bloom himself has raised and introduced more than 100 new varieties. The garden exists side by side with a museum of old railway engines and relics and you can tour large areas of the grounds by steam engine.

Alan Bloom bought the 200 acres of land at Bressingham shortly after the 1939–45 war and following years of hard work, both nursery and farm were set on their feet. The nursery business has flourished and now visitors come from far and wide to the famous plant centre. Robert and Adrian Bloom have extended the range of plants grown and sold and enlarged the nursery to over 100 acres. The informal garden was begun in 1957.

The Dell Garden lies behind Bressingham Hall, to the north. Here, countless hardy plants, shrubs and perennials, are laid out in huge curving island beds, on a gently undulating site, sheltered by mature broad-leaved trees and conifers. Midsummer is the peak time for colour.

The display beds in front of the Georgian house provide an excellent example of Alan Bloom's characteristic style of planting— profuse and varied yet relaxed, without forced 'effects'. He found from the start that open island beds encouraged free and vigorous growth, giving plants more light and space to grow.

Deep blue *Clematis integrifolia* 'Hendersonii', with turned-back petals, one of Alan Bloom's favourite plants, sprawls at its ease in bed 5, near the delightful tall *Iris sibirica* 'Flight of Butterflies', the clear blue delphinium 'Blue Bees' and dianthus 'Constance Finis', with deep pink spotted petals. *Scabiosa graminifolia* makes an attractive carpet, with its silvery grey grass-like foliage and pinkish mauve flowers. In this bed, too, are the very lovely *Roscoea cautleoides* 'Kew Form', with soft yellow, hooded flowers, bright yellow anthemis and the yellow trollius 'Bressingham Sunshine'.

In a nearby bed, note the coral-flame *Heuchera sanguinea* 'Bressingham Blaze' and the unusual red achillea 'Paprika'. Incidentally, it was Alan Bloom who named and introduced the very popular achillea 'Moonshine', canary yellow with greyish leaves.

The display bed behind is given height by pale yellow, pink and white lupins and the bright yellow potentilla *P. recta* 'Warrenii'. Yellow hawkweed (*Hieracium pubescens*) grows wild and weed-like near the blue scabious *S. caucasica* 'Clive Greaves': both these plants are ultra-hardy, as is *Ranunculus acris* 'Flore Pleno', the double form of the common meadow buttercup. Here too is polemonium 'Dawn Flight', tall, white and graceful, pale yellow *Achillea taygetea* and bold red poppies. This gives some idea of the variety and interest pof planting in this area in early summer, and there are many other areas to be explored.

Behind an oak screen and through a holly arch to the north, the garden opens out into a wider and longer grassy area, bounded to one side by the nurseries, to the other by the garden railway and trees screening off the road. Mature oak, beech, ash and silver birch trees stand here and there, interspersed with conifers. The path dips under a small bridge, but before exploring further, walk a little way along the hedge to your right, to see the near-perfect mature specimen of *Cornus kousa chinensis* with its conspicuous white bracts in early summer and rich autumn colouring.

The east and west-facing banks approaching the bridge are planted with bloody cranesbill (*Geranium sanguineum* 'Minuta'), purplish pink, and lilac-pink, red-veined *Geranium cinereum* 'Ballerina', offset by other mauve, pink and blue plants—mauve phlox 'Pilosa', bright pink *Oxalis articulata* and little sky-blue *Viola cornuta* 'Boughton Blue'—sheltered by shrubs and larger perennials such as the ebullient *Euphorbia martinii*, *Viburnum* x *juddii* and *Euonymus fortunei* 'Emerald Gaity'. A tulip tree (*Liriodendron tulipifera*) overhangs the east-facing border. On the other side of the bridge, deep steps lead up through a series of small terraces (wheelchairs can go up the gently sloping grassy bank). *Acer japonicum* 'Aureum' with soft yellow leaves crowns the terraces on one side, and handsome *Rodgersia podophylla* 'Smaragd' flourishes in its shade. Further round, in a lower bed, you can see the Bressingham orchid, *Orchis fuchsii* 'Bressingham Bonus', with spotted leaves and deep mauve flowers.

Proceeding into the main part of the garden, the first curving half-moon bed, overshadowed by an enormous ash, contains a huge variety of shade-loving and moisture-loving plants—*Rodgersia purdonii* and *Rodgersia pinnata* 'Superba' with bright pink flowers, *Hosta sieboldiana* 'Elegans' with great blue-green leaves and *Hosta fortunei* 'Picta', tall feathery goatsbeard (*Aruncus sylvester* 'Plumosus') and *Podophyllum emodi* 'Nanum', to name a few, along with ferns such as the crinkly-leaved royal fern *Osmunda regalis* 'Gracilis' and the plainer soft shield or hedge fern, *Polystichum setiferum divisilobum*. The yellow globe flower *Trollius europaeus* looks very striking beside maroon-pink polygonum 'Milettii' and *Iris sibirica* 'Limeheart'. Blue poppies grow in this bed too—*Meconopsis* x *sheldonii* 'Branklyn'—and look out for *Primula vialii*, with dense spikes of lavender-blue flowers, crimson in bud.

Splendid peonies in nearby beds attract attention in early summer, notably *P. lactiflora* 'Bowl of Beauty', pale pink with a creamy white centre, and deep pink 'Alexander Fleming'—and bold black and white poppies can be seen to the right, near the garden railway. Other plant associations are far too numerous to list; every bed has its particular treasures.

At the back of the Dell Garden, plants grow to gigantic size, masking the wall and the road behind—huge *Crambe cordifolia* with limp heart-shaped leaves and tiny white delicate flowers, and the soaring red spires of *Rheum tanguticum*. In quiet contrast is a little bed almost entirely devoted to hostas—among them 'Golden Medallion', 'Grand Master', 'August Moon' and 'Gold Standard'.

Retracing your steps back down the lawn, you should find directions to the heather and conifer garden. Nearby is a long curving bed of sun-loving plants—including the wonderful *Thymus citriodorus* 'Archer's Gold', geraniums, parahebe 'Miss Willmott' with delicate mauve flowers, viola 'Dwarf Yellow' and many more. A surprising variety of plants can be found in the heather and conifer garden, and many interesting combinations. A red copper beech hedge makes an excellent foil to the white willow *Salix alba* 'Argentea' and a blue fir; while nearby *Berberis thunbergii* 'Dart's Red Lady', *Abies procera* 'Glauca Prostrata' and *Juniperus* x *media* 'Gold Sovereign' make another boldly colourful group. Many lovely bright-leaved trees and shrubs stand out against and among the darker conifers—silver-variegated *Cornus alternifolia* 'Argentea', the golden-yellow currant *Ribes sanguineum* 'Brocklebankii' and *Populus alba* 'Richardii' with golden-yellow leaves, white beneath. There is also a bed of dwarf rhododendrons.

It would be a pity to leave Bressingham without at least one train ride. The two narrow-gauge railways give a fine view of the nursery, woodlands and the two-acre lake; and Alan Bloom may well be driving!

Felbrigg Hall

ADDRESS AND TELEPHONE: The Administrator, Felbrigg Hall, Felbrigg, Norwich, NR11 8PR. Tel. West Runton (026 375) 444

OWNERS: The National Trust

DIRECTIONS: near Felbrigg village, 2 miles SW of Cromer, off A148. Public transport: Cromer station 2¼ miles

OPENING TIMES: 30 March to 27 October, Mon, Wed, Thurs, Sat and Sun 11–5.30. Closed Good Fri. Woodland walks all year (except Christmas Day) daily, dawn to dusk. House open 1.30–5.30 on same days

ADMISSION: house and garden £4; garden only £1.50. Parties £3 (please book with sae to Administrator)

CAR PARKING: yes

TOILETS: yes

REFRESHMENTS: café

SHOP: yes

DOGS: in park only, on lead

WHEELCHAIR ACCESS: yes. Toilets for the disabled: yes, one accessible

PEAK MONTHS: June, September, October

NOTABLE FEATURES: walled garden

The walled kitchen garden was a familiar feature of many large estates from the 17C through to the 19C and often played a vital role in household management, providing fruit and vegetables all year round for family and servants. Nowadays, for reasons of economy and lack of staff, many of these old walled gardens have been converted into car parks or nursery and plant sales areas. At Felbrigg , the National Trust have restored and replanted the walled garden roughly along the lines of a traditional kitchen garden, with wall fruit trees, fruit cages and lean-to glasshouses—but to save labour costs, large areas have been planted ornamentally.

Restoration of the walled garden began in 1972, with the arrival of Mr Ted Bullock, the present head gardener. Originally laid out in the 18C, the garden is arranged on a central north–south axis, on a slight slope to the south for maximum sun and shelter. The red brick walls vary in height, from 9 to 12ft high. The soil is lime-free, except below the walls.

Covering just over 2½ acres, the garden is divided into three sections by two cross walls, but with a long central walk and two side-walks running from north to south. The top section features a huge dovecot, a circular pool, a vegetable area and fruit cage—with cut flower border behind—plenty of wall fruits, a herb bed and two small orchards with white wooden beehives. In the centre section are two lean-to glasshouses, shrub borders, a collection of thorns and lilacs. The southern section was once a tree nursery, but is now laid mainly to grass, with a few specimen trees dotted here and there.

The garden entry lies through a door to the west, at one end of a cross walk in the centre section. Turning left (or northwards) up the west walk, you pass a mixed flower border backed by espalier pears and fan-trained apples. This border is mainly planted with peonies, interspersed with roses on triple supports, such as the purplish-rose rugosa and the magenta-pink musk 'James Mitchell'. Lilies flower later in the year. To your right, by the small propagating glasshouse, is a Californian bay (*Umbellularia californica*), with strongly aromatic leaves. The beds and borders are edged with neat box hedges, narrow at the top, with sloping sides making a wide base. In all, the walled garden contains over half a mile of box hedging.

The west side of the dovecot wall is covered by fig trees, including 'White Genoa', mentioned in an early 19C account of the garden. In front is a herb border, containing a bed of alliums, towering angelica, tall yellow-flowered woad and a variety of other culinary and medicinal herbs—tansy, golden balm, greek valerian, orange thyme, peppermint and pineapple sage, to name just a few.

White doves flutter in the small apple orchard and wildflower area. The dovecot itself is an impressive structure—built in 1680 and restored in 1937, it contains 968 holes and would once have housed several thousand doves. These were a valuable source of fresh meat in winter and would also have provided useful manure. Nowadays the number of birds is strictly limited to a maximum of 50, and the eggs are removed every two weeks. Rose 'Félicité et Perpetue' grows up the dovecot wall.

On the east side of the dovecot, shrub roses are backed by cardoons and espalier pear trees. Among the roses are the hybrid musk 'Penelope' (creamy apricot) and the musk 'Buff Dawn' (apricot yellow). Here too are hibiscus 'Dorothy Crane' (white with a crimson centre), and grapevines trained on wooden pyramids. A potato vine (*Solanum crispum* 'Glasnevin') hangs on the wall, displaying star-shaped purple-blue flowers in late summer.

Directly below is the kitchen garden area, where Mr Bullock and his helpers can often be seen hard at work—no chemical weed-killers are used on the shrub borders and vegetable garden and the beds need constant hoeing in spring and summer. Look out for the old lantern cloches and rhubarb forcing pots. Behind the soft fruit cage is a cut flower border and behind this, the hibiscus and colchicum border. Felbrigg holds, with Wisley, the National Collection of colchicums—often called autumn crocuses or meadow saffrons. In spring you can see, among others, rose-purple *C. giganteum*, rose-pink *C. speciosum*, white *C. speciosum* 'Album' and *C. giganteum* 'Lilac Wonder', purple striped with white; and in autumn, lilac and white *C. autumnale*.

Felbrigg Hall: herb bed in the top section of the walled garden

The circular pond, originally used for water storage, is now planted round with lavender (*Lavandula officinalis* 'Hidcote') and centres on a very unusual stone statue of a boy with two fish tails.

Most traditional kitchen gardens would have contained ornamental flower beds and borders, sometimes on quite an elaborate scale and usually arranged along the central axis. At Felbrigg, double borders are planted on either side of the central cross-path (leading from the entrance) in the middle section. Large shrub roses and buddleias are interspersed with groups of summer-flowering shrubs. The colour scheme is gentle and subtle, with soft mauves, blues, pinks and silvers in mid summer. A collection of lilacs is planted behind, for early colour and fragrance. Among the many varieties to be seen here are creamy-yellow 'Mme Lemoine', rich pink 'Congo' and rose-red 'Paul Thirion'.

The shrub beds are edged with a 1ft-wide border of *Colchicum autumnale tenori*, a rare form of autumn crocus. Tall crown imperials stand at the bed corners, where the paths cross, interplanted with rue (*Ruta graveolens* 'Jackman's Blue').

Of the two lean-to glasshouses, one is a vinery, containing five rods of the grapevine 'Black Hamburgh', as well as grapefruit and lemon trees. All these produce excellent crops on a regular basis, despite the glasshouse being unheated. The other house, a conservatory, features a mimosa (*Acacia decurrens dealbata*), with silvery-green downy leaves and small yellow balls of flowers in April and May—also clumps of sweet ginger (hedychium) and a small border of half-hardy flowering plants.

Two rectangular plots in the lower half of this central section are planted with small ornamental thorns (crataegus species), medlars, and the graft hybrid between them, x *Crataegomespilus dardarii*, the Bronvaux medlar. One west-facing border is filled with dahlias, another devoted mainly to *Carpenteria californica*, which bears anemone-like white flowers from early to mid summer. Gages and plums are fan-trained against the wall behind.

The south section is an open grassy area, well furnished with seats and with specimen trees for interest—two mulberries, Chinese rowans, a Pyrenean oak. In the 18C, this area was sown with turnip seed. Where the thorn hedge now stands, there was once a bamboo screen—a few clumps of bamboo can still be seen. The south-facing walls were used for growing tree fruits, but these have since been replaced with alternate plantings of blue ceanothus and yellow climbing or rambler roses—'Lawrence Johnston', 'Gloire de Dijon', 'Canary Bird', 'Golden Showers', 'Goldfinch' and others.

A great 600-acre wood, planted by William Windham at the end of the 17C, protects Felbrigg from coastal winds—the North Sea is not more than a mile away. If you have time, the woodland is well worth exploring, full of fine old oaks and sweet chestnuts. Not far from the walled garden is a very beautiful and ancient sweet chestnut, planted in about 1680. The walnut (*Juglans regia*) by the western entrance door was felled by a gale many years ago, but is still alive.

Mannington Hall Gardens

ADDRESS AND TELEPHONE: Mannington Hall, Norwich, NR11 7BB. Tel. Saxthorpe (0263 87) 4175

OWNERS: Lord and Lady Walpole

DIRECTIONS: betweem Aylsham and Holt, 18 miles N of Norwich, 9 miles from the coast, 2 miles from Saxthorpe. No public transport available

OPENING TIMES: April, Sun 1–5, May to August, Wed, Thurs and Fri 11–5, Sun 12–5. Hall not open

ADMISSION: £2, OAPs and students £1.50, accompanied children under 16 free. Party rates on request

CAR PARKING: yes

TOILETS: yes

REFRESHMENTS: café

SHOP: yes

DOGS: no, except guide dogs

WHEELCHAIR ACCESS: yes, to main parts of garden. Toilets for the disabled: yes

PEAK MONTHS: summer

NOTABLE FEATURES: Heritage rose garden

Mannington Hall lies 18 miles north of Norwich and 7 miles from the sea, in an area crammed with excellent gardens and nurseries. The gardens of this large estate are still very much in process of development, but there are several interesting areas—the Heritage rose gardens, a scented garden and a wild valley planted with unusual trees. The park, covering about 20 acres, is threaded with nature trails.

The 15C house is very beautiful, with its old flint walls, leaded windows, turrets and battlements and the surrounding moat and nearby lake, both fed by underground springs. Mannington Hall was purchased in the 18C by Horatio, 1st Baron Walpole of Wolterton (brother of Sir Robert Walpole, England's first prime minister) and the Walpole family are still in possession.

Entrance is through the Information Centre, a building with countryside interpretative displays opened in 1989. From the bottom of the main drive, it is a leisurely stroll across wide lawns to the house. The huge cedars here have been badly damaged by recent storms; they are being gradually replaced with new cedars and fast-growing Wellingtonias.

Cross the small drawbridge into the enclosed gardens behind the outer walls of the house and Victorian 'battlements'. Near the old guardhouse (also modified in the last century) is an ancient bell, cast during the Civil Wars, and in the north-west corner, a Venetian lead cistern. The beds hold herbaceous plants, small trees and roses. *R.* 'Canary Bird' shows its small, single, bright yellow flowers in late spring, in the south-facing yellow and orange bed. The front bed is devoted mainly to blues and pinks, and also holds a magnificent silver weeping pear (*Pyrus salicifolia* 'Pendula').

The west-facing bed (beneath the house wall) features peonies and lupins and an interesting three-species-in-one prunus, planted to celebrate Notcutts Nurseries' 75th anniversary. On the walls is the climbing hydrangea *H. petiolaris.*

Continue around the building to the south, where *Rosa banksiae* 'Lutea' climbs vigorously up the wall, producing its double-button shaped yellow flowers early in the season and mingling with a fine mauve wisteria. Enormous mounds of cistus (rock roses) burgeon on the gravel, flowering white and pink from late spring to mid summer.

A formal rose garden to the south, laid out in 1968, features mainly hybrid tea roses grown as bedding plants. The central sundial is surrounded by juniper. This garden commands an excellent view over the moat, past a row of lichen-covered marble busts, to the south lawn, with its shrub and rose beds and small temple. Behind this temple is a collection of Scottish roses, excellent hardy shrubs with small pretty flowers.

Also within the moat area is a small ornamental scented garden. The beds here are cut in an intricate pattern, identical to that of the dining-room ceiling in the house (with a central lime representing the chandelier). This area might have a special appeal for blind people, although it is by no means easy to negotiate the very narrow, curving and twisting grass paths. Many of the beds are planted with herbs, including a collection of sages. Hyacinths fill the urns in spring, replaced in summer by scented pelargoniums. *R. eglanteria*, the wild species rose, can also be found here, included for its strongly fragrant foliage.

The Heritage rose gardens lie due north of the house, in a spacious walled garden, formerly the kitchen garden—the walls, built in 1900, are still well clothed with fruit trees. The garden is now divided into a number of small areas, each representing a particular historical period and planted appropriately. In all, the Heritage gardens contain more than 1000 different roses, including a wide range of wild or species roses (planted in three large beds to the left and right of the entrance).

The Medieval Garden features turf seats, a wattle fence and a small yew tree—also some very old roses such as *R. gallica* 'Officinalis', the apothecary's rose, and creamy-white *R. spinosissima*, one of the Scottish roses. Medieval herbs are cultivated in two beds outside the wattle fence. The 17C style knot garden features circular and semicircular interlocking beds cut into the turf and filled with Scottish roses, moss roses, centifolias and others. The Classical Garden (1700–1836), diagonally above, will eventually be surrounded by hornbeam hedges and already holds a number of very interesting roses, including the unusual Chinese green rose (*R. viridiflora*).

The Victorian Garden takes up a large section and seeks to represent a mixture of styles—the formal, the picturesque, the gardenesque and the rustic. In the Victorian orchard area, below, climbers and ramblers are trained up small fruit trees.

The Trellis Garden (1900–20) is based on a design by Gertrude Jekyll, freely interpreted—it contains roses that she would probably not have chosen. Above is the 1930s or Between the Wars garden, which includes many of the new roses produced at this time.

The Modern Garden—a simple design of circular beds—contains roses introduced since 1945 and associated by colour or breeder. The David Austin bed of old and English roses is particularly lovely. Nearby, below the TRellis Garden, a small bed has been set aside for roses of unknown date.

For a complete change of atmosphere and mood, walk due south (bypassing the horses' graves) and across the road to the Chapel Garden—a wild valley below a ruined Saxon church and free-standing stone arches. Many interesting trees can be found here, notably some seven specimens of *Acer palmatum*, well over 100 years old and probably Korean in origin. Victorian plantings of rhododendrons, now running wild, tower to one side of the chapel; inside are stone coffins and a baptismal font.

Norfolk Lavender

ADDRESS AND TELEPHONE: Caley Mill, Heacham, Norfolk PE31 7JE. Tel. Heacham (0485) 70384

OWNERS: Norfolk Lavender Ltd

DIRECTIONS: on the A419, Heacham

OPENING TIMES: all year, daily except Christmas week

ADMISSION: free. Coach parties telephone Joy Warner to make bookings for tours and meals and guided tours

CAR PARKING: yes

TOILETS: yes

REFRESHMENTS: yes

SHOP: yes

DOGS: yes

WHEELCHAIR ACCESS: yes. Toilets for the disabled: yes

PEAK MONTHS: June, July, August

NOTABLE FEATURES: lavender

If you like lavender, this is definitely the place to come. Billed as the 'home of English lavender', Norfolk Lavender is set in a wide open space near the sea, at Heacham on the north coast of Norfolk. The garden areas are arranged around a 19C corn mill, by the River Hitch (or Hetch) and include the National Collection of lavenders, a 'living dictionary' of many known named varieties, cutting beds, a rose garden and a general herb garden. On a sunny afternoon, you can have tea by the riverside—the air is deliciously scented from early through to late summer—or visit, if the weather is less good, the drying barn and distillery and the large Norfolk Lavender shop, finishing up with a cream tea in the Miller's Cottage tea room. Two guided tours are offered, one of the gardens and distillery, and another longer one, for coach parties, of the lavender fields about 10 miles away.

Norfolk Lavender began as a small two-man enterprise in the 1930s, when Lin (Linnaeus) Chilvers, a former market gardener, and Ginger Dustgate, another local man, began farming lavender on 4 acres of land and making oil from it, following an old George IV recipe. The enormous stills they used are still in good working order and in use, although more than 100 years old. Both men died in the 1950s, and the business was then taken over by the Head family. Now most people in the surrounding community have some connection with Norfolk Lavender, which remains a 'cottage industry' though on a rather grander scale. 100 acres of lavender plants are harvested every summer, providing 150 tons of lavender—of which 100 tons are distilled for oil and 50 tons used for drying.

Caley Mill itself was built in 1836 as a water-powered corn mill, driven by a 12ft iron waterwheel. The wheel is now gone—it was removed in the 1914–18 war and melted down for ammunition—and all that remains of the mill's original workings are the grinding stones, now set in circular beds near the mill, planted round with herbs and bedding plants. The bars on the mill's lower windows date from the time of the bread riots, following the Corn Laws passed 150 years ago—people caught trying to break into the mill were either hung or sent to Australia. After the Industrial Revolution, most small mills fell into disuse, but Caley Mill was used until 1919, for grinding the farmer's own personal supplies of corn.

The building is made of carrstone, a form of sandstone with a very high iron content (accounting for its colour, deep ginger red)—this was quarried locally, just up the road.

Like many other herbs, lavender was introduced to Britain by the

Romans, who enjoyed lavender oil baths and also used it as an antiseptic. The National Collection now contains around 50 different types. Housed here in rectangular wood-edged beds, the flowers range in colour from light grey-blue to deep purple; there are also white and pink varieties. No two lavenders have quite the same scent, and heights and flowering times also vary, but all like a warm sunny spot and light well-drained soil. All the lavender hybrids here are disease-resistant, grown from hardwood cuttings and pruned back hard every year in autumn, to prevent them from getting 'leggy'. Some of the bushes are at least 30 years old, and still in excellent shape. The plants come from all over the country— some supplied by Blooms of Bressingham, some by Culpepers, others by the Chelsea Physic Garden.

Oxburgh Hall

ADDRESS AND TELEPHONE: The Administrator, Oxburgh Hall, Oxborough, near King's Lynn, Norfolk PE33 9PS. Tel. Gooderstone (036 621) 258

OWNERS: The National Trust

DIRECTIONS: at Oxborough, 7 miles SW of Swaffham on S side of Stoke Ferry Road. Signposted off A134 and from Swaffham. Public transport: Downham Market station 10 miles

OPENING TIMES: garden, 30 March to end October, daily except Thurs and Fri 12–5.30. House 30 March to 30 September, Sat to Wed 1.30–5.30 (BH Mon 11–5.30), October, Sat and Sun 1.30–5.30

ADMISSION: £3.30; £2.50 for pre-booked parties of 15 or more (send sae to Administrator)

CAR PARKING: yes

TOILETS: yes

REFRESHMENTS: restaurant

SHOP: yes

DOGS: no, except guide dogs

WHEELCHAIR ACCESS: yes and to ground floor of house. Toilets for the disabled: yes

PEAK MONTHS: mid June to end August

NOTABLE FEATURES: French parterre

This well cared for National Trust garden is laid out around a vast 15C house, originally built to look as much as possible like a castle or fortress and surrounded by a deep moat. For more than five centuries, Oxburgh was the home of the Bedingfelds, an old Catholic family, until the late Dowager Lady Bedingfeld gave it to the National Turst in 1952. The Hall was extensively restored between 1830 and 1870 by the architect J.C. Buckler, who added decorative features such as the tall twisted terracotta chimneys.

The estate covers 36 acres; two full-time members of staff and two trainees are responsible for the gardens and grounds, including upkeep of woods and waterways. My Lady's Wood lies to the south-east, and there is also a Victorian Wilderness.

The formal—and perhaps most interesting—parts of the garden can be found between the Hall and the car park entrance, to the east. Most striking of all is a French *parterre de compartiment*, laid out in immense scrolls and fan-like patterns, with yews at intervals. This is an exact copy of a design illustrated in a 17C French book on gardening and laid out at Oxburgh in 1845. In former times, the box-edged beds would have been filled with coloured stones or coal—and in the last war, they were used for growing potatoes. The parterre then deteriorated, until rescued and restored by the National Trust. The bright green box hedges (of *Buxus semper-virens* 'Suffruticosa') have been retained and are still in excellent condition, although 70–100 years old, but the beds are now lined with perennials—*Cineraria maritima* 'Silver Dust', rue (*Ruta grave-olens* 'Jackman's Blue') and lamb's tongue (*Stachys lanata*)—and filled with bright annual bedding—marigold 'Yellow Boy' and ageratum 'Blue Blazer'. The circular centre bed holds the very old red pelargonium 'Paul Crample', red *Canna indica* and silver-leaved cineraria (*Senecio cineraria*).

Nearby, to the east, is the traditional herbaceous border, 75 yds long, backed by a red brick wall, covered with climbing roses and clematis, bordered with catmint and protected by a long yew hedge. The scheme is simple but effective, with blocks of colour repeated every 6 to 8 yds—yellows, blues, pinks—and a mirror effect at the centre. Yellow Jacob's Rod (*Asphodeline lutea*) is usually the first to flower, followed by blue monkshood. Pinks and reds arrive mid-season and pink tree mallow (*Lavatera olbia* 'Rosea') winds up the year. In all, 35 species are represented here. The wall clematis include blue 'Perle d'Azur', white 'Marie Boisselot' and lavender-blue 'Mrs Cholmondeley'.

Emerging to the south, you enter a grassy area backed by a wide canal. This is the feed stream, used for topping up the moat; levels are controlled by a series of sluice gates. The path above is being renewed and planted with what will eventually be a long undulating hedge of *Taxus baccata*; with red and green-stemmed cornus alternating on the far side of the stream.

The Chelsea border (taken from a design shown at Chelsea) runs parallel to the herbaceous border, between the feed stream and the walled orchard. Among the taller plants here are *Viburnum pli-catum tomentosum*, *V. carlesii* and *V. davidii*; also mahonias and some magnolias. At mid-height are rose-crimson hibiscus 'Wood-bridge' and pink deutzia. Pink spiraea 'Anthony Waterer' and yellow potentilla 'Elizabeth' flower at a lower level, with red and yellow daylilies and crown imperial fritillaries. Hostas are used throughout.

The old Victorian kitchen garden has been replanted as a small formal orchard, surrounded by red brick walls with castellated turrets, and a yew hedge. This grassy area is well stocked with small fruit trees, grown as half-standards or spires—quinces, plums and gages and two medlars (*Mespilus germanica* 'Nottingham').

Roses, clematis and honeysuckle flourish against the walls; also hops and bays, arching sweetspire (*Itea ilicifolia*) and potato vines (purple-blue *Solanum crispum* and white *S. jasminoides* 'Album').

The wire-vine or maidenhair vine (*Muehlenbeckia complexa*) makes dense green ground cover below the west-facing wall—this is recommended by Mr Donachie, the head gardener, as 'something different'.

To the north, near the entrance, are big mounds of white *Hebe rakaiensis*, surrounding *Cistus laurifolius* and bordered with sage. The single pink rose *R. complicata* grows opposite, in a border edged with lavender-blue geranium 'Johnson's Blue'—both flower at the same time, in early to mid summer.

The main south-facing border is dominated by whites and yellows, with one blue ceanothus. Cistus and potentillas mingle with sages (*Salvia officinalis* 'Icterina' and 'Purpurascens'). The hardy or trifoliate orange (*Poncirus trifoliata*) produces white flowers in late spring, before the leaves, but is somewhat unreliable. A large bladder senna (*Colutea arborescens*) flowers yellow all summer; nearby is *Piptanthus laburnifolius*, with yellow laburnum-like flowers. *Vitis coignetiae* grows over the wall, its leaves turning gold in September/October. At the far end of the bed is *Santolina neapolitana*, very quick-spreading and recommended by Mr Donachie over the smaller *S. chamaecyparissus*; also senecio 'Sunshine'.

A cold east-facing border holds philadelphus and viburnum interspersed with potentillas; again, the focus is on light-coloured flowers, anchored by a clump of mauve-flowered *Bergenia cordifolia*. *Epimedium pinnatum* is recommended for its brightly tinted leaves in autumn.

The nursery and greenhouse area to the right is private, but contains one very interesting feature, visible from the gate—a collection of rare 17C striped tulips. Peaches, apricots and nectarines grow against the back wall.

Finally, take a look at the Francham border, just east of the parterre. Polyanthus 'Gold Lace', with its jewel-like yellow and black flowers, was a gift from nearby Felbrigg. Lilies of the valley flower in late spring, and pink and white *Crinum* x *powellii* in summer and early autumn.

Sandringham

ADDRESS AND TELEPHONE: Estate Office, Sandringham, Norfolk, PE35 6EN. Tel. King's Lynn (0553) 772675

OWNER: HM The Queen

DIRECTIONS: off the A149, King's Lynn to Hunstanton road. Clearly signposted

OPENING TIMES: 21 April to 30 September, Mon, Tues, Wed, Thurs 10.30–5, Sun 11.30–5. House also open. Garden closed 26 July to 7 August; house closed 22 July to 10 August

ADMISSION: house and grounds £2.20, OAPs £1.70, children £1.70. Grounds only £1.70, OAPs £1.30, children £1. No reductions for coach parties

CAR PARKING: yes

TOILETS: yes

REFRESHMENTS: café

SHOP: yes, plant sales

DOGS: no

WHEELCHAIR ACCESS: yes. Toilets for the disabled: yes

PEAK MONTHS: June, July, August

Sandringham House and the estate have been owned by the Royal Family for over 100 years. The red-brick house, with decorative gables and imposing chimneys, is surrounded by vast lawns and shrubberies, with two fine lakes to the south-east. While many of the trees and shrubs are long established, special garden features have been added through the years and Mr Fred Waite, the head gardener, is constantly developing new planting schemes with the assistance of his staff of 12–15. Many of the plants and trees are raised in the estate's own private glasshouses.

The approach to the garden, along the perimeter wall, leaves no doubt that you are nearing a sizeable estate. Even the trees in the car park are enormous. The first view from the entrance door confirms the scale of the grounds and sets their style: generous groups of trees set in the lawns; high banks of shrubs—particularly rhododendrons and azaleas—flourishing under conifers and broad leaved trees; and an underplanting of smaller shrubs and herbacous plants.

Imaginative colour combinations are to be seen as soon as you enter: against a background of dark yews and conifers—*Cupressocyparis leylandii* and a gold cupressocyparis 'Castlewellan'. A collection of potentillas flowers surprisingly well out of direct sun. Nearby are two magnolias—*M.* 'Pinkie' and *M. procteriana*, with white, star flowers—and a range of camellias.

On the first bed facing the lawn we saw pinky-white *Viburnum* x *carlcephalum* and the very fragrant *V.* x *burkwoodii* 'Anne Russell', set attractively against *Berberis thunbergii* 'Harlequin' and *Berberis thunbergii* 'Red Chief'; and bright yellow-leaved *Cornus alba* 'Aurea' backed by a dark tree heath.

The trees here are of a great height: mostly pine, yew and spruce, with limes and a metasequoia. Following the path you come to a large bed of lavenders. A sizeable collection of shrub roses stands left of the path and a planting of hydrangeas to the right. Some of the specimen trees here are mentioned in the official guide, including two *Cercidiphyllum japonicum*, with low-branching but upright trunks, and heart-shaped leaves which colour spectacularly in autumn. There is also a colourful group of *Rhododendron kaempferi*; and nearby a very beautiful white camellia, *C. japonica* 'Haku-rakuten' and rhododendron 'Polar Bear', which flowers in summer. A collection of pieris includes the spectacular 'Everest' and the more modest 'Scarlett O'Hara'.

By now you have reached the Norwich Gates, and it is difficult to avoid the word 'majestic' when describing the planting. High banks of rhododendrons edge the drive and groups of bright-leaved acer are set against dark yews and specimens of the purple beech *Fagus sylvatica* 'Riversii'. There are also smaller unexpected pleasures, such as a collection of small thuyas.

Up to now the garden has been planted with carefully planned informality; but at this point you come to the north point of the formal garden laid out for King George VI by Geoffrey Jellicoe (who had also re-designed the royal lodge in Windsor Great Park). Two statues mark the change of style: one is the Chinese Joss, a spectacular gold-plated, bronze figure of the Buddhist divinity Kuvera, presented to the Prince of Wales in 1869. The other is a more restrained grey stone statue of Father Time, winged and carrying an hour glass and scythe. From these markers, avenues of pleached limes stretch towards the north front of the house, their branches entwined overhead as well as at the sides. In the centre are formal beds.

One particularly effective and relatively recent planting stands out across the lawn from the formal garden: bright trees, notably *Acer pseudoplatanus* 'Brilliantissimum' against a background of dark yew and holly; three Himalayan whitebeams (sorbus 'Mitchellii'), a silver lime (*Tilia tomentosa*), three silver weeping pears (*Pyrus salicifolia* 'Pendula') and a snow gum (*Eucalyptus niphophila*) with attractive peeling bark.

From the formal garden, take the path around the house, where a huge wisteria spreads its tendrils around the windows, and downwards over the west lawn to the two lakes. On the west side of the upper lake is a great cliff of rock outcrops planted with dark and gold conifers and acers of contrasting foliage colour. This effective planting can be seen best from the east bank, which slopes down more gently to the lake edge and is bright with polyanthus in the spring. The north bank, where a stream enters the lake, has been planted with damp-loving plants: dark red-leaved rogersias, pink-headed peltiphyllum, and dark red *Rheum palmatum*, with hostas, irises, hemerocallis (day lilies) the bending wands of Solomon's seal and the cream-coloured tufts of false Solomon's seal (*Smilacina racemosa*). There is a gold-leaved tulip tree, *Liquidambar styraciflua* 'Aurea'.

At the head of the lower lake, the stream pours down over the rocks below a striking group of conifers: a golden Himalayan cedar (*Cedrus deodara* 'Aurea Nana'), a feathery *Cryptomeria japonica* and the spreading *Juniperus media* 'Old Gold'. A graceful weeping birch (*Betula pendula* 'Youngii') rises from their midst.

There are many fine trees planted in the area of the lakes and it is pleasant to wander through them: many venerable and knobbly oaks, copper beech, willows, and cedars. Some of the English oaks are said to be over 800 years old. The careful labelling of plants does not always extend to trees and this would add interest to the walks.

NORTHAMPTONSHIRE

Canons Ashby House

ADDRESS AND TELEPHONE: Canons Ashby House, Canons Ashby, Daventry, Northamptonshire NN11 6SD. Tel. (0327) 860044

OWNERS: The National Trust

DIRECTIONS: on B4525 Northampton to Banbury road (Banbury 10 miles). Public transport: not reasonable (Banbury BR 10 miles)

OPENING TIMES: Easter to end October, Wed to Sun and BH Mon 1–5.30. House open

ADMISSION: £2.50, children £1.20. Coach parties by arrangement (reductions)

CAR PARKING: yes

TOILETS: yes

REFRESHMENTS: afternoon teas (light lunches for pre-booked groups)

SHOP: guidebooks, etc

DOGS: on lead in paddock only

WHEELCHAIR ACCESS: limited by steps, good views from top terrace but three steps to negotiate. Telephone for special arrangements. Toilets for the disabled: yes

PEAK SEASON: April and May for bulbs, June to August for flowers

NOTABLE FEATURES: formal garden in style of London and Wise; borders of bulbs, roses and herbaceous plants; formal orchard; 70 acres of parkland

Northamptonshire has many great country houses. Canons Ashby is modest compared to some, but it is one of the oldest. Its name is derived from the priory of Augustinian canons founded here in the 12C; the medieval priory church still survives close to the house.

The house itself was built of ironstone in the 1550s by John Dryden of Cumbria after he married into the Cope family. Later generations of Drydens extended and improved the house but few alterations have been made since the early 18C.

By the 1960s the structure was decaying through lack of attention and in 1980 the property was offered to the National Trust. Duly restored, Canons Ashby was opened to the public in 1984.

The gardens have also undergone a great deal of restoration. The formal design of terraces, high walls set with vases and the axial arrangement of paths reflects the style of London and Wise, although there is no proof of any involvement by this outstanding garden design partnership. The layout is known to date from around 1710 when Edward Dryden, cousin of the poet laureate John Dryden, owned the property.

The garden received a great deal of publicity at the end of the last century with plans and descriptions appearing in several publications—Alicia Amherst's *History of Gardening* (1895), H. Inigo Trigg's *Formal Gardens of England and Wales* (1902) and

Country Life (1904 and 1921)—and it was an important influence on garden designers at that time.

The west door of the house opens onto the Green Court—an intimate, walled courtyard which was used as the main entrance until the mid 19C, when it was turfed over by Sir Henry Dryden. Down the centre of the court four pairs of yews have been cut back and clipped from giant overgrown specimens to an avenue of tall dark green cones. At the end of the avenue stands a lead statue of a Shepherd Boy, attributed to Van Nost who was also responsible for the coat of arms portrayed in lead over the west door.

Beyond the Shepherd Boy, dividing the Green Court from the parkland, the original 1710 gates hang between handsome gate piers capped with obelisk finials. These wooden gates of ornate design were found discarded beneath rubble in the coach house when the National Trust acquired the property. They have been restored using as much of the original oak as possible.

The design of the Green Court is simple. Flowers—mainly white—are restricted to the narrow borders below the enclosing walls. Morello cherries are trained against one wall, and old pear varieties in espalier form along the other.

A doorway in the south wall leads through to the main formal garden lying below the south front of the house. Towering above the wall is a huge cedar tree, at least 210 years old and the only one of six to have survived a disastrous gale in 1947. A sizeable portion of this tree was blown down in the gales of January 1990, damaging one of the clipped yews, the wall and destroying one of the original stone vases.

Four terraces descend to the south, described in 1711 as the 'best garden', the 'upper garden', the 'lower garden' and the 'little one below'. The lowest terrace was also referred to as a 'wilderness'.

During restoration the original symmetrical design of gravel paths was traced and uncovered, dead trees and shrubs were cleared, yews cut back to their intended topiary shapes and a great deal of re-turfing and planting done.

Herbaceous borders of the type probably planted by Sir Henry Dryden have been re-established below the house and along the wall separating the formal garden from the Green Court. This latter border contains daffodils such as the double narcissi 'Cheerfulness' and 'Van Sion'. Tulips include the May-flowering creamy-white 'Niphetos'. There are also numerous varieties of irises.

In summer, the old garden rose 'Cardinal de Richelieu' blooms rich vinous purple and the double 'Tuscany Superba', maroon-violet. Geraniums, lavenders, santolina, germander and other perennials fill in the gaps. Shrubs lend permanence to the border.

Flights of stone steps descend the grassy terraces following the north–south axis. The lowest terrace is planted with old varieties of fruit trees planted in a formal and decorative orchard. Around the perimeter are old varieties of soft fruit—red- and blackcurrants and gooseberries underplanted with primulas.

In the south-west corner of the garden is a garden seat, one of two that have survived from the early 18C. From its timber canopy it looks across the park where some of the formal lime avenues have been reinstated. Another, newly planted, avenue leads across the paddock to the priory church.

Castle Ashby

ADDRESS AND TELEPHONE: Castle Ashby Gardens, near Northampton, Northamptonshire. Tel. Yardley Hastings (060 129) 234

OWNER: The Marquess of Northampton

DIRECTIONS: 7 miles E of Northampton off A428

OPENING TIMES: daily all year round 10–6 or dusk if earlier. House not open

ADMISSION: £1, OAPs/children 50p. Coach parties by arrangement

CAR PARKING: yes

REFRESHMENTS: tea rooms in the village

SHOP: farm shop in the village

DOGS: on lead

WHEELCHAIR ACCESS: yes. Toilets for the disabled: no

PEAK MONTHS: spring

NOTABLE FEATURES: terraces with unique terracotta balustrading; formal Italian garden with orangery and screen by Sir Matthew Digby Wyatt; arboretum; parkland and lakes by Capability Brown; nature trail in woodland. The terraces are *not* open to the public and there is very limited access to the parkland; two guided walks a year

Henry Compton began building the present mansion at Castle Ashby in the 1570s. It would probably have been surrounded by formal Elizabethan gardens but when the diarist John Evelyn visited 'My Lord Northampton's Seat', he found little to interest him except some wrought iron gates: 'They were now inlarging the gardens in which was nothing extraordinary but the Iron gate, opening into the Parke'. However in 1695, perhaps spurred on by a visit from King William, Lord Northampton began creating four large avenues of trees radiating out to the points of the compass.

The avenues are clearly shown on a survey made in 1760. A year later the 7th Earl employed Capability Brown to landscape the grounds. His instructions included 'pulling down the old ice house and building a new one in a very expensive manner and place', and making a sunk fence and wall between the deer park and kitchen garden.

Brown also prepared a 'Great general plan for Castle Ashby' and, although the 7th Earl died abroad in 1763, Brown was able to complete his plans of work for the 8th Earl. So it was that he set about removing the avenues to the north, east and west of the house. Only the south avenue was spared and can be seen today stretching across the landscape for 3½ miles to the deer park at Yardley Chase. To the north and east, Brown created the menagerie and Park Ponds, and he planted many trees—oaks, beeches, chestnuts and a few cedars—in the parkland. On the far side of the Menagerie Pond, to the north of the house, a temple served to screen the menagerie.

Few changes were made to Brown's landscape until the mid 19C when, in keeping with Victorian taste, some formality was brought to bear on the area immediately surrounding the house—until the 1860s, the parkland came right up to the house walls. The terracotta terraces were constructed at this time, to the east, and these remain one of the garden's most magnificent features.

They were designed by the architect Sir Matthew Digby Wyatt on instructions of the 3rd Marquess. In strong contrast to the surrounding parkland, they were ornamented with intricate parterres and topiary works. For reasons of economy, they were grassed over during the 1970s and the topiary removed but they are now undergoing a partial restoration.

The chief attraction of the terraces, however, is the terracotta balustrading by J.M. Blashfield of Stamford. Like the house parapet, this balustrading incorporates a number of biblical messages, running round the terraces: 'Consider the lilies of the field how they grow, they toil not neither do they spin. And yet I say to you that Solomon in all his glory was not arrayed like one of these' and 'The grass withereth and the flower fadeth but the word of God endureth forever'. But sadly, due to the delicate condition of the terracotta balustrading, and its close proximity to parts of the house used for functions and conferences, visitor access to the terraces has had to be restricted, but can be viewed from a distance.

The parish church to the south of the terrace is so close that it almost seems to be part of the garden and the Latin inscription on the balustrading nearby is a dedication to the wife of the 3rd Marquess, who died before the terraces were completed. Translated it reads: 'To Theodosia, sweetest of wives, Douglas Northampton has erected this. Begun in hope, finished in regret'.

To the south of the churchyard is the rectangular Italian garden. Dating from the 1860s, this occupies the site of an 18C kitchen garden. Straight paths, flanked by dumpy shaped topiary cones and large terracotta vases, divide the garden into symmetrical quarters. At the centre are terracotta benches backed by Italian cypresses (*Chamaecyparis lawsoniana* 'Erecta'). Around the garden edges the bosquet planting is dominated by large golden yews surrounded by flowering shrubs.

In the original design the sunken lawns to either side of the paths were laid out with intricate beds, edged with box and filled with coloured gravels and crushed stone. They are now grassed over. The magnificent terracotta vases are still planted each year with spring flowers and summer bedding plants.

Sir Matthew Digby Wyatt designed the orangery and the arched screen at the opposite end of the walk. The orangery faces south, with its tall centrepiece and pavilions at each end. It is home to a wide selection of conservatory shrubs and climbers.

An old mulberry tree stands on the lawn outside the orangery. This is thought to have survived from the kitchen garden. In the woodland to the rear is an old horse chestnut (*Aesculus hippocastanum*), almost 100ft tall and known affectionately as the Family Tree because several of the branches, touching the ground, have layered to produce new offspring.

At the opposite end of the Italian garden from the orangery is Wyatt's Archway, an elaborate arched screen concealing glasshouses. The central arch leads into a further walled garden, divided by tall hedges into several compartments—some with flower borders, others simply grassed and set about with statues. A circular hedge encloses a quiet pool and nearby is a summerhouse. The Victorian kitchen garden, now used by the farm, lies further south. It was designed by E.W. Godwin, who also designed the avenue lodges. To the east, the spring walk, planted with flowering cherries and daffodils, takes you towards the arboretum. Nearby are three large specimens of *Acer cappadocicum*, known for their rich butter-yellow foliage in autumn.

The arboretum was probably begun about the same time as the terraces and the Italian garden, and now contains some very fine trees, including pines, spruces and cryptomerias. There is a young dawn redwood (*Metasequopia glyptostroboides*) with bright green feathery foliage in summer, turning brownish-pink and rich gold in autumn. One of the best trees in the garden is the weeping beech (*Fagus sylvatica* 'Pendula'), now cabled for stability, but a splendid sight, especially in spring when the young fresh green leaves are opening. Also in this area is the tall columnar incense cedar (*Calocedrus decurrens*). The grassland in the arboretum is managed as a hay meadow to encourage a diversity of native wild flowers.

At the eastern edge of the arboretum are the Warren ponds—a string of pools crossed at one end by the Bathstone Bridge and at the other by the 'Terracotta Bridge'. Mixed woodland surrounding the ponds also contains some magnificent trees, including oaks, wellingtonias, Bhutan pines (*Pinus wallichiana*) and horse chestnuts.

From the Terracotta Bridge Brown's Park Pond stretches northwards. Its maker was so pleased with his work that he exclaimed 'Thames, Thames, thou wilt never forgive me!'. This pond is constructed so that it curves away out of sight—suggesting a river or endless stretch of water. It is perfectly situated and contributes greatly to the peace and repose of this typical Brown landscape.

Coton Manor

ADDRESS AND TELEPHONE: Coton Manor, Eaton, Northamptonshire, NN6 8RQ. Tel. Northampton (0604) 740219

OWNER: Commander Pasley-Tyler

DIRECTIONS: near Ravensthorpe, between A50 (Leicester to Northampton road) and A428 (Crick to Northampton road). Well signposted

OPENING TIMES: Easter to end September, Sun and BH 2–6; also June to August every Wed 2–6. Coach parties on other days by appointment. House not open

ADMISSION: £2.50, OAPs £2, children 50p

CAR PARKING: yes

TOILETS: yes

REFRESHMENTS: tea room

SHOP: giftshop and nursery

DOGS: on short lead only

WHEELCHAIR ACCESS: limited (steps). Toilets for the disabled: no

PEAK SEASON: May, June and July for herbaceous borders; October for autumn colours

NOTABLE FEATURES: rose garden; water features and water garden; autumn colours; herbaceous and unusual plants

Coton Manor has a marvellous collection of colourful and unusual birds, including flamingoes, mandarin, pintail and tufted ducks, Ross's snow and emperor geese, demoiselle cranes. The garden is designed to reduce risk of damage to its plants, with terraces, appropriate planting, and where needed, fencing.

Although there has been a manor at Coton since Domesday, the present gardens date entirely from this century. The first manor house was razed to the ground after the Battle of Naseby a few miles away. It was replaced in 1662 with a modest farmhouse constructed of mellow Northamptonshire ironstone, situated on rising ground overlooking farmland. In 1925, the house was bought by Mr and Mrs Harold Bryant, who extended it considerably. No garden existed at that time, except for a kitchen garden, but the Bryants soon transformed the surrounding 6 acres of land.

The kitchen garden was turned into a rose garden and terraces were built around the house, using York stone as paving and local stone for the retaining walls. The spring-fed farm pond, below the house, was shaped to form a large rectangular pool and where it overflowed a water garden was created. Trees were established around the garden perimeter and hedges planted to make a series of interrelated gardens, on different levels. The garden was neglected during the war years, but the basic layout remained intact and a period of restoration followed. In 1950 Commander and Mrs Pasley-Tyler (daughter of the garden's creators) took over Coton Manor. They continued to restore and improve the garden with energy and skill and began to introduce birds—starting with a pair of surface feeding ducks, to tackle algae on the pond.

The garden door leads onto the south-facing terrace, a fine viewing platform. Below, a neatly mown lawn, edged with thickly planted herbaceous borders, slopes down to the pool.

At one end of the terrace, near the garden door, a wall fountain trickles water into a small pool; at the other end is a holly arbour, clipped into a cuboid shape, with seats set in recesses. Round the corner of the house is the rose garden, on the highest of three levels, descending to the pool.

Sheltered by the house, the loggia (built in 1954), and old yew and holly hedges, the rose garden features a circular design of white and pink roses centring on a planting of peonies and edged with silver-leaved plants. More silver-leaved plants, including *Salvia microphylla* (*S. grahamii*) and the pale purple-blue flowering *Abutilon (Corynabutilon) vitifolium* grow in the raised border at the end of the loggia.

Also in the rose garden is a fine *Cestrum parqui*, with yellow-green flowers fragrant at night and *Clerodendrum trichotomum*, with clusters of beautiful starry white flowers.

East of the rose garden is a small informal woodland area, reached through a gateway in the yew hedge. Here is a huge tulip tree (*Liriodendron tulipifera*) which turns rich butter-yellow each autumn; also maples, horse chestnuts and beeches. In the shade of these great trees grow foxgloves, hellebores, hepaticas, wood anemones (*Anemone nemorosa*), trilliums and hostas.

In June and July the garden's herbaceous borders are at their best. The main border with a broad grassy walk lies on the level below the rose garden and is backed by the old holly hedge. Peonies, asphodels, lilies (*Lilium pyrenaicum*), astrantias and phlox fill the border with flowers in mainly pastel shades and good foliage.

The next level down is occupied mainly by the water fowl pool and lawns. On one side of the pool is a large Japanese flowering cherry (prunus 'Kanzan'), dating from the garden's earliest years. In May it is heavily laden with pink blossom.

The pool, being spring fed, overflows at its eastern end, into a water garden. Lush green ferns and hostas line the stream on its way through pools, and many varieties of primula flower in spring. Yellow spathes of the skunk cabbage (*Lysichiton americanus*) and the pink flowers of the umbrella plant (*Peltiphyllum peltatum*) add interest, along with sweet-scented azaleas.

Old orchards and a goose park make up the lower parts of the garden. The orchard is now filled with bird enclosures. The fencing, where possible, has been masked by borders of shrubs and herbaceous plants. A south-facing bank of tender shrubs is planted with eucalyptus, eucryphia, several hebes and so on. Further along the bank are herbs and then lilacs, philadelphus and shrub roses.

The goose park was added in 1971, increasing the size of the garden to 10 acres. A former field, it was transformed by mixed plantings of trees, shrubs and herbaceous plants with the emphasis on late summer flowering and autumn colour. Among the trees are the sweet gum (*Liquidambar styraciflua*), with glorious crimson foliage in autumn, and the paper bark maple (*Acer griseum*), with scarlet autumn colouring, flaky bark and cinnamon coloured underbark. Cherries and viburnums add further interest.

Holdenby House Gardens

ADDRESS AND TELEPHONE: Holdenby House Gardens, Holdenby, Northampton. Tel. (0604) 770786/770241

OWNER: James Lowther, Esq

DIRECTIONS: 7 miles NW of Northampton. Off A428 and A50. Public transport: Northampton BR 7 miles

OPENING TIMES: April to September, Sun and BH Mon 2–6; also Thurs in July and August 2–6. House open by arrangement for pre-booked parties Mon to Fri

ADMISSION: garden £2, OAPs £1.50, children £1. House and garden £3, children £1

CAR PARKING: yes

TOILETS: yes

REFRESHMENTS: café

SHOP: yes, gifts and plants

DOGS: on leads

WHEELCHAIR ACCESS: difficult because of narrow gravel paths. Toilets for the disabled: yes

PEAK SEASON: July and August

NOTABLE FEATURES: replica Elizabethan garden; fragrant borders; shrub borders and border of grey/silver plants; traces of original Elizabethan garden with fish ponds; falconry centre; rare breeds of cattle, pigs and goats

Holdenby House once formed part of a magnificent palace built by Sir Christopher Hatton, Lord Chancellor to Queen Elizabeth I, one of the largest and most lavish houses of its day. Completed in 1583, the palace was built around two courtyards and had 123 huge glass windows. It also had a 20-acre garden and a large deer park. The whole project ruined Sir Christopher financially and when he died in 1591 he was £42,000 in debt. His heir was forced to transfer the property to the crown in lieu of these debts.

Over the following years Holdenby was frequently visited by King James I, and in 1647 Charles I was imprisoned here by Cromwell's army. After Charles's execution the palace was sold to a Parliamentarian, Captain Adam Baynes, for £22,229 6s 10d. Baynes demolished most of the palace and sold the stone. It is said that he sold enough stone to build nearby Coton Manor and a whole street in Northampton. Only the kitchen wing was left standing, which Baynes turned into a manor house. Although mainly Victorian, the present house contains quite a lot of the original Elizabethan stonework.

After the restoration of the monarchy in 1660 Holdenby House reverted to the Crown. Two years later the Crown sold Holdenby to Baron Lewis Duras. In 1709 the estate was purchased by the Dukes of Marlborough and was handed down through the Clifden and Annaly families. In 1945 it was inherited by Captain George Lowther, whose grandson, James Lowther, inherited in 1980.

Although Holdenby House is small in comparison to Sir Christopher's original palace, you can still get an idea of the size of the original building. Two arches, dated 1583, stand in a field to the east; these were the entrance arches to the basecourt of the palace.

There are two garden areas to explore. The inner garden lies around the house and includes Lady Clifden's 19C garden and a garden in Elizabethan style. The outer garden, the original 20 acres planned by Sir Christopher, is now mostly grassed over, but the shape of a 16C plateau and two flanking terraces can still be traced.

The inner garden is reached by passing through the stable courtyard. Lying just west of the house is the Elizabethan garden, enclosed by yew hedges and by the walls of the stables and the kitchen garden. This small garden was planned in 1980 by Mrs Rosemary Verey, its layout being a miniature replica of the beds laid out by Sir Christopher on the plateau in the 16C. Only plants which would have been available in 1580 have been used. The garden focuses on a central sundial surrounded by four varieties of thyme. Four inner beds, edged with santolina and variegated hollies, are each filled with blue flowers — cornflower, clary, echium and love-in-a-mist. The four outer beds contain lavender, rosemary, rue, hyssop, angelica, germander and others.

East of the Elizabethan garden lies a walled kitchen garden, one of two kitchen gardens on the estate; in this one, vegetables are still grown, along with flowers for cutting. There is a 'cuddle farm' for children, with ducks, rabbits and young goats. A herb garden has been established below the lean-to greenhouses.

The outer south-facing side of the kitchen garden wall shelters King Charles's Walk, reputedly Charles I's favourite walk during the time of his imprisonment at Holdenby. A border below the wall is filled with roses and perennials.

King Charles's Walk divides the Elizabethan garden from the Too Too border. Named in memory of a dog belonging to Lady Clifden's daughter, the Too Too border survives from Victorian days. In 1980 Rosemary Verey supervised the border's replanting, selecting plants for fragrance. The result is a mixture of shrubs and herbaceous plants. Phlox, sweet woodruff, night scented stocks and sage grow beneath musk roses, lilacs, philadelphus and buddleia.

More shrubs, rose and herbaceous plants fill the borders beside the croquet lawn, which is sunk in the west wing of Sir Christopher's great palace.

The south front of the present house is clad with wisteria and climbing roses 'Kiftsgate' and 'Wedding Day' and overlooks a gravelled walk and sloping lawns. The lawns descend to Sir Christopher's plateau and beyond that to the Elizabethan fish ponds, close to a 14C church where you can see the tombs of the De Holdenbys.

East of the house, within a yew hedged enclosure, is an ornamental fish pond with a statue of Hermes surrounded by colourful beds of flowers and standard roses. Another very attractive feature is the silver border beneath the south-facing wall of the second kitchen garden, known as the old kitchen garden. The wall marks the northern line of the old palace.

The old kitchen garden has been turned into a falconry centre—appropriate for the period of the estate—and also houses rare breeds of cattle, pigs and goats.

Lamport Hall

ADDRESS AND TELEPHONE: Lamport Hall, Lamport, Northampton NN6 9HD. Tel. (060128) 272

OWNERS: Lamport Hall Preservation Trust

DIRECTIONS: 8 miles N of Northampton on A508 to Market Harborough. Public transport: Northampton BR 8 miles

OPENING TIMES: Easter to end of September, Sun and BH 2.15–5.15; also Thurs in July and August. House also open

ADMISSION: £2.50, OAPs £2, children £1. Group visits by arrangement; prices on request

CAR PARKING: yes

TOILETS: yes

REFRESHMENTS: café

SHOP: yes

DOGS: no

WHEELCHAIR ACCESS: yes. House: ground floor only, including tea room. Toilets for the disabled: yes

PEAK SEASON: July and August

NOTABLE FEATURES: one of the earliest rock alpine gardens created in England, restored 1990; herbaceous borders; Italian garden; rose garden; parkland

Lamport Hall was the home of the Isham family for more than 400 years until Sir Gyles Isham, 12th Baronet, died in 1976 and left the Hall and its contents to the Lamport Hall Trust, which he had established two years earlier.

The Tudor house and grazing land were bought in 1560 by John Isham, a successful wool merchant. Over the centuries the Hall has been extended, altered and redesigned by such famous architects as John Webb (Inigo Jones's principal assistant), Francis and William Smith of Warwick, Henry Hakewill and William Burn. Changes to the house were accompanied by changes in the park and garden.

The west front and balustraded terrace overlook the present arrangement of parkland, which dates from 1823 and was designed by John Webb, a pupil of William Emes. The main area of garden lies to the south-east of the Hall.

The first garden at Lamport was planted by John Isham in the 16C but today's garden owes its basic rectangular layout to Gilbert Clerke, who was entrusted with its development between 1676 and 1679, while Sir Thomas Isham, 3rd Baronet, was in Europe. The raised walk, or terrace, from which perhaps a parterre was viewed, and the stone walls of the kitchen garden, survive from this period.

Much of the garden is now lawned, and divided by broad gravel walks, flanked by vases on pedestals. Towards the centre is a circular stone structure, a cock pit, thought to date from the 17C.

In 1750 Sir Edward Isham planted the lawns with seven groups of shrubs and edged them with box. A hundred years later these had become great 'box bowers' and all but one were removed. The survivor is situated towards the north-eastern boundary of the lawn and hides in its centre a revolving wooden summerhouse.

Sir Charles Isham (1819–1903), 10th Baronet, was a keen gardener and many of the present features date from his time. He planted the Irish yews along the inner side of the raised walk and extending into the Eagle Walk (so called because it led to a cage of eagle owls); and he was also responsible for the Italian garden in front of the drawing room windows. The box-edged beds of this garden were filled until recently with colourful displays of annuals, but these have now been replaced by labour-saving perennial plants. The garden centres on a shell fountain, and stone vases are placed here and there, adding to the formal effect.

Sir Charles's best known creation is the rockery, next to the Italian garden, and also visible from the house. Begun in 1848, this is one of the earliest rock gardens in England and was built to face north, to give the alpine plants a good chance of surviving the mild English climate.

The rockery stands over 20ft tall and is intended to resemble a steep alpine hillside, with miniature rocks, crevices and caves. Sir Charles planted slow-growing conifers, keeping them small by pruning and therefore in keeping with the scale. Some of these are still growing and others have been replanted, as have many varieties of alpines. In Sir Charles's time this rockery also featured a community of little people working in 'mines', thought to be the oldest garden gnomes in this country, imported from Nuremberg. Only one of Sir Charles's gnomes remains, on display in the Library, but replicas can be seen in the rockery.

Next to the rockery is a small rose garden, constructed around a rectangular lily pond. 19C and 20C roses grow in the borders—best seen in June.

There are other good borders below the kitchen garden walls. The section of brick wall dates from the 18C and was constructed on a series of underground arches, so that fruit trained against the south-facing side of the wall could put its roots through to the moist soil of the north side. The fruit trees were replaced during the last century by *Wisteria sinensis*, now of considerable size, with a rich herbaceous border below. Further south, the older stone wall supports another, even larger, wisteria, which was planted by Sir Charles in 1848. There are also splendid specimens of *Magnolia campbellii* and *M. grandiflora* and the border here is gradually being replanted, with the emphasis on blue and white-flowering plants, mostly selected from 19C plant lists.

Rockingham Castle

ADDRESS AND TELEPHONE: Rockingham Castle, Market Harborough, Leicestershire, LE16 8TH. Tel. Rockingham (0536) 770240

OWNER: Commander Michael Saunders Watson RN

DIRECTIONS: 2 miles N of Corby, off A6003 Oakham to Kettering road. Public transport: nearest station Kettering, nearest bus Corby

OPENING TIMES: Easter to end of September, Sun and Thurs, BH and Tues following BH, and Tues in August 1.30–5.30. Other days by appointment. Castle also open

ADMISSION: house and gardens £3, OAPs £2.40, children £1.50; gardens only £1.50. Reduced rates for parties by prior arrangement

CAR PARKING: yes

TOILETS: yes

REFRESHMENTS: tea room

SHOP: yes

DOGS: on lead in gardens

WHEELCHAIR ACCESS: ramp to main terraces, grass slopes to rest of gardens. Toilets for the disabled: yes, in house

PEAK MONTHS: no special peaks

NOTABLE FEATURES: Elephant yew hedge; formal gardens including rose garden; wild ravine garden

Built of a beautiful honey-coloured stone, which catches the sunlight, Rockingham Castle stands on an escarpment overlooking the quiet, green expanse of the Welland Valley—the picture of tranquillity, despite its somewhat turbulent history.

A stronghold in the reign of William the Conqueror, the castle was converted into a private royal residence in the 16C, when it was leased by Edward Watson. In 1619, Edward's grandson, Sir Lewis Watson, bought it from James I, and it has remained in the possession of the Watson family ever since. It was sacked by the Roundheads in the Civil War (as portrayed in the BBC television series *By the Sword Divided*, in which Rockingham Castle appears as Arnescote). The gardens, lying mainly to the west and south of the castle, reflect Rockingham's progress through the centuries.

Probably some form of garden has existed here since Norman times, for the growing of culinary and medicinal herbs and some fruit and vegetables. Records for 1100 show that Henry I spent 20 shillings on the planting of a vineyard. Formal gardens were established by Edward Watson, in the 16C, and have developed since into several distinct areas, with a ravine garden to the south. The present design owes much to the work of Richard and Lavinia Watson, who married in 1839 and were both keen gardeners.

The garden appears in Dickens' *Bleak House*. Staying here as a guest of the Watson family, Dickens imagined the ghost of Lady Dedlock gliding down a walk into the wooded ravine.

One of the Rockingham's most unusual features is the Elephant Hedge. This double row of yews, said to have been planted 400 years ago by Edward Watson, has been shaped over the centuries into a succession of domes, now resembling a herd of elephants.

The flower garden on the terrace beyond the mammoth yew hedge is known as the Cross Garden. Designed by John Codrington for Mrs Wentworth Watson c 1910, it replaced Victorian flowerbeds. Its layout is simple and formal, the lawn being divided by cruciform paths edged with roses and lavender. At the centre is a sundial.

At the eastern boundary of the Cross Garden is the mount. Created possibly in the 16C out of the rubble of the Norman keep, the mount is terraced and covered in spring with daffodils and primroses. A straight gravel path runs below, flanked by a mixture of standard roses, including crimson 'National Trust' and the very fragrant, pearly white 'Margaret Merril'. A flight of steps ascends from the south end of the mount to the gate tower from which there is a glorious view over the castle and across the valley.

Around the corner of the tower is a border of tansy and feverfew, both well known for their medicinal powers, and beyond, the path brings you into a lawned area and the rose garden. Surrounded on three sides by the castle walls, the lawn is fringed by a long herbaceous border.

Circular in design and enclosed by a high yew hedge, the rose garden stands on the site of the old keep. The garden design follows the manuscript plan (on display in the house) of the 17C fortifications during the Civil War, and the statue in the centre marks where a cannon once stood. In summer, hybrid tea roses flower in the concentric beds.

A wooden stile gives access to the large expanse of green lawn, the old Tilting Ground, once used for tournaments and as a training area for the castle's guards. It is bounded to the south-west by a lime avenue, which marks the line of the castle's old ramparts.

Beyond, in a steeply sloping ravine, is the wild garden. This was first planted in the early part of the 19C by Richard and Lavinia Watson, as a typical Victorian shrubbery, with winding gravel paths and beds filled with evergreens and shrubs. It was then called The Grove. By 1965, it was hopelessly overgrown and the owner, Sir Michael Culme-Seymour, with advice from Kew Gardens, undertook to replant the garden with 200 species of trees and shrubs.

Today the wild garden is a very pleasant place to visit, peaceful and secluded, haunted by birdsong. In spring the banks are covered with primroses and daffodils. Among the shrubs are buddleias, mahonias, escalonias and viburnums. There are camellias too, followed in summer by hydrangeas and shrub roses beneath beeches and other trees. Ground cover is provided by dog's mercury.

At the bottom of the ravine are two ponds. These result from a 19C equivalent of a job-creation scheme—George Lewis Watson commissioned unemployed men in the local farming community to dig them. Willows and water plants now grace the pond edges and nearby is a spring-fed well which once provided the castle with water. An earlier design for a water garden by Paxton (on display in the house) was never actually implemented.

A choice of several fairly steep paths ascend from the wild garden, returning by the formal gardens to the castle.

NORTHUMBERLAND

Belsay Hall

ADDRESS AND TELEPHONE: Belsay Hall Castle and Gardens, Belsay, Newcastle upon Tyne, NE20 0DX. Tel. Belsay (0661) 881636

OWNERS: administered by English Heritage

DIRECTIONS: 14 miles NW of Newcastle upon Tyne on A696. Public transport: Newcastle BR 14 miles. Buses from Newcastle to Belsay then ¾ mile walk

OPENING TIMES: Good Fri or 1 April (whichever is earlier) to 30 September, daily 10–6; 1 October to Maundy Thurs or 31 March (whichever is earlier) Tues to Sun 10–4. Closed Mon. Castle, Manor House and Hall all open

ADMISSION: £1.90, OAPs, UB40s and students £1.50, under 16s 95p, under 5s free. Coach parties welcome

CAR PARKING: yes

TOILETS: yes

REFRESHMENTS: yes

SHOP: yes

DOGS: on lead

WHEELCHAIR ACCESS: special garden route to avoid any steps; wheelchairs available. Toilets for the disabled: yes

PEAK MONTHS: good all-year garden, but May/June for rhododendrons, September/October for heathers

NOTABLE FEATURES: terrace garden; magnolia terrace; winter garden; 6-acre quarry gardens; rare trees and shrubs

Not many estates in England can boast a medieval castle, a Jacobean manor house and a Georgian mansion, as well as pleasant and unusual gardens, all within a few hundred yards' walk. Lying less than 15 miles from the centre of Newcastle upon Tyne, on the borders between England and Scotland, Belsay sums up 600 years of Northumbrian history.

The castle, manor house and Hall are all remarkable in their own right, both historically and architecturally, but the landscape around them also has many interesting features and shows the changes in fashions over the centuries.

Much of the surrounding parkland was developed in the 18C—the lake, the folly and the serpentine drive date from this era. Between 1807 and 1815, Sir Charles Monck designed and constructed the Hall, sweeping away a whole village and a chapel in the process. The honey-coloured stone, flecked with iron, was taken from a quarry nearby (planned, and afterwards planted as an informal quarry garden) and the Hall was built on the plan of a perfect square of 100ft. The style strongly echoes Classical Greek architecture, strictly regular, with Doric columns and entablature. Belsay's substantial terraces were constructed around this time, emphasising the Hall's stark grandeur.

Sir Arthur Middleton, a grandson of Sir Charles altered the severe straight lines of the terraces by adding hedges to shelter a rose garden and magnolia terrace.

Today the terraces are definitely Belsay's most formal feature. They lead westwards from the Hall to a series of other gardens, culminating in the famous quarry gardens. The terrace gardens, with stone-edged beds and borders, are now planted in subtle mixtures of shrubs and herbaceous perennials. *Clematis macropetala* drapes over the sides of the steps from the grassed surrounds of the Hall onto the south-facing terrace. Further along another set of steps is flanked by *Hydrangea petiolaris*. In the border beneath the retaining wall, and in the raised stone beds on the terrace, magnolias, cistas, escallonias, pieris, phillyreas, skimmias, garrya, viburnums, acanthas, irises, geraniums and a whole host of other plants serve to provide interest at different times of the year.

Beyond the hedges at the western end of the formal terrace is a small rose garden. Hybrid musk roses such as 'Penelope' enjoy the shelter and seclusion here, along with Lady's mantle (*Alchemilla mollis*) and hosta 'Royal Standard'.

The gravel walk leads on through the magnolia terrace. One side of the walk is bounded by a mixed border of pinks and purples, providing colour and interest for much of the year, while on the opposite side a lawned area is planted with magnolias. Here is the rare *Magnolia fraseri* with its long leaves, and large, slightly fragrant, parchment-coloured flowers in May and June. On the southern edge is *Magnolia acuminata*, the cucumber tree—so named because of the shape and colour of the young fruit.

The Winter Garden, further west, has long parallel borders planted with labour-saving evergreens such as dwarf rhododendrons and heathers. A tall stone wall on the far side of the croquet lawn supports various vines, clematis and climbing roses such as the heavenly scented 'Mme Gregoire Staechelin'. A small doorway in the wall leads out of the winter garden, across the farm track and into the wild garden.

Sir Charles made a Picturesque garden in the old quarry (from which stone was cut to build the house). The 'floor' of the quarry remains level throughout, but the cliff faces get higher as you go deeper into the hillside, and their height is emphasised by a line of dark yews planted along the top. The carefully contrived but rough, uneven stone provides a perfect cool, damp habitat for a wide range of wild flowers and ferns.

More wild flowers can be seen in the meadow garden close to the quarry entrance, including meadow crane's bill, cowslips, colchicums, and fritillaries. Several interesting trees stand in the meadow. There is a pocket handkerchief tree (*Davidia involucrata*) and *Magnolia Kobus* and *Kewensis*, covered in white flowers in April. *Parrotia persica* to the south have attractive flaking bark and splendid crimson and gold leaves in autumn.

Towards the end of the meadow garden, the quarry faces close in on both sides, forming a cool corridor. The graceful tree on the north side is *Fitzroya cupressoides* and close by is a huge *Eucryphia glutinosa* which carries glorious white flowers in July and August.

On the opposite side is *Enkianthus campanulatus*, a small tree which towards the end of May has drooping racemes of coppery lily-of-the-valley-like flowers veined and flushed red. In the autumn it puts on another spectacular display, this time of crimson and yellow foliage.

The path leads through an archway created between the towering cliff faces. Here, tucked into a sheltered corner, is a tall Chusan palm (*Trachycarpus fortunei*). Beyond the archway the quarry opens out again. Fine species of rhododendrons bloom here from December to July, including *R. barbatum* with its delightful plum-coloured bark and blood red trusses of flowers. The quarry garden ends with another 'corridor' and a wooden door, from which a path leads off towards the castle and manor house.

Cragside

ADDRESS AND TELEPHONE: Cragside, Rothbury, Northumberland NE65 7PX. Tel. Rothbury (0669) 20333 (house), (0669) 21051 (country park)

OWNERS: The National Trust

DIRECTIONS: 13 miles SW of Alnwick, 1 mile N of Rothbury on B6341. Public transport: Morpeth BR 15 miles. Buses from Newcastle and Morpeth to Reivers Well Gate then ¾-mile walk

OPENING TIMES: park, 29 March to end October, daily 10.30–7; November to end March, Sat and Sun 10.30–4. House also open

ADMISSION: house and country park £3.50; country park only £2. Coach parties by prior arrangement

CAR PARKING: yes

TOILETS: yes

REFRESHMENTS: café

SHOP: yes

DOGS: yes, in country park

WHEELCHAIR ACCESS: there are special wheelchair routes to several parts but access is limited to others. Toilets for the disabled: yes

PEAK MONTHS: June

NOTABLE FEATURES: woodland with some fine specimen trees; pinetum; rhododendrons; lakes; rock garden (now being restored)

Cragside stands on the southern edge of Alnwick Moor, sur-rounded by the beautiful moorland and wooded dales of Northumbria. It is easy to understand why Sir William Armstrong was so impressed by the area when he visited Rothbury in the 1860s.

Lord Armstrong was a rich industrialist, inventor and engineer and the leading arms manufacturer in the country. He was also a nature lover, and he secured 20 acres of land between Debdon Burn and the River Coquet and built a small house half-way up the craggy hillside. Then he acquired more land, until eventually his estate covered more then 1700 acres.

Richard Norman Shaw was asked to alter the original house to the unique creation you see today, perched on a rocky outcrop and set with gables, towers and chimneys.

Besides building carriageways and paths—some up to 40 miles long—Lord Armstrong dammed streams, created lakes and cleared much heather and scrub. He also planted seven million trees, most of them conifers, to give shelter and protection from the cold east winds sweeping over the Northumbrian moorland.

The enormous rock garden, constructed by Lord Armstrong to look as natural as possible, plunges steeply from the house to the depths of the valley below, where it meets the Debdon Burn. Originally it would have held waterfalls and pools. After years of neglect, the rock garden is now being restored.

Cragside is also famous for its rhododendrons. Lady Armstrong, in 1906, wrote: 'the most striking season is the spring when the azaleas are out and the Rhododendra in full bloom, growing in their thousands right on the hillside, their beauty much emphasised by the huge grey boulders amongst which they flourish'.

The rhododendrons form a dense and sometimes impenetrable undergrowth. *Rhododendron ponticum* keeps the National Trust's Acorn Camp Volunteers very busy, but other rhododendrons and shrubs manage to hold their own, and look splendid in early summer. In September, heathers colour the surrounding moorland and hillsides.

A very pleasant woodland walk passes through part of the valley, roughly following the course of the Debdon Burn as it winds its way towards the River Coquet. Interesting conifers, planted by Lord Armstrong, can be seen on the slopes around the house, including fine examples of western hemlock (*Tsuga heterophylla*), Douglas fir (*Pseudotsuga menziesii*) and noble fir (*Abies procera*), all well over 100ft tall.

In the valley below the house, a gigantic Norway Spruce (*Picea abies*) has reached 150ft—only 6in. short of being the tallest specimen in the United Kingdom. Taller still is the massive Colorado or white fir (*Abies concolor*), growing to the east of the house and on the left of Dunkirk Drive. This specimen is 157ft tall.

The Californian red fir (*Abies magnifica*), Canadian or Eastern hemlock (*Tsuga canadensis*), ornamental tiger tail spruce (*Picea polita*), Nootka or stinking cypress (*Chamaecyparis nootkatensis*), Swiss arolla pine (*Pinus cembra*) and blue Colorado spruce (*Picea pungens glauca*) also do well.

Flowing beneath the woodland canopy, the Debdon Burn is crossed by a rustic bridge. This is a replica of one which existed in Lord Armstrong's day but which was destroyed earlier this century, probably by floods.

A little further along you can see the magnificent iron bridge made at Lord Armstrong's Elswick Works on the River Tyne between 1870 and 1875. This was probably the first structure of its type and scale to be constructed in steel.

Lord Armstrong created a series of lakes to power hydraulic machinery—his was the first house to be lit by electricity from water power. Since the National Trust aquired Cragside in 1977 it has restored much of Lord Armstrong's original machinery and equipment. Today a circular walk, called the Power Circuit, links the Armstrong Energy Centre with Tumbleton Lake, the ram or pump house and the power house where the turbine and dynamo were located.

There are more than 30 miles of footpaths at Cragside—and for motorists, a one-way driveway around the perimeter of the estate, with seven car parks. Trout fishing boats are available on Tumbleton lake.

The country park is jointly managed by the National Trust and the Northumberland County Council and supports a variety of habitats—mainly woodland, lakes, wetland and grassland. Natural flora and many fungi have been noted and the park is renowned for birds. You may also see red squirrels.

Herterton House

ADDRESS TELEPHONE: Herterton House, Hartington, Near Cambo, Morpeth, Northumberland NE61 4BN. Tel. (067) 074 278

OWNERS: Frank and Marjorie Lawley

DIRECTIONS: 2 miles N of Cambo. Off the B6342. No public transport available

OPENING TIMES: mid April to mid October, daily except Tues and Thurs 1.30–5.30. House not open

ADMISSION: £1. Coach parties by prior arrangement

CAR PARKING: yes

TOILETS: yes

REFRESHMENTS: no

SHOP: nursery

DOGS: no

WHEELCHAIR ACCESS: no (paths gravelled and very narrow). Toilets for the disabled: no

PEAK SEASON: June to August

NOTABLE FEATURES: many rare and unusual hardy 'cottage' flowers; physic garden with herbs; small formal garden with topiary

Before 1976 this small but very beautiful garden was a disused farmyard, the house (c 1540) and the outbuildings were derelict, and the land, littered with rubble and broken implements, was waist high in stinging nettles.

In 1975, Frank and Marjorie Lawley began restoring the house, clearing the site and bringing in soil. The result today is a delightful and totally individual garden, with a nursery specialising in hardy cottage garden flowers, including a great many unusual or rare specimens. The plants have to be hardy, to survive the harsh cold winters; the exposed site is 700ft above sea level.

There are three separate garden areas. The tiny formal garden fronts onto the roadside and is a gold and green, evergreen garden. The centrepiece is a range of topiary features—small, in keeping with the scale of the garden and carefully clipped from yew and four different varieties of box.

Box-edged beds of dicentras, lilies and crown imperials add to the beauty of this small garden. The house wall is buried under honeysuckles, ivies, winter and summer flowering jasmines and a sweetly scented form of white *Clematis montana* 'Wilsonii'.

A gravelled walk edged with cream and white 'fumitory' leads into the heart of the old farmyard, now the physic garden. Laid out as a knot, this charming garden contains geometric beds of medicinal herbs such as tansy, southernwood, camphor, hyssop and many more, edged with Elliott's London pride *(Saxifraga* x *urbium* 'Elliott's Variety'). A clipped silver weeping pear stands in the centre. Roses also grow here, and the surrounding walls of the farmhouse and buildings support honeysuckles; in summer, the air is heavy with fragrance.

A walled flower garden to the rear is the largest garden area. Here are more geometric beds, planted to an overall colour scheme, profuse in summer and bounded by neat gravel paths. There is a collection of old-fashioned daisies, also pinks, wallflowers, campions and buttercups. Polemoniums, campanulas, violas, geraniums and geums grow in great variety.

Several hundred plant varieties are available for sale in the adjacent nursery area.

Howick Hall

ADDRESS AND TELEPHONE: Howick Hall, Howick, Alnwick, Northumberland. Tel. Longhoughton (0665) 577285

OWNERS: Howick Trustees Ltd

DIRECTIONS: near Howick (village) 6 miles NE of Alnwick (village of Howick is off the B1339). Public transport: Alnmouth BR 6 miles

OPENING TIMES: Easter to end of October (depending on autumn colours), daily 2–7. House not open

ADMISSION: £1, OAPs and children 50p

CAR PARKING: yes

TOILETS: yes

REFRESHMENTS: no

SHOP: no

DOGS: on lead

WHEELCHAIR ACCESS: with care. Toilets for the disabled: no

PEAK MONTHS: May and June

NOTABLE FEATURES: rhododendrons in woodland garden; terraces; meadows

The east coast of Northumbria is often subjected to freezing winds which sweep in from the North Sea with a penetrating coldness. Yet, only a mile inland stands Howick Hall where woodland shelter provides a sympathetic climate for many tender plants.

Howick Hall, seat of the Grey family, dates from the 18C but its fine woodland garden was not planted until the early 1930s. It is an excellent example of wild gardening after the style of William Robinson.

Although most of the land at Howick Hall is neutral, an acidic area of some 4 or 5 acres was discovered in the woodland, and here Lord Grey decided to plant rhododendrons. A variety of tender trees and shrubs also managed to survive in this sheltered situation.

The result today is a memorable walk through a mature woodland setting, with winding paths opening here and there into pleasant glades. Besides the rhododendrons, there are magnolias and hydrangeas and a collection of acers; underplanted with colchicums, daffodils, primulas, trilliums and meconopsis.

Rhododendrons seem to grow particularly well at Howick. The season starts in February and March with rhododendron 'Praecox' and *R. sutchuenense*. The latter is an outstanding Chinese shrub which makes a magnificent show of pink bell-shaped flowers spotted with purple.

By April many of the rhododendrons are flowering. Particularly noteworthy is *R. williamsianum* with its heart-shaped leaves and splendid bell-like shell-pink flowers. Another which is especially good in woodland conditions is *R. macabeanum*, with handsome shiny dark leaves, often 12in. long, and huge trusses of pale yellow flowers blotched with purple.

By May, the garden is a riot of colour. One of the finest rhododendrons must be the blue flowering *R. augustinii* and *R.a.* 'Electra' which bears clusters of startling violet-blue flowers.

There is a wonderful variety of colours and shades. Pure white 'Loder's White' produces trusses of wide funnel-shaped flowers. Soft pink *Rhododendron Loderi* 'King George', perhaps the best of the Loderi hybrids, is easily identified by its enormous trusses of trumpet-shaped 'tissue pink' flowers. For a stronger pink there is *R. L.* 'Pink Diamond'. The dwarf rhododendron nearby, carrying waxy bells of glistening dark crimson, is 'Carmen'. Yellow is represented by rhododendron 'Yellow Hammer'.

Flowers are not the only part of a rhododendron to bring colour to the garden: there is the plum-coloured bark of *R. macro smithii*. No rhododendron collection is complete without a specimen of *R. decorum* and this large, beautiful, Chinese species can be found showing off its shell-pink fragrant flowers near to *R. macro smithii*. Several pieris can be found in the woodland, especially *Pieris formosa forrestii* with its brilliant red young growths.

Magnolias are well represented at Howick. There are two magnificent specimens of *Magnolia campbellii*, one of which is over 40ft tall while near to the towering *Rhododendron Loderi* 'King George' is *M. campbellii mollicomata* whose flowers are like rose pink water lilies. There are also notable specimens of *M. salicifolia*, *M. sinensis*, *M. watsonii* and *M. kobus*.

Many more flowering trees and shrubs can be enjoyed in the woodland garden. The handsome winter's bark (*Drimys winteri*) carries fragrant, ivory-coloured flowers in May, accompanied by the soft pink flowers of *Sorbus cashmiriana* and the dark purple ones of honey-scented *Pittosporum tenuifolium*. July sees the free-flowering elegance of *Genista aetnensis*, the Mount Etna broom.

Many visitors also come to the woodland garden in the autumn to see the fiery reds and oranges of the acers and other trees. *Acer griseum* is particularly splendid in the fall with red and scarlet leaves as well as flaky, peeling bark. *Acer davidii*, *A. rufinerve* and *Eucryphia glutinosa* also have attractive autumn tints as does *Cercidiphyllum japonicum* with its pale yellow foliage and pungent scent of burnt sugar.

Between the woodland garden and the house lies a meadow, with formal terraces beyond. In early spring, the meadow is flooded with daffodils, followed in April and early May by orange, yellow, red, pink and white tulips, and later in the year by colchicums.

The grand 18C house stands at the top of the terraces, overlooking a shallow valley with a stream at the bottom. These terraces look their best in mid and late summer. The layout of the terraces is formal although the planting itself is quite free. Blue is predominant, with agapanthus in many different shades and varieties of nepeta and lavender.

Central steps lead down from the house to a small circular pool on the lower terrace and then descend again to the sloping meadow. A mown path leads between dancing grasses and flowers to the stream in the lowest part of the valley and then returns back to the house at the furthest end of the terrace. Beyond the house and past the croquet lawn is another woodland area.

Wallington Gardens

ADDRESS AND TELEPHONE: Wallington Garden, Cambo, Morpeth Northumberland NE61 4AR. Tel. Scot's Gap (067 074) 283

OWNERS: The National Trust

DIRECTIONS: 12 miles W of Morpeth off B6342 near Cambo. Public transport: Newcastle BR 19 miles. Buses from Newcastle to Shieldhill Crossroads then 1¾-mile walk

OPENING TIMES: walled garden, 29 March to end September, daily 10.30–7; October to March, daily 10.30–4. Grounds, daylight hours all year. House, mid April to end September, daily except Tues 1–5

ADMISSION: house and garden £3; walled garden and grounds only £1.50. Coach parties by prior arrangement

CAR PARKING: yes

TOILETS: yes

REFRESHMENTS: café

SHOP: yes

DOGS: on lead

WHEELCHAIR ACCESS: apply to car park attendant for special parking for the walled garden. Wheelchair available. Toilets for the disabled: yes

PEAK MONTHS: April to September

NOTABLE FEATURES: walled garden with fine shrubs, herbaceous plants, water garden and conservatory. Also woodland walks

In the conservatory at Wallington is the inscription: 'When wearied and overwrought by study or affairs of business, repair to these haunts and refresh your mind by a stroll amid the flowers.' Translated from a tablet on the Pincian Hill in Rome, this enticing invitation applies particularly to the walled garden, Wallington's most attractive and flowery feature.

The house at Wallington dates from 1688 and was built on the site of Fenwick Castle, which was demolished to make way for it. The landscaping of the estate really began in 1728 when the property was inherited by Sir Walter Calverley Blackett. Little survives today of Sir Walter's garden, but the outline can be seen in the two woods, to the east and west of the house, the ponds in the woods and a former kitchen garden. Further developments took place after the estate passed to Sir George Otto Trevelyan in 1886.

You arrive at the house by passing under the clock tower and crossing the courtyard. The public are allowed into 18 rooms of the house which is particularly known for its Italian plasterwork, porcelain collection and doll's house collection.

Immediately to the east and west of the house are lawns dotted with trees and shrubs, while on the south side a broad gravel terrace provides excellent views over the surrounding Northumbrian countryside. The main garden area lies eastwards, at some distance from the house. A gravelled walk along the mixed border leads to a gateway at the end of the lawn. From here, cross the road to reach the East Wood. Many of the trees in this wood were planted in the 1730s and in the 250 years since then the woodland has hardly altered, only gaining a collection of rhododendrons and azaleas.

Several paths, including a serpentine walk, cut through the East Wood to the walled garden at the most easterly end. A path leads off left near to the road, taking you round by the China Pond—named for the 'Chinese building' which stood at one end in the 1750s but has long since been demolished.

Continuing through the woodland you will see, across the fields, the Arches—a triumphal arch and stone screen which once stood in the courtyard, before it was replaced by the clock tower.

Further east still is the portico wall, running either side of the portico house. Now draped in climbing roses and honeysuckles this wall formed the northern boundary of an earlier kitchen garden. The Garden Pond, dug here in the 1760s, is now surrounded by mature woodland, relaxed and informal—a stark contrast with the lively planting in the walled garden, to the east end of the Garden Pond.

Entering the walled garden through the Neptune Gate, you immediately find yourself on a terrace, overlooking a pool and a water garden. The terrace was designed by Lady Mary Trevelyan in 1938. In the mixed border on the left are many plants which benefit from the shelter of a south-facing wall. The pineapple-perfumed Moroccan broom (*Cytisus battandieri*) is here, along with many flowers—pale pinks, blues and whites predominate with a lot of grey foliage. A row of 18C statues flanks a walk along the terrace to the conservatory, inside which is a marble wall-fountain erected in 1910 and inscribed with the words of wise advice quoted above. Among the conservatory plants are heliotropes, pelargoniums and an enormous fuschia 'Rose of Castile Improved'. The outside lower walls are clothed with various clematis. At the end of the terrace, the path slopes downwards under an archway of *Lonicera periclymenum* and so to the lower level of the garden.

Another mixed border runs along the bottom of the wall to your left—here are many fine shrubs and wall roses such as *Rosa xanthina spontanea*, with large single yellow flowers in late spring and early summer, and the climbing rose 'Cecile Brunner', which displays small pink flowers sporadically throughout the season. Opposite is a large square area enclosed by hedges and containing ornamental trees set out in rows in the style of an orchard. Intersecting the standard trees are rows of cob nut bushes.

One of the walled garden's most exciting features is the stream. It flows down a rocky course, and the whole length is one mass of flourishing waterside vegetation—a blaze of colour in spring and summer.

From the lower level of the garden, you can appreciate the fine shrubs at the base of the high brick retaining wall of the terrace. Roses, clematis, vines and hydrangeas take advantage of the support offered by the wall, while philadelphus, viburnums, junipers and cotoneaster give form to the front of the border.

Returning to the house and terrace, you can turn off down a lime avenue into the West Wood. This mature woodland is threaded with pleasant walks and there are three ponds, one with a boat house.

NOTTINGHAMSHIRE

Clumber Park

ADDRESS AND TELEPHONE: Clumber Park, The Estate Office, Clumber Park, Worksop, Nottinghamshire S80 3AZ. Tel. Worksop (0909) 476592

OWNERS: The National Trust

DIRECTIONS: 4½ miles SE of Worksop. Entrances from A614, A57 and B6005. 1 mile from junction of A1 with A47 and A614. Public transport: Worksop BR 4½ miles; Retford BR 6½ miles. Buses from Worksop and Nottingham to Carburton then 2 mile walk

OPENING TIMES: daily all year round, dawn to dusk. House not open

ADMISSION: pedestrians free. Vehicles £1.50

CAR PARKING: yes

TOILETS: yes

REFRESHMENTS: café

SHOP: yes

DOGS: yes

WHEELCHAIR ACCESS: yes but there are steps along the Lincoln Terrace and paths elsewhere may become muddy. Toilets for the disabled: yes

PEAK MONTHS: no special peaks but good for autumn colour

NOTABLE FEATURES: 4000 acres of parkland; lime avenue; pleasure grounds with formal walk along lake; extensive vine house with collection of old tools; fine trees and shrubs; garden architecture by Stephen Wright

In 1707 the Duke of Newcastle was granted a licence to enclose some 4000 acres of this part of Sherwood Forest as a hunting park for Queen Anne. On the death of the Queen the park became the property of the Duke (although the Crown retained access) and from the 1760s onwards, successive dukes developed the estate.

In 1767 the architect, Stephen Wright, was called in to build a very grand mansion to the north-west of the River Poulter, which flows through the estate. The river was dammed in two places to create a sweeping expanse of lake, today a magnificent centrepiece. Wright built a splendid classical bridge across one end of the lake, a Greek-style temple on the south bank, and a Roman one opposite.

By the 19C, Clumber Park had become the country seat of the Dukes of Newcastle, and towards the middle of the century the gardens were landscaped. Formal terraces with fountains and balustrading were laid out to the front of the house.

In 1879 the house was badly damaged by fire. It was rebuilt to a design by Charles Barry, but demolished in 1938. During the 1939–45 war the estate was requisitioned by the War Department.

The National Trust purchased the estate in 1946, and through repair and improvement programmes have turned Clumber into one of Britain's most visited country parks. Much of the land is woodland, mainly planted with oak, beech, and sweet chestnut. There are also large areas of grassland and heathland, and several Sites of Special Scientific Interest.

The finest entrance to the park is probably the Apleyhead entrance, off the A614. Wright built several gate piers and lodges, and this one is an elaborate classical screen. It is complemented by a magnificent double avenue of lime trees (*Tilia* x *europea*), planted along the driveway in the 1830s. Stretching right across the estate from west to east, the avenue is at its best in autumn, when the fiery golden foliage lights up the driveway. Originally there were 3 miles of avenue, making it the longest in Europe, but only 2 miles are left.

It is more than 2½ miles from the Apleyhead Gate to the old site of the house on the north-western bank of Clumber lake. This magnificent lake is a wildlife sanctuary for large numbers of waterfowl. One of the most dramatic scenes at Clumber is the view from Wright's bridge at the west end of the lake, across the water to the spired chapel (1890).

The spots where the fountains used to stand on the south front are marked by plantings of cotoneasters and fragrant 'Max Graf' shrub roses. The formal terraces were dismantled when the house was pulled down, but the retaining wall of the lowest terrace and a few yews still survive, as do the bastions or gun battery sites which marked the corners of the terrace.

William Sawrey Gilpin was responsible for extending the gardens downstream from the house in the 1830s, creating pleasure grounds and a long formal lakeside walk called the Lincoln Terrace. There were flower beds, vases, seats and a landing stage along this walk, which the National Trust has recently restored. It is gravelled, and passes beneath sturdy cedars, and between lawns and rhododendrons and bamboos. Pairs of stone seats reinforce the Victorian character.

An avenue of cedars of Lebanon links the pleasure grounds with the walled garden or kitchen garden, now being restored to display old varieties of apple trees.

Against the south-facing wall, a long Victorian lean-to structure has recently been renovated, and contains the old palm house and vinery. The central section, the palm house, now holds large specimen conservatory plants in terracotta urns, including the graceful Kashmir cypress (*Cupressus cashmeriana*) with blue-grey pendulous branchlets. The walls of the palm house are richly clothed with plants such as the exotic purple passion flower *Passiflora* x *caerulea-racemosa* and the primrose jasmine (*Jasminum mesnyi*). Fuchsias and citrus species are also on show.

Part of the vinery houses a collection of old kitchen garden equipment, ranging from spades and forks to wheelbarrows and hand carts. There are several wheeled cultivators, some early mowing machines, and an extensive collection of old plant labels together with the original gardeners' mess room. There are also five bays of grape vines and figs. The grape varieties seen today (Foster's Seedling, Madresfield Court, Buckland Sweet Water and Black Hamburgh) are known to have been grown here in the past.

Holme Pierrepont Hall

ADDRESS AND TELEPHONE: Holme Pierrepont Hall, Nottingham. Tel. Nottingham (0602) 332371

OWNERS: Mr and Mrs Robin Brackenbury

DIRECTIONS: 4 miles E of Nottingham off A52. Public transport: Nottingham BR 4 miles. Buses from Nottingham to National Water Sports Centre 1 mile away

OPENING TIMES: June, July and August, Tues, Thurs, Fri and Sun 2.30–6; also Easter, Spring and Summer BH, Sun, Mon, Tues. Groups by appointment throughout the year

ADMISSION: £2.50, children £1

CAR PARKING: yes

TOILETS: yes

REFRESHMENTS: tea room in the Long Gallery

SHOP: gift shop in tea room

DOGS: on lead

WHEELCHAIR ACCESS: yes. Toilets for the disabled: yes

PEAK SEASON: June, July and August

NOTABLE FEATURES: secluded courtyard garden with parterre; developing shrub garden with roses

Holme Pierrepont Hall lies close to the eastern outskirts of Nottingham, separated from the city by mineral extraction sites and the National Water Sports Centre. It covers some 30 acres of land, mostly parkland.

Approaching through the park you get your first view of the Hall, with its adjacent steepled church. A magnificent copper beech spreads its branches over the churchyard railings, contrasting with slender silver birch and sombre yew trees.

The Hall is built around a central courtyard and some parts of it date from late medieval times. The south front is the most striking, with towers flanking the arched entrance doors; built of East Anglian bricks by Sir Henry Pierrepont in the late 15C, this has hardly changed since the days when it served as a moated entrance to the medieval manor house. There is no moat today, and substantial alterations have been made to the rest of the house over the centuries.

The delightful courtyard garden is close by, but well hidden. At the north end is an attractive colonnaded arcade, all that remains of 19C cloisters.

Recently restored, the courtyard garden is still laid out to the original design of 1875, when it was created to mark the coming of age of Charles, Lord Newark (later 4th Earl Manvers). Its main feature, a three-sectioned parterre, is best viewed from the upper rooms of the house. This is believed to have been inspired by the French wife of the 3rd Earl Manvers, daughter of the last Duc de Coigny, who spent her first years of marriage at the Hall.

The intricate patterns of the parterre are edged with box, outlined with gravel and planted with gold and silver-leaved plants such as golden marjoram (*Origanum vulgare* 'Aureum'), lavender and santolina, with wallflowers or antirrhinums for colour. Two of the parterre sections centre on wrought iron trellises smothered with roses and clematis, the third on a stone sundial.

Elsewhere in the courtyard are lawns with beds of old shrub roses, borders of herbaceous plants, and herbs and a shaded border of hostas, ferns and other shade tolerant plants where the south entrance casts its shadow over the courtyard. Clematis, roses and other climbing plants grow up the walls.

Since 1973, a shrub area of garden has been developing to the east of the Hall, on a site occupied by gardens in the 17C. There are two circular lawns with shrub borders backed by yew hedges, and an avenue of clipped yew cones which stretches eastwards to a mature Spanish chestnut (*Castanea sativa*).

The present owners, Mr and Mrs Robin Brackenbury, are responsible for the excellent restoration of the parterre and courtyard garden and the development of the east garden, besides the renovation of the house itself.

Newstead Abbey

ADDRESS AND TELEPHONE: Newstead Abbey, Linby, Nottinghamshire. Tel. Mansfield (0623) 793557

OWNERS: Nottingham City Council

DIRECTIONS: 4 miles S of Mansfield, off the A60 Mansfield to Nottingham road

OPENING TIMES: daily, all year round except the last Fri in November, 10–dusk. House open from Good Fri until 30 September every day 11.30–6 (last admission 5pm)

ADMISSION: garden and grounds £1.20, OAPs and children 60p; house approx. £1.50, OAPs and UB40 cardholders £1, children 50p. Coach parties welcome

CAR PARKING: free

TOILETS: yes

REFRESHMENTS: café

SHOP: yes, 10–6 daily

DOGS: in park on leads

WHEELCHAIR ACCESS: yes, but not to rock garden, Japanese garden or the house. Toilets for the disabled: yes

PEAK MONTHS: July to August

NOTABLE FEATURES: former home of the poet Lord Byron.
Historic house with important collections of Byron's work,
manuscripts, furniture, personal belongings. Variety of gardens:
iris; rose; rock; Japanese garden; extensive park

The long and intriguing history of Newstead Abbey has resulted
in a house of considerable interest and a landscape of great variety.
The estate covers 300 acres, including 25 acres of garden in a
sheltered valley area around the house. In the 12C Henry II founded
a priory in this part of Sherwood Forest, and this was occupied by
Canons of the Order of St Augustine, Black Canons, for nearly 400
years. After the Dissolution of the Monasteries by Henry VIII in the
1530s, it was acquired by Sir John Byron of Colwick. Although most
of the church was then in ruins, Sir John converted the domestic
buildings to the south into a country house and it remained the
Byron family home for nearly 300 years. Byron the poet lived here
in the early part of the 19C.
    The 5th Lord Byron, known as Wicked Lord Byron, was tried for
the murder of a neighbour in 1765, but convicted only of man-
slaughter (and he avoided punishment by virtue of his rank). He
retired to Newstead and towards the end of his life felled the
woodlands surrounding the estate and sold the furniture and
paintings from the house.
    Although he left the estate in a derelict state and with a legacy
of debts, the Wicked Lord also made some positive introductions,
enlarging a pool near the house to form the present upper lake, and
constructing fortresses on the banks so that he and his brother—
an admiral, known as Foul Weather Jack—could stage mock battles
on the water.
    When he died at the end of the 18C the property passed to the
6th Lord, the poet George Gordon Byron. Although he was much
attached to the place, the debts which came with it forced him to
sell Newstead Abbey in 1817.
    The new owner, Colonel Thomas Wildman, had made his fortune
abroad and was able to put the house somewhat to rights, with the
help of the architect John Shaw. Following the Colonel's death in
1860 the property was sold to William Frederick Webb, and in 1931
Webb's grandson sold part of the abbey and estate to Sir Julian
Cahn, who presented it to Nottingham Corporation.
    The entrance to Newstead Abbey is off the Nottingham to Mans-
field road (A60) by a very old oak tree known as the Gospel or
Pilgrim Oak, which tradition says was planted while the canons
occupied the priory. This tree narrowly escaped felling during the
time of the 5th Lord: the local people were so enraged by Byron's
intentions that they purchased the oak in order to preserve it.
    From the entrance a long drive curves through dense plantings
of rhododendrons which date from the end of the last century, and
runs through open heathland of bracken and heather to the car
park, north of the house. From here you can see the upper lake and
the mock fortresses. The group of buildings, complete with spire,
on the eastern bank of the lake, are a stable block built by Webb
in 1862. Of the priory, little remains. The west front, a romantic ruin,

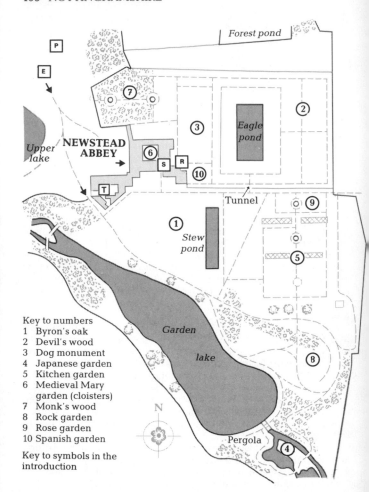

Key to numbers
1 Byron's oak
2 Devil's wood
3 Dog monument
4 Japanese garden
5 Kitchen garden
6 Medieval Mary
   garden (cloisters)
7 Monk's wood
8 Rock garden
9 Rose garden
10 Spanish garden

Key to symbols in the
introduction

dates from about 1290. Visitors to the house see Lord Byron's own
apartments and many other splendid 19C rooms. The Library and
Manuscript Room contain first editions of the poet's work, letters
written by him and a selection of his personal belongings.

From the upper lake water flows via a cascade into the garden
lake. Made by Colonel Wildman in the 19C, the lake is best viewed
from the south front of the house, where it mirrors the surrounding
trees and plantings of dogwood. The south front is ornamented with
scalloped stone-edged beds of spring flowers, followed by summer
bedding. On the walls of the house are climbing plants, including
jasmine and the fragrant yellow-flowering rose 'Golden Showers'.

Between the house and the garden lake is the lawn where the
poet Byron planted an oak tree in 1798, when he first arrived. He
described the event in a poem:

'Young Oak! When I planted thee deep in the ground,
I hoped that thy days would be longer than mine;
That thy dark-waving branches would flourish around,
And ivy thy trunk with its mantle entwine.'

But the tree never grew properly and died some years later—you can still see the stump.

Immediately to the east of the house is the Spanish garden, probably named after its centrepiece, an Iberian well head. It is a parterre of box, edged with brightly planted flower beds.

A long straight gravelled walk leads east from the house, bounded on one side by a tall buttressed stone wall. This is covered in climbing plants such as hydrangeas and honeysuckles, with a border of shade-loving foliage plants in front. On the opposite side is a rectangular stretch of still, dark water surrounded by ancient yews. It may once have been a stew pond where the canons bred fish for the table.

Half-way along the wall, opposite a fine pocket handkerchief tree (*Davidia involucrata*), a dark damp tunnel leads you through the wall to the Eagle Pond. This deep rectangular pool, surrounded by grassy terraces and patches of colourful summer bedding, was probably developed from another of the stew ponds. It was named to commemorate the recovery, in the 18C, of a brass eagle lecturn and two candlesticks, which the canons had hidden in the water at the time of the Dissolution. Today they are safe in Southwell Minster, some 12 miles away.

From the terraces you can see over the walls to other parts of the garden and the parkland beyond. To the west of the pond is the monument which the poet Byron erected to the memory of his Newfoundland dog 'Boatswain', thinking that this was the exact location of the high altar of the priory. (He was probably a little short of the true position.) North-west from the monument lies the Monk's Wood, an area simply planted with trees, daffodils and snowdrops.

The stretches of lawn east of the pond are ornamented by two statues of satyrs. In the days of the Wicked Lord Byron this was an area of dense, dark woodland, known locally as Devil's Wood. Perhaps hoping to add to its satanic atmosphere, he placed the statues here, but the wood has since been felled.

When the poet Byron visited Newstead for the last time in 1814, he found an elm tree in Devil's Wood with two trunks produced from the same root. Feeling this was symbolic of his relationship with his half-sister Augusta, he carved their names on the tree. When the wood was felled the carving was saved and is now housed in the museum.

More formal areas of planting, including an iris garden and rose garden, can be seen in the walled gardens to the south-east of the Eagle Pond, at the end of the long gravel walk. The rose garden, formerly the kitchen garden, displays old-fashioned roses at either end and modern roses in beds in the lawns. A variety of climbers and ramblers grow up the enclosing walls.

South of the rose garden, beyond a corridor of massive yew hedges, is the rock garden, rather wild and overgrown. Further south is Newstead's celebrated Japanese garden—the entrance is by a cascade at the lower end of the garden lake. This garden was commissioned by Miss Ethel Webb, who engaged a Japanese architect to design it in the early years of this century. Stepping stones and hump-backed bridges cross the streams and lead between Japanese ornamentation and plantings of rhododendrons, azaleas, skimmias, mahonias, bamboos and other plants chosen for their foliage or shape.

Where you return to the lake side there is a long pergola smothered in roses and other climbing plants. Looking through its arches, you get one of the best views of Newstead Abbey, across the lake to the house.

The newly-planted garden in the cloister garth has been laid out as a medieval Mary Garden: it contains plants which are symbolic of the Virgin Mary or which share her name. A 16C stone fountain stands at its centre.

Rufford Abbey

ADDRESS AND TELEPHONE: Rufford Country Park, Ollerton, Newark, Nottinghamshire NG22 9DG. Tel. Mansfield (0623) 824153 (rangers) 822944 (craft centre)

OWNERS: Nottinghamshire County Council. The Abbey building is under the guardianship of English Heritage

DIRECTIONS: 4 miles S of Ollerton on A614 Nottingham to Doncaster road. Public transport: the park is served by buses 33 and 36 from Nottingham, Retford and Worksop; 15 from Mansfield connects at Ollerton

OPENING TIMES: park, all year, daily dawn to dusk. Gardens, Mon to Sat 9–5, Sun 9–6. Only undercroft of house open

ADMISSION: free

CAR PARKING: yes, and for coaches

TOILETS: yes

REFRESHMENTS: yes

SHOP: yes

DOGS: on lead

WHEELCHAIR ACCESS: easy. Toilets for the disabled: yes

PEAK MONTHS: no special peaks but particularly fine in July and August

NOTABLE FEATURES: 9 individual formal gardens; small arboretum

The gardens at Rufford Abbey, on the edge of Sherwood Forest, were laid out in 1982 and are now sufficiently well developed to give much pleasure to visitors in this quiet corner of Nottinghamshire.

Cistercian monks from Rievaulx in North Yorkshire founded an abbey at Rufford in 1146. Following the dissolution of the monastery in 1536 the land was granted to Sir John Markham, and a few years later it became the property of George Talbot, the 6th Earl of

Shrewsbury and one of the husbands of Bess of Hardwick (Hardwick Hall stands just across the border in Derbyshire). During this period, many of Rufford's monastic buildings were demolished. They were replaced by a fine hunting lodge.

In 1626 the estate passed, by marriage, to the Savile family, in whose ownership it remained until 1938. The Saviles were responsible for building new wings onto the house and they carried out a great deal of landscaping work on the estate, redesigning the whole grounds on five occasions in order to follow the changes in fashion.

When the estate was sold in 1938 it came into the hands of speculators, who sold off much of the land in small lots and felled many of the trees in the surrounding park and woodland. They also intended to demolish the house but Nottinghamshire County Council opposed this and in 1951 purchased the building and 130 surrounding acres. Unfortunately, half of the house still had to be pulled down, owing to neglect and mining subsidence.

In 1969, Nottinghamshire County Council decided to make Rufford into a country park. The grounds were by then in an unkempt semi-wild state, although some fine trees had survived from earlier days, including several magnificent fern-leaved beech (*Fagus sylvatica heterophylla*) and weeping ash (*Fraxinus excelsior* 'Pendula'). Mining subsidence reduced the size of the lake to the north-east of the house, but work to restore the area was begun in 1970.

Of the former gardens, little remained. A wilderness area lay between the house and the main road, lawns and hedges to the north of the house and further north the Broad Ride, an avenue cutting through woodland, the central *allée* of a 17C radial layout. In short, there was very little to attract the garden visitor until the recent establishment here of a series of formal gardens and informal areas in sympathy with the historic setting.

The nine formal gardens are of different shapes and sizes and contain a great variety of plants. They are laid out as a series of rooms or compartments defined by hedges and walls and linked by paths. Although still quite young, the gardens are beginning to fill out nicely and the paving—mostly herringbone-patterned brick—is mellowing.

Each garden has its own theme. Near the entrance is the Birch Garden where roses, herbaceous and other plants enjoy a sunny warm position within the shelter of walls and specimens of the common white birch (*Betula pubescens*). Stretching eastwards from the Birch Garden the Long Avenue sweeps between smooth lawns studded with unusual sculptures and works of art (Rufford also has an established craft centre). It terminates at a stone seat, with sitting figure. Statues and sculptures also add charm to the formal gardens.

Just off the Long Avenue is the Willow Garden—a small enclosed wild garden dominated by two enormous crack willows (*Salix fragilis*). The herb garden next door is of strictly formal design and contains some 30 varieties of medicinal and culinary herbs, bordered by low clipped box hedges.

The Autumn Garden features plants that flower or colour late in the year, with an emphasis on purple and gold. Plants of many forms and textures fill the Foliage Garden, and the atmosphere is refreshing and cool. White, pink and blue-flowered plants predominate in the Scented Garden.

The orangery at Rufford was formerly used as a bath house by huntsmen; now in need of a great deal of restoration, it serves as a backcloth to the small Orangery Garden. Below the orangery is a disused fountain and an empty canal following the line of the garden wall. Early-flowering shrubs are grouped in the North Wall Garden, to attractive effect in spring. A grotto at the end of the canal has been rebuilt.

The formal gardens are surrounded by informal areas of trees and grass. Oak and birch species are planted in a wild flower meadow, the Reg Hookway Memorial Arboretum which has a shelter for visitors to sit and enjoy the view. Cherries, whitebeams, rowan, crab apples and other trees provide extra protection and add to the variety of leaf form and flower, but many of these will eventually have to be removed to make way for the maturing oak trees.

Near the lake, below, species of trees and shrubs indigenous to Britain form a semi-natural 'wilderness'. Goat willow (*Salix caprea*), guelder rose (*Viburnum opulus*), hawthorn (*Crataegus monogyna*), hazel (*Corylus avellana*) and dog rose (*Rosa canina*) all tangle together, providing excellent cover for wildlife. Brambles and nettles are left undisturbed—management is by coppicing on a seven or 15-year rotation, one third of the area being coppiced at a time.

OXFORDSHIRE

Blenheim Palace

ADDRESS AND TELEPHONE: Administrator's office, Blenheim Palace, Woodstock, Oxford OX7 1PX. Tel. Woodstock (0993) 811325

OWNER: 11th Duke of Marlborough

DIRECTIONS: at Woodstock, 8 miles N of Oxford on the A34 Stratford-upon-Avon road. Public transport: coach services from London (Victoria) to Oxford. Regular bus services from Oxford (Cornmarket Street) to Woodstock, stopping at the park gates

OPENING TIMES: mid March to the end of October, daily 10.30–5.30. Palace also open

ADMISSION: palace and gardens £5.50, OAPs £4.20, children £2.80; gardens only £3, children £1.50. Various group rates

CAR PARKING: yes

TOILETS: yes

REFRESHMENTS: café

SHOP: yes

DOGS: yes, on lead

WHEELCHAIR ACCESS: yes. Toilets for the disabled: yes

PEAK MONTHS: summer

NOTABLE FEATURES: on World Heritage list

This 2000-acre estate was magnificently landscaped in the 18C by 'Capability' Brown. It has many grand features—perhaps the most unforgettable is the Column of Victory, a Doric column 134ft high, supporting Robert Pit's lead statue of John Churchill, 1st Duke of Marlborough, holding a winged Victory aloft. Sir John Vanbrugh designed the palace—an impressive example of English baroque—and the Grand Bridge between two enormous lakes. If you like walking and plenty of space, this is a good place to come and bring a picnic.

A few parts of the estate need attention and replanning, but this is hardly surprising, considering its size. A continual programme of re-planting is underway and plans for the next 40 years have been made under the Park Restoration Scheme.

There are two main avenues, one to the north planted with limes (originally elms) and another to the east with alternating limes and planes. The gardens and terraces around the palace are also well worth visiting, especially the two water terraces to the west. Laid out in 1925 by the 9th Duke of Marlborough and his French landcape architect, Achille Duchene, and completed in 1930, the two terraces are quite different in character—the first stately and graceful, the second smaller and rather overcrowded with statues and fountains—not to mention obelisks, sphinxes and caryatids.

You can admire the first terrace at your leisure from the outdoor restaurant area, while fortifying yourself with tea. On grassy banks to the right stand *Chamaecyparis lawsoniana* 'Erecta Viridis' and golden *Cupressus macrocarpa* 'Lutea'. Box is used throughout, in tall hedges and elaborate scroll patterns set on gravel beds by the waterside. There are five vigorous fountains and a number of classical statues.

The second water terrace features among other items a fountain by Bernini, ornamented with river gods and a drinking lion; six little winged Victories on pillars; a sphinx with the face of the 9th duke's second duchess; and six caryatids, one modelled on a young gardener, Bert Timms of Hanborough. Three-tiered stone fountains fill the spaces between the caryatids. Splendid red-leaved, orange-flowered cannas fill ten vast earthenware pots: and there are some interesting topiary pieces, in box and yew. The bank beneath this terrace is planted with shrub roses and the lake and boathouse lie directly below.

Following the lake south from the palace, we passed the temple of Diana, where Winston Churchill proposed to Clementine Hozier. It was restored in 1975. Many new trees have been planted in this area—we noticed a liquidambar, with maple-like leaves; a silver maple, *Acer saccarinum*, with bright green leaves, silver on the reverse side and turning yellow in autumn; and a silver birch, *Betula pendula*.

It is intented over the next few years to establish an American-style arboretum in this area. The new trees are the initial stages of this scheme and the estate is experiencing problems of tree labels being stolen or damaged. Consequently some trees are without labels.

The drive or Sheep Walk continues past the circular rose garden—another pleasant place to sit and rest, with tall pines and the lake nearby. Two small moose-bark maples guard the entrance and three tulip trees (liriodendron) stand nearby. The roses are a mixture of hybrid teas and floribundas, all well tried and tested varieties— they include 'Iceberg', perhaps the best white floribunda, 'E.H. Morse', a strong red hybrid tea; yellow and pink 'Peace', source of many hybrids, and bright yellow 'Grandpa Dickson'.

Near the rose garden, the Sheep Walk forks into two paths. Either of these will bring you eventually to the Grand Cascade, but the guidebook recommends taking the left fork. The signposting is not very good in this area, and we were distracted by a number of young pheasants, rushing about on their surprisingly long legs and bathing in the dust. (Pheasants are released on the estate in their thousands, to be fattened for shooting.)

Walking across a grassy area, we saw a red horse chestnut (*Aesculus* x *carnea*), a honey locust (*Gleditsia triacanthos*), bright green *Cupressus macrocarpa*, the Monterey cypress, three specimens of the very beautiful small tree *Amelanchier laevis* and an enormous multi-trunked cedar of Lebanon (*Cedrus libani*). The walk was full of interest, but we were very disappointed by the Grand Cascade itself—a quiet trickle rather than, as claimed, a 'deafening roar' of water.

Returning to the east side of the palace, across a vast area of lawn and via the Temple of Health, you'll find the Italian garden tucked between the east wing and the south-facing orangery. This, too, was re-created from a former garden by the 9th Duke and Achille Duchene. Laid out in delightful scrolls and swirls of dwarf box and surrounded by clipped hedges of golden yew, with topiary birds and dogs, and scarlet pelargoniums and pink and purple fuchsias cascading from splendid pots, the garden looks very beautiful on a sunny day. Sadly it is chained off, and can only be fully appreciated from the house windows. In the centre is a very striking black and gold fountain, made by the American sculptor Waldo Storey and featuring a mermaid with a spouting coronet and winged nymphs with tambourines on golden dolphins.

Exploring the Lower Park, to the south-east, we attempted to visit the kitchen garden (praised in glowing terms in the guide booklet), but found it closed. Nearby is a small garden centre, supplying a reasonable selection of plants: also the butterfly house and an adventure play area. Children should enjoy the Narrow Gauge Railway, which connects this part of the estate with the palace.

Oxford College Gardens

ADDRESS AND TELEPHONE: Exeter College, off Turl St; New College, New College Lane, off Catte Street; St Catherine's College, E side of Oxford, off Manor Road, reached from Longwall Street or St Cross Road; Worcester College, off Worcester Street at junction with Beaumont Road

Also: Balliol College, off Broad Street (N side); Christ Church, entrance on Christ Church meadow, through memorial garden on St Aldgates; Holywell Manor (Balliol College), E side of Oxford, at corner of Manor Road and St Cross Road; Keble College, off Parks Road (W side); Lady Margaret Hall, Norham Gardens, 1 mile N of Carfax, from Banbury Road into Norham Road and right into Fyfield Road; Magdalen College, off Magdalen Bridge (N side); Merton College, Merton Street, parallel to High Street; The Queen's College, off High Street (N side); St Hilda's College, below junction of Magdalen Bridge and Iffley Road; St Hugh's College, in St Margaret's Road, near junction with Banbury Road; St John's College, off St Giles Street; Somerville College, off Woodstock Road (W side); Trinity College, off Broad Street (N side); Wadham College, off Parks Road, near Holywell Street; Wolfson College, end of Linton Road, off Banbury Road, between city centre and Summertown shops; Worcester College, off Worcester Street, opposite Beaumont Road

OWNERS: the individual colleges

DIRECTIONS: by the A40 from London. Public transport: BR to Oxford, services from London (Paddington) connections from all major cities

OPENING TIMES: vary. It is safest to check with the individual college

ADMISSION: either small charge (50p–£1) or none

All facilities available in the town, but not in the colleges

DOGS: not usually in formal gardens, though occasionally on lead

WHEELCHAIR ACCESS: after negotiating entrance doors, access through most of the gardens. Toilets for the disabled: in the town

PEAK MONTHS: many colleges have spring bulbs, some herbaceous displays and roses for summer, and there is also autumn colour from shrubs and trees

NOTABLE FEATURES: New College: magnificent herbaceous border under city wall, mount, lawns. Exeter College: quiet, secluded atmosphere, fig trees, pleasant planting. Worcester College: 18C quad, lawns and lake in English landscape style. St. Catherine's College: gardens designed by Professor Arne Jacobsen as integral to the college. Carefully planned juxtaposition of planting with buildings: fine specimen trees and shrubs

Many of the older Oxford gardens lie well concealed from view behind the ancient walls of their colleges. Walking down narrow streets in which a car seems a strange anachronism, you turn in through heavy wooden doors and past porters lodges to find lawns, herbaceous borders, rose gardens, and even lakes. Anticipation is increased when you have to negotiate one or more quadrangles, another set of doors or even a tunnel.

This being said, there are many fine gardens of more open aspect, such as Magdalen, which combines garden quadrangles with parks and river walks; Wolfson, opened in 1974, whose still developing gardens incorporate lawns, shrubberies, borders, woodlands and wild flower meadows by the Cherwell; and St Hughs, whose solid 19C buildings are appropriately enhanced by spacious lawns, shrubberies, extensive borders and vegetable gardens.

College Gardens
Key to numbers

1 **Exeter**
2 **New College**
3 **St Catherine's**
4 **Worcester**
5 Balliol
6 Botanic garden
7 Brasenose
8 Christ Church
9 Christ Church meadow
10 Genetic garden
11 Holywell Manor
12 Keble
13 Lady Margaret Hall
14 Magdalen
15 Merton
16 Nuffield
17 Penicillin garden
18 Queen's
19 Rhodes House
20 St Anne's
21 St Edmund Hall
22 St Hilda's
23 St Hugh's
24 St John's
25 Somerville
26 Trinity
27 University College
28 University parks
29 Wadham
30 Wolfson

◂ Access to garden

Key to symbols in the introduction

OXFORD CITY

Yards
0   500

With 18 gardens to chose from, as well as the Botanic gardens and the University Arboretum nearby at Nuneham Courtenay, the main difficulty is knowing where to start. The standard of planting and upkeep varies, but there is something worthwhile to see in most of the gardens, even apart from their setting. We visited just a few gardens from the long list recommended to us.

We started at **New College**, sited at the end of New College Lane, and opening at 11am. Its name, according to the leaflet guide, is actually 'the St Mary College of Winchester in Oxford' and there is a statue of the Virgin over the doorway. Beyond the doorway is the Founder's Quadrangle—the college was founded in 1379 by William of Wykeham, then Bishop of Winchester. From here you turn back left to enter William of Wykeham's cloisters—a quiet lawn, once a burial ground, surrounded by the covered cloisters themselves and sheltered by a large holm oak (*Quercus ilex*). This 14C quadrangle, the last building in the college to be completed, is an extreme example of a garden enclosed, protected and isolated by its walls. It is overlooked by the bell tower.

The main garden was nearly as secluded as the cloisters until the early 18C, when the fourth wall of the Founder's Quadrangle was taken down and a wrought iron screen substituted. The present screen, a late 19C replica, distances but does not conceal the lawns and gardens beyond. Stepping through a gate in the screen, you find yourself on a terrace overlooking the garden's principal features: a large, wooded mount in the centre of the lawn and on the left a splendid mixed border, a 100 yds long and 20ft deep, sheltered and set off by the high battlemented city wall.

Passing the pink, purples and silvers of the terrace planting (silver and yellow santolina, mauve lavender, pink diascia, purple allium, pale blue teucrium, pink cistus) and three vertical branches of mauve wisteria like a candelabra against the college wall, you come to a gravel path which will lead you down the length of the border. Rich planting themes repeat themselves as you walk along—at the back of the border, the mauve sprays and silver leaves of *Buddleia alternifolia* and the dark leaves of red prunus; huge mounds of purple catmint (nepeta 'Six Hills Giant') spilling out over the path, interspersed with yellow and orange day lilies, and small pink and purple gladioli. There are thickets of acanthus (bears breeches), gold discs of achillea and tall woolly-leaved spikes of yellow flowering mulleins. *Vitis coignetiae* and other climbers scramble up the walls.

Half-way down the border you come level with the mount on your right. Artificial hills, crowned with arbours or banqueting houses, were a standard feature of Tudor gardens, though the fashion dates back to medieval times; one of the finest and most elaborate was raised at Hampton Court in 1533–34. This mount was completed in 1649, although construction began much earlier, at the end of the 16C. It is now being replanted with acer, laburnum, prunus, camellia and lilac, as well as yew, both green and golden, ilex, oaks and sweet chestnuts. In the spring daffodils flower on the lower slopes.

The mount was once shaped like a ziggurat (a pyramid, with a number of storeys), and planted with straight lines of pyramidal-shaped trees, but it gradually fell into disrepair, its outlines softened and it succumbed to invasive sycamore. It was proposed at one time to reinstate the ziggurat shape, but this idea was abandoned in favour of the present, more natural looking scheme.

To your left, a gate in the city wall reveals a striking Barbara Hepworth sculpture seen against the new Sacher building. Further on, herbaceous planting gives way to a rose bed, filled with pink and dark red shrub roses, and at the far end of the lawns, beyond the mount, there is a plantation of fine trees: a huge London plane, a tulip tree and a copper beech, underplanted with hostas and hemerocallis. A theatre area is backed by shrubs on the lower slope of the mount. Golden yew, laburnum and hebe provide convenient entrances for student actors—a perfect setting for 'A Midsummer Night's Dream'. Walking back from here to the garden quadrangle, you get a good view of the terrace planting, backed by the wrought iron screen.

Exeter College in Turl Street has, by comparison, limited space and a correspondingly modest planting scheme. On one side of the main quadrangle is Gilbert Scott's elegant 19C Gothic chapel (modelled on the Sainte Chapelle in Paris). *Magnolia grandiflora* produces its cream-white fragrant flowers from mid to late summer, a magnificent virginia creeper turns fiery colours in autumn and bright annuals in beds and window-boxes flower throughout the season.

If you go through the arch to the secluded Fellows' Garden, open in the afternoons, you will find wisteria on the library walls and a small herbaceous border. There is a pleasant lawn, mostly over-shadowed by chestnut trees, and four venerable figs grow against the main building. Terraced beds at the far end slope up nearly to the top of a battlemented wall, from which, climbing the steps, you can look down unobserved to Radcliffe Square and see the Oxford world, academic and otherwise, going about its business. The terraced beds are peppered with red and yellow tulips in spring.

If possible, you should also visit the well-known gardens at **St John's** and **Trinity**, both planted in the 18C or 19C on land once owned by the Benedictines. St John's in particular offers a variety of interesting features: a long lawn ending in fine trees and shrub-beries; a sizeable and varied rock garden, currently being re-planted; and specially prepared rhododendron beds. Sadly, our schedule did not allow us much time here.

Worcester College garden (open 2pm till dusk in the term time and 9–12 noon as well in the vacations) is, like several other Oxford locations, reputed to have a connection with 'Alice in Wonderland' although Christ Church was Lewis Carroll's college, both as an undergraduate and Student (Fellow). The Worcester College Quadrangle combines the stately Palladian front of the Provost's lodgings to the north with the medieval student lodgings opposite. This sober framework of grey stone surrounds a rectangular lawn cut in precise diamonds, brightened by fuchsias and many-coloured annuals. The north and south walls are hung with climbing roses, jasmine and passion flowers. Wisteria and trumpet creeper (campsis) manage to flourish while facing east—doubtless protected by the enclosed location.

From the north-east corner of the quad, you enter a dark tunnel, said to be the original passage to the garden in 'Wonderland', which Alice could see but found so hard to reach. However, you should find no difficulty in walking through into a spacious arboretum of huge and ancient trees (as well as some of the 'beds of bright flowers' which so fascinated Alice). Here we wandered under another vast London plane, a tulip tree, an Indian bean (*Catalpa bignonioides*) a weeping ash and a Tree of Heaven (ailanthus), among many other specimens. Some trees marked on the college guide as growing near the medieval buildings have been replaced by new planting.

At the far end of the the lawns, gold and silver foliage plants combine in a border with pale flowers against dark ivy, and beyond this, willows hang over what appears to be a long pond. Carefully planned by the Fellows in 1817, this extends into a graceful 'L' of a lake, filled with water lilies and frequented by ducks. Sitting on a stone seat under the willows, you can feel a world away even from Oxford on a busy summer weekend.

A small private garden stretches over Alice's tunnel. The Provost's Garden, also private, forms a triangular promontory into the lake. The orchard and Fellows' Garden are also out of bounds. The lake has been extended to meet the new, award-winning Sainsbury building. A special feature is the prow-shaped terrace, which, when you stand on it, creates the illusion of sailing down the lake.

St Catherine's College, founded in the 19C, was rebuilt on its present site in Manor Road in the 1960s. It is well worth a walk to reach it, via Longwall Street or St Cross Road. The college and garden were conceived as one design by Professor Arne Jacobsen, the Danish architect, and his basic concept remains, although some changes have been made. These include replanting of most of the original trees and shrubs, which did not flourish in their allotted spots. However, the present scheme is well advanced and only awaits the maturity of some specimens to perfect what is already one of the most striking and original of Oxford College gardens. The guide is well worth acquiring at the reception office.

St Catherine's in fact reverses the usual order of things by presenting its landscape first. You come across it almost unawares, as the entrance gate (just on the right beyond Nappers bridge over the Cherwell) is quite easy to pass. Among the trees in this area are a weeping lime (*Tilia petiolaris*), two walnuts (*Juglans regia*) and some graceful Himalayan cedars (*Cedrus deodara*). Once through the gate, pause and look over the low wall to view the full length of the main lawn. The long lines of the college, built of cream brick trimmed with black, are emphasised by the moat, with its water lilies, tall clumps of bullrushes and low, bubbling fountains. Over the wall above the moat hangs tamarisk (*Tamarix pentandra*), feathery pink in late summer, backed by the deeper pink plumes of smoke bushes (*Cotinus coggygria*). Beyond, against the college wall, is a bright *Robinia pseudoacacia* 'Frisia', surprisingly tall for its age (the new planting only began in the 1960s). It is a most satisfactory view.

In the centre of the the the lawn is a striking lyre-shaped statue by Barbara Hepworth and groups of trees and shrubs, including at the far end near the Music House, four Dawyck beeches, which already provide a strong perpendicular line to offset the horizontal buildings. There is a bright yellow-green honey locust (*Gleditsia triacanthos*), and a maidenhair tree (*Ginkgo biloba*).

To enter this area you must now turn right, passing the Alan Bullock Buildings, whose three courtyards are said to contain a 20-year-old dawn redwood, a *Eucryphia* x *nymansensis*, and various acers. These were, however, concealed behind locked gates on our visit. Along the path outside is a pleasant mix of shrubs—the glaucous *Juniperus virginiana* 'Skyrocket' and variegated Norway maples (*Acer platanoides* 'Drummondii') with ground cover. A turn to the left takes you past the bicycle sheds—a challenge to the garden designer, well met by a large firethorn (*Pyracantha watereri*) and a glimpse of a tulip tree behind. A culinary quince hangs over the wall of the Masters garden nearby and there is a varied collection of sorbus. By this time the slow-flowing, willow-edged Cherwell has joined the path to your right.

You are now free to cross the long lawn and the moat and enter the inner, enclosed gardens by way of the lodge—where you can buy the guide. (This records that 25 golden orfe were put into the moat in 1964, and have since populated it, with the help of some unsolicited 'volunteers'.) You step into the main quadrangle, with its two cedars of Lebanon set in a large, circular lawn, and the virginia creeper clothing the walls of the dining hall to your left. Turning this way you pass a bright green pool of prostrate juniper (*J. chinensis* 'Pfitzeriana') and a yew hedge, clipped like a defensive wall. Once through, you are in the Senior Common Room area, its small lawns patterned with stone slabs and specimen shrubs and trees—a prostrate sequoia, a foxglove tree (*Paulownia tomentosa*), and the beautiful, autumn colouring Katsura tree from Japan (*Cercidiphyllum japonicum*), a larger specimen of which adorns the central quadrangle. The Junior Common Room area on the far side of the Great Hall has stone seats decorated with climbing roses and clematis as well as varieties of acer and prunus.

Crossing the quadrangle again, you pass another 'fortified' area, where yew and yellow brick barriers echo and complement each other. On either side of the main central buildings beyond (the library, the Bell Tower and the Bernard Sunley building) you will find an interesting mixture of specimen trees including *Magnolia hypoleuca*, climbers and herbaceous planting; and towards the far end some heather beds.

At this point the level changes and you descend to a lower lawn near the squash courts. Here is a group of trees, including a Swedish whitebeam and two liquidambars, a group of dawn redwoods and cypresses. It is worth noting that the final page of the guide lists some 100 specimens of the principal trees and shrubs in the gardens, leaving aside ground cover, climbers and flowering plants. This is a garden to revisit and appreciate anew, both for its richness of planting and the satisfying juxtaposition of brick and foliage.

Walking around the south side of the Bernard Sunley building to rejoin the main lawn you pass a neat, grassed amphitheatre backed by a low yew hedge. This recalls something of the precision of Hidcote, without that garden's sometimes claustrophobic atmosphere. Once back on the main lawn you can wander in the meadow area near the banks of the Cherwell, reminiscent of the site's flood meadow origins (the area round the Music Room still floods from time to time). There was once a Royalist earthwork near here, and more recently a corporation rubbish dump. The influence of neither remains to disturb the peace of the riverside, or dispel the effect of a remarkable achievement in garden design and planting.

Oxford University Botanic Gardens

ADDRESS AND TELEPHONE: Rose Lane, Oxford OX1 4AX. Tel. (0865) 276920

OWNERS: The University of Oxford

DIRECTIONS: M40, A40 from London. Public transport: BR or coach to Oxford

OPENING TIMES: daily 9–5 (4.30 October to March). Greenhouses open daily 2–4. Nuneham Courtnay: 1 May to 31 October, Mon to Sat 9–5, Sun 2–6. Closed Christmas Day, Good Fri

ADMISSION: usually free, but £1 in July and August

CAR PARKING: no, nearest St Clements car park

TOILETS: nearest in St Clements Street car park, over Magdalen Bridge

REFRESHMENTS: no

SHOP: no

DOGS: no

WHEELCHAIR ACCESS: entrance through river gate or Rose Lane, or ask a member of garden staff to unlock the main gate. Toilets for the disabled: no

PEAK MONTHS: all year round for botanical and horticultural interest

NOTABLE FEATURES: 17C walled garden; glasshouses; herbaceous border; lily ponds and rock garden; bog garden; shrubs

Oxford Botanic Garden, glimpsed from the High Street through the imposing Danby Arch, is an enticing sight. Whatever the season, the view of lawns, trees, walks and flower beds offers a tempting alternative to the crowds pushing over Magdalen Bridge and up the High Street. Moreover, this is a unique refuge, the first Physic Garden in England, created in the early 17C 'for the use of the University and the people'. Its foundation was made possible by a gift of £5000 from Henry Danvers, later Earl of Danby, whose bust can be seen on the north side of the arch named after him, together with those of Charles I and Charles II.

The walled garden was completed in 1633, and first intended for growing 'simples', or medicinal plants. A Professor of Botany was to 'show the use and virtue of them to his Auditors', according to

Anthony Wood, the Oxford historian. This function is still continued in the teaching of botany and biology to undergraduates and the garden remains an important teaching resource for schools and other colleges. Plant material for research is supplied to different departments of the University and the garden is also used as an environment for research into bird life.

Oxford is linked with other botanic gardens through the Botanic Garden Conservation Secretariat throughout the world in a joint effort to preserve endangered plant species, so that any dying out in their natural habitats may be preserved and replanted at a later date.

The post of Professor of Botany was first held by Robert Morison, elected in 1669. William Sherard of St John's College endowed the post from 1734 and the many eminent men who have held it include Dillenius, John Sibthorp (author of the *Flora Graeca*) and Charles Daubeny, who in the 19C established the garden as a botanic garden. The present holder is Professor F.R. Whatley F.R.S.

In addition to a Professor of Botany, the garden has a superintendent (head gardener). The first of these (then known as Horti Praefectus) was Jacob Bobart, an ex-merchant and innkeeper and a somewhat eccentric character, but also a skilled gardener who established the garden on a firm footing. His son, who succeeded him in 1679, made some of the first experiments on sexual reproduction in plants. The most recent superintendent of many to complete a long working life in the garden was Mr J.K. Burras, who retired in 1988.

The serious purposes of the garden by no means prevent it from being a very pleasant place to visit. When you pass through the little gate at the side of the Danby Arch, what is first evident is not the scientific nature of its planting but the splendour of the trees, the shape, form and colour of the shrubs and plants and the variety of the hundred or so climbers on the limestone walls. Although the arrangement of the iris bed just to the left of the entrance is apparently 'in ascending order of chromosome number from 24 to 60' it also provides a marvellous array of colour in June.

The rectangular walled garden is divided into demonstration beds of various plants, set in eight rectangular lawns. Its central walk extends through and beyond the south wall to the triangular garden beyond. The trees (there are well over 300 of them in the whole garden) soften the strictness of this design and, having been planted over the last 350 years, are a living witness to the garden's history. The oldest tree, planted by Jacob Bobart around 1650, is a yew, standing to the western side of the central path near the far end of the garden. The plant catalogue which Jacob Bobart published in 1648 listed 1600 plants, which increased to 2000 over the next ten years. (The present garden contains some 8000 species.) The London plane (*Platanus* x *hispanica*) was probably developed at Oxford, from a hybrid seedling raised by Jacob Bobart the Younger.

If you start your walk near the iris bed at the north-east side of the garden, you come first to a bed of plant crosses between species of the same genera (crosses between different genera are illustrated in the north-west corner). You then start on the rows of family beds, which are continued on the western lawns. In all these beds there are enormous variations between members of each plant family: among the Euphorbiaceae, for instance, between the 4ft tall spurge *E. characias* and the tiny *E. coralloides*, and among the Berberidaceae from the bushy, dense-leaved barberries to the many varieties of epimedium, or barrenwort, which provide such valuable and distinctive ground cover in sun or shade. The euphorbias comprise the NCCPG National Collection.

The bed of Ranunculaceae contains not only the common buttercup and such obvious relatives as the trollius, or globeflower, but less likely ones such as the hellebores (including the Christmas rose and the lent lily) and the peonies and delphiniums. The family of *Solanaceae* boasts not only the common deadly nightshade with its warning black berries, but also its attractive cousin *Atropa belladonna* 'Lutea', whose berries are just as poisonous but more deceptive, being golden, clear and shiny.

There are interesting and ancient trees to see as you move down the eastern lawns: the service tree *Sorbus domestica* f. *pomifera* and the whittypear *S. domestica* f. *pyrifera*, planted in 1790 and 1850 respectively, and near the central pond a manna ash (*Fraxinus ornus*) dating from 1790 and a service tree of Fountainbleau (*Sorbus latifolia*). Near the southern wall there is a weeping ash, (*Fraxinus excelsior* 'Pendula'), planted in 1800.

The west-facing wall is furnished with a variety of shrubs and climbers, including some tender specimens such as the dark mauve *Abutilon* x *suntense* 'Jermyns' and buttercup yellow *Fremontodendron mexicana*, as well as many jasmines, honeysuckles and roses. A large, free-standing *Hoheria sexstylosa* shows its profuse, tiny white flowers and on either side of the central arch is the yellow, spring-flowering *Kerria japonica* 'Pleniflora' and prickly-leaved *Mahonia lomariifolia*, whose flowers, again yellow, appear from autumn to spring. The southern half of this wall contains a splendid range of ivies, which continue along the north face of the southern wall.

The wall borders are devoted to ferns: to the north of the arch garden varieties fashionable in the 19C—part of the Dyer collection—and to the south, native British species. Masses of the horsetail fern *Equisetum telmateia*, grow near the south-east corner—the relic of a prehistoric fern which some 250 million years ago grew to 98ft, with trunks 3ft in diameter.

On the eastern lawns you will find more family beds, and also, near the superintendent's office, a bed illustrating the four types of variegation. Note the 'plastid cimmeras', whose tissue layers consist of different plastids in shades of green or white, such as the attractive, shiny-leaved *Griselinia lucida* 'Variegata'. Near here you will also see an early swamp cypress (*Taxodium distichum*), planted in 1840. Other beds contain lilies, alliums and grasses—outstanding among the latter being the 8ft tall *Arundo donax*—and there are also economic beds, where you can see dye-producing plants such as saffron, and many others grown for spices and flavourings. There is a good range of poisonous plants, including the poison ivy (*Rhus radicans*), with a prudent warning notice attached. Trees in this area include a graceful Persian ironwood (*Parrotia persica*), particularly impressive in autumn, a Turkish hazel (*Corylus colurna*) and, at the south end of the garden, two

Ginkgo biloba, or maidenhair trees, one male and one female.

The east-facing wall is also well hung with climbers, all meticulously listed in the garden guide, and there are many more on its western aspect. Here also, outside the wall, you will find a Corsican and a Bhutan pine (*Pinus nigra maritima* and *Pinus wallichiana*) both planted in the mid 19C, as well as a London plane (*Platanus* x *hispanica*).

Leaving the garden through the southern gate, past Bobart's yew (which in the past was clipped into various topiary designs) and the opposite wall pillar, covered in golden ivy, you step into the new triangle of garden, leased in 1943 from Christ Church. (The older garden is similarly held on lease but from Magdalen College.) Here you will find a lily pond surrounded by a small but attractive rock garden. When we visited, the white water lily *Nymphaea odorata*, the deep pink 'Marliacea Gloriosa', the pale pink 'Marliacea Carnea' and the yellow 'Marliacea Chromatella' were in glorious bloom. The rock slopes support alpine plants which need well-drained soil, and, in one corner, those which look particularly attractive in winter. There are also some shapely small conifers. Miniature poppies, pinks, aquilegias and dicentra make a veil of mauve, pink, purple and yellow.

If you then turn left, you will find a fine herbaceous border beneath the grey stone wall (ornamented not only with golden ivy but with vines, *Magnolia grandiflora*, buddleias and many others). The late flowering herbaceous plants were vigorous in August, particularly red and yellow kniphofias, blue veronica and the charming pale pink mallow *Lavatera olbia* 'Barnsley'.

Just south of the border is a display on the development of roses. This includes beds devoted to the main species and varieties, roses of different periods, and specialities, such as 'first crosses'. Their beauty is equal to their historical interest.

Returning to the main southern path and turning left, you come to the southernmost point of the garden, marked by a grey urn, where two ponds with damp verges make up the bog garden. The great toothed leaves of *Peltiphyllum peltatum*, the umbrella plant, succeed its pale pink heads of flower; gunneras, ligularias and hostas are also in good supply.

Rounding the bend (the garden is here bordered by the river Cherwell) and passing some shrub beds, you come to a series of glasshouses, erected on the banks of the river outside the garden walls by Professor Daubeny. These were rebuilt in steel just after the 1939–45 war and after a flood in 1947 had necessitated the removal of most of the plants. They are the Succulent House, the Palm House, the Orchid House (where the precious sprays can only be seen through glass), the tropical lily house, the fernery, the alpine house (also locked at weekends) and the conservatory.

In the largest, the Palm House, grows the the multi-stemmed, low branching oil palm *Elaeias guheersis*. There are date palms (*Phoenix dactylifera*), coconuts (*Cocos nucifera*) and olives (*Olea europaea*). The great fans and feathery leaves of the various palms give fill the house with verdant, luxuriant growth, in some places almost obscuring the light.

In the Tropical Lily House, the tank which once housed the enormous leaves of the waterlily *Victoria amazonica* now contains a collection of waterlilies growing in wooden boxes. One of these is named after Professor Daubeny, who provided not only the original glasshouses but also the tank. The lilies, purple, pink and white, stick their heads above the water level.

The Succulent House has some spectacularly large desert specimens, pride of place going to *Cereus peruvianus*, an enormous, ancient cactus. There are also examples of carnivorous plants, such as the sun-dews drosera and sarracenia and the floating utricularia.

The conservatory, standing against the southern face of the north wall, contains more palms, including *Chamaerops humilis* the European fan palm, reaching to the roof. There is a graceful Kashmir cypress (*Cupressus cashmeriana*), an Australian honeysuckle (*Banksia integrifolia*), which grows as a small tree, a lemon-scented gum (*Eucalyptus citriodora*) an Australian tree fern (*Dicksonia antarctica*), grown in a pot, many ferns and flowering plants such as fuchsias, pelargoniums and primulas.

Leaving the conservatory, you can see Mediterranean plants growing against the south face of the entrance wall. Outside the garden a plaque has been put up to the developers of penicillin, for whom a garden of largely modern roses has been planted, between yew and box hedges.

Extensions of the botanic garden are the Genetic Garden, half a mile away near the University Parks, and the University Arboretum at Nuneham Courtenay. Besides an area of acid soil where rhododendrons, azaleas, magnolias, camellias and heathers are grown, the arboretum includes a pinetum featuring a fine collection of North American conifers, already in existence when the estate was bought by the university in 1949. The arboretum is a resource for the university, showing species of economic importance, geographic and genetic variations within certain species and groups of species of special botanical and horticultural interest. It is open to the public from May to October.

Waterperry Gardens

ADDRESS AND TELEPHONE: Waterperry Gardens Ltd, Waterperry, near Wheatley, Oxon OX9 1JZ. Tel. (0844) 339254 (office) 226 (shop)

OWNERS: The Fellowship of the School of Economic Science (Registered Charity)

DIRECTIONS: 2½ miles from A40 (M) turn off at Wheatley. 50 miles from London, 9 miles from Oxford. Public transport: buses from Oxford and London stop at Wheatley, which is 2½ miles from Waterperry; no nearer public transport

OPENING TIMES: April to September, weekdays 10–5.30, weekends 10–6. October to March 10–4.30. Closed during Christmas and New Year holidays

ADMISSION: March to October £1.60, OAPs £1.20, children 10–16 80p. November to February: no charge. Coach parties must book in advance. Reductions for parties of 15 and more (March to October)

CAR PARKING: yes

TOILETS: yes

REFRESHMENTS: café

SHOP: yes, and plant centre

DOGS: on leads only

WHEELCHAIR ACCESS: yes, to most of garden. Toilets for the disabled: no, but ramps for wheelchairs at entrance

NOTABLE FEATURES: herbaceous border; display beds; trees; nursery; alpine nursery; riverside walks

Formal and informal elements are combined to pleasing effect in these lovely, varied and spacious gardens, set in 83 acres of grounds, laid out and developed from 1932 onwards. A horticultural school was founded here in that year by two knowledgeable and enterprising women, Miss Beatrix Havergal and her partner Avice Sanders, with the express aim of educating women in all branches of horticulture. The school continued to exist until 1970, and the gardens are still used for day release and amateur courses. The present owner, the School of Economic Science, aims to maintain the original character and intention of the gardens—'peaceful beauty co-existing with a purposeful attitude to practical gardening'.

Until recent years, the garden entrance was approached through the glasshouse and frame area; a path led through the old kitchen garden and between the herbaceous borders into the flower garden. The glasshouses are still a good place to begin your visit, although only the conservatory is open to public. Here you can see a mature orange tree and a lemon tree, along with *Passiflora rubra* draping itself freely here and there, cacti in pots, *Tibouchina semidecandra floribunda* with bright translucent purple flowers and pink-flowered oleander.

Fruit trees are trained against the red brick walls of the old kitchen garden—cordon pears on the east wall and loganberries on the west, also a fig, peaches and morello cherries. There is a shrub nursery here, and a herb bed. To the south, beyond the north wall, lies Waterperry's magnificent herbaceous border, and beyond this lawns shaded by a huge copper beech and set with island beds. To reach this main part of the garden you must first retrace your steps and enter by way of the Virgin's Walk, a little way to the east.

An ancient and shapely yew marks the beginning of the walk, and a shade border runs along its right-hand side. This border contains a number of unusual shade-loving plants, backed by a high wall hung with a variety of clematis, honeysuckles and ivies. The walk leads down to the sculpture of a seated figure by Nathan David, in a meditative pose. You emerge near the rock garden and Sebbs Corner.

Conifers, shrubs and other plants fill the rock garden, and an upper path winds round to Sebbs Corner, a small woodland area where you can see Christmas roses and snowdrops early in the year. The herbaceous border lies just to the west, a magnificent sight in July and August. Just south of the path are the clay bed (opposite the rock garden) and the crab border (roughly opposite the herbaceous border). The crab border contains different varieties of flowering crab apples, such as *Malus floribunda, M. niedzwetzkyana* and *M.* 'Lemoinei', roses such as *R. rubrifolia* and *R. moyesii*, prunus and *Garrya elliptica*. Bearded irises flower along the front of the border in June. The big copper beech is at least 200 years old, and underplanted with spring bulbs and flowers.

Other well established, mature trees can be seen on the lawns below the house, to the west: these include a tree of heaven (ailanthus) given to Beatrix Havergal by Ellen Willmott (the gardener, horticulturist and writer, author of *The Genus Rosa*). A grand cup-and-saucer yew is said to demonstrate the natural shape of yew when left untrimmed. You can also see a lime, a liquidambar, sweet buckeye (*Aesculus octandra* or *A. flava*) and, above the stranvaesia bed, a Scots pine. Two graceful *Robinia pseudoacacia* stand near the copper beech. The park has lost many elms, but has been replanted with Spanish chestnut, cedar of Lebanon and Atlantic cedar.

Turned over to food production during the 1939–45 war, Waterperry is still very much a working garden as well as a pleasure garden; the decorative and the useful can be seen everywhere side by side. Soft fruit—loganberries, raspberries, blackberries, gooseberries, currants—is grown over a large area in the south field, and this is a pleasant place to wander, especially on a hot day. To the west is the herbaceous nursery, and island beds designed by Alan Bloom, as well as a delightful formal garden, recently laid out and featuring intricate beds of period plants and a knot garden. Lines of pyramid pears and escalier apples screen long beds of strawberry plants and young growing seedlings. The Royal Sovereign strawberry, for which Waterperry has won gold medals at Chelsea, is now propagated in pots away from the main soft fruit growing area.

Waterperry also holds the National Collection of kabschia saxifrages (porophylla group); at their best in February and March, these can be seen in the alpine nursery, by the house, which was established by Valerie Finnis, once a student of the school of horticulture. Hundreds of other alpines blossom here in April and May, in raised beds, stock beds and troughs.

Waterperry's shrub borders and mixed borders would be impossible to describe in detail; they are intended to inspire and instruct young gardeners and horticultural students, and designed to provide interest throughout the year. The valley bed and the stranvaesia bed are situated close to each other, leading south-west from the crab border. Near the copper beech is a wide bed filled with many varieties of berberis, and across the path, climbing and rambling roses trained are over hoops. Also of interest is a boomerang shaped conifer bed in the lawn below the house, containing conifers of many shapes and colours and heathers.

The gardens lie close to the little River Thame (to the east) a tributary of the Thames, and there is a winding river walk, especially recommended in spring. Starting not far away from the rock garden, this brings you out at the far corner of the south field, below the main fruit growing area.

Finally, the little parish church is well worth a visit. Just above the alpine nursery and near the tea room, it looks unprepossessing from the outside, but contains a great number of treasures, including a wonderful collection of early glass. A plaque in the church is dedicated in loving memory of Beatrix Havergal MBE VMH, 'who, with her partner Avice Sanders, founded the School of Horticulture. She dedicated her life to imparting to others her great faith, her joy, and her unique skills.'

SHROPSHIRE

Benthall Hall

ADDRESS AND TELEPHONE: Benthall Hall, Broseley, Shropshire, TF12 5RX. Tel. (0952) 882159

OWNERS: The National Trust

DIRECTIONS: 6 miles S of Wellington, 1 mile NW of Broseley, off B4375. Public transport: Telford BR 7½ miles. Buses from Wellington and Telford to Broseley, then 1 mile walk

OPENING TIMES: Easter Sun to end September, Wed, Sun and BH Mon 1.30–5.30. Last admission 5. House also open

ADMISSION: house and garden £2; garden only £1. Coaches by prior arrangement

CAR PARKING: yes

TOILETS: yes

REFRESHMENTS: no

SHOP: no

DOGS: no

WHEELCHAIR ACCESS: to parts of the garden and ground floor of Hall. Toilets for the disabled: yes

PEAK SEASON: spring and early summer

NOTABLE FEATURES: a plantsperson's garden with many unusual species, rockery terraces, remains of Maw's collection of plants and his propagation ditches

Benthall Hall is said to date from 1535, although the general style of the architecture suggests a time nearer to the 1580s. It was built by the Benthall family, whose roots can be traced back to the 11C or 12C, and who lived here until the end of the 18C. In 1844 it was bought by Lord Forester, of the nearby Willey estate.

The Hall stands at around 600ft, on a plateau less than a mile from the Severn Gorge, and is cut off from vehicular access to the north and east by steep-sided valleys.

Local tile manufacturers George Maw and his brother Arthur took the lease in 1860. George Maw was also a keen botanist and gardener, and in 1886 he completed his authoritative work, the classic *A Monograph of the Genus Crocus*, which included his own hand-painted colour plates. Only about 27 copies of the book were issued, making it a priceless rarity.

The enchanting Pixie Garden at Benthall Hall

Maw was also a plant collector and travelled extensively throughout Europe, Turkey and North America. He raised a large number of new species in ditch-like pits which he covered with frames to protect the plants from the cold and wet of this exposed site. One of these pits has survived, although now it is little more than a depression in the ground, and recently several terracotta tablets have been found, once used by Maw to record details of new species.

By 1870 the gardens around Benthall Hall contained several thousand species, especially alpines and bulbs, but after Maw's death, the majority of his plants disappeared. A few species did, however, manage to naturalise themselves in the garden. Among them is *Chionodoxa luciliae*, glory of the snow, which first flowered in Britain at Benthall Hall in 1877. In spring you can see hybrids between *Crocus tomasinianus* and *C. vernus* flowering in rough grass to the east of the Hall, and in autumn, *Crocus speciosus, C. pulchellus* and *C. nudiflorus*. Also naturalised here is the Turk's cap lily (*Lilium martagon*) which flowers in shades from maroon to white in June. Other small bulbous plants appear annually, possible descendants of Maw's original species.

Much of the present garden, however, must be credited to the Bateman family, who rented Benthall Hall from Lord Forester between 1890 and 1906. Robert Bateman (son of James Bateman who created the gardens at Biddulph Grange in Staffordshire) and his wife laid out the rockery terraces or Pixie Garden at the west end of the Hall.

Although nearly 100 years old, the Pixie Garden remains similar in style and planting to that created by the Batemans. The entrance is from the south, just by the house, marked by topiary yew, holly and box shapes; below these are beds of geraniums, dianthus, lavender, peonies, roses and potentillas.

Informal terraces, some cobbled, rise towards the west, away from the Hall. There are numerous beds of alpines and other small plants, roses and shrubs. The long rose bed includes 'Gruss an Aachen', a floribunda-like rose which was raised in 1909. Here too is 'Felicia', a hybrid musk rose with double apricot blooms which flower from June throughout the summer and well into the autumn. The raised scree bed nearby was rebuilt a few years ago, but small rosettes of crepis, sweet-smelling pinks and other alpine plants are fast re-establishing themselves.

The central feature of the Pixie Garden is a small rectangular lily pool, edged with bog myrtle (*Myrica gale*) and other moisture-loving plants. The brick dovecot was built by Robert Bateman.

A brick boundary wall joins the dovecot on each side. The wall plants include several unusual roses and clematises and tree peonies. Shrubby plants and small trees increase in number as you go up the terraces. The top level is dominated by a splendid *Magnolia* x *soulangiana* 'Alba Superba'. Here too is *Dipteronia sinensis*, a large Chinese shrub with inconspicuous flowers, but which in autumn bears clusters of pale green berries, changing to red-brown seeds. At ground level pulmonarias tangle with geraniums. A Victorian-style fernery is being developed in the shade.

Looking over a low wall on the east side of the Hall, you can see the bowling green, bordered by Scots pines, oaks and beech trees. Maw's plant pit survives in a wilder area below the tree screen, together with the remaining species from his collections, but this area is closed to the public.

The Hall itself is built of sandstone and is a good example of late 16C domestic architecture. It has mullioned windows, a gabled roof and attractive 16C chimney stacks. Climbing plants grow up the front, including clematis and wisterias, which frame the lower windows, with a border of fuchsias, sedums and hydrangeas below.

Crossing the carriage turning circle from the Hall, you come to a grassy terrace, which descends to the main south lawn. This terrace commands good views of the countryside beyond the old ha-ha. Bordering the lawn on two sides are rockery banks featuring unusual plants such as *Acanthus balcanicus* with rose-purple flowers, the Indian poke plant or American false hellebore (*Veratrum viride*) with long panicles of yellow-green flowers and the Japanese anglica tree (*Aralia elata*) with prickly stems, large leaves, white flowers and blackberries.

When the property came up for sale in 1934 it was purchased by Mrs Mary Clementina Benthall who gave it to the National Trust in 1958; Sir Paul and Lady Benthall became the Trust's first tenants in 1962. Sir Paul's son James and his wife Jill now hold the tenancy and devote much time, skill and patience to maintaining this plantsperson's garden.

Hodnet Hall

ADDRESS AND TELEPHONE: Hodnet Hall, Hodnet, Market Drayton, Shropshire TF9 3NN. Tel. Hodnet (063 084) 202

OWNERS: Mr and the Hon. Mrs A. Heber-Percy

DIRECTIONS: at end of Church Street, past St Luke's Church, off A53 at Hodnet. 12 miles NE of Shrewsbury

OPENING TIMES: April to end September, daily 2–5. (Sun and BH 12–5.30.) House not open

ADMISSION: £2, OAPs £1.60, children (5–16) £1. Reduced rates for pre-booked parties

CAR PARKING: yes

TOILETS: yes

REFRESHMENTS: café

SHOP: yes

DOGS: on lead

WHEELCHAIR ACCESS: yes, though some gravel paths and steep slopes. There are alternative routes to most parts of the garden avoiding steps. Toilets for the disabled: yes

PEAK MONTHS: May and June but something of interest all seasons

NOTABLE FEATURES: lakes and water garden; shrub planting; camellia garden; wooded walks and meadows

In 1922, when Brigadier A.G.W. Heber-Percy began to create the gardens around Hodnet Hall, there was little more than a small stream in a marshy but sheltered valley. The house, however, must have been a source of inspiration. Built of red bricks in 1870, in Elizabethan style, it stands high on a plateau and commands the views to the south over the valley. It would have been even more impressive in those days—the original roof and top floor have now been removed, to make the building more manageable.

With the assistance of three gardeners, the Brigadier completely transformed the valley. By damming the stream at various points he created a chain of pools, starting in the west and cascading down different levels to the main lake, below the terraces.

The soil at Hodnet Hall is lime free, the rainfall fairly high, and the pools seem to have a moderating effect on the temperature—they rarely freeze over and the warm mists that hang over them keep off severe frosts. The planting is rich and varied, with many unusual specimens, chosen and arranged to provide colour and interest throughout the seasons.

It is best to begin your tour on the forecourt of the north entrance to the Hall. From here the private north drive, flanked by lawns and backed by trees and rhododendrons, connects with the main road. Beyond the road, a stone portico is silhouetted against the skyline. This semi-ruin was brought here by the Brigadier from Apley Castle, near Wellington in Shropshire, which was demolished in 1956.

A path leads westwards from the Hall, passing through a larch wood underplanted with rhododendrons and bulbs. Emerging from the woodland you enter a large grassy meadow set in a light airy clearing above the pools, and fringed with daffodils in early spring.

Retrace your steps to the house and stroll along the Broad Walk below the south front. From this gravelled terrace there are glorious panoramic views over the valley and the main lake to the rolling fields beyond, where a 17C dovecot is the central feature. The slope down to the main lake is planted with a mixture of small trees and shrubs, including *Acer palmatum* 'Dissectum Atropurpureum' with deep purple foliage and *Acer palmatum* 'Dissectum Palmatifidum' which has more finely cut leaves; also *Berberis stenophylla* and *Kalmia latifolia*, and many heather and rose species. In spring the slope is lit with vividly coloured azaleas and rhododendrons. Blue *Rhododendron augustinii* blossoms in April and May, followed by the white of *R.* 'Mrs A.T. de la Mare' and the pink of 'The Master' in mid season.

A flight of stone steps leads down from the Broad Walk through the plantings to the side of the main lake but if you continue along the terrace to the far eastern end you can take another route, which descends past an ivy-clad sandstone cliff face into a formal circular rose garden. Surrounded by tall trees, this garden centres on a stone statue almost enveloped by a ring of *Hydrangea paniculata* 'Grandiflora', *Caryopteris* x *clandonensis* and lavender 'Old English'. The next ring of beds is planted with floribunda roses, while the outer circle contains herbaceous peonies.

Above the rose garden, on top of the sandstone cliff, is an informal camellia garden. This is particularly spectacular in spring when the large camellia 'Cornish Snow', *C.* x *williamsii* 'St. Ewe' and 'Donation' and many more put on a splendid display along with flowering cherries and rhododendrons. The views from the summerhouse in the camellia garden, looking across the circular rose garden to the lake and lawns beyond makes the ascent well worthwhile.

From the rose garden, it is a short step to the lawn by the main lake. The grassy walk along the bank is very pleasant and the mass planting on the slope rising back towards the house is superb when seen from below.

There are five pools, the small Horse Wash Pool being furthest to the east. The main pool, below the house, is followed by an area of water garden and then at higher levels up the valley are the Pike, Heber and Paradise Pools. It is possible to walk around the whole chain of pools and then return along the southern bank through bluebell woods; or you can take a short cut through the water garden, via stepping stones and bridges. Here are mass plantings of candelabra primulas, *Iris kaempferi*, astilbes and gunneras. Also along the water's edge are native ferns, including the Royal fern (*Osmunda regalis*), and kingcups, while clumps of water lilies float between the bright reflections of surrounding rhododendrons and flowering shrubs.

Further along the bank is a collection of cherries, including the pale pink hybrid prunus 'Accolade', shell pink 'Amanogawa' and the profuse pale pink Higan cherry (*Prunus subhirtella*). In spring, naturalised drifts of daffodils flower beneath the trees.

At the east end, a series of streams and cascades connects with the Horse Wash Pool. Laburnums and lilacs flower beneath the larches, and the banks are covered with astilbes, primulas and azaleas. Clumps of *Hydrangea sargentiana* and *H. villosa* provide colour in summer on the lawns nearby, along with the rather tender cape figwort or cape fuchsia (*Phygelius capensis*), and there are more rhododendrons, including various forms of 'Loderi' and many hybrids.

South of the Horse Wash Pool is the Stone Garden, a recent creation which centres on a large glacial boulder of granite retrieved from the Horse Wash Pool in 1960. The surrounding planting consists of roses and conifers. Here you can see *Rosa moyesii* 'Geranium' which has brilliant geranium red blooms in summer and *Rosa* x *cantabrigiensis*, noted for its ferny, fragrant foliage and soft yellow flowers.

Beyond the Stone Garden is a shady Grove of Scots pines, sycamores and oak trees underplanted with daffodils and encircling a summerhouse, once a smoke house.

The stable block has been attractively converted to a tea-house and gift shop. Behind this lies a garden laid out in the winter of 1957–58, which cleverly combines a wide range of plants in informal, curving shrub borders, in a light woodland setting. At one point the shrub borders open out into a lawn with a 17C Italian well head. Rhododendrons, camellias and pieris mix happily with flowering shrubs such as hydrangeas and eucryphias, and with small trees including the mahogany barked *Prunus serrula* 'Tibetica'. There are also herbaceous plants such as *Meconopsis grandis, Gentiana ascelepiadea* and *Euphorbia wulfenii*, and ground cover is provided by hostas, epimediums, ferns, primulas and pulmonarias.

A little futher to the east, a broad magnolia walk leads from an Elizabethan archway, descending a series of low terraces back to the stable block. This was planted in the winter of 1956–57 and despite being exposed to east winds, the magnolias, including *M. officinalis, M. mollicomata, M. sargentiana* and *M. lennei* are doing well. The terraces are planted with Chinese maples, the Cornelian cherry (*Cornus mas*) and the strangely twisted *Corylus contorta*; and for autumn colour, *Liquidambar styraciflua* and *Parrotia persica*.

SOMERSET

Clapton Court Gardens

ADDRESS AND TELEPHONE: Clapton Court Gardens and Plant Centre, Crewkerne, Somerset TA18 8PT. Tel. Crewkerne (0460) 73220/72200

OWNER: Captain S.J. Loder

DIRECTIONS: on the Crewkerne to Lyme Regis road (B3165), about 3 miles S of Crewkerne, signs within a 5-mile radius. Public transport: Crewkerne station (Waterloo to Exeter line), about 2½ miles away

OPENING TIMES: March to October, Mon to Fri 10.30–5 and Sun 2–5, also Easter Sat 2–5

ADMISSION: £3, children £1. Parties must book (reductions)

CAR PARKING: yes

TOILETS: yes

REFRESHMENTS: café

SHOP: plants for sale

DOGS: no

WHEELCHAIR ACCESS: formal garden, glasshouse and tea room are all accessible, but not the woodland garden. Toilets for the disabled: no

PEAK MONTHS: interesting from March to October: bulbs and early rhododendrons in March and April followed by rhododendrons, magnolias and azaleas in May and June, then roses and the herbaceous borders in July and August; finally autumn colours in September and October

NOTABLE FEATURES: planted terraces, woodland garden with rare trees and unusual shrubs

This 10-acre garden, concealed in the depths of rural Somerset, is one of the most lovely in the county. Besides 4 acres of formal gardens and 4 of woodland there is also a nursery and plant sales centre. Many visitors return, sometimes three or four times, especially to see the woodland garden, with its famous ash tree and collection of rare plants.

The existing structure of the formal garden was established by Louis Martineau over nearly 25 years, beginning in the late 1940s. By the late 1970s, the garden had declined, especially the woodland. Captain Simon Loder, the present owner, and one of a very famous gardening family, bought Clapton Court in 1978, restored it to order and greatly extended it, introducing many new and unusual plants, particularly shrubs and trees.

The three terraces are built on a natural slope, facing south-west. They are retained by low walls, probably of Mendip stone (the house is Ham stone): Mr Martineau built them in the early 1950s. Tall pines and other conifers surround and protect the north end of the garden; a tall yew hedge and a fence of *Cotoneaster lacteus* form the right-hand boundary of the terraces. A summerhouse stands on the top terrace, with a spring garden beyond.

Mixed borders lie to the right and left of the bottom two levels, planted in blue, purple, mauve, pink and white. In late July we saw polemonium 'Blue Pearl', mauve catmint, pink sidalcea, the star-like white flowers of astrantia, the flat heads of *Anaphalis triplinervis* and feathery white and pink astilbes. Below the first terrace is a bed of euonymus, including *Euonymus fortunei* 'Sarcoxie', 'Sheridan Gold', 'Silver Queen' and 'Emerald n' Gold' with clematis 'Marie Boisselot' and wisteria clambering over a Scots pine to the left. Other clematis can be seen on the wall behind: 'Perle d'Azur', rampant during summer, and *C. alpina* 'Frances Rivis' in spring.

The second terrace level is planted to magical effect with white, silver and grey plants. Artemisias 'Lambrook Silver' and *A. ludovi-*

ciana grow round the bottom of four standard *Salix hastata* 'Weh-rhahnii', with long grasses arching and waving beside them and masses of the white fosteriana tulip 'Purissima'. Small creeping plants inhabit the terrace walls and steps, including aubrieta and campanulas, followed by china blue *Ceratostigma plum-baginoides*.

On the lawn behind stands a beautiful specimen of silver *Pyrus salicifolia* 'Pendula'; to the left, is a seat in an alcove of clipped 'Pembury Blue' cypress. The next terrace is almost entirely given over to polyantha roses, red and pink: these 25-year-old specimens bloom every summer for many weeks. Two columns of grey-green *Juniperus virginiana* 'Skyrocket' tower 8–10ft high.

In the shrub bed on the middle terrace is a gold-green philadel-phus, pink and white *Berberis thunbergii* 'Rose Glow', *Caryopteris clandonensis* 'Heavenly Blue' and the blue spikes of *Agastache anisata*, the giant hyssop (*Nepeta nervosa*).

The yellow border leads to the summerhouse. Here you can see the only true yellow-flowered lilac, *Syringa vulgaris* 'Primrose', *Acer japonicum* 'Aurem' and *Diervilla* x *splendens* with yellow daylilies swaying among greeny-yellow *Euphorbia cyparissias*, *Santolina neapolitana* 'Edward Bowles' with its pale yellow heads and the bright yellow star-shaped flowers (on tall spikes among delicate foliage) of *Coreopsis verticillata*. *Malus hupehensis* dis-plays white fragrant flowers, followed by yellow fruits. You will also see the very pretty *Jasminium humile* 'Revolutum', peonies 'Ched-dar Cheese' and 'Clair de Lune', spiraeas 'Goldflame' and 'Golden Princess', *Philadelphus coronarius* 'Aureus', yellow violas and tulips in spring.

White and light-flowering shrubs and herbaceous plants—white hydrangeas, philadelphus 'Avalanche', deutzias and escallonia 'Iveyi'—glow incandescent in the shady woodland area behind the summerhouse, beneath a deep canopy of pines and oaks, yew, holly and laurel. There are plenty of camellias too, rhododendrons and mahonias and masses of spring bulbs.

A spacious croquet lawn lies below the spring garden, edged by a rock garden and shrub border: here two *Photinia* x *fraseri* 'Red Robin' make a spectacular show, with olearias, elaeagnus, berberis and viburnums. In the rock garden, *Clematis fargesii souliei* grows attractively over a gold chamaecyparis. Innumerable small creep-ing plants drown the stone, overhung by hypericum, hebes and the hardy *Fuchsia magellanica* 'Variegata'.

A second lawn stretches down below the croquet lawn, bordered by some interesting trees, including *Chamaecyparis nootkatensis* with dark green foliage and blue-grey cones, a stout yew and a pear tree with *Rosa filipes* 'Kiftsgate' scrambling through it. A big lily pond of unusual shape provides the main focus of this lawn area, planted with waterlilies, arum lilies and sibirica irises, and with its plain grey paved surrounds offset by Chinese pots, bronze geese and a stone dog. Nearby stands a high and solid horseshoe-shaped hedge of Pembury Blue cypress, sheltering a semicircular seat.

The rose garden lies just west of this lawn, behind a hornbeam hedge, and planted on the same steep slope. The design has recently been completely changed into four rectangular beds with arbours and seats in each section. Numerous varieities of roses, including polyantha 'Nathalie Nypels' are mixed with perennials, lavender and artemisias. Shrub roses grow in the lower border by the wall, including the clear pink single *Rosa rugosa* 'Frau Dagmar Hastrup' with big hips and white *R. rugosa* 'Blanche Double de Coubert'.

The woodland garden lies to the south east. Having walked round the house, crossing a ha-ha under a big oak, you will come to a meadow area planted with specimen trees and shrubs. This is part of a new link garden, made by Captain Loder in 1980—a pleasant transition between the formal and informal parts of the garden. The trees include 15 different kinds of birch and three kinds of amelanchier. This area has a good view from the house all the year round, even in winter, the white birches standing out against red, yellow and black stems of dogwoods beyond. It is bisected by a stream, planted deeply round with primulas, astilbes, hostas and other water-loving plants. Rhododendron 'Seven Dwarfs' yakushimanum hybrids grow on the far bank, and a bush of *Lonicera periclymenum* 'Belgica', an original seedling of the Early Dutch honeysuckle, first brought to England in the 17C. Just above a pond is *Pyrus salicifolia* 'Pendula' and the wonderful blood-red rambling rose 'Parkdirektor Riggers', which flowers continuously throughout summer.

Cross through the kissing gates into the woodland garden proper. Great Britain's largest ash tree (*Fraxinus excelsior*), over 220 years old, is impossible to miss, with its monstrous knobbly trunk, 23ft round, and great bulging branches.

Here as elsewhere Captain Loder has tried to enhance and enliven rather than conceal the natural contours of the land, integrating new and exotic plants and trees with the existing native woodland. The result is colourful, especially in autumn. Ashes and oaks rub shoulders with a red sycamore, a *Ginkgo biloba, Magnolia campbellii* 'Mollicomata' with mauve-pink flowers, flaky-barked *Parrotia persica, Viburnum sargentii* and the striking *Crinodendron hookeranum* with crimson waxy lantern-shaped flowers in May. The clearings are brightened by groups of day lilies and plentiful astilbes in shades of white and purple, pink and red. *Cornus mas* 'Aurea' is underplanted with white geraniums and orange daylilies: Prunus 'Pink Perfection' (the only prunus not of Japanese origin) and *Tsuga canadensis*, the eastern hemlock, spread themselves above *Helleborus corsica*. There are also many varieties of rhododendrons, magnolias and camellias.

It is a steep climb to the top of the woodland: slices of tree trunk have been placed here and there as seats. A separate woodland 'room' cleared in 1982 was planned for eucalyptus varieties (unfortunately they all died) and now it houses a new collection of styrax.

Exploring the wood in late summer, we also saw pink and white hydrangeas, *Rosa longicuspis* up a tree, displaying its panicles of small white banana-scented flowers and *Clematis flammula* and *Lonicera ledebourii* set against the green leaves of *Cornus controversa, C.* 'Norman Hadden'.

Finally, descending again to the gravel sweep around the front of the house, take a look at the water garden, a string of eight pools—again planted with moisture-lovers and sheltered by mature trees including an 80ft Norway maple. Lovers of fuchsias and pelargoniums should also make haste before closing time to visit the glasshouses in the old kitchen garden, where hundreds of plants are on display and offered for sale, including many rare species.

East Lambrook Manor Garden

ADDRESS AND TELEPHONE: near South Petherton, Somerset TA13 5HL. Tel. South Petherton (0460) 40328

OWNERS: Mr and Mrs Andrew Norton

DIRECTIONS: signposted off A303. 7 miles E of Ilchester, turn N to South Petherton and East Lambrook. Public transport: BR to Yeovil or Crewkerne, then bus to South Petherton (2 mile walk)

OPENING TIMES: Mon to Sat and BH weekends 10–5. Closed Christmas and New Year

ADMISSION: £1.65, OAPs £1.50, children 50p. Coach parties by prior arrangement only

CAR PARKING: yes

TOILETS: yes

REFRESHMENTS: coffee in malthouse; teas for parties by arrangement

SHOP: yes, plant nursery and sales

DOGS: no

WHEELCHAIR ACCESS: most of garden inaccessible. Toilets for the disabled: no

PEAK MONTHS: March to September

NOTABLE FEATURES: traditional cottage style garden created by the late Margery Fish with important collection of plants. National Collection of geraniums (cranesbill)

In 1938 Margery and Walter Fish came to live at East Lambrook Manor and began to make the garden. Walter Fish died in 1947, but Margery Fish continued to improve the garden and collect plants, many of which she saved from extinction. The style of gardening she both practised and inspired is generally described as 'cottage style'. It has its roots in the early 19C, when not only farmers' wives but country-loving gentry (including Dorothy and William Wordsworth) filled their gardens with wild and garden flowers as well as vegetables, and 'florists' (flower enthusiasts rather than flower sellers) cultivated unusual plants and knew their Latin names.

These gardens, which continued to flourish throughout Victorian and Edwardian times, were the inspiration for Gertrude Jekyll when she developed her own very definite schemes of cottage planting on a rather grander scale. Walter and Margery Fish harked back to the beginnings of the cottage garden, but also took took note of the plants that Gertrude Jekyll had popularised when they laid out and planted their smaller area—just over 2 acres—at East Lambrook.

The interest of East Lambrook Manor, both during the time of Mr and Mrs Fish and as it is today, restored and renewed by Mr and Mrs Andrew Norton, is the combination of traditional and unusual plants, and the profusion of the planting, which all but obscures some of the underlying framework of the garden. These elements combine to produce a strongly romantic, nostalgic atmosphere; they also demand continual hard work to maintain the range of plants and hold the fine balance between luxuriance and confusion.

The garden holds the National Collection of geraniums (cranesbill, not pelargonium) amounting to over 200 varieties, some 70 of which are for sale in the plant nursery; and important collections of hellebores, euphorbias, dianthus and lavender. Another speciality are primulas, of which there are over 100 varieties in the gardens, including Jack in the Green, both single and double. As new forms of plants develop, Mr and Mrs Norton are saving them and recording them on computer to make sure that today's varieties will not be lost, as were many in the past.

It is as well, when looking at the map of the garden, to remind yourself that many of the garden features outlined on the garden map are small; it is quite easy to lose your sense of direction, or miss out something altogether, especially as the self-seeding of many flowers, charming in itself, blurs boundaries. After entering through the orchard, you will encounter two particularly small areas, the first, on your left, being the Green Garden, whose freshness is preserved by an Atlantic cedar, a medlar, a Judas tree and a Glastonbury thorn; the latter grown from a cutting of the original tree, which blooms in the winter. Under this shelter, shade-tolerant plants flourish, including bergenias, euphorbias, and several shades of aquilegia, which when we visited, cast a veil of subtle colours over the whole garden. We noticed a white iris, gold-splashed, dark purple *Geranium phaeum*, known as the mourning widow, and *Astrantia major* 'Margery Fish' sometimes called 'Shaggy' on account of its unusually long outer petals.

Opposite this is the lighter Sundial Garden, a small raised bed against the old cowshed, where around the low sundial (almost concealed from view) are crowded a Mexican orange (*Choisya ternata*), a clipped box almost concealed by a scrambling perennial sweet pea, yellow potentilla, dark blue aquilegias and the wild geranium 'Herb Robert', as well as blue and white geranium cultivars, the dark wine-coloured gladiolus 'Byzantinus'and many more. This prolific style of planting is a useful insurance against the effect of over-hot sunshine and the growth of weeds.

Outside the adjoining malthouse is the Knoll, a circle of grass centring on a black mulberry and edged by a border of silver hebe, red helianthemum, a blue centaurea, yellow cistus, a double buttercup and pink geraniums, among others. Nearby, bordering the road, is a shady lawn, with a wall border and mature trees, including the attractive variegated sycamore *Acer pseudoplatanus* 'Leopoldii', a bird cherry (*Prunus padus*) and a sumach. At the end of the lawn, just by the back wall of the manor, lies a herb garden, edged with the shrub honeysuckle *Lonicera nitida* and containing sages (gold, purple and tricolor) lavender, purple basil, green and variegated lovage, and a tall angelica. A beautiful blue mallow grows against the wall of the house.

At this point you change levels, climbing steps between sedate rows of pudding trees—sturdy dark green *Chamaecyparis lawsoniana* 'Fletcheri'. At the farthest point of the avenue in sharp contrast to these slightly dumpy forms, stands a silver weeping pear (*Pyrus salicifolia* 'Pendula'). On your right, towards the south wall of the malthouse, lie the terraces, their outlines in summer almost obscured by trees and plants: a Judas tree, a variegated *Cornus controversa* and a purple-leaved *Corylus maxima* 'Purpurea'—the last grouped with a red berberis, white and mauve thalictrum and a red rose. Yellow day-lilies, mauve scabious, blue aquilegias, cranesbill and the wild red campion abound. Against a stone table a vivid group of large red poppies was in flower when we visited in June, providing a strong contrast to the delicate forms and shades around them. The south wall of the malthouse is well furnished with a wisteria, a fig and a red berberis.

As you reach the top of the path you will find on your left a White Garden, a shady lawn lightened with the silver trunks of birches, and the white double clematis 'Duchess of Edinburgh', which scrambles over a magnolia. There is a *Cornus mas* 'Variegata' with white-edged leaves and a contrasting, wine-coloured clematis 'Margot Koster'. From here you step beneath a white climbing rose, and between borders of *acanthus mollis* into what was once the old nursery and is now a Silver Garden.

In the first section, there is a small silver elaeagnus, the silver-leaved artemisia 'Lambrook Silver', woolly *Stachys lanata* or lambs' ears, white lychnis and pale yellow sisyrinchium. Pink dianthus bloom at the foot of a bird bath, while nearby the pale yellow corymbs of achillea are just visible, as well as budding umbels of allium. Woolly mulleins (verbascums) spread their hairy silver leaves, and the silvery purple foliage of *Rosa argentea* makes a delicate contrast. In the second area, a paved circle with a border, you can see *Artemisia stellerana* which has nearly white leaves, the feathery *A. discolor* and the slashed leaves of *A. ludoviciana*.

Returning through the White Garden, and crossing the upper lawn, past a golden elm, a weeping birch and a red oak, you come to the lido, a dry ditch with steep banks. Here grow the skunk cabbage (*Lysichiton americanus*) Solomon's seal and the huge toothed leaves of the umbrella plant (*Peltiphyllum peltatum*), a large member of the saxifrage family, whose rounded pink inflorescences of flower bloom in spring before its foliage. *Gingko biloba* stands at the top of a bank and nearby is *Acer capillipes*. A rare double white rocket (*Hesperis matronalis*, the dame's violet), shows up boldly.

The ditch leads you round behind the malthouse, where a deep cerise rose was growing on the walls, to the Ditch Garden, edged by pollarded willows. In the ditch itself we saw ferns, and a giant version of the wild geranium, and at the end a silver willow and a plant of the giant hogsweed. The wild takes over here, and you might imagine yourself to be by a shady stream in natural countryside.

This is a garden not to be missed for anyone who enjoys the cottage style and who is interested in the many traditional and rare plants that Mrs Fish was instrumental in reintroducing.

Hadspen Garden and Nursery

ADDRESS AND TELEPHONE: Castle Cary, Somerset BA7 7NG. Tel. Castle Cary (0963) 50939

OWNER: Mr Niall Hobhouse. Garden and nursery managed by Mr and Mrs Pope, Laundry Cottage

DIRECTIONS: 2 miles SE of Castle Cary on the A371. Public transport: BR to Castle Cary 4 miles

OPENING TIMES: beginning of March to end of September, Thurs, Fri, Sat, Sun, BH Mon 9–6. House not open

ADMISSION: £2, children 50p

CAR PARKING: yes. Coach parties by arrangement

TOILETS: yes

REFRESHMENTS: tea Sun only

SHOP: nursery

DOGS: no

WHEELCHAIR ACCESS: to part of garden. Toilets for the disabled: yes

PEAK MONTHS: May to September

NOTABLE FEATURES: south-facing walled garden, with shrub, mixed herbaceous and hosta borders; large lily pond; specimen trees; wild garden; shrubberies; meadow with wild flowers; National Collection of rodgersias

Hadspen is a notable garden, rich in plants and trees, lying concealed by broad-leaved woodlands in the Somerset countryside. The Ham stone manor house was built by the Hobhouse family in the 18C. Mrs Penelope Hobhouse, the respected gardener and garden writer, reclaimed and redesigned the family garden in the 1970s, after 30 years' neglect. The present managers, Mr and Mrs Pope, took over in 1980.

The main garden is now separated from the house and its immediate surroundings, which are private. As if to emphasise this fact, when you visit Hadspen you now enter at what was originally the end of the garden, arriving at its highest point. You find yourself standing at the top of a south-facing slope, a sun-trap protected by trees. To your right is a splendid rectangular lily pond, created by Penelope Hobhouse out of a large water tank, or reservoir. At the foot of a double stone terrace, sun-loving plants surround the pool, while beyond it, near a green cone of dawn redwood (*Metasequoia glyptostropoides*), you can just see the roof of the former gardener's cottage, where tea is provided on Sunday. Around you, in raised beds set in gravel, silver-leaved plants predominate: bold heads of artichokes and the prickly scotch thistle (onopordum), towering above silver *Stachys lanata*, silver thyme and purple sage. Directly below you, through an open doorway in the wall of the old kitchen garden, you can glimpse a double herbaceous border of yellow and gold.

Hadspen has the modern design feature of a number of distinct, small areas—the kitchen garden, for example, forms a separate 'room' within which there are different planting themes. However, the garden retains a unity which enables the visitor to move freely from one feature to the next without being over-conscious of its creators' intentions. It possesses a romantic quality, stemming from its peaceful setting in the Somerset fields, its wild flower meadows, its tangled shrubberies, the profuse banks of flowers and the half-hidden, sometimes overhung Victorian garden buildings.

Romance is seldom achieved without hard work, and there has been plenty of this at Hadspen in recent years. The walled kitchen garden, a 'D' shape set on the steep southerly slope, has been redesigned and planted by the Popes to accommodate predominantly shrubs and herbaceous plants rather than vegetables. A mature border of tall shrubs, interspersed with wall climbers, runs the length of the straight north-east facing wall, leading you downwards into the valley. Here, near a young Caucasian wing nut (*Pterocarya fraxinifolia*) and in a suitably cool and shaded area, you will find several specimens of the Hadspen rodgersia collection such as the dark red *R. pinnata* 'Superba', *R. aesculifolia* and *R. sambucifolia*, with their well defined leaves.

Nearby, a white seat in the Lutyens style faces a steep, upward sloping double border protected by beech hedges. These hedges were built specifically to shade the garden's sizeable collection of hostas, many of which were grown from seed by the former head gardener, Eric Smith. They range from large plants with handsome, deep-veined leaves to tiny circles of delicate foliage; the leaf colour varying from blue-green to light golden. Among them we noticed the cultivars 'Hadspen Blue' and 'Hadspen Heron' and the vivid *H. fortunei* 'Variegata', a blue with a brilliant green edging.

The hosta borders reach half-way up the hill, to where a gravel path, edged with clumps of purple-flowering catmint, bisects the walled garden from south-west to north-east. Beyond and upward of the intersection the borders change to gold and yellow-flowered herbaceous planting, varied from time to time with white and silver: yellow lupins, roses and hypericum, bronze fennel, yellow Jerusalem sage (*Phlomis fruticosa*) and rock roses. If you turn right at the top of the border and follow the curving wall round, the colours change to orange, red, blue and purple. Some vegetables and soft fruits have also been retained, a reminder of the garden's original purpose. A young red oak, (*Quercus robur*) has been planted on the lawn below the vegetable patch.

A border of silver and grey-leaved plants is planted against the outer south-west facing wall of the kitchen garden: artemisias, senecios, santolinas and the morning glory bush (*Convolvulus cneorum*), whose white, pink-flushed flowers are less conspicuous than its silky, glimmering leaves. The graceful silver elaeagnus *E. angustifolia* shelters against the wall. When we visited, a foxglove tree (*Paulownia tomentosa*) had been cut back by a previous spell of frost but was already showing signs of new growth.

This silver border faces the arboretum, where we noticed two swamp cypresses (*Taxodium distichum*) and a group of katsuras (*Cercidiphyllum japonicum*) with their distinctive rounded leaves, bronze when young and turning to bright colours in autumn. A bamboo walk leads you down past the Victorian summerhouse to a small square pond at the foot of the hill flanked by a tulip tree

(*Liriodendron tulipifera*) and a Persian ironwood (*Parrotia persica*). Here you can look out over the peaceful meadow valley.

From this point you move uphill, high Victorian shrubberies masking the walled garden and the entrance area. On your way you pass an ancient meadow, where fritillaries grow in spring and spotted orchids in early summer. The shrubberies are gradually being thinned and cleared by Mr and Mrs Pope (who do all the garden work apart from grass cutting), to allow some original plantings to flourish freely.

At the top of the slope, just inside the boundary fence, is a Victorian fountain, which forms a historical link between the garden and the house (now visible on the slope above). Here a grandmother of the Hobhouse family, influenced by a visit to Italy, created a terrace, adding curved stonework, steps and a pool. Flower beds were then laid out for bedding geraniums and other annuals but the whole area is now being simplified and replanted.

Returning around the shrubberies, you can have tea (on Sundays) in the gardener's cottage which, though small, once housed a family with nine children. There is much to see on the terraces around the rectangular lily pool, including a loquat (*Eriobotrya japonica*), which in favourable years produces orange, pear-shaped fruits, and a variegated buckthorn (*Rhamnus alaterna* 'Argenteovariegata'). We noticed the handsome, blue-leaved, red-fruiting *Berberis temolaica* and the evergreen clematis *C. armandii* scrambling over the wall. There are white and pink water lilies in the pool and damp-loving plants on its verges, as well as silver-leaved plants among the stones and a silver willow marking its western end.

Hadspen is a garden in a constant state of regeneration, retaining important features from each stage of its development, and remaining vividly in the memory. Many plants grown in the garden, some not easily found elsewhere, can be obtained in the nursery at the exit.

Hestercombe House Gardens

ADDRESS AND TELEPHONE: Cheddon Fitzpaine, Taunton, Somerset. Tel. (0823) 337222

OWNERS: Somerset County Council, Fire Brigade HQ

DIRECTIONS: 4 miles from Taunton, close to the village of Cheddon Fitzpaine. Signposted from all the main roads with the Tourist Information Daisy symbol. No public transport

OPENING TIMES: all year, Mon to Fri 9–5, also Sat and Sun 1 May to 30 September 2–5. Parties by prior arrangement only

ADMISSION: a donation of £1 is requested towards the Garden Restoration Fund

CAR PARKING: yes

TOILETS: yes, one

REFRESHMENTS: no

SHOP: no

DOGS: on lead only

WHEELCHAIR ACCESS: partial; entrance is ramped. Toilets for the disabled: yes, possible

PEAK MONTHS: May to August

One of the best surviving examples of the collaboration between Sir Edwin Lutyens and Gertrude Jekyll, this beautiful garden was designed and created by them in the first decade of this century. The house is now the headquarters of the Somerset Fire Brigade; the gardens are managed by a panel chaired by the Chief Fire Officer and cared for by Brigade garden staff.

The word Hestercombe is derived from the Saxon word Hegsteldescumb, meaning Batchelors' Valley. In the 9C, the land formed part of Taunton Deane, the manor of the Bishop of Winchester. The park was developed after around 1750 by Coplestone Warre Bampfylde, and the present house enlarged and remodelled in Victorian times, between 1874 and 1877. The Upper Terrace was introduced during the same period, along with the French Renaissance style tower and the 'New' façades.

The Hon. E.W.B. Portman was given the estate in 1892 as a present, and he commissioned Lutyens to design him a garden in 1903; it was finished in 1908. The garden deteriorated badly during the 1939–45 war, when part of the house was occupied by North American military troops. After Mrs Portman's death in 1951, ownership of the estate passed to the Crown; house, garden and grounds were leased to Somerset County Council and restoration began in 1973.

An architect by profession, and one of the best architects this country has ever produced, Lutyens was an accomplished designer of family houses complemented by beautiful gardens—one of the most famous is Folly Farm in Sulhamstead, Berkshire. At Hestercombe, the house and upper terrace were already in existence and the garden had to be planned accordingly. Lutyens designed a huge sunken plat bounded by terraces—the Grey Walk and the east and west rills—and with a 230ft pergola along the southern end. The orangery terrace runs off at an angle to the north-east, linked to the main garden by the rotunda, a strong pivot set above the eastern end of the Grey Walk. At the far end of the orangery (the only Lutyens building at Hestercombe) is a separate 'garden room', the Dutch garden, providing a subtle design link with the rose garden at the north-west entrance point.

Throughout the garden, Lutyens made use of readily available local materials—Morte slate, a split stone quarried from behind the house and soft yellow Ham stone (quarried from Ham Hill near Yeovil). As well as providing attractive contrasting effects, these local stones helped link the garden with the surrounding landscape; there are beautiful views to the south over Taunton Vale to the Blackdown Hills. He also created a number of excellent vistas— from the rose garden down the west rill, from the rotunda down the east rill, from the rotunda along the orangery terrace and so on. In common with all the best Lutyens gardens, Hestercombe gives an exhilarating sense of spaciousness, achieved through a fascinating combination and manipulation of narrow and wide areas,

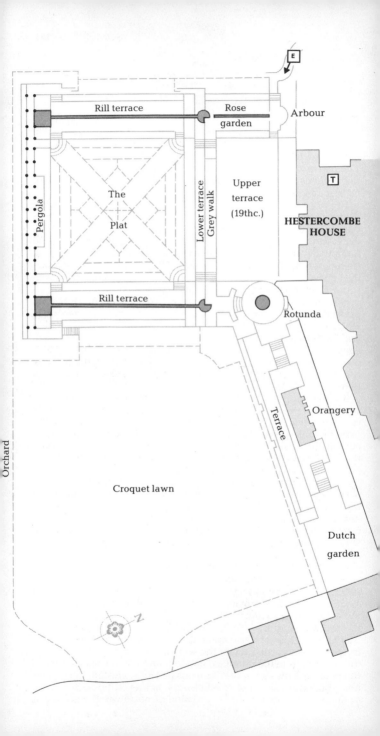

with frequent changes of level. The spreading circular steps are another typical Lutyens touch, as are the water features.

Gertrude Jekyll's planting helps to complete and emphasise the garden's architectural framework—note particularly her use of *Bergenia cordifolia* on the sunken plat. But it also softens the strong lines of the terraces and walls, with splashes and long drifts of colour. As her sight got worse (by her late thirties, she was extremely myopic), Miss Jekyll turned from painting, embroidery and silver-work to designing and planting gardens. As Jane Brown points out in *Gardens of a Golden Afternoon*, Miss Jekyll's distinctive and pioneering approach to gardening and garden design was linked in two important ways to her myopia: 'firstly, because she was most comfortable working in close-up, she appreciated and used the textures and shapes of leaves, the perfumes of flowers, to their greatest advantage; secondly, because much of the distance was a hazy blur, her perception of sweeps of colour, of the habits of light, was uncluttered by details, and therefore the more devastatingly accurate and impressive'.

The Grey Walk, below the top terrace, is a characteristic example. The planting here is on two levels, thanks to a high terrace bed below the balustrade. Soft colours, grey and grey-green, silvers, mauve and white, are used throughout, and there are plenty of scented plants—lavender (*Lavandula spica* 'Munstead') and rose-mary (*Rosmarinus officinalis* 'Jessops Upright'); border pinks (dianthus 'Excelsior') intermingling with catmint (*Nepeta mussinii*); and strongly scented *Choisya ternata* at each end of the border, overflowing the terrace wall. Structural plants include spiky yuccas and the blue thistle *Eryngium oliverianum*. The Grey Walk was the first area tackled by Somerset County Council in 1974.

From the Grey Walk, you get an excellent view over the central sunken plat, with its geometric paving outlining triangular and diamond-shaped beds, and beyond the pergola at the southern end to the fields and woods of Taunton Vale. To your left (facing the plat) is the east rill, with the rotunda above and the orangery terrace beyond; to your right, the west rill and rose garden. The original upper terrace lies directly above, between the Grey Walk and the house; but as Lutyens intended, both house and terrace are easy to ignore, attention being directed strongly southwards.

The garden entrance is to the west, down a flight of circular Lutyens steps and through the rose garden. Note a typical Jekyll detail—a French burr millstone containing clay pots of diminishing size, sunk inside each other. A delightful elm arbour at the top of the rose garden overhangs seats designed by Lutyens—this was intended as a place for Edwardian ladies of the house to take afternoon tea. Old-fashioned pink and white roses grow on the terrace wall beds and in rectangular beds down the garden, running parallel to the central rill. The rill is now full of water and filled with yellow mimulus.

The original water system designed by Lutyens proved difficult to maintain and fell into disrepair with the demise of the gardens. In recent years a new 'natural' water supply has been piped into the gardens, which with the restoration of the rills, channels and pool, means that water will become a vital part of the garden once again. At the head of each rill are very attractive pools where water spouts into semi-spherical pools, reflecting shimmering patterns of light on the recessed walls behind.

The west rill terrace is devoted mainly to shrubs and roses, with two specimens of the Japanese maple *Acer palmatum* 'Dissectum' by the lower end walls. The east rill features herbaceous borders in bright, hot colours, mainly yellow and orange, and including plenty of irises, poppies and red hot pokers, plants favoured by Gertrude Jekyll.

Miss Jekyll's original design for the centre beds of the sunken plat was never implemented. The adopted planting scheme is simple, repetitive and easy to maintain, relying on pink roses (*Rosa chinensis* 'Natalie Nypels'), peonies ('Sarah Bernhardt'), lilies and delphiniums, all surrounded by a thick border of bergenias. Tall purple foxgloves grow in the side border beds, edged with London pride, and there are mounds of *Skimmia japonica*. Various plants have seeded and grow freely in the high south-facing wall, especially pink and white valerian, and there are patches of nepeta and santolina—the overall effect is very lovely and again helps to divert attention from the front of the house. Between the pergola and the plat, to the south, is a border containing roses such as dark purple 'Cardinal de Richelieu' and *R. pimpinellifolia* 'Double White'.

The 230ft pergola provides a delightful shady and scented retreat in summer, being overhung and entwined with climbing roses, Russian vines, honeysuckle and clematis. The slivered stone pillars are alternately round and square, varying the textures of light and shadow; and they support oak crossbeams. Circular windows or *clairvoyées* are cut in the end walls, giving views out over the countryside.

Retracing your steps down the east rill, past a splendid fig tree and through a gate in the wall, you come out by the croquet lawn, with the orangery terrace above. This terrace is set at an angle running north-east from the main garden, on a line relating to a former belt of trees. Stately steps lead down to the orangery—an exemplary Lutyens building, restored in 1974—from the rotunda, and further flights lead down from the terrace to the lawn. East of the orangery, steps lead up to the little Dutch garden, built on the site of an old rubbish tip, with planted beds framed by paving and six Italianate terracotta pots. A sloping red-tiled roof on the east side gives colour and contrast.

Orange trees are overwintered in the orangery and placed in the rotunda in summer, around the circular central pool. The rotunda also provides fine examples of Lutyens' subtle use of stonework and paving, and bold planting beneath the inner walls complements the strong circular structure. You can return from the rotunda to the garden entrance via the Grey Walk, or top terrace.

Montacute House

ADDRESS AND TELEPHONE: Montacute, Somerset TA15 6XP. Tel. Martock (0935) 823289

OWNERS: The National Trust

DIRECTIONS: in Montacute village, 4 miles W of Yeovil, on S side of A3088, 3 miles E of A303 near Ilchester. Public transport: Safeway/Kingston Yeovil to Crewkerne bus (passing close Yeovil Pen Mill BR and Crewkerne). Yeovil Pen Mill station, no practical Sun service, except May to September 5½ miles; Yeovil Junction 7 miles; Crewkerne 7 miles

OPENING TIMES: garden and park open every day except Tues throughout the year, 11.30–5.30 or dusk if earlier. House open at different times

ADMISSION: free to NT members, otherwise house, garden and park £4, parties £3.50. Garden and park only, March to November £2, 4 November to end March £1. Party organiser please book visits, lunches and teas by writing with sae to Administrator

CAR PARKING: yes, free car park opens 11.30

TOILETS: yes

REFRESHMENTS: restaurant

SHOP: yes

DOGS: in park only, on leads

WHEELCHAIR ACCESS: garden, restaurant and shop only. Toilets for the disabled: yes

PEAK MONTHS: June to October

NOTABLE FEATURES: mixed borders, old roses, lily pool; orangery; fine hedges and stonework; historic layout

One of the finest Elizabethan houses in England, Montacute House is surrounded on all sides by beautiful gardens. Unfortunately few records survive of the original Elizabethan planting plans, but the basic shape of the gardens has been retained through the centuries.

In 1587 Sir Edward Phelips inherited the Montacute property jointly with his first wife, Margaret, from his father, Thomas Phelips. Sir Edward was a successful lawyer and eventually became Master of the Rolls. He commissioned William Arnold, a Somerset mason, to design Montacute House, which was probably finished in 1601. Montacute remained in the possession of the Phelips family until 1931, when it was presented to the National Trust.

Much of the present garden dates from the mid 19C, when William Phelips moved here with his newly married wife, Ellen Helyar. Ellen and her gardener, Mr Pridham, replaced the viewing mound in the North Garden with an ornamental pond and planted 44 sentinel Irish yews along the walks. The vast undulating hedges of English yew were planted around a century earlier, although their exact age is uncertain. The original drive had also been replaced, in 1785–87, by the 5th Edward Phelips, who established the west drive leading to a new entrance front.

One important thing to appreciate at Montacute is the quite unusual balance achieved between house and gardens. As Graham Stuart Thomas points out (*Gardens of the National Trust*), the garden is 'much bigger than one can grasp in a short visit—I think this is because the design is so closely allied in scale to the house'.

The entrance to the two car parks is just off the south drive. Created in the old walled kitchen gardens, these car parks have

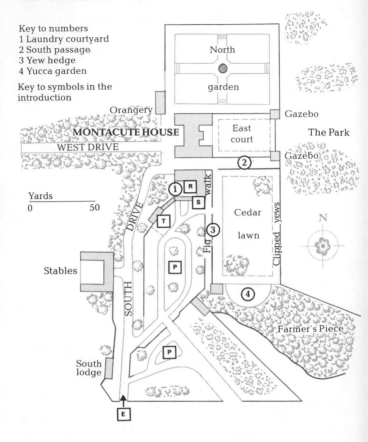

Key to numbers
1 Laundry courtyard
2 South passage
3 Yew hedge
4 Yucca garden

Key to symbols in the introduction

been hailed by Roger Newman (*GC&HTJ Supplement*, July 26, 1985) as 'models of their kind'—they are landscaped with Norway maples and shrubs including weigela, viburnum and ceanothus.

Entry into the garden is through a gate in the north-east corner. This area was once an orchard, known by the curious name of Pig's Wheatie. Now called cedar lawn it was levelled to provide a bowling green in the last century. It features four very fine trees—an Atlas cedar (*C. atlantica*) and a blue cedar (*C. atlantica glauca*) dating from Victorian times and two 250-year-old sweet chestnuts (*Castanea sativa*). The extraordinary yew hedge is worth examining at close quarters—over the centuries it has developed a strange bulging and undulating surface, as if imaginatively sculpted. Young growth in spring gives an attractive two-tone effect; in autumn the surface looks mossy.

The hedge leads down to a 19C arcaded garden house, decorated in the early 20C with an Elizabethan-style façade. Between the hedge and the kitchen garden wall is the fig walk, with its big old mouse-eaten fig trees, probably dating from the last century. The northern part of this walk was replanted recently, with a variety of small trees and shrubs—choisya 'Sundance', *Elaeagnus pungens* 'Gilt Edge', stranvaesia—underplanted with hostas, *Campanula latifolia* and *Iris sibirica*.

Beyond yew arches at the southern end of the cedar lawn is the small semicircular pillar garden or yucca garden, with its two beds of *Yucca recurvifolia*. Further south is Farmer's Piece, a wildish area now planted with daffodils, colchicums, Turk's-cap lilies (*L. martagon*) and other bulbs. A working horse (employed as a lawnmower) was once kept here. The trees are mainly Scots pine and evergreen or holm oak; also a rain tree (*Koelreuteria paniculata*) and a fine Judas tree (*Cercis siliquastrum*).

Walking back towards the house, up the east side of cedar lawn, note the clipped Irish yews, a dominant feature at Montacute. A large number of these yews were planted in the middle of the 19C, of which 96 remain, up to 16ft high. They are pruned every year by hand, with secateurs, a labour-intensive task—one tree takes a minimum of two hours. (The English yew hedges are trimmed with electric clippers.) The white garden seats are from a design by Lutyens, and stand out boldly—'amid so much green, I think it's important to have a contrasting focal point', explains head gardener Graham Kendall. The wildness of the park, beyond the walls, makes a pleasing contrast with the formality of the gardens.

The fine planting of the south passage (*Prunus laurocerasus* 'Otto Luyken', a double-flowered gorse, China tea roses and hebe) is but a prelude to the delights of the east court, below the beautiful east front of the house. This great forecourt was replanted in 1983, on the advice of Jim Marshall, assistant gardens adviser to the National Trust, and keeping to a policy of planting in strong colours—yellows, blues, whites and red—established in the 1950s by Mrs Phyllis Reiss of nearby Tintinhull. (The yellow stone of the house tends to swamp soft colours; Vita Sackville-West's pastel coloured scheme for the borders proved a notable failure.) Aubrieta and alyssum begin the year, followed by *Iris pallida* 'Dalmatica', plume poppies, standard honeysuckles, lupins, delphiniums and penstemons, scarlet Frensham roses and 'Orange Triumph' polyantha roses. Along the north and south walls are clematis (mainly *C. Jackmanii* with three *C. macropetala* and on the gates *C. viticella* 'Royal Velours' and *C. viticella* 'Purpurea Plena Elegans'). The year finishes with fuchsias, late roses and dahlias, which flower until the frosts come.

There are two ornate pavilions or gazebos, with ogee roofs, on either side of the east court. These are Elizabethan, contemporary with the house, and were originally used as lodging houses and to store food. The east court was the original 17C entrance court, although the gatehouse has long since disappeared. The Nine Worthies are carved in stone along the east front of the house.

Leaving this courtyard through a gate to the north (passing rose 'Blanc Double de Coubert'), you come to the magnificent north garden, surrounded on all sides by a raised gravel walk. The central ornamental pond with balustrade was introduced in the 1890s, replacing a viewing mound which disappeared around the 1840s. The rose border below the raised walk nearest the house was planted in the 1950s by Graham Stuart Thomas and Vita Sackville-West. All the roses are labelled—this is the only labelling done at

Montacute. This border was planned for interest throughout the season, with a mixture of old roses and a few species and hybrid musks. They are underplanted to good effect with *Hosta fortunei hyacintha*.

The huge square of this sunken garden is linked with 44 clipped Irish yews, flanked by the round heads of a hybrid thorn, *Crataegus* x *lavallei* (*C.* x *carrierei*). The thorns were planted in 1964, replacing cypresses. Pause on the top steps and look back down through the garden for one of the best vistas at Montacute. A gap in the giant hedge to the west gives access to the ice house.

Below the house to the south, is the orangery, a cold house built in 1848 to an 18C design. Only fan heaters are used, so the plants have to be at least moderately hardy. The vast maidenhair fern on the wall opposite the entrance is watered by a pipe from above; on the same wall are a schizophragma and a scarlet honeysuckle; the Chinese jasmine (*J. polyanthum*) flourishes on the two end walls. Standard fuchsias are grown in raised beds, underplanted with white petunias. African blue lilies (agapanthus 'Headbourne Hybrids') flower in pots outside the house, from late summer to early autumn.

The main entrance was altered to the other side of the house in the late 18C, when Edward Phelips planned the west drive and erected a new ornamental west front (salvaged from Clifton Maybank, a splendid house near Yeovil). A quarter of a mile long, the west drive is bordered by Irish yews, backed by limes, and with evergreens, hydrangeas and specie roses. It was recently renovated and the sides built up. Just below the house to the south is a little planted laundry court, overhung by a cut-leaved beech; watch out for *Salvia microphylla*, a sage with bright cerise flowers, grown as a wall plant.

Retrace your steps and ahead you will see a charming border, featuring foliage plants in a mixture of soft colours—hollies 'Golden King' (male) and 'Silver Queen' (female), cotinus and purple filbert and yellow philadelphus, underplanted with catmint, pink and blue geraniums—*G. endressii* and *G. himalayense* 'Johnson's Blue'. Further on is the 19C stable block, behind large golden yews (*Taxus baccata* 'Aurea'). A record-size Monterey cypress (*Cupressus macrocarpa*) towers above the drive, together with two young ones; opposite are a number of feathery Californian redwood trees, decapitated in the last war.

Further still is south lodge, clothed in wisteria and the rose 'Easleas Golden Rambler'. From here you can see the hill (or 'Mons Acutus'), from which Montacute takes its name, topped with a slender folly tower.

Tintinhull House Garden

ADDRESS AND TELEPHONE: Tintinhull, near Yeovil, Somerset BA22 9PZ. Tel. (0935) 822509

OWNERS: The National Trust

DIRECTIONS: 5 miles NW of Yeovil, ½ mile S of A303, on E

outskirts of Tintinhull. Public transport: Southern National bus 52 from Yeovil (passing close Yeovil Pen Mill BR) (tel. Yeovil (0935) 76233). Yeovil Pen Mill station 5½ miles; Yeovil Junction 7 miles

OPENING TIMES: 30 March to end September, Wed, Thurs, Sat and BH Mon 2–6. House not open

ADMISSION: £2.50 (NT members free). No reduction for parties or children. Coach parties by arrangement with Mrs J.M. Malins

CAR PARKING: yes

TOILETS: yes

REFRESHMENTS: teas at certain times (not NT)

SHOP: no

DOGS: no

WHEELCHAIR ACCESS: yes, to most of garden. Toilets for the disabled: no

This 2-acre Somerset garden is worth visiting many times, for the marvellous range and variety of its planting, flourishing within a series of hedged and walled enclosures. The present tenant is Dr John Malins, who maintains and develops the gardens together with his wife, Penelope Hobhouse, the well-known gardener and garden writer.

Although Tintinhull House was built around 1630 (by the Napper family) and a small walled courtyard garden was planted in the early 18C, the present garden was entirely created during this century. The Rev. Dr S.J.M. Price, who lived at Tintinhull until 1924, was probably responsible for laying the stone paving and perhaps for establishing the enclosed areas to the west. In 1933 the property was bought by Captain and Mrs Reiss. They developed Cedar Court and the Pool Garden to the north, linking them by cross-vistas and paths to the rest of the garden. Mrs Phyllis Reiss lived at Tintinhull for 28 years, from 1933 to 1961 (her husband died in 1947), donating it to the National Trust in 1954. A skilled gardener, she was responsible for much of the planting you see today—'an example of English gardening at its best' (National Trust booklet). From 1954 onwards, she was advised by Graham Stuart Thomas.

As Dame Sylvia Crowe has remarked ('Garden Design', *Country Life* 1958) 'the garden gives the impression of being much larger than it really is, because of the skilful use of space'. Dame Sylvia noted how existing trees had been used as design points—the great cedar of Lebanon in Cedar Court 'sets the pattern for its open asymmetric character', while two holm oaks (*Quercus ilex*) form 'a massive full stop to the south-west and a solid background to the Pool Garden'. The garden's main axis runs from the west front of the house down through three garden compartments to the western boundary and this is crossed (at the fountain) by a path running from the fountain garden through the kitchen garden to the orchard.

The planting is profuse and diverse; Mrs Reiss planned most of the borders for year-round interest and with an eye for colour, shape and the right placing of each plant or grouping of plants. There is plenty of scope, however, for informal effects—blue scillas, anemones and cyclamen flower in spring, periwinkles (*Vinca difformis*) grow thickly under the holm oaks and yellow fumitory (*Corydalis lutea*) makes its home in the steps.

The garden entrance is to the south, off the entrance courtyard. Walk through the house—or around the north front of the house, above Cedar Court—and through an archway to the west front. From here you can look down the long axial path, between spaced domes of clipped box. The five-bayed west front, of golden Ham stone, was completed around 1722, about a century after the house was first built. The walled forecourt dates from the same period and is known as Eagle Court, because of the two stone eagles perched on the gate piers. Note the mullion and transom windows (cross windows) of this west front—by 1722 these were somewhat old-fashioned. The circular window in the pediment was originally solid, and must have been made into a window after 1905.

Four large plots on the west front are planted with July-flowering regale lilies. The patterned path is of local grey stone and was laid before 1920. A 1930 photograph shows the box domes smaller but in their present position, but little else apart from rough grass—Mrs Reiss bought the house and began work on the garden in 1933. The planting has changed since then, but it is difficult to know how much. The massive euphorbias (*Euphorbia characias wulfenii*) are quite recently planted and seed themselves with enthusiasm, shot through by white regale lilies.

Also on the northern side you can see *Choisya ternata*, *Cytisus battandieri*, honeysuckles (*Lonicera splendida* and *L. periclymenum*), clematis 'Perle d'Azur', roses 'Frühlingsgold' and 'Helen Knight', mahonia, rosemary (*R. officinalis* 'Aureus') and the blues of polemonium, agapanthus and ceanothus. To the west are clematis 'Lasurstern', *C. flammula, C. macropetala* and *C. alpina* 'Frances Rivis', rose 'Gloire de Dijon', a white tree peony, the beautiful *Mahonia japonica* and *Mahonia lomariifolia* which only survives in fairly mild climates.

To the south are prunus 'Ukon', philadelphus 'Belle Etoile', hellebores and bergenias, perennial honesty (*Lunaria rediviva*) and others. Below the low wall on the east side grow lavenders 'Hidcote', Twickel Purple' and *Lavandula stoechas*, and an unidentified form of *Clematis montana* on the wall, grown from a Montacute cutting.

The middle garden features eight more box domes, arranged in the same pattern either side of the path. Hydrangeas flourish in the south wall bed—*H. arborescens, H. aspera villosa* and *H. sargentiana*—and ruby-red clematis 'Niobe' grows on the south-east wall, with the Chinese woodbine (*Lonicera tragophylla*) and the orange-yellow climbing honeysuckle *L.* x *tellmanniana*. In the north-east wall bed are roses 'Complicata', 'Fantin Latour', 'Charles de Mills', *R. pimpinellifolia* 'William III' and 'Double Pink'. There are many deutzias at Tintinhull—here you can see *Deutzia* x *rosea* 'Carminea'. A pair of holm oaks dating from 1910 provide necessary shape and structure to the south-west, overhanging a seat.

Azalea beds are planted either side of the path in the next garden. The soil here is rather too dry for azaleas, but the ever-reliable *R. luteum* provides scent in spring and good autumn colour. There are plenty of spring bulbs, including blue *Anemone apennina*, and gold foliage plants such as golden feverfew, gold honeysuckle (*Lonicera japonica* 'Aureo-reticulata') and gold philadelphus (*P. coronarius* 'Aureus').

The area around the circular fountain pool is planted as a white garden, with silver standard willows, white Canterbury bells, white-flowered honesty (*Lunaria annua* 'Alba'), white and pale blue irises and the white roses 'Iceberg' and 'Margaret Merril'—along with *Lychnis coronaria* 'Alba', *Galtonia candicans* and many others. Woodruff makes useful ground cover, with tiny flowers. Venus' fishing rods (*Dierama pulcherrimum*) with delicate shaded bells hang over the lily pond.

Behind the gap in the yew hedge are a number of white oak-leaved hydrangeas (*Hydrangea quercifolia*) with large lobed leaves which turn brilliant colours in autumn—and a range of unusual shade-loving plants. Scotch thistles (*Onopordum acanthium*) flank the entrance to this small enclosure tucked away behind the white garden and cornus stand either side (*C. controversa* 'Variegata').

Rosa gallica 'Officinalis' flowers light crimson in June in two long rectangular beds between the fountain garden and the kitchen garden. These beds are also planted with blue scillas (flowering at the end of March) and *Leucojum aestivum* 'Gravetye Giant', which grows to 2–3ft in April and May. The crab apple at the far end is malus 'John Downie'. Daphnes in the small borders include *D. pontica* and *D. x Burkwoodii* 'Somerset', which flowers profusely without getting leggy. A yellow tree lupin, grown from seed, spills over the gravel path.

The large rectangular kitchen garden—directly to the north, on a lower level from the rest of the garden—has been used for growing fruit, vegetables and herbs since around 1900. Vegetables are still grown in traditional fashion, but shrub roses and other decorative plants have been introduced around the edges. A haze of mauve catmint lines the central gravel path, which leads down to a gate and a small apple orchard beyond. Fastigiate pears stand either side of the path, with *Salix elaeagnus* below making a nice contrast. A cross path half-way down is bordered by espalier pear trees, with roses 'Else Poulsen' and the china rose 'Nathalie Nypels' and blue-flowered *Caryopteris clandonensis*. Many plants in this garden are both useful and ornamental/structural—fennel, angelica, Swiss chard, artichokes. The roses include sweet-smelling pink 'Isfahan', *R. moyesii* 'Geranium', the rugosa rose 'Fru Dagmar Hastrup' and many others. The tree peony *Paeonia suffruticosa* grows to the west, and huge magenta *P. suffruticosa* 'Norah Warre' at the bottom of the garden, near *Rosa villosa* 'Duplex' and another tree peony, 'Duchess of Kent'. Red-flowered *Eccremocarpus scaber* is draped over the yew hedge, which separates this garden from the Pool Garden to the east.

In 1947, Mrs Reiss built a summerhouse and laid out this Pool Garden on the site of a former tennis court, in memory of her nephew, killed as a fighter pilot in the 1939–45 war. The main borders—on opposite sides of the garden, backed by yew hedges—are described in detail by Penelope Hobhouse in *The National Trust: a Book of Gardening*. The west (east-facing) border is planted mainly in hot, bright, clear colours; the east border in softer colours linked by grey and silver foliage. Both borders contain a mixture of shrubs and small trees, foliage plants and flowering plants, with bulbs to begin the season, which extends well into October. Rose 'Allen Chandler', *Vitis vinifera* 'Purpurea' and *Clematis* x *jackmanii* grow over the summerhouse. Tall clumps of yellow irises look very effective at the corners of the lily-filled pool.

Cedar Court, below, takes its name from the huge cedar of Lebanon in the north-east corner. It also features magnolias, including *M.* x *soulangiana* set in the grass near the cedar, *M.* x *soulangiana* 'Lennei' in an island bed to the south, underplanted with yellow poppies, and *M. grandiflora* against the south-facing wall. By the entrance is a box, said to be the oldest tree in the garden, and a big yew, perhaps 400 years old. The north wall of the house is brightened by *Rosa pimpinellifolia* 'Double White', *R. pimpinellifolia* 'Williams' Double Yellow', the climbing rose 'Madame Grégoire Staechelin' and the flame creeper, *Tropaeolum speciosum*. The broad path between this north wall and the cedar lawn gives you a last delightful view down through the garden, before you leave it through the courtyard to the east. Teas are provided in the stablehouse, just off the courtyard.

STAFFORDSHIRE

Alton Towers

ADDRESS AND TELEPHONE: Alton Towers, near Alton, Staffordshire. Tel. Oakamoor (0538) 702200

OWNERS: Tussauds Group

DIRECTIONS: signposted on M1 and M6 motorways and fully signposted from exits. Off B5032 4½ miles E of Cheadle. Public transport: BR offer excursion trips from many parts of the country to include train and coach travel and admission. From London, Green Line operate daily trips during the height of the season

OPENING TIMES: late March to early November, daily 10–5, 6, or 7, depending on the time of the year. Gardens open in winter. House also open

ADMISSION: approx. £9.50 per person. Reductions and discounts for school parties, coach parties and senior citizens. Price includes admission to grounds and rides. Much reduced charge in winter for gardens only

CAR PARKING: yes

TOILETS: yes

REFRESHMENTS: café

SHOP: yes

DOGS: on lead

TOILETS FOR THE DISABLED: yes

PEAK MONTHS: June

NOTABLE FEATURES: rock garden; Italian and Dutch gardens; Pagoda Fountain; water features such as Corkscrew Fountain;

monuments and follies such as Stonehenge; Chinese Temple;
Grotto; Roman Colonnade and Swiss Cottage; woodland walk

Alton Towers is well known as an amusement park with its numerous rides and attractions, including the famous 'corkscrew' roller coaster—no wonder they call a day out here 'The Alton Towers Experience'. Don't be put off—the garden is a major attraction in itself, one of the largest and most fantastic landscape creations in the country and a showpiece of Romanticism.

Standing above the rock garden and looking down the valley, it is hard to believe that this was just a steep, rugged slope when in 1814 Charles Talbot, the 15th Earl of Shrewsbury, decided to put his dreams into reality.

The Earl was 60 when he moved to this quiet part of Staffordshire from the family seat at Heythrop in Oxfordshire. A man of considerable wealth, he was determined to spare no expense to create an enchanting and mysterious garden, full of replicas of ancient buildings and other objects from distant lands and days long past.

Besides hiring an army of labourers and gardeners, the Earl brought in specialists, including Thomas Allason and Robert Abraham, to design buildings such as the Conservatory, the Gothic Tower, the Grotto, the Pagoda Fountain, the Swiss Cottage and the very strange 'Stonehenge'. Water was diverted from a spring 2 miles away to feed all the streams, cascades and fountains. And trees were planted everywhere. It must have been a very peculiar sight—a valley clothed in young trees and set around with huge architectural features.

In 1827 Charles Talbot was succeeded by his nephew John, the 16th Earl—another flamboyant character, who also liked to do things on a grand scale, and who engaged A.W.N. Pugin to design the big house overlooking the valley. This mysterious, dark mansion with its many towers and turrets is now a ruin—and as such very effective and atmospheric—but in its day it would have crowned the valley like a fairy-tale castle. The garden below was an example of Romanticism at its most passionate and the effect was so garish that Loudon in 1833 wrote that the garden was 'in excessively bad taste, or rather, perhaps, as the work of a morbid imagination joined to the command of unlimited resources'.

With the passage of time, Alton Towers has changed beyond recognition. After 170 years the trees now fill the valley with a sea of foliage, washing over and in some instances almost swallowing up the various monuments which now act as focal points rather than intruding eye-sores.

The steep sides of the Churnet Valley are terraced with the head of the valley, beneath the causeway, transformed into a huge rock garden. This part of the garden is relatively new: the central, more fertile area was constructed in 1928, using stone from a local quarry and the shady section added in the 1930s.

Dwarf conifers, spiraeas, sedums and saxifrages seem to cling to the sides as the rock garden tumbles into the valley below. In May and June it is a mass of colour, with rhododendrons and azaleas flowering among the light and dark shades of conifers. Water tumbles down through the rock garden to the canal, which then winds away out of sight.

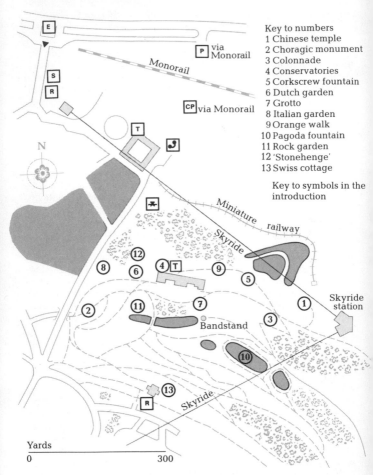

Key to numbers
1 Chinese temple
2 Choragic monument
3 Colonnade
4 Conservatories
5 Corkscrew fountain
6 Dutch garden
7 Grotto
8 Italian garden
9 Orange walk
10 Pagoda fountain
11 Rock garden
12 'Stonehenge'
13 Swiss cottage

Key to symbols in the introduction

Standing on a knoll above the rock garden is the Choragic Monument. This was erected by the 16th Earl as a memorial and tribute to his uncle. The inscription on its walls read: 'He made the desert smile'.

The Italian garden, north-east of the rock garden, is watched over by statues of the apostles, perched on a high wall. Formal beds of roses enjoy the sun at this high level, and autumn colour is provided by acers. Not far away you can find the Dutch garden and conservatory.

Higher up the bank and hidden by the trees, is the monument known as Stonehenge. Unlike the original on Salisbury Plain, this Stonehenge is built in a straight line! The domed conservatory, designed by Robert Abraham, was heated by underground ovens, the entrance to which is clearly visible on the terrace below.

The Swiss Cottage stands on the hillside across the valley, commanding a magnificent view over the trees to the conservatory and terraces. Now converted to a restaurant, it was originally the home of a blind Welsh harp player, who was employed to fill the valley with music.

Outside the conservatory is a temple, with a grotto below. From here the Orange Walk leads off towards the Corkscrew Fountain, recently restored. Not far away is the Chinese temple, with lovely views across the garden. Terrace walls in the valley below provide shelter for magnolias and an old gnarled Judas Tree (*Cercis siliquastrum*), whose flowers appear in May on the joints of branches and the trunk.

Following the path down, past Roman colonnades, more pools and fountains and a summerhouse, you will eventually reach the valley floor, and the Pagoda Fountain, perhaps the most fascinating monument in the garden. Again designed by Abraham, this is a copy of the To Ho Pagoda in Canton. A brightly painted three-storey structure, it sits on a little island in the centre of a pool, and a jet of water shoots 70ft into the air from the roof.

Splendid trees can be found everywhere throughout the garden—tulip trees, the fern-leafed beech, oaks, chestnuts, sycamores, cedars and Wellingtonias to mention but a few. And at the lower end of the valley are miles of footpath through beautiful woodland. Venture into the ruins of the mansion to investigate two further areas of garden—Her Ladyship's Garden and the Star Garden.

The leisure park sky ride passes silently over the gardens, giving an aerial view not to be missed.

The Dorothy Clive Garden

ADDRESS AND TELEPHONE: The Dorothy Clive Garden, Willoughbridge, near Market Drayton, Staffordshire TF9 4EU. Tel. Pipegate (063 081) 237

OWNERS: The Willoughbridge Garden Trust

DIRECTIONS: 9 miles SW of Newcastle-under-Lyme. 1 mile E of Woore on A51

OPENING TIMES: Easter to October, daily 10–5.30

ADMISSION: £1.50, children 50p

CAR PARKING: yes and for coaches

TOILETS: yes

REFRESHMENTS: tea room

SHOP: no

DOGS: on lead

WHEELCHAIR ACCESS: yes, also special parking near entrance to quarry garden. Toilets for the disabled: yes

PEAK MONTHS: May and June for rhododendrons and azaleas

NOTABLE FEATURES: woodland/quarry garden with rhododendrons; scree garden with pool; fine shrubs in landscaped setting; camellia trials

The Dorothy Clive Memorial Garden consists of some 7 acres of garden set in the rolling countryside of the Staffordshire–Shropshire borders. There is no grand mansion, but the garden features woodland and rhododendrons, rock and scree gardens, shrub roses and rare trees. The richness of planting here will delight keen plantspeople and garden enthusiasts alike, and the atmosphere is both tranquil and intimate.

The garden was created in the late 1930s by Colonel Harry Clive. He and his wife, Dorothy, lived in the large house known as Elds Gorse (still standing but now privately owned). Failing health meant that Dorothy Clive could only walk circuits of the lawn near the house—even her dogs grew bored of the routine and eventually refused to accompany her. Hoping to make life more pleasant for his wife, Colonel Clive decided to build her a garden in the woodland above the house.

The 1½-acre site had originally been a gravel pit but left undisturbed for 20 years had become an impregnable mass of pines, larches, small oaks, silver birches, mountain ash, brambles, holly and elderberry bushes. Paths were cut into the undergrowth and slowly the woodland garden took shape.

The quarry offered good shelter from bitter winds and the gravel screenings from the pit, combined with the rich leaf mould, made a good well-drained soil capable of supporting a wide range of plants. Rhododendrons grew particularly well. Frank Knight, a director of the Royal Horticultural Society's Garden at Wisley, and a friend of the Colonel, helped to choose the plants. The garden gave Dorothy Clive much pleasure during the last years of her life. She died in 1942 and her ashes were scattered from a path above the quarry—a stone marks the site.

After her death, Colonel Clive sold Elds Gorse and built a bungalow at the entrance to the quarry. In 1958 he set up The Willoughbridge Garden Trust in order to preserve the garden for the enjoyment of the public. At 80, the Colonel was still an active man and he began developing the sloping field between the bungalow and the main road. He planted a collection of Exbury azaleas and his grandchildren celebrated his birthday by planting two blue cedars (*Cedrus atlantica glauca*).

Harry Clive died in 1963 and since then many people have been involved in developing and improving the site and ensuring that this garden, a memorial to Dorothy Clive, is well preserved.

A rock and scree garden have recently been constructed, with a pool, and a great many bulbs are planted here. There are several dwarf tulips, including *Tulipa tarda* which has white star-shaped flowers with large yellow centres.

Around the pool, irises thrive among primulas. In mid summer you can see *Dierama pulcherrimum*—the wandflower or angel's fishing rod—with its wiry arching stems bearing dangling deep purplish-red trumpet-shaped flowers.

The planting in the scree garden is carefully orchestrated for colour throughout the season. Once the candelabra primulas are past their best, the ligularias start showing off their orange and yellow flowers against green and purple foliage.

Island beds in the lawns around the scree garden display an enormous selection of shrubs, roses and herbaceous plants. The heather beds look very effective beneath silver birches. Along the western boundary is a collection of camellias, donated by the International Camellia Society in 1978. Over 80 varieties of camellia are currently being tested here.

Sun-loving plants bask on a terrace higher up the slope, and further on, past a bungalow, you arrive at the entrance to Colonel Clive's original creation. Rhododendrons shelter beneath mature trees, a breathtaking sight in May and June when viewed from the higher perimeter path. Every shade of pink, red, purple and mauve can be seen here, together with creamy yellows. Noteworthy species include the blood-red *Rhododendron thompsonii*, the rose-pink flowered *R. orbiculare* which has heart-shaped leaves, and the pale yellow *R. campylocarpum elatum*. Among the hybrids are *R.* 'Goldsworth Yellow', the white- flowered *R.* 'Sappho' and the blue, compact *R.* 'Blue Tit'.

As the rhododendrons begin to fade, the hybrid azaleas, including Ghent, Exbury and Knaphill cultivars blossom in bright pinks, reds, oranges, and yellows and fill the air with scent.

Visitors to this garden can always expect to find something of interest, no matter what the season. Winter aconites are among the first flowers to show, followed by bulbs such as *Crocus tomasinianus* with its slender lavender-coloured flowers. Some of the rhododendrons are early flowerers too—rhododendron 'Christmas Cheer', for example, produces white flowers in March. By May there is a rich display of spring flowers, beneath flowering cherries and crab apples. Shortly afterwards the rhododendrons reach their peak, and then come the shrub roses, accompanied by a huge variety of summer flowers. With the coming of summer a different range of flowers takes over—including gazanias, osteospermums and crocosmias among them.

Dahlias and chrysanthemums provide the colour as autumn approaches and from September to November the garden offers autumnal tones and tints, along with bright fruits and seeds. There are some late flowering bulbs too, such as *Nerine bowdenii*, a moderately hardy plant with large elegant pink flowers.

Conifers provide interest in winter and form a backdrop throughout the year—some are features in their own right. No matter in which direction you look, whatever the time of year, there is always something to catch your attention. This is a garden in which Dorothy Clive—and her dogs—would have delighted.

Moseley Old Hall

ADDRESS AND TELEPHONE: Moseley Old Hall, Moseley Old Hall Lane, Wolverhampton, Staffordshire, WV10 7HY. Tel. Wolverhampton (0902) 782808

OWNERS: The National Trust

DIRECTIONS: 4 miles N of Wolverhampton, between A449 and A460. Public transport: Wolverhampton BR 4 miles. Midland Red Buses, Wolverhampton to Cannock, alight Bognop Road, then ¾ mile walk

OPENING TIMES: mid March to end October, Wed, Sat, Sun and BH Mon 2–5.30; also Tues in July and August. House also open

ADMISSION: house and garden £2.50, family ticket £6.25. Parties by prior arrangement

CAR PARKING: yes

TOILETS: yes

REFRESHMENTS: café

SHOP: yes

DOGS: no

WHEELCHAIR ACCESS: yes (ground floor of house). Toilets for the disabled: yes

PEAK SEASON: July and August

NOTABLE FEATURES: reconstruction of a mid-17C garden, including knot garden, arbour, hornbeam tunnel and nut walk; orchard

Two days after his defeat at the Battle of Worcester in September 1651, Charles II took refuge in the half-timbered Tudor house of Moseley Old Hall. The house has since (c 1870) been clad in dull blue-grey bricks, giving it a 19C appearance, apart from its high pointed gables and Elizabethan chimneys.

Moseley Old Hall was given to the National Trust in 1962, by the Wiggin family. The house was then virtually empty and in a bad state of repair, having suffered mining subsidence in the 1920s. Of the garden, about an acre in extent, nothing remained except for the surrounding walls, a few old fruit trees, some misshapen yews and a variegated holly. Pigsties, hen houses and broken cloches lay abandoned. It was decided to construct a garden in mid-17C style, using plants known to have been cultivated at that time. Graham Stuart Thomas took charge of the reconstruction, helped by advice from garden historian Miles Hadfield and using money raised by the Wolverhampton Centre of the National Trust. By spring 1963 most of the work was completed.

The knot garden, the principal feature, lies south of the Hall and is best viewed from the upper rooms. It is a copy of one designed in 1640 by the Rev. Walter Stonehouse, Rector of Darfield in Yorkshire; the original design is kept in the Library of Magdalen College, Oxford.

The Moseley knot comprises 11 neatly clipped spheres of box standing on 3ft stems, giving the garden a vertical dimension. Each sphere is surrounded by a circular bed of large pebbles and contained within dwarf box hedging.

Along one side of the knot garden is a wooden arbour, its design inspired by one in *A Gardener's Labyrinth*, 1577, by Thomas Hills. It is now well covered with the white-flowering virgin's bower (*Clematis flammula*)—one of the few clematis with a scent—and *Clematis viticella*, contrasting with the deep purple Teinturier Grape (*Vitis vinifera* 'Purpurea'). Narrow borders beneath the arbour are filled with fragrant lavender (*Lavandula angustifolia*).

Beyond the arbour is a leafy walk through a hornbeam tunnel, which changes direction to lead west through a nut walk lined with varieties of hazel. Snowdrops (*Galanthus nivalis*), winter aconite (*Eranthis hyemalis*) and the Siberian squill (*Scilla siberica*) flower in winter and early spring, in the grass beneath the garden wall to one side of the walk. These are followed by stinking hellebore (*Helleborus foetidus*) and snake's head fritillary (*Fritillaria meleagris*), and in autumn by the autumn crocus (*Colchicum autumnale*) and pink-flowering *Cyclamen hederifolium*.

At the end of the nut walk is the King's Gate, by which Charles II is said to have entered Moseley, stealing in secretly from the surrounding fields. The Long Walk beyond was originally a sweet chestnut avenue; now only one of the original trees remains, but the walk has been replanted with young trees. A flagged path leading from the nut walk to the back door of the house divides the knot garden from the orchard and is lined with morello cherries (*Prunus cerasus austera*), quinces (*Cydonia oblonga*), black mulberries (*Morus nigra*) and medlars (*Mespilus germanica*).

Close to the King's Door, as the back door is now known, is a small box-edged herb garden. The orchard is planted with varieties of fruit trees known to have been cultivated in the mid 17C, and shrub roses grow against the boundary wall. Further along, by the barn, now a tea room, you can see niches or 'bee boles' set into the wall. These once sheltered straw bee skeps—small conical hives.

The front garden, to the east of the Hall can be reached via a wrought iron gate at the end of the timber arbour. On the neat lawns are small spirals and cones of clipped box, in keeping with the scale of the garden. There are two beds of tutsan (*Hypericum androsaemum*) edged with wall germander (*Teucrium chamaedrys*).

Against the walls is one of the oldest roses known to cultivation, the apothecary's rose (*Rosa gallica* 'Officinalis') and its pink and white-striped sport *R. gallica* 'Versicolor'; also the white rose of York or Jacobite Rose (*R.* x *alba* 'Maxima') and the eglantine or sweet briar (*R. rubiginosa*).

Among herbaceous plants in the borders is bouncing Bet or soapwort (*Saponaria officinalis*), pink and white forms of *Paeonia officinalis*, Solomon's seal (*Polygonatum* x *hybridum*), red valerian (*Centranthus ruber*) and Cupid's dart (*Catananche caerulea*). In spring there are striped tulips and crown imperials (*Fritillaria imperialis*).

The planting at Moseley Old Hall is exceptional, but even more successful is the design and layout, with various elements skilfully linked to create a convincing picture of a mid-17C garden.

Shugborough

ADDRESS AND TELEPHONE: Shugborough, Milford, near Stafford ST17 0XB. Tel. Little Haywood (0889) 881 388

OWNERS: The National Trust, but leased to and administered by Staffordshire County Council

DIRECTIONS: 5½ miles SE of Stafford off A513 at Milford. Public transport: Stafford BR 6 miles. Buses from Stafford, Tamworth and Lichfield

OPENING TIMES: Good Fri 29 March to 27 October, daily 11–5. 28 October to 31 December, daily 11–4. Note: 2 January to 27 March 1992 booked parties only

ADMISSION: parking, which includes admission to park and gardens, £1 per car. House, museum and farm: £6.50 (otherwise £2.50 per site), OAPs, children and UB40 holders £3. Family ticket £12. Parties should book in advance

CAR PARKING: yes, see above

TOILETS: yes

REFRESHMENTS: café

SHOP: yes

DOGS: on lead in grounds only

WHEELCHAIR ACCESS: yes. Toilets for the disabled: yes

PEAK MONTHS: spring for daffodils, early June for rhododendrons, October for autumn colours

NOTABLE FEATURES: monuments throughout park and garden; wild garden, terraces and rose garden; Chinese House with Chinese plantings; museum and rare breeds farm

The magnificent mansion at Shugborough, ancestral home of Lord Lichfield, lies in a broad, flat valley beside the River Sow where it meets the River Trent. The surrounding land rises gently to form a wooded boundary of towering beeches and other mature native species underplanted with masses of *Rhododendron ponticum*. More fine trees are scattered over the valley floor. A unique collection of buildings and monuments of the 'Greek Revival'—indulgences of 18C owners—make this estate of special interest to historians.

In 1744, Admiral Lord George Anson returned from a 4-year voyage around the world. He brought back a fortune in the form of a captured Spanish galleon and with this wealth he and his brother, Thomas, were able to enlarge the family home and set about landscaping the park and gardens. Anson also introduced *Lathyrus nervosa* or Lord Anson's Blue Pea, to England, and this fragrant blue flower is still cultivated at Shugborough.

Many of the monuments at Shugborough were designed by Thomas Wright of Durham or by James 'Athenian' Stuart—so nicknamed because of his fondness for Greek architecture. Since 1748, a considerable number of the original monuments, such as a Pagoda, Palladian Bridge, Cascade, Colonnade and a Ladies Seat have disappeared. The remaining eight are excellent examples of 18C fantastical architecture.

You can view most of the monuments on the special routed tour of the garden. For those with more stamina there is an additional tour covering 2 miles of the parkland to take in the Tower of the Winds, Triumphal Arch and the Lanthorn of Demosthenes.

The gardens surrounding the house—some 22 acres—are basically Georgian but show considerable Victorian influence with features such as the formal terraces and rose garden. A wild garden to the south of the house leads into landscaped and formal areas.

A path gently meanders through the wild garden, among tall beeches, limes and yews. There are masses of purple rhododendrons and yellow azaleas and the arresting scent of several osmarea. *Buddleia alternifolia*, with its graceful arching branches, displays fragrant lilac flowers in June. A number of young viburnums are also beginning to make their mark, such as *Viburnum rhytidophyllum* with its creamy-white flowers in May.

The wild garden also holds many species roses—*Rosa rubiginosa* with clear pink fragrant flowers, *R. rugosa* 'Alba'—a vigorous grower with beautiful white flowers—and *R.r.* 'Scabrosa' which is known for its excellent foliage and huge crimson flowers followed by tomato-red hips in the autumn.

The ground cover planting in the wild garden includes some fine herbaceous plants such as the attractive salmon coloured *Geranium endressii* 'Waldegrave Pink', and dicentras, with their nodding heart-shaped flowers. At the south end, the path doubles back on itself to follow the River Sow along the bank—a mass of daffodils in spring, followed by bluebells. Nearer to the mansion, the path passes more plantings of rhododendrons, and groups of rugosa roses—the pale pink ground cover rose 'Nozomi' and the shrub rose 'Nevada' which has creamy-white semi-double highly fragrant flowers on almost thornless branches. An invaluable small tree in this border is *Acer palmatum* 'Senkaki', the coral bark maple, which has attractive coral red younger branches and canary yellow leaves in autumn.

The formal part of the garden, Victorian in layout, is sited on the west side of the house. Broad grass terraces, hedged round with lavender, rise from the river to the house. A central path is flanked by golden yews clipped into huge dome shapes. A somewhat discordant note is struck by Thomas Wright's 18C mock ruin—erected on the bank of the River Sow for picturesque effect.

The planting on the right of the terrace (as you face the house) reaches full splendour in late summer. It is a combination of variegated foliage cornus and the large-flowered yellow shrub rose 'Golden Wings', with the attractive *Hydrangea paniculata*, groups of buddleia 'Lochinch' and potentilla 'Primrose Beauty'.

Beds on the top terrace hold some 500 yellow roses and another 500 roses can be found beyond the house, in the Victorian-style rose garden. Designed by Graham Stuart Thomas in 1966 this rose garden features mainly Victorian roses, and other types for contrast and association.

The central sundial is surrounded by intricate beds of bush roses. There are standard roses too, and roses growing up pillars and hoops, climbing over arched entrances and clinging to ropes. This garden is a spectacular sight in summer, the beds filled with pink, crimson, mauve and white blossoms, the rambling roses entwined with clematis and set in pools of cotton lavender (*Santolina chamaecyparissus*).

From the nearby Doric Temple, you get an excellent view of Shugborough's 72ft yew. It is the largest in the British Isles, possibly in Europe. The golden yew, near to the Victorian rose garden, is splendidly 'architectural'.

The path along the river bank leads on towards the picturesque Chinese House which Admiral Lord Anson had erected in 1747; it was copied from sketches made by one of his officers at Canton. The surrounding planting is mainly of Chinese origin, with groups of bamboos to either side of the house. In front are fine shrubs, including *Osmanthus delavayi*, tree peonies, groups of bamboos; recently planted *Ligustrum quihoui* has heavily scented flowers in August and September. The picturesque Chinese red lacquer bridge over the river and Chinese house complete the scene.

Across the bridge stands the Cat's Monument. Dating from the 18C, this was possibly built to commemorate a cat which accompanied the Admiral on his voyage around the world, or it may be a memorial to the last of a breed of Persian cats kept by Thomas Anson.

Further down the bank is the Shepherd's Monument, with its intriguingly cryptic incription, D. OUOSVAVV M., the source of much speculation.

Continue along the river bank to the grey stone Essex Bridge, which commands splendid views of the river. You can return to the house by way of a rhododendron walk and the Doric Temple.

A number of major developments are planned for the gardens over the next few years: a large herbaceous border is to be planted in the spring of 1991, to be followed by an increase in plants of Chinese origin near to the Chinese House. Rhododendron ponticums are to be replaced in some cases with Victorian hybrids. There are also plans to establish a wild flower meadow.

Trentham Gardens

ADDRESS AND TELEPHONE: Trentham Gardens, Stoke-on-Trent, Staffordshire. Tel. (0782) 657341

OWNERS: Leased by Country Sports International

DIRECTIONS: 3 miles S of Stoke-on-Trent on A34. Public transport: Stoke BR 3 miles. Buses from Stoke

OPENING TIMES: daily except 25 December and 1 January. 9.00am to dusk

ADMISSION: £2.50, OAPs and children £1.50. Reduced rates for pre-booked coach parties

CAR PARKING: yes

TOILETS: yes

REFRESHMENTS: café

SHOP: no

DOGS: on lead

WHEELCHAIR ACCESS: yes. Toilets for the disabled: yes in complex (reached by lift)

PEAK MONTHS: July and August for bedding displays on terraces

NOTABLE FEATURES: terraces originally laid by Barry and Nesfield; splendid lake by Capability Brown; good trees in wood and parkland

It may seem unlikely that anyone would want to create an Italianate paradise in the heart of Staffordshire Potteries; and Trentham is indeed the only known example. The estate's history was made clearer in the 1960s when literally tons of paper work—invoices, letters, plans and surveys—relating to the house and gardens, were taken from the estate office to the Staffordshire County Records Office where they were sorted and catalogued. A little knowledge of Trentham's origins and development is a great help when visiting the gardens and attempting to visualise their former splendour.

There is no longer a grand house on the site although several have been built through the centuries. The mansion that stood here at the turn of the century was developed from an earlier 17C house with additions by Brown and Holland, and later by Sir Charles Barry; this was an immense residence, spacious and gracious, handsome and elegant. The gardens evolved alongside the house. Early 18C plans show the house with parterres on either side of a long walk which leads to a small lake and continues through the woods beyond.

In 1759, Capability Brown was called in to soften this formality. He created parkland and meadows, and enlarged the lake and brought it much closer to the house. However, the estate's greatest period of development was in the 1830s and 1840s when the 2nd Duke of Sutherland commissioned Barry and Nesfield to lay out prestigious terraces with parterres, topiary and statuary. Disraeli described what must have been a magnificent sight in Lothair (1870): 'It would be difficult to find a fairer scene than Trentham, especially in the lustrous effulgence of a glorious English summer. It was an Italian palace ... rising itself from statued and stately terraces. At their foot stood a gardened demain of considerable extent, bright with flowers, dim with coverts of rare shrubs, and magical with fountains.' He also described the park, 'with timber such as the midland counties can produce' and the waters of 'a broad and winding lake'.

Early this century, however, disaster struck—not one of the usual family misfortunes, but pollution. The River Trent close by became so heavily contaminated with sewage from Stoke-on-Trent that the house had to be abandoned and then demolished. Fortunately the garden was not lost, although periods of neglect and the need to make economies (particularly in staffing levels) have brought about several changes and reduced the lavish effect.

More recently Trentham has been well known as a centre of entertainment, with attractions including miniature train rides, an adventure playground, boating on the lake and a night club. These delights have now been replaced by a conference centre and exhibition complex and the company, Country Sports International, which currently leases the property, has implemented a vast scheme to reinstate the gardens and has introduced outdoor sports and country leisure activities.

The spirit of the old garden lingers in the terraces, which still present a noble formality to the eye. The simplifications to the design are in excellent taste—indeed, some visitors would probably find the terraces as seen today more acceptable and satisfying than the highly elaborate formal design created by Barry and Nesfield.

Barry submitted estimates to the 2nd Duke of Sutherland in 1843 for work to the house and garden totalling £40,000 of which nearly £15,000 was spent on the garden and pleasure grounds. Two large, level terraces were laid out between the house and the lake and framed with balustrading, topped with rows of vases and urns planted with bright flowers. The upper level of the terrace was ornamented with flower beds in a circular design. The lower level consisted of a long broad walk, flanked by elaborate sunken parterres and topiary. The walk ended with a cast of Cellini's Perseus in front of the lake and pavilions were constructed at the garden corners.

The essence of this Italian-style formal garden remains, although the gravel walks have been tarmaced over in a somewhat unsympathetic, but no doubt functional manner. Barry's balustrading stretches for many yards, separating the two levels of terracing, the vases and urns have now disappeared. The upper level retains its circular design, but the beds are now planted with roses. Numerous cone-shaped clipped yews decorate this terrace, arranged in regular patterns, and many more decorate the lower level.

From the steps of the rose terrace the central walk marches straight across the large expanse of the lower terrace to the statue of Perseus on the lake edge. Barry's parterres, either side of the walk, have now been replaced by a simpler arrangement of geometric beds, filled with rows of bright seasonal plants. In the centre of each planted area are two large ornamental pools, and until recently these held musical, floodlit fountains.

In dramatic contrast to the stiff formality of the terraces and the regimentation of the clipped yews, is the irregular 'natural' beauty of Brown's extensive lake with its tree-covered islands, stretching away into the valley.

The woodland to the right of the lake and the terraces contains a good mixture of deciduous and coniferous trees, while on the other side of the formal gardens there are areas of lawn with informal shrubberies and a small rock and peat garden. A clematis walk runs along the eastern edge of the lower terrace. Here clematis and roses are trained over a series of iron arches, which are badly in need of repair. Pleasant as these parts of the garden are, the formal terraces and Capability Brown's lake steal the show.

SUFFOLK

Akenfield

ADDRESS AND TELEPHONE: Akenfield, 1 Park Lane, Charsfield, Woodbridge, Suffolk IP13 7PT. Tel. Charsfield (047 337) 402

OWNER: Mrs Peggy Cole

DIRECTIONS: 3 miles W of Wickham Market on B1078; turn N to Charsfield

OPENING TIMES: end of May to September, daily 10–7. House not open

ADMISSION: £1. Coach parties by appointment only

CAR PARKING: yes

TOILETS: no

REFRESHMENTS: no

SHOP: no

DOGS: no

WHEELCHAIR ACCESS: no. Toilets for the disabled: no

PEAK MONTHS: July to September

NOTABLE FEATURES: vegetable plot and separate garden rooms, combined in a ¼-acre garden

In 1958, Mrs Peggy Cole and her husband, Mr Ernie Cole, began to plan a garden in the ¼ acre of waste ground behind their small semi-detached house in Charsfield, Suffolk. In 1971 they opened the resulting garden to the public for one day—500 people came and £25 was raised for the St. John's Ambulance. Now over 10,000 people visit every summer and more than £33,000 has been given to various charities. Since Mr Cole's death in 1980, Mrs Cole has been helped in the garden by her brother, Mr Ron Balls.

What makes Mrs Cole's garden outstanding among many other small gardens created and cared for by enthusiasts? Part of the answer lies in the thorough realisation of the initial plan, which allotted just over half the space for vegetables and the remainder for flowers and shrubs—balancing pleasure and practicality. Included in this scheme was a change in levels between the two areas, which Mrs Cole feels is important for the small garden. She also envisaged the division of the 'pleasure garden' into several garden rooms, to give an element of surprise and change.

Just as important as the overall design, however, is the quality of Mrs Cole's planting. She is both a practical and an imaginative gardener; well rehearsed in traditional methods of growing but also well read. She counts foliage as important as flowers, and one of her earliest ambitions was to have a shrub garden. A wide variety of climbers is used throughout, which give some of the shrubs a double flowering season; and she has some original as well as traditional ways of displaying annuals.

It must be said that the front garden, though it immediately catches the eye, does not give much idea of what is to come. There is a steep front bank planted with African marigolds and crowned by a row of dwarf conifers—gold green and variegated; beds of roses, including the scarlet floribunda 'Evelyn Fison' and several standard bushes, and hanging baskets of fuchsias on the house. These last indicate one of Mrs Cole's great enthusiasms—she grows fuchsias of every shade and shape and has had one named after her.

The first small garden room, reached through the side gate, attracts attention by the quantity of its man-made features: a comfortable garden seat and table, a wishing well, a sundial and a small pool with a tortoise bridge and a small wheel providing a pleasant sound of running water.

The flowering cherry overhanging the pool has variegated ivy trained up it; hostas and rushes edge the pool, with *Astrantia major* 'Sunningdale variety', whose creamy yellow leaves are splashed with two shades of green. In the garden's border there is a gold *Choisya ternata* 'Sunburst' (a recent innovation); a deep red smoke bush (*Cotinus coggygria*) and a tall plume poppy (*Macleaya cordata*). By the seat we noticed a Chinese lantern (*Abutilon thompsonii*), with orange-yellow bells of flowers, mottled red. Clematis 'Nelly Moser' and a gold-leaved honeysuckle decorate the entrance arch to the garden.

Having walked past two greenhouses, filled with small plants for restocking the garden, it is a good idea to continue on up the main path (one of many paved and grassed paths originally laid out by Mr Cole) to the end of the garden, so that you can get an idea of the overall layout. Looking through the end gate, you get a very pleasant view, for Mr and Mrs Cole were fortunate in their site, and there is an orchard on two sides of the garden. Here too you will find a most practical and attractive garden feature: a neat henhouse with a strutting black-tailed cock and hens of various shades, shiny and contented. Mrs Cole lets some of the eggs 'run on' each year to provide chickens and keep up the stock of hens.

From this point the vegetable plot stretches almost to the house, providing runner beans, lettuces, celery, perpetual spinach, several varieties of onion, including Japanese, sprouts, and the striking red orach, which can be cooked like spinach or eaten in salad. There are rows of flowers for cutting: delphiniums, two kinds of everlastings, scabious and many others. We noticed a plant of Our Lady's milk thistle, an annual, with blue-green leaves splashed white. There is also a strawberry tower: a green painted petrol drum with strawberries sprouting from holes and filling the top.

You can return to the top of the garden by walking along the side fence adjoining the neighbouring garden. Here Mrs Cole has made a basic design of hanging baskets of fuchsias alternating with upended bottles trailing different varieties of pelargoniums. In between, rising from the border, are many climbing plants; we saw clematis 'Dr. Ruppel' (rose pink with a deep carmine bar), the 'blue rose' (*R*. 'Weilchenblau'), the gold variegated, white-flowered summer jasmine and the brilliant scarlet flowers of the Chilean glory vine (*Eccremocarpus scaber*).

Crossing back to the 'pleasure garden' area, you will find, at the north end, beds of dahlias and Icelandic poppies. Turning right, you step suddenly into a small grassed garden room where, in June, we encountered three delighted visitors resting on a seat, marvelling at the ingenuity of the design and admiring an apple tree decorated, in between flower and apple, with hanging fuchsia baskets. The apple blossom is preceded in spring by a *Clematis montana*.

The small centre bed here is filled with conifers—glaucous, bright green and gold—with flowering mauve alliums and blue lobelia. We noticed in the surrounding border, hibiscus, a wine-red *Rosa rugosa* 'Roseraie de l'Hay', a tree mallow (*Lavatera arborea* 'Variegata'), red berberis glowing against golden privet, white rose 'Penelope', a white philadelphus and a blue-green *Eucalyptus gunnii* in the early stages of growing to fill one of the very small gaps in this prolific garden. There were purple foxgloves and sweet rocket, pink aquilegias, and over the arch leading to the next room, the climbing roses 'Handel' and 'Golden Showers'. The bed bordering the path contained a striking combination of *Buddleia davidii* 'Harlequin', deep purple with variegated leaves; also *Pinus pungens glauca* and *Spiraea* x *arguta* underplanted with yellow pansies, golden feverfew and calceolaria.

In the third garden room, beyond the rose arch, we saw the beautiful dark red foliage and tiny pink flowers of the shrub rose *R. rubrifolia*; variegated holly and weigela and the twisted hazel (*Corylus avellana* 'Contorta'), whose shape is seen to best advantage in winter. Against the greenhouse there was a tree peony, the sweet-smelling *Viburnum opulus* 'Sterile', a glossy leaved *Fatsia japonica* and the poached egg plant, (*Limnanthes douglasii*), also known as meadow foam, with white, yellow-centred flowers.

Mrs Cole likes to talk to visitors when she can: her wish is for people to visit her garden and escape from the bustle of life for a short time; she also hopes that it will show others what can be achieved in a small area, without any help. For nearly 30 years, Mrs Cole, with her husband and then her brother, has dug, fed and constantly renewed their garden, in winter as well as summer; the results speak for themselves.

Netherfield Herbs

ADDRESS AND TELEPHONE: Rougham, near Bury St Edmunds, Suffolk. Tel. Beyton (0359) 70452

OWNERS: Lesley Bremness and Roger Lowe

DIRECTIONS: S of Bury St Edmunds, off the A134 or A45. Ask at Rougham post office for directions as difficult to find

OPENING TIMES: daily 10.30–6

ADMISSION: free. Guided tours £2.50 per person, only by prior arrangement

CAR PARKING: no

TOILETS: no

REFRESHMENTS: no

SHOP: plants for sale

DOGS: no

WHEELCHAIR ACCESS: yes. Toilets for the disabled: no

PEAK MONTHS: May to September

NOTABLE FEATURES: herb garden

This small herb garden in the depths of the Suffolk countryside contains an enormous selection of herbs, both common and unusual, planted in knot beds, demonstration beds and ornamental borders, each with its own distinctive fragrance and fascinating history. Lesley Bremness, the owner, has now been growing herbs and researching into them for more than 20 years, and has written several books on the subject. You may be surprised to learn the many uses—culinary, medicinal, cosmetic—of even the most ordinary garden plants, not usually thought of as 'herbs', such as

Netherfield Herbs: visitors are welcome to sit on this camomile seat with thyme armrests

alchemilla (lady's mantle). The garden was featured in the Channel 4 'The World of Herbs' series, broadcast in 1990.

Tucked well away from main roads, in a pleasant leafy country lane, and unsignposted, the garden is extremely difficult to find—look out for a small herb stall by the roadside. The herb garden lies at some distance from the entrance, at the far side of the house, a 16C thatched cottage. On the hillside behind is a small nursery area, with green net and polythene tunnels. The garden as a whole is pleasantly ramshackle and casual, with various 'problem areas'—a sunken and almost-vanished stream, a huge murky pond. Lesley Bremness and her husband Roger Lowe moved here from London in the late 1960s, to start a small- holding and breed Tamworth pigs.

To your left, immediately on entering, is a small enclosure containing two herb wheels, one featuring varieties of thyme and the other mints. This old-fashioned way of growing herbs, between the spokes of a cartwheel, is both decorative and economical on space—unfortunately cartwheels are not so easy to find nowadays. More herbs are ranged round the sides of the enclosure, all well labelled with their various uses carefully listed—lovage (*Levisticum officinalis*) is good for applying to wounds, being antiseptic, and the tea stimulates digestion, while the roots of musk mallow will cure coughs, urinary complaints and sprains. Ordinary parsley, besides being a rich source of vitamins A, B and C, also stimulates the digestive system and kidneys, and the leaves may be used as a breath sweetener to neutralise garlic.

Walk across the front of the house to find the herb garden proper. Here, Lesley has planted two box-edged knot gardens, in triangular and circular patterns. Silver curry plants (*Helichrysum angustifolium*), willow green santolina (*S. incana* 'Lemon Queen') and bright green germander (teucrium) provide the three main foliage colours. One has a golden bay in the centre, the other a 'willowleaf' bay.

Although not enormous in size (roughly 60ft x 40ft), the herb garden is very densely planted, full of interesting ideas, suggestive combinations and varieties not commonly seen. Four demonstration beds in the centre are devoted respectively to sages, rosemaries, oreganos and marjorams and creeping thymes. In addition, Lesley has planted one variety of mint in each bed—perhaps an unwise idea, considering mint's rapid spreading powers. Prostrate sage (*S. officinalis* 'Prostratus') keeps its leaves and pleasant balsamic medicinal smell late into the year, while the less hardy pineapple sage and *Salvia officinalis* 'Tricolor', variegated yellow, white and pink/purple, are overwintered indoors and brought out in summer. Lesley thinks that sage is underused as a flowering plant: it is excellent for attracting butterflies and bees.

Five-leaf akebia (*Akebia quinata*), a vigorous twining and very hardy evergreen, overhangs a small arbour and seat. This plant has a very lovely smell and its dark purple-red flowers later turn to edible fruits. To one side of the akebia is a soft pink damask rose, the petals of which are used to make attar of roses—unfortunately it has a very short flowering season—and at the back of the arbour the modern shrub rose 'Bloomfield Abundance'. Although not a climber, this rose has very lax stems, which can easily be encouraged up trellis, and true to its name it produces an abundance of pale shell-pink tiny blossoms.

Next to the damask is an eglantine rose, with deliciously apple-scented leaves, arching over soft apricot coloured foxgloves. Unusual foxgloves are dispersed throughout the garden, including the perennial *Digitalis grandiflora*, bearing masses of pale yellow flowers, marked with brown.

In the far left-hand corner, a golden hop has been trained up a cherry tree, and below this grows elecampane (*Inula helenium*), a hardy perennial with elephantine leaves. The aromatic root of this plant was once used to make sweetmeats, and Helen of Troy is supposed by legend to have been collecting it when she was abducted. Its large leaves make echoing 'music' in the rain—for this reason, Lesley recommends planting it under a window, as banana trees are often planted in China. Nearby grow mauve sweet rocket, or dame's violet, a good cottage-garden standby, and towering angelica. Lesley suggests putting a leaf of angelica in your car—it freshens the air and helps to prevent nausea.

Sweet Joe Pye (*Eupatorium purpureum*) can be recognised by its vanilla-scented leaves and clouds of pink flowers borne from mid to late summer. Named after a Native American medicine man, it was once used to break fevers. Like many other plants with purple in their stems, it is reliably healthy, strong and hardy.

To celebrate the age of the cottage, Lesley has planted two 'Sixteenth Century' beds, one for salad herbs—orach, purslane, salad rocket—and one for medicinal herbs including blue and pink comfrey. Visitors are welcome to sit on the camomile seat, behind. Lesley opted for a seat rather than a lawn, due to difficulties of upkeep—camomile easily gets infested with weeds. Nearby is tall *Lobelia syphilitica*, with pale green leaves and clear blue flowers: this was used by Native Americans against syphilis. Wild strawberries flourish in the shade—Francis Bacon noted their scented leaves, which colour in autumn.

On the right-hand side of the garden, a small statue of Pan shelters under a weeping silver-leaved pear (*Pyrus salicifolia* 'Pendula'). The colour scheme here is white and silver, with white and crimson roses—the apothecary's rose and *Rosa mundi*. On a moonlit night, this small area looks eery and magical, with the white and silver plants glowing iridescent around the statue (Lesley recommends a full moon in May).

The garden is crammed with excellent culinary herbs, such as sweet cicely, with its new seeds like soft aniseed-flavoured nuts, good for eating raw or scattering on fruit salads; tansy, once a popular seasoning and wrapped around meat to keep the flies away; broad-leaved sorrel (try a leaf to quench your thirst on a hot day); and costmary or bible herb (*Chrysanthemum balsamita*), which has a strong Wrigley chewing gum flavour and was used to flavour ale before the discovery of hops.

Many of the plants are labelled but the labels are not always easy to find. You might find an identification book useful.

Somerleyton Hall

ADDRESS AND TELEPHONE: Somerleyton Hall, Lowestoft, Suffolk NR32 5QQ. Tel. Lowestoft (0502) 730224

OWNERS: Lord and Lady Somerleyton

DIRECTIONS: 5 miles NW of Lowestoft, off B1074. Public transport: 1 mile from Somerleyton station

OPENING TIMES: Easter Sun to end September, Sun, Thurs and BH 2–5.30; also 2 July to 29 August, Tues and Wed. House also open

ADMISSION: £3, OAPs £2.40, children £1.65. Reductions for parties

CAR PARKING: yes

TOILETS: yes

REFRESHMENTS: café

SHOP: yes

DOGS: no

WHEELCHAIR ACCESS: yes. Toilets for the disabled: yes

PEAK MONTHS: May, June and August

NOTABLE FEATURES: maze, fine trees, Paxton greenhouses

This lovely and peaceful 12-acre garden is full of fine features, including several of special interest to children, such as the huge maze and the ¼-mile long miniature railway. Since Victorian times, Somerleyton has always been a popular place for a family outing—even in the 1920s, around 8000 people visited every year.

Now the home of Lord and Lady Somerleyton, the splendid Victorian mansion was remodelled from 1843 onwards from an earlier Elizabethan manor house, by Sir Morton Peto, a leading building contractor, self-made man and great public benefactor. Peto employed the architect John Thomas, better known as a sculptor and ornamental mason, to make what was later described (in the sale particulars of 1861) as a 'princely residence with solid magnificence and a grand elevation exhibiting one of the finest examples of Anglo-Italian architecture to be met with in the Kingdom'. Unfortunately, Thomas chose soft Caen stone, easily damaged by harsh winds and sea air, for the house facings and sculptures; a great deal of renewal and restoration work has been carried out in recent years.

W.A. Nesfield was employed as garden designer, and much of his work can still be seen today, although his original splendid parterre has been replaced with rose beds.

In Victorian times, Somerleyton was especially famous for its extraordinary Winter Garden, a giant domed glasshouse, 126ft by 136ft, and ornamented with sculpture and vases from Italy and Germany. Most of this was dismantled in 1914 and all that now remains is the splendid reglazed loggia, around the sunken garden.

The car park and ticket office are on the north side, at some distance from the house. The delightful greenhouse entrance is filled in late spring and early summer with *Schizanthus pinnatus* 'Giant Hybrids' in many shades. A tulip-bordered path leads down to the old walled kitchen garden, a spacious and relaxed area, now containing a small ornamental orchard, play areas for children, glasshouses and herbaceous borders. The glasshouses here are of unusual and very attractive design, with ridged roofs—they were designed by Joseph Paxton, of Crystal Palace fame. Originally used for growing vines, they are now planted ornamentally, with citrus trees and a wonderful variety of flowering plants.

The left-hand glasshouse contains a selection of beautiful abutilons, trained against the south-facing wall—among them, puce-coloured *Abutilon* x *hybridum* 'Ashford Red' and graceful *A. megapotamicum* with red and yellow, lantern-like flowers. In the narrow bed opposite, *Abutilon* x *milleri* shows its bell-shaped, orange flowers, in company with deep rose *Buddleia colvilei*. Olearia, datura (angel's trumpets) and lilies scent the air, but none of these can match the astonishing fragrance of the huge jasmine (*Jasminum officinale*) in the right-hand greenhouse, with its glorious sprays of pink buds opening to white.

Lovely *Diplacus glutinosus*, with trumpet-shaped orange flowers, grows next to the jasmine, mingling on the other side with strange and sinister looking *Kennedia nigricans*, a member of the pea family; opposite, a huge broom, cytisus 'Porlock', flowers bright yellow, and nearby is a small goldfish pool, planted with waterlilies.

In mid summer, this wonderful display of colour and fragrance is echoed by the herbaceous borders in the lower part of the walled garden. The emphasis here is on height and a strong mixture of bright, bold colours—the tall columns of delphiniums and phlox are used at intervals throughout, accompanied by yellow heliopsis, rosy-lilac heads of giant allium, golden *Achillea filipendulina* 'Cloth of Gold' and pink *A. millefolium* 'Roseum', light pink toadflax

(*Linaria purpurea* 'Canon Went'), lupins, sidalceas, lilies, plume poppies and many others—a brilliant show backed by long lines of espalier fruit trees.

The old red-brick walls are clothed with clematis, not looking quite so happy as the greenhouse plants: the violet-blue species clematis *C. macropetala* and rose pink *C. macropetala* 'Markhamii', both flowering from late spring to summer; the large-flowered hybrid *C.* 'Ville de Lyon', carmine edged with crimson and very late-flowering; the white summer-flowering species *C. montana* 'Wilsonii' and *C. chrysocoma sericea.* These are interspersed with climbers including *Hydrangea petiolaris* and variegated ivy. Fig 'Brown Turkey' hangs on the west-facing wall, a sister to the fig house specimen. The small orchard is well stocked with flowering fruit trees—medlars, crab apples and pears.

East of the walled garden, in a wide lawn area, stands a 300ft-long iron pergola. Covered with Italian vines and white, pink and mauve wisteria, the pergola is especially beautiful in spring and autumn, but also pretty in summer, when the climbing roses flower. More superb climbers and shrubs cover the east-facing wall—brilliant crimson *Chaenomeles* x *superba* 'Rowallane', yellow forsythia and *Kerria japonica* 'Pleniflora', mauve *Wisteria sinensis* and lilac-purple *Buddleia davidii,* the butterfly bush.

The excellent maze is nearby: designed by William Nesfield and planted in 1846, this is claimed to be one of the finest in Britain and certainly seems in rather better condition than the famous maze at Hampton Court. The hedges are of neatly clipped and smoothly rounded yew, the entrance through a huge yew arch. At the centre—about 400 yds from the entrance, if you don't take any wrong turnings—is a small pagoda, raised on a grassy mound.

You may prefer to forgo these excitements and head straight for the house and tea rooms. Continue along the path, through rhodo-dendron plantings and past huge 200-year-old cedars. To your right is a small garden surrounded by yew hedges and centring on a statue of Mercury, with cherubs—the head gardener's cottage once stood here. Storms have devastated much of the planting in this area. An eastern hemlock (*Tsuga canadensis*) was blown down in October 1987, but winched and guyed back up. Further along the path is an enormous Monterey cypress (*Cupressus macrocarpa*) and across the lawn, a fine specimen of *Eucalyptus gunnii.*

Monkey puzzles and cedars tower above the lawns, framing a graceful bronze statue of Atlanta (see if you can pick up the 'golden' apple!). Many other interesting statues can be found in the garden, including classical figures in the loggia, outside the conservatory (now, with the loggia, converted into a tea room). Nearby, aviaries house the Chinese painted quail and white crested jay thrush.

West of the house is a formal lawn area, laid out in 1846 and decorated with an equatorial sundial, planted basins and troughs, huge clipped yews, rose beds and rhododendrons grown as stand-ards. Looking south into the park, you can see an avenue of 250-year-old lime trees, flanking the former main driveway—un-fortunately these, too, have been badly damaged by storms. Red deer can now be seen grazing in the park to the west of the gardens, for the first time since 1935. The herd will eventually total 100.

The path winds back northwards through the gardens, towards

the walled garden and car park. Among the many lovely trees are a stout copper beech (*Fagus sylvatica* 'Cuprea'), a sweet gum (*Liquidambar styraciflua*) and a pocket handkerchief tree (*Davidia involucrata*). A vast Wellingtonia (*Sequoiadendron giganteum*) stands near the entrance to the walled garden, with monkey puzzles nearby, and a shrub bed planted with *Pieris floribunda*, berberis, yellow bush honeysuckle (*Lonicera nitida* 'Baggesen's Gold'), skimmia and a small specimen of *Acer pseudoplatanus* 'Brilliantissimum'.

Glass peach cages line the outer walls of the kitchen garden: these contain not only peaches but apricots, plums, tayberries and some early-blossoming roses.

SURREY

Claremont Landscape Garden

ADDRESS AND TELEPHONE: Claremont Landscape Garden, Portsmouth Road, Esher, Surrey KT10 9JG. Tel. (0372) 69421/67806

OWNERS: The National Trust

DIRECTIONS: just S of Esher, off A307. Public transport: Esher BR 2 miles (not Sun) or Hersham 2 miles. Buses from Kingston-upon-Thames pass Esher BR

OPENING TIMES: daily, March 9–5, April to end October 9–7 (or sunset whichever is earlier). 10–14 July garden closes at 4. November to end March 9–5 (or sunset if earlier). Closed 25 December and 1 January. Last admission 30 minutes before closing. House not open

ADMISSION: Sun and BH £2, Mon to Sat £1.20; children under 17 years half price (under 5 free). Coach parties by prior arrangement only and not on Sun. Tel. (0372) 69421

CAR PARKING: yes

TOILETS: yes

REFRESHMENTS: tea room

SHOP: yes

DOGS: not between April and October and on leads from November to end of March

WHEELCHAIR ACCESS: yes around lake. Toilets for the disabled: yes

PEAK MONTHS: no peaks

NOTABLE FEATURES: historically important landscape garden; large grassed amphitheatre; lake with island; grotto; camellia terrace; belvedere; fine views, good walks and some splendid trees

Situated on the outskirts of Esher, in the gently rolling hills of Surrey, Claremont is one of the earliest examples of a landscape garden to have survived to the present day: it predates Stourhead by some 20 years. Laid out between 1715 and 1726 for Thomas Pelham-Holles, Duke of Newcastle, it was created as a pleasure garden where the owner and his guests could stroll in 'natural' surroundings and admire the various views. These views were carefully planned so as to awaken different moods and sensations—surprise, joy or melancholy—in the viewer.

Many famous gardeners and garden designers have worked at Claremont, beginning with Vanburgh and Bridgeman. Kent and Brown added their own distinctive touches. By 1727 Switzer was already describing the garden as 'noblest of any in Europe'. It must have been spectacular with its huge amphitheatre, round pond and majestic garden architecture. Unfortunately, from the 1920s onwards the garden suffered decades of neglect. The lake silted up, garden buildings and ornaments fell into ruin and the entire garden—including the amphitheatre and bowling green—disappeared beneath a mass of laurels, rhododendrons and trees.

When the National Trust took the garden on in 1949 the finances for the vast amount of restoration just were not available. It was only in 1975, with help from the Slater Foundation and other donations and grants, that work could begin.

Today, you can see the gardens fully restored. The most striking and impressive feature at Claremont is the huge curved grassed amphitheatre. Covering more than 3 acres and rising high above the lake, this is the only surviving example of its kind in Europe. It was designed by Charles Bridgeman in the 1720s but was never intended as the scene for plays or musical performances. The sweeping, semicircular layers of banks were created purely to complement a round pond below.

William Kent altered the round pond in the 1730s—enlarging it, giving it a more natural appearance and creating an island on which he built a pavilion with a pyramidal roof. Although mainly intended for ornament, this was also used by fishing parties and for picnics. Kent also planted beech trees, chestnuts and yews and laid out wandering paths through the garden.

South of the lake, it is still possible to make out the old course of the London to Portsmouth road. Following the death of the Duke of Newcastle in 1768, the estate was purchased by Lord Clive who had returned from India with a vast fortune. It was he who commissioned Capability Brown to alter the course of the Portsmouth road, re-routing it out of sight through a cutting in the hillside.

No landscape garden would have been complete without a grotto at the edge of the lake. Claremont's grotto is a typical rock-like structure, designed to look like a natural ruin and with an interior encrusted with shells and minerals. The grotto dates from around 1770 and replaces an earlier cascade built by Kent.

From the grotto and lakeside a winding path passes through groves of trees on its way towards a camellia terrace higher on the hillside. At one point the path comes close to Kent's ha-ha—now a shallow ditch—which separated the garden from the pastureland beyond. On the opposite side of the path, nestling in the trees, is a small thatched building. Octagonal in shape, this little house is believed to date from the last century but it stands on the site of an earlier 18C thatched house.

The camellia terrace occupies what was once the site of a menagerie, until 1824, when J.B. Papworth designed and built a heated camellia house for Prince Leopold of Saxe-Coburg, who had moved to Claremont with his new wife, Princess Charlotte of Wales, in 1816. At that time, camellias were believed to be tender plants, unable to survive the British winter without heated protection. Today, as you can see, they still flourish—surrounded by the foundation of the greenhouse once thought to be so vital for their survival. Prince Leopold's cypher is included in the terrace railing— two letter 'Ls' back to back.

Beyond the camellia terrace is the belvedere, best viewed from the bowling green. Like the mansion house of Claremont, the belvedere is now privately owned by the Claremont Fan Court School. The tower was designed by Sir John Vanburgh and stands on a little knoll called the mount. The Duke of Newcastle was also Lord Clare, hence the name Claremont.

No doubt Lord Clare's guests enjoyed the fine views from the first floor of the tower, looking across the garden and the gentle, rolling Surrey countryside. Behind the belvedere, which was originally painted white and housed a games room, a series of large grassed steps rises into the distance and forms a backcloth against which the belvedere looks even more impressive.

Between the bowling green and the amphitheatre is the site of the nine-pin or skittle alley. This was housed in a Tuscan-style temple, probably a design by Kent, but which was unfortunately demolished in the 1920s. Another of Kent's items of garden architecture—a small classical building—once stood at the side of the bowling green, but this too has been lost.

Before returning down the hillside to the lake, follow the path to the terrace above the amphitheatre. Here you can see the foundations of a mausoleum—a small Gothic building, constructed to a design by Papworth and Pugin and intended as a teahouse for Princess Charlotte. The Princess did not live to see her first wedding anniversary, so her husband, Prince Leopold, dedicated the building as a shrine to her memory.

The scale of the amphitheatre can best be appreciated from this terrace, with the lake and island below. Around the lake there are some exceptional trees, most notably several massive cedars of Lebanon. Although oaks and beeches dominate much of the garden there are also some good examples of Japanese Cedar (*Cryptomeria japonica*), Chinese fir (*Cunninghamia sinensis*) and redwoods (*Sequoia sempervirens*). There are many tall yews and hollies. Flowers really have no place in a garden like this and the most you can expect to see are daffodils under the trees and along the walks.

Now that this remarkable garden—where Queen Victoria used to play as a child—has been restored, it is a delightful place to spend a morning or afternoon.

Painshill Park

ADDRESS AND TELEPHONE: Painshill Park, Portsmouth Road, Cobham, Surrey KT11 1JE. Tel. (0932) 868113

OWNERS: Painshill Park Trust

DIRECTIONS: entrance A245 beside Cobham Bridge

OPENING TIMES: Sun, mid April to mid October 2–6. House closed

ADMISSION: £2.50, OAPs and children £1.50. Includes free
optional guided tour. Coach parties by prior arrangement, Mon
to Sat for more than 10 people. No reductions

CAR PARKING: yes

Toilets: yes

REFRESHMENTS: café

SHOP: yes

DOGS: no

WHEELCHAIR ACCESS: yes, to most parts. Toilets for the disabled:
yes

NOTABLE FEATURES: exceptional 18C ornamental landscape
garden, with restored buildings and planting

This magical landscape garden, well known and much visited in
the 18C, is being restored on a grand scale. It was created by
Charles Hamilton, penniless ninth son of the 6th Duke of Abercorn,
a knowledgeable gardener with the inspiration of an artist. 'I must
tell you it beggars all description, the art of hiding art is here in
such sweet perfection, that Mr. Hamilton cheats himself of praise,
you thank Nature for all you see, tho' I am informed all has been
reformed by Art.' wrote Elizabeth Montagu, on visiting Painshill in
1755—and her words hold true today.

Hamilton had virtually no income or expectations, but he borrowed money from friends, and with this, in the late 1730s, he began
to acquire land at Painshill in Surrey. His 250-acre property was
bounded to the north-west by the road from London to Guildford
(now the A3) and included, to the south-west, a steep escarpment
overlooking the River Mole.

For the next 30 or so years, Hamilton cleared the land and
planted—receiving seeds and plants from Peter Collinson (who ran
a nursery at Mill Hill, London, and was agent for John Bartram's
nursery outside Philadelphia in North America) and from John
Bartram (owner of a nursery in Pennsylvania) and exchanging
seeds, plants and advice with Abbé Nolin, inspector of the royal
nurseries for the French kings Louis XV and XVI.

He created garden buildings and features using the cheapest of
materials—a five-arched bridge of wood made to look like stone,
a Gothic temple made of plaster and lathe. Placed as focal points
in a careful design, these appear and disappear at intervals as you
walk around the garden. A serpentine lake was created to look like
a river, its beginning and end hidden from sight.

Hamilton planted vineyards on the south-facing slope and sold
wine to the inns of Cobham; he also made some small profit from
a brick and tile works. But in the end his debts were called in and
in 1773 he was forced to sell Painshill. He moved to Bath, where
he married for the third time and kept up his interest in gardening—he helped, for instance, to design the grotto and cascade at
Bowood.

Painshill Park: the Chinese bridge from the south

At 75, Hamilton was, according to Jeremy Bentham at Bowood, 'the oracle for the gardening works that are carried on here, he has been mainly employed in undoing what Capability Brown had done.' Hamilton's ideas on natural landscape and his appreciation of the land's natural contours and wildness, were before his time, and heralded the Romantic movement in England. He died in 1786.

Painshill remained in good repair for 170 years, until the 1939–45 war. It was divided up and sold in 1948, and the gardens fell into a very neglected state. Elmbridge Borough Council bought 47 acres of the site in 1975, and a further 106 in 1981. The Painshill Park Trust was formed in 1981, to restore and maintain the ornamental gardens around the lake, reaching to the Gothic Tower in the west. Funding and labour for this project came mainly from a National Heritage Memorial Fund grant of £1 million, announced in 1984, to be spread over three years, and from an MSC scheme.

The original Painshill is recorded in many diaries, letters and commentaries written by 18C visitors, as well as drawings, paintings and engravings; these have assisted the work of restoration as have archaeological excavations and a detailed survey. The Gothic temple has been fully restored, with its view over the hillside and the lake (now dredged). The amphitheatre and Chinese bridge peninsula have been cleared and replanted. The Chinese bridge, ruined abbey and Gothic tower are now restored and work on the grotto is continuing. Plenty of work remains to be done, but the essence of Hamilton's vision is now clearly visible; his garden has reappeared.

The 3-mile historic circuit walk begins at the visitor centre; from here, you proceed southwards, up Wood Hill, to the bastion. The wood is mainly beech (*Fagus sylvatica*) and sweet chestnut (*Castanea sativa*). About 160 trees originally planted by Hamilton (between 1738 and 1773) survive in the grounds; these are marked with green tabs and listed in a useful leaflet, available at the centre. The gales of 1987 destroyed nearly 1000 trees at Painshill and those of winter 1990 destroyed or damaged another 200, but many of the original trees were left untouched. At the foot of Wood Hill are two of Hamilton's false acacias, and a cedar of Lebanon (*Cedrus libani*) stands at the top.

The bastion is the first viewing point, overlooking a steep south-facing slope (on which Hamilton planted his Burgundy vines) with the lake and the river below and the North Downs beyond. Nearby, to the west, is the restored Fir Walk, planted with a mixture of northern pitch pine (*Pinus rigida*), red spruce (*Picea rubens*), Norway spruce (*Picea abies*) and Scotch pine (*Pinus sylvestris*). The first two species are from north-east America; Hamilton made pioneering use of American trees and plants in his landscape, planting them as freely as if they were native species.

Behind the fir walk is the wide grassed amphitheatre, once surrounded by evergreens planted thickly in tiers, and now being replanted using as many of the original species as possible. These include exotics from north-east America—Hamilton was one of the first gardeners in England to use rhododendrons including *Rhododendron maximum*, *Magnolia grandiflora* and the calico bush, *Kalmia latifolia*. The cork oak (*Quercus suber*), an original Hamilton tree, is of particular interest to children and school parties—its bark is cork, and may have been used by Hamilton to cork his own wine bottles. Matthew Arnold is said to have sat under this tree, writing—he rented a house in the village at one time.

The amphitheatre planting includes a sunny south-facing area of Mediterranean plants such as rock roses (*Cistus ladanifer*) and *Artemisia arborescens*. There are different varieties of hollies—Hamilton grew around 30—some with gold or silver-edged leaves. Note also the curious way in which some trees in the amphitheatre are shaved of branches almost to their tops—this was a fashion in Hamilton's time.

At the eastern end of the amphitheatre is a plinth that once supported a lead statue, a copy of Giambologna's Rape of the Sabines. This was melted down in 1952, after vandals had broken off the arms; it will be replaced with a duplicate statue.

The trees converge to the west, as you approach the Gothic temple, creating a nave-like effect. The temple commands an excellent view down the hill to the lake and is itself delightful—built in the early 1750s, it is a perfect example of 'Georgian Gothic', with its ogee arches, quatrefoil windows, buttresses and painted fan-vaulted plaster ceiling. To the left is an effective planting of orange berried rowans and silver birches.

Following a path leading southwards through a gate and past a red oak (*Quercus rubra*), you glimpse through trees to your left the ruined abbey, a Gothic folly built as a ruin in 1770, from brick plastered to simulate stone, and concealing Hamilton's brick and tile kilns. It was in process of reconstruction when we visited. A little way to the east is the Chinese bridge peninsula, planted with a mixture of evergreens and deciduous trees and shrubs, including a great number of Hamilton's favourite North American trees and shrubs, such as Cockspur thorn (*Crataegus crus-galli*), the tulip tree (*Liriodendron tulipifera*) and maples.

The Chinese bridge is the only one that survives of three original bridges to the double kidney shaped Grotto Island. On the island side of the bridge is a wellingtonia (*Sequoiadendron giganteum*). There is no access to the island except with a trust guide, at present, as the grotto is in process of restoration—a massive project which may take up to five years. The grotto was originally built by Joseph Lane in the 1760s, and is made of limestone quarried near Cirencester.

From the grotto island, it is a cool, dark walk to the mausoleum, bordered by yew trees. On your way, note a beech and London plane (the latter a Hamilton tree) with their branches fused together. To the right are two swamp cypresses (*Taxodium distichum*). Like the abbey, the mausoleum was built as a romantic ruin. It is in the form of a Roman triumphal arch, with niches designed to hold antique busts and urns.

The River Mole is noticeably lower than the lake, by about 12ft. Hamilton used a wooden water wheel to raise water to the lake— this was replaced in the 1830s by a cast iron wheel, which you can see across the fields. Hamilton's Cascade, fed by the water wheel, was not working on our visit. Designed to look 'natural', the structure was built from boulders, roots and fallen tree trunks.

The path between the cascade and the water wheel runs below the aptly named Hanging Wood, where you can see two trees planted by Hamilton, a beech and a false acacia, as well as a very old yew. The waterwheel is well worth visiting. Beyond to the west are Tower Hill and the hermitage, and the gothic tower on the western boundary of the estate.

On your way back to the visitor centre, along the north side of the lake, note one of Hamilton's original and magnificent cedars of Lebanon; this one is said to be the largest in England (120ft x 32ft). There are many other interesting and beautiful trees in this area, including a mountain ash (*Sorbus aucuparia*) growing out of the trunk of a pencil cedar (*Juniperus virginiana*).

Polesden Lacey

ADDRESS AND TELEPHONE: Polesden Lacey, near Dorking, Surrey RH5 6BD. Tel. Bookham (0372) 458203/452048

OWNERS: The National Trust

DIRECTIONS: 5 miles NW of Dorking. 1½ miles S of Great Bookham. Off Leatherhead to Guildford road (A246). Public transport: nearest BR station is Boxhill and Westhumble, leaving a 2 mile walk. Or BR Bookham and 2½ mile walk. Buses from Croydon and Guildford stop at Great Bookham

OPENING TIMES: daily, all year round, 11.00am to sunset. House open March and November, Sat and Sun 1.30–4.30. April to end October Wed to Sun 1.30–5.30.

ADMISSION: garden only, April to October £2. Other times £1.20.

House £2 Wed to Sat and Sun and BH £3

CAR PARKING: yes

TOILETS: yes

REFRESHMENTS: café

SHOP: yes

DOGS: not allowed in formal garden or on lawns

WHEELCHAIR ACCESS: to many parts of the garden. Toilets for the disabled: yes

PEAK MONTHS: May to August

NOTABLE FEATURES: rose garden; lavender and iris gardens; herbaceous borders; winter garden

Situated on a chalk ridge overlooking the Surrey countryside, the garden at Polesden Lacey is best described as typically English. Its history can easily be traced back to the late 18C and early 19C when the playwright Richard Brinsley Sheridan lived here, in an earlier house; he is believed to have lengthened the Long Walk, south-east of the house.

Two years after Sheridan's death in 1816, the property was purchased by Joseph Bonsor who set about building a new house and planted some 20,000 trees on the estate. However, it was not until 1906, when Captain Ronald Greville and his wife took over that the gardens as they exist today were developed. Mrs Greville, in particular, enriched the garden with a wealth of plant life.

The mansion house is set just below the brow of the hill, with a large gravel forecourt to the east, surrounded by clipped domes of golden English yew. The walls of the house provide support for several climbing plants such as winter jasmine (*Jasminum nudiflorum*) and *Wisteria sinensis*, intertwined with clematis. Summer bedding adds a splash of colour all round the house walls.

The south front of the house is particularly impressive, with its Ionic colonnade, and the terrace here offers marvellous, restful views over the grand sloping south lawn and across the valley to the farmland and woods on the opposite hillside.

West of the house lies a series of formal gardens, some enclosed and some open. The enclosed plots include rose, iris and lavender gardens and a peony border, all flanking a central path. Close by, near to the house, is a simple grassed burial plot surrounded by yew hedges and ornamented by statues. Here is Mrs Greville's grave.

The entrance to the formal gardens is through a wrought iron gateway in the brick wall, guarded by a pair of stone griffins. This brings you into a large enclosed formal rose garden, originally the site of the 19C kitchen garden. Some 2400 roses are planted here and the colour scheme is distinctively Edwardian—mainly pinks, crimson, white and creamy yellows.

Long pergolas draped with rambler roses divide the garden into quarters, and a Venetian well-head forms a central feature. Each quarter is lawned, with formal rose beds cut into the grass. There are many lovely hybrid roses in these four sections, including, among the hybrid teas, 'Red Planet', 'Crimson Glory' and 'Peace', and among the floribundas, the beautiful crimson flowering 'Frensham' and white 'Iceberg'. It is worth noting that the shallow chalk soil at Polesden Lacey is not particularly suited to rose growing and Mrs Greville established the rose garden by digging beds to a depth of 18in. and infilling with best quality loam.

A selection of ramblers on the pergola all have *Rosa wichuraiana* in their parentage. There is 'Crimson Shower', the double rose pink 'Dorothy Perkins', rosy crimson 'Excelsa' with a white centre, 'Sanders White Rambler', deep pink and white 'American Pillar', the fragrant shell pink 'New Dawn', the glorious double cream scented 'Alberic Barbier' and pale pink deeply perfumed 'Albertine'. The borders surrounding the rose garden hold many excellent shrub roses and climbing roses are supported on the wall. There are several specimens of 'Mermaid'—a great climber with large beautiful and fragrant blooms of primrose yellow.

Further formal gardens lie beyond the rose garden. A wall dating from 1910 forms the southern boundary of this area and also provides a home for aubrieta and other wall plants; at the base grow Japanese anemones and deep red fuchsias. Just adjacent to the rose garden is a narrow garden containing two parallel borders of peonies. A thick hedge of yew separates this from the next garden, where formal beds full of bearded irises are cut into the lawn.

A further enclosure is devoted to lavender. Several different kinds of lavender are grown here to produce a hazy cloud of purple, grey and blue flowering stems in summer.

Each of the formal gardens at Polesden Lacey has its own distinct character and is self-contained and yet at the same time harmonises with the rest.

The main element in the winter garden is the Persian ironwood tree (*Parrotia persica*), which overhangs a collection of winter and early spring bulbs and small shrubs. The boundary for public access at this end of the garden is marked by the unusual roofed bridge which passes over an estate road in a deep cutting below.

The long herbaceous border is a notable feature. Divided into four sections, the border runs the entire length of the wall enclosing the formal gardens.

Originally this was a double border, the other section lying on the opposite side of the gravel walk, but during the 1939–45 war this second border was given over to vegetables. Many early-flowering shrubs enjoy the shelter of the south-facing wall, and give interest to the border before the main shrubs and herbaceous plants bloom in summer; backed by various clematis and ceanothus.

Beyond the yew hedge lies the croquet lawn, with a lead statue of Diana at the far end. Having crossed this, you climb down through a rocky bank of Westmorland limestone to the sunken garden. The steep slope is smothered in shrubs, including an enormous wide-spreading specimen of *Juniperus* x *media* 'Pfitzerana'. There is also a fine smoke bush (*Cotinus coggygria*).

Set in the lawn below is *Pyrus nivalis*, noted for its attractive silvery foliage, and shrubs such as *Viburnum rhytidophyllum*—particularly suited to chalk soils. Lilacs also love chalk and there is a massed bank of these, with hydrangeas.

Cross the south lawn and walk eastwards, away from the house.

A pair of stone columns and griffins marks the entrance to the Long Walk or Sheridan's Walk. The Nun's Walk runs parallel to this but is a little to the north and there are some fine specimens of trees that do well in chalky soil in the nearby pinetum.

At the far end of Sheridan's Walk are six Doric columns from the portico to the house. Close by is *Acer cappadocium* and beyond a rough lawn speckled with wild flowers leads to the open air theatre.

Try if possible to visit Polesden Lacey when the spectacular rose garden is in bloom, although this garden has something of interest in all seasons.

A considerable number of mature trees were lost in the storms of October 1987 and January 1990 resulting in several new views and vistas. Replanting has begun.

Winkworth Arboretum

ADDRESS AND TELEPHONE: NT Regional Office, Polesden Lacey, Dorking, Surrey RH5 6BD. Tel. Bookham (0372) 53401 (Office 048632 477)

OWNERS: The National Trust

DIRECTIONS: near Hascombe, 2 miles SE of Godalming on E side of B2130. Public transport: Godalming station 2 miles. Bus: Tillingbourne 33 Godalming to Guildford (passing close BR Godalming) (Tel. Cranleigh 0483 276880)

OPENING TIMES: all year, daily during daylight hours

ADMISSION: £1.50, children free. No reduction for parties

CAR PARKING: yes. Coach parties must book to ensure parking space

TOILETS: yes

REFRESHMENTS: tea room for light refreshments near upper car park

SHOP: yes

DOGS: must be kept under control

WHEELCHAIR ACCESS: limited; viewpoint and lake from lower entrance are accessible. Toilets for the disabled: no

PEAK MONTHS: autumn and spring

NOTABLE FEATURES: rare trees and shrubs; autumn colour; fine views; spring bluebells; azaleas; National Collection of *Sorbus aria*. 86 species of birdlife recorded in 1987

This beautiful arboretum suffered heavy losses in the storms of October 1987 and January 1990 but there has since been large-scale replanting and the basic structure remains intact and the views if anything have improved.

Planted mainly on steep hillside above two lakes, Winkworth covers nearly 100 acres. The soil is sandy and dries out easily, so the plants are particularly vulnerable to drought; but these conditions encourage magnificent autumn colours and the lime-free topsoil favours azaleas and other ericaceous plants. Autumn and spring are the best times to visit, but there is plenty to see even in winter.

The arboretum was established from the late 1930s onwards by Dr Wilfrid Fox, who bought the land, including two lakes, by auction from Lady Peel (the actress Beatrice Lillie). A doctor and skin specialist by profession, Dr Fox was knowledgeable about trees and enthusiastically set about clearing and planting the land, assisted by one employee and with help from friends, including the invaluable Mrs Madeline Spitta. Many of the trees Dr Fox planted in the early years still remain, notably maples to the south, near Winkworth Hill, and Japanese maples on the slope. During the 1939–45 war, he established a collection of sorbus, and then planted dwarf evergreen azaleas and maples in a grassy glade leading up the slopes (now Azalea Steps). He introduced a huge variety of species to the Foliage Glade and the Bowl, and planted Magnolia Wood. In 1952 he donated 62 acres to the National Trust, and a further 35 acres in 1957. Dr Fox died in 1962.

The main car park lies just below Rhododendron Wood, an oak wood underplanted with rhododendrons and daffodils, which provides a pleasant setting for the tea room and National Trust shop. Just over the main walk is the Winter Garden, planted with witch-hazels (hamamelis spp), viburnums, prunus and *Symplocos paniculata*, with deep blue fruits, for winter interest. Camellias blossom here in spring.

Turning right off the main path, past the camellias, you can see evidence of considerable storm damage and tree felling, and of recent replanting. The young trees in this area include hornbeam (*Carpinus betulus* 'Incisa'), oak (*Quercus* x *hispanica* 'Diversifolia'), an umbrella pine, and small attractive trees such as *Nyssa sinensis* with rich red autumn tints and *Styrax japonica* with pure white pendulous flowers in late spring and summer.

Just past the damaged larch wood is the Summer Garden. Among the summer-flowering trees and shrubs here is an eye-catching group of *Stewartia pseudocamellia* with flaking pinky bark and white flowers produced in succession through several weeks in July and August. Sorbus 'Wilfred Fox' stands next to the memorial to Dr Fox, with two *Eucryphia nymansensis* 'Nymansay' to either side. Here too are abelias, clethras, eucryphias and an enormous tree heath. Wood anemones and primroses bloom in spring, followed by sheets of bluebells.

Beyond, to the south, is Magnolia Wood, planted with many different types of magnolia, including a lovely specimen of magnolia 'Kewensis', with delicate white flowers produced before the leaves in April and a less healthy looking one of M. *salicifolia*, the willow-leaved magnolia. M. *sieboldii* flowers intermittently throughout the summer and the popular M. x *soulangiana* offers large tulip-shaped white flowers, stained purple at the base, from April to May. Note also the very rare M, *cylindrica*, whose white flowers appear in April on bare stems.

Following the diagonal path through this wood, you emerge above the Slopes and get your first magnificent view down over the tree-clad escarpment to the upper lake. Both lakes are artificial, made by damming the stream that runs through the valley from Hascombe to Bramley. The upper lake, or Rowe's Flash (flash is an old word for sluice) was constructed in 1896; the lower, Phillimore Lake, at a much earlier date. In autumn the whole hillside is aflame with bright-coloured acers, some of the best being *A. japonicum*, *A. palmatum* and *A. rubrum*; also *Cornus kousa*, cotinus, enkianthus, liquidambars, malus species, *Parrotia persica*, rhus, stewartias, vacciniums and many other species, against a background of dark green conifers, blue cedars and broadleaved trees.

Walking southwards up the path until you reach two handsome specimens of fragrant winter-flowering *Viburnum* x *bodnantense* 'Dawn', you come to a steeply curving path of steps, leading down the hillside into the Bowl. To your right is Sorbus Hill, and in autumn you should take the high level path along the top of this hill, to see the many varieties of whitebeam (*Sorbus aria*) and rowans or mountain ash (*Sorbus aucuparia*) with their rich autumn foliage and many-coloured berries. Filling the hollow Bowl are acers, prunus, sorbus, liquidambars and *Parrotia persica*. Witch-hazels (hamamelis) blossom in late winter and horse chestnuts in late spring, accompanied by a large group of deciduous azaleas to the south.

At the bottom of the steps, turn right and follow the path down to a semicircular wooden bench. Here you can rest and appreciate the beauty of the lake in its woodland setting. Canada geese are usually to be seen on the water, besides mallards, tufted ducks, moorhens and coots; and cows graze peacefully on the far banks.

To the left of the lakeside path is a group of larches, followed by an area of about 2 acres which is still being developed, with new plantings of sorbus, malus and acer. North of these is the Memorial Glade, dedicated to Dr Fox.

The lakeside path leads to a decorative boathouse and to the left, the foot of Azalea Steps. Beyond is a marshy area, the bluebell woods and Phillimore Lake. Evergreen azaleas surge up the steps, a mass of bright colours in late spring and backed by maples, *Magnolia* x *veitchii*, an excellent specimen of the madrona (*Arbutus menziesii*) and *Davidia involucrata* by the log cabin.

By turning left, you can reach the Memorial Glade, planted with maples and azaleas, and a group of tall columnar *Chamaecyparis lawsoniana*. Above, to the west, is the quarry, and then the Foliage Glade. This area features trees and shrubs with unusual foliage and a magnificent grouping of pieris. You now rejoin the main path, leading back to the car park and shop.

For a more detailed listing of the plants in the foliage glade and throughout the arboretum, the reader is referred to the National Trust's own leaflets, the *Autumn Walk* and the *Spring Walk*.

Wisley

ADDRESS AND TELEPHONE: Wisley Garden, near Ripley, Surrey GU23 6QB. Tel. Guildford (0483) 224234

OWNERS: The Royal Horticultural Society

DIRECTIONS: M25 Junction 10 (Wisley RHS Garden). Public transport: London to Wisley; Green Line Coach 715 from Oxford

Circus/Upper Regent Street (opposite Polytechnic), or 740 from
Victoria (Eccleston Bridge). Guildford to Wisley; Green Line
Coach 715 and 740 from Friary bus station, Guildford. Waterloo
BR (or Clapham Junction) to Esher. Green Line Coach 715 to
Wisley. Waterloo (or Clapham Junction) to West Byfleet. Taxi
service is sometimes available at station, the journey to Wisley is
4 miles.

OPENING TIMES: all year round except 25 December. Mon to Sat,
February to October 10–7 (or sunset if earlier); November,
December and January, 10–4.30 (or sunset if earlier). Sun,
members of the Royal Horticultural Society only

ADMISSION: £3.50, children £1.50. Reductions for pre-booked
parties of 20 or more (write 14 days in advance)

REFRESHMENTS: café

SHOP: gifts and books. Plant centre with wide range of hardy
plants

DOGS: no

WHEELCHAIR ACCESS: yes, wheelchairs available and a special
route constructed. Toilets for the disabled: yes

PEAK MONTHS: peaks throughout the year

NOTABLE FEATURES: almost every style of garden is displayed
here; all types of ornamental, fruit and vegetable production
practised; enormous variety of plants displayed and trialled,
woodland, wild, rock, water, heather, rose gardens, herbaceous
borders, model gardens

In 1878 a very keen amateur gardener and former treasurer of the
Royal Horticultural Society, Mr George F. Wilson, purchased a
60-acre estate at Wisley near Ripley in Surrey and began creating
settings to display a variety of flowering shrubs and other plants
and developing a 6-acre woodland garden which still exists today
in the centre of this much larger garden.

When Wilson died the estate was purchased by Sir Thomas
Hanbury, who in 1903 gave the garden in trust for use by the Royal
Horticultural Society 'for the purpose of an Experimental Garden
and the Encouragement and Improvement of Scientific and Practical Horticulture in all its branches'. In the following spring the
Society moved from its former gardens at Chiswick to Wisley and
over the next 80 years it developed the now world-famous garden.

Today there are about 250 acres of garden under cultivation.
Nowhere else can you see such a variety of gardening styles,
ornamental as well as practical and productive. Rock and water
gardens, formal gardens and herbaceous borders—everything is
here on one site.

In accordance with the terms of the trust the garden is maintained
to show as wide a range of ornamental plants as possible; to provide
advice on horticultural problems; to carry out trials and form
collections of new varieties of flowers, fruit and vegetables; to train
young gardeners in the skills and practices of horticulture; and to
carry out research into horticultural and related subjects.

The scientific laboratory is housed in a beautiful half-timbered
building. Although old-fashioned in style, this building was in fact
erected in 1915. Ornamented with rambling roses, ceanothus and

magnolias, it provides the perfect setting for terraced lawns and a formal garden laid out to the west.

The formal garden, designed by Lanning Roper and Sir Geoffrey Jellicoe, has a long canal pool as its central feature, flanked by stretches of neat lawn and with a pergola on one side. A mixture of summer-flowering shrubs and foliage provides a background and the pool ends in front of an open pavilion or loggia, through which you can see the walled garden.

This garden is divided into two compartments by yew hedges; the first part features beds set in brick paving, with bulbs, pansies and wallflowers in spring followed by summer bedding displays. The second compartment is laid out in much the same way, but with permanent plantings of roses, small shrubs and perennial plants, especially grey or silver foliaged types. The walls support ivies, clematis, roses and other climbing plants.

A small pinetum lies south of the formal and walled gardens, then a broad grass walk ascends a hill between colourful mixed borders. Backed by hornbeam hedges, the borders are 18ft wide and 420ft long and are filled with herbaceous plants, shrubs, ornamental grasses and annuals. The effect is spectacular in summer. Two borders running at right-angles to the central path provide colour from late summer through to autumn.

In the enclosures to the west of the mixed borders you will find the summer garden and the garden for new rose introductions. The summer garden is filled with plants that flower from June onwards, and has many delightful old-fashioned and shrub roses. On the western boundary, cultivars such as 'Buff Beauty' and 'Zephirine Drouhin' are trained along post and wire fences. The new rose garden, another large area, is planted with over 200 different bush, miniature and climbing rose cultivars —all introduced over the last five years. To guard against soil sickness, which often occurs when roses are continually replanted on the same site, the beds are always sterilised before new cultivars are introduced.

At the top of the hill, known as Battleson Hill, is a lightly wooded area of Scots pines, sweet chestnuts, oaks and birches where trials of hybrid rhododendrons and evergreen azaleas are conducted. This area was damaged in the storm of 1987 and is being restored.

Trials of flowers and vegetables can be seen in Portsmouth Field, beyond Battleston Hill. Carnations, irises, dahlias and delphiniums, and many other flowers, as well as vegetables are grown here, and their various characteristics assessed and compared.

Wisley's main glasshouse complex lies to the west of Battleston Hill. The large display house is divided into cool, intermediate and warm temperature zones, to accommodate a very wide range of plants. At the far end of the complex is a demonstration area of hedging and ground cover plants, showing possible combinations, such as beech and box hedging with ivy and Pachysandra for ground cover, and to the north-west is a series of model gardens.

The model gardens may be a good source of ideas and inspiration for your own garden. They show how ornamental plants can be planted for best effect in small gardens and how to incorporate fruit trees and bushes and vegetable beds. One rectangular area of 72 x 24ft is laid out as a typical small town garden, another shows how to make space for children in a family garden and a third gives some ideas on how to use a small plot (82 x 54ft) to display a range of gardening styles and a variety of plants. Another garden, across the service road, was planted for the television series *Gardeners Calendar*.

Disabled gardeners are made particularly welcome at Wisley with wheelchairs available at the gate and a route laid out around the gardens. The model gardens include a plot of special interest to disabled and elderly gardeners: planned in association with the Disabled Living Foundation, this shows a selection of paving styles, ramps and raised beds. Next door is the herb garden, also paved in a variety of styles and with geometric beds containing all kinds of culinary and medicinal herbs.

Model fruit gardens show fruit trees trained in cordons, espaliers, fans and dwarf pyramids, along with a good selection of soft fruits. The main fruit collection at Wisley lies further to the west in a 16-acre field: here you can see 670 cultivars of apples divided into dessert and culinary, 90 cultivars of pear and 90 of plums and gages, along with strawberry, blackcurrant, quince, nuts and other collections.

The model vegetable garden lies north-west of the other model gardens, past long rose borders planted with bush hybrid tea and floribunda roses. The vegetable garden measures 90 x 30ft and would provide enough vegetables to keep an average size family going through most of the year. There are two small greenhouses, for tomatoes and cucumbers.

A short distance to the west are two larger houses sheltering early flowering alpines. These are at their best between February and May, but there is nearly always something of interest to see. The newer house has been laid out as a scree garden, its outside walls clad with stone and wall plants.

Standing at the top of Wisley's marvellous rock garden, you can look down towards the alpine meadow. The rock garden itself dates from 1911 although it has been enlarged and altered over the years. A path zig-zags through the Sussex sandstone rock formation, crossing streams and waterfalls en route.

The rock garden is at its most colourful in April and May but there are interesting things to see even in winter, such as dwarf irises and snowdrops. Water is used to good effect and flows at the bottom into a pool fringed with aquatic perennials and moisture-loving plants.

The alpine meadow makes a stunning sight in early spring, filled with *Narcissus bulbocodium* and *N. Cyclamineus*. Later *N. triandrus* mixes with wood anenomes and dog's-tooth violets, followed in June by spotted orchids and in autumn by purple autumn crocuses (*Crocus nudiflorus*). Rock outcrops built on the grassy slope help to link the meadow with the rock garden.

Across the path from the alpine meadow is one of the oldest gardens at Wisley, G.F. Wilson's wild garden. Pathways made of log rounds lead through the woodland, where you can see many fine trees and shrubs, including an Umbrella pine (*Sciadopitys verticillata*), its leaves arranged like the spokes of an umbrella. The moist peaty soil here suits rhododendrons, magnolias, camellias and other shrubs; among the smaller herbaceous plants are primulas, lilies and meconopsis.

Walking north-east from the wild garden you come to lawns and the round pond—especially attractive in autumn—and to the north is an area known as Seven Acres. A gravel pit was converted into a lake here in 1915 and large beds of flowering shrubs have been planted, to give interest from March to late summer. The heather garden is well worth a visit, and contains an extensive collection of heathers, planted in informal curved beds. Wisley also boasts excellent collections of trees in its arboretum and pinetum.

EAST SUSSEX

Great Dixter

ADDRESS AND TELEPHONE: Great Dixter, Northiam, East Sussex TN31 6PH. Tel. (0797) 253160. Plant nursery: (0797) 253107

OWNERS: Christopher and Quentin Lloyd and Mrs O. Lind

DIRECTIONS: 12 miles N of Hastings on A28: follow signposts from Northiam. Public transport: buses infrequent nos 340, 342, 348, Hastings and District. Alight Northiam post office 500yds

OPENING TIMES: 29 March to mid October, Tues to Sun and BH Mon 2–5; some Sats and Suns in late October 2–5; garden opens at 11 some days in May, Sun in July and August and August BH Mon. House also open

ADMISSION: house and garden £3, children 50p. OAPs and NT members (Fri only) £2.50; gardens only £2, children 25p. Coach parties by appointment, reduced rates

CAR PARKING: yes

TOILETS: yes

REFRESHMENTS: teas

SHOP: no

DOGS: no

WHEELCHAIR ACCESS: no. Toilets for the disabled: no

The medieval manor of Dixter and its surrounding farmyards were bought by Nathaniel Lloyd in 1910: Edwin Lutyens, who was commissioned to design the gardens, retained many of the original farm buildings, but added several features distinctively his own, such as the steps and terraces. Nathaniel Lloyd himself designed the sunk garden and oversaw the planting and training of yew and box hedges and topiary pieces. The wild moat garden was the inspiration of Mrs Daisy Lloyd, who continued to develop the planting after her husband's death, in partnership with her son Christopher.

Christopher Lloyd is a well-known gardening writer and has written a lot about Great Dixter, especially the long border. Having studied and taught horticulture for seven years at Wye College in Kent, he returned to Dixter in 1954, to start a nursery and devote himself full-time to the garden. He is now helped by three full-time

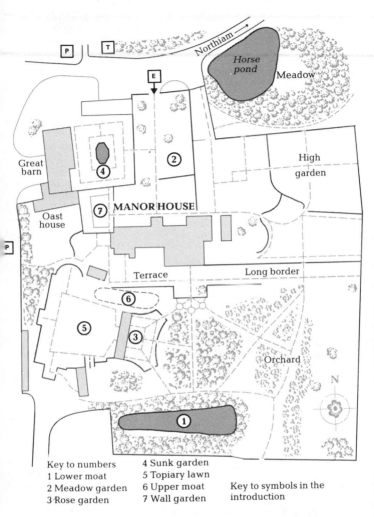

Key to numbers
1 Lower moat
2 Meadow garden
3 Rose garden
4 Sunk garden
5 Topiary lawn
6 Upper moat
7 Wall garden

Key to symbols in the
introduction

and three or four part-time staff: and his brother Quentin Lloyd manages the estate.

The gardens cluster round the house, surrounding it on all sides. The Great Barn and oast houses lie to the north, just behind the sunk garden and walled garden; orchards stretch to the south, below the terrace and long border. The design is strongly centred but not inward-looking: structured round the house, yet retaining strong links with the surrounding Sussex countryside.

A lane from Northiam brings you to the main entrance, a long straight path leading through a very attractive meadow area to the north-east front of the house. The large flagstone paving is slippery in wet weather.

You can catch a first glimpse of the sunk garden through a yew arch to your right. The house porch and right-hand part of the building date from the mid 15C. Pots of plants stand either side of the porch, looking bright and welcoming. On our visit in July we saw orange lily 'Orestes', yellow lily 'Phoebe', and a splendid blue-green succulent, *Cotyledon obtusa*, trailing fat leaves to the ground. Ferns grow below the house windows. Left of the porch is a wing added by Lutyens, before the 1914–18 war; the lawn is dominated by *Chusquea culeou*, a Chilean bamboo, backed by *Pyrus communis*, an enormous and very old wild pear, growing through a yew hedge.

Head straight away for the sunk garden, just around to your right and an unforgettable sight in summer. Entering through an arch in the stone wall, you look down over an octagonal stone pool, surrounded by flagstones and a drystone wall, with a sloping strip of lawn, a path and borders above. Barn walls and a yew hedge form the other three garden boundaries.

As a gardener, Christopher Lloyd is remarkably open-minded, prepared to wait on and work with Nature, rather than impose his own rigid plans. The plants obviously appreciate this, self-seeding freely and flourishing. Thistly *Acaena novae-Zealandiae*, the New Zealand burr, spreads over the paving in wide pools, covered with rusty pink heads in July and interspersed with self-seeded bird's-foot trefoil and wild orchids. Ferns and ivy grow in and from all available crevices in the low walls, along with *Cymbalaria muralis*, the miniature wild toadflax, geraniums and lavender.

The north bed, by the entry arch, is a splendid tangle of bright and delicate flowers—mauve and white campanulas, marigolds, waving astrantia and the lovely silver-blue thistle 'Miss Wilmott's Ghost' (*Eryngium giganteum*). The variegated euonymus 'Emerald Gaiety' was also in flower, unusual for July.

The border planting is rich almost beyond description—a real treasure-trove for plant lovers. Besides plentiful foliage plants and grasses, there are many flowers—orange and yellow day lilies, pink and red lychnis, blue polemonium.

Pots stand on the paving, planted the year we visited with silver *Helichrysum petiolare*, red pelargonium, blue lobelia and orange *Mimulus glutinosus*. *Verbena bipinnatifida*, with very pretty tiny mauve flowers and leaves, decorated two stone troughs, accompanied by diascia. In an upper bed, bright blue *Brodiaea laxa* leaned over yellow and orange violas; behind, against the barn, grew a magnificent *Schisandra rubriflora*, with trusses of green berries, later turning red.

One 'special effect' that must be mentioned is the flooding juniper, pouring from the terrace wall to the paving in two green waterfalls, spiked through with tree peonies.

The walled garden is just adjacent: unfortunately this is rather a thoroughfare, but it's worth pausing for more than a few minutes, especially to look at *Clematis* x *jouiniana praecox*, amid a heavy thicket of shrubs. Nearby are pink mallow, blue thistles and orange and pink alstroemeria. *Euphorbia griffithii* grows in great mounds by the south wall, underplanted with tiny bright flowers of leptosiphon; pears and honeysuckle behind.

Leaving past a handsome *Fatsia japonica*, you descend by curving semicircular steps, designed by Lutyens, to a pleasant transitional area. With risers made from layers of red tiles or sandstone, topped by York stone, the steps are an ideal breeding place for small plants—ferns, alchemilla and even yellow poppies. A big bed of hydrangeas (lilac to red), rodgersias and pink geraniums, leads along to the loggia, with topiary lawn below.

Giant yew birds with tiny wings and several strange abstract shapes stand here and there on the topiary lawn: viewed for best effect on a winter morning through mist. Just along from here is the delightful moat garden—an old moat now drained and seeded with grasses and wildflowers—moon daisies, purple knapweed, yellow bird's-foot trefoil, pink clover and some irises; stonecrop, aubrieta and white and pink valerian grow in the wall. *Magnolia* x *soulangiana* 'Lennei' makes an impressive show on the south-west terrace, just above, bearing rose-purple, goblet-shaped flowers in mid spring.

The famous long border now comes into view, but pause first to admire another flight of Lutyens steps, swirling in circles and half moons. The hedged rose garden lies to your right, surrounded by grassland and trees, and an orchard, with the long border lying directly above. Wild and formal features combine everywhere here with great success.

The long border is familiar to most keen gardeners and especially Christopher Lloyd's readers. The general effect is stimulating rather than harmonious: the planting is intensive and adventurous, and some of the colour combinations very daring. Golden sambucus (elder) makes a bright beginning; nearby *Genista aetnensis*, the Mount Etna broom, incredibly light and delicate, grows through mahonia and white *Hydrangea paniculata* 'Praecox'. Here too is *Hosta ventricosa* 'Aureovariegata', with glaucous leaves edged with gold, and the red rose 'Florence May Morse'.

Blue-stemmed sea holly, *Eryngium* x *oliverarianum*, appears throughout the garden, but looks especially lovely here, with the two blues of *Campanula lactiflora*, gold-green euonymus 'Silver Queen' and a spread of pink diascia ('Ruby Field'), the miniature twin-spur, a tiny relative of the snapdragon.

Dickson's golden elm makes a magnificent half-way mark to the border, surrounded by silvery-grey willows (*Salix alba* 'Argentea'), underplanted with blue veronica and purple everlasting peas: in front is a purple smoke bush (*Cotinus coggyria*).

Christopher Lloyd obviously likes big, bold-growing and colour-ful plants—phlox, yellow daisies, purple clematis—and these are well served by the strong foliage structure, including many small trees and plants of tree-like size.

You must explore the long border for yourself (preferably in high summer), since each visitor will notice and remember different things. Most people seem attracted like bees to the 'hot' end, where orange-red helenium 'Moerheim Beauty' and bright orange-red *Lychnis chalcedonica* clash wonderfully, offset by blue *Salvia nemerosa* 'Superba'.

You may be glad to relax, in the plain oak seat (designed by Lutyens) at the top of the border, and admire the delicate quivering deep pink heads of astrantia, underneath hydrangeas. *Alchemilla mollis* spills over the paving, backed by white *Viola cornuta*.

The high garden lies directly above the long border: a large area enclosed by yew hedges, and originally designed as a kitchen garden with narrow flower borders. Nowadays it supplies plants for bedding out and cutting and for sale in the nursery. There is plenty of interest here, including wonderful lupins and tree lupins, many varieties of poppy, shrub and climbing roses. Also conifers and a surprising amount of topiary, at least as good as the topiary on the main lawn.

The horse pond and meadow above are an ideal relaxing spot, abundant with wildflowers. Yellow flag irises, wild broom and golden sedge grow near the water, lighting it with bright reflections, and pink and red water lilies bloom throughout June and July.

Sheffield Park Garden

ADDRESS AND TELEPHONE: Sheffield Park Garden, Uckfield, East Sussex TN22 3QX. Tel. Danehill (0825) 790231

OWNERS: The National Trust

DIRECTIONS: midway between East Grinstead and Lewes, 5 miles NW of Uckfield, on E side of A275. Public transport: ½ mile from Sheffield Park station (Bluebell line), 7 miles from Haywards Heath BR. Southdown buses 720, 769 from Haywards Heath and Brighton BR, peak days: otherwise 781 from Haywards Heath and Uckfield BR, alight Chailey crossroads, 1¾ miles

OPENING TIMES: 30 March to 10 November, Tues to Sat (closed Good Fri) 11–6, Sun and BH Mon (closed Tues following BH) 2–6 or sunset if earlier. October and November, open Sun 1pm to sunset. Last admission 5pm

ADMISSION: March, April and June to end September £3.10, parties £2, children £1.60. May, October and November £3.60, parties £2.50, children £1.30. No reduction for parties on Sat, Sun and BH Mon

CAR PARKING: yes

TOILETS: yes

REFRESHMENTS: café

SHOP: yes

DOGS: no

WHEELCHAIR ACCESS: yes, to most parts. Toilets for the disabled: yes

PEAK MONTHS: autumn and spring

NOTABLE FEATURES: 5 lakes; landscaping by Capability Brown; mature trees, rare shrubs and water lilies, spring blossom, foliage effects and autumn colour

Since 1775, when Lancelot 'Capability' Brown laid out two lakes in the valley for the 1st Earl of Sheffield—a design to be extended a century later by James Pulham's addition of two upper lakes and a waterfall—there has been a notable landscape garden at Sheffield

Park. The basic structure remains the same as its designers intended, and it is still ornamented by many of the exotic trees and shrubs planted for the 3rd Earl at the end of the 19C and those added by Mr Arthur G. Soames between 1904 and 1934.

The garden's own excellent guide maps outline two separate tours of the park—one figure of eight around the lakes and a longer more leisurely inspection of the outer areas of the garden. You can also pick out for yourself to the south-east a variety of walks suited to different seasons—the Red Walk for autumn colour, and the conifer, kalmia, gentian or griseum walks at appropriate seasons. On the north-west slopes you will also find the Big Tree Walk, Queen's Walk, Palm Avenue, Himalaya, Coronation and Jubilee Walks, each focusing on different types of tree.

Deciding on the figure of eight to begin with, we descended the hill to the head of the first lake, walking between carpets of bluebells and groups of brilliant red and white rhododendrons. To the left lies Sheffield Park House, no longer linked to the garden as it is privately owned, but adding, with its neo-Gothic castellations and turrets, a romantic focus to the scene. There are several venerable sweet chestnuts near the path, which may have been there before Capability Brown's time. On our way we also passed sweet smelling *Azalea lutea* and bushes of the swamp or highbush blueberry (*Vaccinium corymbosum*), with clusters of white flowers and leaves which colour bright red in autumn. Nearby are the white bottle-brush flower heads of fothergillas, whose leaves produce spectacular variations of autumn colour and tulepo trees (*Nyssa sylvatica*), also brilliant in autumn. A blue cedar (*Cedrus atlantica glauca*) on the shores of the Ten Foot Pond (the first lake) makes a striking contrast with these reds and oranges.

In springtime, the colour round the first lake is more delicate, with pink and white-flowered rhododendrons spilling over into the water and blue-grey clumps of pampas grass. Despite a few losses during the storms of recent years, there are many fine conifers to be seen—including the view of a conical noble fir (*Abies procera*) across the lake and a dawn redwood (*Metasequoia glyptostroboides*). Nearby there are also mature broad-leaved trees—a beautiful low branching tall beech, a tall lime and a weeping birch. We noticed a group of distinctive Swedish birches with drooping habit and finely dissected leaves.

The Top Bridge, which was built in 1880, to provide a crossing between the upper and lower lakes, offers views back to the house and down over the falls to the second lake. There are some interesting trees here including the coffin juniper (*Juniperus recurva coxii*), favoured by the Chinese for burials. From the bridge we walked down to below the rocky waterfall—designed and constructed by Pulham in 1895—where a group of Chusan palms add distinction to the grass verge. There are also royal ferns (*Osmunda regalis*) giant leaves of *Gunnera manicata*, the yellow spathes of the skunk cabbage (*Lysichiton americanus*), the blue flowers of pickerel weed (*Pontederia cordata*) and clumps of iris.

It is tempting to remain by the lakes, enjoying the beautiful shapes and subtle colouring of the planting on the surrounding banks, but there are other areas to visit. On the south side of the park, as well as the speciality walks criss-crossing the slopes, a stream garden has been planted which you can follow along to the fourth lake, or Lower Woman's Way pond.

The curving sides of the stream are planted with drifts of bright green hostas, spikes of iris and candelabra heads of primula for spring, with feathery heads of astilbe to follow in autumn. From here we followed the shores of the Lower Woman's Way Pond to the cascade that separates it from the third lake, or Upper Woman's Way Pond. According to local legend, the woman who gave her name to these lakes used to cross the water below the present cascade via some stepping stones. She now appears from time to time as a headless ghost, vanishing if approached.

From this point you can cross the isthmus between the second and third lakes, and enjoy the Queen's Walk which leads you past conifers and a Caucasian oak (*Quercus macranthera*) to a conservation area for wild flowers, where spotted orchids grow in July.

Returning to the junction of the second and third lakes you turn north to the Big Tree Walk, featuring three majestic Wellingtonias (a Nootka cypress was lost in 1987). Huge clumps of rhododendrons grow in this area, especially the Loderi varieties. The pale pink *R. Loderi* 'King George' is particularly fragrant, but other Loderi varieties—'Venus', 'Sir Edmond' and 'White Diamond'—are also in evidence. There are also 'Angelo' hybrids in purple and yellow—a complete list of these is given in the guide. Further on the Palm Walk curves away to the right—the Windmill palms (*Trachycarpus fortunei*) with their grey hairy stems, lend an exotic touch to the landscape. Here there are also spring flowering camellias and late summer flowering hydrangeas, large-leaved rhododendrons and clumps of bamboo.

This route returns you down the hillside to the starting point at the head of the first lake. It would take many visits fully to appreciate the diversity of trees and shrubs as well as the lilies and water plants around the lakes at Sheffield Park. The harmonious design of the garden and its variation of colour and form, however, will always give pleasure. While the garden is particularly spectacular in the autumn, there is no season when it is dull. The vigorous programme of new planting everywhere is a guarantee that Sheffield Park will continue to delight and interest visitors for many more years to come.

WEST SUSSEX

Borde Hill Garden

ADDRESS AND TELEPHONE: The Secretary, Borde Hill Garden, Haywards Heath, West Sussex RH16 1XP. Tel. Haywards Heath (0444) 450326

OWNERS: The Stephenson Clarke family. Leased to Borde Hill Garden Ltd (a charitable company)

DIRECTIONS: 1½ miles N of Haywards Heath, West Sussex, on the Balcombe Road. Public transport: 1 mile from Haywards Heath BR. No bus

OPENING TIMES: 10–6, daily from Good Fri to the last weekend in October inclusive; also weekends in March. House closed

ADMISSION: £2, children 75p, OAPs and parties of 20 or more £1.25

CAR PARKING: yes

TOILETS: yes

REFRESHMENTS: 2 restaurants

SHOP: plants for sale

DOGS: yes, on lead

WHEELCHAIR ACCESS: yes, two wheelchairs available. Toilets for the disabled: yes

PEAK MONTHS: March, April and May

NOTABLE FEATURES: rhododendrons, azaleas, camellias, mahonias. New lake below the car park to be landscaped. Children's adventure playground

Borde Hill is famous for its magnificent rhododendrons, azaleas and camellias, which come into their full glory in April and May. The 40-acre gardens are part of a 3000 -acre traditional, agricultural estate, including parkland and some beautiful woods.

Borde Hill is quite exposed, standing on a narrow ridge with the north park garden and woods lying below and the land beyond sloping gradually to the floor of the Upper Ouse Valley. It suffered badly in the storms of 1987 and 1990, losing approximately 300 trees and leaving the rhododendrons badly exposed, and it is planned to move the rhododendrons to more sheltered woodland areas.

The south walled garden, near the car park, is a convenient place to start. There is a good (but not cheap) tea room here, as well as a licensed restaurant and conference centre. A fishpond, rose garden and small orchard have recently been established here. High walls, built in 1906, still support and shelter plants put in before the 1914–18 war, along with more recent introductions. Three big spiky *Phormium tenax*, or New Zealand flax, are difficult to miss outside the tea room. The herbaceous and shrub borders are thoughtfully planted, containing many lovely foliage plants (anthemis, helichrysum, euphorbia, lavender) and flowers (rock roses and true geraniums). A specimen of ceanothus, the Californian lilac, with clusters of pale blue tiny flowers, makes a bright contrast with orange/yellow *Spiraea* x *bumalda* 'Goldflame'.

However, the most interesting and oldest planting lies outside the garden walls. *Magnolia delavayi*, a tender species from south China, has managed to survive since 1910, spreading above the west wall. An impressive array of mahonias, hardy evergreen berried shrubs with spiky leaves, grows just outside the entrance gate, to the left. There are 70 species of mahonia and Borde Hill hopes to make a complete collection. It is fascinating to see their variations—*Mahonia aquifolium* 'Moseri' with bronze-red young leaves, turning apple green, then dark green, bold M. *acanthifolia*, with deeply cut leaves somewhat similar to acanthus, and two M. *rotundifolia*, with (as might be guessed) rounded leaves.

Right of the gate stands a Japanese *Wisteria venusta*, arthritic in shape like all wisterias, and some handsome camellias. Lower down is an unusually big specimen of *Viburnum cinnamomifolium*, underplanted with frothing skimmia. Round the corner, along the south wall, maintenance has obviously been less of a priority— nettles grow freely—but there are many fine shrubs and trees. Notably the astonishing *Stuartia sinensis*, with its stone-coloured wrinkled trunk, more like a huge carved limb than a tree, sprouting low branches. Further up, the bark is peeling away, revealing lovely snake-like patterns. This stuartia, planted in 1914, was raised from seed collected by E.H. Wilson in China. *Lindera megaphylla*, which grows nearby, is described somewhat unkindly in the guide booklet as 'rare but uninteresting'. Certainly *S. sinensis* is a hard act to follow. As if the bark were not enough, it also produces white camellia-like flowers, 2in. across, and its leaves turn red in autumn. Further on sprawls *Osmanthus delavayi*, with fragrant tubular flowers in April, and along the east wall are several good-sized magnolias. An adventure playground has been constructed using timber from the October 1987 gale in just south of the walled garden, with an adjacent picnic area.

The azalea ring is pretty in late April, bordering on an open lawn once sheltered by the 150-year-old Turkey oak which was lost in a storm in March 1987. Here again are some good magnolias. The old rhododendron garden, with plant sales area nearby, comes next, with many Himalayan species or hybrids, including *R. campylocarpum*, with lemon-yellow, bell-shaped flowers. The success or otherwise of this part of the garden depends entirely on your feelings for rhododendrons: it is rather dismal out of season, brightened only by the whip-like red stems of *Cornus alba*. A grassy glade leads through it, named Jack Vass walk in honour of a retired head gardener. Here are viburnum, pieris, more mahonias and a solid mass of dark red bergenias, favoured by Gertrude Jekyll, who used their big leaves in flower borders to 'root the eye'.

A nursery garden lies just north of Jack Vass Walk, sheltering old shrub roses and herbs. The long herbaceous border is planted with sedums and *Alchemilla mollis*, both full of diamond lights after rain; also blue polemonium and grey woolly *Stachys lanata* (lambs ears).

Borde Hill House looks out over the south lawn, rather grim and formal with its upright Jacobean architecture and dark narrow windows. The south lawn is wide, and waterlogged at the time we visited, ending in a ha-ha with wooded parkland beyond. It was lowered and levelled at the end of the last century, to give a better view. At the same time, a fine specimen of *Magnolia* x *soulangiana* was brought in by horse and cart and planted at the west corner of the house, which it now covers. On the nearby wall is the aptly named *M. Grandiflora* 'Goliath'.

The whole west side of Borde Hill is fascinating, with many unusual features: a lovely place to wander round, particularly on a windy day with the pines sighing above (although many of these have been blown down in the storms). A flagged stone path along the west terrace leads to the marble Bride statue.

Umbellularia californica, the headache tree, stands not far away, a member of the laurel family, introduced from North America by David Douglas. Do not sniff the leaves, as they may give you a headache, or make you sneeze violently. Luckily, the branches are placed high up. Another interesting tree is *Cercis siliquastrum*, the Judas tree, a native of the eastern Mediterranean, and reputed by legend to be the tree on which Judas hanged himself. This speci men would not be ideal for the purpose: twice broken by winds in the 1930s, and again in October 1987, it is now growing again from its base. It still determinedly produces its purple pea flowers, followed by distinctive heart-shaped leaves.

The ruined cottage just below the terrace is steadily being swallowed up by ivy and climbers. Corylus grows in front, with its very pretty delicate small yellow flowers, and plentiful hydrangeas, including the venerable *H. sargentiana* from Central China, more than 60 years old. Rhododendrons crowd round the porch and the back walls. Round the other side of the terrace, steps lead down to a rectangular pool, its flagged surrounds edged with sun-loving plants—hebes, sage, rue and cineraria. In summer, this part of the garden is particularly charming, with its somewhat formal design, like a Spanish courtyard.

For a complete contrast, follow the Long Walk along the edge of the South Park to the Round Dell, a damp-pit garden featuring Chusan palms, bamboos and yellow bog arum. Kingcups grow plentifully around the pool and a wide variety of day lilies (hemerocallis) flourish in the rock bank. With pines above and laurel overhanging, the Round Dell gives an impression of careless luxuriance.

The path now leads back towards the North Garden, taking you past the Long Dell, an old quarry now full of chestnut trees and early flowering pale pink and red rhododendrons.

North Park Garden was separated off from the park around 1925. It contains rhododendrons raised from seed collected by Kingdon Ward in the 1920s, on his explorations through the Himalayas and Burma, and others introduced by Forrest and Rock. The guide booklet provides good historical notes. From the terrace above, you can get a fine view over parkland and countryside, and down to Warren Wood. A small and unexpected tombstone marks the grave of Flora Macdonald Chisholm Fraser Clarke, who died in 1927, aged 14.

The woodland walks are recommended, but wear stout water-proof boots!

Denmans

ADDRESS AND TELEPHONE: Denmans Ltd, Clock House, Denmans Lane, Fontwell, near Arundel, West Sussex BN18 0SU. Tel. Eastergate (0243) 542808

OWNER: Mrs Joyce Robinson. Manager: John Brookes

DIRECTIONS: turn into Denmans Lane off the A27 near Fontwell racecourse. Public transport: Barnham BR, then taxi or possibly bus

OPENING TIMES: early March to mid December, daily 9–5. House not open

ADMISSION: £1.80, OAPs £1.60, children £1. Coach parties by appointment, groups of 12 or more £1.50

CAR PARKING: yes

TOILETS: yes

REFRESHMENTS: café

SHOP: yes

DOGS: no

WHEELCHAIR ACCESS: yes. Toilets for the disabled: no

PEAK MONTHS: May, June, July

NOTABLE FEATURES: walled garden; tree planting; shrub and perennial planting

This beautiful 3½-acre garden, set in the Sussex countryside just off a busy A road, has been a source of inspiration to many gardeners, both amateur and professional. Like all the best gardens, it is still changing, developing and maturing, so it is a place to keep visiting and learning new lessons from. Since 1985 it has been managed by John Brookes, landscape designer and author, who also runs garden design courses here.

Mrs Joyce Robinson and her husband bought the estate in 1946, after the war. With the help of one gardener, they grew flowers, fruit and vegetables for the London market, including strawberries in the walled garden and salad crops in a large Dutch light greenhouse. After 1970, Mrs Robinson began to grow herbs in the walled garden and train climbers up the walls. Apart from a cedar of Lebanon, planted in 1800, and some old pear trees near the cottage, most of the trees at Denmans were introduced by Mrs Robinson. They form a very important part of the garden's design, inspiring in their marvellous groupings and contrasts.

A gravel path leads from the car park down to the old conservatory, the former Dutch greenhouse, where you pay your entrance money (and may buy plants). Plants spill over from the beds and grow up through the gravel. They are encouraged to self-seed, planted close together and rarely staked. An enormous clump of brilliant green euphorbia sprouts outside the tea shop; nearby is a shrub bed, with *Rosa Chinensis mutabilis*, plentiful viburnum, a variegated weigela and thick-spreading laurel. Achilleas, purple sage backed by grey senecio and *Alchemilla mollis* (lady's mantle) provide interest at a lower level, while golden feverfew flourishes in the gravel. *Silybum marianum* (Our Lady's milk thistle, or blessed thistle) recurs through the garden, with its spiky acanthus-like leaves, marbled green and white, and deep violet flowers in summer.

Four small square foliage beds have been planted in a grassy area to the left, like a colour key to the main map of the garden—one made up mainly of grey, silver and white plants, another red and purple, the third gold and the fourth devoted to variegated grasses. In the first bed, lamium 'Molten Silver' (light silver-green leaves, splashed with burgundy) mingles with white spikes of hebe 'Pagei', backed by rue, and alongside woolly ballota, *Stachys lanata* and achillea 'Moonshine'. Nepeta 'Six Hills Giant' lives up to its name, extending 6in. spikes of lavender flowers. Here too is silvery branching *Verbascum bombyciferum*: verbascums self-seed all over the garden, shooting up their spikes of yellow flowers like sky rockets from the borders. In the red bed, *Berberis thunbergii* and 'Red Pillar', *Rosa rubrifolia*, *Weigela florida* 'Foliis Purpureis', a dark-leaved bergenia and an elder make a bold contrast to the silver.

The low-roofed conservatory houses frost-tender species. Climbing plants grow everywhere up and around the supports: clematis 'Vyvyan Pennell', producing very showy big mauve flowers in spring, both single and double (single only in autumn), variegated golden summer jasmine, *Rosa fortuniana banksiae laevigata*, with variegated leaf, and two lovely abutilons, peach and red. Near the centre twines *Acacia pravisima*, its branches trained out in all directions, with fronds of tiny heart-shaped leaves raining down. There is a small water tank, with fountain jet. At ground level grow red and cream spiky phormiums, and agaves with their two-tone fleshy sword-like leaves.

The walled garden lies just adjacent, with *Clematis montana* 'Rubrum' cascading over the arched entrance. In the 19C, this was a soft fruit garden, supplying nearby Westergate House, owned by Lord Denman. The planting here must be seen to be believed. We visited in late spring, following a few weeks of rain and mild temperatures, when the plants were looking marvellously healthy and vigorous. Here as elsewhere, Mrs Robinson has established a strong basic structure of trees and perennial shrubs, with a designer's eye for shape and gradations of height. The planting is intense but never messy: exuberant within well established lines. It is possible to lose sight of your companions and wander alone, always a pleasant sensation: but they can be retrieved without too much difficulty. Gravel paths snake between the wall beds and large curving irregular island beds. The second bed to the left is dominated by a tall *Eucalyptus gunnii*, with its many-coloured subtle foliage, and golden-yellow *Robinia pseudoacacia* 'Frisia', underpinned with a cluster of bushes—gold bush honeysuckle, a purple rose, golden philadelphus and purple lilac. A big peony, robust yellow *Paeonia lutea ludlowii*, stands at the other end of the bed, together with a fine purple weeping beech.

Herbs and other small delicate plants grow around and between large square paving stones, with some squares left open: this gives the effect of 'stepping stones' leading deep into the heart of the bed. Here are chives, lavender, purple sage, creeping gold and silver thymes and the decorative mauve and pink umbels of small alliums: also blue-flowered bugle (*Ajuga reptans*), silver hebe and low mounds of bright green alchemilla.

The flint and brick walls are covered in climbing plants, including *Clematis montana* 'Elizabeth', mauve *C. heraclifolia* 'Juliana', wisteria, variegated ivy and climbing roses. The many lovely old-fashioned roses come into full bloom and fragrance in summer, from June to August.

The main garden slopes gently to the south, catching the sun, with views of the cornfields and a distant line of poplars. The grass is mown at two levels, leaving curving raised areas of meadow height, like thick carpets to walk across—a very effective way of lending interest to a large lawn. A two-branched 'gravel stream', filled with bright pebbles, runs down to a pond. At the top, near the walled garden, is a graceful group of trees: a tall birch, over-hanging a prunus and *Sorbus aria* (whitebeam). Low stone bridges cross the 'stream' and there are naturalistic plantings of grasses, bugles, bamboo and shrubby willows, besides some handsome viburnums and such exotica as phormiums and *Choisya ternata*, the Mexican orange blossom. The pond is filled with real water (rather than pebbles), water lilies and goldfish.

Among the trees in this area are *Cupressus arizonica*, with ball-shaped leathery fruits, *Metasequoia glyptostroboides* (dawn redwood) a ginkgo and a tulip tree. Two red oaks (*Quercus rubra*) stand guard over a miniature orchard.

One of the best places from which to observe the garden at your leisure is a small wooden seat, set far back in a sunny corner by the walled garden. However, the far side of the garden is hidden from this point, including a wild area full of bulbs and shade-loving plants.

A very striking blue spruce—unnamed: it was originally bought in a mix of seedlings—stands above the wild garden. From here, follow the path up to Mrs Robinson's house and the south garden. A bed of *Romneya coulteri* (tree poppy) blooms dazzling white in summer. Passing stone seats, an urn and *Magnolia wilsonii*, the path leads to a peculiar small rectangle of grass, like a rug laid on the gravel, backed by three dark conifers, one with golden ivy growing through it. Right of the house is one of the old glasshouses, artistically arranged inside. The yellow abutilon is especially eye-catching, trained along wires: also the potted pelargoniums, pink mallow and *Streptosolen jamesonii*, a tender evergreen shrub with bright orange flowers.

The Clock House lies behind Mrs Robinson's house, beyond a lawn, some very fine shrub planting and a number of tastefully placed sculptures. Here John Brookes runs garden design courses.

Highdown

ADDRESS AND TELEPHONE: Highdown, near Worthing, West Sussex.

OWNERS: Worthing Borough Council

DIRECTIONS: take the A24 to Worthing, then turn W along the A2032. Signposted. Public transport: nearest BR station Goring by Sea. 30-minute walk, N 400 yds to roundabout, then W 400 yds. Garden is N of the dual carriageway, up a private drive

OPENING TIMES: Mon to Fri 10–4.30. Also weekends and BH from April to October, 10–8. House not open

ADMISSION: free

CAR PARKING: yes

TOILETS: yes

REFRESHMENTS: café

SHOP: no

DOGS: yes, on a lead

WHEELCHAIR ACCESS: poor: woodchip paths and slopes, difficult for wheelchairs. Toilets for the disabled: yes

NOTABLE FEATURES: chalk pit garden

This fascinating and unusual garden was created in the early part of this century by Sir Frederick Stern and given to Worthing Corporation, now Worthing Borough Council, after his death. It lies 100ft above sea level on Highdown Hill, the nearest of the South Downs to the sea.

Stern took over Highdown House (now a clubhouse) in 1820, but did not begin gardening until 1909, nearly 30 years later. The site was unpromising—a chalk pit, a grass paddock and not much growing but beech trees and ilex oaks. Indeed it was doubtful whether anything much would flourish in solid chalk, or in the very chalky Downs soil. Many eminent gardeners of the time thought not: but Arthur Hill, then director of Kew, encouraged the experiment.

The first plantings were made north-east of the pit, in Musgrave's corner, named for another famous gardener, Stern's friend Charles Musgrave of Hascombe. *Cupressus macrocarpa*, the Monterey cypress, was planted along the top of the pit, to shelter it from the salt sea winds: lilacs and cherries below. Like all pioneer gardeners, Stern learnt by his mistakes—plants would grow in chalky soil, but could not develop healthy root systems until the hard under-layer of chalk was broken up.

The success of Stern's endeavours is evident today. Hart's tongue ferns and ivies grow up the walls of the chalk pit; trees grow out at daring angles; *Cotoneaster horizontalis* and prickly berberis hang on the lower slopes; exuberant viburnums tangle with masses of yellow forsythia. Junipers and grey osmanthus provide subtle colour contrasts, along with the herbaceous plantings of grey-green cistus, irises and sedum, and the dark reds and pinks of the houseleek (sempervivum).

Chalk shines bare in occasional smooth bright patches, or crumbling into shining trails of rubble. And far above, along the top rim of the pit, lending a Mediterranean quality to the skyline, tower Monterey cypress, *Quercus ilex* and Australian pines, protective overseers. Indeed one of the great pleasures of visiting this garden is the feeling you get of being, like the plants, guarded, watched over and sheltered.

The base of the chalk pit is now divided into two big lawn areas, gently sloping between long planted beds. The first lawn is reached by a path through beech woodland, where in early spring hundreds of tiny blue scillas and white and blue windflowers bloom in the moist shade, interspersed with bright patches of polyanthus and closely followed in mid spring by narcissi and bluebells. A blue cedar, *C. atlantica glauca*, stands to the right, and further down is a paulownia, *P. tomentosa*, mauve-flowering in May. These and other similarly sizeable trees are in their element at Highdown, profiting from the sheltered scooped-out bowl of the chalk pit with its 'sun trap' effect, and the well-drained soil. Only the beech roots have proved a nuisance, intruding under the rose garden.

Peonies grow in the woodland too—*P. lutea*, blossoming yellow in June with a lily-like fragrance. Indeed peonies grow everywhere. in colours ranging from yellow to white to deep red or scarlet. *P. suffruticosa* 'Rock's Variety' is one to watch out for, with its white single flowers, about 6in. across, a maroon-crimson blotch at the base of each petal; also semi-double scarlet 'Sybil Stern', bred at Highdown, and single yellow 'Argosy'. Stern was an avid collector and hybridiser of peonies. They are astonishing plants, fiercely energetic, rushing up from the ground in spring, and with their tight, perfectly spherical buds exploding into flower.

Highdown was created for enjoyment and recreation—the chalk pit was initially converted into a tennis court. As Stern's interest in plants grew, and his expertise, it became a working experimental garden, but lost nothing of its original spirit-refreshing qualities. It is a peaceful, gentle place to be, alternating shady areas with sunny open spaces. *Euphorbia wulfenii*, with its lovely mixture of dark and light green, grows in deep shade near a yew, or enjoys fuller sun, sheltered by tall *Juniperus cedrus*. Green-flowered hellebores, winter-flowering members of the buttercup family, share a bed with wine-red peony shoots, *Hydrangea villosa* and lilacs at the southern end of the second lawn: while further up, alongside the lawn, *Helleboris orientalis*, with its variegated flowers of purple, pink and white, makes a beautiful sunlit spread among daffodils.

A deep fish pool and water-filled grotto (once a lime kiln) stand south of the first lawn. The pond was built in 1920, with Horsham stone and cement-lined. Clarence Elliott, a famous rock garden enthusiast, helped landscape the surrounding area. The rock garden beds are filled with small-flowered, interesting plants—dianthus, *Incarvillia grandiflora*, carpenteria—interspersed with dwarf conifers such as *Chamaecyparis pisifera* 'Boulevard' and *Picea glauca albertiana* 'Conica', perfect for rockeries. Shallow steps lead down from the central ridge to the pool, accompanied by a stream, which is cleverly diverted from side to side of the path, through a progression of stone basins. Small children are immediately attracted by the shallow steps and running water, but should be guarded near the fishpond.

The second lawn is almost concealed from the first by a clump of trees—a Swedish whitebeam (*Sorbus intermedia*) with its white flowers and red berries, a big holly and a yew. These are underplanted with hellebores, day lilies and the silvery dead nettle, lamium, so useful for ground cover. Nearby stands an attractive *Berberis* x *lologensis*, with clusters of yellow flowers in spring followed later by purple-blue fruits.

The second lawn also has a pond, a shallower overflow from the first, criss-crossed with twine to keep herons off. There is a bog area, containing single and double kingcups (*Caltha palustris*), bog irises, bergenia and pink glyceria (flote grass). The pond surrounds an island of tall bamboo, myriad long slender grey stems topped with delicate light green foliage. A palm and more forsythia grow behind. A wide bed contains snowdrops, then day lilies (hemerocallis); *Choisya ternata*, the Mexican orange blossom, grows to one side.

Next along is a limestone rock garden with its full complement of cistus, aubrieta, sempervivum, epimedium (good for leaf colour all through the year), thyme, primroses, soft lamium and yellow butterflies.

Highdown grew in piecemeal fashion, not according to any grand design, but to accommodate Stern's rapidly growing obsession with new species and plants in general. In 1912, E.H. Wilson was selling off plants collected in China, which Stern was able to buy through the nurseryman James Veitch of Combe Wood. Many of Wilson's tree and shrub trophies still flourish in the garden, such as *Magnolia delavayi, Acer griseum* with its amazing peeling bark and wonderful autumn colour, and *Viburnum henryi.* Stern also sponsored plant-hunting expeditions to south-east Asia, including Farrer's trips in 1914, and in return received a share of the seedlings and plants.

Meanwhile, Stern himself continued to adventure and experiment on home grounds, raising and hybridising plants which he would show in London (he was at one time RHS president). Some of his daffodils are named after places nearby, such as Broadwater and Goring. He raised roses *R. highdownensis* and 'Wedding Day', the classic summer-flowering *Magnolia* x *highdownensis* (white with crimson stamens) and *Helleborus sternii.*

So it is certainly worth venturing south, below the beeches, into the tree and shrub garden. The southern lawns are generously filled with seats, making this an ideal place in fine weather to admire the distant, sparkling sea. It has seen considerable changes since Stern's time, with much replanting of trees and reshaping of the beds—originally squared off, allotment-style, and each devoted to a single species, these are now much freer in outline, filled with mixed herbaceous plants and spring bulbs among trees and shrubs. The long row of pittosporum, of unusual height, was once a solid hedge. Berberis, mahonia and *Choisya ternata* can be found in plenty here, also lilacs, prunus, tree peonies and roses. There are several striking groups of golden and green conifers. Among the rarer trees are *Chionanthis retusis*, the Chinese fringe tree, with its downy shoots and white corymbs, and a sophora with white and purple pea-like flowers. Another member of the pea family, *Indigofera pseudotinctoria*, offers contrasting pink blossoms.

At the far end of the lawn, shaded by huge *Quercus ilex*, a log-edged raised bed displays rhodendrons and azaleas, lovers of acid soil and for this reason impossible to grow in the main planting areas.

A small rose garden crowns the central ridge, overshadowed and sapped by beech trees; turned over to vegetables during the last war, as part of the 'Dig for Victory' campaign, it now has six oblong rose beds, two round beds of lavender and a curving pergola.

Your way out leads through an avenue of *Prunus serrula*, banded with shining pink bark, and past more pittosporum. Before you go, take a wander through the grassy hyacinth glade near the car park, splendid in spring with pink, blue and white hyacinths and daffodils and planted with a variety of lovely and colourful shrubs—lilacs, sorbus, a sea buckthorn, abelia, viburnum and maple. To the right of the path is a small orchid and cacti house and planting frames for replenishing garden stock.

Highdown is not a museum to Stern's memory: it has seen many alterations since his death in 1967 and new plants are still being introduced and propagated. However, Chris Beardsley, the nursery manager, says 'We try to follow the spirit of his gardening and to keep it the kind of garden he wanted it to be, a place for people to enjoy themselves.'

Leonardslee Gardens

ADDRESS AND TELEPHONE: The Secretary, Leonardslee Gardens, Lower Beeding, near Horsham, West Sussex. Tel. Lower Beeding (0403) 891212

OWNERS: The Loder family

DIRECTIONS: M23/A23 to Handcross, then A279 (3 miles) to village of Lower Beeding or 4½ miles SE of Horsham, Sussex, at the junction of the A279 and A281. Public transport: Horsham BR. Take bus 107 southbound (4½ miles, bad at weekends, stops at the entrance)

OPENING TIMES: mid April to mid June, daily 10–6; in July, August and September, weekends only 12–6; October weekends 10–5. House not open

ADMISSION: £3 (May Sun and BH £4); April, June and October £2.50, July, August and September £2. Children £1 (May £2). Season ticket £10. Pre-booked coach parties welcome at reduced rates

CAR PARKING: yes

TOILETS: yes

REFRESHMENTS: café and licensed restaurant

SHOP: yes, plants for sale and sundries in café

DOGS: not in gardens (but may be walked in grass car park)

WHEELCHAIR ACCESS: yes, at top of valley (best in mid May): but the valley slopes down very steeply. Electric wheelchair users report favourably. Toilets for the disabled: yes

PEAK MONTHS: spring and autumn

NOTABLE FEATURES: 70 acres set in 200 acres of parkland; rhododendrons, azaleas, magnificent trees, lakes

Set in a deep forest valley, Leonardslee is perhaps the most breathtakingly spectacular garden in Sussex, an area not short on scenic beauty. Although famous for its collection of rhododendrons and azaleas, Leonardslee is lovely in all seasons, with its magnificent trees, chain of lakes and long open views across deer parks and forest to the South Downs. Visitors should take heed of its scale: covering 70 acres and set in parkland of 200 acres this is not really a good place to bring small children—although they may enjoy seeing the wallabies, the Sika deer and the swans.

Sir Edmund Loder created Leonardslee gardens in the last part of the 19C, having purchased the estate from his wife's family, the Hubbards. Rhododendrons from the Himalayas and surrounding regions were then flooding into Britain. Sir Edmund's skills in planning and landscaping were luckily equal to his financial means—he planted thousands of rhododendrons and azaleas in large groups, not swamping the woodland but enhancing its natural beauty. He was also an expert plant breeder, responsible for hybridising the Loderi group of rhododendrons. The most outstanding of these are 'King George' (pink buds turning white in flower), 'Pink Diamond' and 'Venus' (both delicate shades of pink), 'Sir Edmund' (pink-white) and 'Sir Joseph Hooker'. They are all richly fragrant. At their best from early to mid May, they can be found in the Loderi garden, not far from the car park, and many others are planted around the garden.

Sir Giles Loder inherited the estate after his grandfather's death; camellias were his particular interest. There is a camellia walk just south of the house and a camellia grove down by the lakes. These bloom in April, following the magnolias. In 1981, Sir Giles handed over the running of the gardens to younger members of his family. With quite a small staff, considering the acreage—four full-timers, three part-timers and occasional help—the garden is extremely well maintained, its vistas kept open and its plants regularly thinned and replaced.

For a first taste of the variety of planting, walk down below the café area. On the right-hand side of the lawn stands a lovely umbrella-shaped cherry tree with a stout trunk. This is still unidentified—even the late Collingwood Ingram, the world-renowned cherry expert, was puzzled by it. Another flowering cherry grows nearby (*Prunus sargentii*). Further down, *Cornus nuttallii* sports its creamy-white bracts, which look confusingly like big rounded petals, each ring of bracts surrounding a small central knob of tiny flowers. Here too is *Magnolia wilsonii*, with its striking white flowers, like upside-down saucers. A sizeable Japanese maple, *Acer palmatum* 'Elegans purpureum', branching from just above the ground, displays its purple-red and indeed very elegant foliage. There are also several tall rhododendrons, a promise of the woodland walk to come. A fine young pocket handkerchief tree (*Davidia involucrata*) stands next to the acer 'Prinz Handjery' with its salmon-coloured spring foliage. A superb collection of *R. yakushimanum* hybrids are a riot of colour at the bottom of the lawn. All this against a stunning backdrop: bright splashes of colour on the lower valley slopes, then the lakes and a sea of trees and flowers beyond.

An evergreen azalea, blooming bright cerise in May, opens the woodland walk, dazzlingly partnered by greeny-yellow *Acer palmatum* 'Senkaki'. Just opposite is a vast specimen of *R. Loderi* 'Glamour'. The Loderi crosses are at their best in May: other particularly appealing rhododendrons here are 'Carita Charm' with its offbeat subtle colouring, pink with a suggestion of yellow, and further along the lovely pale yellow *R. campylocarpum*. *R. Williamsianum*, spreading delicate branches and sparse pale pink flowers, crouches near an enormous tree of *R. fictolacteum*, hung with clusters of bell-shaped white flowers, but more interesting for its big leathery green leaves with brown felted undersides.

Sir Edmund was also very fond of conifers, and they have repaid his efforts with interest. Enormous sequoias (*S. sempervirens*, the Californian redwood) soar above the woodland path. Redwoods are the world's tallest trees and a great tourist attraction in the western USA, where they originate. *S. giganteum*, the Wellingtonia, grows near the woodland steps. They seem entirely at home here and the latter appears hurricane-proof. Camellias in the woodland include *C. japonica* 'Donckelarii', with its semi-double stars of red flowers, dappled white, and 'Duchess of Normandy'. Quite a number of camellias have been named for high-born ladies and it is easy to see why. There are some beautiful magnolias here too, some growing very high—starry *M. stellata* and *M. denudata*, its pure white flowers blossoming on bare branches. Many magnolias of splendid size grace the gardens, including varieties and hybrids of *M. campbellii*, *M. mollicomata* and *M. sprengeri diva*.

Sedate groupings of palms, *Trachycarpus fortunei*, stand at intervals, contentedly maintaining a more modest height. The very rare clump-forming variety 'Surculosa' can also be seen at Leonardslee: it grows very slowly but occasionally seeds itself. Climbers grow everywhere with great enthusiasm. *Hydrangea petiolaris* climbs 60ft up the larches and clematis reaches almost as high up oak trees.

For an unsurpassable view, follow the woodland path north to the memorial table (dedicated to Edmund Loder 'who made and loved these gardens'). Standing in a wide clearing surrounded by towering Sussex beeches and larches, you can look right down through the valley. An exotic clump of gunnera stands to the right, rhododendrons ramble down wooded slopes and the lakes wind their way into the distance. Although they look totally natural, these were originally 'hammer ponds', constructed to provide power for the Sussex iron industry.

The path continues on downwards (very steeply—impossible for wheelchairs), bringing you to a stream, source of the lakes. Here is a pleasantly sheltered boggy area, scattered with bright yellow patches of kingcups and the bog arum, *Lysichiton americanus*.

Continue walking round the lakes, or as we did, return to the café for refreshment and then approach the gardens from a different angle. The shrubberies and lawns near the café and old house are well worth exploring, dotted with fine specimen conifers. Here too is the plant sales house, a temperate greenhouse.

The rock garden, like the lakes, looks deceptively natural, but in fact it was entirely man-made, by Messrs Pulham in about 1900, largely using Pulhamite, their patent artificial stone. Originally constructed for cultivation of alpines, it is now mainly stocked with less labour intensive azaleas, conifers and small shrubs. There is a wishing well below the waterfall: proceeds go to the Gardeners Royal Benevolent Fund. You can get a good overall view of the rock garden by taking one of the side paths, past old specimens of dwarf spruces (forms of *Picea abies*). The rock garden is at its very best in early May.

Walk round behind the house for another fine prospect of lakes, parkland and forest. Dark conifers spike up through a sea of luminous green deciduous trees and the effect is completed by a big clump of red copper beeches to one side. On the lawn nearby is *Betula pendula* 'Youngii', a weeping birch, and another copper beech. A low-growing blue spruce *Picea pungens* 'Glauca Procumbens', has striking foliage and small pinkish cones.

Follow the steep path down through Wallaby Park—the wallabies are quiet, self-effacing creatures, very good at camouflage, but you may spot one. Here rhododendrons grow in towering banks, fronted by a wide border of deciduous azaleas. Close by the dam stands an extraordinarily ugly tree, *Picea abies* 'Virgata', the snake spruce, probably the biggest of its kind in the country. As Robin Loder points out, few other people would ever want to plant one!

A charming subsidiary valley, with its own stream, lies north of the lakes: this is known as the Mossy Ghyll. 'Ghyll' is a Victorian spelling of the Sussex word for valley (also 'gill'). The deciduous azaleas here are pruned right down to ground level approximately every 15 years. The larger rhododendrons appear to very good effect in the ghyll, glimpsed through the trees. They also produce superb colours in the autumn.

The garden suffered badly from the gales of October 1987, but the disaster has been turned to advantage. The total area open to the public has been extended by over 100 per cent. In Robin Loder's words 'Although we were saddened at the loss of so many fine old trees, their removal all in one night has given us wonderful new planting opportunities and the chance to extend and replan the valley for the next century. Do come and visit the garden and give us the encouragement to make this vision a reality.'

Nymans

ADDRESS AND TELEPHONE: Handcross, near Haywards Heath, West Sussex RH17 6EB. Tel. Handcross (0444) 400321/400002

OWNERS: The National Trust

DIRECTIONS: on B2114 at Handcross, 4½ miles S of Crawley, just off London to Brighton M23/A23. Public transport: Brighton and Hove/Greenline bus 773 Brighton to Gatwick BR (passing Crawley BR), alight Handcross ¼–¾ miles according to direction. Balcombe station 4½ miles, Crawley 5½ miles

OPENING TIMES: Good Fri 29 March to end October, daily except Mon and Fri (but open BH Mon and Good Fri) 11–7 or sunset if earlier. Last admission 1 hour before closing. House not open

ADMISSION: £2.80, parties £2.30. Parking space limited, so coaches must book

CAR PARKING: yes

TOILETS: yes

REFRESHMENTS: café

SHOP: yes

DOGS: in car park only

WHEELCHAIR ACCESS: yes, special wheelchair route indicated. Toilets for the disabled: yes

PEAK MONTHS: April/May

Nymans is a fine, diverse garden of some 30 acres, set on a rise in the Sussex Weald. Developed over 100 years by the level-headed but enterprising Messel family, it must be visited several times and in different seasons for full appreciation of its variety and subtlety.

The walled garden, converted from an old orchard, is the true heart of Nymans. Visible from the wood through a stone arch, a spectacular old-fashioned double summer border stretches from end to end. The beds were laid out by William Robinson, drawing on ideas of Gertrude Jekyll, and modulating from the heights of mauve and white acanthus, blue echinops and orange-red cannas, through roses, red dahlias, mixed statices, pink hydrangeas, oriental poppies and delicate green nicotiana, to the dwarf annuals—vivid purple heliotrope, yellow violas and two forms of blue ageratum. Just before the Italian fountain is a fine specimen of *Cornus kousa*, flowering white in July. Plentiful magnolias, hamamelis, corylopsis, camellias and rhododendrons grow behind, and some splendid trees. Climbing plants include *Hydrangea petiolaris*, clematis and roses.

The pinetum was the first part of Nymans to be developed by Ludwig Messel, when he bought the estate in 1890. Planted in horseshoe fashion round a paddock, cedars, cypresses, junipers, hemlock spruces and redwoods were planted to shield the garden from north and east winds. Colonel Leonard Messel inherited in 1916: he interplanted the trees with evergreens, including *Eucryphia* x *nymansensis*, hybridised here in the 1920s, azaleas and hydrangeas. Unfortunately this area was very badly hit by the storm of October 1987; Nymans lost 80 per cent of its trees at this time, including tall cedars and an enormous monkey puzzle tree on the main lawn and a laurel walk. However, replanting has been under way since April 1990.

Colonel Messel's Jacobean-style house, built according to Walter Tapper's design from soft grey stone, was devastated by fire in 1947. Several magnificent trees and climbers somehow managed to survive and now twine among the ruins—*Magnolia grandiflora* 'Goliath', a double yellow Banksian rose, wisterias and clematis. A bed of herbs is laid out below, fronted by topiary birds and a tortoise. The main lawn is surrounded by beds of hydrangeas and fuchsias.

The smaller lawns are largely hidden from the house. To the west lies a long grey stone pergola, supporting massive wisterias with twisted trunks almost as thick as the pillars, and clematis. Massed plantings of creamy-white *Hydrangea arborescens* 'Grandiflora' give onto the croquet lawn.

Across the road, you can catch some intriguing glimpses of the reserve garden, forged from the wilderness by Colonel Messel to accommodate hundreds of specimens brought back from plant-hunting expeditions of the 1920s. Colonel Messel also set up a nursery here—but the trees are no longer 'babies'. They grew large during the war years and could not safely be moved.

A Japanese temple crowns the rock garden, which is planted with small, many-coloured specimens of conifer. Behind this, crossed by winding grass paths, is one of the first heather gardens to be developed in England, containing many rare heaths. Among rocks and boulders flourish pinks, geraniums, primulas and gentians. A tennis lawn lies beyond, bordered by a bed of comparatively new planting—a green-gold elaeagnus, blue ceanothus, agapanthus and perovskias and silver artemisia.

In the sunken garden, formal beds of snapdragons edged with agerati, complement a central Byzantine vase and an Italian stone loggia hung with Dundee rambler roses and *Clematis* x *jackmanii*.

The rose garden, north-west of the walled garden, was planted in the 1920s by Mrs Leonard Messel and developed by her daughter, Lady Rosse. Old-fashioned English, French and Italian shrub roses are arranged on arches and pillars around a wishing well and underplanted with deep blue nepeta. The rose garden was completely replanted in 1989 with a new layout of paths. A bronze fountain in the form of a single rose was added in 1990. Set in a wooded area nearby, we also saw a clump of Himalayan lilies, whose enormous seed pods in autumn are nearly as impressive as their white flowers in July.

It is almost a relief to turn from this intensive planting and walk down to the Prospect: to look out over fields to Balcolmbe Forest and the hills, and to feel again the estate's connection with the countryside from which it grew.

Parham Park

ADDRESS AND TELEPHONE: The Administrator, Parham Park, Pulborough, West Sussex. Tel. Storrington (0903) 742021

OWNER: Mrs P.A. Tritton

DIRECTIONS: main gate is on A283, Pulborough to Storrington road. Public transport: Pulborough BR 3 or 4 miles away. No buses

OPENING TIMES: open Sun, Wed, Thurs and all BH from Easter Sun to first Sun in October, 1–6 (last admission 5.30). House also open

ADMISSION: house and garden £3.20, OAPs £2.50, children £1.50; gardens only £1.60, children 75p. Coach parties welcomed on open afternoons, by prior appointment. Also guided tours for groups, by appointment, on Wed and Thurs mornings. Season tickets available

CAR PARKING: yes

TOILETS: yes

REFRESHMENTS: café

SHOP: yes

DOGS: yes, in gardens, on leads

WHEELCHAIR ACCESS: yes, in gardens. Ground floor of house accessible by arrangement. Toilets for the disabled: no

Parham Park is a very lovely Elizabethan house, once owned by the Palmer family and now the home of Mrs Veronica Tritton (but maintained and administered by a charitable trust). There are 11 acres of gardens, including a 4-acre walled garden and 7 acres of pleasure grounds with a lake. The setting is spacious, the atmosphere peaceful and relaxed: this is the ideal place to while away a sunny summer day. Good provision has been made for children,

Parham: the densely planted herb garden,
surrounded by yew hedges, inside the walled
garden

with a discreet play area by the lake and a Wendy House in the walled garden.

The estate lies on a plateau beneath the South Downs. A long, gently curving drive leads through the deer park from the east, bending around the foot of Windmill Hill. You may have to queue at the car park entrance and ticket office on busy Sundays.

You enter the garden through Fountain Court, on the east side of the house. It is always pleasant to be greeted by water—in this case, pouring into a raised circular stone pool filled with pink water lilies. On the south-facing wall are pairs of climbing roses, red 'Allen Chandler', dark red 'Etoile d'Hollande', yellow noisette 'Gloire de Dijon' and the single 'Mermaid', dating from 1911.

Steps lead from the courtyard to the main garden (there is also wheelchair access), where you can see fruit trees growing on a wall to your right, interspersed with lead statues. To your left, just before the walled garden, is a handsome catalpa, and a lime leaning languidly against a copper beech. Two specimens of *Actinidia chinensis*, the Chinese gooseberry, sport their hairy leaves on either side of the wrought iron gate, above two affronted-looking white stone lions with plentiful manes.

Peter Coats, the garden architect who redesigned and planted the main borders in 1982, has used many shrubs and herbaceous plants of good structure for easy maintenance and all-year-round colour. They are interesting even in January, but magnificent in summer. Mirror planting, very difficult to achieve, has been managed here: at least, the two borders reflect and complement each other. On either side you can see the gold-green pinnate leaves of *Robinia pseudoacacia* 'Frisia' and the purple foliage of *Cotinus coggyria* 'Foliis Purpureis' with its smoke-like plumes. Yellow *Potentilla fruticosa* and phlomis, the Jerusalem sage, contrast with pink-flowered and golden-leaved *Spiraea bumaldi*, the silvers of *Hebe pagei* and *Stachys lanata* and golden and purple berberis. The planting is repetitive, in mounds and clumps, but the foliage mixture is satisfyingly rich. Flowers are not in short supply either— pink geraniums, purple fuchsias and blue salvia and the white purple-splashed flowers of philadelphus 'Belle Etoile'. Alchemilla and rue spill over the path and creeping acaena 'Novae Zealandii' with its rust-red burrs. This is a stimulating prelude, but there is plenty to follow. The walled garden is largely planned around herbaceous and flower borders: though it also includes a greenhouse and a small herb garden.

Reaching the end of the main borders, marked by big mounds of tree peonies, you are faced by a very difficult choice: either turn right along the gold borders or left between beds of delicate purples, blues and pinks. Dazzlingly bright and splendid, the gold borders seem to radiate sunlight and warmth, even on the dullest day. Shrubs include the golden elder, *Sambucus nigra* 'Aurea'; *Weigela florida* 'Variegata' with its leaves edged creamy white; *Lonicera nitida* 'Baggeson's Gold' the shrub honeysuckle; and the golden privet, *Ligustrum ovalifolium* 'Aureum'. These are fronted by bright flowers, mainly yellow—helenium, lysimachia and potentilla, *Achillea filipendulina* with wide flat heads of bright yellow flowers and the pale sulphur-yellow *A. taygetea* 'Moonshine', with silver-grey pinnate leaves. Also many cheerful marigolds, apricot-tinted hemerocallis, blue *Vinca major* and the red tubular flowers of *Phygelius capensis*. Herbs carpet the ground and encroach on the path—golden sage, oregano and variegated mint.

The left-hand borders are far quieter and less immediately riveting, but have their own charm. Blue delphiniums, silver *Eryngium giganteum* and tall white spikes of galtonia and phlox provide focus and structure among clouds of soft blues and pinks—powdery blue ageratum, plentiful mauve-blue scabious, purple and pink sage, alstroemeria, polemonium and pink mallow.

Standing here at the centre of this astonishing garden, you can see borders leading off seemingly in all directions, along cross paths and beneath the great weather-beaten red brick walls. To relieve your eyes, take a walk around the small lawn areas, liberally scattered with daisies and clover, and bordered by well-established fruit trees. The lead pumps are an attractive feature with their accompanying semicircular brick wells.

A very long border runs beneath the right-hand wall—itself well covered with roses, clematis, climbing hydrangea, Mexican orange blossom (*Choisya ternata*) and the ubiquitous golden hop (very well used here, with purple clematis growing through it). The garden designer was obviously not afraid of repetition, but this gives pleasure in itself, and the plant combinations are stimulating and interesting. Looking to your right up this border, past an elegant lead pump, you can see a vivid grouping of yellow genista, gold *Robinia pseudoacacia* 'Frisia', bright blue delphiniums, white phlox, salmon hemerocallis 'Iuna' and deep blue salvia.

Blue and white *Aconitum napellus* 'Bicolor' is underplanted with silver *Anaphalis triplinervis* (pearl everlasting) and pink sedum. To your left is a clump of scarlet bergamot, waving its red coxcombs, purple phlox, white astilbe and bronze helenium, wedded together by clusters of lavender and anaphalis at the front of the border.

The walled garden also contains a densely planted herb garden, surrounded by yew hedges. Useful kitchen herbs grow here in profusion, along with three types of santolina (cotton lavender) and a trough of apricot violets. Take a walk also through the passage-like greenhouse, past pots of bedding and through trailing curtains of fuchsias.

For a complete change of scene, step outside the walled garden (retracing your steps along the gold and blue borders). Wide lawns slope down to a stone balustrade and the lake; in the distance you can see a cricket ground and the South Downs beyond.

The walks here are very pleasant, underneath vast trees—limes, beeches, yews and planes (now reduced in numbers, owing to the storms). A lead river god (similar to one at Ham House in Surrey) surveys the prospect, reclining at his ease by the wall. Further back towards the house is a children's play area, complete with swings, slides, a seesaw and hopscotch.

Finally, you may like to take tea in the old kitchen, off the main courtyard.

Standen

ADDRESS AND TELEPHONE: East Grinstead, West Sussex, RH19 4NE. Tel. East Grinstead (0342) 323029

OWNERS: The National Trust

DIRECTIONS: 2 miles S of East Grinstead, signposted from B2110 (Turners Hill road). Public transport: East Grinstead BR 2 miles. Occasional buses from East Grinstead to house, otherwise London & Country SW 434/474E Grinstead to Crawley, alight Saint Hill, ½ mile on 474, Saint Hill Turn, 1½ miles on 434

OPENING TIMES: 29 March to end October, Wed to Sun and BH Mon 12.30–5.30, house 1–5.30, last admission 5pm

ADMISSION: house and garden £3.20; garden only £1.60, children half price. Coach parties on weekdays by arrangement with the Administrator (reductions)

CAR PARKING: yes

TOILETS: yes

REFRESHMENTS: café

SHOP: yes

DOGS: no, in car park and woodland walks only

WHEELCHAIR ACCESS: yes, to parts of garden

PEAK MONTHS: May and June

NOTABLE FEATURES: hillside garden, fine views

This 12-acre garden around a remarkable late Victorian 'Arts and Crafts movement' country house was developed from 1890 onwards by Margaret and James Beale. It is set on a comfortable rise above woodland and fields, with views south-east across the Medway Valley to Ashdown Forest. The planting is interesting, but takes second place to the views and the birdsong.

A London landscape gardener, G.B. Simpson, was commissioned to design the garden from scratch and choose a suitable position for the house: but two years later the Beales changed their minds and consulted the architect Philip Webb. These two experts had quite different ideas on gardening. Simpson liked the prim and decorative 'gardenesque' style of John Claudius Louden; Webb, a lifelong friend of William Morris, liked simple, formal effects near the house, combined with stretches of grass and groupings of native trees. The two styles were never quite reconciled, but the result was a perfectly adequate family garden. Margaret Beale did the planting on a grand scale, introducing a great range of shrubs and trees and lots of colourful exotic plants and hybrids and establishing a series of garden enclosures or compartments. Today Standen retains a comfortable 'lived in' feel.

Standen House is the only Philip Webb house still virtually intact and a fine example of his work. A medieval timbered farmhouse was sensitively incorporated into the design: a member of the Arts and Crafts Movement, Webb was very reluctant to destroy old buildings. The entrance drive was made through an old sandstone quarry; another quarry by the house was converted into a heather and conifer rock garden.

When the National Trust took over in 1972, the gardens were very overgrown, with jungle-like shrubberies. A National Trust gardener now manages them almost single-handedly. No significant features have been added, apart from a box walk leading to Webb's summerhouse (above the south lawn) and a formal rose garden, planted in the old kitchen garden but all the ground cover is new and much new planting has been carried out.

A sheltered courtyard by the main entrance is attractively planted with quinces, roses and ivy, with buddleia spilling over from the top terrace. The narrow beds are crammed with bergenias—*B. crassifolia* and *B. cordifolia*—excellent for low-maintenance ground cover. Make your way out again past Hollybush farmhouse and a stretch of grass (Goose Green), sheltered by London planes, and continue clockwise around the house to mulberry lawn. The old mulberry (*Morus nigra*) was lost in the gales and has been replaced. Nearby is a yew, the only remaining tree dating from before the house (the ancient oak was lost in the gales). On the house walls near mulberry lawn are *Magnolia grandiflora*, evergreen clematis and the Banksian rose.

Originally Standen was a spring garden, though the National Trust has been working to increase its year-round interest. Above the south lawn slopes a small wildflower meadow, planted with fritillaries and other native species, and some cultivated flowers such as lupins.

The long arcaded conservatory is an impressive sight, running half the length of the terrace; inside grow palms, *Jasminum polyanthum* with white and pale pink flowers, blue plumbago, ferns and begonias. Fuchsias in big pots decorate the terrace. The spiky plants surrounded with lavender are yuccas (*Yucca gloriosa*): behind them lurk artichokes, introduced in a spirit of fun by the gardener. *Ceanothus impressus* 'Puget Blue' and the Chilean *Azara microphylla* (a small tree with delicate yellow vanilla-scented flowers) make a lovely show in spring, at the east end of the terrace.

The trellis above the south-facing border was designed by Webb—who incidentally also designed some of the house wallpaper. Mainly alba roses and 'Old Blush China' are trained along here, and sweet-smelling white *Clematis flammula*, also in the border you can see mauve and white Japanese anemones and large peonies in pastel shades. Buttresses of osmanthus have developed a striking variety of shapes, battered by wind and weather—the gardens are quite exposed, especially since the hurricane of 1990 removed the shelter belt of Austrian pines.

The quarry is perhaps the most striking part of the garden, certainly the most intensely planted. Stepping stones lead through from the terrace to a pool and fountain and the deep bowl of scooped-out sandstone, now planted with many kinds of fern—beech ferns, oak ferns and royal ferns (*Osmunda regalis*), which can grow up to 10ft in the wild. There are plentiful mollis azaleas, and magnolias fringing the bowl edge. *Hydrangea petiolaris*, the self-clinging climber, grows around. The miniature ravine is best viewed from the top walk above.

Children love this garden, with its winding steps, long paths and hidden corners. A box walk above the south lawn leads to Webb's summerhouse, where you can sit and gaze across the meadow, or down over the lawn.

Plentiful ground cover, including cotoneaster, variegated ground elder and geraniums, makes for easy maintenance and there are few bare spaces in the borders. Mr Ludman encourages wildflowers, especially foxgloves, and likes plants to grow through and among each other, in profusion. Beside the woodland steps to the top walk, some tall self-seeding yellow evening primroses spike up through geranium groundcover, with a white rambling rose above; further down in a border, clematis tangles with pernettya, cotoneaster and tufted vetch.

Japanese maples are a feature of the garden, providing glorious autumn colour. Look out for *A. japonicum* with its soft green foliage colouring brilliantly in autumn and *A. palmatum*, including *A. p.* 'Heptalobum Elegans Purpureum', with deeply divided dark bronze crimson leaves. You will also find many camellias, *Magnolia* x *soulangiana* and at least one pieris. Amelanchiers and cherries blossom in spring: Ghent azaleas from late May to mid June.

The woodland walks have been thoughtfully planned for views. To the south-east you can see Weirwood reservoir (this used to be the River Medway, but was dammed in 1955 to provide water for Crawley) and Ashdown forest. Crowborough beacon is visible from the top terrace. Directly below, across a field, you can see Hollybush wood, on the site of ancient woodland. There is a walk of about a mile around this area.

Several paths lead back to the main garden, so you can walk just so far as you wish; and benches appear at strategic points.

The garden is based on fertile greensand, over sandstone rock: a moderately acid soil. Unfortunately this does not suit lilies, the obvious flowers to put in an 'Arts and Crafts' garden, but it is ideal for rhododendrons. Banks of hardy hybrid rhododendrons stand below the south lawn, including some supplied by Messrs Waterer towards the end of the last century, and a rhododendron dell below the south garden features tender Loderi varieties.

In the circular bamboo garden you can see all kinds of bamboo, besides wild broom and yellow azaleas. Especially striking is *Nandina domestica*, called sacred bamboo, but in fact a shrub related to berberis.

The croquet lawn, formerly a tennis court, lies just adjacent: you can play croquet (mallets and balls provided). This area is subject to floods in winter, so the borders have been replanted with damp-loving plants, including irises. Clethra fills the air with fragrance in July and August. Small amelanchiers and *Prunus sargentiana* stand on the lawn. By the path leading towards the rose garden is the rare *Acer palmatum* 'Corallinum', with shrimp-pink young leaves turning green. White wisteria covers an old holly stump at the back of the garden: behind lies a solid bank of hardy rhododendrons, mainly in shades of red.

The orchard area below is planted up with 17C and 18C varieties of apples, pears and quinces—trees lovely for shape and blossom, but not so good for fruit. This area, now so neat and orderly, was a sea of brambles when the National Trust took over.

The rose garden was a kitchen garden in Victorian times: you can still see the stout espalier apple trees, 100 years old. This is a pleasant place to sit and rest, sheltered by yew and beech hedges. The simple square beds contain catmint, small junipers and rugosa hybrids. Pear trees have been planted for autumn colour.

Standen is one of the few National Trust gardens where fruit trees are still cultivated. On your way out, note the figs and gages along the huge north walls, and perry pears in the car park.

You could also take a walk through Hollybush wood. This is mainly oak, underplanted with hazel and sweet chestnut coppice, and filled with bluebells in spring. The large clay pits date probably from the 17C, when farmers spread marl or clay over their sandy soil, as a fertiliser.

Wakehurst Place

ADDRESS AND TELEPHONE: Ardingly, Haywards Heath, West Sussex RH17 6TN. Tel. Ardingly (0444) 892701

OWNERS: leased to the Ministry of Agriculture by the National Trust and administered and maintained by the Royal Botanic Gardens, Kew

DIRECTIONS: just N of Ardingly, above Haywards Heath, off the

B2028. (Junction 10 to East Grinstead from M23). Public transport: bus 473 from Haywards Heath BR. Infrequent service

OPENING TIMES: daily (except Christmas Day and New Year's Day) from 10am. Closing hour varies from 4pm in mid-winter to 7pm in summer. Visitors are allowed entry to within 30 minutes of closing time. Ground floor of house also open, with restaurant, bookshop and exhibition rooms

ADMISSION: £3, OAPs and students £1.50, children (up to 15) £1. Season tickets available

CAR PARKING: yes

TOILETS: yes

REFRESHMENTS: restaurant, Easter to mid October and at weekends throughout the winter. Other times light refreshments from bookshop

SHOP: yes, bookshop open all year

DOGS: no, except guide dogs

WHEELCHAIR ACCESS: yes, but uneven ground and not all areas practical for wheelchairs. Toilets for the disabled: yes

PEAK MONTHS: all year round

NOTABLE FEATURES: fine collection of exotic trees, shrubs and other plants; rock walk, water garden, heath garden, walled garden and winter garden, pond, lakes, Himalayan Glade; exceptional natural topography

Kew Gardens began to run Wakehurst in 1965, leasing it from the National Trust. In many respects it is like a second Kew, but set in much less polluted and more beautiful surroundings. The soil is more water retentive, the climate is damper and the air is considerably fresher. Magnificent though it is, the world-famous Kew Gardens is limited by its flat terrain. Wakehurst is comparatively secluded and sheltered and boasts an exciting natural landscape.

Before Kew took over, Wakehurst was already a garden of stature. Lord Wakehurst, Gerald Loder (brother of Edmund Loder, who created Leonardslee) spent over 30 years developing the gardens and estate, in the early part of this century. He planted specimen trees and shrubs from all over the world, including a magnificent collection from Australasia and Latin America, still flourishing in the heath garden. Sir Henry Price continued Gerald Loder's work after his death (in 1936) and bequeathed the gardens of Wakehurst in their entirety to the National Trust. The gardens are now a reservoir of superb trees and shrubs, including a number of species collections.

Apart from its established and growing reputation as a botanic garden, Wakehurst is an exciting place to explore, adventurously landscaped and planned, with narrow walks leading through steep wooded slopes and valleys and a number of very impressive natural features. Alternative, gentler paths are provided for people in wheelchairs or pushing prams.

A ravine walk begins about 700 yds from the entrance, leading west from the water garden (with giant Himalayan lilies, *Cardiocrinum giganteum*, and blue poppies, *Meconopsis betonicifolia*) and emerging onto a steep drop, Rock View, by the Himalayan

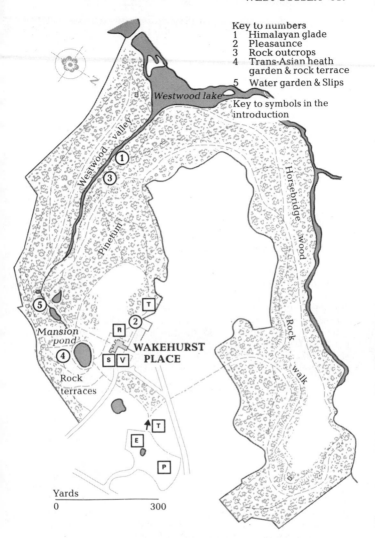

Key to numbers
1   Himalayan glade
2   Pleasaunce
3   Rock outcrops
4   Trans-Asian heath
     garden & rock terrace
5   Water garden & Slips

Key to symbols in the
introduction

Westwood lake

Westwood valley

Horsebridge wood

Pinetum

Rock walk

T

R
②
S V   **WAKEHURST
         PLACE**
④

*Mansion
pond*

Rock
terraces

T
E
P

Yards
0   300

Glade. Nearby is the pinetum, containing conifers from all parts of
the world (but badly affected in the storm of October 1987); further
downhill, Westwood Valley and a big artificial lake. Horsebridge
woods follow, and then the three-quarter mile Rock Walk, featuring
great sandstone outcrops enveloped by weird contorted tree roots.

The size of the gardens is considerable, with about 180 acres of
the total 462 acres open to the public, and it may be unwise to bring
very young children too far. They should enjoy the picturesque
Rock Walk, however, and the lushly planted pools in the water
garden at the foot of the Slips. The woods are lovely in spring,

carpeted with bluebells and full of gigantic trees—redwoods, native oak and some very tall conifers, including *Tsuga heterophylla*, 135ft high.

Believing that 'any plant worth seeing is worth walking to', Gerald Loder planted many interesting, exotic species at the very furthest reaches of the garden. But there is plenty to be seen and enjoyed within more reasonable walking distance, close by the Elizabethan mansion, café and car park. The south-east side of the mansion is extended by a hedge of mixed yew and variegated holly with a doorway cut through it. Thick-stemmed *Schizophragma integrifolia*, from central China, snakes up the nearby wall, beside *Parthenocissus henryana*, the Chinese Virginia creeper, its vigorous foliage, variegated silvery white and pinky bronze along the midrib, especially brilliant in autumn. Further along is *Ceanothus impressus*, with its deep blue flower clusters, overhung by graceful wisteria.

An impressive specimen of *Magnolia grandiflora* grows along the west wall, fronted by thick-leaved clumps of verbascum. Here too are several shrubby potentillas, *P. fruticosa*, including 'Tilford Cream' and 'Tangerine'. Potentillas recur throughout the upper gardens, waving in a yellow sea above the Slips and in shrub beds adjoining the heath garden. Gerald Loder often experimented by placing a number of plants of the same species in different soils, aspects and exposures, to see which proved most suitable, and this custom is still followed. Potentillas clearly enjoy the sun; they will flower in partial shade, but less freely. Wakehurst holds a key collection of hypericum and reference species collections of a number of deciduous trees—especially those of the genus Betula. A selection of monocotyledons (one main group of flowering plants: dicotyledons form the other) flourish to the west of the mansion, including some quite rare species. Behind this border lies the Sir Henry Price Memorial Garden and the Pleasaunce. Mellow sandstone and Horsham stone walls offset the soft colours and subtle foliage of planting in the memorial garden. Some of the best foliage plants are common garden herbs—here are purple sage, nepeta (catmint), hyssop, plenty of lavenders and various thymes, including 'Silver Posie'. All hard colours, such as scarlet, orange and yellow, have been purposefully excluded (although the very pretty creeping *Veronica cineraria* comes perilously near true blue). Instead, the emphasis is on grey and silver-leaved plants, interspersed with gentle pinks, purples and mauves—the hardy shrub *Weigela florida* 'Foliis Purpureis', with purple leaves and pink flowers, mauve-flowered *Geranium phaeum* 'Reflexum' with star-shaped leaves, *Syringa meyeri* 'Palibin', a miniature purple lilac.

Just inside the south gate grows lovely *Camassia leichtlinii* 'Eve Price', its purple-blue flowers clustered like thin stars on tall racemes: and nearby, dicentra 'Bacchanal' suspends its wine-red, bell-shaped flowers above light green, deeply dissected foliage. Several Australasian species have been incorporated into the planting, including leptospermums, but the overall effect is of a tranquil English cottage garden. Behind the two weeping pears, *Pyrus salicifolia* 'Pendula', stands a distinctive 17C lead cistern, decorated with fleurs-de-lis, suns and faces.

Geranium renardii grows by the west gate, its pale lavender flowers veined with purple. Here is the entrance to the Pleasaunce, a peaceful and secluded small garden with a raised terrace and lawn area, centring on a fountain of Pan. The tall yew hedges were planted at the turn of this century.

A short walk brings you from the Pleasaunce to the Mansion Pond, past open lawns and the 60ft-long low hedge of *Lavandula angustifolia* 'Hidcote'. South-east of the house, beyond the yew and holly hedge, is a very attractive grouping of trees: a sequoiadendron, and a recently planted collection of fastigiate trees including all three forms of the dawyk beech. Wakehurst has a wonderful collection of acers. Big soft mounds of *Acer dissectum* squat further down: and just around the water is *A. dissectum* 'Atropurpureum', the purple version. *A. shirasawanum* 'Aureum', quite different in shape and bearing, stands mid-way between them on the lawn: and across the water a magnificent specimen of gold-green *A. pseudoplatanum* 'Prinz Handjery' stands out amidst a variety of attractive trees and shrubs (including Chusan palms, *Trachycarpus fortuneii*, magnolias and rhododendrons). *Taxodium distichum*, the swamp cypress, dominates the small island.

An artificial sandstone outcrop stands left of the pond, home of many small prostrate and creeping plants. Conifers include *Tsuga canadensis* 'Pendula', the eastern hemlock, hunched up and many-fingered.

The rhododendron walk was flattened by the storm of October 1987 and has been replaced by the Trans-Asian Heath Garden which contains 'heath' rhododendrons, grouped to give an impression of their natural habitat with gaultherias, cotoneasters and junipers.

Continue round behind the pond to the Heath Garden, the heart and focus of Gerald Loder's Wakehurst. This opens through a series of interesting tree and shrub beds. Some particularly rare and fine specimens of Australasian and South American plants are identified in the guidebook: you should not miss the vivid red Chilean firebush, *Embothrium coccineum*. Wakehurst's own pieris (*Pieris formosa* var. forrestii 'Wakehurst') also stars here and in many other parts of the garden.

The variety of heathers is fascinating—*Erica vagans*, growing in hedgehog-like mounds, tiny *Erica tetralix* and the spreading variegated carpet of *Calluna vulgaris* 'Ruth Sparkes'. There are also many dwarf and sun-loving rhododendrons and a strong display of conifers and maples.

Across the long lawn there is a copse of rare and unusual trees such as bitternut hickory, *Carya cordiformis* black oak, *Quercus velutina* and hornbeam-leaved maple *Acer carpinifolium*.

Above the Slips, a steep, planted with magnolias and pieris and including natural vegetation, stands a stone sundial dedicated to the memory of Gerald Loder and his great head gardener, Alfred Coates. It bears the following quotation:

> 'Give fools their gold and knaves their power,
> Let fortunes bubbles rise and fall,
> Who sows a field or trains a flower
> Or plants a tree, is more than all'

Gerald Loder was lucky enough to have everything—gold, power, good fortune and a passion for plants. He was also fortunate in his successors and the present standard of Wakehurst is a tribute to the talents and dedication of them all.

West Dean Gardens

ADDRESS AND TELEPHONE: The Edward James Foundation, West Dean, Chichester, West Sussex. Tel. Singleton (024363) 301

OWNERS: The Edward James Foundation

DIRECTIONS: above Chichester, 5 miles S of Midhurst, just on the A286. Public transport: Chichester BR. Take bus 260 to Midhurst. It stops close to the garden gates

OPENING TIMES: 1 March to 31 October, daily 11–6 (last admission 5pm). House not open

ADMISSION: £2, OAPs £1.75, children £1. Parties by appointment at £1.50 per person

CAR PARKING: yes

TOILETS: yes

REFRESHMENTS: at certain times

SHOP: yes

DOGS: no

WHEELCHAIR ACCESS: yes, though many parts of the garden hard to cover by wheelchair. Toilets for the disabled: yes, one

PEAK MONTHS: May and July

NOTABLE FEATURES: cedars and other trees, pergola and gazebo

The students and staff of West Dean College of Arts and Crafts are privileged in their lovely surroundings: 35 acres of lawns and gardens, set in a gently sloping Sussex valley. When the college was set up in 1971, West Dean House and stableyards were sensitively adapted and their character preserved. It is good to feel the still living connection between house and gardens: although normally only the gardens are open to the public.

West Dean began to enter its full glory in the mid 19C, when many trees and shrubs new to this country were planted. However, gardens in some form or another had existed here since 1622, taking on new aspects according to whatever might be in fashion— whether the grand avenues of the Restoration, the 18C 'natural' landscape style or the Gothic 'picturesque'. The present result is surprisingly harmonious and well integrated, perhaps due to the vast size of the gardens, or the softening effects of time. Some of the trees have lived through centuries. Unfortunately the great gale of October 1987 resulted in the loss of many specimen trees and caused considerable destruction to the garden. However, the majority of the trees remain and large-scale replanting and restoration work has been carried out.

A majestic cedar of Lebanon (*Cedrus libani*) stands near the main drive, its dark foliage rising layer upon plate-like layer, high into the sky. Braced in places with steel cables, it looks otherwise remarkably intact—unlike its two ancient companions, which fell in the 1987 storms. No less impressive, though quite different in colour and shape, are the two blue cedars (*Cedrus atlantica glauca*). The three cedars round the car park were planted by 'visiting royalty', the Duke and Duchess of York in 1899 and King Alphonso XIII of Spain in 1907. The guide booklet marks these and other royal trees with stars.

Near the garden shop grow three liquidambars (*L. styraciflua*), more modest in proportion but very striking in autumn, when their maple-like leaves turn rich colours of red, purple and gold.

Walking north, roughly parallel to the entrance drive, you reach the rectangular sunken garden, built on two levels, its mossy stone banks planted with spring bulbs such as dwarf narcissi and grape hyacinths, among reliable rockery perennials such as aubrieta and many cistus, and in the spring, dwarf narcissi. Though basically in good order, the sunken garden has a wildish feel to it: the grass is thick with daisies and forget-me-nots grow freely in the rose beds. The pond is a most unusual crooked arrow shape (and deep), planted behind with *Alchemilla mollis* and more bulbs.

A vast pergola stretches its widely spaced stone columns right across the north lawns, from the sunken garden to a gazebo in the far west—in all, a magnificent 300ft. Commissioned in 1911 by William James (who bought West Dean in 1891), it cost £1,754 19s 3d to build. It was designed by the architect Harold Peto, in the Italianate style so popular at the time. Peto was an expert in all things Italian, a collector of Italian statues and ornaments, which he stored at Iford Manor in Wiltshire.

Many subtle and lovely foliage plants grow just under the pergola—silver artemisia, grey-green *Stachys lanata* and lamiums, catmint (nepeta) with its blue flowers, purple sage and verbascums. Roses, clematis, honeysuckle and euonymus grow up the pillars. Half-way along, the pergola expands into a paved rectangle around a small pond. There are two stone benches, supported by winged gryphons, and this is a pleasurable place to rest, in the dappled sunlight.

As you approach the gazebo, prepare for a grisly shock—the unusual floor decoration includes converging lines of horses' molars. The Rustic style was very popular from the mid 19C onwards—sheep's vertebrae and sections of antlers were used in similar period structures. You may perhaps be more interested by the modern engraved glass windows, or indeed (since gazebos are meant to be gazed from) by the views. There is a lovely long perspective down through the pergola: or looking westwards, you can glimpse the 11C church of St Andrews behind tall hedges.

The north lawns boast many fine trees, most notably the astonishing *Cryptomeria japonica* 'elegans', a cultivar of the Japanese cedar, with young green needles blending to bronze and purple: in shape, more like a snake or a sea monster than a tree. One specimen arches and bends to the ground; another, nearer to the pergola, launches itself forwards and upwards. These are certainly far more exciting and interesting than the Dragon's Grave, an overgrown mound above the sunken garden.

Two big spreading fern-leaved beeches (*Fagus sylvatica hetero-phylla*), grafted onto common beeches, stand either side of the pergola: and nearby is another vast cedar of Lebanon.

Proceeding down across the palm house lawn, passing two sizeable mixed borders and the orangery, follow the path round to the west lawn. A very tall (at least 30ft high) yew hedge growing between St Andrews Church and West Dean House is overhung by *Clematis montana rubens*, like a casually draped pale pink curtain.

The house, or college, walls are worth examining, for their intricate grey and white flint patterning. In fact, West Dean House is built entirely from flint: knapped or split flints arranged in small squares, filled in with little flint spikenels. The construction process must have been labour intensive, to say the least, and when William James was altering the house in 1891 he had trouble finding skilled 'galleters': but at least flint endures, and requires very little maintenance. Knapped flints can also be seen on the Gazebo floor and exterior walls.

The topiary mounds outside the west front look like big green bubbles blown together. There are more alongside the south front. *Vitis coignetiae* grows up the wall, displaying its pretty heart-shaped leaves, offset by the rounded grey-green foliage of *Eucalyptus gunnii*. Nearby on the west lawn is a tulip tree, so called because of its tulip-shaped, greenish yellow flowers, produced in June and followed in autumn by yellow leaves.

An avenue of rustling bamboos leads into the spring garden. A stream rises here, flowing down under low footbridges and over water falls to join the River Lavant. Some years, however, it does not appear: as the guide booklet points out, it is dependent on the water table in the chalk. Chusan palms (*Trachycarpus fortunei*) stand on the banks, well protected from wind and cold by the thick fibre covering their trunks: and just as well, as this garden has suffered many losses.

Approaching the summer borders, you may be puzzled by two grey truncated 'trees', apparently decapitated in their prime. Closer examination reveals a small plaque—'Ralph Burton sculp. fecit'—these are in fact real beech trees, but encapsulated in glass fibre and resin. It is an odd idea. The herbaceous borders hold more conventional attractions: two irregularly shaped beds either side of the path, filled with bright and delicate summer colour—potentilla, foxgloves, delphiniums, irises, aquilegias, poppies, daylilies and peonies. Gertrude Jekyll's original choice of plants has not been strictly adhered to. Commissioned in 1898, by Mrs James, to redesign the wild garden, she proposed a stylised layout, including a circular rose garden, with a path leading on to the herbaceous borders. Sadly, her plans were largely ignored; but given time, the Edward James Foundation hopes to replant in the Jekyll spirit.

The wild garden, too, has lost many mature trees, but retains considerable charm. This is an enjoyable place to walk, especially on a hot day, with its very successful deep planting, conifers and deciduous trees overhanging the water. People congregate by the bridges to chat and sketch, but you can walk alone through the woodland. South of the river, a sundial stands in deep grass; beyond are ploughed fields and the hills. On your way back towards the west lawn, take a short detour through the magnolia garden, where *Magnolia* x *soulangiana* and other species—some planted by 'visiting royalty' grow in oblong and moon-shaped beds, underplanted with big clumps of primroses. Here is another chusan palm and two big dark yews.

The lower west lawns are rich in oaks—red oak, scarlet oak, Hungarian oak. Two small 'pocket handkerchief trees' (*Davidia involucrata*) stand by a weeping variegated holly: and close by are a couple of unmistakable corkscrew hazels, their extraordinary squiggly branches writhing like heads of gorgon's hair.

More beautiful magnolias can be found below the front of the house—*M. grandiflora, M. denudata* and *M.* x *soulangiana*. A climbing hydrangea (*H. petiolaris*) grips fiercely to the top turrets. There is also a weeping silver lime (*T. petiolaris*). The view is sublime.

If you have time, visit the well-stocked sales centre in the walled garden, where you can buy your own small *Cryptomeria japonica* or *H. petiolaris*: and see an exhibition on the garden's history from 1622 in the fig house.

TYNE AND WEAR

Jesmond Dene

ADDRESS AND TELEPH0NE: Millfield House Visitor Centre, Jesmond Dene, Newcastle NE7 7BQ. Tel. (091) 2810973

OWNERS: City of Newcastle Council

DIRECTIONS: about 1¼ miles NE of centre of Newcastle. Entered at S end off A1058 at Jesmond. Public transport: Newcastle BR 1½ miles. Buses from city centre

OPENING TIMES: daily all year round, dawn to dusk (not closed at any time)

ADMISSION: free

CAR PARKING: some parking on edges of Dene. Coaches may park on E side of Armstrong Bridge

TOILETS: yes, in Millfield House

REFRESHMENTS: café in Millfield House where there is also a visitor centre

SHOP: yes

DOGS: yes

WHEELCHAIR ACCESS: yes, most paths tarmaced, some routes steep but avoidable. Toilets for the disabled: yes

PEAK SEASON: no special peaks. Busy during July and August

NOTABLE FEATURES: wooded valley park; fine trees and shrubs; buildings and ruins; Victorian style planting; ecological planting

Jesmond Dene acts as a 'green lung' to the City of Newcastle and an important corridor for wildlife. A deep wooded valley, it runs north to south for well over a mile, from Benton Bank to South Gosforth. Along its length flows the Ouseburn, a glacial stream which rises on Callerton Fell near Ponteland (8 miles away) and journeys to the Tyne. Before the mid 1800s the valley was wooded with native species, mostly oak, ash, and hazel, with a thick undergrowth of brambles and gorse.

The armament manufacturer William George Armstrong (later Lord Armstrong and associated with the development of Cragside, Northumbria) acquired the land now known as the Dene in the 1850s. Besides enclosing it, laying out paths and building bridges across the stream, he carried out extensive clearing programmes, replanting the land with a great variety of exotic trees and shrubs. The garden was opened to the public twice a week.

In 1883, Lord Armstrong presented the main part of the Dene to the Corporation of Newcastle for the benefit of the people of the city. The Prince and Princess of Wales formally opened the park in 1884 and in commemoration of the occasion planted the (now large) Turkey oak (*Quercus cerris*) by the banqueting hall on the west bank. The smaller tree here was planted in 1933 by Alderman H. Benson to mark the 50th anniversary of the Dene, and in 1936 the park was extended to the north.

A great number of fine trees can be seen at Jesmond Dene, although many are now over-mature (a balanced felling and re-planting programme is in process). Species include oak, sycamore, ash, lime, chestnut and cherry, growing along the banks of the Ouseburn and up the steep sides of the valley. You may also see Californian redwood (*Sequoia sempervirens*), blue cedar (*Cedrus atlantica glauca*), Austrian pines (*Pinus nigra*), cut-leaved beech (*Fagus sylvatica heterophylla*) and purple beech (*F. s. purpurea*).

Near the fisherman's lodge, now a restaurant, towards the centre of the Dene, are a tulip tree (*Liriodendron tulipifera*) and Japanese cedar (*Cryptomeria japonica*). Acers have been planted on the opposite bank of the river, to replace lost elms. The Picnic or Maypole Field, one of the few open spaces, is surrounded by broadleaves including mature Spanish chestnuts (*Castanea sativa*), oaks, Norway maples (*Acer platanoides*), London planes and silver birches. Trees and shrubs line the banks of the Ouseburn, here and there forming green tunnels over the swift-flowing clear water.

Himalayan balsam (*Impatiens grandulifera*) shows its purple and pink flowers from July onwards along parts of the water's edge; elsewhere there are ramsons (*Allium ursinum*), bamboos and drooping sedges (*Carex pendula*). Gunneras flourish in the damp soil of the Old Mill Leat.

Several of the walks feature typical Victorian planting— cherry laurels, hollies, yews and rhododendrons—all dark sombre colours. More rhododendrons can be seen in dense planting along sections of the valley sides and around Pet's Corner there are plantings of the early flowering rhododendron 'Praecox', with glistening rosy-purple wide funnel shaped flowers appearing in February and March.

Wood anemones (*Anemone nemorosa*) appear in spring in several parts of the Dene as do the lesser celandine (*Ranunculus ficaria*) and dog violet (*Viola riviniana*). Excellent shrub planting can be seen, for instance around the Old Mill, where cotoneasters, mahonias and yew grow with a dense carpet of the bright yellow summer flowering rose of Sharron (*Hypericum calycinum*). By the North Lodge the buttercup-flowering potentilla forms an unusual hedge and beyond the lodge, in winter, you can see the white stems of the ghost bramble (*Rubus cockburnianus*).

A quarry to the north, once worked for its sandstone, has been converted into a secluded garden, its steep ivy-clad sides sheltering viburnums, pieris and magnolia. A stand of bamboos in this garden is all that remains of an earlier Chinese Garden. Mosses and ferns flourish in rock outcrops. Buildings and other constructions are scattered through the valley. To the south is Armstrong Bridge, a lattice girder bridge spanning the Ouseburn Valley, a distance of 500ft, and carrying a 25ft wide carriageway some 50ft above the valley floor. The bridge was presented to the citizens of Newcastle by Lord Armstrong and officially opened on 30 April 1878.

Millfield House also stands close to the south end. Formerly a flour mill, some parts of this building are over 200 years old. It has been restored and converted for use as administration offices, interpretation centre and café.

A third mill, towards the centre of the Dene, dates from the 14C. This mill was originally used for grinding flour and later for grinding flints for use in the pottery industry. Now in ruins, it looks picturesque against the great waterfall created by Lord Armstrong. Not far away is a grotto, partially hidden by wild growth of bracken, sycamore saplings, ivy and brambles.

Of especial architectural interest is the preserved ruin of the banqueting hall, which stands on the West Bank beyond Millfield House. Built in 1865 to an Italian design by John Dobson, this was used for many years for grand functions and balls, and boasted one of the country's few water-driven organs. But dry rot set in, the roof collapsed and in 1964 the hall was closed. It is now used as an outdoor workshop by local sculptors.

The ruins of St Mary's Chapel can be seen in a small wooden grove west of the banqueting hall. Built in the first quarter of the 12C, these are the oldest ecclesiastical remains in Newcastle. The chapel can be reached by a tunnel under the road. It has associations with a holy well where various miracles are said to have been performed.

St Mary's Holy Well lies 200 yds west of the chapel, off Reid Park Road and bears the inscription GRATIA. This well was renovated in 1982 and archaeological investigations at that time revealed that it probably dates from the 17C or later.

Future development of Jesmond Dene will take account of its value as a wildlife refuge. The Friends of Jesmond Dene, established in 1976, works with the City Council to preserve the character of this beautiful area under increased pressure of use.

Seaton Delaval Hall

ADDRESS AND TELEPHONE: Seaton Delaval Hall, Whitley Bay, Tyne and Wear, NE26 4QR. Tel. (091) 237 1493 2373040

OWNER: Lord Hastings

DIRECTIONS: 1½ miles NE of Seaton Delaval, on A190 to Seaton Sluice. Public transport: Northumbrian bus routes 363 and 364 (half hourly)

OPENING TIMES: May to end of September, Wed, Sun and BH Mon 2–6. House also open

ADMISSION: Hall and garden £1, OAPs and children 50p. Coach parties by prior arrangement

CAR PARKING: yes

REFRESHMENTS: no

SHOP: guidebooks, etc

DOGS: no

WHEELCHAIR ACCESS: special access on request to avoid steps. Toilets for the disabled: no

PEAK SEASON: July and August

NOTABLE FEATURES: sunken garden with parterre; formal rose garden; herbaceous borders; 250-year-old weeping ash tree; splendid Hall built by Sir John Vanbrugh

Seaton Delaval Hall has been described as 'one of the glories of the North', 'Vanbrugh's masterpiece' and a 'great theatrical pile'. Certainly this imposing mansion is one of Sir John Vanbrugh's (1664–1726) finest achievements, a superb piece of architecture built between 1718 and 1728 for Admiral George Delaval.

Twice gutted by fire, left roofless for 50 years and requisitioned during both wars, the Hall came close to dereliction and was occupied by hundreds of pigeons, which roosted on the charred rafters. It was first opened to the public in 1950 after an initial phase of restoration involving re-roofing both east and west wings, replacement of woodwork and ceilings and redecoration of some rooms. The main central block with its turrets and towers was restored in two phases (1959 and 1962).

The Hall is approached from the north, the driveway passing between large lawns to arrive in the gravelled court in front of the north façade of the main block. The long, arcaded, east and west wings enclose the court on two sides, leaving open the view northwards to the industrial port of Blyth and the North Sea.

To reach the garden, visitors must ascend the steps, go through the great hall and gallery and leave by the opposite door, which brings you out onto the great portico of the south front overlooking rolled parkland beyond the garden lawn. To the south-west, visible between mature chestnut, oak and beech trees, is the early Norman church of Delaval, thought to have been built by Hubert de la Val in the first half of the 12C.

The most impressive part of the garden is the long rectangular sunken garden to the west of the Hall. It is enclosed with yew and beech hedges along the top of its banks and features a parterre designed by James Russell of Sunningdale in 1950. The sunken garden is best viewed from the stone balustraded platform close to the house; access is via twin flights of stone steps. This stonework is matched by a screen at the opposite end of the garden.

The parterre is mirrored across a central lawn; box hedging creates circular, square and segmented compartments. Each section is filled with block planting—some contain hypericum, silver-leaved plants, golden privet or fuchsias.

Elsewhere at Seaton Delaval are both formal and informal gardens, mostly made this century. The garden's oldest plant is a weeping ash tree (*Fraxinus excelsior* 'Pendula'), reputed to be at least 250 years old, on a lawn close to the south front of the Hall.

To the right of the ash is a formal rose garden, its beds edged with golden box.

Part of the west wing and an old brick wall border the rose garden and provide support for a range of climbing plants including roses, ceanothus and jasmines. These rise from a border of herbaceous plants, also edged with golden box.

A long curving border of shrubs and plants lies to the north, beneath the tall trees surrounding Delaval church. Here are irises, hostas, foxgloves, ornamental grasses, geraniums and pulmonarias backed by a thick planting of azaleas, shrub roses and hydrangeas.

More azaleas and a selection of rhododendrons are planted informally in a lawn further west, beside the churchyard. Adjoining this rhododendron lawn is a small garden with a formal water lily pool and another herbaceous border.

WARWICKSHIRE

Arbury Hall

ADDRESS AND TELEPHONE: Arbury Hall, Nuneaton, Warwickshire. Tel. (0203) 382804

OWNER: the Rt Hon. the Viscount Daventry

DIRECTIONS: 2 miles SW of Nuneaton. Off B4102. RAC signposted. No public transport

OPENING TIMES: Sun from Easter to end of September, 2–5. Also BH Mon. House also open

ADMISSION: house and garden £2.70, children £1.40; gardens and park only £1.40, children 70p. Coach parties by appointment for parties of 25 or more

CAR PARKING: yes

TOILETS: yes

REFRESHMENTS: café (upstairs)

SHOP: yes, for souvenirs

DOGS: no

WHEELCHAIR ACCESS: yes to much of garden, but house and café upstairs difficult. Toilets for the disabled: no

PEAK SEASON: July and August

NOTABLE FEATURES: newly established arboretum; rose garden and rose lawn; herbaceous and shrub borders; wild and woodland garden with spring flowers and rhododendrons; lakes

Situated close to the industrial edges of Nuneaton and Bedworth, Arbury Hall attracts many visitors each year and is one of the best examples of an early Gothic Revival house in the country. The novelist George Eliot (born Mary Ann Evans) was the daughter of the estate bailiff, and Arbury Hall features under the name Cheverel Manor in her *Scenes of Clerical Life*.

The house was built in the 1580s by Sir Edmund Anderson, Lord Chief Justice to Queen Elizabeth I, but in 1586 a property exchange was arranged with John Newdegate, in whose family it remains today. Sir Roger Newdegate, founder of the Newdegate Prize for Poetry at Oxford, commissioned Sanderson Miller and others to redesign the house in the Gothic style in the latter part of the 18C. Sir Roger was also responsible for the basic layout of the gardens that surround the Hall.

The gardens are well designed and very well maintained. There are excellent herbaceous and shrub borders, a fine rose garden, well placed lakes, mature woodland, lawns, a variety of trees and a newly established arboretum.

In the courtyard opposite the stable block is a large round pond, in which you can see the Cape pondweed or African water hawthorn (*Aponogeton distachyus*), which bears waxy white spiky flowers throughout the summer.

Behind the stable block is the old walled kitchen garden; previously run on a commercial basis, this is now planted as an arboretum. A small hop tree (*Ptelea trifoliata*) bears pleasantly aromatic leaves and clusters of small yellow/green flowers in mid summer, succeeded by winged pale green fruit. The dazzling white bark of *Betula jacquemontii* contrasts with red *Prunus tibetica*. The sweet gum (*Liquidambar styraciflua*) and the lovely snake bark maple *Acer grosseri hersii* are particularly attractive for their foliage at the end of summer. Notable among the conifers are *Cedrus atlantica glauca* and *Cedrus deodara*.

Outside the east wall of the walled garden is one of Arbury's superb mixed borders, containing a rich variety of species. There are shrub roses such as the fragrant pale apricot 'Buff Beauty' and the hybrid musk 'Felicia', which bears apricot pink flowers over a long period. A huge bush of the bright yellow rose 'Canary Bird' flowers in May at the far end of the border. On the wall behind are roses including the rambler 'Albertine', with very fragrant pale pink flowers, as well as vines and clematis.

Lavenders grow well in this border, along with a good selection of potentillas and berberis. *Hydrangea arborescens* 'Grandiflora' bears large creamy-white flowers from July to September. There are also hebes, fuchsias, hostas, geraniums and many other herbaceous plants.

The wild garden lies to the east, across a grassy ravine, shaded by mature woodland trees. It is best seen in spring, for the daffodils and primroses. Rhododendrons flower in May and June.

Within this wooded area lies another walled garden, planted as a formal rose garden in the Italian style—its entrance lies close to a magnificent fern-leaved beech (*Fagus sylvatica heterophylla*). A gravel path leading through the garden is flanked by with beds of hybrid tea roses such as 'Peace', 'Fragrant Cloud', 'Dutch Gold' and 'Whisky Mac' and floribundas 'City of Leeds', 'Glenfiddich' and

'Iceberg'. Around the central, circular and very ornate lily pool are 'Pink Parfait', 'Blessings' and the fragrant, rich red, 'Ernest H. Morse'. 'Pink Favourite' and 'Grandpa Dickson' then lead on towards the far end of the garden, where a pergola standing on a terrace marks the site of an earlier orangery.

In the woodland beyond the rose garden more rhododendrons grow beneath mature oaks and beech trees and a splendid tulip tree (*Liriodendron tulipifera*) produces its peculiar tulip-shaped flowers in June and July.

The southern boundary of the gardens is marked by two lakes. These once formed part of a canal system joining the estate to the Grand Union Canal, but the water levels changed in the 1930s, due to subsidence following coal mining, and the canal no longer functions. The higher of the two lakes, Hall Pool, is connected to the lower by a cascade and elaborate piece of rockwork dating from the late 18C. Close by are *Tilia platyphyllos* 'Laciniata', a lime with deeply and irregularly cut leaves, and the Glastonbury thorn (*Crataegus monogyna* 'Biflora'). The pocket handkerchief or ghost tree (*Davidia involucrata*) was planted about 20 years ago.

Overlooking the lily covered expanse of Hall Pool, to the west is a wall clothed in wisteria, a large fig and *Chimonanthus praecox*, which bears sweetly scented pale yellow waxy flowers on leafless branches in winter. The climbing rose 'Mme Gregoire Staechelin' arches over a recessed seat in the wall, covered in June with fragrant pink flowers. The Maidenhair trees (*Ginkgo biloba*) and swamp cypresses (*Taxodium distichum*) stand on the lawn above Hall Pool, and beyond lies the west garden, walled on three sides.

A yew hedge divides the west garden into two parts. The first is of simple design—a large lawn with two rows of whitebeams (*Sorbus aria* 'Lutescens'). Climbing roses such as the pale yellow 'Leverkusen' and 'Handel', the star of climbers, blossom against the old walls in summer.

Beyond the yew hedge is a rose lawn, planted in a formal design with beds of hybrid tea roses and domes of clipped golden yew. There are also some splendid magnolias, and below the walls, borders of shrubs such as daphne 'Somerset', pineapple-scented broom *Cytisus battandieri*, the bright blue summer flowering *Caryopteris* x *clandonensis* 'Heavenly Blue' and the smoke tree *Cotinus coggygria* 'Royal Purple'.

Farnborough Hall

ADDRESS AND TELEPHONE: Farnborough Hall, near Banbury, Oxfordshire/Warwickshire OX17 1DU. Tel. (0295) 89202

OWNERS: The National Trust

DIRECTIONS: 6 miles N of Banbury. Signposted off the A423, ½ mile. Public transport: Banbury BR 6 miles. Buses from Banbury

OPENING TIMES: house, grounds and terrace walk, April to end of September, Wed and Sat 2–6. Terrace walk only, Thurs and Fri 2–6. Also house and grounds May BH weekend 2–6. NOTE: the tenants, Mr and Mrs G. Holbech, are responsible for opening arrangements

ADMISSION: house, grounds and terrace £2.20; garden and terrace £1.30. Terrace walk only (Thurs and Fri) 80p. Coach parties by prior arrangement, no reductions

CAR PARKING: yes

TOILETS: yes

REFRESHMENTS: no

SHOP: no

DOGS: on lead, grounds only

WHEELCHAIR ACCESS: house and garden (terrace very steep)

PEAK SEASON: no peak but formal garden best in summer. Terrace best mid-April with daffodils

NOTABLE FEATURES: ¾ mile terrace walk with 18C temples and obelisk; lakes and woodland; formal garden; views

As you enter the gate and driveway of Farnborough Hall, you get a splendid view of the Hall's north front, framed by spreading trees. Farnborough was bought by Ambrose Holbech in 1683 and his family have lived there ever since. The house was altered and extended during the 18C and is currently occupied by Mr Geoffrey Holbech, who gave the property to the National Trust in 1960. The house is notable for its rococo plasterwork.

To the left of the drive are two lakes, created by Sanderson Miller, who lived at nearby Radway. Between 1730 and 1750, Miller helped William Holbech to landscape the grounds. The upper lake is known as the Island Pool. The lower, more formal and rectangular lake, is the Lady Pool and is set off by a splendid mature tulip tree (*Liriodendron tulipifera*), beautiful in autumn when the leaves turn rich butter yellow.

In front of the Hall is a walled forecourt, surrounding a gravel carriage-turning circle around a circular lawn. In mixed borders below the surrounding walls you can see lady's mantle (*Alchemilla mollis*), hypericum, fuchsias, peonies, potentillas, phlox, sedums, geraniums, snapdragons and other summer-flowering plants.   To the right of the house, an archway covered in *Hydrangea petiolaris* brings you onto the main lawn, which is dominated by a very fine cedar of Lebanon.

Beyond the ha-ha and pastureland lies Sourland Pool, a lake backed by mixed woodland. Sourland Pool was originally part of the garden; the road which now divides it was constructed in the mid 19C by Archdeacon Holbech. The lake is connected by a stream passing under the road to a second lake known as 'the river', best viewed from the terrace.

The terrace was planned by William Holbech (c 1740) as a broad grassy sward between shrubs and trees, linking the estate with nearby Mollington, where Holbech's brother lived. It rises upwards for 800 yds, following the curves of the hilly ridge. The terrace edge is scalloped with a series of promontories hedged about with laurel. The laurels are thought to have been planted c 1905. Trees and other shrubs were also planted along the edge, but many of these were removed in 1975 and the rest have been cut hard back in recent years, robbing the terrace of much of its shelter. However, the laurels are now being grown much higher, which will not only protect the daffodils from winds in spring, but will also help to obscure the new M40 being constructed through the valley.

The other side of the terrace is still backed by a woodland strip of beech, sweet and horse chestnuts, oaks, limes, sycamore, holly and yew, as well as snowberry-cherries and some rhododendrons.

An Ionic temple stands half-way along the terrace, on the right and almost hidden by a thick growth of hollies. A little higher up the walk, on the left and on the edge of woodland, is another temple, oval in shape, with an upper room beneath a domed roof. The upper room features exquisite plaster work and can be reached by an external staircase. An obelisk, dated 1751, marks the end of the terrace.

Returning through the woodland, you may see the Turk's cap lily (*Lilium martagon*), spurge laurel (*Daphne laureola*), butcher's broom (*Ruscus aculeatus*) and the giant bellflower (*Campanula latifolia*) with purple blue flowers in mid summer; besides plenty of naturalised winter aconites, daffodils, bluebells and wood anemones in spring.

A door in a wall at the lower end of the terrace gives access to the game larder—a small building set in its own tiny garden overlooking the Island and Lady pools. In spring this garden is filled with snowdrops and daffodils.

West of the house, across the main lawn, is a small formal garden on two levels. Until 1960 the upper level was partly occupied by an orangery, housing camellias, but the structure was damaged by successive gales and eventually it had to be demolished. It has been replaced by circular beds of small pink roses ('The Fairy') set in stone paving. The lower garden is reached by a flight of steps and has eight formal beds edged with low box and filled with roses—mostly floribunda but with old-fashioned roses in two outer beds. In the centre is a large urn. Smaller urns decorate the top of the low wall surrounding this garden, filled in summer with pale pink geraniums, blue lobelia and grey-leaved helichrysums.

Grannie's Walk continues down towards the Cascade, under an almost-arch of ancient yews. There are plans to extend this walk along the edge of the field.

Packwood House

ADDRESS AND TELEPHONE: Packwood House, Lapworth, Solihull, Warwickshire B94 6AT. Tel: Lapworth (0564) 782024

OWNERS: The National Trust

DIRECTIONS: 11 miles SE of Birmingham, 2 miles E of Hockley Heath. Off B4439 at Lapworth. Public transport: Lapworth BR 1½ miles, not Sun. Midland Red buses Birmingham to Stratford-upon-Avon, alight Hockley Heath then 1¾ mile walk

OPENING TIMES: 30 March to end September, Wed to Sun, 2–6. October, Wed to Sun, 12.30–4. House also open

ADMISSION: house and garden £2.50, family tickets £6.90; garden only £1.70. Pre-booked parties of 15 reduced rates

CAR PARKING: yes

TOILETS: yes

REFRESHMENTS: no

SHOP: yes

DOGS: no

WHEELCHAIR ACCESS: to part of garden and ground floor of house. Toilets for the disabled: yes

PEAK MONTHS: no special peak

NOTABLE FEATURES: unusual yew garden; Carolean garden with flower borders

Packwood is well known for its unusual yew garden, a feature which by its size and solemn grandeur tends to dominate the 5 acres of garden surrounding the house. But there is much else to be explored.

The house, a timber-framed building set in the fields and woodland of the Forest of Arden, was built during Elizabethan times for the Fetherston family, who lived here for 300 years. John Fetherston enlarged the building in the 17C, and was also involved in laying out some of the garden you see today. In 1869, the property was bought by George Oakes Arton and following his death it was auctioned in 1905 and came into the ownership of Mr Alfred Ash. His son, Graham Baron Ash, donated the property to the National Trust in 1941.

There are two main areas of garden. The first, reached through a gated archway south of the entrance courtyard, is the south or Carolean Garden. The other is the Yew Garden, whose towering masses of clipped yews can be seen beyond the raised terrace.

Old brick walls enclose the Carolean Garden on three sides, the fourth being bounded by the raised walk, and in each corner is an elegant brick-built gazebo. These little buildings are all quite similar in appearance, but were in fact constructed at different times. The oldest is situated in the north-east corner and dates from about 1680. It incorporates a small furnace and flues, one used to heat the adjacent south-facing wall, against which tender fruit was grown.

The gazebo in the south-west corner, diagonally opposite, is thought to originate from the early 18C, while that in the north-west has been rebuilt in a style shown in a mid-18C drawing of the garden. The gazebo in the south-east corner was built quite recently, but is on the site of an earlier construction.

The walls of the Carolean garden provide a home for a range of climbing shrubs and below the south-facing wall is a herbaceous border combining perennials with a mixture of seasonal plants, massed for colour. The border below the west-facing wall is divided into compartments by thick buttresses of yew, and planted with roses.

The large expanse of lawn was once bright with flowerbeds, but these had to be removed during the 1939–45 war, owing to lack of staff. There is, however, a sunken garden set into the eastern part

The Yew Garden at Packwood House

of the lawn. Created by Baron Ash, this little self-contained garden is girded by a yew hedge and consists of a small rectangular pool surrounded by steep banks of flowers.

The raised terrace walk separating the Carolean from the yew garden can be reached by walking through the gazebos nearest to it, or from the lawn via an elliptical flight of brick steps. A stone path runs along the top of the terrace, flanked by plantings of dianthus, peonies, geraniums and a host of other flowering plants, providing a colourful contrast to the dark green yews beyond. An elaborate 18C wrought iron gateway gives access from the raised walk into the yew garden.

Before venturing off among the tall clipped yews, look back at the retaining wall of the raised walk. Along its length are 30 arch-shaped recesses, set in pairs. These are called bee boles and once housed a colony of bee skeps. A few mock hives have been set up, to give an impression of the original arrangement.

It has been said that the yew garden portrays the Sermon on the Mount, with Christ represented by a yew crowning the summit of a grassy mount. A further 12 yews planted in two straight lines are said to symbolise the apostles, the four largest being known as the evangelists, while the 'multitude' stands all around.

Unfortunately this tradition is cast into some doubt by the fact that the yews are not of the same age, the planting having been done in two quite separate phases. It was probably John Fetherston who, between 1650 and 1760, planted the Christ and apostles yews. Whether he intended the symbolism is not known. The Multitude was not assembled until the 19C, when they were planted as small specimens to surround a newly planted orchard —an older orchard having first been removed. Mr Baron Ash took out the remaining fruit trees to leave the yew garden as you now see it.

A spiral path, edged with box hedging, ascends the mount to the single yew specimen, 'the master', sometimes called the Pinnacle of the Temple. From here there are good views of the house across the 'multitude'.

It is worth noting that the yews are growing in a heavy clay soil—not the perfect choice for them—and while the Trust has drained and aerated the soil around them, a number of strong young specimens are kept in readiness in case any should fail.

Having explored the gardens to the south visit the area to the west of the house, via a gateway in the north-west corner of the Carolean Garden. In the 18C, this side of the house was the main entrance, the driveway being along the causeway of the lake.

The west front of the house looks out onto a gravelled court, surrounded by yew hedges and featuring a sundial decorated with the arms of the Fetherston family. In another yew enclosure, a little to the north, is a cold plunge bath dating from 1680. This west face of the house is also graced by two beautiful specimens of *Magnolia denudata* (*conspicua*), the Yulan or lily tree, which bear fragrant white cup-shaped flowers in early spring.

Ragley Hall

ADDRESS AND TELEPHONE: Ragley Hall, Alcester, Warwickshire B49 5NJ. Tel. (0789) 762090/762455

OWNERS: Marquess and Marchioness of Hertford

DIRECTIONS: 2 miles SW of Alcester (8 miles from Stratford-upon-Avon) on the A435 Alcester/Birmingham to Evesham road. No public transport

OPENING TIMES: Easter to October, daily except Mon and Fri, but open BH Mon, 12–5. Park and gardens open 10–6

ADMISSION: house, gardens and park £4, OAPs, children and groups of 20 £3; garden and park only £3, children £2

CAR PARKING: yes

TOILETS: yes

REFRESHMENTS: café

SHOP: yes

DOGS: on lead in park only

WHEELCHAIR ACCESS: limited

PEAK SEASON: June to August

NOTABLE FEATURES: rose garden with some unusual varieties; circular herbaceous garden; parkland

Ragley Hall, the Warwickshire home of the Marquess and Marchioness of Hertford, was designed by Robert Hook in 1680 but was not fully furnished and decorated until the middle of the 18C. The present owner, Hugh, 8th Marquess of Hertford, inherited the estate at the age of nine in 1940; but it needed restoration, which, together with his wife, he began in 1956. The Hall and gardens were first opened to the public in 1958.

The gardens lie largely to the west and south of the Hall, the west terrace overlooking a delightful rose garden, with open parkland beyond and an avenue cut through woodland on a distant hill.

In contrast to the bare, architectural east front, the west front of the Hall is softened by climbing plants such as the deep-purple flowering clematis 'The President', the very fragrant climbing roses 'Ena Harkness' (crimson) and 'Compassion' (pink), and the climbing hydrangea (*Hydrangea petiolaris*).

Below the retaining wall of the terrace is a border planted with many types of rose. Here are hybrid perpetuals such as 'Reine de Violette', albas including 'Semi-Plena', cabbage and moss roses such as the old *R.* x *centifolia* 'Tour de Malakoff' (1856), a mix of lilac-purple shades, and hybrid musks including the fragrant pale apricot coloured 'Buff Beauty'. A few modern shrub roses are also included.

A broad gravel walk leads from the centre of the terrace down flights of steps and across the rose lawn to the rose garden, which is a formal circular design of beds set into turf, around a large urn. The hybrid tea rose 'Heart of England' blooms at the base of the plinth on which the urn stands. Set in the surrounding lawns are radiating beds, each of a single variety. Many well known hybrid tea roses are incorporated in the display, including the beautifully formed coral pink 'Blessings', rich red fragrant 'Ernest H. Morse', 'Lady Sylvia', and the very fragrant 'Mister Lincoln', 'Silver Jubilee' and 'Troika'.

Below another terrace on the south side of the Hall is a colourful mixed border of shrubs and herbaceous plants overlooking a sloping lawn. Again a central view to the parkland is left open, and informal planting of trees and shrubs kept to the edges of the lawn, to frame the view.

Ragley's unusual herbaceous garden is situated beyond woodland south-east of the Hall, in a glade surrounded by magnolias and other spring flowering trees. The garden is circular and enclosed by a tall hedge of Leyland's cypress. It contains a rich mixture of anemones, asters, campanulas, lupins, erigerons and others in four radiating beds around a central bed of lavender. A bed of azaleas has recently been established outside the herbaceous garden, to give colour and interest in spring and early summer.

The 400 acres of parkland offer many good walks, including farmland and woodland trails. For children there is a woodland maze play area and picnic site by the side of a large lake.

Upton House

ADDRESS AND TELEPHONE: Upton House, Banbury, Oxfordshire, OX15 6HT. Tel. (029 587) 266

OWNERS: The National Trust

DIRECTIONS: 7 miles NW of Banbury, 12 miles SE of

Stratford-upon-Avon. On A422 Banbury to Stratford road. Public transport: Banbury BR 7 miles

OPENING TIMES: 30 March to end April and October, Sat, Sun and BH Mon 2–6; May to end September, Sat to Wed including BH Mon 2–6. House also open

ADMISSION: house and garden £3.10; garden only £1.80. Coach parties by prior written arrangement

CAR PARKING: yes

TOILETS: yes

REFRESHMENTS: yes

SHOP: yes

DOGS: no

WHEELCHAIR ACCESS: golf buggy available to assist access to lower part of garden. Ground floor rooms of house. Toilets for the disabled: yes

PEAK SEASON: June to October (October for aster collection)

NOTABLE FEATURES: terraced walled garden; valley bog garden; fine trees; vegetable garden

Upton House is well known for its outstanding collection of works of art, particularly paintings and porcelain, acquired by Lord Bearsted. The 19 acres of garden make full use of the natural lie of the land and contain some surprises.

The garden keeps its secrets well—at first sight there are no hints of hidden glories or concealed valleys. The straight driveway passes through a dark avenue of Scots pines, leading up to the north front of the long house, which was built of local golden-brown Hornton sandstone in the 1690s for Sir Rushton Cullen.

The south front is graced by two terraces, built in 1927, when the house was extended—shortly after the 2nd Viscount Bearsted purchased the property in 1927. The designer was Percy Morley Horder.

Constructed of the same Hornton stone as the house, the terraces are set off by borders of shrub roses and catmint. Climbing roses, wisteria and clematis partially cover the house walls. Flanking the central flights of steps in summer are the very fragrant pale pink blooms of rambler rose 'Albertine'. At the west end of the terrace are two small formal paved gardens.

Standing on the centre of the terraces, you could be forgiven for thinking this a typical English park-style garden. The broad level lawn stretches away towards the hills and the whole view is framed by large cedars of Lebanon (*Cedrus libani*) on the right and a planting of native trees, with a rock garden below, on the left. Now walk southwards across the lawn. It comes to a very abrupt end, and you find yourself above a valley. A long rectangular stretch of water lying in the bottom of the valley is first to appear; then gradually, the terraced banks of the south-facing slope.

This warm sunny site was originally laid out as a walled kitchen garden, providing fruit, vegetables and cut flowers for the house. A rich and varied mixture of plants now grows on the descending terraces, despite the shallow and stony soil.

You can enter the valley from the east corner of the lawn, via a path and steps which curve round and down to the first terrace level. On the opposite side of the lawn, beneath the magnificent cedars, is a grand stairway, with landings, and balustrading, constructed from local stone in the 1930s.

The first terrace, a broad grassy walk, runs along the foot of the high retaining wall which supports the lawn above and which is thought to date from Rushton Cullen's time. Various climbing plants and shrubs grow against the wall, including summer flowering ceanothus 'Topaz' which has attractive light indigo blue flowers, and the deeper, violet blue ceanothus 'Henri Desfosse'. The lower side of the walk is edged with lavender and grey-leaved plants.

The second level is dominated by a steep dry bank of shrubs and plants selected for flower and autumn colour. Here are mahonias, berberis, brooms, laburnums and acers, with irises, narcissi and small tulips.

On the next terrace, a long border houses the National Collection of asters—notably *A. amellus, A. cordifolius* and *A. ericoides* cultivars and hybrids—a splendid sight in autumn. In spring and summer this terrace is brightened by lilacs, brooms, buddleias, potentillas, hypericums and shrubs growing in a dry bank on the opposite side of the grass walk.

For 300 years the south-facing slope was used for the cultivation of early crops of fruit and vegetables, so it is not inappropriate that much of the remainder of this garden is planted with neat rows of vegetables and soft fruit between old apple trees.

East of the kitchen garden, a yew hedge separates the vegetables from a double herbaceous border. On the opposite side (west), are three small formal gardens within yew hedges. This area at the foot of the stairway, was occupied earlier in the century by greenhouses and frames.

The first of the small formal gardens is the Hibiscus Garden, comprising borders of standard hibiscus 'Bluebird' underplanted with steel blue *Eryngium bourgattii* and small bulbs. The next, Her Ladyship's Garden, is planted with a variety of soft pastel flowers and the third with roses around a small statue of Pan.

Another valley runs below the western edge of the lawn and once contained three stew ponds. One of these remains but has been made more informal with the planting of marginals. The southernmost pond has been drained and planted with flowering cherries while the third has been made into a bog garden with water courses fed by the Monk's Well. There are plenty of bamboos, primulas and moisture-loving plants, and the surrounding lawns are planted with flowering trees and shrubs.

A lake lies some distance to the east and can be reached by the public footpath off the main Banbury Road. The small 18C classical temple is thought to be the work of Sanderson Miller from nearby Radway.

WILTSHIRE

Bowood House

ADDRESS AND TELEPHONE: Bowood Estate Office, The Bowood Estate, Calne, Wiltshire SN11 0LZ. Tel. Calne (0249) 812102

OWNER: Earl of Shelburne

DIRECTIONS: off the A342 Chippenham to Devizes road mid-way between Derry Hill and Sandy Lane Villages

OPENING TIMES: mid March to early November, daily 11–6. House also open

ADMISSION: £4, OAPs £3.30, children £1.90. Reductions for parties of 20 or more. Full details, booking forms and party catering menus on application to the House Administrator

CAR PARKING: yes

TOILETS: yes

REFRESHMENTS: café

SHOP: yes

DOGS: in car park only

WHEELCHAIR ACCESS: yes. Toilets for the disabled: yes

NOTABLE FEATURES: landscaped park, collection of trees and shrubs

Bowood is the home of the Earl and Countess of Shelburne and has been owned by the same family since 1754. 'We arrived at Bowood and were delighted to find it in so much verdure and beauty', wrote Lady Shelburne, wife of the 2nd Earl, in her diary, 1 June 1769. Her sentiments were echoed in the next century (December 1841) by one of Bowood's many guests, the six-year-old daughter of Fanny Kemble the actress. On seeing the park, the little girl exclaimed 'Well, this is my idea of heaven! I do think this might be called Paradise, or that garden Adam and Eve were put into...'

The 100 acres of park and pleasure grounds have been open to the public since 1975 (and a separate woodland garden with rhododendrons is open from mid May to mid June). The 2000-acre park was landscaped by Lancelot 'Capability' Brown between 1762 and 1768 and now includes a lake with Doric temple, a cascade, caves and grottoes, besides an outstanding plant collection—more than 400 trees and 300 shrubs and climbers.

Families are well catered for at Bowood—the adventure playground, near the car park entrance, features a life-size pirate galleon complete with crow's nest and rigging, along with treetop cabins, rope bridges and trampolines. The playground is supervised at weekends and during the school holidays, so you can leave the children here while exploring the grounds.

Follow the winding path from the car park entrance (Temple Gate) past the tea rooms and adventure playground, passing on your left a group of pink-flowered *Indigofera pseudotinctoria* and elaeagnus. The path descends through a collection of lilacs and you cross an access road to reach the house. Before venturing onto the west end of the upper terrace, note the handsome sycamore (*Acer pseudoplatanus* 'Prinz Handjery') above the small concealed lawn area to your right. The lawn is pleasantly shady and secluded, planted with prunus and a good place to rest in hot weather.

The stately terraces provide an excellent setting for the Georgian house with its pale stone and high arched glass windows. Stout clipped yews on the terraces lean at gracious angles over the rosebeds. The house is fronted to the south by an orangery and sculpture gallery. *Fremontodendron californicum* climbs up past the first storey, clad with yellow cup-shaped flowers from late spring through summer. Other climbers include the pale pink rambler rose 'Albertine', jasmine, *Rosa banksiae* 'Lutea', *Rosa moyesii*, *Pyracantha atalantioides*, a splendid *Magnolia grandiflora*, *Rosa longicuspis* and *Wisteria sinensis*.

The terrace statues include two delightful pairs of stone lions and deer with branching antlers. The top wall of the lower terrace is covered with climbing roses such as deep pink 'Etoile de Hollande', pink 'Shot Silk' and 'Crimson Glory' and clematis including 'Daniel Deronda' and 'Madame le Coultre'. Long stone seats are set into the balustrade below and from here you can gaze over a picturesque landscape, with sheep grazing and the distant lake.

Two yew arches give access to the east terrace, with its open views over Lake Field to Bowood Lake and the Doric temple. A few yards from the east terrace steps is a sweet chestnut tree planted by Louisa, Marchioness of Lansdowne, in 1825. Varied tree planting around the lake includes tall Lombardy poplars (*Populus nigra* 'Italica'), an enormous lime tree (*Tilia europaea*) and its close neighbour, a plane (*Platanus* x *acerifolia*), a cedar of Lebanon, taxodiums, oaks, ash, thorns, a tulip tree (*Liriodendron tulipifera*), a Californian redwood (*Sequoia sempervirens*) and Wellingtonias (*Sequoiadendron giganteum*).

On lake field, which slopes gently downward from the house to the lake, are beech (*Fagus sylvatica*), oak (*Quercus robur*) and a variegated Turkey oak (*Quercus cerris* 'Variegata'), horse chestnut (*Aesculus hippocastanum*), walnut (*Juglans regia* and *Juglans ailantifolia*) and others.

Following the line of the lake northwards, you arrive at the cascade and cave area, set in a darkened valley. The splendid cascade was constructed in the mid 1780s by Josiah Lane of Tisbury, to a design by the Hon. Charles Hamilton, the creator of Painshill in Surrey. The lake path continues past the Hermit's Cave—lined with fossils and mineralogical specimens collected by the Reverend Joseph Townsend of Pewsey—and ends at the Doric temple. The cascade, the caves and the Doric temple were added after Brown's time—the caves are known oddly as Crooked Mustard.

Retracing your steps and striking west across the path, you reach Archery Lawn and then the pinetum, with the House Hollow below. The pinetum, once a tree nursery, was first planted up in the late 1820s by the 3rd Lord Lansdowne—a few cedars survive from this time. From 1848 to 1849, trees were planted in a geographical pattern according to their countries of origin, but this plan has now been abandoned.

For a complete list of trees, the reader is referred to *A guide to*

Bowood Trees and Shrubs by Allen J. Coombes. The range of species and varieties is vast and includes *Catalpa bignonioides* 'Aurea', *Fagus sylvatica* 'Riversii', maples such as *Acer saccharinum, A. palmatum, A. griseum* and *A. pseudoplatanus* 'Brilliantissimum', cedars, liriodendrons, sorbus, *Parrotia persica* and a great many others. The tallest tree in the collection is a giant fir (*Abies grandis*), 137ft high, but this is challenged in eminence by the limes (*Tilia* x *europaea*) and by a fine group of redwoods (*Sequoia sempervirens*). To the west is a lovely grouping of silver birch trees, underplanted with laurel; and in an isolated position near the car park, a lime pergola, established by the 6th Lord Lansdowne in 1936.

Rhododendrons are planted here and there under the trees, but rhododendron enthusiasts should make every effort to visit the separate woodland garden, with rhododendron walks and mausoleum—approached through Kennels Lodge on the A342 between Sandy Lane and Derry Hill.

Heale House

ADDRESS AND TELEPHONE: Middle Woodford, near Salisbury, Wiltshire, SP4 6NT. Tel. Middle Woodford (0722 73) 207 and 504

OWNER: G.M.C. Rasch, Esq

DIRECTIONS: 4 miles from Salisbury, Wilton and Stonehenge, on the Woodford Valley Road between the A360 and A345. Public transport: Wiltshire and Dorset bus 1 from Salisbury

OPENING TIMES: daily throughout the year, 10–5. House open by arrangement, for groups of 20 or more

ADMISSION: £2, children under 14 free

CAR PARKING: yes

TOILETS: yes

REFRESHMENTS: no

SHOP: gift shop and plant centre

DOGS: yes, on lead

WHEELCHAIR ACCESS: yes. Toilets for the disabled: no

PEAK MONTHS: April to September

NOTABLE FEATURES: varied plant and shrub collection; roses; river walk; Japanese tea house and watergarden

This 8-acre garden could hardly fail to give pleasure, having so many natural advantages. Lying by the River Avon at Middle Woodford, just north of Salisbury, it is surrounded by wide water meadows, fields and woods and the softly sloping hills of the West Country. The house, of mellow red brick, dates from the 16C.

The garden is a relaxing, continually interesting blend of informal and formal features—a walled garden, terraces and borders, framed by lawns and wilder areas. Harold Peto, the classical landscape architect, had a hand in contriving the views—and many of the balustrades are his, including the long balustrade on the east side—but with the passing of time and reductions in staff, his scheme proved impossible to maintain faithfully. The planting is now geared for low maintenance, with plenty of shrubs and perennials and variegated and coloured foliage providing year-round interest. Shrub roses appear everywhere, along with huge bushes of variegated weigela and golden philadelphus, red-leaved cotinus and purple-leaved plums (*Prunus cerasifera* 'Pissardii'). Many varieties of clematis, peonies and honeysuckle blossom through spring and summer.

Having entered through the plant sales and nursery area, you come out immediately above the river and part of the wild or Japanese garden, with water meadows beyond. Huge tangled bush roses overhang the water. You can cross here by a wooden plank bridge, to explore the far side; or take the path to your left for the tunnel garden.

Originally planted as a formal rose garden, the tunnel or walled garden underwent a complete change during the war, when the house was requisitioned as a convalescent home and all the beds were replanted with vegetables. Flowers, fruiting trees and vines, vegetables and herbs now co-exist in relaxed abundance. The garden's simple but very attractive design is aided by strong structural features—three long apple tree tunnels converging to a central lily pond, and a huge wooden pergola running along the south side. On the pergola, a crimson glory vine (*Vitis coignetiae*), crimson and scarlet in autumn, mingles with a deep purple grape vine (*Vitis vinifera* 'Purpurea'). Roses and clematis grow here too—including roses 'Easlea's Golden Rambler' and 'Maigold', white clematis 'Wada's Primrose' and deep purple 'The President'.

The walled garden is walled only on three sides: left open to the south, it commands an excellent view over the lawn to the wild or Japanese garden and the river.

The square lily pond is surrounded by huge rounded bushes of box, dating from the turn of the century, and still in very good health. These are enclosed within a narrow circular strip of lawn, planted round with herbs and flowers. Ornamental beds border the grassy paths and line the apple tree tunnels with soft colours of mauve, blue, pink and silver. Visiting in early June, we saw plenty of silver-leaved plants such as artemisia and *Stachys lanata*, mauve-blue violas, mauve irises and tall mauve, pink and white foxgloves.

This delicate planting is complemented by bold and striking effects in the wall borders—pink and yellow standard honeysuckles, huge bushes of golden *Philadelphus coronarius* 'Aureus' and Mexican orange blossom (*Choisya ternata*), an enormous variegated weigela, tall creamy-yellow spikes of *Sisyrinchium striatum*, standing out against a purple-leaved hebe. Woolly-leaved mulleins shoot up like fireworks from early to mid summer. Here too are honesty (*Lunaria annua*), with purple flowers and variegated seed heads, tall variegated Russian comfrey, plenty of variegated rue and nepeta, and again irises and a great variety of foxgloves.

The walls are clad with fruit trees, clematis and roses—among the roses, light cerise 'Californica Plena' and the magnificent white 'Mme Alfred Carrière' draped over a long stretch of wall. The pale mauve-blue clematis 'Mrs Cholmondeley' backs a summer bed of roses and delphiniums.

Stepping out of the walled garden through a gate to the north-east, you enter what might be described as a 'transitional area', or nowhere place, a steep path leading down to a ramshackle court-yard. Turn right for the toilet or left (up the path) and around to your right for the top terrace. Screened by a huge yew hedge, clipped into giant cubes and cones on stilts, this terrace is a surprise to discover and a pleasure to explore. Wide and generous in its proportions, paved with well-weathered and irregular York stone slabs, it commands a fine view over lawns down to the house. The planting too is generous, with trees and shrubs for foliage interest and rugosa roses in abundance. Purple cotinus and bright-leaved *Philadelphus coronarius* 'Aureus' grow intricately intertwined; a very tall weeping pear (*Pyrus salicifolia* 'Pendula') pours like a silvery waterfall over viburnum, buddleia and white rugosa roses. A spreading tree wisteria overhangs a group of white delphiniums; while across the path, another wisteria mingles with the white rose 'Nevada'. See if you can spot the monkey!

A broad central path links the upper and lower terrace and the lawn area between. Although, looking down from the top terrace, the house seems very far away, it is in fact surprisingly close—a feat of perspective achieved by Peto, who was a great admirer of gardens of the Italian Renaissance. The balustraded lower terrace is planned around two wide stone fishponds. Along the west side, roses including deep pink 'Zephirine Drouhin' are trained over pyramid supports, along with clematis 'Nelly Moser'. The planting is familiar—standard honeysuckles, foxgloves, tall variegated com-frey, underplanted with small and delicate plants, such as pinks, violas and London pride. The narrow side beds are stocked with *Iris reticulata*, cyclamen, *Anemone pulsatilla* and autumn crocuses, for interest from autumn through to spring, followed by a multitude of delicate aquilegias, amidst white-flowered, bright-leaved fever-few.

A River Walk begins at the eastern end of the house, leading southwards to a small and charming boat terrace and the south lawn just beyond. Some of the rambler roses along the balustrade date from 1920. A low wall to the right supports flowering Japanese quinces (*Chaenomeles japonica*) —red, white and pink varieties—with polyanthus below.

Two enormous specimens of *Magnolia grandiflora*, planted in 1910, dominate the south front of the house, winding around and above the French windows; below, sisyrinchium, *Alchemilla mollis*, rue and purple sage flourish between the cracks in the paving stones, set about with small box trees in tubs. Follow the long lavender border down to a thick hedge of hybrid musk roses, underplanted with bright green sedum: this marks a change in level and the break between the two lawns. From this point you get another excellent view of the house, with its mellow, pale red brick, greyish stone facings and red tiled roof.

A deep herbaceous border runs across the top of the lower lawn, planted in characteristic style, relaxed but well-kept. Irises do well in this very hot south-facing spot; also melissa, rue and other herbs, purple thalictrum, honesty and foxgloves, tall delicate maroon gladioli, delphiniums, achillea and campanulas. To the west is an ancient cob wall, with the sundial garden beyond. Once, like the walled garden, planted with roses, this is now a pleasant orchard area, with a sloping bed at the far end. Here old roses including the lovely 'Constance Spry' tower above white peonies.

Having now come in a complete circle back to the walled apple tunnel garden, you can wander southwards over the lawn to the explore the Japanese or wild water garden. Planted at the turn of the century by four Japanese gardeners hired by Louis Greville (a former owner), this garden ran wild during the 1939–45 war and has only recently (in the last 20 years) been reclaimed. The Japanese tea house, the bridge and some remarkable lanterns survived, along with many trees—a towering poplar, a tulip tree, acers, walnuts and cherries. The streamside planting is bold and garish, with tall yellow irises and glorious orange, red and maroon primulas.

Iford Manor

ADDRESS AND TELEPHONE: Iford Manor, near Bradford-on-Avon, Wiltshire. Tel. Bradford-on-Avon (02216) 3146 or head gardener 2840

OWNERS: Mr and Mrs J.J.W. Hignett

DIRECTIONS: 2½ miles SW of Bradford-on-Avon. Entrance through gates at Iford Bridge by the lanes from Westwood, or from A36 6 miles S from Bath. Public transport: only by bus to Westwood, BR to Freshford

OPENING TIMES: May to end September, Tues, Wed, Thurs, Sat and Sun 2–5. April and October Sun only. House not open

ADMISSION: £1.50, OAPs and children £1. Coach parties by prior arrangement

CAR PARKING: yes

TOILETS: yes

REFRESHMENTS: teas Sun 3–5

SHOP: guidebooks/cards for sale at ticket point

DOGS: yes, but must be well controlled and on a lead

WHEELCHAIR ACCESS: not easy. Toilets for the disabled: no

PEAK MONTHS: May/June

NOTABLE FEATURES: Italian-style garden created by Harold Peto

This is a garden of great atmosphere and charm, not large but extensively terraced, planted in a valley overlooking the River Frome and sheltered by beech woods. Although the setting is typically English, the garden is laid out in Italian style, with terraces, broad walks and pools and filled with ancient statues and fragments. Its creator was Harold Peto, the architect and garden designer, who was very influential in promoting the Italian style in English gardening at the turn of this century.

Iford Manor was laid out in the Italian style by Harold Peto. (F.A.H. Bloemendal)

The ticket office and entry point is by the loggia, at the south-east corner of the Tudor house. To your right, across a small courtyard, is a semicircular pool, fed by a lion's head fountain. The decorative wrought iron balconies above the loggia date from the mid 15C. The loggia itself includes an Italian Renaissance window and various marble ornaments dating from the same period; also Byzantine roundels of animals and birds, a theme throughout the garden. Worn stone steps lead up to the small first terrace and from here to the second terrace and conservatory. 18C vases (from Church House in Richmond) crown the pillars of the steps. Two ancient fluted columns can be seen near the conservatory; that on the right dates from the 6th or 7C BC and the left-hand one is described as 'a fine example of Roman spiral fluting'.

At the far end of the terrace is a 15C Italian well head, flanked by 15C carved saints from Siena. The curious marble lions supporting pillars date from about 1200 and are also Italian. Here, as throughout the garden, the planting is discreetly planned to offset the stonework and drystone walls, with plenty of wisterias and climbing plants, along with pungent blue-flowering and purple sage. There are warm, bright colours too—deep pink roses and pink-flowering escallonia and bright reddish purple *Gladiolus byzantinus*, the soft red foliage of *Cotinus coggygria*, the Venetian sumach or European smoke bush and the yellow flowers of St John's wort. The Chilean glory flower (*Eccremocarpus scaber*) grows on the steps.

Light and shade are combined everywhere in this garden to fine effect and there are plenty of cool secluded places to rest. A small pool overhung by burgeoning potentillas flows down alongside shallow steps to a small paved area thickly planted with *Alchemilla mollis* and shaded by weeping birch. Sisyrinchium grows here, with its tall spikes of pale creamy yellow flowers, and bright yellow day lilies (hemerocallis). These hidden shady places add to the garden's character and charm, but sadly the many changes of level (and uneven paving) make it unsuitable for visitors in wheelchairs.

To your left are further shallow terraces, below the Great Terrace with its imposing colonnade. A small paved court features various panels of arms and a pair of Italian stone figures; and further up the steps is the Blue Pool, lined with blue mosaic, beneath a delightful bas-relief of a woman riding a lion. The pool is surrounded by jasmine, honeysuckle and a pink rose; ajuga 'Burgundy Glow' flourishes in the paving.

Peto's Great Terrace, above, stretches from a curved seat at the western end to a little 18C teahouse in the east. The curved stone seat overlooks a small apple orchard with the hills beyond. Senecio floods over the paving and a small rosemary bush is set to good effect in the centre of a millstone. The nearby wellhead is Byzantine and thought to have been made for the Church of St Andrew of the Goths at Ravenna, built in 534. A French stone lion is set on a Roman column, one of Peto's many inspired combinations.

The Casita, on the far side of the terrace, contains many fascinating features, such as a 14C Venetian Gothic wheel window; note the carved woodwork below the roof and the pink marble Verona columns (dating from about 1200). In the courtyard of the Casita grow lavender, rosemary, artemisia and phlomis. Two small formal courts are being created at the back of the Great Terrace, below the huge yew hedge. On the south side of the terrace is a bronze wolf suckling Romulus and Remus, made from a mould taken from the original in the Capitol museum in Rome. This is set in a deep bed containing fluffy pink thalictrum, irises, red berberis and another pink rose.

Just to the north, in woodland beyond the yew hedge, is a Japanese water garden in process of reconstruction, with *Acer palmatum* and bamboo already well established. Harold Peto began the Japanese garden on this site, which the present owners are completing; the elements of water and stone, lanterns and tower are placed in accordance with the customs of the Heian era, c 8–12 AD.

Returning to the Great Terrace, you soon reach a broad flight of stairs leading up into the wood, crowned at the top by a column placed here during the 1914–18 war and dedicated to King Edward VII. The stone hounds on plinths by the colonnade—one alert, one scratching a flea—are 18C German work; not far away to the left is a Roman sarcophagus.

The 18C garden house was moved to its present position by Peto—it originally stood on a mount, at the end of what is now the kitchen garden. Beyond this the path continues above smooth lawns and areas of long grass, with Martagon lilies, through an arbour of berberis, under beeches and laburnum and huge chestnut trees, to the cloisters. Built by Peto in 1914, in the Italian Renaissance style of about 1200, the cloisters are crammed with ancient fragments (for a complete listing, see the garden guidebook). Replacing the immense lime that was a victim of the 1990 gale is a golden elm, standing above the path, which leads you back to the main part of the garden.

If you have time, visit the lily pond, set in the lawn above the rockery; and see its fountain—a 16C figure of a huntsman. Curving steps lead up from this pond to the Great Terrace.

Stourhead

ADDRESS AND TELEPHONE: the Administrator, Stourhead House, Stourton, near Warminster, Wiltshire BA12 6QH. Tel. Bourton (Dorset) (0747) 840348

OWNERS: The National Trust

DIRECTIONS: in the village of Stourton just off B3092, 3 miles NW of Mere (A303), 10 miles S of Frome. Public transport: Southern National bus 59 from Gillingham BR, alight Zeals, 1¼ miles. Gillingham BR 6 miles; Bruton 7 miles

OPENING TIMES: garden, all the year daily 8–7, or dusk if earlier. Different times for house

ADMISSION CHARGE: free to NT members. Garden, March to 30 October £3.50, children £1.70, parties £3. November to end February, £2.30, children £1.20, no reductions for parties

CAR PARKING: yes

TOILETS: yes

REFRESHMENTS: café

DOGS: in garden, November to end February only, in woods throughout year

WHEELCHAIR ACCESS: yes, wheelchair route round garden with access to grotto. Iron bridge can be slippery. Please telephone the administrator before visiting to arrange car parking. Toilets for disabled: yes, adapted for wheelchairs at Spread Eagle Inn yard beside NT shop

NOTABLE FEATURES: lake and temples; grotto; rare trees and plants

Stourhead defies all classification: an 18C century landscape garden existing entirely on its own magnificent terms, a world in itself. Graham Stuart Thomas (*Gardens of the National Trust*) has described it as 'a unique work of art ... precious, involved and all-embracing'. The landscape is both 'natural' and in an important sense 'artificial', a living picture—temples and other architectural features are strategically placed around the enormous lake and the trees are arranged with magnificent artistry.

Stourhead House was built in the 1720s for Henry Hoare, a banker and son of the Lord Mayor of London. His son, Henry Hoare II (1705–85), succeeded to the banking business when he was only 19, on his father's death. In 1741, the young man returned from three years' travelling and living abroad, mainly in Italy, and took up residence at Stourhead. Left a widower at the age of 38, with three young children, he began to take an active interest in planting and developing the landscape. Helped and advised by the architect

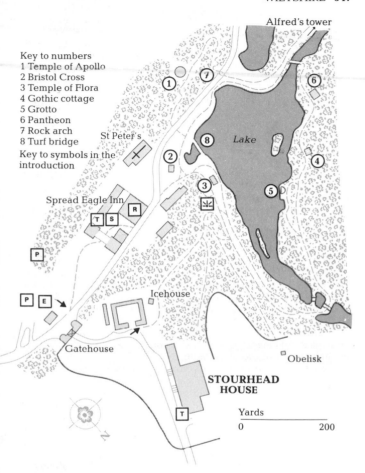

Key to numbers
1 Temple of Apollo
2 Bristol Cross
3 Temple of Flora
4 Gothic cottage
5 Grotto
6 Pantheon
7 Rock arch
8 Turf bridge
Key to symbols in the introduction

Alfred's tower

Lake

St Peter's

Spread Eagle Inn

Icehouse

Gatehouse

Obelisk

STOURHEAD HOUSE

Yards
0   200

Henry Flitcroft, he erected classical buildings beginning with the little Temple of Flora (then called the Temple of Ceres) and constructed the lake, by damming medieval fishponds.

Tragedy entered Henry Hoare's life again in 1751, when his son died in Naples at the age of 21—'a grief I never expected or wished to have survived', he wrote to his brother. Nevertheless much of his life's work lay ahead—he was to live until 1785, surviving all three of his children. He found consolation in planning the marriages of his daughters and continued building and planting—sustained also by his love of classical literature and philosophy. The Pantheon (then called the Temple of Hercules) was built from 1753 to 1756 and the lake finished by 1757.

Henry Hoare's younger daughter Anne (called Nanny) died in childbirth in 1759, also aged 21. Her son, Richard Colt Hoare, was later to inherit Stourhead and proved a worthy successor to Henry—

a keen plantsman, he made considerable changes and additions to the landscape.

Stourhead remained in the same family's possession until 1946–47, when Sir Henry Hoare, the 6th Baronet, gave 3000 acres to the National Trust (his only son had died of wounds in Egypt in 1917).

As a memorial to one family and their achievements through generations, Stourhead is unsurpassed. Kenneth Woodbridge (*The Stourhead Landscape*, The National Trust) describes the gardens and park as 'an outstanding example of a landscape garden showing the influence of William Kent in the use of buildings, and intermediate at the time of its conception between Kent and Capability Brown'. Ideas were changing, as Woodbridge says, even as the garden was being made, and it continues, inevitably, to grow and develop; but all new planting is carried out with sensitive deference to the 'genius of the place', Stourhead's original and lasting spirit.

One of the best times to visit is early spring, when the woods are lit with narcissus, especially the native *Narcissus pseudonarcissus* species. Rhododendrons and azaleas, all planted in this century, thrive in the woodland and around the lake, especially sweet-smelling yellow *R. luteum*, rampant purple *R. ponticum*, giant *R. arboreum* and its hybrids, *R. cinnabarium* and *R. yunnanense*. However, it is worthwhile visiting at any time of year, to see the excellent and varied tree planting, the temples and of course the huge lake itself. The best approach is by a route leading from the gatehouse around the house—from here you get an excellent first view across to the Temple of Apollo—but this entrance to the gardens is not clearly indicated and you may find it easier to enter by the gate near Spread Eagle Inn.

This alternative route brings you out above the Bristol High Cross and the Turf Bridge, with a clear view across the water to the Pantheon; other buildings and architectural features will be revealed as you follow the 2-mile circuit route anti-clockwise round the lake. The cross, a medieval monument, decorated with statues of British kings and queens, once stood at the junction of High Street and Broad Street in Bristol; it was dismantled in 1762 and erected at Stourhead in 1765.

A number of winding paths lead through the woodland along the eastern shore of the lake, and you can wander from one to the other as you please without fear of losing your way. The first lakeside building to the east, below, is the Temple of Flora, designed by Henry Flitcroft in 1744 and built by William Privet in Chilmark stone, a type of limestone. The four columns of the portico are of Tuscan Doric order and the Latin inscription over the door is from the *Aeneid*. It translates as 'Begone, you who are uninitiated! Begone!'—the warning spoken by the Cumaean Sybil as Aeneas was preparing to enter the underworld.

An excellent tree list is available, which details the most important and eye-catching trees at Stourhead. Some ancient trees, especially oak, beech and sycamore, survive from the time of Henry Hoare II or before. Hoare was concerned mainly to achieve an artistic contrast between dark and light green shades; his grandson, Richard Colt Hoare, was more adventurous in his selection of species, planting variegated sycamore, tulip trees, an Indian bean tree, six weeping ash, a locust tree and others. A variety of conifers was introduced in the 19C, and the 6th Baronet added 71 types, along with numerous broad-leaved trees and masses of azaleas and rhododendrons.

Only a few trees can be mentioned here individually. The striking gold tree on the bottom path leading to Flora's temple is the variegated tulip tree *Liriodendron tulipifera* 'Aureomarginatum', one of the largest in the British Isles. Also along this eastern shore, we noted a variegated sycamore (*Acer pseudoplatanus* 'Variegatum') planted at Stourhead in 1791; and further on a weeping ash (*Fraxinus excelsior* 'Pendula')—though this is much younger than the six weeping ash planted by Richard Colt Hoare. Below is *Thuja plicata* 'Zebrina', a golden variegated form of the western red cedar, and on the lower path a black walnut (*Juglans nigra*). A London plane (Platanus acerifolia) overhangs the water and further on to the right of the path is a monkey puzzle (*Araucaria araucana*) planted around 1852.

Among the many other interesting trees in this area are maples including the grey-budded snake-bark maple (*Acer rufinerve*) and the Japanese maple *Acer palmatum*. There is a purple-leaved sycamore (*Acer pseudoplatanus* 'Purpureum') along the top path, a tree of heaven (*Ailanthus altissima*), and conifers including the coast redwood (*Sequoia sempervirens*), a Wellingtonia (*Sequoiadendron giganteum*) planted in 1861, and Forrest's Silver Fir (*Abies delavayi forrestii*).

Rounding the north arm of the lake, you pass under a spreading Turkey oak (*Quercus cerris*) and a grey poplar (*Populus canescens*), one of the tallest specimens in Britain. The path continues along this side of the lake to the Pantheon, passing on its way the grotto and Gothic cottage. Pause by the lovely *Fagus sylvatica* 'Purpurea Tricolor', a rare variety of purple beech, with pink-striped, narrow leaves. Further along, what appears to be a waterside grove of western red cedar (*Thuja plicata*) is in fact just one tree.

The grotto is wheelchair accessible, although it has a rather bumpy cobbled floor. It is lined with tufa, waterworn limestone deposit, and lighted from above by an opening in the dome. In a recess with a cold bath (fed by the springs of the Stour) a nymph lies sleeping—a lead copy of the sleeping Ariadne. The inscription, cut in marble below the bath, is Pope's translation of a pseudo-classical poem forged in the 15C:

> Nymph of the Grot these sacred springs I keep
> And to the murmur of these waters sleep;
> Ah! spare my slumbers, gently tread the cave,
> And drink in silence or in silence lave.

A white lead statue of the River God can be seen in a separate cave.

The Gothic Cottage is of uncertain age, but certainly dates at least from 1806, when Richard Colt Hoare added the Gothic seat and porch.

Approaching the Pantheon, you pass a manna ash (*Fraxinus ornus*), recorded as planted at Stourhead in 1791. The Pantheon, designed by Henry Flitcroft and first called the Temple of Hercules, was being overhauled when we visited, its interior having been badly damaged by condensation. You are invited to throw donations to the gods through the gate—taking care to throw them beyond the metal strip, lest they fall into the hands of the underworld. The classical statues include Michael Rysbrack's statue of Hercules (facing the entrance) and Flora. The god Hercules was associated with gardens in Roman times, and earlier with the sacred gardens of Greek mystery cults.

A rock bridge across the Zeals road, constructed at some time between 1760 and 1765, meets a steep path leading up to the Temple of Apollo, from which you get a magnificent view over the whole garden. Unfortunately, it is not possible to reach the temple by wheelchair. The temple niches are now empty, their statues transferred to the roof of Stourhead House.

Along this south side of the lake, the trees include a huge tulip tree (*Liriodendron tulipifera*), the largest broad-leaved tree at Stourhead and the tallest tulip tree in the British Isles. It was planted in 1791 by Richard Colt. There is also a considerable collection of magnolias, including two specimens of *Magnolia* x *soulangiana* 'Alexandrina', *M.* x *soulangiana* 'Lennei', a small *Magnolia kobus* and the Japanese big leaf magnolia, *M. hypoleuca*.

Passing on your left the Turf Bridge, you now return to the starting point, and can proceed from here back along the entrance path to Spread Eagle Inn, the café, lavatories and National Trust shop.

While you are in the neighbourhood, it is also worth visiting King Alfred's Tower, a red-brick folly 160ft high, built in 1772 by Flitcroft at the edge of the estate. This gives fine views over three counties —Somerset, Dorset and Wiltshire.

Stourton House Garden

ADDRESS AND TELEPHONE: Stourton, near Warminster, Wiltshire (immediately adjacent to Stourhead car park). Tel. (0747) 840417. Look for the blue signs

OWNERS: Col.onel Anthony and Mrs Elizabeth Bullivant

DIRECTIONS: off B3092, 3 miles NW of Mere. Public transport: not convenient. Southern National bus 59 from Gillingham BR, alight Zeals, then 1 mile. Gillingham BR 6½ miles, or, between May and September, Bruton station 7 miles

OPENING TIMES: 1 April to end November, or from Easter Mon if earlier, Sun, Wed, Thurs and BH Mon 11–6. Parties on other days by appointment. House not open

ADMISSION: £2, children 50p

CAR PARKING: yes, in Stourhead car park and for disabled people in the farmyard

TOILETS: yes

REFRESHMENTS: café

SHOP: home propagated plants, dried flowers, and over 200 varieties of hydrangea for sale

DOGS: no

WHEELCHAIR ACCESS: yes to most of garden. Toilets for the disabled: no, but facilities available at Stourhead 300 yds away

PEAK MONTHS: April (daffodils, narcissi and other spring bulbs) May/June (rhododendrons and azaleas, roses), June to November (hydrangeas and herbaceous plants)

NOTABLE FEATURES: wide variety of garden plants and vegetables grown for drying; unusual varieties of daffodils and narcissi; very large collection of hydrangeas, woodland garden

Stourton is a garden with an underlying purpose: the production of flowers and foliage for drying. In one sense, the rich planting of the garden is a by-product of the dried flower industry; in another, the industry benefits from the generosity and variety of the planting. Whichever way you view it, Stourton is a rewarding place to visit.

In late Georgian times, a parson of Stourton married one of the Miss Hoares of Stourhead, and some of the Stourhead money went to building the Stourton house and garden. The Victorian greenhouse, still standing in the vicinity of the house, is a legacy of that period. The garden's transformation to its present shape, however, began more than 30 years ago when Colonel and Mrs Bullivant came to live there; the main gardens are laid out to the east side of the house and 70 per cent of the plants grown end up as dried flowers. The public were first admitted to Stourton in 1982 and from 1983 the gardens have opened on a regular basis, owing to popular demand. Mrs Bullivant's drying of flowers, carried out with the assistance of her husband and local 'pickers and strippers', has grown steadily, and in 1989 she published a book on the drying process. It is appropriate that this was on the 200th anniversary of Sir Joseph Banks' introduction of the hydrangea to England— being, as it is, a flower much favoured for drying and a speciality of the Stourton House garden.

The recommended route begins with the kitchen garden: beds contain not only artichokes, radishes and leeks, but a range of flowers suitable for drying: the tassel flower (*Amaranthus caudatus*) statice, poppies and delphiniums (2500 spires of delphiniums have been dried at Stourton). The leeks are also encouraged to burst into blossom, since their flower heads look well in the dried bouquets, as do the seed heads of radishes. There are Chinese lanterns (*Physalis alkekengi*), teasels, golden rod and achillea, all of which are dried by the water heating plant in the cellars. The kitchen garden also contains some of Stourton's 200 varieties of hydrangea, the shades ranging through many blues and pinks as well as creams and whites.

The vegetable beds are partly concealed by the 'Twelve Apostles': *Chamaecyparis Lawsoniana Glauca columnaris* which stand on either side of the path. This avenue leads down to the Lily Pond garden, which is itself surrounded by a tall and undulating hedge of Leyland cypresses (*Cupressulyparis leylandii*). This forms a graceful and unusual boundary for the garden, which consists of a central pool surrounded by island beds of small shrubs and herbaceous plants.

The centrepiece of the lily pond is a 'flower fountain'—a large stone dish filled with many unusual plants. Outstanding among the pond planting are the carnivorous pitcher plants (nepenthes) which Colonel and Mrs Bullivant manage to grow in the open throughout the year. Their technique is to grow the plants above water level, with a 'wick' of peat connecting them to a secondary container underwater, thus avoiding direct contact with icy water. Flies are snared by the honey contained in the 'pitchers' and then devoured by the plant. There are also flowering rushes, whose buds resemble alliums, including one striped variety. Clumps of yellow and purple water iris, and a double orange mimulus grow on the verges, with an edging of orange cistus, red helianthemum and pink dianthus.

The surrounding beds are filled to overflowing with standard roses, tree peonies, and of course, hydrangeas, including the lilac blue *H. villosa* and the porcelain blue *H. aspera*. Blue delphiniums and pink, white and purple aquilegias abound, as well as silver thistles and many colours of sweet pea. One group combines a climbing blue clematis, red lupins, and small yellow poppies. Huge red poppies flourish beneath a twisting Chinese gooseberry (*Actinidia chinensis*). Perennial honesty (*Lunaria rediviva*) whose seed heads feature in dried flower bouquets, seeds itself throughout and many beds are edged with *Limnanthes douglasii*, the meadow foam, or poached egg plant. This is a delightful garden in spring, summer or autumn.

To the west of this garden is a shady area where many hydrangeas are being reared. A path towards the house is flanked by two enormous mauve rhododendrons, two Mount Etna brooms (*Genista aetnensis*) and two circular troughs dated 1757 and decorated with sailing ships, mermaids, anchors and starfish. Nearby are two *Styrax japonica* planted in 1988, to bloom in 1991.

South of the Pool Garden is the Lower Pond Garden, a less formal area, where daffodils and narcissus flourish in spring. Many of these have been exhibited at London flower shows, including a unique striped narcissus. There is a *Davidia involucrata*, known as the pocket handkerchief tree because of the pairs of white, drooping bracts which surround its heads of blossom and the beautiful, purple-flowered *Magnolia liliiflora* 'Nigra'. A crimson perennial nasturtium (*Tropaeolum speciosum*) clambers up the shady side of one of the boundary hedges.

The water supply for the lower pond, which looks as if it occurred naturally in the meadow, is ingeniously drained from the flat roof at the side of the house and piped across beside the main lawn. A cotoneaster and a weeping birch stand near the water's edge, with rodgersias, iris and seakale (*Crambe cordifolia*). Yellow Turk's cap lilies grow wild, and Himalayan poppies have set seed in the grass. Ponies graze in the fields beyond, and the area has the relaxed feeling of a place where cultivated garden and meadow meet.

From the Lower Pond Garden you cross the south lawn, past the Victorian greenhouse, with a fine view over the Wiltshire countryside. (On a clear day, you can see four church spires.) Against the house, a wisteria shelters a red cestrum.

To the west of the lawn a woodland garden has been created, shaded by trees under planted with blue hydrangeas, the white lacecap ('Veitchii') and huge hostas, with a 'secret garden' to shelter some of the more tender specimens. As you enter this inner circle, there is a large magnolia (*M. wilsonii*) with saucer-shaped white flowers and red stamens. Besides the many rhododendrons and azaleas, we saw *Viburnum plicatum* 'Pink Beauty', whose white heads of flower not only turn a delicate pink but are produced throughout the summer. Nearby grow two specimens of the pink lacecap hydrangea 'Tricolor', which has yellow, grey and green leaves, and 'Quadricolor', whose leaves are white, yellow, grey and green.

You can now finish your visit in the tea gardens in the nearby verandah or inspect the plants for sale. Hydrangea enthusiasts will find at least 200 of the garden's varieties among them.

NORTH YORKSHIRE

Beningbrough Hall

ADDRESS AND TELEPHONE: Shipton-by-Beningbrough, York YO6 1DD. Tel. York (0904) 470666

OWNERS: The National Trust

DIRECTIONS: 8 miles NW of York, 2 miles W of Shipton, 2 miles SE of Linton-on-Ouse (A19). Public transport: Yorkshire Pullman bus from York (passing close York BR), to within 1 mile (tel. York 0904 622304). York BR 8 miles

OPENING TIMES: Good Fri 29 March to end October, daily except Mon and Fri (open BH Mon) 12–6 or dusk if earlier. Also Fri in July and August. Last admission 5.30

ADMISSION: house and garden £3.40, children £1.70, family ticket £8.50, parties £2.80. Garden and exhibitions only £2.20, children £1.10

CAR PARKING: yes

TOILETS: yes

REFRESHMENTS: café

SHOP: yes

DOGS: no

WHEELCHAIR ACCESS: yes. Toilets for the disabled: yes

This well maintained 7-acre garden belongs to an imposing Baroque house, built by John Bourchier in 1716, and which is now the 'northern branch' of the National Portrait Gallery in London, housing over 100 pictures on long-term loan. Although not large, the garden gives a pleasant feeling of spaciousness, with its big walled garden, smaller formal gardens and flower borders and the surrounding 365 acres of parkland.

Walking across the courtyard from the entry and ticket office, you soon come to the walled garden. Once a kitchen garden, this is now a relaxed, informal area, lawned over and with seats for visitors. An unusual avenue of ancient pears runs down the centre from north to south—espalier pear trees, trained overhead on hoops to form six archways. The pears include 'Pitmaston', 'Conference',

'Black Worcester' and 'Marie Louise', underplanted with herbs and scented foliage plants—lavender, artemisia, marjoram, sage, lad's love and rue.

The high kitchen garden walls were once heated from inside, to ensure the survival of wall fruits, and you can still see the little grates set into the bricks. Fruit trees, vines and figs are still grown against the walls, along with golden hops (*Humulus lupulus* 'Aureus'), clematis, ivies and climbing hydrangeas.

The south border lies directly below the kitchen garden. This sheltered position under a high south-facing wall suits species vulnerable to the north-east Yorkshire climate—Mexican orange (*Choisya ternata*), bay, huge bushes of hebe, the wine grape *Vitis vinifera* 'Purpurea', ceanothus, the Chinese gooseberry (*Actinidia chinensis*), white *Jasminum officinale* and mauve-pink *Jasminum beesianum*.

Not far away to the east is the American garden, featuring ericaceous trees and shrubs, many brought back from plant-hunting expeditions in North America, and spring bulbs. Among the trees are snowy mespilus (*Amelanchier canadensis*), with abundant sprays of white flowers and richly coloured trees in autumn, the distinctive tulip tree (*Liriodendron tulipifera*), the paper birch or canoe birch (*Betula papyrifera*) with papery white bark and yellow autumn leaves and the American crab *Malus coronaria* 'Charlottae', which bears large, shell-pink, fragrant flowers.

Retracing your steps westwards, you arrive below the main garden, with its flower borders and lawns. The double border, running 150ft from north to south, is planned for colour throughout the summer, but especially in early mid summer and again at the beginning of early autumn. Shrubs, roses and herbaceous plants are arranged in two parallel borders, the wider one to the east backed by the kitchen garden wall, the other by a box hedge. The wall clematis include beautiful lavender-blue 'Mrs Cholmondeley', blue 'Perle d'Azur', cerise-pink *C. texensis* 'Etoile Rose' and pinkish-mauve 'Comtesse de Bouchard'. Roses grow here too, trained along wires, and vigorous Japanese honeysuckle (*Lonicera japonica* 'Halliana'), semi-evergreen with sweet-smelling pale yellow flowers. Dark purple buddleia 'Dartmoor' is repeated down the border, as are shrub roses, shrubs with interesting foliage such as berberis and cotinus and fine flowering shrubs such as deutzia and philadelphus. This still leaves room for an enormous range of perennials, of all sizes and contrasting shapes. Among the taller perennials at the back are bugbane (*Cimicifuga cordifolia*) with shiny dark leaves, some heart-shaped, and creamy-green flowers; variegated silver grass (*Miscanthus sinensis* 'Variegatus'), thalictrum and *Geranium psilostemon*, which has eye-catching magenta flowers, centred with black. Tall spikes of flag irises (*Iris germanica*)—yellow, purple/maroon and mauve—give structure to the middle of the border, accompanied by *Crambe cordifolia* with huge heart-shaped leaves and tiny white flowers, blue *Campanula persicifolia*, rich violet *Campanula glomerata dahurica*, pale rose-pink *Geranium endressii* and white madonna lilies (*Lilium candidum*). In the foreground are hostas including *H. fortunei hyacinthina* and *H. sieboldiana elegans*, geranium 'Johnson's Blue', *G. endressii* and blue-purple *G. pratense* or meadow cranesbill, catmint (*N.* x *faassenii*), penstemons and many other border plants. This superb display is excellently framed by views of open parkland to the south.

The main border, leading towards the house, takes precedence at the height of summer with its 'hot' and 'cool' ends and cleverly manipulated perspective—the cool-coloured far end seems to fade away into the distance, making the border seem longer. This border was designed in the 1970s by Graham Thomas, one of the National Trust's most famous and influential gardens advisers. Around the hot end you can see red rose 'City of Belfast', the vigorous butter-yellow rose 'Graham Thomas' (raised by David Austin), peony 'Lady Alexandra Duff', yellow and dark red lilies, yellow hypericum and yellow-flowered senecio, red-leaved heuchera, shrubby and herbaceous potentillas. A huge Mount Etna broom (*Genista aetnensis*) flourishes against the wall, and clematis hang all the way down. At the cool end is a pool of silver *Stachys lanata*, rose 'Gruss an Aachen', pearly pink fading to creamy white, and silver artemisia backed by variegated ivy.

Continuing westwards, you arrive at two small formal gardens, on either side of the conservatory and house steps. Surrounded and secluded by yew hedges, these are peaceful places to sit and relax. The east garden is cool in its colour scheme, with white regale lilies, peonies and anemones, *Euphorbia myrsinites* with blue-grey leaves and greenish-yellow bracts, lavender-blue *Aster thomsonii* 'Nanus', pale yellow achillea and phlomis, tall bearded irises—and painted wooden tubs filled with purple cherry pie (heliotrope) and white woolly ballota. Against the south-facing wall grows an enormous Banksian rose (*Rosa banksiae lutea*), which bears large sprays of very small yellow flowers, and further along, the lemon-yellow, lemon-scented climbing rose 'Leverkusen'. The small pond contains water lilies and white arums.

The west formal garden is planted with low interlacing box hedges and bright bedding, in traditional knot garden style. The colours here are hot and flamboyant—marigolds, orange-red calceolaria 'Kentish Hero', mahogany-red potentilla 'M. Rouillard', red heuchera interplanted with the small orange-red rose 'Anna Ford', red verbena 'Peruviana' and others. Against the wall is bright yellow *Clematis tangutica* and the brilliant orange-scarlet modern climber 'Danse du Feu'.

Turning right up a sloping ramp, planted either side, you enter the cobbled laundry courtyard, its high walls bordered with plenty of strong foliage plants, including a splendid fig, and clothed with clematis, roses and a Morello cherry. To your left is a wooded Wilderness and adventure play area; or by turning right, past the clock tower, you can return to the restaurant and entrance.

On your way back, note the trellis lawn, where pink and yellow roses ('Katherine Harrop' and 'Leverkusen') alternate on wooden trellis supports, and the Santa Barbara ceanothus (*Ceanothus impressus*) makes a magnificent show, with its dark green leaves and deep blue flowers.

Mr Michael Walker, the head gardener, recommends a visit to the potting shed, which houses a collection of old garden tools; or if you would prefer a woodland walk, continue past the car park and old skating pond to Pike Ponds.

Castle Howard

ADDRESS AND TELEPHONE: Castle Howard, Coneysthorpe, York
YO6 7DA. Tel. Coneysthorpe (065 384) 333

OWNERS: The Howard family

DIRECTIONS: by road 15 miles from York, off the A64. Public
transport: train to Malton. Bus from York

OPENING TIMES: 25 March to end October, daily 10–4.30. Castle
open

ADMISSION: Castle and grounds £5, OAPs £4, children £2;
grounds only £3, children £1.50

CAR PARKING: yes, and for coaches

REFRESHMENTS: café

SHOP: yes

DOGS: on lead

WHEELCHAIR ACCESS: yes. Toilets for the disabled: yes

PEAK MONTHS: July/August

Everything at Castle Howard is on a grand scale—the magnificent
House, the fountains, lakes and parterres, the temple and mausoleum. This vast estate has impressed visitors for almost 300 years:
'I have seen gigantic palaces before, but never a sublime one' wrote
Horace Walpole, also noting 'the noblest lawn in the world fenced
by half the horizon, and a mausoleum that would tempt one to be
buried alive.'

During the 1939–45 war, the house was used as a girl's boarding
school, and was badly damaged by fire; it remained empty from
1940 to 1950. Restoration of both house and gardens has been going
on since then, aided in the 1980s by considerable financial input
from Granada Television— 'Brideshead Revisited' was filmed here.

The main framework of the estate was established by Charles,
3rd Earl of Carlisle (1669–1738). In 1699 John Vanbrugh was
commissioned to design and build the house and lay out the
surrounding landscape, helped by Nicholas Hawksmoor. Among
the oldest features, dating from Vanbrugh's time or not long after,
are the Temple of the Four Winds, the South Lake, the Pyramid,
the Mausoleum and the New River Bridge. However, the Great
Lake, to the north, was not constructed until the very end of the
18C. Ray Wood, to the east, was filled with fountains, temples, pools
and statues by Carlisle, but within a century it had returned to its
original wild state.

The approach to the estate is very impressive—a long narrow
straight avenue bordered with beeches and limes, with architectural features marking the entrance and crossroads. The gatehouse,
with its massive centre arch and pyramid, was designed by Vanbrugh in 1719 and the wings added 30 years later, to provide
temporary accommodation for sightseers. Under Rosalind, 9th
Countess of Carlisle, the rooms were made available to ill and
debilitated women from the West Riding, Sheffield and Newcastle
upon Tyne. The 100ft obelisk was built even earlier, in 1714, to

celebrate the Duke of Marlborough's military victories; it also bears an inscription by the 3rd Earl of Carlisle commemorating his own labours as the builder of Castle Howard.

The best place to start your tour is south of the house, below the parterres and the magnificent Atlas Fountain. Designed by W.A. Nesfield in 1850 and carved by the London sculptor John Thomas, the fountain is now restored to working order and operates on Sundays and Bank Holidays—fed by huge volumes of water from a reservoir in Ray Wood. Surrounded by four tritons with carved shells concealing water jets, Atlas bends under the weight of his globe, gilded with signs of the zodiac. Nesfield's original Italian-style parterres, ornate and intricate, were not to the taste of the 9th Countess, who replaced them in the 1890s with lawns and yew hedges.

A long balustrade to the south divides this strictly formal area from fields and countryside. In the distance you can see the Pyramid, looking rather odd in an English landscape. Designed by Hawksmoor in 1728, this holds an enormous bust of the 3rd Earl's ancestor, Lord William Howard. The south parterre is screened on either side by mature trees —to the west, cedars and yews, backed by limes, and to the east, copper beeches, cedars, pines and holm oaks. Beyond, to the west, lies the walled garden; to the east, the south lake, with the statue terrace above, leading to the Temple of the Four Winds.

Retrace your steps to the beginning of the terrace, marked by a circular gravel path surrounding a small lawn. A time capsule was buried here on 17 November 1982, by George Howard, then chairman of the BBC—not to be opened until 3982. In spring, the lawns are carpeted with daffodils, around the house and along the outskirts of Ray Wood. sited along the route of the main street of the old village of Henderskelfe, which was demolished by the 3rd Earl, the terrace to the temple is marked by a series of statues and pedestals. The slopes down to the lake are planted with white-beams. At the eastern end, in Temple Hole, is a shrub and wild garden, with plenty of rhododendrons, azaleas and eucryphias. New River Bridge and the mausoleum are visible in the distance. The south lake was restructured by W.A. Nesfield in the 1860s. In recent years it has been drained and dredged and in the process the lower pipes of a 100-year-old fountain were uncovered. Known as the Prince of Wales fountain, this is now restored to full working order, and plays, like the Atlas fountain, on Sundays and Bank Holidays.

A vast area of woodland, Ray Wood, lies above statue terrace, and is well worth exploring, although you may easily get lost or discouraged—the undergrowth is wild and deeply entangled, the paths hard to follow. This ancient woodland was filled with statues, pools and fountains by the 3rd Earl, but of his design, only the main paths and rides now survive. It was completely replanted with hardwoods in the 1940s, and planting of ornamentals began in 1975. Here you can see collections of nothofagus (southern beech), acers, arbutus, styrax and magnolias, along with more than 900 rhododendron species and hybrids and cherries and liquidambars along the top ride. From the overgrown ruins of the Temple of Venus, in the north-east corner of the wood, built by Hawksmoor in the 1730s, an avenue of pyramid hornbeam, leads southwards to the Statue Walk and the Temple of the Four Winds.

This very striking Italianate building was Vanbrugh shortly before his death in 1726. The porticoes are decorated with statues of the four sibyls, carved in 1731. Rescued from dereliction in the 1950s, the temple was given a new dome and the floor inlaid with marble from an old reredos from St Paul's Cathedral. Once the trees have been cleared, you will get a clear view south-east from here over New River Bridge (1744) to the magnificent mausoleum. Designed by Hawksmoor between 1726 and 1729, and thought to be one of his finest buildings, it was completed after his death and that of the 3rd Earl, in 1742. The mortuary chapel is surrounded by a colonnade of 20 pillars; below lies the crypt, where members of the family have been buried for more than nine generations.

Retracing your steps westwards, along the terrace towards the house, you can take a break for tea. Afterwards explore the grounds to the north, by the Great Lake, which dates from the end of the 18C when the 5th Earl banked and flooded the area. The smaller ponds on the shores of the lake were restructured in 1989, and near the boathouse a new lakeside adventure playground has been built.

The 11-acre walled gardens must not be missed. Once a kitchen garden and private garden, these are now filled with roses, both old and modern. The various collections are displayed in a number of separate walled enclosures—Lady Cecilia's Garden, the Sundial Garden, the Pyramid Garden and the Statue of Venus Garden.

Lady Cecilia's Garden is dedicated by an Latin inscription to the memory of Lady Cecilia Howard, who died in 1974: 'Ad memoriam Ceciliae amatae rosarum amatrices' (To the memory of loved Cecilia, lover of roses). Designed around an 18C gardener's house, it contains a great many beautiful old roses—moss roses· and gallicas in the lower section and centifolias, damasks and mosses around the pool and fountain. The garden is divided by yew hedges, with long alleys on either side, and the central circle is surrounded by a low box hedge.

The exuberance of the planting is contained within a strict formal structure—clematis and roses are trained up trellis supports, while massed silver weeping pears and Lawson's cypresses provide height in the beds surrounding the pool. Lime and hornbeam arbours stand on either side and a curving stilt hedge of hornbeam encloses the lawn by the house. The colour scheme is gentle, with plenty of soft blues and pinks, mauves and silver.

The Pyramid Garden features modern roses and a long border running from this garden to the Satyr Gate is planted with brilli-ant-coloured modern floribundas and hybrid teas, interplanted with purple-leaved (corylus). Here you can see, among others, the stunning orange-red 'Fred Loads', yellow 'Mountbatten', light red 'Memento' and 'Eye-paint', an orange-red floribunda with a white eye and yellow stamens. The Satyr Gate itself commands attention, with its ornate carvings—grinning satyrs on the inside and lions on the outside, and stone baskets overflowing with fruit and flowers.

In the Sundial Garden, old favourites such as 'Rambling Rector' and 'Treasure Trove' drape themselves over apple trees. The seg-mented beds contain over 90 hybrid tea and floribunda varieties.

Just above this garden, over the yew hedge, is the delphinium border. Close by is the broad walk, and a south-facing border containing tea roses, china roses, hybrid musks and modern shrub roses, interplanted with lilies and galtonias.

In the Statue of Venus garden (the statue was transferred from the Temple of Venus), to the east, rose beds are edged to interesting effect with *Berberis thunbergii* 'Atropurpurea' and hebes. Among the many hybrid perpetuals in this garden is the lovely pale pink 'Baronne Natalie de Rothschild'. Wooden pergolas on two sides are covered with honeysuckle and climbing hybrid perpetuals and noisette roses. There are fuchsia borders, too.

The plant centre lies just adjacent and beyond this are the car park and exit.

Fountains Abbey and Studley Royal

ADDRESS AND TELEPHONE: Fountains, Ripon, HG4 3DZ. Tel. Sawley (0765) 86333

OWNERS: The National Trust

DIRECTIONS: 4 miles W of Ripon off B6265 to Pateley Bridge. Public transport: United bus 145 from Ripon (with connections from Harrogate BR) Thurs and Sat only (tel. Darlington 0325 468771); Dalebus 806 from Leeds, summer only (passing close Harrogate BR) (tel. Leeds 0532 442621)

OPENING TIMES: deer park, all year during daylight hours. Abbey and grounds, all year daily except 24 and 25 December and Fri in November, December and January. January to end March and November to end December 10–5 or dusk if earlier. April to end June and September 10–7. July and August 10–8. October 10–6 or dusk if earlier. Fountains Hall open April to end September daily 11–6. October to end March daily 11–4.

ADMISSION: abbey and garden, winter £2.40, summer £2.70

CAR PARKING: yes

TOILETS: yes

REFRESHMENTS: café

SHOP: yes

DOGS: on leads only

WHEELCHAIR ACCESS: yes. Toilets for the disabled: yes

PEAK MONTHS: all year round

NOTABLE FEATURES: spectacular formal water garden with temples and other classical buildings; romantic vista of Fountains Abbey

It is ironic that the serene and symmetrical water garden at Studley Royal in North Yorkshire should have been created by an ambitious, devious, failed politician, who had been sent to the Tower of London for receiving bribes during his term as Chancellor of the Exchequer. This was at the time of the bursting of the 'South Sea Bubble'. John Aislabie, the disgraced Chancellor, took advantage of his retirement to his Yorkshire estate in 1723 to excavate the valley of the

River Skell near his house at Studley Royal and to create the amazing grand design you see today.

It would be pleasant to discover that the nobility of the project, undertaken over some 30 years, was accompanied by a corresponding metamorphosis in the character of its architect and creator. It seems, however, that he remained the opinionated, parsimonious man that he had always been, hiring and firing architects, mean with workmen and not above quarrelling with the neighbouring landowner who was preventing him from constructing his cherished project of a view down the river to the ruins of Fountains Abbey. Vision, nevertheless, he had in abundance, and a tenacity which eventually gave him the place in the history of garden design that he had failed to achieve in public life and financial affairs.

As well as vision, John Aislabie had enough fundamental knowledge of water gardens and architecture to give him a clear idea of what he wanted to achieve. He had previously acquired an estate in Buckinghamshire (Hall Barn) which reflected the influence of French and Dutch gardens of the period (as did many English gardens owned by returning exiles after the Restoration). Hall Barn was a 'mature garden of long canals, avenues and vistas terminating on garden buildings'.

Aislabie also had some knowledge of the Loire area of France and the work of the French gardener designer Le Nôtre. Moreover, he was well acquainted with the work of many contemporary architects, including Wren and Vanbrugh, and garden designers such as Stephen Switzer. However, he apparently sought little if any advice on his own project, hiring mainly local workmen, and employing architects only for some of the individual buildings. As it turned out, the garden had in the end two architects, for his son, William Aislabie, took over the project after John's death in 1742, and finally achieved his father's dream of a distant prospect of Fountains Abbey.

The gardens now have two approaches. You can enter from Fountains Abbey itself and walk through to Studley Royal Park, where in the grass slopes above the small lake John Aislabie's manor house once stood, or begin at the lake, walking up river to Fountains. In either case, there are two levels for viewing: a path running along the side of the valley, which gives the best prospect of the water gardens, and the steep hill walk through the woods with its panoramic vistas. You can also wander along the paths beside the pools enjoying the sounds of the falls and cascades.

Beginning, as we did, at the entrance for Fountains Abbey, a Cistercian monastery located strategically near sources of water (hence 'Fountains') you will find Fountains Hall immediately on your left. This is an early 17C building, bought by William Aislabie in 1768 but not maintained by him to any high standard. It was restored in 1926 by C.G. Vyner and is now used as a resource centre by the National Trust. Maps and photographs of the present restoration of the gardens are on display, and a model of the abbey is shown in the Abbey museum. Like most of the architecture in the neighbourhood, Fountains Hall is built of the local limestone, in this case salvaged from the abbot's house and monks infirmary nearby.

Taking the level path along the north side of the valley (and walking eastwards) you pass on your right the great ruins of the abbey, dwarfing its tiny river. Enough remains of the abbey's fabric—tower, nave, cloisters, refectory, undercroft—to justify its 18C description of 'The most spectacular Gothic view in Christendom'. The gold and grey shades of the limestone harmonise admirably with the green lawns and wooded heights ahead.

Past the abbey, the river meanders through peaceful flat pasture between wooded slopes. The National Trust is undertaking a massive restoration programme of the whole area, and in 1988 replanting of the valley slopes with beech, ash and English yew was already under way. There is a wide variety of broad-leaved trees on either side of the valley, including oak, lime and sweet chestnut, with smaller specimens such as *Sorbus torminalis*, the wild service tree, which colours red and yellow in autumn; the snowberry (*Symphoricarpos albus laevigatus*), with white fruits, and the common spindle (*Euonymus europaeus*). On the height of the slopes tower Scots pines, adding greatly to the dramatic effect of the steep valley.

As the river curves to the left under Tent Hill, the main path cuts through the wood on the promontory, leaving the Half Moon Pond, backed by its semicircle of trees, for later viewing. You emerge to find a junction of paths, where a rustic bridge leads across to the opposite woodland. A yew hedge conceals the river beyond this point, so that the sudden sight of the Moon Pond, with its two adjoining crescents and the graceful cream-coloured Temple of Piety on the far bank is breathtaking. In the summer of 1988 it was all the more so as the waters had recently been drained, the banks strengthened, and the grass just resown under the National Trust's restoration programme.

The pristine simplicity of the still ponds, cut out of green lawns against the backdrop of the woods, must have seemed to John Aislabie ample justification of his years of effort, and still provides an unforgettable sight. Three statues—of Neptune in the Moon Pond, and Endymion and Bacchus beside the crescent ponds—provide a focus for the eye without in any way distracting from the view. Below, the river pours in a neat comb over the Drum Fall, which although aptly named does not disturb the peaceful scene.

On the hill opposite can be glimpsed the curious 'Gothick' Octagon Temple, and in the woods behind you stands the Banqueting House. This building, by the architects Colen Campbell and Roger Morris, was originally planned as an orangery but changed function during the course of its construction. It can now be hired out on request.

The river now continues as a long canal among the lawns until the end of the formal gardens. Here there is another spectacular set piece, the Grand Cascade into the lake, which lies within the deer park. On either side of the cascade are Fishing Tabernacles originally designed by Roger Morris—but their shape was altered many times by John Aislabie during construction. The final effect, however is both distinctive and harmonious.

At this point you may leave by the canal gates to wander in the deer park. There are walks around the lake, ice houses in the hillside, and St Mary's Church, a late 19C 'ecclesiastical masterpiece' designed by the architect William Burges and built by the

Marchioness of Ripon in 1871–78. It displaced the obelisk of 1805 which in turn supplanted a funerary pyramid put up by William Aislabie in 1742 as a memorial to his father. You can also walk up the hill to the site of Studley Royal House, which was gutted by fire in 1946, leaving the stables as the only remaining inhabited building (in private hands). After all this you may be glad to have a drink or a meal in the National Trust restaurant in the steward's house.

When you are ready to pursue the way back, you should cross over the cascade and walk back to the Moon Pond, enjoying a closer view of the Temple of Piety. This was John Aislabie's last work, built in 1740–42 with the interior completed in 1948. It was at first dedicated by him to Hercules (possibly because of his own Herculean efforts in completing the garden) but later re-dedicated by his son to Piety—the Roman virtue of Pietas, or duty to the gods, to country and to family, both living and dead.

There is a steep ascent here through a tunnel grotto, carefully devised so that just as you think you will have to step into complete darkness, the light appears round the bend. You come out at the foot of the Octagon Tower, the classical summerhouse 'gothicked' in 1728 with parapet, pinnacles, quatrefoil piercings in the parapet and the addition of a 'gothick' porch. From here you can clearly see the Banqueting House on the opposite hillside. Below, the slope has been newly planted with yew, wild roses and butcher's broom. The walk along the top of the woods will then lead you on to the Temple of Fame, another splendid look-out point over the valley and the water gardens.

Finally, the path leads you to Anne Boleyn's Seat and from here you can look right back to Fountains Abbey: the 'surprise view', which although very thoroughly documented is still a surprise, because of its unexpected angle. The effect is entrancing, and completes the whole in just the way John Aislabie intended.

After climbing down again to the Moon Pond, you can wander back to the abbey, and if you wish study its layout in detail with the help of the available guide. A second tea shop and National Trust shop are located at this end of the estate.

Harlow Carr Gardens

ADDRESS AND TELEPHONE: Crag Lane, Harrogate, North Yorkshire. Tel. (0423) 565418

OWNERS: The Northern Horticultural Society

DIRECTIONS: on Crag Lane off the B6126 Harrogate to Otley road. Public transport: BR to Harrogate

OPENING TIMES: 9–7.30 or sunset if earlier. Old Bath House often open for exhibitions and displays

ADMISSION: £2.50. OAPs £2. Free admission for accompanied children

CAR PARKING: yes

TOILETS: yes

REFRESHMENTS: café

SHOP: yes

DOGS: guide dogs only

WHEELCHAIR ACCESS: yes. Toilets for the disabled: yes

PEAK MONTHS: April to October

NOTABLE FEATURES: trials and demonstration grounds; five
National Plant Collections: hypericum; rock and heath gardens;
rose and bulb gardens; herbaceous beds, foliage garden; peat
terraces and streamside garden; arboretum, woodland 'winter
garden', museum of gardening

It is no accident that the list of notable features given above for
Harlow Carr Gardens is unusually long; according to the official
guide they were designed as a comprehensive model 'to help
gardeners cope successfully with the often hard, if not always harsh,
growing conditions of the north'. In 1948, the Northern Horticultural
Society leased 40 acres of mixed woodland, pasture and arable land
from Harrogate Corporation for trial grounds; since then, the site
has been extended to 68 acres and includes examples of every type
of garden in which northern, or indeed any gardeners might be
interested. What makes it particularly relevant to the North is the
fact that it is high, exposed to the north-west wind, in an area of
heavy snowfall and with a high rainfall (average 27½in.). In
addition, the soil is heavy clay (a problem not confined to northern
areas) and very acid (pH 4.8–5.6).

Harlow Carr is above all a delightful place to visit: full of variety
and a constant pleasure to the eye. Part of the reason for its success
is the site itself, however exposed: a valley running from north-west
to south-east with a small stream at its foot. From the entrance you
can look down over pools, rock gardens and shrub beds and across
to the arboretum on the opposite hillside. As you explore further,
different features reveal themselves gradually and new vistas open.

The illustrated guide indicates an energetic approach—a descent
down the length of the Broad Walk, the central axis of the garden,
and a return by way of the lower and upper lawns before starting
on any detailed study. You may, however, content yourself with a
look down the Broad Walk to the focal point of a southern beech
(*Nothofagus obliqua*), and proceed straight to the display areas.

The first demonstration consists of a hedge and ground cover
display, useful for any gardener. Within a framework of lawson
cypress and beech are hedges of the daisy bush (*Olearia* x *haastii*),
variegated holly (*Ilex aquifolium*), gold Leyland cypress (x *Cupressocyparis leylandii* 'Castlewellan'), *Cotoneaster simonsii*, a gold
privet (*Ligustrum ovalifolium* 'Aureum') and a shrubby honeysuckle (*Lonicera nitida* 'Baggesen's Gold'). Ground cover includes
the blue spikes and wine red leaves of a bugle (*Ajuga reptans*
'Burgundy Glow'), the invasive bright yellow creeping Jenny or
moneywort (*Lysimachia nummularia*), a silver dwarf hebe (*H.
pinguifolia* 'Pagei') and the prostrate *Juniperus horizontalis*.
Nearby are beds of heaths and heathers, beds with shrubs needing
different types of pruning and displays of different clones.

The miniature rock gardens here are very attractive, with their
plantings matched to different types of stone. Mid-grey limestone
from the Forest of Dean shows off mauve thyme, pink dianthus and

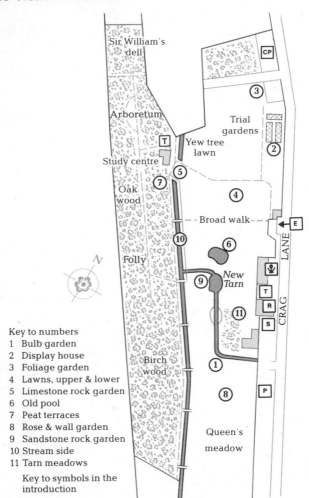

Key to numbers
1 Bulb garden
2 Display house
3 Foliage garden
4 Lawns, upper & lower
5 Limestone rock garden
6 Old pool
7 Peat terraces
8 Rose & wall garden
9 Sandstone rock garden
10 Stream side
11 Tarn meadows

Key to symbols in the
introduction

white and blue dwarf campanula; dark Westmorland slate makes
a striking background for a bright orange heath (*Erica carnea* 'Anne
Sparkes') and a purple sedum (*S. spathulifolium* 'Purpureum').
Nearby, silver-grey waterstone shows off the tiny mauve bells of
Parahebe catarractae 'Diffusa' and a blue juniper (*J. squamata*
'Blue Spray'). In an adjacent area, rock beds are combined with
planted stone troughs: in one, a 4ft high silver-blue cork fir (*Abies
lasiocarpa arizonica* 'Compacta') is well matched with yellow-
flowered hypericum and a mixture of heaths.

Nearby are silver foliage and Mediterranean beds, containing
some striking specimens: tall *Allium siculum*, a variety with drooping green and purple bell-shaped flowers teamed with a Corsican

rue; pink *Diascia rigescens* with delicate pink flowers and tiny sculptured leaves; and *Onopordum arabicum*, a grey-green, spiny-leaved cardoon with pink stems and burrs.

The cool greenhouse is crowded with exotic blossoms: the double purple bells of *Rhodochiton atrosanguineum*, the red/orange bells of an abutilon (*A. mulleri*) the tubular flowers of the Cape fuchsia (*Phygelius capensis*) and many others.

A Time Walk beside the greenhouse shows shrub and plant introductions from the 16C to the 20C; more could be added to indicate the vast expansion of plant discoveries in the 19C. Nearby, a small but charming rose garden has been laid out with a central path and arches. Here examples of the early rose families predominate. More modern hybrid musks, hybrid teas and climbers can also be found here, all successfully combined with tree peonies and shrubs in beds edged with mauve nepeta.

It is worth a slight detour to your right at this point to see the Foliage Garden, where there are some eye-catching associations: the bright lime-green honey locust (*Gleditsia triacanthos* 'Sunburst') providing a background for the grey-green foliage and white daisy flowers of an olearia and Bowles' golden grass (*Milium effusum* 'Aureum'); *Spiraea bumaldi* 'Gold Flame' combined with blue-green rue and a white-flowering tree heath; the cream and pink splashed leaves of a poplar (*Populus candicans* 'Aurora') set against red-fruiting, bronze-leaved *Berberis ottawensis* 'Superba' and gold-leaved *Philadelphus coronarius* 'Aureus'.

The Trial Gardens slope down hill from here. They include a comparison of different vegetables, a display of new vegetables, varieties of sweet pea and a demonstration of chemical tests on garden pests. There is also a Winter Garden (contributed by Bridgmere Garden World from Cheshire) which makes good use of foliage contrast, berried shrubs, winter-flowering plants and early spring bulbs.

At the foot of the slope, near the study centre in the old bath house, is the limestone rock garden, the stones donated by an RHS member. There are several outcrops, many crowned by conifers. We also noticed, in late summer, the bright orange flowers of an edelweiss (*Leontopodium sibiricum*), helianthemum 'Cerise Queen' and one of the tiny prostrate New Zealand burrs (*Acaena saccaticupula* 'Blue Haze'). A group of orange yellow and pink 'Harlow Carr' primulas showed up vividly against a dark yew. In spring this area is bright with crocus and narcissus, while in the autumn colchicum and schizostylis flourish. By the edge of the woodland are terraced peat beds, holding spectacular acers, including *A. shirasawanum* 'Aureum', its gold leaves contrasting with red *A. palmatum* 'Atropurpureum'. Behind are banks of rhododendrons and azaleas, vivid in the spring.

· You are now beside the pleasant, winding stream, whose banks are luxuriant with damp loving plants such as the bog arum (*Lysichiton americanus*); the umbrella leaves and hairy stems of *Gunnera tinctoria*; the multi-coloured trumpets of day lilies; abundant plantings of primula; deep red, pink and white astilbes; green, gold, blue and variegated hostas. There are clumps of bamboo, sturdy silver willow (*Salix lanata*) and many specimen small trees both coniferous and broad-leaved, including a weeping beech, swamp cypresses and the blue Atlas cedar *C. atlantica glauca*. This is a relaxing place to wander, between the vivid and varied gardens and the arboretum on your right.

From half-way along the Stream Garden, the Sandstone Garden stretches up the hill towards the Old Pool: among these rocks grow many striking acers and conifers and a multitude of rock plants such as the brilliant lithospermum 'Heavenly Blue'; tiny pink *Sedum hispanicum* and yellow-flowered variegated *Aubrieta deltoidia* 'Aurea Variegata'.

Above, a beautiful grouping of trees and shrubs has been set around the Old Pool, near Tarn Meadows, where a new heath and heather garden, with ericas, callunas and daboecias selected for year-round interest. Near here too are beds for hybrid tea and climbing roses.

For those with time to spare, there are woodland walks through the arboretum. At the furthest point of the Broad Walk you will find a folly—a classical portico transferred from a building in the the town centre and set down among the woods. Greek pillars and melancholy stone lions gleam among fine specimens of native and foreign trees.

There is far more to Harlow Carr Gardens than can be experienced in one visit. It is a place to return to many times and at all seasons of the year. In the 40 odd years of its life, it has flourished and matured on its challenging site, with the support of the local gardening community. Like the southern RHS garden at Wisley, it is both related to its area and wide in its appeal.

Newby Hall

ADDRESS AND TELEPHONE: The Estate Office, Newby Hall, Ripon, North Yorkshire HG4 5AE. Tel. Boroughbridge (0423) 322583

OWNERS: R.E.J. Compton, Esq

DIRECTIONS: between Ripon and Boroughbridge on the B6265, well signposted from the A1, Boroughbridge and Ripon. Public transport: bus from York to Ripon, stops in Skelton village (1 mile away). Alternatively, stop in either Boroughbridge or Ripon and take a taxi

OPENING TIMES: daily except Mon, but including all BH, 1 April to end of September, 11–5.30. House open Tues to Sun and BH Mon 12–5

ADMISSION: house and garden £4.50, OAPs £3.60, disabled/children £2.50; garden only £2.50, OAPs £2.30, disabled/children £1.80

CAR PARKING: yes

TOILETS: yes

REFRESHMENTS: café

SHOP: yes

DOGS: no, except in area adjoining picnic area

WHEELCHAIR ACCESS: yes. Toilets for the disabled: yes

PEAK MONTHS: June to August

NOTABLE FEATURES: a classic example of formal layout, enhanced by rare and beautiful trees and shrubs including the National Collection of cornus (dogwoods)

Designed over a period of 50 years, from 1921 onwards, by the late Major Edward Compton, and restored and replanted from 1977 by his son and daughter-in-law, Robin and Jane Compton, Newby has been considerably replanted in recent years and reduced from 40 acres to 25 and simplified for ease of maintenance, but remains one of England's notable gardens.

The original Victorian layout was haphazard and fragmented—two parterre gardens to the south and west of the house and the Statue Walk linking a kitchen garden to the south-east with an enormous rock garden (designed by Ellen Willmott) to the south-west. Major Compton's design gave the garden unity and a strong 'backbone'—a main axis of twin herbaceous borders, running at right angles to the Statue Walk, in a line south from the house down to the River Ure. A number of small separate gardens—Sylvia's garden, the rose garden, the autumn garden, circular garden, tropical garden, orchard gardens and white garden—provide variety and interest throughout the year.

Starting at the information pavilion and walking north towards the house, you soon arrive at the Statue Walk, which spans the garden from east to west. Planned by the Victorian architect William Burges, this walk is decorated with Venetian statues—effectively backed by a red *Prunus pissardii* hedge—and ornate curving stone seats at either end, one from Italy and one from Caen in Normandy. The Italian seat (with stone animals) is overhung by a magnificent copper beech. Irish yews and other conifers make an excellent backdrop.

Half-way along this walk, you join the garden's main axis: the house (south front) and lily pond appear directly above, and below, to your left, the huge sweep of the double herbaceous borders runs down to the river. Backed by a 6ft yew hedge, the borders are a splendid sight in mid summer. Well established viburnums provide solid resting points for the eye, and many other plants have reached an impressive height and size—delphiniums, thalictrum, eryngiums, achillea, mallow, monkshood, campanulas and towering clumps of yellow *Cephalaria gigantea*. The colours are gloriously mixed, with certain plants mirrored on either side for symmetry and recurring combinations and themes. Red and pink rose bushes appear at intervals all the way down and at the bottom are beds of white roses edged with pale yellow sisyrinchium. Glance to your right and left before crossing over the narrow garden railway track, which runs alongside the river. The little miniature railway is great fun for children and Newby is a favoured venue for local school outings.

Retracing your steps up towards the house, passing the rose garden entrance to your left and the autumn garden to your right, cross Statue Walk and turn left just below the lily pond for Sylvia's garden. Named for the present owner's mother, this spring and

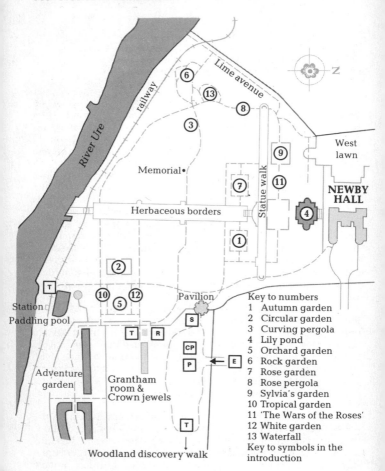

River Ure

railway

Lime avenue

⑥

⑬

⑧

③

Memorial•

⑨

⑪

Statue walk

West lawn

⑦

NEWBY HALL

Herbaceous borders

④

①

②

T

Station

Paddling pool

⑩ ⑤ ⑫

Pavilion

S

T R

Adventure garden

Grantham room & Crown jewels

CP

P ← E

Woodland discovery walk

T

Key to numbers
1 Autumn garden
2 Circular garden
3 Curving pergola
4 Lily pond
5 Orchard garden
6 Rock garden
7 Rose garden
8 Rose pergola
9 Sylvia's garden
10 Tropical garden
11 'The Wars of the Roses'
12 White garden
13 Waterfall
Key to symbols in the introduction

summer garden has been completely replanted in recent years by Mrs Jane Compton, and is now well stocked with foliage plants for year-round interest—including artemisias, sage and other herbs, and the silver-leaved alpine chrysanthemum *Tanacetum densum*.

The rose-lined approach, known as 'The Wars of the Roses', features the red rose of Lancaster, *Rosa gallica* 'Officinalis', and the white rose of York, *Rosa* 'Alba Semi-Plena', with the red and white striped *Rosa mundi* 'keeping the peace' between them. Japanese and weeping cherries blossom in spring, pale yellow and pink, and a group of splendid cedars—Lebanon, Deodar and *C. Atlantica glauca*—stand to the right.

The garden is a square surrounded by yew hedges, descending in shallow terraces, divided into paths and long planted beds, to four square beds and the central feature, an old Byzantine corn grinder. Symmetrical in architecture and planting, with the soft bright colours of its flowers and foliage and mellow brick and stone, Sylvia's garden is a very lovely sight from early spring all the way through summer. Tulips and gentians in spring are followed by a profusion of summer flowers and herbs.

Emerging from Sylvia's garden, you join the western end of Statue Walk; from here you can see a lime avenue, one of Newby's oldest features, possibly dating back to the early 18C. A straight pergola clothed with climbing and rambler roses and underplanted with alchemilla and peonies leads down from here to the rock garden; further to the south is a curving pergola, covered with laburnum, clematis and Japanese quinces.

The huge rock garden was designed by Ellen Willmott c 1900; it incorporates a waterfall, a stone bridge and a great many damp-loving plants. Near the curving pergola is a strange coffin-like object—in fact a Cheshire well head—and not far away an unusual memorial, commemorating the untimely deaths of six keen fox hunters, including Sir Charles Slingsby, in 1869. All were drowned in what has since become known as the Newby Ferry Disaster, while attempting to cross the flooded River Ure by boat in pursuit of a fox—the fox survived.

From the memorial, take the path to your right (south-west towards the river); then turn left where the paths meet for a magnificent vista across the borders, focussing on a huge copper beech. White-barked Himalayan birch (*Betula jacquemontii*) stand to your left and rhododendrons to your right. In spring, continue to the main borders, turn right for 50 yards and then left down the rhododendron walk; the small circular garden directly above is also worth visiting early in the year, being crammed with camellias, dwarf rhododendrons and, in the centre, *Magnolia stellata*.

A river walk takes you round the garden's outer circumference, above the railway and river; many splendid trees and shrubs are to be found here, including Japanese maples, a huge silver maple (*Acer saccharinum*) the Chilean flame tree (*Embothrium longifolium*) and a Scots pine blasted by lightning in 1930. Continue along the walk to reach the tropical garden, orchard gardens and white garden (leading to the cafeteria) or strike north again up between the herbaceous borders for a closer look at the rose and autumn gardens.

The sunken rose garden is surrounded by a copper beech hedge, strengthened with holly; a bold foil to four silver weeping pears, one at each inside corner, and old-fashioned shrub roses in many shades of pink, mauve and red. The roses are underplanted with many unusual plants, mainly blue or white. Two Italian oil jars dating from 1820 stand above the steps—an especially attractive feature.

The autumn garden—designed in 1939, when it replaced an old croquet lawn—balances the rose garden on the other side of the herbaceous borders. Profusely planted with buddleias, hydrangeas and fuchsias and shot through with fiery red hot pokers and yellow and white spikes of lysimachia, this garden positively radiates warmth and cheer as the weather grows colder. The wattle fence is covered with clematis, roses and honeysuckle, the central urn surrounded by purple, white and pink clary and lavender. Among the many eye-catching smaller plants are *Sedum maximum*

'Atropurpureum', with fleshy purple-red stems and leaves, and showy *Nepeta nervosa*, which bears blue flowers in dense spikes.

The tropical garden is planted in very English style, but with plants of bold and striking appearance, including large-leaved rheum and *Rodgersia podophylla*. A splendid collection of magnolias flanks the path, blossoming white, purple and pink in spring. Just before you reach the wrought iron gate, turn left into the orchard garden—a spacious area, thoughtfully designed and planted, with its central urn surrounded by clouds of silvery *Santolina incana* and graceful apple trees at intervals along the neat lawn. Here as elsewhere, boundaries have been subtly indicated with two different levels of grass, achieved by careful mowing—a less labour-intensive method than hedging. A white bench (from a design by William Kent) stands against the south-facing wall, backed by *Ceanothus impressus* and yellow *Rosa banksiae* 'Lutea'; further along the wall, *Carpenteria californica* displays its fragrant anemone-like white flowers from early to mid summer.

The White Garden, above, flanks a walk leading to the café area; it includes white rugosa and other roses and white delphiniums.

The cafeteria provides excellent refreshment in pleasant surroundings—or if you should feel in need of further exercise, there is always the Woodland Discovery Walk, through Bragget Wood.

Rievaulx Terrace

ADDRESS AND TELEPHONE: The Administrator, Rievaulx Terrace and Temples, Helmsley, North Yorkshire YO6 5LJ. Tel. Bilsdale (043 96) 340

OWNERS: The National Trust

DIRECTIONS: 2½ miles NW of Helmsley on B1257. Public transport: United bus 294 from Middlesbrough (passing close BR Middlesbrough), Fri only; occasional summer service from Middlesbrough, otherwise Scarborough and District 128 Scarborough to Helmsley, then 2½ miles

OPENING TIMES: 29 March to end October; daily 10.30–6 or dusk. Last admission 5.30

ADMISSION: £1.70, children 80p. Parties £1.50, children 70p

CAR PARKING: yes, at reception, also coach park 200yds away

TOILETS: yes

REFRESHMENTS: no

SHOP: yes, small

DOGS: yes, on lead

WHEELCHAIR ACCESS: yes, to terrace (not temples). Powered 'Runaround' available. Toilets for the disabled: yes, unadapted

NOTABLE FEATURES: ½ mile long grass-covered terrace, bordered by woodland; views; temples

This serpentine terrace, half a mile long, commands fine views over the North Yorkshire countryside and the distant hills, with Rievaulx

Abbey, a Cistercian ruin, in the foreground. The Picturesque movement and the paintings of Poussin, Claude and Salvator Rosa had brought views very much into fashion by the mid 18C, when Rievaulx was planned and constructed. The landscape of Italy had so much influenced styles of painting that painting in its turn began to influence the scenery—landscapes were now treated like pictures, to be skilfully framed and composed by artistic arrangement of trees etc.

Roman and Greek temples and rotundas were placed at strategic points to recall past civilisations and ideals, and genuine ruined buildings such as abbeys and chapels were also much in demand, for romantic atmosphere. One of the best examples is Fountains Abbey in North Yorkshire, used by John Aislabie as a magnificent scenic focal point for his huge landscaped estate, Studley Royal.

The main predecessor of Rievaulx was Duncombe Terrace nearby, a curved terrace overlooking the Rye Valley, with a temple at either end. This was laid out by Thomas Duncombe II, whose son, also called Thomas Duncombe, built Rievaulx terrace around 1758, possibly intending at one stage to link the two terraces by a 3-mile viaduct.

Although Duncombe terrace was remarkably informal for its date, Rievaulx, built 40 years later, is far more 'Natural' in style, with the emphasis on landscape rather than ornamental buildings. The Tuscan temple and Ionic temple are important landmarks (and described in detail in the guidebook) but they take second place to the gently serpentine walk, the fine trees and magnificent views. The National Trust bought Rievaulx from the Feversham (Duncombe) family in 1972. Rievaulx Abbey, acquired by the Duncombes in 1689, is now managed and opened to the public by English Heritage.

You approach the terrace by a woodland walk leading southwards from the entrance and emerging near the Tuscan temple. Much felling and replanting has been done in this area following outbreaks of Dutch elm disease and beech bark disease, but you can see plenty of oaks, beeches, sycamores, ash and newly planted larches and wildflowers such as bluebells, wood anemones and early purple orchids. Emerging from dank shady woodland onto the smooth lawned terrace, you immediately get a wonderful sense of spaciousness and a feeling of being 'on top of the world'. The terrace is very exposed, but the Tuscan temple offers a degree of shelter on windy or rainy days. Unfortunately visitors are not allowed inside, as the fragile floor is made up of original tiles from Rievaulx Abbey, but through the windows you can see the beautiful round ceiling, with its painting of a winged goddess.

Wooden seats are placed at intervals along the terrace, and behind is a marvellous backdrop of many-shaded hardwood trees, including variegated sycamore and rowan. These were originally mixed with flowering shrubs. The steep slope is well wooded, with viewpoints at intervals. The first of these is a view from the temple down to an 18C bridge (a reconstruction of an original medieval bridge) crossing the river Rye. Wild roses flourish on the rim of the precipice, and wild grasses on the slope, along with plentiful knapweed, harebells and clover. Cowslips, primroses, forget-me-nots and wild violets can be seen here in May.

The views continue as you progress along the terrace, until soon you catch your first glimpse of the magnificent abbey, with hills, woods and a head of moorland beyond. The church is seen at different angles from each clearing, until finally you reach the Ionic temple, and the steepest drop—and most breathtaking view—of all: here, to quote the guidebook, we look 'down, almost vertically, to the north transept of the Abbey, where the great length of the nave is at last apparent'.

Half-way along the terrace, note a pair of well-weathered 19C pedimented gate piers, marking the approach from Duncombe Park. This was the original entrance to the terrace for the Duncombe family and friends, who would have arrived by carriage to walk and picnic on the terrace.

The Ionic temple has antique shoe-cleaning implements outside and a very beautiful and ornate interior. Like the Tuscan temple, it was originally made entirely of York sandstone, soft and vulnerable to the elements, but the columns are now French stone. A guide can usually be found sitting inside, who will answer questions about the banqueting hall with its brilliant-coloured, intriguing paintings of goddesses and gods and scenes from mythology. 'Upon the whole, this elegant little room in respect of proportion and ornament, is the most pleasing one I remember to have seen in any temple', wrote Arthur Young, after his visit in the late 18C (*Six Months Tour of the North*, 1779–71). It certainly must have been a delightful place to banquet, while servants prepared food in the basement below. The basement now houses two exhibitions, one of Victorian photographs from the Duncombe family albums, the other on the formal terrace and its origins.

Ripley Castle

ADDRESS AND TELEPHONE: Ripley Castle, Ripley, near Harrogate, North Yorkshire. Tel. (0423) 770152

OWNER: Sir Thomas Ingilby, Bt

DIRECTIONS: from London M1 or A1, 4 hours. From Edinburgh A1, 3¼ hours. Motorway: M1, 18 miles S; M62, 20 miles S. Public transport: bus to Ripley, or take a Blueline taxi (Harrogate 503037)

OPENING TIMES: April to mid October, daily 11–5.30. Castle open at restricted times

ADMISSION: castle and gardens £2.75, children £1.25; gardens only £1, OAPs 75p, children 50p. Phone for group rates, details of guided tours and to book refreshments

CAR PARKING: yes

TOILETS: yes

REFRESHMENTS: café

SHOP: yes

DOGS: no

WHEELCHAIR ACCESS: yes. Toilets for the disabled: not up to disabled standard, but can be used

PEAK MONTHS: end of July and throughout August

NOTABLE FEATURES: herbaceous borders, walled garden, parkland

Home of the Ingilby family for over 600 years, Ripley Castle is a solid and peaceful edifice, built on a hill overlooking a Capability Brown landscaped park and two huge lakes. The grounds encompass extensive walled gardens and a wooded pleasure park.

Ripley village, which lies close by the castle, is interesting in itself. In the 1820s it was entirely rebuilt, on the orders of Sir William Amcotts Ingilby, after the style of a French village in Alsace-Lorraine. Sir William also drew up plans for the walled garden and laid out the adjacent pleasure grounds. Not all of Sir William's grand gestures and schemes were entirely successful—some, like the walled garden hothouses, he later greatly regretted.

From the west and north terraces of the castle, you get a splendid view of the Capability Brown park, with its gently sloping hills, lakes—one serpentine and one widely spreading—and clumps of trees set at artistic intervals. The cascade pours down to the north, focussing a long vista across the wider lake. Walk across the north terrace and down the steps to join the path leading round to the walled garden and pleasure grounds. Towering mature trees line the way, including yews, copper beech and variegated sycamore (*Acer pseudoplatanus* 'Leopoldii') and huge golden yews crowd near the walled garden entrance.

The walled garden covers 4 acres, surrounded by 9ft-high brick and stone walls and subdivided by walls and hedges. The larger area is a formal flower garden; other parts are devoted to vegetables, herbs and roses. The south-facing boundary wall was entirely covered, in Sir William's time, by garden rooms, two ranges of hothouses (each nearly 60 yds long) and the central orangery/palmhouse. The orangery remains, as does a stone gazebo at the far end and one range of hothouses, looking rather unbalanced—Sir William himself came in later life to dislike the hothouses and advised his successor to knock the whole lot down—'You would do well to upset my folly and houses, etc, and make a clearance of that stupid range of hothouses. I have often been about doing it, but like an Ass, at great cost I have maintained it …'.

Roses feature throughout the walled garden: hybrid teas in large circular beds on the lawn and blush pink climbers all along the inside entrance wall. The second lawn also features herbaceous plants: a raised stone-edged circular bed flowers through the summer in all shades of pink, red, blue, mauve and purple—salvias, knotweed, geraniums, astilbe, carnations and many others jostle each other for space here, with a great tangle of phlox in the centre. However, nothing can match the magnificence of the huge herbaceous borders, 6 yds deep and running the length of the garden beneath the hothouse wall—these borders, at least, Sir William had just cause to be proud. Prominent in mid summer are giant scabious (*Cephalaria gigantea*) with creamy yellow flowers on branching stems; also clumps of yellow achillea, blue delphiniums, pink sidalcea and bright pink lychnis. The high wall behind is hung with wisteria, flowering pale blue early in the year, and *Clematis tangutica* with yellow lantern flowers and fluffy seed heads. The thick writhing arms of another ancient wisteria bar the entrance to a gazebo in Greek architectural style at the far end of this wall.

The north-facing border on the opposite side of the garden is planted along more sombre lines, with shade-loving plants—hostas, hydrangeas, Solomon's seal and plentiful aruncus, rodgersias and podophyllums, but the picture is lightened by a silver eucalyptus, in the centre of the left-hand bed, underplanted with bright green striped grass and red cotinus and clusters of lilies—orange 'Enchantment' and pale *Lilium regale*. Also included in these borders are a number of interesting alpine plants—a speciality of David Woolveridge, the head gardener.

A surging sea of golden Irish yews makes an excellent focal point to the east, against dark yews and a young robinia, with a copper beech behind. The yews conceal an extraordinary fountain (now dry) of an upended boar's head in a huge circular basin. Another stouter robinia stands on the lawn, while to the west majestic dark yews form an arch over the central gateway into the vegetable, fruit and herb gardens.

Many ancient and still fruitful apple and pear trees are cultivated in this part of the garden—some grown from cuttings sent from Switzerland in the early 19C by a former owner (living in exile), Sir John Ingilby, others planted comparatively recently, in late Victorian times or this century. A great many varieties of pear flourish against the south-facing wall in the third section—'Louise Bonne of Jersey', 'Conference', 'William's Bon Chrétien', 'Doyenne de Comice' and many others.

Box-edged formal beds in the second section are thickly planted with herbs, notably sage, while huge clumps of fennel and lovage tower above the path. Collections of peonies (mostly double varieties, pink, red and white) and tall blue delphiniums feature in the surrounding beds. The central pergola stands in a direct line with the orangery/palmhouse; its well-weathered red brick supports are clothed with the bright pink rambler rose 'American Pillar' and another pale pink climbing rose, not identified. *Humulus lupulus* 'Aureus' rushes up either side of the entrance arch into the yews, golden yellow against dark green, and nearby the crimson glory vine (*Vitis coignetiae*) is trained up wooden supports, either side of the path. Beyond a hornbeam hedge to the east are plentiful old roses—mosses, bourbons, centifolias and rugosas.

For longer walks, and views over the valley and deer park, follow the central path through the orangery into the 8-acre Pleasure Grounds. Although rather overgrown and gloomy, these are lightened in late winter and early spring by thousands of snowdrops, followed by daffodils and bluebells and then in late spring by deciduous azaleas, brightly coloured and filling the air with delicious scent. The trees include sequoiadendrons, with soft red bark, and a mature specimen of *Abies koreana*, at least 100 years old, with violet-purple, cylindrical cones.

As you leave, note the unusual sight of a maidenhair tree (*Ginkgo biloba*), trained up the castle wall, and now at least 30ft high.

Sutton Park

ADDRESS AND TELEPHONE: Sutton on the Forest, York YO6 1DP. Tel. (0347) 810249

OWNER: Mrs Nancy Sheffield

DIRECTIONS: 8 miles N of York on the B1363. Public transport: bus service to Sutton Park daily except Sun. Tel. York (0904) 768262 for details

OPENING TIMES: gardens only, Easter to October 11–5.30, last admission 5. House open 1.30–5.30, Wed and BH Mon and also for private pre-booked parties

ADMISSION house and garden £2.50, OAPs £2, children £1.20, coaches £2; gardens only £1, OAPs 75p, children 50p

CAR PARKING: yes

TOILETS: yes

REFRESHMENTS: tea room

SHOP: yes

DOGS: no, not in garden, but allowed in woodland

WHEELCHAIR ACCESS: to garden but woodland would be difficult. Toilets for the disabled: no

PEAK MONTHS: mid June to end July

NOTABLE FEATURES: terraces on the south front of the house with beautiful and original planting; specimen trees, woodland walks to temple

It is a challenge to the capacities and power of any garden to visit it in bad weather. To view it during a heavy downpour but still be absorbed and intrigued must mean it has considerable fascination. This was our experience during a wet July at Sutton Park and it is a tribute to the garden's creators that the visit was, even at the time, such a positively enjoyable experience.

Sutton Park is an elegant Georgian house with a three-storey central block and two wings with balustrades terminated by pavilions. It was built in in 1730 by Thomas Atkinson, and looks out beyond its terraces to parkland which may have been landscaped by Capability Brown.

From the main, north entrance, a short drive curves between ancient cedars and yews to the house. On the lawns, shrub and climbing roses mingle with new plantings of yew, prunus and elaeagnus. This shrubbery shelters a Georgian ice house sited near the north wall whose beehive brick dome protrudes above the ground. Like an iceberg, some two thirds lie underground: it is perhaps 20ft from floor to ceiling and 12ft in diameter. It must have provided an efficient refrigeration system, except in the warmest summers.

On the west side of the house, roses and lavender flourish on a paved area, even though shaded by the shrubs and trees. Later in the year these are supplanted by tubs of blue hydrangeas, a foil to a nearby bed of bright dahlias. However, this is only a prelude to the three splendid terraces to the south, laid out in the 1960s by Percy Cane, and planted by Mrs Sheffield herself.

The south front of the house provides a perfect backdrop for the garden. The neat rectangles of window, the triangles of pediment, the twin rows of balustrade on the wings of the house are an effective foil to the luxuriant planting below. Against the house grow wisterias and jasmine and in the border bush honeysuckles show their pink tubular flowers, joined in late summer by the white cones of *Hydrangea grandiflora*. Pale aquilegia, pink heuchera and penstemon are interspersed with pink and white foxgloves and the dark leaves of red orach. From among the York paving stones spring the spiky leaves of sisyrinchium, with mounds of silver thyme and woolly leaves of *Stachys lanata*. Two stone vases spill over with pink geranium, silver helichrysum and blue lobelia.

Flanking the steps down to the centre terrace, two substantial blue-green conifers lend an attractive Mediterranean air to the scene. The silver and purple leaves of *Vitis vinifera* 'Brandt' spill over the steps towards a pair of stone vases filled with pelargoniums and helichrysum.

The lawns of the central terrace are divided into symmetrical island beds filled with a delicate and enchanting display of flowers and foliage. The centrepiece of the design is a large octagonal stone urn decorated with eight figures of bearded saints. Surrounding this striking centrepiece are eight beds: four L-shaped, two rectangular and two square, with a linked yet varied planting scheme.

Each of the corner beds contains a standard bush of *Pyrus salicifolia* 'Pendula'. Each bed also has standard bushes of species or polyantha roses in pink or yellow, and a choice of herbaceous plants in pink or mauve. In the main these are geranium, fuchsia, potentilla and penstemon, accompanied by spikes of iris and globes of allium. The edges are carpeted with with gold sage or marjoram, blue *Festuca glauca*, silver santolina or hebe.

The square and rectangular beds also display pink and yellow standard roses, and mirror the former planting scheme, though new elements are introduced, such as bright blue delphiniums, yellow *Phlomis fruticans*, the Jerusalem sage and pink dianthus.

This felicitous combination of geometrical shapes and profuse planting is enhanced by the borders at the back of the terrace: to the west, a double pink rose clambers over shrubs near the statue of a boy with grapes; nearby tall blue delphiniums and lupins are set off by orange crocosmia, silver eryngiums, mauve acanthus and lilies. There is a line of early flowering iris and an edging of silver sunloving plants: anaphalis, rosemary, lavender and artemisia.

On the west side we saw the tall plume poppy *Macleaya cordata* near blue campanula, red penstemon and the tiny silver pink heads of astrantia. This border ends with a group of fine trees : a cedar of Lebanon, with a companion blue Atlas cedar (*Cedrus atlantica glauca*) and a yew.

Ten pillars of *Chamaecyparis lawsoniana* 'Allumii' stand at the south front of the terrace; to either side of them are pink and yellow shrub roses, with a white species rose rampaging up into a larch tree.

If the centre terrace offers the richest of planting, the bottom terrace is effective in its simplicity: a rectangular lily pool set in lawns, with specimen shrubs and trees to either end, as well as a mature cedar of Lebanon. At the western end of this lawn we noted a group composed of a red weeping beech, the graceful spreading shape and delicately varied leaves of *Parrotia persica* and two shades of berberis. As we walked out the opposite way we noticed a Katsura tree (*Cercidiphyllum japonicum*) near a young ginkgo, a twisted willow (*Salix tortuosa*) and a blue chamaecyparis.

Further on we saw a circular pergola hung with the brilliant leaves of the golden hop *Humulus lupulus* 'Aureus', with a tulip tree and a spreading cedar nearby.

The rain still persisting, we decided not to follow the nature trail that day, there are walks in the woods, where there is a temple, for clearer weather. The garden would repay visiting more than once, preferably in finer weather, to appreciate all it has to offer.

Thorp Perrow Arboretum

ADDRESS AND TELEPHONE: R.A. Watson, Curator, Thorp Perrow Arboretum, Thorpe Perrow, Bedale, North Yorkshire DL8 2PR. Tel. Bedale (0677) 25323

OWNER: Sir John Ropner, Bt

DIRECTIONS: Thorp Perrow is 2½ miles S of Bedale, 4 miles from Leeming Bar on the A1. The arboretum entrance is off the Bedale to Well to Ripon road. No public transport

OPENING TIMES: daily throughout the year dawn to dusk. House not open

ADMISSION: £1.50, OAPs and children £1. Tours for parties by arrangement with the curator

CAR PARKING: yes

TOILETS: yes

REFRESHMENTS: no

SHOP: no

DOGS: yes, on lead

WHEELCHAIR ACCESS: about two-thirds of the arboretum is wheelchair accessible. Toilets for the disabled: no

PEAK MONTHS: May/early June for spring blossom, October/early November for autumn colour

NOTABLE FEATURES: fine collection of trees and shrubs, including many rare specimens; spring flowers; autumn colour

Praised by tree expert Alan Mitchell as a collection of European if not world importance, this Yorkshire arboretum was created single-handed by Colonel Sir Leonard Ropner, Bt, between 1931 and his death in 1977. Now the property of Sir John Ropner, Bt, it survives and flourishes through the well-informed care of Bob Watson, who took on the job of curator after the retirement of John Beach in 1990.

The arboretum contains over 1000 different species, including many rare and notable trees from all over the world. (Seeds are sent from the National Arboretum in the USA and from collectors in Mexico, China and Japan.) A programme of judicious thinning and pruning has greatly improved their chances of survival—Sir Leonard would never have any felling or thinning done in his lifetime—and replanting goes on all the time.

For full appreciation of the range and variety of trees here, you should if possible go on one of the excellent guided tours. However, the catalogue is comprehensive and detailed and includes a useful plan of the arboretum—divided for convenience into sections representing the main collections of the various genera. Confusingly, you have to work backwards through the alphabet, starting at the entrance between sections X and Z and walking north-east to section A, before crossing back in front of the house, round the lake and through Spring Wood. Daffodils flank every walk from mid March through to May: there are also primroses and bluebells in spring, followed by foxgloves, campions and forget-me-nots.

Starting then in section X, you can see around 60 different kinds of lilac, along with plums, cherries, birches and firs. The Japanese cherries make a lovely sight in spring; they include the dazzling great white cherry (prunus 'Tai Haku') with coppery red young leaves and brilliant white blossom. The Fuji cherry (*Prunus incisa*), another Japanese species, is smaller, with small white flowers which appear pink from a distance. The bird cherry (*Prunus padus*) produces drooping racemes of almond-scented white flowers in May, after the leaves. *Prunus subhirtella* 'Autumnalis' provides winter interest, flowering white between November and March.

A laburnum walk crosses this section. Here, besides the common laburnum, Scotch laburnum, weeping laburnum and golden laburnum, you can see the very unusual and interesting + *Laburnocytisus adamii*, Adam's laburnum, a hybrid between laburnum and broom, which displays both sorts of leaves—the laburnum leaves appear higher up. Not far behind this is a noble fir (*Abies procera*) from the western USA. This specimen grew from a rooted side branch, so the cones are borne very low—usually they are far more difficult to spot, hanging 50ft or more above ground. Nearby are various cotoneasters, the pink and orange fruiting spindle tree (*Euonymus europaeus*, very showy in winter) and *Rosa moyesii* which bears bright single red flowers in early and mid summer, followed by huge post office red hips. Young Korean firs (*Abies koreana*) produce masses of little violet-purple cones.

Walking north from here, you enter a peaceful glade (Y), well stocked with Japanese maples, which turn glorious colours in autumn, against a backdrop of green oaks, blue spruces and various forms of Lawson's cypress. The intricately cut leaves of *A. japonicum* 'Aconitifolium' change from bright green to clear yellow. *A. palmatum* 'Heptalobum Osakazuki' is acclaimed in the Hillier *Manual of Trees and Shrubs* as probably the most brilliant of all Japanese maples, with its green leaves, turning fiery scarlet in autumn, but it has many rivals, not least the brilliant *A. japonicum* 'Vitifolium'. *A. j.* 'Aureum' remains a soft yellow all through the seasons. Here too is *A. palmatum* 'Ribesifolium', rather curious in shape, upright with a broad crown and dark green, deeply cut leaves, turning gold in autumn.

Several varieties of cedars can be seen in this area, including the weeping form of the Mount Atlas cedar, *C. atlantica* 'Pendula' (best planted at the top of a bank and allowed to ramble down) and a rare Cyprian cedar, *Cedrus brevifolia*. There are magnolias too, notably *Magnolia officinalis biloba*, a very rare tree, with large, pale green, deeply indented leaves, and pale, strongly fragrant flowers with a purple centre. This tree has been used in medicine by the Chinese for centuries: it was thought lost until rediscovered growing in one Chinese temple garden. Hilliers got seed from the Botanic Garden, Lusham, in 1936. Other magnolias in this area were grown from seed by John Beach.

From the Monument, near the western boundary of the arboretum, you can look down a long avenue, formerly of stately elms (killed by Dutch Elm disease) and now replanted with young tulip trees. The Monument, with its stone pillars and wrought iron roof, is an attractive memorial to Sir Leonard, and is inscribed with a fitting tribute, 'If you seek his monument, look around' (translated from the Latin of Sir Christopher Wren's memorial in St Paul's Cathedral). To your left is an avenue of huge cypresses—a photo of 1931 shows these when they were about 1ft high. You are now in section W. The Japanese cherries in this area have passed their best years and will soon be replaced.

Taking the Wiggly Waggly Walk north from the Monument, you enter section V. Note the Mexican white pine (*Pinus ayacahuite*) with its long thin curved cones, which open and shed seed while still on the tree. This tree is surviving very well in Yorkshire conditions, although it normally grows best in the south and west. Beware of picking up the cones—they are smeared with white sticky resin.

Rare digger pines (*Pinus sabiniana*) from California can be seen nearby—native Americans used to gather their large edible seeds, to store for the winter. The digger pine is related to the big-cone pine (*Pinus coulteri*), which also grows in this area, along with Corsican pines, Crimean or 'church organ' pines, Western yellow pines, limber pines, maritime pines and many other types; and the Weymouth pine (*Pinus strobus*), so named after Lord Weymouth, who introduced it from eastern North America in the early 1700s. The British Navy favoured this tree, with its straight tall trunks, for ships' masts, and marked huge numbers of young trees for cutting, so that American settlers with considerable resentment had to plough around them. The innocent Weymouth pine was thus one of the main causes of the American War of Independence!

Crab apples also flourish here in great variety, including the Siberian crab (*Malus baccata*), rare Chinese crabs (*Malus hupehensis*), Japanese crabs (*Malus floribunda*) and the very rare and distinctive *Malus trilobata* from the eastern Mediterranean, with white flowers, yellow fruits and maple-like, deeply lobed leaves, a sheet of port wine red in early November. *Malus kansuensis* from western China turns butter yellow in autumn and its little currant-like fruits turn from translucent white to pink.

A row of witch-hazels runs up to the east (and section V), backed by snowdrop trees (*Halesia monticola*). In late May/early June, the latter produce snowdrop-like flowers on naked branches, followed by woody green, winged fruits. Further along the path is a rarely seen specimen of the tree mallow *Hoheria glabrata*: free-flowering but very tender, this has been cut down to the ground three times in nine years because of frost damage. Next to it is *Holodiscus discolor*, with long white sweet-smelling flower panicles like bunches of lace in mid summer (July) and just along from this, the Judas tree (*Cercis siliquastrum*), a great rarity in the north.

You now arrive at the top of the cherry avenue. Although the Japanese cherries here are reaching the end of their lifetime, they are fortunately interplanted with flowering crabs (malus spp). Nearby is a small wood of ancient beech trees—the ground here is a mass of bluebells in spring, followed by forget-me-nots. In the background (section S) is a collection of 42 different kinds of Lawson's cypress (*Chamaecyparis lawsoniana*), all planted at the same time (1939), so you can observe their relative rates and different habits of growth.

Areas N, O and P are known as the Autumn Bays, having been planted mainly for autumn colour effect. Scarlet oaks, Chinese rowans, purple-leaved plums, yellow-woods and blue birches can all be found here, and even common golden privet is used to amazing effect. Paper-bark and snake-bark maples turn brilliant colours in autumn and their bark is fascinating in all seasons. The Persian ironwood (*Parrotia persica*) turns crimson and gold, above flaking bark.

A long avenue of limes leads up to the north. This boasts 19 species and varieties of lime and one or two are the biggest of their kind in Britain. The very rare Mongolian lime (*Tilia mongolica*) has grown to unusual height, at least 70ft, with an elegant, open crown and attractive, delicate, ivy-like foliage.

Following the path leading off north-east between sections M and J, you pass a medlar, quinces (with lemon yellow, huge fruits) and maples, with a collection of walnuts beyond. In a clearing to your left is the Caucasian wing-nut (*Pterocarya fraxinifolia*), a handsome specimen, and further on a huge cricket-bat willow (*Salix alba* 'Caerulea'). Beyond the broad walk, you can see the poplar avenue, where the handsome poplar 'North-west', planted in 1953 and now about 100ft high, stands between an American balsam poplar and a European black poplar. To your right, you may spot an unusual beech (*Fagus sylvatica* 'Rotundifolia'), with small rounded brown leaves, the size and colour of an old penny.

Now you join the broad walk, one of six avenues which converge on a central grass circle and the majestic Jubilee oak (sown in situ in 1935). (One more avenue is shown on the map, but has been left unmown.) In section A, to the north, are rare hazels, including the Chinese hazel (*Corylus chinensis*) and the Turkish hazel (*Corylus colurna*), also the varnish tree (*Rhus verniciflua*), which you should avoid touching or it may give you a bad rash—it belongs to the same family as poison ivy. In section B are beeches, including handsome *Nothofagus obliqua* from Chile, yews and sweet chest-nuts, and section C features junipers, rowans, whitebeams and rare thorns. The 'white walk' in section C is stocked with a fine collection of viburnums, besides other white-flowered or pale-leaved/barked shrubs and trees.

Many rare sorbus species are planted here too, such as the service tree (*Sorbus domestica*)—from south-eastern Europe although it was reckoned native British for 300 years—*Sorbus bristolensis*, which only grows wild in the Avon Gorge, Bristol, and the extremely rare *Sorbus keissleri*. *Sorbus prattii* is notable for its masses of pure white, glistening berries, and *Sorbus vilmorinii* for its fern-like leaves, which turn a multitude of brilliant colours in autumn—this tree colours even as a young seedling.

Spring Wood spans a sizeable area beneath the lake and the house. This is ancient woodland, now planted with a very wide variety of trees, both native and exotic. Rhododendrons and azaleas have been tried here, but failed to flourish in the alkaline soil. Next to a Hungarian oak (*Quercus frainetto*) with huge leaves grows *Cercidiphyllum japonicum*, which never colours the same two years running. Near the lake is sorbus 'Joseph Rock', which bears lemon yellow berries and colours coral pink to red in autumn.

Finally, on your way back to the entrance and car park, you can admire the shimmering silver, white and gold foliage plants in section Z, the silver glade.

WEST YORKSHIRE

Bramham Park

ADDRESS AND TELEPHONE: Wetherby, West Yorkshire LS23 6ND. Tel. Boston Spa (0937) 844265

OWNERS: Mr and Mrs George Lane Fox

DIRECTIONS: main drive opens off A1 travelling N—entry signposted after crossing over the A64. Terrylug entrance off Leeds to Thorner to Bramham road. Public transport: take the Leeds to Wetherby bus 41 from market bus station, Leeds

OPENING TIMES: house and gardens, mid June to end August, Sun, Tues, Wed and Thurs. Gardens only, Easter weekend and Spring BH (Sat to Mon)

ADMISSION: house and gardens £2, OAPs £1.50, children £1; gardens only £1.50, OAPs £1, children 50p. Reduced admission for parties of 20 or more; contact the house opening manager, estate office

CAR PARKING: yes

TOILETS: yes

REFRESHMENTS: no (picnics allowed in grounds)

SHOP: no

DOGS: on lead only

WHEELCHAIR ACCESS: yes, to most of formal gardens. Toilets for the disabled: yes

PEAK MONTHS: June and July

NOTABLE FEATURES: unspoilt early 18C formal gardens laid out in the style of Le Nôtre: enclosed *allées*, long vistas, water gardens, classical temples, woodland rides designed as part of total garden plan

Britain is fortunate in having many fine examples of 18C landscape gardens, created by designers such as William Kent and Lancelot

Brown and preserved to a great extent as they were originally conceived. Much rarer are examples of the earlier formal gardens against which the landscape gardeners reacted and many of which they were instrumental in destroying. Some Tudor knot gardens and 17C parterres have been carefully recreated on their original sites using contemporary plants but it is very unusual to discover a complete early 18C formal garden that reproduces the long straight walks and symmetrical water gardens of late 17C taste, in the French style. One of these few is Bramham Park in Yorkshire, which is said to draw its inspiration from the work of Le Nôtre, creator of the gardens at Versailles. Bramham now belongs to the Lane Fox family, who open it to the public for a part of the summer.

As with Studley Royal, an inspired and determined owner was responsible for the overall design. Robert Benson, the son of a self-made man who had flourished under the Commonwealth, himself rose to be Chancellor of the Exchequer after the Restoration. He was created Lord Bingley on becoming Ambassador to Madrid and later became Treasurer to King George II's household.

Around 1699–1700, he began to build Bramham House, which remains today much the same building that he planned, although it was badly damaged by fire in 1828 and stood empty for some years. No professional architect is associated with it, so it seems likely that Benson, a recognised architectural expert and adviser, designed both house and gardens. Owing either to the preferences of various succeeding members of the family, or to their collective indifference, the gardens were left alone, the original grand design allowed to remain intact.

Bramham Park (again like Studley Royal) was created just as 'irregularity' in garden design was beginning to encroach on strict formality. One indication of this change is that the main axis of the garden does not branch out from the house, but cuts across the south west front. As you emerge through a flagged hall (where a hospitable open fire burns on the colder days in summer) you are momentarily at a loss as to which way to go. Not for long however, for the rose garden, created out of the original parterre, is in sight. Eight yew cones map out the beds of red, pink and yellow hybrid tea bushes: Peace, Apricot Silk, Beauté and Blessings. At the far end of the parterre a dragon's head is set into the wall—probably once the fountainhead of a cascade. Now rock plants cover a mound beneath and urns filled with pelargoniums stand on the wall behind. In the spring, the lawns stretching beyond and to either side of the parterre are flooded with daffodils.

It would take several hours to see everything in this garden, but a number of short cuts can be taken. The garden guide recommends you to begin by turning north-east into the Broad Walk and proceeding down it to the chapel, actually an Ionic temple designed by Paine between 1750 and 1762, and only consecrated in the earlier part of this century. From the chapel you can gaze over distant ponds and cascades, and beyond the garden proper to the Black Fen pleasure grounds, and the distant obelisk, three quarters of a mile away.

You now turn away from the Broad Walk down a grass avenue, between impressive beech hedges, clipped as smooth as walls. These hedges are a feature throughout the gardens, sometimes as high as 20ft. The first *allée* is a secluded area, designed as a private retreat for members of the household and their friends. At the next 'crossroads' you can turn right to the North Terrace, between massive beech trees and look out over the fields towards the Terry Lug gate. Many beeches fell in this exposed corner during the 1962 gales. To the left is the Queen's (Queen Anne's) Hollow, where springs once rose to fill the waterfall into the parterre/rose garden. It is now a pleasant open meadow, newly planted with shrubs, species roses and bulbs.

The next focal point of the enclosed *allée* is a stone nymph standing in the centre of a diamond shaped hedged 'salon'. The *allée* at this point is rather gloomy and dark, and it is a relief when you come to a five-way crossroads marked by a stone urn with carved heads of the four seasons. From here you can look towards the distant cascades of the water garden, or along to the 'T' pond. Thus lured on, but not cutting corners, we sped along, under threat of rain, to an open temple where we could sit in shelter looking down the Quarter Mile Walk in the direction of the house.

It is interesting to speculate whether Robert Benson and his friends planned their walks according to the seriousness of the matters under discussion. A full-scale political debate might be held on one of the longer expeditions, perhaps with a pause for refreshment brought by a servant to the temple. If still half-way through the argument, they could then have continued on around the periphery to a semicircular ha-ha wall looking out over the fields to the south, near the foot of the 'T' pond. Here there is an opportunity to turn northwards between newly planted woodland along the long stretch of the 'T' pond to its shorter crosspiece. At this point you can look back to the Four Faces urn or in the other direction to the Lead Lads' temple in the Pleasure Grounds. At least, so said the guidebook—our view in this direction was rather obscured by branches. We had been much impressed by this stage, however, not only by Benson's well-integrated overall design and the many vistas which it affords but by the faithful way in which most of his intended effects have been preserved.

Having now reached open meadowland, you can explore among young magnolia and ilex to find the family dog memorials: from a miniature 19C obelisk dedicated to Jet and Daisy to stone lettering marking the grave of Wizza, the 'faithful and beloved friend' of the Lane Fox family from 1939 to 1952. Nearby stands the Octagon, a 'Gothic' temple once used as a summerhouse and still furnished with 18C stools and a table. Honeysuckle and roses clamber over the mellow limestone.

A short walk over lawns takes you to the Obelisk Ponds and Cascades, one of the garden's main features. Here a dragon's mouth spews water into a semicircular pool; this semicircle feeds the main rectangular pool, which in its turn empties into a wide cascade. A second set of dragon's heads, pools and cascades, drops down the steep hill leading out of the garden proper in the direction of the obelisk. At the time we visited there were no cascades in the direction of the house, but it looked as though these might be restored in future. This is a delightful place to sit in summer, with the sound of the water and fine views in every direction, and horses grazing peacefully in the nearby fields.

You now have to decide whether you are energetic enough to tackle the pleasure grounds. If so, you should remember their other name of Black Fen and take a pair of stout waterproof shoes or boots in all but the driest weather. Descending the cascade steps you follow a track through open fields which continues the line of the Broad Walk. The woods are enclosed by a ha-ha and stone wall but there are gates to give access to the Round House, a temple probably modelled by William Paine on William Kent's design for the temple of Ancient Virtue at Stowe. Cedars of Lebanon flank the temple.

Beyond the temple, a *patte d'oie* of five rides fans out through the woods. The Weymouth ride, rather boggy at the time of our visit, leads to the temple of 'Leod Lud' or Lead Lads' temple. Disappointingly, there are now no lads and the temple itself has fallen into some disrepair.

The determined visitor can now walk on round the periphery of the wood along Lord Bingley's Walk, where new trees are being planted, but deciding, on a wet summer's day, that the ground conditions were against us, we opted to head for the obelisk along the Douglas Fir Ride. This turned out to be almost impassible because of mud and undergrowth; the weather is beyond control, but some woodland clearing in most of the rides would have helped us to identify the drier areas.

As we neared the obelisk, we were able to see the remains of the original arboretum: yews, pines and a monkey puzzle. The obelisk itself is a memorial to 36-year-old Robert Fox Lane, son of 'George Fox Lane, and Harriet Benson his wife ... heir to Herbert Benson, Lord Bingley' who died in 1768 and whose memory is 'worthy to be revered by Posterity'. From the obelisk, 10 rides branch out into the woods, each originally planted with one particular species of tree, but now a mixture of oak, ash, beech, birch lime and sycamore. Bearing in mind the conditions underfoot, we headed back across the field path, to the cascades.

It took some searching past the cascades, to the left of the Broad Walk, to discover the last architectural feature, the folly. After several false starts we slipped through a narrow gate in the beech hedges, coming suddenly, across an aged tennis court, in sight of the folly, which turned out to be another, larger, Gothic summer-house. This has apparently been used within living memory for the family to enjoy meals brought out by the servants from the house. The enclosed area has a somewhat romantic air, confined as it is within its high beech hedges.

Approaching the exit (through the house), we came across a well designed and tended herbaceous border, with a circular lily pond and fish fountain in the centre. Delphiniums and tall blue eryngiums back the beds, with climbing roses on supports and two daturas dangling their yellow trumpet heads. In front of them achillea, astilbe and heleniums make bold groups of colour, with silvery *Stachys lanata*, artemisia and anaphalis providing an edging carpet for pink geraniums. It was an enjoyable reminder of present day planting skills, as were the rock plants growing attractively among the paving stones in the front courtyard, which you cross to leave the garden.

For those willing to bring their own supplies, picnics are allowed in the grounds, and a whole day might be spent here exploring the formal mown *allées*, admiring the water gardens and browsing the more unpredictable tracks of the pleasure grounds. It would take many hours fully to appreciate the variety of sights line and vistas which Robert Benson conceived and which have so happily remained exactly where he planned they should be.

Harewood House

ADDRESS AND TELEPHONE: Harewood Estate Office, Harewood, Leeds, West Yorkshire LS17 9LQ. Tel. (0532) 886225

OWNERS: The Earl and Countess of Harewood

DIRECTIONS: on the main A61 road between Harrogate and Leeds; easily reached from the A1, M1, M62 and M18

OPENING TIMES: April to October, daily from 10am. Sun in February, March and November. House also open

ADMISSION: house, garden and bird garden £5, children £2.50; garden only £2, children £1. Various admission Coach parties and guided tours by prior arrangement

CAR PARKING: yes

TOILETS: yes

REFRESHMENTS: café

SHOP: yes

DOGS: yes, on lead

WHEELCHAIR ACCESS: yes. Toilets for the disabled: yes

PEAK MONTHS. May to October

NOTABLE FEATURES: Capability Brown landscaped hills and lake—terraces below south front of house, woodland walks, rock and rose gardens, bird sanctuary

In his foreword to the Harewood House guide, Lord Harewood, the 7th Earl, acknowledges that the estate can only be maintained by a sizeable portion of public money, as well as a considerable amount of his own. Like many another owner of a stately home, he is in the business of marketing his assets to survive, and must attract enough interest to make the project viable.

Lord Harewood started his venture with some strong advantages, including a house to which Robert Adam contributed important elements of design, modifying John Carr's Palladian design with his own lighter neo-classical contributions. Much of the furniture is by Chippendale and there are notable works of art. For our purposes, however, the third genius of the place, Capability Brown, who worked for nine years to create a 'natural' landscape of hills, lake and woodland, is of most importance.

It is reassuring to discover that the original view over valley, lake and hills from the south front of the house has not been meddled with by man, although it has been ravaged by nature: in 1962 gales destroyed over 20,000 trees throughout the estate. Replanting over

The rock garden at Harewood House. (T.C. Photography)

26 years has restored the woodlands, if not to what they were before, to a very satisfactory state, and when you look out over the serene and graceful landscape, you still see the view that Brown planned for Edwin Lascelles in 1772.

The balustraded terrace gardens in the front of the house, built in 1840, are also well laid out and planted. When we visited in July the stone baskets along the south front were replete with dahlias and ageratum. On the main, centre, terrace, a modern black/bronze statue of Orpheus carrying a leopard cub stands in the centre of the main pool, woven around with a parterre of box scrolls on gravel. To either side lie star-shaped beds, planted urns, and stone statues of playing children.

This terrace is backed by a lengthy herbaceous border of drought-tolerant plants, designed to show blue in June, pink in July and a mixture from then on.

From the Archery Border an enormous *Eucryphia* x *nymansensis* 'Nymansay' pushes its branches over the balustrade, its profuse white flowers scenting the air in late summer. Here too are the fan-leaved maidenhair tree (*Ginkgo biloba*), a bright blue early-flowering *Ceanothus* x *veitchianus*, a butter-yellow *Fremontodendron californicum* and a wisteria, besides delphiniums, roses, and lilies. Below in the meadow graze St Kilda sheep.

In 1947, after the death of the 6th Earl, 20,000 acres of the estate had to be sold off to meet £1,000,000 of estate duty. There still remain 7000 acres, however, of which 75 acres are open to the public. You must be persistent and enterprising if you want to explore the lake and its surrounding woodland, the rock and water gardens and the promised but elusive rose garden, as there is a distinct lack of clear directions. Harewood House likes to let its visitors 'discover' the garden for themselves. Opposite the playground for children is a hinged gate to a leafy path.

A variety of broad-leaved and coniferous trees can be seen in the woodland: oak, beech, yew, larch, chestnut and many more. A white climbing rose, displayed on a dark Irish yew and the late-flowering white rhododendron 'Polar Bear' caught our attention. There are newly planted specimen trees and shrubs: round-leaved *Cercidiphyllum japonicum* 'Katsura' colours brilliantly in autumn, as does the subtle and elegant *Parrotia persica*. Between purple and variegated acer and fastigiate beech you can catch glimpses of the green lake below. The wood is conveniently furnished with roofed shelters, where you can sit in peace, safe from the inevitable summer showers. Swamp cypresses grow close to the the water, unmistakable with their near-conical shapes and knobbly roots.

On reaching the head of the lake, overhung by willows, you are rewarded with a long view back towards the house and the bird gardens. Rhododendrons edge the lake, reflecting brightly in the water in spring. The Harewood collection of rhododendrons is now an interesting mixture of hybrids and species plants from the wild, which have all been catalogued by the head gardener. Here the river leaves the lake and cascades down under a wooden bridge into a lush valley. Tall silver willows and oak thrust upwards to the light.

Do not be deterred by the continuing lack of directions, for it is worth pursuing the path through the woods on the far side of the lake. Apart from many varieties of chaemaecyparis and rhododendron, we noticed the variegated green and cream poplar *P. candicans* 'Aurora', a striking red acer (*A. palmatum* 'Bloodgood') and a blue pine, underplanted with pink polygonum. The wood is in excellent order and full of new planting.

You are now heading towards the Bothy, a pleasant rustic brick house with its own green and garden, which used to be occupied by unmarried gardeners on the estate. There are beds of old fashioned roses, in beds edged with black stone, backed by a stone wall, a miniature temple and a seat with classic frieze. Among the rose bushes we saw the gallicas 'Belle de Crécy' (cerise), the crimson and white striped 'Rosa Mundi' (*R. gallica versicolor*) and the maroon 'Tuscany Superb'. The walled garden was shut, but we were able to wander along the shore of this secluded part of the lake, the only visitors within sight.

This is a good point at which to retrace your steps round the lake. In the stable courtyard there is a tea room, where you can sit either indoors or at tables in the open air.

Temple Newsam

ADDRESS AND TELEPHONE: Parks Department, Leeds City Council, Selectapost 10, 19 Wellington Street, Leeds LS1 4DG. Tel. (0532) 463504 or 463000

OWNERS: Leeds City Council

DIRECTIONS: signposted off the A63 Selby Road, 5 miles E Leeds Centre. Public transport: bus 47 from City Square, Leeds

OPENING TIMES: daily, dawn to dusk. Different times for house and farm

ADMISSION: free

CAR PARKING: yes

TOILETS: yes

REFRESHMENTS: café

SHOP: yes

DOGS: yes, under control

WHEELCHAIR ACCESS: yes. Toilets for the disabled: yes

PEAK MONTHS: May to October

NOTABLE FEATURES: National Collections of phlox and asters. The largest municipally owned park in Europe

This huge 1000-acre estate belongs to the City of Leeds and is deservedly popular with both local people and tourists. Besides its extensive gardens, it has a Home Farm, the largest rare breed centre in England—with cattle, pigs, sheep, horses, goats, ducks, geese and turkeys—golf courses and woodland areas. Yet however many people come, Temple Newsam never seems crowded—the wide green lawns and open parkland (landscaped by Capability Brown) always give a sense of openness and freedom.

The large Tudor mansion dates from about 1500, but the estate goes back to Saxon times. Recorded as NEUHUSU ('new houses') in the Domesday Book of 1086, it was held by Norman families after the Conquest and given in about 1160 to the Knights Templar, an order of religious knights who protected pilgrims (hence the name 'Temple'). The Knights Templar's cross can still be seen in various places on the estate, set in paving and displayed on gates.

In its turbulent history, Temple Newsam has seen several forced changes of ownership. Henry VIII seized it from Thomas Darcy in 1537, and beheaded Darcy for treason at the Tower of London. In 1544 it was granted to Margaret Douglas and her husband Matthew Stuart, 4th Earl of Lennox, whose son Henry Lord Darnley unwisely married Mary Queen of Scots. Queen Elizabeth I confiscated Temple Newsam in 1565 and it remained crown property until restored by King James (son of Mary and Darnley) to Ludovick, Duke of Lennox. In 1622 it was sold to Sir Arthur Ingram, a financier who owned considerable property in Yorkshire, and the gardens grew and developed from this period onwards.

In the 18C, Temple Newsam's formal gardens were swept away in favour of natural landscaping. William Etty of York was employed by Edward Ingram, 4th Viscount Irwin, between 1710 and 1715, to construct the East Avenue, with three artificial lakes and cascades (now silted up) and ornamental bridges. Plantations of oak, elm and beech were established in the park around this period and fish and swans introduced to the lakes.

Capability Brown drew up new landscape plans for Temple Newsam in 1762 and 1770. Some—although by no means all—of Brown's ideas were adopted, such as the ha-ha or broken wall, parts of which still survive, and the Little Temple on the hillside. Much of Brown's work to the south-east has been destroyed in this century by open-cast mining.

The rhododendron walk is a spectacle of colour in late spring, leading from below the house and home farm to sloping lawns and the lakes. On your way down, note the magnificent iron Sphinx Gates to your left—based on Lord Burlington's design for Chiswick House, these were erected by Brown in 1768. Beyond the ha-ha is a stretch of azaleas, with young ginkgos at intervals; and beyond the azaleas, a wild grassy area flooded with daffodils in early spring. Specimen trees grace the lawns, including many mature conifers. Rhododendrons and azaleas overhang the lake, casting brilliant reflections in the water. The lakeside verges are thickly planted with hostas, gunnera, astilbes, primulas and other moisture-lovers, beneath swamp cypresses and willows.

Crossing a wooded bridge over the lake, follow a steep path upwards through woodland to the old kitchen gardens, now completely replanted as modern rose gardens, with display glass-houses along the top south-facing wall. The garden itself is on a steep incline—difficult but not impossible for wheelchairs. Note the Knights Templar's cross set in the central path. Splendid herbaceous borders line all four walls, a magnificent sight in mid summer. In the very deep south-facing border you can see enormous clumps of plume poppies (*Macleaya microcarpa*, pale coral), eryngiums and campanulas and many others; while the north-facing border, far below, is brightened in mid summer by delphiniums, sweet peas, acid yellow *Thalictrum speciosissimum* and scarlet *Lychnis chalcedonica*.

The lean-to glasshouses are very well stocked and maintained to the highest standards by Leeds City Council. Wonderful fuchsias are trained across the inside roof—including the lovely 'Florence Turner' with pale purple sepals and deep pink petals—and pelargoniums grow 10–15ft up the wall. Many tender and semi-hardy plants flourish here under glass, including plumbago (cape leadwort), the semi-hardy South African climber with panicles of pale blue primrose-shaped flowers; showy *Bougainvillea glabra* with bright purple bracts and sweetly scented Chinese jasmine (*Jasminum polyanthum*). Set in the paving is a huge bottlebrush (*Callistemon citrinus*) with deliciously lemon-scented leaves and bright crimson flowers borne in distinctive bottlebrush-shaped clusters; also the Swiss cheese plant, *Monstera deliciosa*, which has large holes in its huge shiny leaves, to let the tropical rain through.

One section of the glasshouses is entirely devoted to different kinds of ivy, trained up pillars; and the next 'room' along features an impressive variety of cacti.

More display areas can be found just outside the kitchen garden walls—the phlox and delphinium gardens to the south and east. These are only open in the early afternoon (1–3) from Monday to Friday. Among the many spectacular varieties of border phlox are amethyst-blue 'Hampton Court', mauve dark-eyed 'Fairy's Petticoat' and one pink specimen oddly labelled 'Blue Lagoon'. Even more dazzling in mid summer are the massed ranks of towering delphiniums ascending the eastern slope—bright blue 'Pericles' and 'Loch Leven', pale cream 'Sungleam', mauve 'Garden Party', white 'Olive Poppleton', mulberry-pink 'Ruby' and many others.

Retracing your steps to the house, you have a choice of pleasures to explore. An unusual brick maze, recently created, lies to the east, a formal garden to the south and a modern herb garden, pleached lime tree tunnel and lily ponds to the west. The south garden was redesigned and replanted in 1977, although you can still see the remains of a Tudor mound in the south-west corner and cast iron fountains and urns dating from Victorian times. The design incorporates clipped yews, laburnum walkways and a hornbeam stilt hedge and box-edged flower beds filled with bedding plants. These beds repeat the shape of the fountain pool, a square within four semicircles.

The west garden was at one time a bowling green, according to Kip's engraving of 1699. This area is especially pleasant on a hot day, with its pleached lime tree tunnel, shady and cool, and rectangular brick-edged lily ponds, crossed by wise stepping stones. The neat herb garden includes a springy camomile lawn (*Anthemis nobilis* 'Treneague') and a camomile seat—the ideal place to sit and rest.

SHORTER DESCRIPTIONS

AVON

Bath Botanical Gardens

ADDRESS AND TELEPHONE: Royal Victoria Park, Bath. Managed by Bath City Council, Parks Section, 15A Milsom Street, Bath BA1 1DE. Tel. (0225) 448433

DIRECTIONS: within the Royal Victoria Park, N of A431 in Bath, at the junction of Marlborough Road and Upper Bristol Road. Public Transport: BR to Bath; bus to Victoria Park

OPENING TIMES: 9am until dusk throughout the year, including Christmas Day and Boxing Day

ADMISSION: free

Wheelchair access and toilets for the disabled in main park. Dogs on short lead

Bath Botanical Gardens provide 7 acres of peace within the Royal Victoria Park, in the west part of the city. Within this relatively small area, you can see a remarkable number of specimen trees, shrubs and flowering plants.

The gardens were originally designed in 1887 to house the collection of Mr E. Broome of Batheaston—later bequests extended the range. Forming a rough rectangle, running from east to west and sloping towards the south, the gardens consist largely of lawns, well furnished with trees and intersected by winding paths. A stream bisects the rectangle, providing a waterfall, a pond and a deep channel filled with damp-loving plants. There are sizeable rock gardens and an herbaceous border, but the main interest lies in the fine collection of trees and shrubs. Near a bridge, note the small *Salix matsudana* 'Tortusa' or dragon's claw willow, planted by Amnesty International to commemorate the Universal Declaration of Human Rights. Amnesty's barbed wire motif reflects the twisted habit of the willow.

Clevedon Court

ADDRESS AND TELEPHONE: The National Trust, Clevedon Court, Clevedon BS21 6QU. Tel. Clevedon (0272) 872257

DIRECTIONS: 1½ miles E of Clevedon on Bristol Road (B3130)

OPENING TIMES: 31 March to end September, Wed, Thurs, Sun and BH Mon 2.30–5.30. House open at same times

ADMISSION: charged

The 14C manor house at Clevedon, home of the Elton family, conceals a distinctive south-facing terraced garden protected by a shelter belt of trees.

The top terrace, or Esmond Terrace, where Thackeray is said to have begun *Henry Esmond*, is home to an arbutus, a Judas tree and dwarf palms, and provides a view down over the Pretty Terrace, where many tender shrubs and plants flourish, and which is flanked by an octagonal 18C garden house at one end and a Gothic garden shelter at the other.

The lower garden, sheltered by Monterey pines, holds a fine collection of magnolias.

Dyrham Park

ADDRESS AND TELEPHONE: The National Trust, Dyrham Park, Dyrham, near Chippenham SN14 8ER. Tel. Abson (027582) 2501

DIRECTIONS: 8 miles N of Bath, 12 miles E of Bristol: approached from Bath to Stroud road (A46) 2 miles S of Tormarton interchange with M4 exit 18

OPENING TIMES: park all year, daily 12–5.30 or dusk. House and garden, 30 March to 3 November, daily except Thurs and Fri 12–5.30

ADMISSION: charged.

Restaurant

Visitors are welcome to picnic in Dyrham's 263 acres of beautiful landscaped parkland, home to a famous herd of fallow deer.

Near the Manor House, built between 1691 and 1710, for William Blathwayt, Secretary of State to William III, are herbaceous borders and climbing plants. The sheltered lawns are furnished with trees and shrubs and contain formal ponds and cascades, an echo of the large formal gardens that existed in earlier days. The 18C orangery contains citrus fruit and tender plants.

BEDFORDSHIRE

Woburn Abbey

ADDRESS AND TELEPHONE: Trustees of the Bedford Estates, Woburn Abbey, Woburn, Bedfordshire MK43 0TP. Tel. (0525) 290666

DIRECTIONS: 13 miles SW of Bedford on A4012

OPENING TIMES: 1 January to 24 March 10.30–3.45, 25 March to 3 November 10–4.45 (Sun to 5.45) House open 11–5

ADMISSION: charged

This magnificent 3000-acre parkland was landscaped by Humphry Repton in the 19C and features many lakes, specimen trees and shrubs.

The house is surrounded by 40 acres of pleasure grounds—mainly lawn but with several interesting trees and shrubs and a bog garden area.

There is also an orangery and a maze with a beautiful pagoda in the centre.

BERKSHIRE

The Old Rectory

ADDRESS AND TELEPHONE: Mr and Mrs Ralph Merton, The Old Rectory, Burghfield, Reading, Berkshire

DIRECTIONS: 5 miles SW of Reading. Off A4 in Burghfield village

OPENING TIMES: February to October, last Wed in each month 11–4

ADMISSION: charged

Parking (coaches by arrangement). Toilets. Plants for sale. No dogs

The 6 acres of 'cottage' garden have been created since 1950, when Mr and Mrs Ralph Merton began designing and planting the garden.

Mrs Merton could be described as a compulsive plant collector and has made this garden particularly attractive to plantspeople. There are fine displays of shrubs and climbing roses—selected and planted for variety and blend of colour. Azaleas and ericaceous plants also do well in the garden, among other plants brought from Japan and China.

A south-east-facing vista is created by the long double herbaceous border, in which many rare and unusual plants provide a succession of flowers against dark yew hedges from spring to the end of summer.

There is a swimming pool surrounded by climbing roses—many of them old-fashioned varieties—a spring garden with drifts of daffodils around a pond completed by a statue of Antinous, and an area planted with rhododendrons and azaleas.

The urns at the side of the house contain beautiful and distinctive arrangements of tender plants and in the paved area near the back, stone sinks show a collection of alpines and other miniatures.

Stratfield Saye House

ADDRESS AND TELEPHONE: the Duke of Wellington, The Wellington Office, Reading, Berkshire. Tel. (0252) 882882

DIRECTIONS: between Reading and Basingstoke, 1 mile off A33 (turn by the Wellington Arms)

OPENING TIMES: May to end September, daily except Fri 11.30–5. House also open

ADMISSION: charged.

Refreshments. Toilets. Wheelchair access. Dogs on leads

The grounds include a Victorian walled kitchen garden, rose garden, American garden, with many unusual shrubs, the Paxton Camellia House, herbaceous borders and pleasure grounds with specimen trees including many fine wellingtonias. The Wellington Country Park is a few miles away and provides a range of leisure activities.

BUCKINGHAMSHIRE

Stowe Landscape Gardens

ADDRESS AND TELEPHONE: National Trust, Stowe Landscape Gardens, Buckinghamshire MK18 5EH. Tel. (0280) 822850

DIRECTIONS: 3 miles NW of Buckingham via Stowe Avenue, off A422 Buckingham/Banbury road

OPENING TIMES: 1–5 January, 23 March to 14 April, 29 June to 1 September, 18–27 October, 14–24 and 27–31 December, daily 10–6

ADMISSION: charged

The National Trust acquired Stowe Landscape Gardens from Stowe School in July 1989. Following 18 months' exhaustive architectural and and garden surveys, the Trust is now carrying out a massive £11 million restoration project, with the aim of returning this classic 18C landscape to its former glory.

17C formal gardens (with buildings by Vanbrugh, Kent and Gibbs) were transformed over 75 years by a succession of great garden landscapers, from Bridgeman to Brown; but William Kent's style prevailed. The huge mansion overlooks serpentine lakes and a cascade. A grand avenue ends in a Corinthian arch, set on a hill. The landscape is well supplied with monuments, temples, pavilions and other architectural features.

CAMBRIDGESHIRE

Wimpole Hall

ADDRESS AND TELEPHONE: The National Trust, Wimpole Hall, Arrington, Royston, Hertfordshire SG8 0BW. Tel. (0223) 207257

DIRECTIONS: 8 miles SW of Cambridge, 6 miles N of Royston, off A603

OPENING TIMES: Easter to end October, daily except Mon and Fri 1–5 but open BH Mon 11–5. House also open

ADMISSION: charged

This grand house, built in 1640 but later altered, was shown in an engraving by Kip as surrounded by formal gardens and avenues. Charles Bridgeman, Sanderson Miller, Capability Brown, William Emes and Humphry Repton all worked here or produced designs for the gardens.

The North Garden today features formal lawns and gravel paths separated from the parkland by Repton's railings. An old Indian bean tree and a huge bush of common box are worth noting. Around the west corner of the house is a small rose garden but more interesting is the Victorian shrubbery to the east where several splendid conifers are mixed with native trees. The whole is underplanted with different kinds of narcissus.

CHESHIRE

Little Moreton Hall

ADDRESS AND TELEPHONE: The National Trust, Little Moreton Hall, Congleton, Cheshire, CW12 4SD. Tel. (0260) 272018

DIRECTIONS: 4 miles SW of Congleton on A34

OPENING TIMES: March and October weekends 1.30–5.30, April to end September, daily except Tues 1.30–5.30 (BH Mon 11.30–5.30). House also open

ADMISSION: charged

Probably the best-known example of timber-framed architecture in the country, the Hall dates from the mid 15C.

A moat surrounds the Hall, taking in about an acre of land to the north and west, where a knot garden was laid out in 1975, under the guidance of Graham Stuart Thomas. Based on a design in *The English Gardener* (1688), Little Moreton's knot is of open form with gravel filling in the dwarf box patterns. Flowers, herbs and vegetables known to have been available in the 16C and 17C have been planted in surrounding borders. Nearby is a mount.

Peover Hall

ADDRESS AND TELEPHONE: Mr Randle Brooks, Peover Hall, Over Peover, near Knutsford, Cheshire. Tel. (0565) 722404

DIRECTIONS: 4 miles S of Knutsford, off A50

OPENING TIMES: May to October, Mon and Thurs 2–5. Hall on Mon

ADMISSION: charged

The series of room-like gardens around Peover Hall are enclosed by walls and hedges and include a box-hedged herb garden, a knot-style rose garden, white and pink gardens and a lily pond garden.

Topiary features strongly.

The wilderness garden and dell are best seen in late spring when rhododendrons, azaleas and magnolias are blooming. The surrounding parkland inlcudes lakes and woodland.

CLEVELAND

Ormesby Hall

ADDRESS AND TELEPHONE: The National Trust, Ormesby Hall, Middlesbrough TS7 9AS. Tel. (0642) 324188

DIRECTIONS: 3 miles SE of Middlesbrough off B1380 in Ormesby village

OPENING TIMES: 30 March (Easter Sat) to 2 April 2–5.30; April to October, Wed, Sat, Sun and BH Mon 2–5.30; also Thurs July to September. House also open

ADMISSION: charged but free to NT members.

No dogs

The main features of this small but attractive garden are formal flower beds, rose beds and shrub borders; a Victorian holly walk; a woodland area with spring flowers; croquet lawns and a magnificent copper beech. Two large 'cubes' of yew overlook the lawn, both embroidered in summer with the scarlet flowers of *tropaeolum speciosum*.

The Hall dates from c 1740 and was the home of the Pennyman family.

CORNWALL

Antony House

ADDRESS AND TELEPHONE: The National Trust, Antony House, Torpoint, Plymouth PL11 2QA. Tel. (0752) 812191

DIRECTIONS: 5 miles W of Plymouth via Torpoint Ferry, or 16 miles SE of Liskeard off A374

OPENING TIMES: 1 April to end October, Tues, Wed, Thurs and BH Mon 2–6; also Sun in June, July and August 2–6

ADMISSION: charged.

No dogs

The Victorian flower beds which once surrounded this early 18C house have been replaced by extensive lawns, but a clipped yew cone designed as a garden pavilion and several garden ornaments remain from the days when the Carew family lived here.

There are some interesting trees, including a large shagbark hickory (*Carya ovata*), and excellent borders of hemerocallis—once forming part of one of the largest collections of hemerocallis in the country and a speciality of the late Lady Carew Pole.

Around the edge of the estate is a privately owned woodland garden with rhododendrons, camellias and magnolias. This part of the garden is open mid March to mid June and again 1 August to end of October, daily except Sat 11–5.30; Sun and BH Mon 2–5.30.

County Demonstration Garden—Probus

ADDRESS AND TELEPHONE: Cornwall County Council Education Committee, County Demonstration Garden, Probus, near Truro, Cornwall. Tel. (0872) 74282

DIRECTIONS: at Probus, 6 miles E of Truro on A390

OPENING TIMES: October to April, Mon to Fri 10–4.30; May to September daily 10–5

ADMISSION: charged

No dogs

Established in the early 1970s, this 7½-acre garden serves as the education, demonstration and advisory centre for Cornwall. It comprises numerous display plots of small garden layouts such as the patio and labour-saving gardens, as well as demonstrating gardening principles and practices for vegetable, fruit and flower production, lawn care, pruning and shrub planting. In the glasshouses are displays showing propagation techniques, and comparisons of labelling and mulching materials.

The Fox-Rosehill Garden

ADDRESS AND TELEPHONE: Carrick District Council, Falmouth, Cornwall. Tel. (0872) 78131

DIRECTIONS: Melvill Road (B3290) towards centre of Falmouth

OPENING TIMES: all year round daily, dawn to dusk

ADMISSION: free

Yet another garden made by the Fox family of Falmouth. Now a public park but extremely interesting for its attractive layout and number of fine sub-tropical plants—many of which are labelled.

Around the lawns and in the shelter of pines are embothriums, acacias, cordylines, griselinias, palms and tree ferns as well as camellias, rhododendrons and magnolias. Many tender shrubs and many rarities.

Long Cross Victorian Garden

ADDRESS AND TELEPHONE: Mr and Mrs R. Warrillow, Long Cross Victorian Hotel, Long Cross, Trelights, near Port Isaac, North Cornwall, PL29 3TF. Tel. (0208) 880243

DIRECTIONS: 7 miles NE of Wadebridge. Off B3314 between Port Isaac and Port Quin

OPENING TIMES: Easter to October, daily 11–5.30

ADMISSION: charged

Much renovation and reconstruction work in the last decade has brought this once neglected garden back under control. Overlooking open countryside with fine sea views of Port Isaac and Port Quin, the garden comprises 2 to 3 acres of pathways, Victorian style.

The charm of this garden is the maze-like effect created by the wind-breaking hedges. The house is now a hotel.

Penjerrick

ADDRESS AND TELEPHONE: Rachel Morin, Penjerrick Gardens, Budock, Falmouth, Cornwall. Tel. (0326) 250074. Contact Mrs Bird for information and guided tours

DIRECTIONS: 3 miles SW of Falmouth, near Budock

OPENING TIMES: March to September, Sun and Wed 1.30–4.30

ADMISSION: charged

This 15-acre garden is of historical and botanical interest for growing the 'Barclayi' and 'Penjerrick' rhododendron hybrids. The upper garden with lovely views to the sea, contains many rhododendrons, camellias, magnolias, azaleas, bamboos, tree ferns as well as magnificent trees. The lower, luxuriant valley garden features ponds in a wild woodland setting.

Trerice

ADDRESS AND TELEPHONE: The National Trust, Trerice, near Newquay, Cornwall, TR8 4PG. Tel. (0637) 875404

DIRECTIONS: 3 miles SE of Newquay via A392 and A3058

OPENING TIMES: Easter to end October, daily except Tues 11–6 (5 in October). House also open

ADMISSION: charged

The terraces and small gardens surrounding this Elizabethan house have been replanted by the National Trust. The borders of the front courtyard are particularly attractive in summer, filled with purple or gold-flowering plants.

The bowling green is thought to have been created c 1818, and there is an orchard planted with Cornish fruit trees.

Trerice's collection of more than 70 lawnmowers, some dating from the last century, is also worth a visit.

CUMBRIA

Brantwood

ADDRESS AND TELEPHONE: Brantwood Educational Trust, Brantwood, Coniston, Cumbria. Tel. (05394) 41396

DIRECTIONS: E of Lake Road, head of Conistan Water

OPENING TIMES: mid March to mid November, daily 11–5.30; winter Wed to Sun 11–4. House open

ADMISSION: charged

Superbly sited house and garden overlooking Coniston Water. The Victorian artist and critic John Ruskin settled here in 1872 and planted hundreds of rhododendrons and azaleas in a woodland garden. A major restoration project is now underway.

Brockhole, Lake District National Park Centre

ADDRESS AND TELEPHONE: Lake District National Parks Authority, Brockhole Lake District National Park Centre, Windermere, Cumbria, LA23 1LJ. Tel. (09662) 6601

DIRECTIONS: 2 miles N of Windermere on A591

OPENING TIMES: late March to early November, daily from 10am

ADMISSION: charged

The Lake District National Park Visitor Centre is set in 32 acres of garden and park overlooking Lake Windermere. Excellent terraced garden designed by Thomas Mawson in the late 1890s to exploit the magnificent views. Rhododendrons, azaleas and acid-loving plants are well represented here; there is a rose garden with disabled access, a scented garden close to the orangery, a recently restored kitchen garden, and many rare and unusual plants.

Exhibitions are staged at the centre and audio visual theatres provide information about the Lake District.

Garden tours are available May to September.

Corby Castle

ADDRESS AND TELEPHONE: Sir John Howard-Lawson, Bt and Lady Howard-Lawson, Corby Castle, Great Corby, Carlisle, Cumbria. Tel. (0228) 60246

DIRECTIONS: at Great Corby. 1½ miles S of Warwick Bridge on B6258

OPENING TIMES: April to end October, daily 1–5

ADMISSION: charged

Walks along the River Eden were laid out in 1720. Many interesting architectural features including a tempietta, caves and cascade. Fine trees in the woodland setting.

Rydal Hall

ADDRESS AND TELEPHONE: The Diocese of Carlisle, Rydal Hall, Ambleside, Cumbria, LA22 9LX. Tel. (05394) 32050

DIRECTIONS: 1½ miles NW of Ambleside off A591 at Rydal

OPENING TIMES: all year round

ADMISSION: donations welcome

There has been a garden at Rydal Hall since the mid 17C although the present layout of landscaped grounds dates from the 18C and the formal gardens around the house were laid out by Thomas Mawson c 1909. The rose garden with fountain, double terrace with balustrading, steps and topiary are typical of Mawson's work.

Also a rockery garden with pool and a grotto thought to have been built by Daniel le Fleming in 1668–69.

DEVON

Buckland Abbey

ADDRESS AND TELEPHONE: managed by the National Trust and Plymouth City Council, Yelverton, Devon PL20 6EY. Tel. Yelverton (0822) 853607

DIRECTIONS: 6 miles S of Tavistock, 11 miles N of Plymouth, turn off A386 ¼ mile S of Yelverton. Public transport: Western National bus 55 from Yelverton (with connections from Plymouth BR) (tel. Plymouth 0752 664011). Bere Alston station, not Sun, except May to September, 4½ miles

OPENING TIMES: 29 March to end October, daily except Thurs 10.30–5.30 (October 10.30–5). Last admission 45 minutes before closing. November to end March, Sat and Sun 2–5, Wed for pre-arranged parties only. Abbey at same times

ADMISSION: charged

Car park 150 yds. Refreshments. Toilets. Partly accessible to wheelchairs; toilets for the disabled. Shop. No dogs

Now known principally as the home of Sir Francis Drake, Buckland Abbey was originally a Cistercian monastery, founded in 1273 by Amicia, Dowager Countess of Devon. Amicia's daughter Isabella, Countess of Devon, provided the land, and the monastery was dedicated to Our Lady and St Benedict. Buckland was the fourth and last Cistercian abbey founded in Devon, and the one furthest to the west.

The main interest here for garden visitors is the herb garden, planted on gently sloping and curving ground under the west wall of the medieval Great Barn. The garden contains over 40 kitchen herbs, within a free-flowing and pleasingly irregular pattern of box hedges—a mixed bed of thymes, tall fennel, heartsease, sweet cicely (*Myrrhis odorata*), elecampane (*Inula helenium*), horehound (*Marrubium vulgare*), evening primrose (*Oenothera biennis*) and many others. The site is sheltered but sunny and the plants lush and thriving. On the grey stone walls behind you can see wisteria and actinidia. There is more planting around the abbey and on the lawns, including huge magnolias and ancient yews.

Saltram

ADDRESS AND TELEPHONE: The National Trust, Plympton, Plymouth, Devon PL7 3UH. Tel. (0752) 336546

DIRECTIONS: 2 miles W of Plympton, 3½ miles E of Plymouth city centre, between Plymouth to Exeter road (A38) and Plymouth to Kingsbridge road (A379); take Plympton turn at Marsh Mills roundabout. Public transport: Plymouth Citybus 20/A, 21, 22/A, 51 from Plymouth, alight Plymouth Road/Plympton Bypass Junction, ¾ mile footpath (tel. Plymouth 0752 222221). Plymouth BR station 3½ miles

OPENING TIMES: Good Fri 29 March to end October, Sun to Thurs and Sat of BH weekends 11–6 (October 11–5). Last admission 30 minutes before closing.

ADMISSION: charged

Car parking 500 yds. Refreshments. Toilets. Wheelchair access. Toilets for the disabled. Shop. Dogs on lead

Saltram House and its garden stand high above the River Plym (from which Plymouth takes its name) on pleasant well wooded terrain. Saltram Wood itself slopes steeply from the north boundary to the river, protecting the garden from northerly winds. Between 45 and 55 trees were lost in the gales of January 1990, including eight limes from the avenue. An extensive replanting programme has begun.

Accepted by the Treasury in lieu of death duties, after the death of the 5th Earl of Morley, Saltram was given to the National Trust in 1957. The garden dates back to 1770, but was greatly altered and replanted during the 19C. Its present design owes much to the efforts of the 3rd Earl of Morley, who lived at Saltram from 1884 to 1905, and to his son, who died at Saltram in 1951.

The garden's most striking and original feature is a 77ft long lime avenue. Probably planted by the 3rd Earl in the late 19C, this avenue flanks the long walk, which leads westwards from the house, parallel to the southern boundary. Above the avenue are glades and walks, with the castle to the far west. Wide lawns stretch east and west of the house, and various garden buildings and features are within easy walking distance—the chapel gallery, the orange grove, the orangery. Fanny's Bower, a small mid 18C classical garden house, can be found to the far north, on a path above the orangery.

Tapeley Park

ADDRESS AND TELEPHONE: Mrs Rosamund Christie, Tapeley Park, Instow, near Bideford, Tel: Instow (0271) 860528

DIRECTIONS: 1½ miles S of Instow on A39 (¾ mile from public transport)

OPENING TIMES: Good Fri to end October, daily except Sat (open BH Sat and Mon), 10–6. (Check times for November to April)

ADMISSION: charged

Interesting gardens dating from Victorian/Edwardian times, including Italian terraced gardens, sundial garden, shell house, ice house, walled kitchen garden with vine house, herbaceous borders and shrubs.

There are mature native and sub-tropical trees and a woodland walk takes you to a lily pond.

Family features include pets (chickens, geese, ducks), a putting green, play areas and picnic places. Teas are also provided. Jousting.

Vicar's Mead

ADDRESS AND TELEPHONE: Mr and Mrs H.J.F. Read, Vicar's Mead, Hayes Lane, East Budleigh, Devon. Tel. (03954) 2641

DIRECTIONS: from A376, Newton Poppleford to Budleigh Salterton, turn off W for East Budleigh. Hayes Lane is opposite 'Sir Walter Raleigh'. Garden 100 yds W of public car park

OPENING TIMES: April to 8 September, Sun afternoons and BH Mon 2–6

ADMISSION: charged

Rare and unusual plants are displayed in this 3½-acre garden, which has been created since 1977 on an unpromising but distinctive north-facing red sandstone escarpment.

Specialities include tender plants, mainly from Chile, in a sheltered border, and four National Collections: dianella, libertia, liriope and ophiopogon.

Not to be missed if you are visiting Bicton Park, ¾ mile to the north.

DORSET

Athelhampton

ADDRESS AND TELEPHONE: The Cooke family, Athelhampton, Puddletown, near Dorchester. Tel. (0305) 848363

DIRECTIONS: 5 miles NE of Dorchester, on A35 ½ mile E of Puddletown

OPENING TIMES: Easter to early October, Wed, Fri, and BH, Mon and Tues in August 2–6

ADMISSION: charged

Although the present house at Athelhampton was built in the 15C and 16C, the 20 acres of formal gardens date only from the late 19C and were laid out in sharp contrast to the freer styles of 'cottage' and 'wild' gardens which were then coming into vogue. The design, by Francis Inigo Jones, includes a Great Court with terrace, pavilions, pool, fountain and yew obelisks. Also outstanding are the circular corona and the private garden with its rectangular lawn and long pool.

There are also cloister, White and walled kitchen gardens and many vistas, as well as access to the river by way of sloping lawns.

Compton Acres

ADDRESS AND TELEPHONE: The Secretary, Compton Acres, Canford Cliffs Road, Poole, Dorset BH13 7ES. Tel. Canford Cliffs (0202) 708036

DIRECTIONS: 2 miles W of Bournemouth on A35, turn left to Canford Cliffs. Wiltshire and Dorset Red buses 147, 150 and 151 from Poole, Bournemouth and Swanage. Yellow Buses 11 and 12 (summer) from Christchurch, Southbourne, Boscombe and Bournemouth stop at Canford Cliffs

OPENING TIMES: daily from 1 April, or Good Fri if earlier, to end October, 10.30–6.30

ADMISSION: charged

Café/crêperie. Toilets. Wheelchair access to gardens. Toilet for the disabled. Plant sales.

The many visitors to Compton Acres are offered a tour of ten linked but separate gardens, each illustrating a different style. These include an Italian garden with pool, temple, fountain and much valuable statuary, and a Japanese garden, constructed under the direction of a Japanese architect, where every detail is said to have a special traditional significance (see the lavishly illustrated guide).

The scheme was conceived by Thomas William Simpson and executed immediately after the 1914–18 war. It entailed excavation of the heathland, landscaping, planting and the collection of expensive ornaments.

The gardens fell into disrepair during the 1939–45 war, but were restored and re-opened in 1952. The garden guide now describes them as 'reputed to be the finest in Europe'.

For these writers the most enjoyable aspect of these gardens was the presence of many mature cedars, yews, broadleaved and ornamental trees, as well as rhododendrons and other flowering shrubs. The rock and water garden features 30-year-old carp, and conveys a sense of calm and repose, not present in some of the more densely ornamented areas.

Forde Abbey

ADDRESS AND TELEPHONE: Mr M. Roper, Forde Abbey, near Chard, Dorset. Tel. South Chard (0460) 20231

DIRECTIONS: 4 miles SE of Chard, 7 miles E of Crewkerne. Signposted off A30

OPENING TIMES: daily, throughout the year 10–4.30

ADMISSION: charged

Plants for sale. Teas

The present Hamstone manor house, built on the site of an original Cistercian abbey, is surrounded by 30 acres of gardens which are mainly informal, but include rock gardens, herbaceous borders and kitchen gardens.

Redwoods and cedars and other fine specimen trees, planted in Victorian times, provide shelter for flowering trees and shrubs such as magnolias, rhododendrons and pieris. The largest of four ponds, joined by cascades, has a flourishing bog garden, which includes an unusually large collection of Asiatic primulas.

An arboretum, begun in 1947, stands to the north-east beyond the main gardens, and this is well worth visiting.

Minterne

ADDRESS AND TELEPHONE: Lord Digby, Minterne Magna, Dorset. Tel. Cerne Abbas (0300) 341370

DIRECTIONS: 3 miles N of Dorchester, on A352 at Minterne Magna.

OPENING TIMES: daily 1 April to 31 October, 10–7

ADMISSION: charged

Landscape garden dating from 18C with rare trees and cascaded river.

Beeches and pines shade an outstanding woodland garden, mainly planted in the 19C. Here the acid soil provides ideal conditions for rhododendrons, azaleas and camellias together with swamp cypress, clumps of bamboo and many other fine specimens.

Moisture-loving plants flourish in the woodland and on the verges of pools.

Parnham House

ADDRESS AND TELEPHONE: Mr and Mrs J. Makepeace, Parnham House, Beaminster, Dorset. Tel. Beaminster (0308) 862204

DIRECTIONS: ½ mile S of Beaminster on A3066; 5 miles N of Bridport

OPENING TIMES: 1 April to 31 October every Wed, Sun and BH, including Good Fri 10–5. House open at same times. Listed

Grade 1 building, includes John Makepeace furniture workshops

ADMISSION: charged, children under 10 free.

This hamstone Tudor manor, dating from 1540 with additions by John Nash, was purchased by John Makepeace in 1976 as a home and business and school for the making of fine 20C furniture.

There are 14 acres of gardens, those in front of the house reconstructed in the early part of this century, probably by Inigo Thomas or Harold Peto. Here a balustraded upper terrace, with stone gazebos, looks down on to a grassed terrace with 50 conical yews and parallel stone rills. The lowest terrace is separated from parkland by a ha-ha wall.

Since 1979, Mrs Makepeace has replanned and planted the gardens to the north of the house. These include a silver garden with Mediterranean plants, a shade garden and an Italian garden incorporating herbaceous borders in contrasting colours—one in delicate shades of blue, mauve pink and white and one in stronger colours: yellows, bronzes, oranges, reds.

The eastern forecourt with shrub and climbing roses, the woodland garden and walled kitchen garden complete a most enjoyable tour.

COUNTY DURHAM

University of Durham Botanic Garden

ADDRESS AND TELEPHONE: University of Durham Botanic Garden, Hollinside Lane, Durham DH1 3TN. Tel. (091 374) 2670

DIRECTIONS: Hollinside Lane, Durham. 1 mile SE of city centre

OPENING TIMES: all year round, daily 10–4

ADMISSION: free

No dogs

The Botanic Garden is planted on 18 acres of south-west-facing hillside among extensive mature woodland to the south of Durham City. The mature trees provide shelter for some of the more unusual trees and shrubs collected from all over the world.

Small 'gardens within gardens' make features from roses or woodland primulas, or heathers. By the rose garden two small greenhouses contain tropical and acid zone plants.

ESSEX

The Magnolias

ADDRESS AND TELEPHONE: Mr and Mrs R.A. Hammond, The Magnolias, 18 St Johns Avenue, Brentwood.

DIRECTIONS: from A1023 turn S on A128, after 300 yds right at traffic lights and over railway bridge. St Johns Avenue third on right

OPENING TIMES: 1991: 31 March, 14 and 28 April, 12 and 26 May, 9 June, 14 July, 11 and 25 August, 8 September, 13 October, 10–5. Also by appointment

ADMISSION: charged

Tea. No dogs

This comparatively small (½ acre) garden holds not only a fine collection of magnolias, but the National Collection of arisaema. Many small specimen trees can be seen here, as well as rhododendrons, camellias and pieris. Foliage plants include 80 varieties of hosta and many kinds of fern. Among the plentiful spring bulbs are some rare snowdrop varieties.

Without appearing overcrowded, the garden also incorporates raised fish ponds and two water gardens, with Japanese temple and bridge and a greenhouse. It is well worth visiting, to see what gifted gardeners can make of a limited space.

Saling Hall

ADDRESS AND TELEPHONE: Mr and Mrs Hugh Johnson, Great Saling, Braintree, Essex.

DIRECTIONS: midway between Braintree and Dunmow, turn off N at the Saling Oak. No public transport available

OPENING TIMES: May to July, Wed 2–5, also parties by appointment. House not open

ADMISSION: £1 in aid of National Gardens Scheme, children free. Coach parties by appointment only

Car parking. Toilets. Wheelchair access. No toilets for the disabled. No dogs

Saling Hall is the garden of Hugh Johnson, who for 15 years has written 'Trandescant's Diary' in the RHS monthly journal *The Garden* and is the author of a number of books on gardening and trees. He and his wife Judy began to restore the garden in 1972, following the basic plan established by a previous owner, Lady Carlisle, after the 1939–45 war. Much of the background planting dates from 1959, but there are many new things, including a young arboretum. The walled garden is excellently designed and profusely planted. Booked parties only.

GLOUCESTERSHIRE

Misarden Park

ADDRESS AND TELEPHONE: Maj. and Mrs M.T.N.H. Wills, Misarden Park, Misarden, near Stroud. Tel. Misarden (028 582) 309/303

DIRECTIONS: 7 miles NE of Stroud in Misarden village

OPENING TIMES: late April to end September, 10–4.30 every Wed and Thurs. Other days by appointment for charity. House closed

ADMISSION: charged

Delightful gardens, including some designs by Edwin Lutyens, laid out around a stone Elizabethan manor house.

Terraces near the house contain topiary, a scented garden and herbaceous borders. The rose gardens have lately been replanted.

The lawns below lead to pleasure grounds with specimen trees and spring bulbs. There is a walk through woods to the lake.

Painswick Rococo Garden

ADDRESS AND TELEPHONE: Lord and Lady Dickinson, The Stables, Painswick House, Painswick. Tel. (0452) 813204

DIRECTIONS: on B4073 ½ mile from Painswick

OPENING TIMES: 1 February to mid December, Wed to Sun and BH Mon 11–5. House closed

ADMISSION: charged.

Restaurant. Shop. Wheelchair accessible

These gardens are of great historical interest, having been laid out by Benjamin Hyett, the then owner, between 1738 and 1748 and combining formal features of the preceding centuries with the landscaping of the 18C. Lord and Lady Dickinson are now restoring the gardens, which lie below the Palladian mansion, according to a picture of 1848 by Thomas Robins.

The replanting of the formal gardens, kitchen garden and orchard is of the original period. The 18C buildings, allées, woodland paths and pools are undergoing extensive renewal, and already present an impressive picture.

Westbury Court Garden

ADDRESS AND TELEPHONE: The National Trust, Westbury Court, Westbury on Severn, Gloucestershire GL14 1PD. Tel. Westbury on Severn (045 276) 461

DIRECTIONS: 9 miles SW of Gloucester on A48. Bus: Gloucester to Cardiff (passing close BR Gloucester and Newport)

OPENING TIMES: 30 March to end October, Wed to Sun and BH Mon 11–6. Closed Good Fri. Other months by appointment only. House closed

ADMISSION: charged

Car park. Picnic area. Wheelchair accessible. No dogs

Westbury Court is the earliest formal water garden in England and was laid out in the Dutch style between 1698 and 1705. It was taken over by the National Trust between 1967 and 1971.

The main features are canals, yew hedges, topiary, and a walled garden featuring over 100 species of plants grown in England before 1700, wall fruits and roses.

Westonbirt Arboretum

ADDRESS AND TELEPHONE: The Forestry Commission, Westonbirt, near Tetbury, Gloucestershire. Tel. Westonbirt (066 688) 220

DIRECTIONS: 3½ miles SW of Tetbury on A433

OPENING TIMES: daily all year 10–8 or sunset when earlier

ADMISSION: charged

The Forestry Commission has been restoring and replanting this 500-acre arboretum since 1956.

The original planting, begun in 1829 by Robert Holford, features many of the outstanding conifers then being discovered by David Douglas in North America.

Among these mature trees, many smaller trees and shrubs, such as the

Hillier glade of flowering cherries, provide variety. Carpets of flowers brighten the woodland in spring, and the autumn foliage colour is outstanding.

HAMPSHIRE

Bramdean House

ADDRESS AND TELEPHONE: Mr and Mrs H Wakefield, Bramdean House, Bramdean, near Alresford. Tel. (0962) 771214

DIRECTIONS: in Bramdean village on A272

OPENING TIMES: one Sun or Mon each month from March to August (see National Gardens Scheme for dates in any particular year) or by appointment. House closed

ADMISSION: charged

Bramdean is a connoisseur's garden: not unduly large (4 acres) but planned and planted by owners of distinctive taste.

The long borders within sight of the 18C house contain plants of all heights and habits in purples, mauves, yellows and blues and immaculate lawns surround a central lily pond. There is a working kitchen garden of vegetables and fruit as well as some flower beds surrounding a sundial.

The orchard, still within sight of the house, is ornamented by many bulbs in spring and in summer by climbing roses and clematis. Unusual plants are to be found throughout the garden.

Furzey Gardens

ADDRESS AND TELEPHONE: Furzey Garden Charitable Trust, Minstead, near Lyndhurst, Hampshire. Tel. (0703) 812464

DIRECTIONS: 2 miles N of Lyndhurst, turn W to Minstead. (1 miles S of A31 2 miles W of Cadnam and end of M27)

OPENING TIMES: all year except 25 and 26 December, daily 10–5. House at more limited hours

ADMISSION: charged

No dogs

Eight acres of beautiful, informal gardens laid out on a south-facing slope in the 1920s. Fine collections of rhododendrons, azaleas, camellias and heathers flourish in the acid soil.

Magnolias, acers and other trees and shrubs valuable for their spring flowers or autumn colour can also be found here, together with water gardens and a fernery.

Hinton Ampner

ADDRESS AND TELEPHONE: Bramdean, near Alresford
Hampshire SO24 0LA. Tel. Winchester (0962) 771305/771023

DIRECTIONS: on A272 1 mile W of Bramdean village, 8 miles E of Winchester. Hampshire bus 67 Winchester to Petersfield. Station: Alresford 4 miles; Winchester 9 miles

OPENING TIMES: good Fri 29 March to end September, Sat, Sun, Tues, Wed, also Good Fri 1.30–5.30. House open in August

ADMISSION: charged

Teas

An impressive garden laid out in a strongly architectural style in the early 1930s by Lord Sherbourne. The estate was acquired by the National Trust in 1985 and is in process of renovation.

Formal walks hedged with yew or box and informal paths link a variety of garden rooms filled with flowering shrubs and roses. There are many vistas throughout, with focal points marked by architectural features and statuary.

HEREFORD AND WORCESTER

Dinmore Manor

ADDRESS AND TELEPHONE: Mr R.G. Murray, Dinmore Manor, Wellington, Hereford and Worcester. Tel. (0432) 71322

DIRECTIONS: 6 miles N of Hereford, off A49

OPENING TIMES: daily 10.30–6

ADMISSION: charged

No dogs

Dinmore Manor occupies a serene and splendid position at the head of a valley. A chapel remains from the 12C when the Order of the Knights Hospitaller based its county headquarters here. The manor house dates from the end of the 16C with later additions.

In 1927 the manor was purchased by Richard Hollins Murray, who built a medieval-style music room and cloisters, which now look out onto a small and charming garden. A roof walk gives panoramic views of the gardens and countryside.

Rockeries occupy much of this garden, following a narrow stream down to a pool. There is an excellent selection of acers, their colourful foliage contrasting with the green ferns along the water course. Other borders are planted with shrubs and roses, and spring flowers surround the chapel.

Eastnor Castle

ADDRESS AND TELEPHONE: James Hervey-Bathurst Esq, Eastnor Castle, Ledbury, Hereford and Worcester HR8 1RN. Tel. (0531) 2305/2304

DIRECTIONS: 2½ miles NE of Ledbury on A3438 Tewkesbury road

OPENING TIMES: mid May to end September, Sun and BH Mon, also Wed and Thurs in July and August 2.15–5.30. House also open

ADMISSION: charged

Eastnor Castle was built in 1812, but looks like a medieval fortress. It was designed by Robert Smirke for the 1st Earl Somers. Around it flourishes one of the greatest 19C pinetums. There are redwoods, Wellingtonias and incense cedars as well as the only recorded American beech (*Fagus grandifolia*) in the country.

Other interesting trees include *Abies bracteata*, grown from the original seed first imported in 1854, and several *Cedrus atlantica* grown from seed collected by the 2nd Earl Somers in 1845.

A terraced garden below the south-east front of the castle contains many fine shrubs and herbaceous plants and offers good views of the lake and parkland beyond.

Hanbury Hall

ADDRESS AND TELEPHONE: The National Trust, Hanbury Hall, Droitwich, Hereford and Worcester WR9 7EA. Tel. (0527) 84214

DIRECTIONS: 4½ miles E of Droitwich, 1 mile N of B4090

OPENING TIMES: likely opening times in 1991 are 29 June and subsequent Sat, Sun and Mon until end October, 2–6. House also open

ADMISSION: charged

No dogs

George London was commissioned to lay out a formal garden to the south of the Hall. A perspective view by Joseph Dougharty (1732) shows extensive parterres and compartments of box and yew in the Dutch style. These formal features were swept away in the 18C and the gardens now consist mainly of lawns and trees, with a fine forecourt, a rose garden and orangery.

The forecourt, with Victorian gates and gazebos, features an interesting selection of climbing plants (especially clematis), shrubs and flowers. The orangery, thought to have been built shortly after 1732, is covered with wisteria and overlooks a small lavender garden.

Also noteworthy—a Primrose Walk, and a Cedar Walk leading to ice house. Fine parkland.

Stoke Lacy Herb Garden

ADDRESS AND TELEPHONE: Mrs Madge Hooper, Stoke Lacy Herb Garden, Stoke Lacy, near Bromyard, Hereford and Worcester HR7 4HJ. Tel. (0432) 820232

DIRECTIONS: 4 miles S of Bromyard on A465, 10 miles N of Hereford

OPENING TIMES: mid May to mid September, Sat only 10–1, 2–4.30. No parties

ADMISSION: donations to charity welcomed

The herb garden, with skilful and attractive layout, contains up to 200 different herbs. The owner is knowledgeable about herb traditions and experienced in growing herbs. The original herb farm, on 6½ acres of land, was established in 1939, producing bulk crops of culinary and medicinal herbs for drying. The existing small garden also features old roses and unusual shrubs.

HERTFORDSHIRE

Ashridge Management College

ADDRESS AND TELEPHONE: Ashridge Management College, Berkhamsted. Tel. Little Gaddesdon (044284) 3491

DIRECTIONS: 4 miles N of Berkhamsted on B4506

OPENING TIMES: April to October, most weekends and BH, 2–6. House open at selected times. (Dogs on lead)

Ashridge College was originally a monastery: it passed into royal possession during the Tudor period and then into private ownership in the early 17C. In the early 19C the Bridgwater family built the present Gothic-style mansion and employed Humphry Repton to design the gardens. At their request, Repton included small formal gardens as well as landscape. The generous overall design and two of the formal gardens remain of his work.

From the terrace by the house, with its box-edged plant beds and clipped cubes of yew, there is a fine view over the lawns and specimen trees—mature beeches, Wellingtonias, cedars and evergreen oaks. In May, this view is enhanced by masses of flowering rhododendrons.

The smaller formal gardens include a rose garden (by Repton), a grotto, a Monks' Garden with clipped box hedges and old fashioned roses, a Bible garden with incense cedars, a heather garden and two unusual beech tree houses in a pink and grey garden.

Benington Lordship

ADDRESS AND TELEPHONE: Mr and Mrs C.H.A. Bott, Benington Lordship, Benington, Hertfordshire. Tel. Benington (043885) 668

DIRECTIONS: 5 miles E of Stevenage, in Benington village

OPENING TIMES: BH Mon 12–5; April to end September, Wed 12–5; April to end August, Sun 2–5

ADMISSION: charged

Benington Lordship, which has been in the ownership of the same family since early this century, is a beautiful and diverse plantsperson's garden surrounding an 18C house and adjacent to a Saxon church. A Victorian flint folly marks the site of an ancient castle.

The main features include grass terraces overlooking lakes, masses of snowdrops filling the dry moat in February, formal sunken rose gardens, a dell, a walled, productive kitchen garden and outstanding double herbaceous borders.

Knebworth House

ADDRESS AND TELEPHONE: Lord Cobbold, Knebworth House, near Stevenage. Tel. Stevenage (0438) 812661

DIRECTIONS: 28 miles N of London, direct access from A1(M) at Stevenage. Station and bus Stevenage 3 miles

OPENING TIMES: 1991: 22 March to 19 May, Sat, Sun and BH Mon; 25 May to 8 September, daily except Mon unless a BH; 8 September to 29 September, Sat and Sun. Park open 11–5.30; house and garden 12–5

ADMISSION: charged

Knebworth House was remodelled by Edward Bulwer-Lytton in Edwardian times into a Gothic-style mansion with battlements and heraldic beasts. He did better by the garden, persuading his brother-in-law, Edwin Lutyens, to lay out formal beds, while he himself was responsible for the overall design.

Avenues of pleached limes mark out the grassed terrace in front of the house and surround the rectangular pool. The rose garden is flanked by two long herbaceous borders, designed by Lutyens and originally planted by

Lady Bulwer-Lytton. These, together with the square formal garden, are now being restored for Lord and Lady Cobbold by Ms Sophie Piebenga, the Head Gardener. Much of the new planting is inspired by Gertrude Jekyll and the herb garden has recently been reconstructed from a design she made for Knebworth.

HUMBERSIDE

Burton Constable Hall

ADDRESS AND TELEPHONE: Mr J.R. Chichester-Constable, Burton Constable Hall, near Hull, North Humberside. Tel. (0964) 562400

DIRECTIONS: 7½ miles NE of Hull, off B1238

OPENING TIMES: Easter Sun and Mon; May BH Sun and Mon; Spring BH Sun and Mon; Sun in June and July and from 21 July to 1 September inclusive 1–5. House also open

ADMISSION: charged

The gardens immediately surrounding the Hall have been kept simple—large expanses of lawn with shrubs—to emphasise the striking architecture of this magnificent Elizabethan house.

The attractive orangery was designed by Thomas Atkinson in 1780. In the parkland are 22 acres of lakes, designed by Lancelot 'Capability' Brown in 1770. His plans for the landscape can be seen in the Hall.

Sledmere House

ADDRESS AND TELEPHONE: Sir Tatton Sykes, Sledmere House, Sledmere, near Driffield, North Humberside. Tel. (0377) 86208

DIRECTIONS: 24 miles E of York, 3 miles NW of Driffield, in Sledmere village at the junction of B1251 and B1252

OPENING TIMES: Easter weekend 1.30–5.30; April Sun 1.30–5.30; May to end of September, daily except Mon and Fri 1.30–5.30. House also open

ADMISSION: charged

Lancelot 'Capability' Brown worked here, but left no lake as the soil was too chalky. He moved the village so that the house could enjoy uninterrupted views of the parkland. Brown's plans can be seen in the Exhibition Room. A knot garden has recently been laid out below the west front of the house, using dwarf box hedging and variegated ivies. Sheltered by the walls of the old kitchen garden are a rose garden and a selection of fruit trees.

KENT

Bedgebury National Pinetum

ADDRESS AND TELEPHONE: The Forestry Commission, Research Division, Goudhurst, Kent. Tel. Goudhurst (0580) 211044

DIRECTIONS: 7 miles E of Tunbridge Wells on A21 turn N on to B2079 for 1 mile

OPENING TIMES: daily from 10am until dusk

ADMISSION: charged.

Bedgebury is reputed to have the largest collection of conifers in Europe. It was begun in 1925, by the Royal Botanic Gardens, Kew, and the Forestry Commission, on an estate already planted with some conifers. The original hillside, valleys and lake have been greatly enhanced by sweeping rides and long vistas.

The planting includes every type of conifer, from vast Wellingtonias to a mixed dwarf collection, supplemented by many broad-leaved trees as well as rhododendrons, cornus and other shrubs. The autumn colouring is outstanding.

Emmetts Garden

ADDRESS AND TELEPHONE: The National Trust, Emmetts, Ide Hill, Sevenoaks, Kent TN14 6AY. Tel. Ide Hill (073 275) 367/429

DIRECTIONS: 1½ miles S of A25 on Sundridge to Ide Hill road. 11 miles N of Ide Hill off B2042. Kentish Bus 24 from Sevenoaks (passing close Sevenoaks BR). Tel. Gravesend (0474) 321300. Sevenoaks station, 4½ miles; Penhurst station, 5½ miles

OPENING TIMES: April to end October, Wed to Sun and BH Mon 2–6. Last admission 5

ADMISSION: charged

Tea room. Toilets. Toilets for the disabled. Garden mainly wheelchair accessible. Dogs on lead only

One of the highest gardens in Kent, giving a fine view over the Weald, Emmetts' 6½ acres are notable for their fine specimen trees and shrubs. These are laid out in an informal style, owing much to the influence of William Robinson on the garden's creator, Frederick Lubbock.

As well as the now mature trees, there are rhododendrons, azaleas, pieris and other shrubs as well as a rose garden, fountain and waterfall. The garden is well worth visiting in spring for early flowers and autumn for foliage colour.

Northbourne Court

ADDRESS AND TELEPHONE: Lord Northburne, Northbourne Court, Northbourne, Deal. Tel. Deal (0304) 360813

DIRECTIONS: W of Deal off A258 to Northbourne (signposted from village)

OPENING TIMES: 26 and 29 May, 9 and 23 June, 7 and 21 July, 4, 25 and 28 August, 15 September, 2–5 or 6.

ADMISSION: charged

Although the present house was built in the 18C and 19C, the three large terraces, an outstanding feature, date from Elizabethan times.

The late Lord Northbourne filled the gardens with Mediterranean plants as well as native specimens which would flourish in the chalk soil in dry conditions. There is much silver foliage, brightened by the flowers of peonies, fuchsias and geraniums and by the roses and other climbers that decorate the house walls.

LANCASHIRE

Gawthorpe Hall

ADDRESS AND TELEPHONE: The National Trust, Gawthorpe Hall, Padiham, near Burnley, Lancashire, BH12 8UA. Tel. (0282) 78511

DIRECTIONS: on eastern outskirts of Padiham on A671

OPENING TIMES: Good Fri 29 March to 3 November, daily except Mon and Fri 1–5. Also open BH Mon

ADMISSION: charged

No dogs

The present layout dates from the mid or late 19C. Sir Charles Barry made the high sloping terrraced banks, now planted with Irish yews and clipped box, as a surround to the principal parterre, which was removed in the 1950s. It is the long-term intention of the Trust to reinstate this feature. The circular rose garden to the east of the house is a simpler form of an earlier design.

Rufford Old Hall

ADDRESS AND TELEPHONE: The National Trust, Rufford Old Hall, Rufford, near Ormskirk, Lancashire L40 1SG. Tel. (0704) 821254

DIRECTIONS: 7 miles N of Ormskirk in Rufford village on A59

OPENING TIMES: 30 March to 3 November, daily except Fri 1–5

ADMISSION: charged

The garden around this late medieval half-timbered Hall is being developed in the Victorian style and is planted with many rhododendrons and azaleas. Old-fashioned roses also feature and there are good displays of topiary leading to the Hall. Daffodils, crocus and snowdrops bloom in spring beneath mature trees on the garden outskirts.

LONDON AND GREATER LONDON

Kensington Gardens and Hyde Park

OWNERS: The Department of the Environment

DIRECTIONS: off Kensington High Street, Kensington Grove, Bayswater Road and Park Lane. Frequent bus services

OPENING TIMES: daily, all year round

ADMISSION: free

Restaurant. Toilets. Most walks and paths accessible for wheelchairs

These 600 acres were a royal hunting ground until opened to the public by James I and Charles I in the 17C. The Serpentine lake and the Long Water were later created by William Kent for Caroline, George II's queen.

Just over half of the remaining parkland now forms Hyde Park, well furnished with oak, beech, plane, and a few rarer specimens. Swimming, boating, and fishing (with a licence) are permitted on the Serpentine, with cycling and riding on specially laid out tracks, including the famous Rotten

Row (or *Route du Roi*) for horses. Most visitors come in search of a welcome green space near the busy shopping streets.

Kensington Gardens has, as its name suggests, a greater element of garden proper. An Italian water garden provides fountains and a falls at the head of the Long Water. The beautiful and well tended Flower Walk stretches eastwards from the Albert Memorial, where the solemn Prince sits beneath Gothic pinnacles, towards the Broad Walk. Even at the height of summer the well tended beds of annuals and perennials, backed by ornamental trees and shrubs and protected by sheltering woodland, remain colourful and refreshing to the eye.

Beyond the Round Pond, Kensington Palace has a Sunken Garden, hedged with pleached limes. Special viewing windows capture a charming sight: the rectangular lily pond with its fountains and neat clipped cones of yew and bay, surrounded by banks of flowers. This garden was planted for Queen Anne, for whom Sir John Vanbrugh and Nicholas Hawksmoor later added the nearby orangery.

Kensington Roof Garden

ADDRESS AND TELEPHONE: Kensington Roof Garden,
99 Kensington High Street. Tel. (071) 937 7994

DIRECTIONS: on the 6th floor of British Home Stores and Marks & Spencer in Kensington High Street. Entrance through a side door of BHS, adjacent to Barkers. Near Kensington High Street underground station and buses.

OPENING TIMES: from 10am daily throughout the year, when no privte function is taking place. Check by telephone or enquire at the entry desk

ADMISSION: free

Many people will be surprised to find that 'Derry and Toms Roof Gardens' still exists and pleased to discover that under new ownership it is well maintained and open on most occasions to those who seek it out.

It is startling to leave the lift at the 6th floor and step out into a mature woodland garden, where streams flow beneath birch, bamboo, chestnut, cedar and yews—and flamingo, duck and other waterfowl appear perfectly at home chimney height. An inner brick wall, with occasional windows, fosters the illusion of a normal garden, obscuring the Kensington roof-scape. Set in the wall is a plaque commemorating Trevor Bowen, Chairman of the (Derry and Toms) Company 1941-57 'who inspired this garden in the sky'.

Two more garden rooms lie on the opposite side of the central restaurant (for private functions only). The first of these is a Tudor Garden with herringbone brick paths and raised beds, well stocked with herbs, shrubs and climbers. The Spanish/Moorish garden is the most unusual: decorative tiles appear among the vines and flowering climbers which scramble over arches, pillars and the surrounding walls.

Osterley Park

ADDRESS AND TELEPHONE: The National Trust, Osterley Park,
Isleworth, Middlesex TW7 4RB. Tel. (081) 560 3918

DIRECTIONS: from A4 (Great West Road) turn N into Jersey Road, near Osterley underground station. Public transport: Osterley station (Piccadilly line)

OPENING TIMES: park, daily, all year round 9–7.30 or sunset if earlier

ADMISSION: free

Tea room. Toilets. Wheelchair access to most of park

Coming from the rush of the Great West Road, Osterley's 140 acres, now being restored by the National Trust, seem another world. Mature cedars (both Lebanon and Atlantic blue), planes, limes, ash, oak, beech and hornbeam have grown to great height and girth, and the three lakes created in the 18C when the park was landscaped are edged with silver and weeping willows, alders and Lombardy poplars.

Robert Adam's great house, remodelled from Sir Thomas Gresham's Elizabethan mansion, has a semicircular summer house on its north-west side, where lemons shine against their dark green leaves. Opposite stands a Temple of Pan with plaster reliefs symbolising Art and Science.

Magnolia grandiflora flourishes alongside the Elizabethan stable block nearby, and against the house. Herons stalk on the verges of the lakes.

St James's Park and Green Park

OWNERS: The Department of the Environment

DIRECTIONS: entry from Piccadilly, Queen's Walk, Constitution Hill, The Mall (Green Park) The Mall, Horse Guards Parade and Birdcage Walk (St James's Park). Frequent bus services and underground from Green Park and Hyde Park stations (Green Park) and St James's Park

OPENING TIMES: daily

ADMISSION: free.

Restaurant in St James's Park. Toilets

Green Park, of no particular interest to gardeners, is a pleasant expanse of grass and trees which forms a link in the chain of parks between Kensington and Westminster.

St James's Park, the smallest of the four central parks, stretching between Buckingham Palace and Westminster Palace, was opened to the public by Charles II, who had the deer park transformed into a French-style garden, with an avenue of trees and a canal complete with duck island.

George IV employed John Nash to transform Charles's formal design into a landscape park with a lake and a bridge.

The well cultivated landscape has many mature trees, including swamp cypresses and willows near the Victoria Memorial. A rose walk was created in 1980 for the Queen Mother and there are spring bulbs and bedding plants near the lake. Pelicans are the most spectacular of the many species of water-birds that crowd the lake and its verges.

MERSEYSIDE

Speke Hall

ADDRESS AND TELEPHONE: The National Trust, Speke Hall, The Walk, Liverpool L24 1XD. Tel. (051) 427 7231

DIRECTIONS: 8 miles SE of Liverpool city centre off A561. On N bank of River Mersey, next to Liverpool Airport

OPENING TIMES: garden, 30 March to 1 November, daily except Mon (but open BH Mon) 1–5.30; 2 November to March, daily except Mon 12–4. Closed 24–26 December, 31 December and 1 January. House also open

ADMISSION: charged

No dogs

Surrounding this lovely timber-framed Tudor house are herbaceous borders in the moat garden, a Victorian-style rose garden, shrubberies and extensive woodland. A raised walk gives views across the River Mersey.

WEST MIDLANDS

Wightwick Manor

ADDRESS AND TELEPHONE: The National Trust, Wightwick Manor, Wightwick Bank, Wolverhampton, WV6 8EE. Tel. (0902) 761108

DIRECTIONS: 3 miles W of Wolverhampton town centre on A454 (Wightwick Bank)

OPENING TIMES: garden, March to 31 December (closed 25–26 December), Thurs, Sat and BH Sun and Mon 2.30–5.30. House also open

ADMISSION: charged

The horticultural artist Alfred Parsons was responsible for designing the upper part of this garden but Thomas Mawson also worked here.

Particularly noteworthy is the rose garden, with a circular clematis-clad arbour in the centre, topiary and good herbaceous borders flanking the entrance.

Ponds and rhododendron plantings add to the interest of this small garden.

NORFOLK

Sheringham Park

ADDRESS AND TELEPHONE: The National Trust, Sheringham Park, Upper Sheringham, Sheringham, Norfolk NR26 8TB. Tel. Sheringham (0263) 823778

DIRECTIONS: 2 miles SW of Sheringham. Access for cars off A148 Cromer to Holt road. 5 miles W of Cromer, 6 miles E of Holt. Station: Sheringham 2 miles

OPENING TIMES: all year round, dawn to dusk

ADMISSION: charged

Raised walkway for wheelchairs from car park to park viewpoints. Toilets for the disabled. Dogs on lead. Refreshments at nearby Felbrigg Hall

Humphry Repton laid out the park at Sheringham late in the early 19C and considered it to be his masterpiece. He also, with his eldest son, designed the neo-classical house, which is set for protection among hills; out of sight of the sea, but with a fine prospect of the hills themselves, crowned by woods. A recently restored temple and the windmill at Weybourne are focal points in the landscape.

Camellias, rhododendrons and azaleas were planted behind the house in the 1950s, when lawns, shrub borders and a small lake were also made between the house and the original walled kitchen garden.

Way-marked walks lead through the extensive wooded areas of the park, where rhododendrons were planted in the late 19C. There are also many acres of open parkland to enjoy.

NORTHAMPTONSHIRE

Delapre Abbey

ADDRESS AND TELEPHONE: Northamptonshire Borough Council, London Road, Northampton. Tel. (0536) 520070

DIRECTIONS: 1 mile S of Northampton city centre on A508

OPENING TIMES: March to end October, daily dawn to dusk

ADMISSION: free

An abbey was founded on this site, on the south bank of the River Nene, in 1145. After the Dissolution of the Monasteries, Delapre was rebuilt as a country house and in 1946 it was purchased by the then Northampton Corporation, becoming the County Records Office in 1958.

The present approach is through parkland with many fine trees. To the east of the building is a walled garden—once the kitchen garden but now partly occupied by a herb garden and displays of summer bedding, with herbaceous borders beneath the walls.

The woodland garden features varied shrubs and rhododendrons, and there is a small bog garden. In spring there are fine bulb displays.

OXFORDSHIRE

Brook Cottage

ADDRESS AND TELEPHONE: Mr and Mrs D. Hodges, Brook Cottage, Alkerton. Tel. Edgehill (029587) 303 or 590

DIRECTIONS: from A422, Banbury to Stratford, turn W at sign to Alkerton, then left opposite Alkerton war memorial and right at fork

OPENING TIMES: April to end October, Mon to Fri also occasional weekends and by appointment. House closed

ADMISSION: charged

This distinguished 4-acre private garden was constructed around a 17C cottage some 25 years ago and has been constantly developed and enriched by the owners.

A strong design, with terraces and a variety of garden rooms and water features, on different levels, is complemented by rich and varied planting.

Shrub and climbing roses, clematis, single colour borders and many flowering shrubs are displayed among lawns and framed by contrasting types of hedge.

Broughton Castle

ADDRESS AND TELEPHONE: Lord Saye and Sele, Broughton Castle, Broughton, near Banbury, Oxfordshire. Tel. Banbury (0295) 262624

DIRECTIONS: 2½ miles W of Banbury on B4035

OPENING TIMES: mid May to mid September, Wed and Sun, also Thurs and BH Mon in July and August 2–5. Occasional other days and parties by appointment

ADMISSION: charged. Extra for house

Tea room

Old castle walls, moat and parkland form a perfect background for the 1-acre garden, which contains carefully planned shrub and flower borders and a variety of climbers.

Particularly appropriate to the setting is the walled knot garden. Its box edged beds contain lavender and rosemary and other sweet smelling plants.

Buscot Park

ADDRESS AND TELEPHONE: The National Trust, Faringdon Oxfordshire SN7 8BU. Tel. Faringdon (0367) 240786 (not weekends)

DIRECTIONS: between Lechlade and Faringdon, astride A417

OPENING TIMES: Easter weekend to end September, Wed to Fri and every 2nd and 4th Sat and Sun 2–6. House open

ADMISSION: charged

The extensive gardens surrounding 18C house include a formal water garden with pools, rills and fountains, designed by Harold Peto, as well as beech and lime avenues.

The formal gardens near the house include beds illustrating the four seasons, recently designed by Peter Coates.

Greys Court

ADDRESS AND TELEPHONE: The National Trust, Greys Court, Henley-on-Thames, Oxfordshire. Tel. (049 17) 529

DIRECTIONS: 3 miles W of Henley-on-Thames, S of A423. BR Henley-on-Thames. Bee-line bus 136/7 from Reading, alight Peppard Common

OPENING TIMES: end March to end September, garden Mon, Tues, Wed, Fri and Sat 2–6 (not Good Fri). House, Mon, Wed and Fri

ADMISSION: charged

Teas

The 8-acre garden around a Jacobean house contains the ruins of a 14C manor, now used as a setting for formal garden 'rooms'.

A White Garden, a garden devoted to old-fashioned roses and another to wisteria can be seen in the ruins, together with apple and cherry tree walks and a kitchen garden. Beyond is the Archbishop's Maze, laid out in 1980. The Tudor donkey-wheel well-house is an interesting historical feature.

Kingston Bagpuize House

ADDRESS AND TELEPHONE: Lady Tweedsmuir, Kingston Bagpuize House, Kingston Bagpuize, near Abingdon, Oxfordshire. Tel. (0865) 820259

DIRECTIONS: 10 miles SW of Oxford, 5½ miles W of Abingdon on A420

OPENING TIMES: April to end September, Sun and BH, 2.30–5.30. Groups by appointment weekdays. House open

ADMISSION: charged

Teas

The extensive gardens around this Charles II manor house include formal terraces of the period, Victorian shrubberies, many spring flowering bulbs and a woodland garden.

Rousham Park

ADDRESS AND TELEPHONE: Mr C. Cottrell-Dormer, Rousham Park, Steeple Aston, Oxfordshire. Tel. Steeple Aston (0869) 47110

DIRECTIONS: 14 miles N of Oxford, turn E on B4030 to Steeple Aston

OPENING TIMES: daily, 10–4.30 (no children under 15)

ADMISSION: charged

Rousham is an important historical landscape garden, laid out by William Kent in 1738 around a house that predates it by a century. Kent embellished the house with battlements and a cupola to achieve a Gothic effect, furthered by an eye-catcher (three arches on the opposite hill) and the Temple of the Mill within the gardens.

The gardens, which slope down to the river Cherwell, take the visitor by paths that offer a series of romantic vistas, inspired by the then fashionable paintings of Claude and Poussin. The Venus Vale provides pools and cascades, a lime walk leads to the statue of a dying gladiator on the 7-arched portico or Praeneste; other garden features include an amphitheatre, a pyramid and a statue of Apollo.

SHROPSHIRE

Dudmaston

ADDRESS AND TELEPHONE: The National Trust, Dudmaston, Quatt, near Bridgnorth, Shropshire. Tel. (0746) 780866

DIRECTIONS: at Quatt, 4 miles SE of Bridgnorth on A442

OPENING TIMES: end March to end September, Wed and Sun 2.30–6. House also open

ADMISSION: charged

Grass terraced slopes link this 17C mansion to a fine lake, which was formed by joining several small pools together.

To one side of the lake is a small rock garden, on the other, a well planted bog garden.

An American garden is planted with magnolias, kalmias and other trees and shrubs. Splendid mature cedars and woodland form a backdrop.

Weston Park

ADDRESS AND TELEPHONE: Weston Park Foundation, Weston Park, Shifnal, Shropshire. Tel. (095 276) 207

DIRECTIONS: Telford 6 miles, M54. Station: Shifnal 2 miles. Bus: Telford to Tong, then 2 miles

OPENING TIMES: Easter weekend 11–7; April and May weekends and BH Mon 11–7; June and July, daily except Mon and Fri 11–7; August, daily 11–7; September weekends 11–7. House also open

ADMISSION: charged

The house, dating from 1671, sits very comfortably in almost 1000 acres of park. In the 1760s, Lancelot 'Capability' Brown contoured the landscape, added lakes and planted trees in the parkland.

Temple Wood is particularly noteworthy, especially in early summer when rhododendrons add colour beneath chestnuts and oaks. On the edge of the woodland is the domed Temple of Diana designed by James Paine. Within the wood is Temple Pool, overlooked by another smaller temple and with a Roman bridge at one end.

Around the house are balustraded terraces and in front of the orangery is an Italianate garden.

Fine conservatory with birds; also a butterfly garden.

SOMERSET

Lytes Cary Manor

ADDRESS AND TELEPHONE: The National Trust, Lytes Cary Manor, near Somerton, Somerset. Tel. (045822) 3297

DIRECTIONS: 1 mile N of Ilchester bypass A303; signposted from roundabout at junction of A303, A37 and A372

OPENING TIMES: end March to 30 October, Mon, Wed and Sat 2–6 or dusk if earlier. House not open

ADMISSION: charged.

No toilets. No dogs. Plants for sale

The Manor house, dating from the 14C, 15C and 16C, provides a perfect backdrop to yew-hedged gardens laid out in the early part of this century.

Many different garden areas have been incorporated in the garden's 3 acres: these include, as well as the formal lawns and topiary in front of the house, an orchard with medlars and quinces, a pool, a white garden and a long colourful mixed border by Graham Thomas.

STAFFORDSHIRE

Biddulph Grange

ADDRESS AND TELEPHONE: The National Trust, Stoke-on-Trent, Staffordshire ST8 7SD. Tel. (0782) 517999

DIRECTIONS: 10 miles N of Stoke-on-Trent, off A527

OPENING TIMES: 1 May to 3 November, Wed to Fri 12–6. Sat, Sun and BH Mon 11–6. Also 9 November to 18 December, Sat and Sun 12–4

ADMISSION: charged

An important and impressive Victorian garden with surprise elements. Recently restored by the National Trust. It comprises 20 acres designed in 1842 by the then owner, James Bateman.

In the centre, reached by a secret passage, is a garden known as China, featuring a Chinese bridge, temple and joss house surrounded by acers, willows and bamboos. In another part of the garden, Egypt, clipped yews and sphinxes guard the entrance to what appears to be a tomb, but is found to be a cottage.

SUFFOLK

Helmingham Hall

ADDRESS AND TELEPHONE: Lord Tollemache, Helmingham Hall, Stowmarket, Suffok. Tel. Helmingham (047339) 363

DIRECTIONS: 9 miles N of Ipswich on B 1077

OPENING TIMES: Sundays May to end September 2–6; parties at other times by appointment. House closed

ADMISSION: charged

Refreshments

The moated Hall and garden date from Elizabethan times, though some alterations have been made through the years. There is a charming parterre, and a walled flower and kitchen garden with a wild flower garden beyond.

Wild flower plantings also surround the clipped yews above the moat, and stretch down to the water's edge. This is a most peaceful garden to visit

Ickworth

ADDRESS AND TELEPHONE: The National Trust, Ickworth, The Rotunda, Bury St Edmunds IP29 5QE. Tel. Horringer (0284) 735270

DIRECTIONS: in Horringer, 3 miles SW of Bury St Edmunds on W side of A143. Eastern Counties bus 141–4 Bury St Edmunds to Haverhill (passing close BR Bury St Edmunds). Bury St Edmunds BR, 3 miles

OPENING TIMES: garden and house 30 March to end April, Sat, Sun and BH Mon 1.30–5.30; May to end September, Tues, Wed, Fri, Sat, Sun and BH Mon 1.30–5.30; October, Sat and Sun 1.30–5.30. Park all year, daily 7,196.7

ADMISSION: charged

Wheelchair access to much of garden (not shop or restaurant). Toilets for the disabled. Braille guide

The main gardens were laid out at the beginning of the 19C around the newly built Italianate manor, with its massive rotunda, pillared portico and long curved wings to either side, each culminating in a pavilion.

There is a strong formal structure of spacious terraces, lawns, clipped hedges and walks with groupings of cedars and other specimen trees. The woodland contains many walks, one of which—the Albana woodland walk, named in memory of the wife of the 1st Marquis—has recently been restored.

Gold and silver foliage gardens have been created and the flower planting in the long borders is imaginative and effective.

SURREY

Chilworth Manor

ADDRESS AND TELEPHONE: Lady Heald, Chilworth Manor, Surrey. Tel. Guildford (0483) 61414

DIRECTIONS: 3½ miles SE of Guildford. From A248 at centre of Chilworth, up Blacksmith Lane. LC bus 425, Guildford to Dorking, alight Blacksmith Lane. Station: Chilworth

OPENING TIMES: Sat to Wed for one weekend each of April, May, June, July, August under National Gardens Scheme (see Gardens of England and Wales)

ADMISSION: charged

Teas

The original 17C manor was added to in the 18C by Sarah, Duchess of Marlborough, whose walled, terraced garden still remains to the north of the house. The terraces are grassed and planted with fruit trees; there are herbaceous borders at the top of the retaining walls.

Other features in this varied garden are a mixed border, many climbing plants and roses, a paved court, and stew ponds dating from 1000.

Ramster

ADDRESS AND TELEPHONE: Mr and Mrs P. Gunn, Ramster, Chiddingfold, Surrey. Tel. Haslemere (0428) 4422

DIRECTIONS: on A283 1½ miles S of Chiddingfold

OPENING TIMES: late April to mid June, daily 2–6

ADMISSION: charged

20 acres of woodland garden, laid out by Gauntlett nurseries in 1904, and restored and developed by the present owners. Camellias, rhododendrons and azaleas flourish under the shelter of larch and oak and spring flowers decorate the grass slopes. There are many mature specimen trees, and a well stocked bog garden.

Vann

ADDRESS AND TELEPHONE: Mr and Mrs M.B. Caroe, Vann, Hambledon, Surrey. Tel. Wormley (0428) 683413

DIRECTIONS: 6 miles S of Godalming, take A283 to Chiddingfold, turn off at head of green, take first left past Post Office, signed Vann Lane, house 2 miles on right

OPENING TIMES: 1991: 14 April 2–7, 15–20 April 10–6, 6 May 2–7, 7—12 May 10–6, 23 June 2–7, 24–29 June 10–6. At other times by appointment

ADMISSION: charged.

Teas

The 4½ acres of garden around the 17C and 18C house were laid out by Mr and Mrs W.D. Caroe in the early part of this century. The water garden was designed by Gertrude Jekyll along a stream that flows out of the ¼-acre pond. Here many spring bulbs flourish under flowering cherries and acers and wild flowers grow in grassy meadows.

As well as the woodland, orchard and kitchen garden, there are more formal gardens nearer the house, which W.D. Caroe altered between 1907 and 1909 to incorporate the barn and outbuildings. Features here include a yew walk, arches of yew and hornbeam, a pergola with varied climbers and distinctive mixed borders.

EAST SUSSEX

Bateman's

ADDRESS AND TELEPHONE: The National Trust, Bateman's, Burwash, Etchingham, East Sussex TN19 7DS. Tel. Burwash (0435) 882302

DIRECTIONS: ½ mile S of Burwash A265. Approach by road leading S from W end of village or N from Woods Corner (B2096). Etchingham station, 3 miles

OPENING TIMES: Good Fri 29 March to end October, daily except Thurs and Fri (open Good Fri) 11–6. Last admission 5

ADMISSION: charged

Wheelchair accessible. Toilet for disabled in car park. Refreshments

Rudyard Kipling lived in the Jacobean house from 1902 to 1936 and added several features to the existing 10-acre garden. To the south of the house are mixed borders, lawns and a rose garden with a pool made by Kipling. He also planted the yew hedges that divide the garden 'rooms' and laid the stone paths that lead from one to the other.

The lawns stretch down to the river, and a pleasant walk along to the mill—still used occasionally to grind flour. In spring the river banks are bright with bulbs and in summer wild flowers grow in the long grass. The gardens to the north of the house include an orchard and a vegetable garden.

Cobblers

ADDRESS AND TELEPHONE: Mr and Mrs Furniss, Cobblers, Mount Pleasant, Jarvis Brook, Crowborough. Tel. Crowborough (08926) 55969

DIRECTIONS: A26 to Crowborough Cross, B2100 to Crowborough Station, at 2nd crossroads turn into Tolworth road for ¼ mile

OPENING TIMES: some Sundays between late May and late August. House closed

ADMISSION: charged for National Gardens Scheme. (Teas)

The garden at Cobblers has been designed and planted by Mr and Mrs Furniss since 1968. The 2-acre sloping site features terraces, lawns and two pools, all skilfully designed to give an impression of a far larger space, and incorporating an enormous number of plants, many of which are unusual and rare.

This is a notable small garden which should be seen by anyone interested in garden design or creative plant association.

WEST SUSSEX

Gravetye Manor

ADDRESS AND TELEPHONE: Mr Peter Herbert, Gravetye Manor, Sharpthorne, near East Grinstead, West Sussex. Tel. East Grinstead (0342) 810 567

DIRECTIONS: take A22 from East Grinstead, at Wych Cross turn right for Sharpethorne, or from M23 leave at Exit 10, take A264 for ½ mile to East Grinstead, turn right down B 2028 then left to West Hoathly and Sharpthorne

OPENING TIMES: Tues and Fri 10–5. House closed

ADMISSION: free

Limited wheelchair access. Dogs on lead only

Gravetye, an Elizabethan manor house, was bought by William Robinson, author of *The English Flower Garden*, in 1885. Here he developed the informal type of gardening he preferred, with emphasis on plant associations and wild areas. The garden, which fell into disrepair after his death in 1935, is now being renewed by the owner, Mr Peter Herbert, and under the guidance of a new young head gardener, Ms Helen Greenwood.

Near the lake are a fine 4-acre wild flower meadow, a 'wild garden' containing hardy exotic plants, a walled kitchen garden, herbaceous borders, and shrubs, including rhododendrons. The formal gardens near the manor (now a hotel and country club) are not open to the public.

Heaselands

ADDRESS AND TELEPHONE: Mrs Ernest Kleinwort, Heaselands, Haywards Heath, West Sussex. Tel. Haywards Heath (0444) 454181

DIRECTIONS: 1 mile SW of Haywards Heath, on A273 to Burgess Hill

OPENING TIMES: 3 Sundays and 3 Wednesdays in May. Parties by appointment at other times, including in October for autumn colour. House closed

ADMISSION: charged, for National Gardens Scheme

Teas. No dogs

This beautiful 30-acre garden is well worth seeking out, even though its times of opening are limited. It has a series of distinctive walled or hedged gardens—rock garden, paved herbaceous garden and swimming pool garden—each lavishly planted. From the terrace behind the house, which features beds of annuals, a pool and a blue Atlas cedar, there is a fine view over the informal gardens.

The main feature here is a skilfully cultivated woodland garden, largely

devoted to rhododendrons and azaleas: the garden holds the National Collection of Knap Hill hybrids. Added pleasures are the water plants flourishing by ponds and streams, spring bulbs and wild flowers.

The High Beeches

ADDRESS AND TELEPHONE: Mr and Mrs E. Boscawen, The High Beeches Garden Conservation Trust. Handcross, near Crawley. Tel. (0444) 400589

DIRECTIONS: on B2110, 1 mile E of Handcross, 4 miles S of Crawley

OPENING TIMES: Easter Mon to 15 June and 7 September to end October, daily 1–5, except Wed, Sun and BH Mon, when 10–5. Also a few days under NGS and for organised parties by arrangement at any time. House not open

ADMISSION: charged

The outstanding woodland garden at The High Beeches was planted in the early part of the century by Colonel Giles Loder, nephew to Gerald Loder of Wakehurst Place and Edmund Loder of Leonardslee, and has been maintained and developed by Mr and Mrs Boscawen. Colonel Loder benefited, as did his uncles, from the influx of shrubs and plants from the East, which had begun in the later half of the previous century.

On a south-facing slope at some distance from the house, mature specimen trees shade camellias, rhododendrons, magnolias and azaleas, which give a magnificent display of flowers in spring. Ornamental trees and shrubs, many of which provide spectacular autumn colour, are enhanced by streams and a pool, encircled with damp-loving plants.

Of particular interest is a 'Loderi' walk, featuring the hybrid rhododendrons developed by the Loder family. The garden also holds the National Collection of pieris, stuartias and styrax.

Petworth House and Park

ADDRESS AND TELEPHONE: The National Trust Petworth House, Petworth West Sussex GU28 0AE. Tel. Petworth (0798) 42207

DIRECTIONS: in centre of Petworth (A272/A283) car park well signposted. Pulbrough station, 5¼ miles

OPENING TIMES: garden, Good Fri 29 March to end October, daily except Mon and Fri (open Good Fri and BH Mon, closed Tues following) 12.30–5.30; park, all year, daily 8 to sunset (closed 28–30 June)

ADMISSION: charged

Refreshments

Grand 17C house, with notable landscaped park by Capability Brown. including serpentine lake and groups of trees.

The pleasure grounds near the house, laid out by Brown on site of an earlier formal garden, lost many trees in the 1987 gales, but replanting is now in progress.

WARWICKSHIRE

Charlecote Park

ADDRESS AND TELEPHONE: The National Trust, Charlecote Park, Wellesbourne, Warwickshire CV35 9ER. Tel. (0789) 840277

DIRECTIONS: 5 miles E of Stratford-upon-Avon, 1 mile W of Wellesbourne

OPENING TIMES: Easter Sat to end October, daily except Mon and Thurs (but open BH Mon) 11–6. House also open

ADMISSION: charged

No dogs

Home of the Lucy family since 1247, Charelcote Park is where the young Shakespeare was caught poaching.

The present house is a little over a hundred years old, although the gatehouse dates from 1550. The park was landscaped by Lancelot 'Capability' Brown. He altered the River Hale, which is today linked to the house by balustraded terraces, but was not allowed to remove the fine lime avenue—once an approach to the house from the east.

In the North Garden is an interesting border containing plants mentioned in Shakespeare's plays—heartease, columbine, saffron and others. The forecourt borders are planted with many good shrubs and the charming woodland garden features both wild and cultivated plants.

Shakespeare Gardens, Stratford-upon-Avon

SHAKESPEARE'S BIRTHPLACE: Henley Street

ANNE HATHAWAY'S COTTAGE: Shottery

HALL'S CROFT: Old Town (home of Shakespeare's daughter, Susanna, when marrid to Doctor John Hall)

NASH'S HOUSE, NEW PLACE: Chapel Street (home of Shakespeare's grandaughter and foundation of Shakespeare's last home)

MARY ARDEN'S HOUSE: Wilmcote (Shakespeare's mother's house)

ADDRESS AND TELEPHONE: Shakespeare's Birthplace Trust, Stratford-upon-Avon, Warwickshire. Tel. (0789) 204016

DIRECTIONS: in and around Stratford-upon-Avon

OPENING TIMES: April to end of October, weekdays 9–6, Sun 10–6, November to end of March, weekdays 9–4.30. Shakespeare's Birthplace and Anne Hathaway's Cottage only, Sun 1.30–4.30

ADMISSION: charged. Inclusive ticket admits to all five properties

no dogs

The garden at Shakespeare's Birthplace features a collection of plants mentioned in his plays and sonnets.

A knot garden is laid out at New Place, in the foundations of Shakespeare's last home. Also arboured walk of crab-apple trees and laburnums.

Anne Hathaway's Cottage features an attractive cottage-style garden and the recently planted Shakespeare's Tree Garden; in contrast, Hall's Croft is surrounded by a formal walled garden with terrace, lawns and herbaceous borders.

Box hedges and old-fashioned roses can be seen at Mary Arden's House.

Warwick Castle

ADDRESS AND TELEPHONE: Tussaud's Group, Warwick Castle, Warwick, CV34 4QU. Tel. (0926) 495421

DIRECTIONS: centre of Warwick

OPENING TIMES: daily (except Christmas Day), 10–5 (November to February inclusive 10–4.30). Castle open

ADMISSION: charged

No dogs

The grounds around Warwick Castle consist mainly of parkland with many fine trees. The general layout is attributed to Lancelot Brown and is believed to have been his first independent venture.

Attractive formal Victorian rose garden in a secluded setting. Reconstructed from the original 1864 designs of Robert Marnock, the rose garden is best viewed in late June and July. A small rock garden with cascade and pond is sited close by and in front of the Conservatory (1786) is another larger formal summer garden—the Peacock Garden—featuring topiary work. An area of woodland has recently been planted (rhododendrons, camellias and magnolias) on the perimeter of the grounds.

WILTSHIRE

Corsham Court

ADDRESS AND TELEPHONE: Lord Methuen, Corsham Court, Corsham, near Chippenham, Wilts. Tel. Corsham (0249) 712214

DIRECTIONS: 4 miles W of Chippenham, S of A4

OPENING TIMES: 1 January to Maundy Thurs, Tues, Wed, Thurs, Sat and Sun 2–4.30; 29 March to 30 September, Tues, Wed, Thurs, Sat and Sun 2–6; October and November, Tues, Wed, Thurs, Sat and Sun 2–4. Also open Fri in summer

ADMISSION: charged

Corsham Court has been in the possession of the Methuen family since 1745, when they employed Capability Brown and Humphry Repton to design the park and gardens.

As well as the landscaped park, planted with fine chestnuts and other trees, there are walled gardens, herbaceous borders, an avenue of pleached hornbeams and flowering trees, including prunus 'Kanzan' and some rarer specimens.

The Courts

ADDRESS AND TELEPHONE: The National Trust, The Courts, Holt, near Trowbridge, Wiltshire BA14 6RR. Tel. (0225) 782340

DIRECTIONS: 3 miles SW of Melksham, 3 miles N of Trowbridge, 2½ miles E of Bradford-on-Avon on S side of B3107. Badgerline bus 237 Chippenham to Trowbridge. Bradford-on-Avon BR, 2½ miles; Trowbridge BR, 3 miles

OPENING TIMES: end March to end October, daily except Sat 2–5. Out of season by appointment

ADMISSION: charged

The Courts was a wool mill until the 1880s and some of its functional features, such as fleece washing pools, were incorporated by Lady Goff when she added a series of separate 'rooms' to the garden designed by Sir George Hastings early in this century.

The formal gardens include terraces and herbaceous borders, a rectangular lily pond, roses and a fern garden, as well as a Venetian gate and stone ornaments. A large part of the garden's 7 acres is taken up by an arboretum and wild flower garden, planted by Miss E.M. Goff.

Sheldon Manor

ADDRESS AND TELEPHONE: Maj. M.A. Gibbs, Sheldon Manor, Allington, Wiltshire. Tel. Chippenham (0249) 653120

DIRECTIONS: 1½ miles W of Chippenham, turn S off A420 at Allington crossroads. Eastbound traffic signposted from A4

OPENING TIMES: Easter Sun and Mon, then Sun, Thurs, and BH May to end June (closed July), 1 August to 6 October 12.30–6

ADMISSION: charged

Refreshments

Picturesque, old-fashioned garden surrounding a 13C house. The many shrub roses of early European origin, clematis and climbing roses, rare flowering trees and shrubs make this a rewarding garden to visit. The availability of lunches and cream teas is an added inducement.

NORTH YORKSHIRE

Parcevall Hall Gardens

ADDRESS AND TELEPHONE: Walsingham College (Yorkshire Properties) Ltd, Parcevall Hall, Skyreholm, near Skipton, North Yorkshire. Tel. Burnsall (0756) 72 311 or 214

DIRECTIONS: 12 miles N of Skipton. From Grassington on B6265 turn S at Hebden crossroads, follow signs to Burnsall, through Appletreewick to Parcevall Hall

ADMISSION: charged

Teas

The 16C farmhouse and 20 acres of land were bought in 1927 by Sir William Milner, who laid out these unusual gardens, first planting a shelter belt of trees and diverting a stream.

Fine trees provide autumn colour. From the terraces there are vantage points to look out across marvellous moorland scenery. The wild garden includes camellias, rhododendrons, azaleas and magnolias.

You may picnic in the orchard, where there are old varieties of apple.

University of York Gardens

ADDRESS: The University of York

DIRECTIONS: in Heslington, in the SE outskirts of the city of York; follow signs from A64, avoiding city centre.

OPEN: daily

ADMISSION: free

Refreshments

In 1950 when the University campus was built, an integral water garden was designed by Frank Clark of Edinburgh University, thus cleverly solving the problem of boggy terrain while providing an imaginative and beautiful landscape.

The main feature is a 14-acre lake, linked to the Elizabethan Heslington Hall by a canal pool, and surrounded by the new campus buildings—the hexagonal Great Hall rising directly from its waters. There are bridges and covered walks, and inlets, well patronised by ducks between the lower buildings.

Vertical interest is given to the landscape by groups of ornamental trees, while willows and water plants decorate the verges of the lake, pools and waterways.

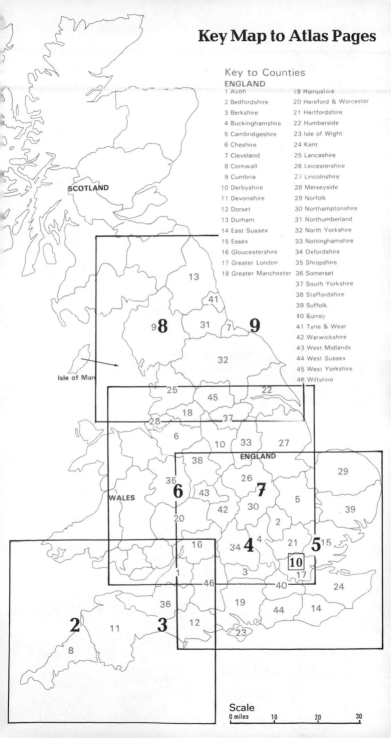

Key Map to Atlas Pages

Key to Counties
ENGLAND

1 Avon	19 Hampshire
2 Bedfordshire	20 Hereford & Worcester
3 Berkshire	21 Hertfordshire
4 Buckinghamshire	22 Humberside
5 Cambridgeshire	23 Isle of Wight
6 Cheshire	24 Kent
7 Cleveland	25 Lancashire
8 Cornwall	26 Leicestershire
9 Cumbria	27 Lincolnshire
10 Derbyshire	28 Merseyside
11 Devonshire	29 Norfolk
12 Dorset	30 Northamptonshire
13 Durham	31 Northumberland
14 East Sussex	32 North Yorkshire
15 Essex	33 Nottinghamshire
16 Gloucestershire	34 Oxfordshire
17 Greater London	35 Shropshire
18 Greater Manchester	36 Somerset
	37 South Yorkshire
	38 Staffordshire
	39 Suffolk
	40 Surrey
	41 Tyne & Wear
	42 Warwickshire
	43 West Midlands
	44 West Sussex
	45 West Yorkshire
	46 Wiltshire

SCOTLAND

Isle of Man

WALES

ENGLAND

Scale
0 miles   10   20   30

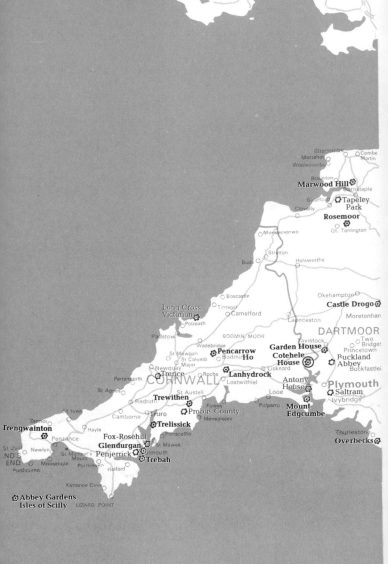

2

Ilfracombe   Combe
Mortehoe   Martin
Woolacombe

Braunton
Marwood Hill
Bideford   Barnstaple
Clovelly   **Tapeley Park**
Rosemoor
Gt. Torrington

Morwenstowe

Stratton   Holsworthy
Bude

Boscastle   Okehampton
Long Cross   Tintagel   **Castle Drogo**
Victorian   Camelford   Moretonhan
Polzeath   Launceston
Padstow   BODMIN MOOR   Tavistock   **DARTMOOR**
Wadebridge   **Garden House**   Two
St Mewgan   **Pencarrow**   Bridge
Newquay   St Columb   Bodmin Ho   **Cotehele**   Princetown
Major   **House**   Buckfastleigh
Perranporth   **Trenice**   Roche   **Lanhydrock**
St Agnes   Lostwithiel   **Antony**   **Plymouth**
CORNWALL   St Austell   **House**   Saltram
Redruth   Looe   Ivybridge
Trewithen   Truro   Foway
Camborne   **Probus County**   Polperro   **Mount**
St Ives   Mevagissey   **Edgcumbe**
Trengwainton   Hayle   **Trelissick**   Thurlestone
Zennor   Penzance   Fox-Rosehill   Portscatho   **Overbecks**
St Just   Newlyn   **Glendurgan**   St Mawes
ND'S   St Michael's   **Penjerrick**   Falmouth
END   Mousehole   Mount   **Trebah**
Porthcurno   Porthleven   Halford
Kynance Cove
Abbey Gardens
Isles of Scilly   LIZARD POINT

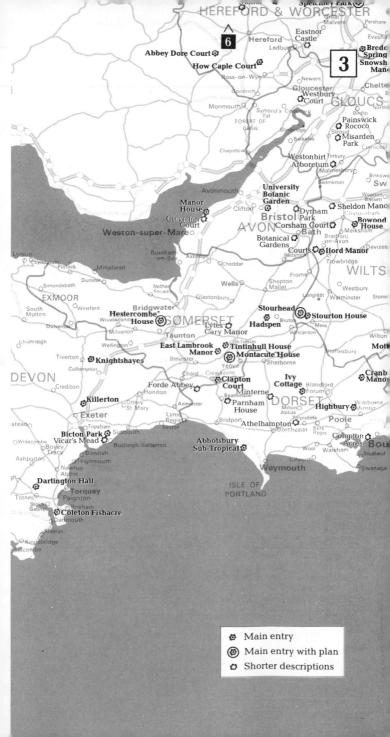

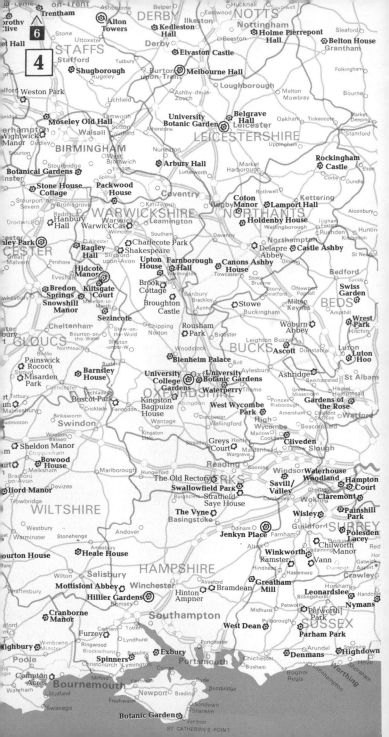

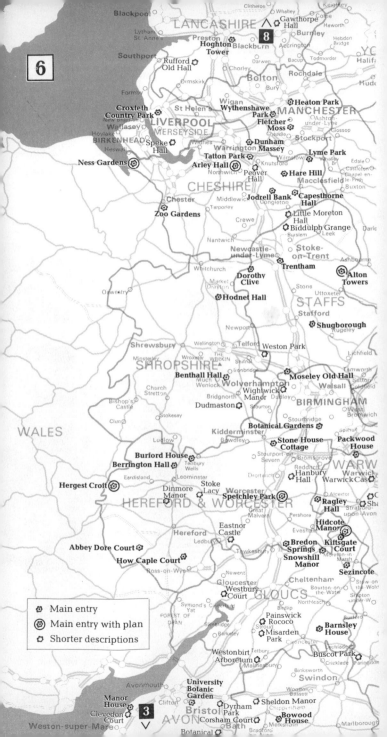

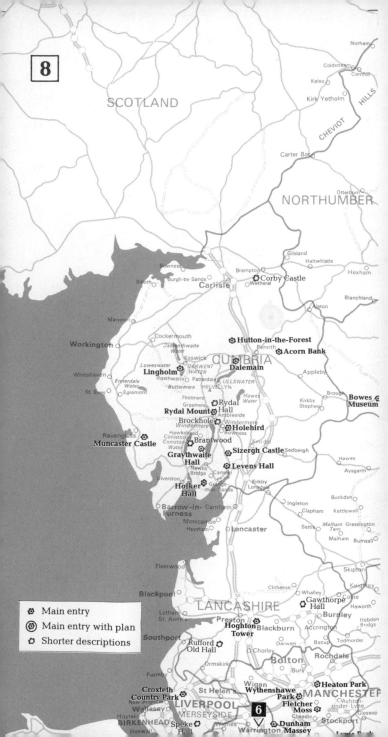

9

Berwick-upon-Tweed

HOLY ISLAND

FARNE ISLANDS

Chillingham

Kirknewton

Bamburgh

Wooler

Seahouses

Howick Hall ✿

Craster

Alnwick

✿ Cragside

Alnmouth

Rothbury

Warkworth

LAND

✿ Herterton House

Morpeth

Newbiggin-

by-the-Sea

✿ Wallington

Bedlington

Belsay

Hall

Ponteland

Blyth

✿ Seaton Delaval Hall

✿ Jesmond Dene

Whitley Bay

Corbridge

Tynemouth

TYNE &

Newcastle

upon Tyne

WEAR

Jarrow

South Shields

Gateshead

Chester-

le-Street

Washington

Sunderland

Stanhope

Durham ✿

University

Botanic Garden

Brancepeth

DURHAM

Bishop

Auckland

West Hartlepool

Raby

Castle

Sedgefield

✿ Hartlepool

Barnard

Castle

Staindrop

Aycliffe

CLEVELAND

Redcar

Stockton-

on-Tees

Ormesby Hall

Darlington

Middlesbrough

Staithes

Croft

Yarm

Guisborough

Loftus

Scotch Corner

Stokesley

Great

Ayton

Whitby

Richmond

Catterick

Egton

Robin Hood's

Bay

Goathland

Leyburn

✿ Thorp Perrow

Wensley

Middleham

Northallerton

Hawnby

Rievaulx Terrace ✿

Thirsk

Kirkbymoorside

Scarborough

NORTH

Helmsley

Pickering

YORKSHIRE

Oswaldkirk

Kirby

Misperton

Filey

Fountains Abbey/

Ripon

Castle Howard

Staxton

Studley Royal ✿

Boroughbridge

Malton

Humber

✿ Parcevall

Hall

Newby Hall

Easingwold

Sewerby Hall ✿

Flamborough

Ripley Castle ✿

✿ Sutton Park

Sledmere

✿ Bridlington

Harrogate

Knaresborough

House

Beningbrough

Burton Agnes Hall ✿

✿ Harlow Carr

Hall

Ilkley

Wetherby

York

Stamford

Bridge

Great

Driffield

Otley

✿ Harewood

House

University

of York

Tadcaster

✿ Stewart's Burnby Hall

✿ Bramham Park

Bradford

WEST

Leeds

Market

Weighton

Beverley

Hornsea

Burton Constable Hall ✿

YORKSHIRE

Selby

HUMBERSIDE

Halifax

Batley

✿ Temple Newsam

Howden

Hull

Dewsbury

Brough

Hedon

Huddersfield

✿ Wakefield

Goole

Barton-upon-

Humber

Patrington

Pontefract

Barnsley

Scunthorpe

SOUTH

✿ Elsham Hall

Immingham

YORKSHIRE

Doncaster

Grimsby

Conisbrough

Brigg

Cleethorpes

Rotherham

Bawtry

Reepham

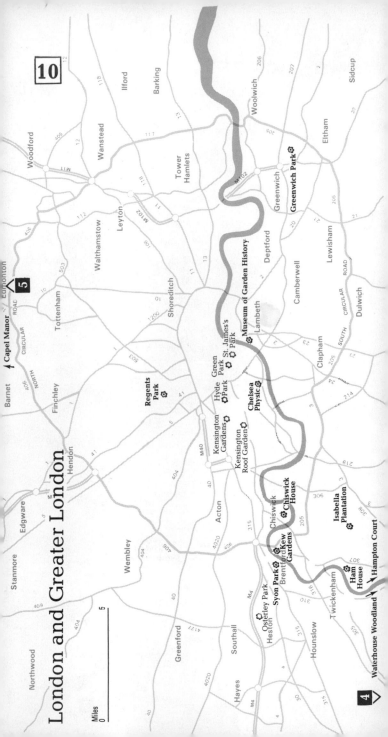

London and Greater London

10

Miles
0 —————— 5

Capel Manor / Edmonton **5**

Northwood

Stanmore

Edgware

Hendon

Wembley

Finchley

Barnet

Tottenham

Woodford

Ilford

Barking

Wanstead

Leyton

Walthamstow

Shoreditch

Tower Hamlets

Regents Park

Kensington Gardens

Hyde Park

Green Park

St. James's Park

Museum of Garden History

Lambeth

Greenwich

Greenwich Park

Woolwich

Eltham

Sidcup

Lewisham

Camberwell

Dulwich

Clapham

Chelsea Physic

Kensington Roof Garden

Acton

Chiswick

Chiswick House

Kew Gardens

Brentford

Syon Park

Osterley Park

Heston

Hounslow

Southall

Greenford

Hayes

Twickenham

Isabella Plantation

Hampton Court

Ham House

Waterhouse Woodland **4**

Deptford

Woodford

Northwood